Praise for *OpenGL® Shading Language*

"As the 'Red Book' is known to be the gold standard for OpenGL, the 'Orange Book' is considered to be the gold standard for the OpenGL Shading Language. With Randi's extensive knowledge of OpenGL and GLSL, you can be assured you will be learning from a graphics industry veteran. Within the pages of the second edition you can find topics from beginning shader development to advanced topics such as the spherical harmonic lighting model and more."

—David Tommeraasen
CEO/Programmer
Plasma Software

"This will be the definitive guide for OpenGL shaders; no other book goes into this detail. Rost has done an excellent job at setting the stage for shader development, what the purpose is, how to do it, and how it all fits together. The book includes great examples and details, as well as good additional coverage of 2.0 changes!"

—Jeffery Galinovsky
Director of Emerging Market
Platform Development
Intel Corporation

"The coverage in this new edition of the book is pitched just right to help many new shader-writers get started, but with enough deep information for the 'old hands.'"

—Marc Olano
Assistant Professor
University of Maryland

"This is a really great book on GLSL—well written and organized, very accessible, and with good real-world examples and sample code. The topics flow naturally and easily, explanatory code fragments are inserted in very logical places to illustrate concepts, and, all in all, this book makes an excellent tutorial as well as a reference."

—John Carey
Chief Technology Officer
C.O.R.E. Feature Animation

OpenGL®
Shading Language
Third Edition

OpenGL® Shading Language
Third Edition

Randi J. Rost
Bill Licea-Kane

**With contributions by
Dan Ginsburg,
John M. Kessenich,
Barthold Lichtenbelt,
Hugh Malan, and
Mike Weiblen**

✦Addison-Wesley

Upper Saddle River, NJ • Boston • Indianapolis • San Francisco
New York • Toronto • Montreal • London • Munich • Paris • Madrid
Capetown • Sydney • Tokyo • Singapore • Mexico City

Many of the designations used by manufacturers and sellers to distinguish their products are claimed as trademarks. Where those designations appear in this book, and the publisher was aware of a trademark claim, the designations have been printed with initial capital letters or in all capitals.

The authors and publisher have taken care in the preparation of this book, but make no expressed or implied warranty of any kind and assume no responsibility for errors or omissions. No liability is assumed for incidental or consequential damages in connection with or arising out of the use of the information or programs contained herein.

The publisher offers excellent discounts on this book when ordered in quantity for bulk purchases or special sales, which may include electronic versions and/or custom covers and content particular to your business, training goals, marketing focus, and branding interests. For more information, please contact:

U.S. Corporate and Government Sales
(800) 382-3419
corpsales@pearsontechgroup.com

For sales outside the United States, please contact:

International Sales
international@pearsoned.com

Visit us on the Web: informit.com/aw

Library of Congress Cataloging-in-Publication Data

Rost, Randi J., 1960-
  OpenGL shading language / Randi J. Rost, Bill Licea-Kane ; with contributions by
Dan Ginsburg ... [et al.]. — 3rd ed.
      p.   cm.
  Includes bibliographical references and index.
  ISBN 978-0-321-63763-5 (pbk. : alk. paper) 1. Computer graphics. I. Licea-Kane, Bill.
II. Title.
  T385.R665 2009
  006.6'86—dc22

                                                                    2009019529

Pearson Education, Inc
Rights and Contracts Department
501 Boylston Street, Suite 900
Boston, MA 02116
Fax (617) 671-3447

ISBN-13: 978-0-321-63763-5
ISBN-10:   0-321-63763-1
Text printed in the United States on recycled paper at Edwards Brothers in Ann Arbor, Michigan.
First printing, July 2009

*To Baby Cakes, Baby Doll, Love Bug, and
Little Zooka—thanks for your love and support*

To Mom and Pop—my first and best teachers

Contents

Foreword to the Second Edition

To me, graphics shaders are about the coolest things to ever happen in computer graphics. I grew up in graphics in the 1970s, watching the most amazing people do the most amazing things with the mathematics of graphics. I remember Jim Blinn's bump-mapping technique, for instance, and what effects it was able to create. The method was deceptively simple, but the visual impact was momentous. True, it took a substantial amount of time for a computer to work through the pixel-by-pixel software process to make that resulting image, but we cared about that only a little bit. It was the effect that mattered.

My memory now fast-forwards to the 1980s. Speed became a major issue, with practitioners like Jim Clark working on placing graphics algorithms in silicon. This resulted in the blossoming of companies such as Evans & Sutherland and Silicon Graphics. They brought fast, interactive 3D graphics to the masses, but the compromise was that they forced us into doing our work using standard APIs that could easily be hardware supported. Deep-down procedural techniques such as bump mapping could not follow where the hardware was leading.

But the amazing techniques survived in software. Rob Cook's classic paper on shade trees brought attention to the idea of using software "shaders" to perform the pixel-by-pixel computations that could deliver the great effects. This was embodied by the Photorealistic RenderMan rendering software. The book *RenderMan Companion* by Steve Upstill is still the first reference that I point my students to when they want to learn about the inner workings of shaders. The ability to achieve such fine-grained control over the graphics rendering process gave RenderMan users the ability to create the dazzling, realistic effects seen in Pixar animation shorts and TV commercials. The process was still miles away from real time, but the seed of the idea of giving an *interactive* application developer that type of control was planted. And it was such a powerful idea that it was only a matter of time until it grew.

Now, fast-forward to the start of the new millennium. The major influence on graphics was no longer science and engineering applications. It had become games and other forms of entertainment. (Nowhere has this been more obvious than in the composition of the SIGGRAPH Exhibition.) Because games live and die by their ability to deliver realistic effects at interactive speeds, the shader seed planted a few years earlier was ready to flourish in this new domain. The capacity to place procedural graphics rendering algorithms into the graphics hardware was definitely an idea whose time had come. Interestingly, it brought the graphics community full circle. We searched old SIGGRAPH proceedings to see how pixel-by-pixel scene control was performed in software then, so we could "re-invent" it using interactive shader code.

So, here we are in the present, reading Randi Rost's *OpenGL Shading Language*. This is the next book I point my shader-intrigued students to, after Upstill's. It is also the one that I, and they, use most often day to day. By now, my first edition is pretty worn.

But great news—I have an excuse to replace it! This second edition is a *major* enhancement over the first. This is more than just errata corrections. There is substantial new material in this book. New chapters on lighting, shadows, surface characteristics, and RealWorldz are essential for serious effects programmers. There are also 18 new shader examples. The ones I especially like are shadow mapping, vertex noise, image-based lighting, and environmental mapping with cube maps. But they are all really good, and you will find them all useful.

The OpenGL Shading Language is now part of standard OpenGL. It will be used everywhere. There is no reason not to. Anybody interested in effects graphics programming will want to read this book cover to cover. There are many nuggets to uncover. But GLSL is useful even beyond those borders. For example, we use it in our visualization research here at OSU (dome transformation, line integral convolution, image compression, terrain data mapping, etc.). I know that GLSL will find considerable applications in many other non-game areas as well.

I want to express my appreciation to Randi, who obviously started working on the first edition of this book even before the GLSL specification was fully decided upon. This must have made the book extra difficult to write, but it let the rest of us jump on the information as soon as it was stable. Thanks, too, for this second edition. It will make a significant contribution to the shader-programming community, and we appreciate it.

—Mike Bailey, Ph.D.
Professor, Computer Science
Oregon State University

Foreword to the First Edition

This book is an amazing measure of how far and how fast interactive shading has advanced. Not too many years ago, procedural shading was something done only in offline production rendering, creating some of the great results we all know from the movies, but were not anywhere close to interactive. Then a few research projects appeared, allowing a slightly modified but largely intact type of procedural shading to run in real time. Finally, in a rush, widely accessible commercial systems started to support shading. Today, we've come to the point where a real-time shading language developed by a cross-vendor group of OpenGL participants has achieved official designation as an OpenGL Architecture Review Board approved extension. This book, written by one of those most responsible for spearheading the development and acceptance of the OpenGL shading language, is your guide to that language and the extensions to OpenGL that let you use it.

I came to my interest in procedural shading from a strange direction. In 1990, I started graduate school at the University of North Carolina in Chapel Hill because it seemed like a good place for someone whose primary interest was interactive 3D graphics. There, I started working on the Pixel-Planes project. This project had produced a new graphics machine with several interesting features beyond its performance at rendering large numbers of polygons per second. One feature in particular had an enormous impact on the research directions I've followed for the past 13 years. Pixel-Planes 5 had programmable pixel processors—lots of them. Programming these processors was similar in many ways to the assembly-language fragment programs that have burst onto the graphics scene in the past few years.

Programming them was exhilarating, yet also thoroughly exasperating.

I was far from the only person to notice both the power and pain of writing low-level code to execute per-pixel. Another group within the Pixel-Planes team built an assembler for shading code to make it a little easier to write, although it was still both difficult to write a good shader and ever-so-rewarding once you had it working. The shaders produced will be familiar to anyone who has seen demos of any of the latest graphics products, and not surprisingly you'll find versions of many of them in this book: wood, clouds, brick, rock, reflective wavy water, and (of course) the Mandelbrot fractal set.

The rewards and difficulties presented by Pixel-Planes 5 shaders guided many of the design decisions behind the next machine, PixelFlow. PixelFlow was designed and built by a university/industry partnership with industrial participation first by Division, then by Hewlett-Packard. The result was the first interactive system capable of running procedural shaders compiled from a high-level shading language. PixelFlow was demonstrated at the SIGGRAPH conference in 1997. For a few years thereafter, if you were fortunate enough to be at UNC-Chapel Hill, you could write procedural shaders and run them in real time when no one else could. And, of course, the only way to see them in action was to go there.

I left UNC for a shading project at SGI, with the hopes of providing a commercially supported shading language that could be used on more than just one machine at one site. Meanwhile, a shading language research project started up at Stanford, with some important results for shading on PC-level graphics hardware. PC graphics vendors across the board started to add low-level shading capabilities to their hardware. Soon, people everywhere could write shading code similar in many ways to that which had so inspired me on the Pixel-Planes 5 machine. And, not surprisingly, soon people everywhere also knew that we were going to need a higher-level language for interactive shading.

Research continues into the use, improvement, and abuse of these languages at my lab at University of Maryland, Baltimore County; and at many, many others. However, the mere existence of real-time high-level shading languages is no longer the subject of that research. Interactive shading languages have moved from the research phase to wide availability. There are a number of options for anyone wanting to develop an application using the shading capabilities of modern graphics hardware. The principal choices are Cg, HLSL, and the OpenGL Shading Language. The last of which has the distinction of being the only one that has been through a rigorous multivendor review process. I participated in that process, as did more than two dozen representatives from a dozen companies and universities.

This brings us back full circle to this book. If you are holding this book now, you are most likely interested in some of the same ideals that drove the creation of the OpenGL Shading Language, the desire for a cross-OS, cross-platform, robust and standardized shading language. You want to learn how to use all of that? Open up and start reading. Then get shading!

—Marc Olano
University of Maryland
Baltimore County, MD
September 2003

Preface

For just about as long as there has been graphics hardware, there has been programmable graphics hardware. Over the years, building flexibility into graphics hardware designs has been a necessary way of life for hardware developers. Graphics APIs continue to evolve, and because a hardware design can take two years or more from start to finish, the only way to guarantee a hardware product that can support the then current graphics APIs at its release is to build in some degree of programmability from the very beginning.

Until recently, the realm of programming graphics hardware belonged to just a few people, mainly researchers and graphics hardware driver developers. Research into programmable graphics hardware has been taking place for many years, but the point of this research has not been to produce viable hardware and software for application developers and end users. The graphics hardware driver developers have focused on the immediate task of providing support for the important graphics APIs of the time: PHIGS, PEX, Iris GL, OpenGL, Direct3D, and so on. Until recently, none of these APIs exposed the programmability of the underlying hardware, so application developers have been forced into using the fixed functionality provided by traditional graphics APIs.

Hardware companies have not exposed the programmable underpinnings of their products because of the high cost of educating and supporting customers to use low-level, device-specific interfaces and because these interfaces typically change quite radically with each new generation of graphics hardware. Application developers who use such a device-specific interface to a piece of graphics hardware face the daunting task of updating their software for each new generation of hardware that comes along. And forget about supporting the application on hardware from multiple vendors!

As we moved into the 21st century, some of these fundamental tenets about graphics hardware were challenged. Application developers pushed the envelope as never before and demanded a variety of new features in hardware in order to create more and more sophisticated onscreen effects. As a result, new graphics hardware designs became more programmable than ever before. Standard graphics APIs were challenged to keep up with the pace of hardware innovation. For OpenGL, the result was a spate of extensions to the core API as hardware vendors struggled to support a range of interesting new features that their customers were demanding.

The creation of a standard, cross-platform, high-level shading language for commercially available graphics hardware was a watershed event for the graphics industry. A paradigm shift occurred, one that took us from the world of rigid, fixed functionality graphics hardware and graphics APIs to a brave new world where the graphics processing unit, or GPU (i.e., graphics hardware), is as important as the central processing unit, or CPU. The GGU is optimized for processing dynamic media such as 3D graphics and video. Highly parallel processing of floating-point data is the primary task for GPUs, and the flexibility of the GPU means that it can also be used to process data other than a stream of traditional graphics commands. Applications can take advantage of the capabilities of both the CPU and the GPU, using the strengths of each to optimally perform the task at hand.

This book describes how graphics hardware programmability is exposed through a high-level language in the leading cross-platform 3D graphics API: OpenGL. This language, the OpenGL Shading Language, lets applications take total control over the most important stages of the graphics processing pipeline. No longer restricted to the graphics rendering algorithms and formulas chosen by hardware designers and frozen in silicon, software developers are beginning to use this programmability to create stunning effects in real time.

Intended Audience

The primary audience for this book is application programmers who want to write shaders. This book can be used as both a tutorial and a reference book by people interested in learning to write shaders with the OpenGL Shading Language. Some will use the book in one fashion, and some in the other. The organization is amenable to both uses and is based on the assumption that most people won't read the book in sequential order from back to front (but some intrepid readers of the first edition reported that they did just that!).

Readers do not need previous knowledge of OpenGL to absorb the material in this book, but such knowledge is very helpful. A brief review of OpenGL is included, but this book does not attempt to be a tutorial or reference book for OpenGL. Anyone attempting to develop an OpenGL application that uses shaders should be armed with OpenGL programming documentation in addition to this book.

Computer graphics has a mathematical basis, so some knowledge of algebra, trigonometry, and calculus will help readers understand and appreciate some of the details presented. With the advent of programmable graphics hardware, key parts of the graphics processing pipeline are once again under the control of software developers. To develop shaders successfully in this environment, developers must understand the mathematical basis of computer graphics.

About This Book

This book has three main parts. Chapters 1 through 8 teach the reader about the OpenGL Shading Language and how to use it. This part of the book covers details of the language and details of the OpenGL commands that create and manipulate shaders. To supply a basis for writing shaders, Chapters 9 through 19 contain a gallery of shader examples and some explanation of the underlying algorithms. This part of the book is both the baseline for a reader's shader development and a springboard for inspiring new ideas. Finally, Chapter 20 compares other notable commercial shading languages, and Appendixes A and B contain reference material for the language and the API entry points that support it.

The chapters are arranged to suit the needs of the reader who is least familiar with OpenGL and shading languages. Certain chapters can be skipped by readers who are more familiar with both topics. This book has somewhat compartmentalized chapters in order to allow such usage.

- Chapter 1 reviews the fundamentals of the OpenGL API. Readers already familiar with OpenGL may skip to Chapter 2.

- Chapter 2 introduces the OpenGL Shading Language and the OpenGL entry points that have been added to support it. If you want to know what the OpenGL Shading Language is all about and you have time to read only two chapters of this book, this chapter and Chapter 3 are the ones to read.

- Chapter 3 thoroughly describes the OpenGL Shading Language. This material is organized to present the details of a programming language. This section serves as a useful reference section for readers who have developed a general understanding of the language.

- Chapter 4 discusses how the newly defined programmable parts of the rendering pipeline interact with each other and with OpenGL's fixed functionality. This discussion includes descriptions of the built-in variables defined in the OpenGL Shading Language.

- Chapter 5 describes the built-in functions that are part of the OpenGL Shading Language. This section is a useful reference section for readers with an understanding of the language.

- Chapter 6 presents and discusses a fairly simple shader example. People who learn best by diving in and studying a real example will benefit from the discussion in this chapter.

- Chapter 7 describes the entry points that have been added to OpenGL to support the creation and manipulation of shaders. Application programmers who want to use shaders in their application must understand this material.

- Chapter 8 presents some general advice on shader development and describes the shader development process. It also describes tools that are currently available to aid the shader development process.

- Chapter 9 begins a series of chapters that present and discuss shaders with a common characteristic. In this chapter, shaders that duplicate some of the fixed functionality of the traditional OpenGL pipeline are presented.

- Chapter 10 presents a few shaders that are based on the capability to store data in and retrieve data from texture maps.

- Chapter 11 is devoted to shaders that are procedural in nature; that is, effects are computed algorithmically rather than being based on information stored in textures.

- Chapter 12 presents several alternative lighting models that can be implemented with OpenGL shaders.

- Chapter 13 discusses algorithms and shaders for producing shadows.

- Chapter 14 delves into the details of shaders that implement more realistic surface characteristics, including refraction, diffraction, and more realistic reflection.

- Chapter 15 describes noise and the effects that can be achieved with its proper use.

- Chapter 16 contains examples of how shaders can create rendering effects that vary over time.

- Chapter 17 contains a discussion of the aliasing problem and how shaders can be written to reduce the effects of aliasing.

- Chapter 18 illustrates shaders that achieve effects other than photorealism. Such effects include technical illustration, sketching or hatching effects, and other stylized rendering.

- Chapter 19 presents several shaders that modify images as they are being drawn with OpenGL.

- Chapter 20 compares the OpenGL Shading Language with other notable commercial shading languages.

- Appendix A contains the language grammar that more clearly specifies the OpenGL Shading Language.

- Appendix B contains reference pages for the API entry points that are related to the OpenGL Shading Language.

- Finally, the Glossary collects terms defined in the book, Further Reading gathers all the chapter references and adds more, and the Index ends the book.

About the Shader Examples

The shaders contained in this book are primarily short programs that illustrate the capabilities of the OpenGL Shading Language. None of the example shaders should be presumed to illustrate the "best" way of achieving a particular effect. (Indeed, the "best" way to implement certain effects may have yet to be discovered through the power and flexibility of programmable graphics hardware.) Performance improvements for each shader are possible for any given hardware target. For most of the shaders, image quality may be improved if greater care is taken to reduce or eliminate causes of aliasing.

The source code for these shaders is written in a way that I believe represents a reasonable trade-off between source code clarity, portability, and performance. Use them to learn the OpenGL Shading Language, and improve on them for use in your own projects.

I have taken as much care as possible to present shaders that are done "the right way" for the OpenGL Shading Language rather than those with idio-syncrasies from their development on specific implementations of the OpenGL Shading Language. Electronic versions of most of these shaders are available through a link at this book's Web site at http://3dshaders.com.

Errata

I know that this book contains some errors, but I've done my best to keep them to a minimum. If you find any errors, please report them to me (randi@3dshaders.com), and I will keep a running list on this book's Web site at http://3dshaders.com.

Typographical Conventions

This book contains a number of typographical conventions to enhance readability and understanding.

- SMALL CAPS are used for the first occurrence of defined terms.

- *Italics* are used for emphasis, document titles, and coordinate values such as *x*, *y*, and *z*.

- **Bold serif** is used for language keywords.

- Sans serif is used for macros and symbolic constants that appear in the text.

- **Bold sans serif** is used for function names.

- *Italic sans serif* is used for variables, parameter names, spatial dimensions, and matrix components.

- `Fixed width` is used for code examples.

About the Authors

Randi Rost is currently the external manager at Intel Corporation, where he manages relationships with a variety of game developers and other software developers. He also directs Intel's visual computing university research program.

Before joining Intel, Randi was the director of developer relations at 3Dlabs. In this role, he led a team that educated developers and helped them take advantage of the new graphics hardware technology. He led a team that produced development tools, documentation, and white papers; and contributed to standards and open source efforts.

Before his developer relations role, Randi was the manager of 3Dlabs' Fort Collins, Colorado, graphics software team. This group drove the definition of the OpenGL 2.0 standard and implemented OpenGL drivers for 3Dlabs' graphics products. Before joining 3Dlabs, Randi was a graphics software architect for Hewlett-Packard's Graphics Software Lab and the chief architect for graphics software at Kubota Graphics Corporation.

Randi has been involved in the graphics industry for more than twenty-five years and has participated in emerging graphics standards efforts for more than twenty years. He has been involved with the design and evolution of OpenGL since before version 1.0 was released in 1992. He is one of the few people credited as a contributor for each major revision of OpenGL, up through and including OpenGL 2.0. He was one of the chief architects and the specification author for PEX, and he was a member of the Graphics Performance Characterization (GPC) Committee during the development of the Picture-Level Benchmark (PLB). He served as 3Dlabs' representative to the Khronos Group from the time the group started in 1999 until the OpenML 1.0 specification was released, and he chaired the graphics subcommittee of that organization during this time. He received the National Computer Graphics Association (NCGA) 1993 Achievement Award for the Advancement of Graphics Standards.

Randi has participated in or organized numerous graphics tutorials at SIGGRAPH, Eurographics, and the Game Developer's conference since 1990. He has given tutorials on the OpenGL Shading Language at SIGGRAPH 2002 and SIGGRAPH 2003 and made presentations on this topic at the Game Developer's Conference in 2002 and 2003. In 2004, Randi taught OpenGL Shading Language MasterClasses across North America, Europe, and Japan.

Randi received his B.S. in computer science and mathematics from Minnesota State University, Mankato, in 1981 and his M.S. in computing science from the University of California, Davis, in 1983.

On a dreary winter day, you might find Randi in a desolate region of southern Wyoming, following a road less traveled.

Bill Licea-Kane is currently a principal member of technical staff at AMD. There he is a contributor to the OpenGL ARB and is chair of the OpenGL Shading Language Technical Subcommittee. Prior to his work at AMD, Bill worked at Digital Equipment Corporation (DEC), Compaq, 3Dlabs, and ATI. Bill has a B.S. in mechanical engineering from Cornell University.

About the Contributors

Dan Ginsburg has been working on developing 3D computer graphics software for more than ten years. He is currently a software engineer at Still River Systems where he is developing OpenGL-based image registration software for the Monarch250 proton beam radiotherapy system. Before joining Still River Systems, Dan was a senior member of technical staff at AMD where he worked in a variety of roles including developing OpenGL drivers, creating desktop and handheld 3D demos, and leading the development of handheld GPU developer tools. Prior to working for AMD, he worked for n-Space, Inc., an Orlando-based game development company. Dan has a B.S. in computer science from Worcester Polytechnic Institute and an MBA from Bentley College.

John Kessenich, a Colorado native, has worked in Fort Collins as a software architect in a variety of fields including CAD applications, operating system kernels, and 3D graphics. He received a patent for using Web browsers to navigate through huge collections of source code and another for processor architecture. John studied mathematics and its application to computer graphics, computer languages, and compilers at Colorado State University, receiving a bachelor's degree in applied mathematics in 1985. Later, while working at Hewlett-Packard, he earned his master's degree in applied mathematics in 1988. John has been working on OpenGL drivers since 1999 at 3Dlabs and led the 3Dlabs shading language compiler development effort. John was the lead author for the OpenGL Shading Language specification, and in this role he was one of the leaders of the technical effort to finalize and standardize it as part of core OpenGL. Currently, John is a senior staff architect at Intel, and he continues to work as spec editor for the OpenGL Shading Language.

Barthold Lichtenbelt received his master's degree in electrical engineering in 1994 from the University of Twente in the Netherlands. From 1994 to 1998, he worked on volume rendering techniques at Hewlett-Packard Company, first at Hewlett-Packard Laboratories in Palo Alto, California, and later at Hewlett-Packard's graphics software lab in Fort Collins, Colorado. During that time, he coauthored the book *Introduction to Volume Rendering*, and wrote several papers on the subject. He was awarded four patents in the field of volume rendering. In 1998, Barthold joined Dynamic Pictures (subsequently acquired by 3Dlabs), where he worked on both Direct3D and OpenGL drivers for professional graphics accelerators. Since 2001, he has been heavily involved in efforts to extend the OpenGL API and was the lead author of the three ARB extensions that support the OpenGL Shading Language. Barthold also led the implementation of 3Dlabs' first drivers that use these extensions. He is currently a senior OpenGL manager at NVIDIA and is also chair of the OpenGL Architecture Review Board.

Hugh Malan is a computer graphics programmer currently working for Real Time Worlds in Dundee, Scotland. In 1997, he received B.S. degrees in mathematics and physics from Victoria University in Wellington, New Zealand, and followed that with a year in the honors program for mathematics. He subsequently received an M.S. in computer graphics from Otago University in Dunedin, New Zealand. After receiving his M.S., Hugh worked on 3D paint and UV mapping tools at Right Hemisphere, then joined Pandromeda, Inc., and currently works at Realtime Worlds.

Michael Weiblen received his B.S. in electrical engineering from the University of Maryland, College Park, in 1989. Mike began exploring computer graphics in the 1980s and developed 3D renderers for the TRS-80 Model 100 laptop and Amiga 1000. Using OpenGL and IrisGL since 1993, he has developed global-scale synthetic environments, visual simulations, and virtual reality applications, which have been presented at such venues as the United States Capitol, EPCOT Center, DARPA, NASA, and SIGGRAPH. He has been awarded two U.S. patents and has published several papers and articles. In 2003, Mike joined 3Dlabs in Fort Collins, Colorado, where he was an engineer with the 3Dlabs Developer Relations group, focusing on applications of hardware-accelerated rendering using the OpenGL Shading Language. Mike is currently senior software engineer at Zebra Imaging, and he contributes to several open source software projects, including spearheading the integration of OpenGL Shading Language support into OpenSceneGraph.

Acknowledgments

John Kessenich of Intel was the primary author of the OpenGL Shading Language specification document and the author of Chapter 3 of this book. Some of the material from the OpenGL Shading Language specification document was modified and included in Chapters 3, 4, and 5, and the OpenGL Shading Language grammar written by John for the specification is included in its entirety in Appendix A. John worked tirelessly throughout the standardization effort discussing, resolving, and documenting language and API issues; updating the specification through numerous revisions; and providing insight and education to many of the other participants in the effort. John also did some of the early shader development, including the very first versions of the wood, bump map, and environment mapping shaders discussed in this book. Since August 2005, John has been working at Intel, where he is editor of the OpenGL Shading Language Specification and is active in several standardization efforts at the Khronos Group.

Barthold Lichtenbelt of Nvidia was the primary author and document editor of the OpenGL extension specifications that defined the OpenGL Shading Language API. Some material from those specifications has been adapted and included in Chapter 7. Barthold worked tirelessly updating the specifications; discussing, resolving, and documenting issues; and guiding the participants of the ARB-GL2 working group to consensus. Barthold is also the coauthor of Chapter 4 of this book. Since August 2005, Barthold has been working at NVIDIA, where he is involved in OpenGL standardization efforts.

The industrywide initiative to define a high-level shading effort for OpenGL was ignited by a white paper called *The OpenGL 2.0 Shading Language*, written by Dave Baldwin (2001) of 3Dlabs. Dave's ideas provided the basic framework from which the OpenGL Shading Language has evolved. Publication of this white paper occurred almost a year before any publication of information on competing, commercially viable, high-level shading languages. In this respect, Dave deserves credit as the trailblazer for a standard high-level shading language. Dave continued to be heavily involved in the design of the language and the API during its formative months. His original white paper also included code for a variety of shaders. This code served as the starting point for several of the shaders in this book: notably, the brick shaders presented in Chapter 6 and Chapter 17, the traditional shaders presented in Chapter 9, the antialiased checkerboard shader in Chapter 17, and the Mandelbrot shader in Chapter 18. Steve Koren of 3Dlabs was responsible for getting the aliased brick shader and the Mandelbrot shader working on real hardware for the first time.

Mike Weiblen developed and described the GLSL diffraction shader in Chapter 14, contributed a discussion of scene graphs and their uses in Chapter 8, and contributed to the shadow volume shader in Section 13.3. Philip Rideout was instrumental in developing frameworks for writing and testing shaders. Many of the illustrations in this book were generated with Philip's **GLSLdemo** and **deLight** applications. Philip also contributed several of the shaders in this book, including the shadow shaders in Chapter 13 and the sphere morph and vertex noise shaders in Chapter 16. Joshua Doss developed the initial version of the glyph bombing shader described in Chapter 10. He and Inderaj Bains were the coauthors of **ShaderGen**, a tool that verified the fixed functionality code segments presented in Chapter 9 and that can automatically generate working shaders from current fixed functionality state. Teri Morrison contributed the OpenGL 1.5 to 2.0 migration guide that appears in Appendix B. Barthold Lichtenbelt took the pictures that were used to create the Old Town Square environment maps.

Hugh Malan of Realtime Worlds contributed the initial version of the shadow volume shader discussed in Section 13.3.

Bert Freudenberg of the University of Magdeburg developed the hatching shader described in Chapter 18. As part of this effort, Bert also explored some of the issues involved with analytic antialiasing with programmable graphics hardware. I have incorporated some of Bert's diagrams and results in Chapter 17. The stripe shader included in Chapter 11 was implemented by LightWork Design, Ltd. Antonio Tejada of 3Dlabs conceived and implemented the wobble shader presented in Chapter 16.

William "Proton" Vaughn of Newtek provided a number of excellent models for use in this book. I thank him for the use of his Pug model that appears in Color Plates 19 and 22 and the Drummer model that appears in Color Plate 20. Christophe Desse of xtrm3D.com also allowed me to use some of his great models. I used his Spaceman model in Color Plate 17, his Scout-walker model in Color Plate 18, and his Orc model in Color Plate 21. Thanks are owed to William and Christophe not only for allowing me to use their models in this book, but for also contributing these models and many others for public use.

I would like to thank my colleagues at 3Dlabs for their assistance with the OpenGL 2.0 effort in general and for help in developing this book. Specifically, the 3Dlabs compiler team has been doing amazing work implementing the OpenGL Shading Language compiler, linker, and object support in the 3Dlabs OpenGL implementation. Dave Houlton and Mike Weiblen worked on RenderMonkey and other shader development tools. Dave also worked closely with companies such as SolidWorks and LightWork Design to enable them to take full advantage of the OpenGL Shading Language. Teri Morrison and Na Li implemented and tested the original OpenGL Shading Language extensions, and Teri, Barthold, and Matthew Williams implemented the official OpenGL 2.0 API support in the 3Dlabs drivers. This work has made it possible to create the code and images that appear in this book. The Fort Collins software team, which I was privileged to lead for several years, was responsible for producing the publicly available specifications and source code for the OpenGL Shading Language and OpenGL Shading Language API.

Dale Kirkland, Jeremy Morris, Phil Huxley, and Antonio Tejada of 3Dlabs were involved in many of the OpenGL 2.0 discussions and provided a wealth of good ideas and encouragement as the effort moved forward. Antonio also implemented the first parser for the OpenGL Shading Language. Other members of the 3Dlabs driver development teams in Fort Collins, Colorado; Egham, U.K.; Madison, Alabama; and Austin, Texas have contributed to the effort as well. The 3Dlabs executive staff should be commended for having the vision to move forward with the OpenGL 2.0 proposal and the courage to allocate resources to its development. Thanks to Osman Kent, Hock Leow, Neil Trevett, Jerry Peterson, Jeff Little, and John Schimpf in particular.

Numerous other people have been involved in the OpenGL 2.0 discussions. I would like to thank my colleagues and fellow ARB representatives at ATI, SGI, NVIDIA, Intel, Microsoft, Evans & Sutherland, IBM, Sun Microsystems, Apple, Imagination Technologies, Dell, Compaq, and HP for contributing to discussions and for helping to move the process along. Evan Hart, Jeremy

Sandmel, Benjamin Lipchak, and Glenn Ortner of ATI also provided insightful review and studious comments for both the OpenGL Shading Language and the OpenGL Shading Language API. Steve Glanville and Cass Everitt of NVIDIA were extremely helpful during the design of the OpenGL Shading Language, and Pat Brown of NVIDIA contributed enormously to the development of the OpenGL Shading Language API. Others with notable contributions to the final specifications include Marc Olano of the University of Maryland/Baltimore County; Jon Leech of SGI; Folker Schamel of Spinor; Matt Cruikshank, Steve Demlow, and Karel Zuiderveld of Vital Images; Allen Akin, contributing as an individual; and Kurt Akeley of NVIDIA. Numerous others provided review or commentary that helped improve the specification documents.

I think that special recognition should go to people who were not affiliated with a graphics hardware company and still participated heavily in the ARB-GL2 working group. When representatives from a bunch of competing hardware companies get together in a room and try to reach agreement on an important standard that materially affects each of them, there is often squabbling over details that will cause one company or another extra grief in the short term. Marc Olano and Folker Schamel contributed enormously to the standardization effort as "neutral" third parties. Time and time again, their comments helped lead the group back to a higher ground. Allen Akin and Matt Cruikshank also contributed in this regard. Thanks, gentlemen, for your technical contributions and your valuable but underappreciated work as "referees."

A big thank you goes to the software developers who have taken the time to talk with us, send us e-mail, or answer survey questions on http://opengl.org. Our ultimate aim is to provide you with the best possible API for doing graphics application development, and the time that you have spent telling us what you need has been invaluable. A few ISVs lobbied long and hard for certain features, and they were able to convince us to make some significant changes to the original OpenGL 2.0 proposal. Thanks, all you software developers, and keep telling us what you need!

A debt of gratitude is owed to the designers of the C programming language, the designers of RenderMan, and the designers of OpenGL, the three standards that have provided the strongest influence on our efforts. Hopefully, the OpenGL Shading Language will continue their traditions of success and excellence.

The reviewers of various drafts of this book have helped greatly to increase its quality. Thanks to John Carey, Steve Cunningham, Bert Freudenberg, Michael Garland, Jeffrey Galinovsky, Dave Houlton, John Kessenich, Slawek

Kilanowski, Bob Kuehne, Na Li, Barthold Lichtenbelt, Andy McGovern, Teri Morrison, Marc Olano, Brad Ritter, Philip Rideout, Teresa Rost, Folker Schamel, Maryann Simmons, Mike Weiblen, and two anonymous reviewers for reviewing some or all of the material in this book. Your comments have been greatly appreciated! Clark Wolter worked with me on the design of the cover image, and he improved and perfected the original concepts.

Thanks go to my three children, Rachel, Hannah, and Zachary, for giving up some play time with Daddy for a while, and for the smiles, giggles, hugs, and kisses that helped me get through this project. Finally, thank you, Teresa, the love of my life, for the support you've given me in writing this book. These have been busy times in our personal lives too, but you have had the patience, strength, and courage to see it through to completion. Thank you for helping me make this book a reality.

Chapter 1

Review of OpenGL Basics

This chapter briefly reviews the OpenGL application programming interface to lay the foundation for the material in subsequent chapters. It is not an exhaustive overview. If you are already extremely familiar with OpenGL, you can safely skip ahead to the next chapter. If you are familiar with another 3D graphics API, you can glean enough information here about OpenGL to begin using the OpenGL Shading Language for shader development.

Unless otherwise noted, descriptions of OpenGL functionality in this book are based on the OpenGL 3.1 specification. However, in this chapter, we will also include OpenGL functionality included in the ARB_compatibility extension.

1.1 OpenGL History

OpenGL is an industry-standard, cross-platform APPLICATION PROGRAMMING INTERFACE (API). The specification for this API was finalized in 1992, and the first implementations appeared in 1993. It was largely compatible with a proprietary API called Iris GL (Graphics Library) that was designed and supported by Silicon Graphics, Inc. To establish an industry standard, Silicon Graphics collaborated with various other graphics hardware companies to create an open standard, which was dubbed "OpenGL."

The evolution of OpenGL is controlled by the OpenGL Architecture Review Board, or ARB, created by Silicon Graphics in 1992. This group is governed by a set of by-laws, and its primary task is to guide OpenGL by controlling the specification and conformance tests. In September

1

2006 the OpenGL ARB became a workgroup of the Khronos Group. This enabled closer working opportunities with the OpenGL ES workgroup. The original ARB contained representatives from SGI, Intel, Microsoft, Compaq, Digital Equipment Corporation, Evans & Sutherland, and IBM. The ARB currently has as active promoters and contributors AMD, Apple, ARM, Blizzard, IBM, Intel, NVIDIA, S3 Graphics, and TransGaming.

OpenGL shares many of Iris GL's design characteristics. Its intention is to provide access to graphics hardware capabilities at the lowest possible level that still provides hardware independence. It is designed to be the lowest-level interface for accessing graphics hardware. OpenGL has been implemented in a variety of operating environments, including Macs, PCs, UNIX-based systems, game consoles, and phones. It has been supported on a variety of hardware architectures, from those that support little in hardware other than the framebuffer itself to those that accelerate virtually everything in hardware.

Since the release of the initial OpenGL specification (version 1.0) in June 1992, nine revisions have added new functionality to the API. The current version of the OpenGL specification is 3.1. The first conformant implementations of OpenGL 1.0 began appearing in 1993.

- Version 1.1 was finished in 1997 and added support for two important capabilities—vertex arrays and texture objects.

- The specification for OpenGL 1.2 was released in 1998 and added support for 3D textures and an optional set of imaging functionality.

- The OpenGL 1.3 specification was completed in 2001 and added support for cube map textures, compressed textures, multitextures, and other things.

- OpenGL 1.4 was completed in 2002 and added automatic mipmap generation, additional blending functions, internal texture formats for storing depth values for use in shadow computations, support for drawing multiple vertex arrays with a single command, more control over point rasterization, control over stencil wrapping behavior, and various additions to texturing capabilities.

- The OpenGL 1.5 specification was published in October 2003. It added support for vertex buffer objects, shadow comparison functions, occlusion queries, and nonpower-of-2 textures.

- OpenGL 2.0 was finished in September 2004. In addition to OpenGL Shading Language Version 110 for programmable vertex and fragment shading, OpenGL 2.0 added multiple render targets, nonpower-of-2 textures, point sprites, separate blend equation, and separate stencil.

- Version 2.1 was released in August 2006. OpenGL Shading Language Version 120 added support for nonsquare matrices, promoted arrays to first class objects, allowed limited type conversion, and introduced centroid and invariant qualifiers. OpenGL 2.1 also added support for nonsquare matrices, pixel buffer objects, and sRGB textures.

- OpenGL 3.0 was released in August 2008. OpenGL Shading Language 130 added many new features including the following:

  - Native signed and unsigned integer

  - Texture functions for size query, explicit LOD, offset, and gradient

  - Texture arrays

  - Switch/case/default

  - In, out, centroid, flat, smooth, invariant, noperspective

  - Special variables *gl_VertexID*, *gl_ClipDistance*

  - Hyperbolic, **isinf**, **isnan**, and additional rounding functions

  OpenGL 3.0 also added integer and unsigned integer texture formats, conditional rendering, buffer object subrange mapping and flushing, float-point color and depth formats for textures and renderbuffers, framebuffer objects, half-float vertex array and pixel data formats, multisample stretch blit, nonnormalized integer color internal formats, one-dimensional and two-dimensional texture arrays, packed depth-stencil formats, separate blend enables, RGTC compressed textures, one and two channel texture formats (R and RG), transform feedback, vertex array objects, and sRGB framebuffer.

- OpenGL 3.1 followed shortly after in March 2009. OpenGL Shading Language 140 added uniform blocks, rectangular textures, texture buffers and gl_InstanceID. OpenGL 3.1 also added instanced rendering, copying data between buffer objects, primitive restart, texture buffer objects, rectangle textures, uniform buffer objects, and signed normalized texture formats.

All versions of OpenGL from 1.0 through 1.5 were based on a fixed-function configurable pipeline—the user could control various parameters, but the underlying functionality and order of processing were fixed.

OpenGL 2.0, finalized in September 2004, opened up the processing pipeline for user control by providing programmability for both vertex processing and fragment processing as part of the core OpenGL specification. With this version of OpenGL, application developers have been able to implement their own rendering algorithms, using a high-level shading language. The addition of programmability to OpenGL represents a fundamental shift in its design, which is why the version number changed from 1.5 to 2.0.

OpenGL 3.0, finalized in August 2008, brought another fundamental shift in its design. For the first time, portions of OpenGL were marked "deprecated," setting the stage for future streamlined specifications. In March 2009, OpenGL 3.1 moved much of the deprecated functions into the ARB_compatibility extension.

1.2 OpenGL Evolution

Because of its fundamental design as a fixed-function state machine, before OpenGL 2.0, the only way to modify OpenGL was to define extensions to it. Therefore, a great deal of functionality is available in various OpenGL implementations in the form of extensions that expose new hardware functionality. OpenGL has a well-defined extension mechanism, and hardware vendors are free to define and implement features that expose new hardware functionality. Since only OpenGL implementors can implement extensions, there was previously no way for applications to extend the functionality of OpenGL beyond what was provided by their OpenGL provider.

To date, more than 400 extensions have been defined. Extensions that are supported by only one vendor are identified by a short prefix unique to that vendor (e.g., SGI for extensions developed by Silicon Graphics, Inc.). Extensions that are supported by more than one vendor are denoted by the prefix EXT in the extension name. Extensions that have been thoroughly reviewed by the ARB are designated with an ARB prefix in the extension name to indicate that they have a special status as a recommended way of exposing a certain piece of functionality. Extensions that achieve the ARB designation are candidates to be added to standard OpenGL. Published specifications for OpenGL extensions are available at the OpenGL extension registry at www.opengl.org/registry/.

The extensions supported by a particular OpenGL implementation can be determined by calling the OpenGL **glGetStringi** function with the symbolic constant GL_EXTENSIONS with an index indicating which extension to query. The returned string contains the name of the extension supported by the implementation. Some vendors currently support more than 100 separate OpenGL extensions. It can be a little bit daunting for an application to try to determine whether the needed extensions are present on a variety of implementations and what to do if they're not. The proliferation of extensions has been primarily a positive factor for the development of OpenGL, but in a sense, it has become a victim of its own success. It allows hardware vendors to expose new features easily, but it presents application developers with a dizzying array of nonstandard options. Like any standards body, the ARB is cautious about promoting functionality from extension status to standard OpenGL.

Before version 2.0 of OpenGL, none of the underlying programmability of graphics hardware was exposed. The original designers of OpenGL, Mark Segal and Kurt Akeley, stated, "One reason for this decision is that, for performance reasons, graphics hardware is usually designed to apply certain operations in a specific order; replacing these operations with arbitrary algorithms is usually infeasible." This statement may have been mostly true when it was written in 1994 (there were programmable graphics architectures even then). But today, all of the graphics hardware that is being produced is programmable. Because of the proliferation of OpenGL extensions and the need to support Microsoft's DirectX API, hardware vendors have no choice but to design programmable graphics architectures. As discussed in the remaining chapters of this book, providing application programmers with access to this programmability is the purpose of the OpenGL Shading Language.

1.3 Execution Model

The OpenGL API is focused on drawing graphics into framebuffer memory and, to a lesser extent, in reading back values stored in that framebuffer. It is somewhat unique in that its design includes support for drawing three-dimensional geometry (such as points, lines, and polygons, collectively referred to as PRIMITIVES) as well as for drawing images and bitmaps.

The execution model for OpenGL can be described as client-server. An application program (the client) issues OpenGL commands that are interpreted and processed by an OpenGL implementation (the server). The application program and the OpenGL implementation can execute on a single computer or on two different computers. Some OpenGL state is stored in the address space of the application (client state), but the majority of it is stored in the address space of the OpenGL implementation (server state).

OpenGL commands are always processed in the order in which they are received by the server, although command completion may be delayed because of intermediate operations that cause OpenGL commands to be buffered. Out-of-order execution of OpenGL commands is not permitted. This means, for example, that a primitive will not be drawn until the previous primitive has been completely drawn. This in-order execution also applies to queries of state and framebuffer read operations. These commands return results that are consistent with complete execution of all previous commands.

Data binding for OpenGL occurs when commands are issued, not when they are executed. Data passed to an OpenGL command is interpreted when the command is issued and copied into OpenGL memory if needed. Subsequent changes to this data by the application have no effect on the data that is now stored within OpenGL.

1.4 The Framebuffer

OpenGL is an API for drawing graphics, and so the fundamental purpose for OpenGL is to transform data provided by an application into something that is visible on the display screen. This processing is often referred to as RENDERING. Typically, this processing is accelerated by specially designed hardware, but some or all operations of the OpenGL pipeline can be performed by a software implementation running on the CPU. It is transparent to the user of the OpenGL implementation how this division among the software and hardware is handled. The important thing is that the results of rendering conform to the results defined by the OpenGL specification.

The hardware that is dedicated to drawing graphics and maintaining the contents of the display screen is often called the GRAPHICS ACCELERATOR. Graphics accelerators typically have a region of memory that is dedicated to maintaining the contents of the display. Every visible picture element (pixel) of the display is represented by several bytes of memory on the graphics accelerator. A color display might have a byte of memory for each of red, green, and blue in order to represent the color value for each pixel. This so-called DISPLAY MEMORY is scanned (refreshed) a certain number of times per second in order to maintain a flicker-free representation on the display. Graphics accelerators also typically have a region of memory called OFFSCREEN MEMORY that is not displayable and is used to store things that aren't visible.

OpenGL assumes that allocation of the display memory and offscreen memory is handled by the window system. The window system decides which portions of memory may be accessed by OpenGL and how these portions are structured. In each environment in which OpenGL is supported, a small set of function calls tie OpenGL into that particular environment. In the Microsoft Windows environment, this set of routines is called WGL (pronounced "wiggle"). In the X Window System environment, this set of routines is called GLX. In the Macintosh environment, this set of routines is called NSOpenGL, CGL, or AGL. In each environment, this set of calls supports such things as allocating and deallocating regions of graphics memory, allocating and deallocating data structures called GRAPHICS CONTEXTS that maintain OpenGL state, selecting the current graphics context, selecting the region of graphics memory in which to draw, and synchronizing commands between OpenGL and the window system.

The region of graphics memory that is modified as a result of OpenGL rendering is called the FRAMEBUFFER. In a windowing system, the OpenGL notion of a default framebuffer corresponds to a window. Facilities in window-system-specific OpenGL routines let users select the default framebuffer characteristics for the window. The windowing system typically also clarifies how the OpenGL default framebuffer behaves when windows overlap. In a nonwindowed system, the OpenGL default framebuffer corresponds to the entire display.

A window that supports OpenGL rendering (i.e., a default framebuffer) may consist of some combination of the following:

- Up to four color buffers
- A depth buffer
- A stencil buffer
- A multisample buffer
- One or more auxiliary buffers

Most graphics hardware supports both a front buffer and a back buffer in order to perform DOUBLE BUFFERING. This allows the application to render into the (offscreen) back buffer while displaying the (visible) front buffer. When rendering is complete, the two buffers are swapped so that the completed rendering is now displayed as the front buffer and rendering can begin anew in the back buffer. When double buffering is used, the end user never sees the graphics when they are in the process of being drawn, only the finished image. This technique allows smooth animation at interactive rates.

Stereo viewing is supported by having a color buffer for the left eye and one for the right eye. Double buffering is supported by having both a front and a back buffer. A double-buffered stereo window will therefore have four color buffers: front left, front right, back left, and back right. A normal (non-stereo) double-buffered window will have a front buffer and a back buffer. A single-buffered window will have only a front buffer.

If 3D objects are to be drawn with hidden-surface removal, a DEPTH BUFFER is needed. This buffer stores the depth of the displayed object at each pixel. As additional objects are drawn, a depth comparison can be performed at each pixel to determine whether the new object is visible or obscured.

A STENCIL BUFFER is used for complex masking operations. A complex shape can be stored in the stencil buffer, and subsequent drawing operations can use the contents of the stencil buffer to determine whether to update each pixel.

Normally, when objects are drawn, a single decision is made as to whether the graphics primitive affects a pixel on the screen. The MULTISAMPLE BUFFER is a buffer that allows everything that is rendered to be sampled multiple times within each pixel in order to perform high-quality full-screen anti-aliasing without rendering the scene more than once. Each sample within a pixel contains color, depth, and stencil information, and the number of samples per pixel can be queried. When a window includes a multisample buffer, it does not include separate depth or stencil buffers. As objects are rendered, the color samples are combined to produce a single color value, and that color value is passed on to be written into the color buffer. Because multisample buffers contain multiple samples (often 2, 4, 8, or 16) of color, depth, and stencil for every pixel in the window, they can use up large amounts of offscreen graphics memory.

AUXILIARY BUFFERS are offscreen memory buffers that can store arbitrary data such as intermediate results from a multipass rendering algorithm. A framebuffer may have 1, 2, 3, 4, or even more associated auxiliary buffers.

In addition to the default framebuffer, OpenGL provides framebuffer objects. These are application-created framebuffers and are much more flexible than the window system default framebuffer. Framebuffer objects may have several buffers of different formats, including normalized formats (storing numbers in the range 0.0 to 1.0), signed normalized formats (storing numbers in the range −1.0 to 1.0), signed and unsigned integers, and floating-point numbers.

1.5 State

OpenGL was designed as a state machine for updating the contents of a framebuffer. The process of turning geometric primitives, images, and bitmaps into pixels on the screen is controlled by a fairly large number of state settings. These state settings are orthogonal to one another—setting one piece of state does not affect the others. Cumulatively, the state settings define the behavior of the OpenGL rendering pipeline and the way in which primitives are transformed into pixels on the display device.

OpenGL state is collected into a data structure called a GRAPHICS CONTEXT. Window-system-specific functions create and delete graphics contexts. Another window-system-specific call designates a graphics context and an OpenGL framebuffer that are used as the targets for subsequent OpenGL commands.

Quite a few server-side state values in OpenGL have just two states: on or off. To turn a mode on, you must pass the appropriate symbolic constant to the OpenGL command **glEnable**. To turn a mode off, you pass the symbolic constant to **glDisable**. You enable client-side state (such as pointers that define vertex arrays) with **glEnableClientState** and disable it with **glDisableClientState**.

glGet is a generic function that can query many of the components of a graphics context. Symbolic constants are defined for simple state items (e.g., GL_CURRENT_COLOR and GL_LINE_WIDTH), and these values can be passed as arguments to **glGet** to retrieve the current value of the indicated component of a graphics context. Variants of **glGet** return the state value as an integer, float, double, or boolean. More complex state values are returned by "get" functions that are specific to those state values, for instance, **glGetTexParameter**. Error conditions can be detected with the **glGetError** function.

1.6 Processing Pipeline

For specifying the behavior of OpenGL, the various operations are defined to be applied in a particular order, so we can also think of OpenGL as a GRAPHICS PROCESSING PIPELINE.

Let's start by looking at a block diagram of how OpenGL was defined up through OpenGL 1.5. Figure 1.1 is a diagram of the so-called FIXED FUNCTIONALITY of OpenGL. This diagram shows the fundamentals of how OpenGL has worked since its inception and is a simplified representation of how OpenGL still works with the ARB_compatibility extension. It shows the main features of the OpenGL pipeline for the purposes of this overview. Some new features were added to OpenGL in versions 1.1 through 1.5, but the basic architecture of OpenGL remained unchanged through OpenGL 3.0. We use the term *fixed functionality* because every OpenGL implementation supporting the ARB_compatibility extension is required to have the same functionality and a result that is consistent with the OpenGL specification for a given set of inputs. Both the set of operations and the order in which they occur are defined (fixed) by the OpenGL specification.

It is important to note that OpenGL implementations are not required to match precisely the order of operations shown in Figure 1.1. Implementations are free to modify the order of operations as long as the rendering results are consistent with the OpenGL specification. Many innovative software and hardware architectures have been designed to implement OpenGL, and most block diagrams of those implementations look nothing like Figure 1.1. However, the diagram does ground our discussion of the way the rendering process *appears* to work in OpenGL, even if the underlying implementation does things a bit differently.

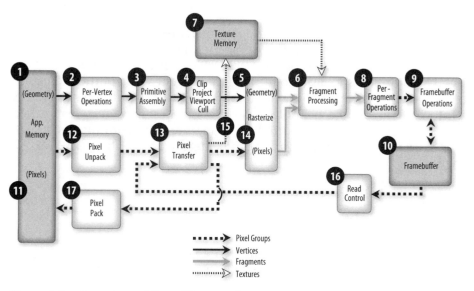

Figure 1.1   Overview of OpenGL operation

1.7   Drawing Geometry

As you can see from Figure 1.1, data for drawing geometry (points, lines, and polygons) starts off in application-controlled memory (1). This memory may be on the host CPU, or, with the help of some recent additions to OpenGL or under-the-covers data caching by the OpenGL implementation, it may actually reside in video memory on the graphics accelerator. Either way, the fact is that it is memory that contains geometry data that the application can cause to be drawn.

1.7.1   Geometry Specification

The geometric primitives supported in OpenGL are points, lines, line strips, line loops, polygons, triangles, triangle strips, triangle fans, quadrilaterals, and quadrilateral strips. There are four main ways to send geometry data to OpenGL. The first is the deprecated, but still available with ARB_compatibility, vertex-at-a-time method, which calls **glBegin** to start a primitive and calls **glEnd** to end it. In between are commands that set specific VERTEX ATTRIBUTES such as vertex position, color, normal, texture coordinates, secondary color, edge flags, and fog coordinates, using calls such as **glVertex**, **glColor**, **glNormal**, and **glTexCoord**. (A number of variants of these function calls allow the application to pass these values with various data types as well as to pass them by value or by reference.) Up through version 1.5 of OpenGL, there was no way to send arbitrary (user-defined) per-vertex data. The only per-vertex attributes allowed were those specifically defined in the OpenGL specification. OpenGL 2.0 added a method for sending arbitrary per-vertex data; that method is described in Section 7.7.

When the vertex-at-a-time method is used, the call to **glVertex** signals the end of the data definition for a single vertex, and it may also define the completion of a primitive. After **glBegin** is called and a primitive type is specified, a graphics primitive is completed whenever **glVertex** is called enough times to completely specify a primitive of the indicated type. For independent triangles, a triangle is completed every third time **glVertex** is called. For triangle strips, a triangle is completed when **glVertex** is called for the third time, and an additional connecting triangle is completed for each subsequent call to **glVertex**.

The second deprecated method of drawing primitives is to use vertex arrays. With this method, applications store vertex attributes in user-defined arrays, set up pointers to the arrays, and use **glDrawArrays**, **glMultiDrawArrays**,

glDrawElements, glMultiDrawElements, glDrawRangeElements, or **glInterleavedArrays** to draw a large number of primitives at once. Because these entry points can efficiently pass large amounts of geometry data to OpenGL, application developers are encouraged to use them for portions of code that are extremely performance critical. Using **glBegin** and **glEnd** requires a function call to specify each attribute of each vertex, so the function call overhead can become substantial when objects with thousands of vertices are drawn. In contrast, vertex arrays can be used to draw a large number of primitives with a single function call after the vertex data is organized into arrays. Processing the array data in this fashion can be faster because it is often more efficient for the OpenGL implementation to deal with data organized in this way. The current array of color values is specified with **glColorPointer**, the current array of vertex positions is specified with **glVertexPointer**, the current array of normal vectors is specified with **glNormalPointer**, and so on. The function **glInterleavedArrays** can specify and enable several interleaved arrays simultaneously (e.g., each vertex might be defined with three floating-point values representing a normal followed by three floating-point values representing a vertex position.)

The preceding two methods are referred to as drawing in IMMEDIATE MODE because primitives are rendered as soon as they have been specified. The third deprecated method involves storing either the vertex-at-a-time function calls or the vertex array calls in a DISPLAY LIST, an OpenGL-managed data structure that stores commands for later execution. Display lists can include commands to set state as well as commands to draw geometry. Display lists are stored on the server side and can be processed later with **glCallList** or **glCallLists**. This is not illustrated in Figure 1.1, but it is another way that data can be provided to the OpenGL processing pipeline. The definition of a display list is initiated with **glNewList**, and the display list definition is completed with **glEndList**. All the commands issued between those two calls become part of the display list, although certain OpenGL commands are not allowed within display lists. Depending on the implementation, DISPLAY LIST MODE can provide a performance advantage over immediate mode. Storing commands in a display list gives the OpenGL implementation an opportunity to optimize the commands in the display list for the underlying hardware. It also gives the implementation the chance to store the commands in a location that enables better drawing performance, perhaps even in memory on the graphics accelerator. Of course, some extra computation or data movement is usually required to implement these optimizations, so applications will typically see a performance benefit only if the display list is executed more than once.

The fourth method, now strongly preferred, added in version 1.5 of OpenGL permitted vertex array data to be stored in server-side memory. This mechanism typically provides the highest performance rendering because the data can be stored in memory on the graphics accelerator and need not be transferred over the I/O bus each time it is rendered. The API also supports the concept of efficiently streaming data from client to server. The **glBindBuffer** command creates a buffer object, and **glBufferData** and **glBufferSubData** specify the data values in such a buffer. **glMapBuffer** can map a buffer object into the client's address space and obtain a pointer to this memory so that data values can be specified directly. The command **glUnmapBuffer** must be called before the values in the buffer are accessed by subsequent GL rendering commands. **glBindBuffer** can also make a particular buffer object part of current state. If buffer object 0 is bound when calls are made to vertex array pointer commands such as **glColorPointer**, **glNormalPointer**, **glVertexPointer**, and so on, the pointer parameter to these calls is understood to be a pointer to client-side memory. When a buffer object other than 0 is bound, the pointer parameter is understood to be an offset into the currently bound buffer object. Subsequent calls to one of the vertex array drawing commands (e.g., **glMultiDrawArrays**) can thus obtain their vertex data from either client- or server-side memory or a combination thereof.

OpenGL supports the rendering of curves and surfaces with evaluators. Evaluators use a polynomial mapping to produce vertex attributes such as color, normal, and position that are sent to the vertex processing stage just as if they had been provided by the client. See the OpenGL specification for a complete description of this deprecated functionality.

1.7.2 Per-Vertex Operations

No matter which of these methods is used, the net result is that geometry data is transferred into the first stage of processing in OpenGL, VERTEX PROCESSING (2). Fixed-function vertex processing is deprecated but still available with the ARB_compatibility extension. At this point, vertex positions are transformed by the modelview and projection matrices, normals are transformed by the inverse transpose of the upper leftmost 3×3 matrix taken from the modelview matrix, texture coordinates are transformed by the texture matrices, lighting calculations are applied to modify the base color, texture coordinates may be automatically generated, color material state is applied, and point sizes are computed. All of these things are rigidly defined by the OpenGL specification. They are performed in a specific order, according to specific formulas, with specific items of OpenGL state controlling the process.

Because the most important things that occur in this stage are transformation and lighting, the vertex processing stage is sometimes called TRANSFORMATION AND LIGHTING, or, more familiarly, T&L. There is no application control to this process other than modifying OpenGL state values: turning lighting on or off with **glEnable/glDisable**; changing lighting attributes with **glLight** and **glLightModel**; changing material properties with **glMaterial**; or modifying the modelview matrix by calling matrix manipulation functions such as **glMatrixMode**, **glLoadMatrix**, **glMultMatrix**, **glRotate**, **glScale**, **glTranslate**. At this stage of processing, each vertex is treated independently. The vertex position computed by the transformation stage is used in subsequent clipping operations. The transformation process is discussed in detail in Section 1.9.

Lighting effects in OpenGL are controlled by manipulation of the attributes of one or more of the simulated light sources defined in OpenGL. The number of light sources supported by an OpenGL implementation is specifically limited to GL_MAX_LIGHTS. This value can be queried with **glGet** and must be at least 8. Each simulated light source in OpenGL has attributes that cause it to behave as a directional light source, a point light source, or a spotlight. Light attributes that can be adjusted by an application include the color of the emitted light, defined as ambient, diffuse, and specular RGBA intensity values; the light source position; attenuation factors that define how rapidly the intensity drops off as a function of distance; and direction, exponent, and cutoff factors for spotlights. These attributes can be modified for any light with **glLight**. Individual lights can be turned on or off by a call to **glEnable/glDisable** with a symbolic constant that specifies the affected light source.

Lighting produces a primary and secondary color for each vertex. The entire process of lighting can be turned on or off by a call to **glEnable/glDisable** with the symbolic constant GL_LIGHTING. If lighting is disabled, the values of the primary and secondary color are taken from the last color value set with the **glColor** command and the last secondary color set with the **glSecondaryColor** command.

The effects from enabled light sources are used in conjunction with surface material properties to determine the lit color at a particular vertex. Materials are characterized by the color of light they emit; the color of ambient, diffuse, and specular light they reflect; and their shininess. Material properties can be defined separately for front-facing surfaces and for back-facing surfaces and are specified with **glMaterial**.

Global lighting parameters are controlled with **glLightModel**. You can use this function to

- Set the value used as the global ambient lighting value for the entire scene.

- Specify whether the lighting calculations assume a local viewer or one positioned at infinity. (This affects the computation of specular reflection angles.)

- Indicate whether one- or two-sided lighting calculations are performed on polygons. (If one-sided, only front material properties are used in lighting calculations. Otherwise, normals are reversed on back-facing polygons and back material properties are used to perform the lighting computation.)

- Specify whether a separate specular color component is computed. (This specular component is later added to the result of the texturing stage to provide specular highlights.)

1.7.3 Primitive Assembly

After vertex processing, all the attributes associated with each vertex are completely determined. The vertex data is then sent on to a stage called PRIMITIVE ASSEMBLY (3). At this point the vertex data is collected into complete primitives. Points require a single vertex, lines require two, triangles require three, quadrilaterals require four, and general polygons can have an arbitrary number of vertices. For the vertex-at-a-time API, an argument to **glBegin** specifies the primitive type; for vertex arrays, the primitive type is passed as an argument to the function that draws the vertex array. The primitive assembly stage effectively collects enough vertices to construct a single primitive, and then this primitive is passed on to the next stage of processing. The reason this stage is needed is that at the very next stage, operations are performed on a set of vertices, and the operations depend on the type of primitive. In particular, clipping is done differently, depending on whether the primitive is a point, line, or polygon.

1.7.4 Primitive Processing

The next stage of processing (4), actually consists of several distinct steps that have been combined into a single box in Figure 1.1 just to simplify the diagram. The first step that occurs is clipping. This operation compares each primitive to the view volume, and with the ARB_compatibility extension, any user-defined clipping planes set by calling **glClipPlane**. If the primitive is completely within the view volume and the user-defined clipping planes, it is passed on for subsequent processing. If it is completely outside the view volume or the user-defined clipping planes, the primitive is rejected, and no further processing is required. If the primitive is partially in and partially out, it is divided (CLIPPED) in such a way that only the portion within the clip volume and the user-defined clipping planes is passed on for further processing.

Another operation that occurs at this stage is perspective projection. If the current view is a perspective view, each vertex has its x, y, and z components divided by its homogeneous coordinate w. Following this, each vertex is transformed by the current viewport transformation (set with **glDepthRange** and **glViewport**) to generate window coordinates. Certain OpenGL states can be set to cause an operation called CULLING to be performed on polygon primitives at this stage. With the computed window coordinates, each polygon primitive is tested to see whether it is facing away from the current viewing position. The culling state can be enabled with **glEnable**, and **glCullFace** can be called to specify that back-facing polygons will be discarded (culled), front-facing polygons will be discarded, or both will be discarded.

1.7.5 Rasterization

Geometric primitives that are passed through the OpenGL pipeline contain a set of data at each of the vertices of the primitive. At the next stage (5), primitives (points, lines, or polygons) are decomposed into smaller units corresponding to pixels in the destination framebuffer. This process is called RASTERIZATION. Each of these smaller units generated by rasterization is referred to as a FRAGMENT. For instance, a line might cover five pixels on the screen, and the process of rasterization converts the line (defined by two vertices) into five fragments. A fragment comprises a window coordinate and depth and other associated attributes such as color, texture coordinates, and so on. The values for each of these attributes are determined by interpolation between the values specified (or computed) at the vertices of the primitive. At the time they are rasterized, vertices have a primary color and a secondary color. The **glShadeModel** function specifies whether these color values are interpolated between the vertices (SMOOTH SHADING) or whether the color values for the last vertex of the primitive are used for the entire primitive (FLAT SHADING).

Each type of primitive has different rasterization rules and different OpenGL state. Points have a width controlled by **glPointSize** and other rendering attributes that are defined by **glPointParameter**. OpenGL 2.0 added the ability to draw an arbitrary shape at each point position by means of a texture called a POINT SPRITE. Lines have a width that is controlled with **glLineWidth** and a stipple pattern that is set with **glLineStipple**. Polygons have a stipple pattern that is set with **glPolygonStipple**. Polygons can be drawn as filled, outline, or vertex points depending only on the value set with **glPolygonMode**. The depth values for each fragment in a polygon can be modified by a value that is computed with the state set with **glPolygonOffset**. The orientation of polygons that are to be considered front facing can be set with **glFrontFace**. The process of smoothing the jagged appearance of a primitive is called ANTIALIASING. Primitive antialiasing can be enabled with **glEnable** and the appropriate symbolic constant: GL_POINT_SMOOTH, GL_LINE_SMOOTH, or GL_POLYGON_SMOOTH.

1.7.6 Fragment Processing

After fragments have been generated by rasterization, a number of operations occur on fragments. Collectively, these operations are called FRAGMENT PROCESSING (6). Fixed-function fragment processing has been deprecated, but remains available with the ARB_compatibility extensions. Perhaps the most important operation that occurs at this point is called TEXTURE MAPPING. In this operation, the texture coordinates associated with the fragment are used to access a region of graphics memory called TEXTURE MEMORY (7). OpenGL defines a lot of state values that affect how textures are accessed as well as how the retrieved values are applied to the current fragment. Many extensions have been defined to this area that is rather complex to begin with. We spend some time talking about texturing operations in Section 1.10.

Other operations that occur at this point are FOG (modifying the color of the fragment depending on its distance from the view point) and COLOR SUM (combining the values of the fragment's primary color and secondary color). Fog parameters are set with **glFog**, and secondary colors are vertex attributes that can be passed in with the vertex attribute command **glSecondaryColor** or that can be computed by the lighting stage.

1.7.7 Per-Fragment Operations

After fragment processing, fragments are submitted to a set of fairly simple operations called PER-FRAGMENT OPERATIONS (8). These include tests like the following:

- PIXEL OWNERSHIP TEST—Determines whether the destination pixel is visible or obscured by an overlapping window

- SCISSOR TEST—Clips fragments against a rectangular region set with **glScissor**

- ALPHA TEST—Decides whether to discard the fragment on the basis of the fragment's ALPHA value and the function set with **glAlphaFunc**

- STENCIL TEST—Compares the value in the stencil buffer with a reference value, using a comparison set with **glStencilFunc** and **glStencilOp**, by which it decides the fate of the fragment

- DEPTH TEST—Uses the function established with **glDepthFunc** to compare the depth of the incoming fragment to the depth stored in the frame-buffer

Blending, dithering, and logical operations are also considered per-fragment operations. The blending operation calculates the color to be written into the framebuffer using a blend of the fragment's color, the color stored in the framebuffer, and the blending state as established by **glBlendFunc**, **glBlendColor**, and **glBlendEquation**. Dithering is a method of trading spatial resolution for color resolution, but today's graphics accelerators contain enough framebuffer memory to make this trade-off unnecessary. The final fragment value is written into the framebuffer with the logical operation set by **glLogicOp**.

Each of the per-fragment operations is conceptually simple and nowadays can be implemented efficiently and inexpensively in hardware. Some of these operations also involve reading values from the framebuffer (i.e., color, depth, or stencil). With today's hardware, all these back-end rendering operations can be performed at millions of pixels per second, even those that require reading from the framebuffer.

1.7.8 Framebuffer Operations

Things that control or affect the whole framebuffer are called FRAMEBUFFER OPERATIONS (9). Certain OpenGL state controls the region of the framebuffer into which primitives are drawn. OpenGL supports display of stereo images as well as double buffering, so a number of choices are available for the rendering destination. Regions of the framebuffer are called BUFFERS and are referred to as the front, back, left, right, front left, front right, back left, back right, front and back, and aux0, aux1, and so on, up to the number of auxiliary buffers supported minus 1. Any of these buffers can be set as the destination for subsequent rendering operations with **glDrawBuffer**. Multiple buffers can be established as the destination for rendering with **glDrawBuffers**. Regions within the draw buffer(s) can be write protected. The **glColorMask** function determines whether writing is allowed to the red, green, blue, or alpha components of the destination buffer. The **glDepthMask** function determines whether the depth components of the destination buffer can be modified. The **glStencilMask** function controls the writing of particular bits in the stencil components of the destination buffer. Values in the framebuffer can be initialized with **glClear**. Values that will be used to initialize the color components, depth components, stencil components, and accumulation buffer components are set with **glClearColor**, **glClearDepth**, **glClearStencil**, and **glClearAccum**, respectively. The accumulation buffer operation can be specified with **glAccum**.

For performance, OpenGL implementations often employ a variety of buffering schemes in order to send larger batches of graphics primitives to the 3D graphics hardware. To make sure that all graphics primitives for a specific rendering context are progressing toward completion, an application should call **glFlush**. To make sure that all graphics primitives for a particular rendering context have finished rendering, an application should call **glFinish**. This command blocks until the effects of all previous commands have been completed. Blocking can be costly in terms of performance, so **glFinish** should be used sparingly.

The overall effect of these stages is that graphics primitives defined by the application are converted into pixels in the framebuffer for subsequent display. But so far, we have discussed only geometric primitives such as points, lines, and polygons. OpenGL also renders bitmap and image data.

1.8 Drawing Images

As mentioned previously, OpenGL has a great deal of support for drawing images in addition to its support for drawing 3D geometry. Although deprecated, they remain in the ARB_compatibility extension. In OpenGL parlance, images are called PIXEL RECTANGLES. The values that define a pixel rectangle start out in application-controlled memory, as shown in Figure 1.1 (11). Color or grayscale pixel rectangles are rendered into the framebuffer with **glDrawPixels**, and bitmaps are rendered into the framebuffer with **glBitmap**. Images that are destined for texture memory are specified with **glTexImage** or **glTexSubImage**. Up to a point, the same basic processing is applied to the image data supplied with each of these commands.

1.8.1 Pixel Unpacking

OpenGL reads image data provided by the application in a variety of formats. Parameters that define how the image data is stored in memory (length of each pixel row, number of rows to skip before the first one, number of pixels to skip before the first one in each row, etc.) can be specified with **glPixelStore**. So that operations on pixel data can be defined more precisely, pixels read from application memory are converted into a coherent stream of pixels by an operation referred to as PIXEL UNPACKING (12). When a pixel rectangle is transferred to OpenGL by a call like **glDrawPixels**, this operation applies the current set of pixel unpacking parameters to determine how the image data should be read and interpreted. As each pixel is read from memory, it is converted to a PIXEL GROUP that contains either a color, a depth, or a stencil value. If the pixel group consists of a color, the image data is destined for the color buffer in the framebuffer. If the pixel group consists of a depth value, the image data is destined for the depth buffer. If the pixel group consists of a stencil value, the image data is destined for the stencil buffer. Color values are made up of a red, a green, a blue, and an alpha component (i.e., RGBA) and are constructed from the input image data according to a set of rules defined by OpenGL. The result is a stream of RGBA values that are sent to OpenGL for further processing.

1.8.2 Pixel Transfer

After a coherent stream of image pixels is created, pixel rectangles undergo a series of operations called PIXEL TRANSFER (13). These operations are applied whenever pixel rectangles are transferred from the application to OpenGL (**glDrawPixels**, **glTexImage**, **glTexSubImage**), from OpenGL back to the application (**glReadPixels**), or when they are copied within OpenGL (**glCopyPixels**, **glCopyTexImage**, **glCopyTexSubImage**).

The behavior of the pixel transfer stage is modified with **glPixelTransfer**. This command sets state that controls whether red, green, blue, alpha, and depth values are scaled and biased. It can also set state that determines whether incoming color or stencil values are mapped to different color or stencil values through the use of a lookup table. The lookup tables used for these operations are specified with the **glPixelMap** command.

Some additional operations that occur at this stage are part of the OpenGL IMAGING SUBSET, which is an optional part of OpenGL. Hardware vendors that find it important to support advanced imaging capabilities will support the imaging subset in their OpenGL implementations, and other vendors will not support it. To determine whether the imaging subset is supported, applications need to call **glGetString** with the symbolic constant GL_EXTENSIONS. This returns a list of extensions supported by the implementation; the application should check for the presence of the string "ARB_imaging" within the returned extension string.

The pixel transfer operations that are defined to be part of the imaging subset are convolution, color matrix, histogram, min/max, and additional color lookup tables. Together, they provide powerful image processing and color correction operations on image data as it is being transferred to, from, or within OpenGL.

1.8.3 Rasterization and Back-End Processing

Following the pixel transfer stage, fragments are generated through rasterization of pixel rectangles in much the same way as they are generated from 3D geometry (14). This process, along with the current OpenGL state, determines where the image will be drawn in the framebuffer. Rasterization takes into account the current RASTER POSITION, which can be set with **glRasterPos** or **glWindowPos**, and the current zoom factor, which can be set with **glPixelZoom** and which causes an image to be magnified or reduced in size as it is drawn.

After fragments have been generated from pixel rectangles, they undergo the same set of fragment processing operations as geometric primitives (6) and then go on to the remainder of the OpenGL pipeline in exactly the same manner as geometric primitives, all the way until pixels are deposited in the framebuffer (8, 9, 10).

Pixel values provided through a call to **glTexImage** or **glTexSubImage** do not go through rasterization or the subsequent fragment processing but directly update the appropriate portion of texture memory (15).

1.8.4 Read Control

Pixel rectangles are read from the framebuffer and returned to application memory with **glReadPixels**. They can also be read from the framebuffer and written to another portion of the framebuffer with **glCopyPixels**, or they can be read from the framebuffer and written into texture memory with **glCopyTexImage** or **glCopyTexSubImage**. In all of these cases, the portion of the framebuffer that is to be read is controlled by the READ CONTROL stage of OpenGL and set with the **glReadBuffer** command (16).

The values read from the framebuffer are sent through the pixel transfer stage (13) in which various image processing operations can be performed. For copy operations, the resulting pixels are sent to texture memory or back into the framebuffer, depending on the command that initiated the transfer. For read operations, the pixels are formatted for storage in application memory under the control of the PIXEL PACKING stage (17). This stage is the mirror of the pixel unpacking stage (12), in that parameters that define how the image data is to be stored in memory (length of each pixel row, number of rows to skip before the first one, number of pixels to skip before the first one in each row, etc.) can be specified with **glPixelStore**. Thus, application developers enjoy a lot of flexibility in determining how the image data is returned from OpenGL into application memory.

1.9 Coordinate Transforms

The purpose of the OpenGL graphics processing pipeline is to convert three-dimensional descriptions of objects into a two-dimensional image that can be displayed. The ARB_compatibility extension retains many of the transformation functions. In many ways, this process is similar to using a camera to convert a real-world scene into a two-dimensional print. To accomplish the transformation from three dimensions to two, OpenGL defines several coordinate spaces and transformations between those spaces. Each coordinate space has some properties that make it useful for some part of the rendering process. The transformations defined by OpenGL afford applications a great deal of flexibility in defining the 3D-to-2D mapping. For success at writing shaders in the OpenGL Shading Language, understanding the various transformations and coordinate spaces used by OpenGL is essential.

In computer graphics, MODELING is the process of defining a numerical representation of an object that is to be rendered. For OpenGL, this usually means creating a polygonal representation of an object so that it can be drawn with the polygon primitives built into OpenGL. At a minimum, a polygonal representation of an object needs to include the coordinates of each vertex in each polygon and the connectivity information that defines the polygons. Additional data might include the color of each vertex, the surface normal at each vertex, one or more texture coordinates at each vertex, and so on.

In the past, modeling an object was a painstaking effort, requiring precise physical measurement and data entry. (This is one of the reasons the Utah teapot, modeled by Martin Newell in 1975, has been used in so many graphics images. It is an interesting object, and the numerical data is freely available. Several of the shaders presented in this book are illustrated with this object; see, for example, Color Plate 24.) More recently, a variety of modeling tools have become available, both hardware and software, and this has made it relatively easy to create numerical representations of three-dimensional objects that are to be rendered.

Three-dimensional object attributes, such as vertex positions and surface normals, are defined in OBJECT SPACE. This coordinate space is one that is convenient for describing the object that is being modeled. Coordinates are specified in units that are convenient to that particular object. Microscopic objects may be modeled in units of angstroms, everyday objects may be modeled in inches or centimeters, buildings might be modeled in feet or meters, planets could be modeled in miles or kilometers, and galaxies might be modeled in light years or parsecs. The origin of this coordinate system (i.e., the point (0, 0, 0)) is also something that is convenient for the object being modeled. For some objects, the origin might be placed at one corner of the object's three-dimensional bounding box. For other objects, it might be more convenient to define the origin at the centroid of the object. Because of its intimate connection with the task of modeling, this coordinate space is also often referred to as MODEL SPACE or the MODELING COORDINATE SYSTEM. Coordinates are referred to equivalently as object coordinates or modeling coordinates.

To compose a scene that contains a variety of three-dimensional objects, each of which might be defined in its own unique object space, we need a common coordinate system. This common coordinate system is called WORLD SPACE or the WORLD COORDINATE SYSTEM, and it provides a common frame of reference for all objects in the scene. Once all the objects in the scene are transformed into a single coordinate system, the spatial relationships between all the objects, the light sources, and the viewer are known. The units of this coordinate system are chosen in a way that is convenient for describing a scene. You might choose feet or meters if you are composing a scene that represents one of the rooms in your house, but you might choose city blocks as your units if you are composing a scene that represents a city skyline. The choice for the origin of this coordinate system is also arbitrary. You might define a three-dimensional bounding box for your scene and set the origin at the corner of the bounding box such that all of the other coordinates of the bounding box have positive values. Or you may want to pick an important point in your scene (the corner of a building, the location of a key character, etc.) and make that the origin.

After world space is defined, all the objects in the scene must be transformed from their own unique object coordinates into world coordinates. The transformation that takes coordinates from object space to world space is called the MODELING TRANSFORMATION. If the object's modeling coordinates are in feet but the world coordinate system is defined in terms of inches, the object coordinates must be scaled by a factor of 12 to produce world coordinates. If the object is defined to be facing forward but in the scene it needs to be facing backwards, a rotation must be applied to the object coordinates. A translation is also typically required to position the object at its desired location in world coordinates. All of these individual transformations can be put together into a single matrix, the MODEL TRANSFORMATION MATRIX, that represents the transformation from object coordinates to world coordinates.

After the scene has been composed, the viewing parameters must be specified. One aspect of the view is the vantage point (i.e., the eye or camera position) from which the scene will be viewed. Viewing parameters also include the focus point (also called the LOOKAT POINT or the direction in which the camera is pointed) and the up direction (e.g., the camera may be held sideways or upside down).

The viewing parameters collectively define the VIEWING TRANSFORMATION, and they can be combined into a matrix called the VIEWING MATRIX. A coordinate multiplied by this matrix is transformed from world space into EYE SPACE, also called the EYE COORDINATE SYSTEM. By definition, the origin of this coordinate system is at the viewing (or eye) position. Coordinates in this space are called EYE COORDINATES. The spatial relationships in the scene remain unchanged, but orienting the coordinate system in this way makes it easy to determine the distance from the viewpoint to various objects in the scene.

Although some 3D graphics APIs allow applications to separately specify the modeling matrix and the viewing matrix, OpenGL combines them into a single matrix called the MODELVIEW MATRIX. This matrix is defined to transform coordinates from object space into eye space (see Figure 1.2).

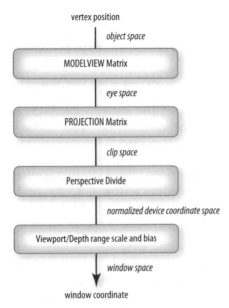

vertex position
object space
MODELVIEW Matrix
eye space
PROJECTION Matrix
clip space
Perspective Divide
normalized device coordinate space
Viewport/Depth range scale and bias
window space
window coordinate

Figure 1.2   Coordinate spaces and transforms in OpenGL

You can manipulate a number of matrices in OpenGL. Call the **glMatrixMode** function to select the modelview matrix or one of OpenGL's other matrices. Load the current matrix with the identity matrix by calling **glLoadIdentity**, or replace it with an arbitrary matrix by calling **glLoadMatrix**. Be sure you know what you're doing if you specify an arbitrary matrix—the transformation might give you a completely incomprehensible image! You can also multiply the current matrix by an arbitrary matrix by calling **glMultMatrix**.

Applications often start by setting the current modelview matrix to the view matrix and then add on the necessary modeling matrices. You can set the modelview matrix to a reasonable viewing transformation with the **gluLookAt** function. (This function is not part of OpenGL proper but is part of the OpenGL utility library that is provided with every OpenGL implementation.) OpenGL actually supports a stack of modelview matrices, and you can duplicate the topmost matrix and copy it onto the top of the stack with **glPushMatrix**. When this is done, you can concatenate other transformations to the topmost matrix with the functions **glScale**, **glTranslate**, and **glRotate** to define the modeling transformation for a particular three-dimensional object in the scene. Then, pop this topmost matrix off the stack with **glPopMatrix** to get back to the original view transformation matrix. Repeat the process for each object in the scene.

At the time light source positions are specified with the **glLight** function, they are transformed by the current modelview matrix. Therefore, light positions are stored within OpenGL as eye coordinates. You must set up the modelview matrix to perform the proper transformation before light positions are specified, or you won't get the lighting effects that you expect. The lighting calculations that occur in OpenGL are defined to happen on a per-vertex basis in the eye coordinate system. For the necessary reflection computations, light positions and surface normals must be in the same coordinate system. OpenGL implementations often choose to do lighting calculations in eye space; therefore, the incoming surface normals have to be transformed into eye space as well. You accomplish this by transforming surface normals by the inverse transpose of the upper leftmost 3×3 matrix taken from the modelview matrix. At that point, you can apply the per-vertex lighting formulas defined by OpenGL to determine the lit color at each vertex.

After coordinates have been transformed into eye space, the next thing is to define a viewing volume. This is the region of the three-dimensional scene that is visible in the final image. The transformation that takes the objects in the viewing volume into CLIP SPACE (also known as the CLIPPING COORDINATE SYSTEM, a coordinate space that is suitable for clipping) is called the PROJECTION TRANSFORMATION. In OpenGL, you establish the projection transformation by calling **glMatrixMode** to select the projection matrix and then setting this matrix appropriately. Parameters that may go into creating an appropriate projection matrix are the field of view (how much of the scene is visible), the aspect ratio (the horizontal field of view may differ from the vertical field of view), and near and far clipping planes to eliminate things that are too far away or too close (for perspective projections, weirdness will occur if you try to draw things that are at or behind the viewing position). Three utility functions set the projection matrix: **glOrtho**, **glFrustum**, and **gluPerspective**. The difference between these functions is that **glOrtho** defines a parallel projection (i.e., parallel lines in the scene are projected to parallel lines in the final two-dimensional image), whereas **glFrustum** and **gluPerspective** define perspective projections (i.e., parallel lines in the scene are foreshortened to produce a vanishing point in the image, such as railroad tracks converging to a point in the distance).

FRUSTUM CLIPPING is the process of eliminating any graphics primitives that lie outside an axis-aligned cube in clip space. This cube is defined such that the x, y, and z components of the clip space coordinate are less than or equal to the w component for the coordinate, and greater than or equal to $-w$ (i.e., $-w \leq x \leq w$, $-w \leq y \leq w$, and $-w \leq z \leq w$). Graphics primitives (or portions thereof) that lie outside this cube are discarded. Frustum clipping is always performed on all incoming primitives in OpenGL. USER CLIPPING, on the other hand, is a feature that can be enabled or disabled by the application. Applications can call **glClipPlane** to specify one or more clipping planes that further restrict the size of the viewing volume, and each clipping plane can be individually enabled with **glEnable**. At the time user clipping planes are specified, OpenGL transforms them into eye space using the inverse of the current modelview matrix. Each plane specified in this manner defines a half-space, and only the portions of primitives that lie within the intersection of the view volume and all of the enabled half-spaces defined by user clipping planes are drawn.

The next step in the transformation of vertex positions is the perspective divide. This operation divides each component of the clip space coordinate by the homogeneous coordinate w. The resulting x, y, and z components range from $[-1,1]$, and the resulting w coordinate is always 1, so it is no longer needed. In other words, all the visible graphics primitives are transformed into a cubic region between the point $(-1, -1, -1)$ and the point $(1, 1, 1)$. This is the NORMALIZED DEVICE COORDINATE SPACE, which is an intermediate space that allows the viewing area to be properly mapped onto a viewport of arbitrary size and depth.

Pixels within a window on the display device aren't referred to with floating-point coordinates from -1 to 1; they are usually referred to with coordinates defined in the WINDOW COORDINATE SYSTEM, where x values range from 0 to the width of the window minus 1, and y values range from 0 to the height of the window minus 1. Therefore, one more transformation step is required. The VIEWPORT TRANSFORMATION specifies the mapping from normalized device coordinates into window coordinates. You specify this mapping by calling the OpenGL functions **glViewport**, which specifies the mapping of the x and y coordinates, and **glDepthRange**, which specifies the mapping of the z coordinate. Graphics primitives are rasterized in the window coordinate system.

1.10 Texturing

The area of texture mapping is one of the more complex areas of the OpenGL API. It has been extended more often than most of the other areas of OpenGL primarily because this was the area of graphics for which hardware was the least mature when OpenGL was defined in the early 1990s. The programmability added through the OpenGL Shading Language in OpenGL 2.0 makes this area much more straightforward, but the existing OpenGL APIs are still used to create, modify, and define the behavior of textures. This section describes the texturing functionality as it existed for OpenGL 1.5. Some significant changes have been made to this model by OpenGL 2.0, particularly to the concept of texture units, and are described later in this book. Additional texture maps were added in OpenGL 2.1, OpenGL 3.0, and OpenGL 3.1.

OpenGL currently supports eight basic types of texture maps: one-dimensional, two-dimensional, three-dimensional, cube maps, one-dimensional array, two-dimensional array, texture buffer, and rectangle. (Only one- and two-dimensional textures were supported in OpenGL 1.0.) A 1D TEXTURE is an array containing *width* pixel values, a 2D TEXTURE is an array containing *width* × *height* pixel values, and a 3D TEXTURE is an array containing *width* × *height* × *depth* pixel values. A CUBE MAP TEXTURE contains six two-dimensional textures: one for each major axis direction (i.e., ±*x*, ±*y*, and ±*z*).

OpenGL has the notion of a TEXTURE UNIT. A texture unit corresponds to the underlying piece of graphics hardware that performs the various texturing operations. With OpenGL 1.3, support was added for multiple texture units. Each texture unit maintains the following state for performing texturing operations:

- Enabled/disabled state of the texture unit

- Texture matrix stack that for transforming incoming texture coordinates

- State used for automatic texture coordinate generation

- Texture environment state

- Current 1D texture

- Current 2D texture

- Current 3D texture

- Current cube map texture

Commands to set the state in the preceding list operate on the ACTIVE TEXTURE UNIT. Texture units are numbered from 0 to GL_MAX_TEXTURE_UNITS – 1 (a value that can be queried with **glGet**), and the active texture unit can be set with **glActiveTexture** with a symbolic constant indicating the desired texture unit. Subsequent commands to set state in the preceding list operate on only the active texture unit. A texture unit can be enabled for 1D, 2D, 3D, or cube map texturing by calling **glEnable** with the appropriate symbolic constant.

The active texture unit specifies the texture unit accessed by commands involving texture coordinate processing. Such commands include those accessing the current texture matrix stack (if GL_MATRIX_MODE is GL_TEXTURE), **glTexGen**, and **glEnable/glDisable** (if any enumerated value for texture coordinate generation is selected), as well as queries of the current texture coordinates and current raster texture coordinates. The active texture unit selector also selects the texture unit accessed by commands involving texture image processing. Such commands include all variants of **glTexEnv**, **glTexParameter**, and **glTexImage** commands; **glBindTexture**; **glEnable/glDisable** for any texture target (e.g., GL_TEXTURE_ 2D); and queries of all such state.

A TEXTURE OBJECT is created as follows: call **glBindTexture** and provide a texture target (a symbolic constant that indicates whether the texture will be a 1D, 2D, 3D, or cube map texture) and a previously unused texture name (an integer other than zero) that can be used to refer to the newly created texture object. The newly created texture object also becomes active and is used in subsequent texturing operations. If **glBindTexture** is called with a texture name that has already been used, that previously created texture becomes active. In this way, an application can create any number of textures and switch between them easily.

After a texture object has been created, the pixel values that define the texture can be provided. Pixel values for a 3D texture can be supplied by **glTexImage3D**, pixel values for 2D or cube map textures can be provided by **glTexImage2D**, and pixel values for a 1D texture can be specified by **glTexImage1D**. In versions 1.0–1.5 of OpenGL, when any of these three commands was used, each dimension of the texture map had to be a size that was a power of 2 (including the border width). OpenGL 2.0 allows textures to have sizes that are not restricted to being powers of 2. These functions all work in the same way as **glDrawPixels**, except that the pixels constituting a texture are deposited into texture memory before rasterization. If only a portion of a texture needs to be respecified, the **glTexSubImage1D/2D/3D** functions can be used. When any of these three commands is used, there is no power-of-2 restriction on the texture size. Textures can be created or modified with values copied from framebuffer memory by **glCopyTexImage1D/2D** or **glCopyTexSubImage1D/2D/3D**.

OpenGL also provides a method for specifying textures with compressed image formats. Applications can use the commands **glCompressedTexImage1D/2D/3D** and **glCompressedTexSubImage1D/2D/3D** to create and store compressed textures in texture memory. Compressed textures may use significantly less memory on the graphics accelerator and thereby enhance an application's functionality or performance. Standard

OpenGL does not define any particular compressed image formats, so applications need to query the extension string in order to determine the compressed texture formats supported by a particular implementation.

Each of the preceding texture creation commands includes a LEVEL-OF-DETAIL argument that supports the creation of MIPMAP TEXTURES. A mipmap texture is an ordered set of arrays representing the same image. Each array has a resolution that is half the previous one in each dimension. The idea behind mipmaps is that more pleasing final images will result if the texture to be used has roughly the same resolution as the object being drawn on the display. If a mipmap texture is supplied, OpenGL can automatically choose the appropriately sized texture (i.e., MIPMAP LEVEL) for use in drawing the object on the display. Interpolation between the TEXELS (pixels that comprise a texture) of two mipmap levels can also be performed. Objects that are textured with mipmap textures can therefore be rendered with high quality, no matter how they change size on the display.

After a texture object has been defined and bound to a texture unit, properties other than the pixels that define the texture can be modified with the command **glTexParameter**. This command sets parameters that control how the texture object is treated when it is specified, changed, or accessed. Texture object parameters include

- The wrapping behavior in each dimension—Whether the texture repeats, clamps, or is mirrored when texture coordinates go outside the range [0,1]

- The minification filter—How the texture is to be sampled if the mapping from texture space to window space causes the texture image to be made smaller than a one-to-one pixel mapping in order to be mapped onto the surface

- The magnification filter—How the texture is to be sampled if the mapping from texture space to window space causes the texture image to be made larger than a one-to-one pixel mapping in order to be mapped onto the surface

- The border color to be used if the wrapping behavior indicates clamping to a border color

- The priority to be assigned to the texture—A value from [0,1] that tells OpenGL the importance of performance for this texture

- Values for clamping and biasing the level-of-detail value that is automatically computed by OpenGL

- The level that is defined as the base (highest-resolution) level for a mipmap texture

- The level that is defined as the maximum (lowest-resolution) level for a mipmap texture

- Depth comparison values—Whether a comparison operation should be performed when the texture is accessed, what type of comparison operation should be performed, and how to treat the result of the comparison (these values are used with depth textures to implement shadowing)

- A value that signifies whether mipmap levels are to be computed automatically by OpenGL whenever the base level is specified or modified

The manner in which a texture value is applied to a graphics primitive is controlled by the parameters of the texture environment, which are set with the **glTexEnv** function. The set of fixed formulas for replacing an object color with a value computed through texture access is rather lengthy. Suffice it to say that texture functions include replacement, modulation, decal application, blending, adding, enabling point sprites, and even more complex combining of red, green, blue, and alpha components. A wide variety of texturing effects can be achieved with the flexibility provided by the **glTexEnv** function. This function can also specify an additional per-texture-unit level-of-detail bias that is added to the per-texture-object level-of-detail bias previously described.

OpenGL supports the concept of multitexturing, by which the results of more than one texture access are combined to determine the value of the fragment. Each texture unit has a texture environment function. Texture units are connected serially. The first texture unit computes a fragment value by using the texture value that it reads from texture memory and its texture environment function, and passes on the result to be used as the input fragment value for the second texture unit. This fragment value is used together with the texture environment function for the second texture unit and the texture value read from texture memory by the second texture unit to provide the input fragment value for the third texture unit. This process is repeated for all enabled texture units.

After texture objects have been defined and one or more texture units have been properly set up and enabled, texturing is performed on all subsequent graphics primitives. Texture coordinates are supplied at each vertex with **glTexCoord** or **glMultiTexCoord** (for use with vertex-at-a-time entry points) or as an array indicated by **glTexCoordPointer** (for use with vertex array commands). The **glMultiTexCoord** command specifies texture coordinates that are to be operated on by a specific texture unit. This command specifies the texture unit as well as the texture coordinates to be used. The command **glTexCoord** is equivalent to the command **glMultiTexCoord** with its texture parameter set to GL_TEXTURE0. For vertex arrays, it is necessary to call **glClientActiveTexture** between each call to **glTexCoordPointer** in order to specify different texture coordinate arrays for different texture units.

Texture coordinates can also be generated automatically by OpenGL. Parameters for controlling automatic texture coordinate generation are set on a per-texture unit basis with the **glTexGen** command. This function lets the application select a texture generation function and supply coefficients for that function for the currently active texture unit. Supported texture generation functions are object linear (useful for automatically generating texture coordinates for terrain models), eye linear (useful for producing dynamic contour lines on moving objects), and sphere map (useful for a type of environment mapping that requires just one texture).

When texture coordinates have been sent to OpenGL or generated by the texture unit's texture generation function, they are transformed by the texture unit's current texture transformation matrix. The **glMatrixMode** command selects the texture matrix stack for modification, and subsequent matrix commands modify the texture matrix stack of the currently active texture unit. The current texture transformation matrix can translate the texture across the object, rotate it, stretch it, shrink it, and so on. Both texture generation and texture transformation are defined by OpenGL to occur as part of vertex processing (i.e., they are performed once per-vertex before rasterization).

TEXTURE ACCESS is the process by which the texture coordinates are used by a texture unit to access the enabled texture for that unit. It occurs after rasterization of the graphics primitive and interpolation of the transformed texture coordinates. The texture access is performed according to the bound texture object's parameters for filtering, wrapping, computed level-of-detail, and so on.

After a texture value has been retrieved, it is combined with the incoming color value according to the texture function established by calling **glTexEnv**. This operation is called TEXTURE APPLICATION. This computation produces a new fragment color value that is used for all subsequent processing of the fragment. Both texture access and texture application are defined to occur on every fragment that results from the rasterization process.

1.11 Summary

This chapter has briefly reviewed the fundamentals of the OpenGL API. In it, we've touched on some of the deprecated OpenGL function calls still available with the ARB_compatibility extension. If you haven't used OpenGL for quite some time, the hope is that this review chapter has been enough to orient you properly for the task of using the OpenGL Shading Language to write shaders. If you have been using another 3D graphics programming API, the hope is that this short overview is enough to get you started using OpenGL and writing your own shaders. If not, the next section lists a number of resources for learning more about OpenGL.

1.12 Further Information

The Web site http://opengl.org has the latest information for the OpenGL community, forums for developers, and links to a variety of demos and technical information. OpenGL developers should bookmark this site and visit it often.

The standard reference book for the OpenGL API is the *OpenGL Programming Guide, Seventh Edition* (2010) by Dave Shreiner and the Khronos OpenGL ARB Working Group. Another useful OpenGL book is *OpenGL SuperBible, Fourth Edition,* by Richard S. Wright Jr., Benjamin Lipchak, and Nicholas Haemel (2008).

A good overview of OpenGL is provided in the technical paper *The Design of the OpenGL Graphics Interface* by Mark Segal and Kurt Akeley (1994). Of course, the definitive document on OpenGL is the specification itself, *The OpenGL Graphics System: A Specification (Version 3.1)*, by Mark Segal and Kurt Akeley, edited by Jon Leech (2009).

The OpenGL.org Web site, http://opengl.org, is also a good source for finding source code for OpenGL example programs. Another useful site is Tom Nuyden's site at http://delphi3d.net. The hardware vendors that support OpenGL typically provide lots of example programs, especially for newer OpenGL functionality and extensions. The AMD and NVIDIA Web sites are particularly good in this regard.

[1] *AMD developer Web site.* http://developer.amd.com

[2] *NVIDIA developer Web site.* http://developer.nvidia.com

[3] *Delphi3D Web site.* http://delphi3d.net

[4] OpenGL Architecture Review Board, *OpenGL Reference Manual, Fourth Edition: The Official Reference to OpenGL, Version 1.4*, Editor: Dave Shreiner, Addison-Wesley, Reading, Massachusetts, 2004.

[5] *OpenGL, official Web site.* http://opengl.org

[6] Segal, Mark, and Kurt Akeley, *The OpenGL Graphics System: A Specification (Version 2.0)*, Editor (V1.1): Chris Frazier, (V1.2–V3.1): Jon Leech, (V2.0): Jon Leech and Pat Brown, March 2009. www.opengl.org/documentation/specs/

[7] Segal, Mark, and Kurt Akeley, *The Design of the OpenGL Graphics Interface*, Silicon Graphics Inc., 1994. wwws.sun.com/software/graphics/opengl/OpenGLdesign.pdf

[8] Shreiner, Dave, and the Khronos OpenGL ARB Working Group, *OpenGL Programming Guide, Seventh Edition: The Official Guide to Learning OpenGL, Versions 3.0 and 3.1*, Addison-Wesley, Boston, Massachusetts, 2010.

[9] Wright, Richard, Benjamin Lipchak, and Nicholas Haemel, *OpenGL SuperBible, Fourth Edition,* Sams Publishing, 2008. www.starstonesoftware.com/OpenGL/opengl_superbbile.htm

Chapter 2

Basics

This chapter introduces the OpenGL Shading Language to get you started writing your own shaders as quickly as possible. When you finish reading this chapter, you should understand how programmability has been added to OpenGL and be ready to tackle the details of the shading language description in the next three chapters and the simple example in Chapter 6. After that, you can learn more details about the API that supports the shading language or explore the examples contained in the later chapters.

2.1 Introduction to the OpenGL Shading Language

This book helps you learn and use a high-level graphics programming language formally called the OPENGL SHADING LANGUAGE. Informally, this language is sometimes referred to as GLSL. This language has been made part of the OpenGL standard as of OpenGL 2.0 and has since further evolved through OpenGL 3.0.

The recent trend in graphics hardware has been to replace fixed functionality with programmability in areas that have grown exceedingly complex. Two such areas are vertex processing and fragment processing. Vertex processing involves the operations that occur at each vertex, most notably transformation and lighting. Fragments are per-pixel data structures that are created by the rasterization of graphics primitives. A fragment contains all the data necessary to update a single location in the framebuffer. Fragment processing consists of the operations that occur on a per-fragment basis, most notably reading from texture memory and applying the texture value(s) at each fragment. With the OpenGL Shading Language, the fixed functionality stages for vertex processing and fragment processing have been replaced with programmable stages that can do everything the fixed functionality stages could do—and a whole lot more. The OpenGL Shading Language allows application programmers to express the processing that occurs at those programmable points of the OpenGL pipeline.

The OpenGL Shading Language code that is intended for execution on one of the OpenGL programmable processors is called a SHADER. The term OPENGL SHADER is sometimes used to differentiate a shader written in the OpenGL Shading Language from a shader written in another shading language such as RenderMan. Because two programmable processors are defined in OpenGL, there are two types of shaders: VERTEX SHADERS and FRAGMENT SHADERS. OpenGL provides mechanisms for compiling shaders and linking them to form executable code called a PROGRAM. A program contains one or more EXECUTABLES that can run on the programmable processing units.

The OpenGL Shading Language has its roots in C and has features similar to RenderMan and other shading languages. The language has a rich set of types, including vector and matrix types to make code more concise for typical 3D graphics operations. A special set of type qualifiers manages the unique forms of input and output needed by shaders. Some mechanisms from C++, such as function overloading based on argument types and the capability to declare variables where they are first needed instead of at the beginning of blocks, have also been borrowed. The language includes support for loops, subroutine calls, and conditional expressions. An extensive set of built-in functions provides many of the capabilities needed for implementing shading algorithms. In brief,

- The OpenGL Shading Language is a high-level procedural language.

- As of OpenGL 2.0, it is part of standard OpenGL, the leading cross-platform, operating-environment-independent API for 3D graphics and imaging.

- The same language, with a small set of differences, is used for both vertex and fragment shaders.

- It is based on C and C++ syntax and flow control.

- It natively supports vector and matrix operations since these are inherent to many graphics algorithms.

- It is stricter with types than C and C++, and functions are called by value-return.

- It uses type qualifiers rather than reads and writes to manage input and output.

- It imposes no practical limits to a shader's length, nor does the shader length need to be queried.

The following sections contain some of the key concepts that you will need to understand in order to use the OpenGL Shading Language effectively. The concepts are covered in much more detail later in the book, but this introductory chapter should help you understand the big picture.

2.2 Why Write Shaders?

Until recently, OpenGL has presented application programmers with a configurable but static interface for putting graphics on the display device. As described in Chapter 1, you could think of OpenGL as a sequence of operations that occurred on geometry or image data as it was sent through the graphics hardware to be displayed on the screen. Various parameters of these pipeline stages could be configured to select variations on the processing that occurred for that pipeline stage. But neither the fundamental operation of the OpenGL graphics pipeline nor the order of operations could be changed through the OpenGL API.

By exposing support for traditional rendering mechanisms, OpenGL has evolved to serve the needs of a fairly broad set of applications. If your particular application was well served by the traditional rendering model presented by OpenGL, you may never have felt the need to write shaders. But if you have ever been frustrated because OpenGL did not allow you to define area lights or because lighting calculations are performed per-vertex rather than per-fragment or, if you have run into any of the many limitations of the traditional OpenGL rendering model, you may need to write your own OpenGL shader.

The OpenGL Shading Language and its supporting OpenGL API entry points allows *application developers* to define the processing that occurs at key points in the OpenGL processing pipeline by using a high-level programming language specifically designed for this purpose. These key points in the pipeline are defined to be programmable in order to give developers complete freedom to define the processing that occurs. This lets developers utilize the underlying graphics hardware to achieve a much wider range of rendering effects.

To get an idea of the range of effects possible with OpenGL shaders, take a minute to browse through the color images that are included in this book. This book presents a variety of shaders that only begin to scratch the surface of what is possible. With each new generation of graphics hardware, more complex rendering techniques can be implemented as OpenGL shaders and can be used in real-time rendering applications. Here's a brief list of what's possible with OpenGL shaders:

- Increasingly realistic materials—metals, stone, wood, paints, and so on

- Increasingly realistic lighting effects—area lights, soft shadows, and so on

- Natural phenomena—fire, smoke, water, clouds, and so on

- Advanced rendering effects—global illumination, ray-tracing, and so on

- Nonphotorealistic materials—painterly effects, pen-and-ink drawings, simulation of illustration techniques, and so on

- New uses for texture memory—storage of normals, gloss values, polynomial coefficients, and so on

- Procedural textures—dynamically generated 2D and 3D textures, not static texture images

- Image processing—convolution, unsharp masking, complex blending, and so on

- Animation effects—key frame interpolation, particle systems, procedurally defined motion

- User programmable antialiasing methods

- General computation—sorting, mathematical modeling, fluid dynamics, and so on

Many of these techniques have been available before now only through software implementations. If they were at all possible through OpenGL, they were possible only in a limited way. The fact that these techniques can now be implemented with hardware acceleration provided by dedicated graphics hardware means that rendering performance can be increased dramatically and at the same time the CPU can be off-loaded so that it can perform other tasks.

2.3 OpenGL Programmable Processors

The introduction of programmable vertex and fragment processors is the biggest change to OpenGL since its inception and is the reason a high-level shading language is needed. In Chapter 1, we discussed the OpenGL pipe-line and the fixed functionality that implements vertex processing and fragment processing. With the introduction of programmability, the fixed functionality vertex processing and fixed functionality fragment processing are disabled when an OpenGL Shading Language program is made current (i.e., made part of the current rendering state).

Figure 2.1 shows the OpenGL processing pipeline when the programmable processors are active. In this case, the fixed functionality vertex and frag-ment processing shown in Figure 1.1 are replaced by programmable vertex and fragment processors, as shown in Figure 2.1. All other parts of the OpenGL processing pipeline remain the same.

This diagram illustrates the stream processing nature of OpenGL made possible by the programmable processors that are defined as part of the OpenGL Shading Language. Data flows from the application to the vertex processor, on to the fragment processor, and ultimately to the framebuffer. The OpenGL Shading Language was carefully designed to allow hardware implementations to perform parallel processing of both vertices and frag-ments. This gives graphics hardware vendors the opportunity to produce faster graphics hardware with more parallel processors with each new gen-eration of hardware.

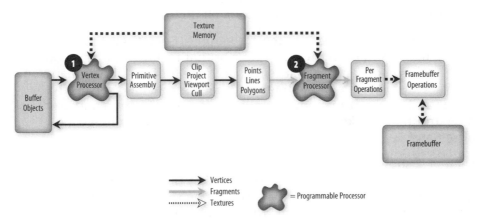

Figure 2.1   OpenGL logical diagram showing programmable processors for vertex and fragment shaders rather than fixed functionality

2.3.1 Vertex Processor

The traditional VERTEX PROCESSOR is a configurable unit that operates on incoming vertex values and their associated data. The vertex processor usually performs traditional graphics operations such as the following:

- Vertex transformation

- Normal transformation and normalization

- Texture coordinate generation

- Texture coordinate transformation

- Lighting

- Color material application

The vertex processor has evolved from a configurable unit into a programmable unit. Because of its general-purpose programmability, this processor can also be used to perform a variety of other computations. Shaders that are intended to run on this processor are called VERTEX SHADERS. Vertex shaders can specify a completely general sequence of operations to be applied to each vertex and its associated data. Vertex shaders that perform some of the computations in the preceding list must contain the code for all desired functionality from the preceding list. For instance, it is not possible to have the existing fixed functionality perform the vertex and normal transformation but to have a vertex shader perform a specialized lighting function. The vertex shader must be written to perform all three functions.

The vertex processor does not replace graphics operations that require knowledge of several vertices at a time or that require topological knowledge. OpenGL operations that remain as fixed functionality in between the vertex processor and the fragment processor include perspective divide and viewport mapping, primitive assembly, frustum and user clipping, frontface/backface determinaton, culling, polygon mode, polygon offset, and depth range.

Figure 2.2 shows the data values that are used as inputs to the vertex processor and the data values that are produced by the vertex processor. Vertex shaders express the algorithm that executes on the vertex processor to produce output values based on the provided input values. Type qualifiers that are defined as part of the OpenGL Shading Language manage the input to the vertex processor and the output from it.

Global variables defined in a vertex shader can be qualified as IN VARIABLES. These represent values that are frequently passed from the application to the

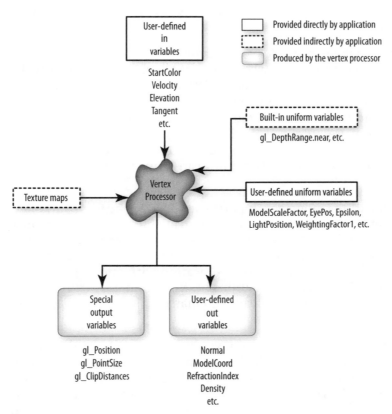

Figure 2.2 Vertex processor inputs and outputs

vertex processor. Because this type of variable is used only for data from the application that defines vertices, it is permitted only as part of a vertex shader.

In the OpenGL API these are called GENERIC VERTEX attributes. (Historically, generic vertex attributes replaced the now deprecated SPECIALIZED vertex attributes such as **glColor, glNormal, glMultiTexCoord,** and **glVertex.**) Applications can provide attribute values with vertex array calls, so they can change as often as every vertex. Generic vertex attributes are defined and referenced by numbers from 0 up to some implementation-dependent maximum value. The command **glVertexAttrib** sends generic vertex attributes to OpenGL by specifying the index of the generic attribute to be modified and the value for that generic attribute.

Vertex shaders can access these generic vertex attributes through user-defined in variables. Another OpenGL command, **glBindAttribLocation,** allows an application to tie together the index of a generic vertex attribute to the user-defined in variable.

Global variables that are available to either the vertex processor or the fragment processor are UNIFORM VARIABLES. Uniform variables typically provide values that change relatively infrequently. A shader can be written so that it is parameterized with uniform variables. The application can provide initial values for these uniform variables, and the end user can manipulate them through a graphical user interface to achieve a variety of effects with a single shader. But uniform variables cannot be specified within **glDrawArrays** or other OpenGL drawing commands, so they can change at most once per primitive.

The OpenGL Shading Language supports user-defined uniform variables. Applications can make arbitrary data values available directly to a shader through user-defined uniform variables. **glGetUniformLocation** obtains the location of a user-defined uniform variable that has been defined as part of a shader. Data can be loaded into this location with another new OpenGL command, **glUniform**. Variations of this command facilitate loading of floating-point, integer, Boolean, and matrix values, as well as arrays of these.

Another new feature is the capability of vertex processors to read from texture memory. This allows vertex shaders to implement displacement mapping algorithms, among other things. For accessing mipmap textures, level of detail can be specified directly in the shader. Existing OpenGL parameters for texture maps define the behavior of the filtering operation, borders, and wrapping.

Conceptually, the vertex processor operates on one vertex at a time (but an implementation may have multiple vertex processors that operate in parallel). The vertex shader is executed once for each vertex passed to OpenGL. The design of the vertex processor is focused on the functionality needed to transform and light a single vertex. Output from the vertex shader is accomplished partly with special output variables. Vertex shaders must compute the homogeneous position of the coordinate in clip space and store the result in the special output variable *gl_Position*. Values to be used during user clipping and point rasterization can be stored in the special output variables *gl_ClipDistances* and *gl_PointSize*.

Global variables that define data that is passed from the vertex processor to the rasterizer are called OUT VARIABLES. They may be further qualified with one of the interpolation qualifiers smooth, noperspective, and flat. If qualified smooth (the default), the out values are gathered together by the rasterizer, and perspective-correct interpolation is performed to provide a value at each fragment for use by the fragment shader. For noperspective, the values are interpolated without perspective correction. A flat qualified out tells the rasterizer to pass only the value of the provoking vertex to the fragment shader. A vertex shader can use a user-defined varying variable to pass along anything that needs to be interpolated: colors, normals (useful for per-fragment lighting computations), texture coordinates, model coordinates, and other arbitrary values.

There is actually no harm (other than a possible loss of performance) in having a vertex shader calculate more varying variables than are needed by the fragment shader. A warning may be generated if the fragment shader consumes fewer varying variables than the vertex shader produces. But you may have good reasons to use a somewhat generic vertex shader with a variety of fragment shaders. The fragment shaders can be written to use a subset of the varying variables produced by the vertex shader. Developers of applications that manage a large number of shaders may find that reducing the costs of shader development and maintenance is more important than squeezing out a tiny bit of additional performance.

The vertex processor output (special output variables and user-defined out variables) is sent to subsequent stages of processing that are defined exactly the same as they are for fixed-function processing: primitive assembly, user clipping, frustum clipping, perspective divide, viewport mapping, polygon offset, polygon mode, and culling.

2.3.2 Fragment Processor

The FRAGMENT PROCESSOR is a programmable unit that operates on fragment values and their associated data. The fragment processor usually performs traditional graphics operations such as the following:

- Operations on interpolated values

- Texture access

- Texture application

- Fog

- Color sum

- Alpha Test

A wide variety of other computations can be performed on this processor. It is easy to implement some traditional vertex operations such as lighting in a fragment shader. Shaders that are intended to run on this processor are called FRAGMENT SHADERS. Fragment shaders express the algorithm that executes on the fragment processor and produces output values based on the input values that are provided. A fragment shader cannot change a fragment's x/y position. Fragment shaders that perform some of the computations from the preceding list must perform all desired functionality from the preceding list. For instance, it is not possible to use the existing fixed functionality to compute fog but have a fragment shader perform specialized texture access and texture application. The fragment shader must be written to perform all three functions.

The fragment processor does not replace graphics operations that require knowledge of several fragments at a time. To support parallelism at the fragment-processing level, fragment shaders are written in a way that expresses the computation required for a single fragment, and direct access to neighboring fragments is not allowed. An implementation may have multiple fragment processors that operate in parallel.

The fragment processor can perform operations on each fragment that is generated by the rasterization of points, lines, and polygons. If images are first downloaded into texture memory, the fragment processor can also be used for pixel processing that requires access to a pixel and its neighbors. A rectangle can be drawn with texturing enabled, and the fragment processor can read the image from texture memory and apply it to the rectangle while performing traditional operations such as the following:

- Pixel zoom
- Scale and bias
- Color table lookup
- Convolution
- Color matrix

The fragment processor does not replace the fixed functionality graphics operations that occur at the back end of the OpenGL pixel processing pipeline such as coverage, pixel ownership test, scissor test, depth test, stencil test, alpha blending, logical operations, dithering, and plane masking.

Figure 2.3 shows the values that provide input to the fragment processor and the data values that are produced by the fragment processor.

The primary inputs to the fragment processor are the interpolated varying variables (both built in and user defined) that are the results of rasterization. User-defined varying variables must be defined in a fragment shader, and their types must match those defined in the vertex shader.

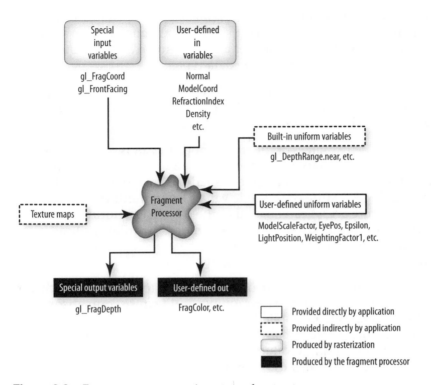

Figure 2.3   Fragment processor inputs and outputs

Values computed by fixed functionality between the vertex processor and the fragment processor are made available through special input variables. The window coordinate position of the fragment is communicated through the special input variable *gl_FragCoord*. An indicator of whether the fragment was generated by rasterizing a front-facing primitive is communicated through the special input variable *gl_FrontFacing*. The point sprite coordinate position of the fragment is communicated through the special input variable *gl_PointCoord*.

Global variables that define data that is passed from the vertex processor through the rasterizer into the fragment processor are called IN VARIABLES. They may be further qualified with one of the interpolation qualifiers smooth, noperspective, and flat. The name, type and interpolation qualifier of the fragment shader's IN VARIABLE must match the corresponding vertex shader's OUT VARIABLE. A fragment shader can use a user-defined in variable to read interpolated: colors, normals (useful for per-fragment lighting computations), texture coordinates, model coordinates, and other arbitrary values.

User-defined uniform variables allow the application to pass relatively infrequently changing values to a fragment shader. The same uniform variable can be accessed by both a vertex shader and a fragment shader if both shaders declare the variable using the same data type.

A small amount of OpenGL state for depth range is accessible to a fragment shader through built-in uniform variable *gl_DepthRange*. This OpenGL state is available to both vertex and fragment shaders.

One of the biggest advantages of the fragment processor is that it can access texture memory an arbitrary number of times and combine in arbitrary ways the values that it reads. A fragment shader is free to read multiple values from a single texture or multiple values from multiple textures. The result of one texture access can be used as the basis for performing another texture access (a DEPENDENT TEXTURE READ). There is no inherent limitation on the number of such dependent reads that are possible, so ray-casting algorithms can be implemented in a fragment shader.

The OpenGL parameters for texture maps continue to define the behavior of the filtering operation, borders, wrapping, and texture comparison modes. These operations are applied when a texture is accessed from within a shader. The shader is free to use the resulting value however it chooses. The shader can read multiple values from a texture and perform a custom filtering operation. It can also use a texture to perform a lookup table operation.

The fragment processor defines almost all the capabilities necessary to implement the fixed-function pixel transfer operations defined in OpenGL, including those in the imaging subset. This means that advanced pixel processing is supported with the fragment processor. Lookup table operations can be done with 1D texture accesses, allowing applications to fully control their size and format. Scale and bias operations are easily expressed through the programming language. The color matrix can be accessed through a built-in uniform variable. Convolution and pixel zoom are supported by accessing a texture multiple times to compute the proper result. Histogram and minimum/maximum operations are left to be defined as extensions because these prove to be quite difficult to support at the fragment level with high degrees of parallelism.

For each fragment, the fragment shader may also compute a replacement depth writing to the special output variable *gl_FragDepth*, or completely discard the fragment. If the fragment is not discarded, the results of the fragment shader are sent on for further processing.

Global variables that define data that is passed from the fragment processor to the fixed-function per-fragment pipeline are called OUT VARIABLES. Another OpenGL command, **glBindFragDataLocation**, allows an application to tie together the user-defined out variable to an index of a drawbuffer.

The remainder of the OpenGL pipeline remains as defined for fixed-function processing. Fragments are submitted to coverage application, pixel ownership testing, scissor testing, stencil testing, depth testing, blending, dithering, logical operations, and masking before ultimately being written into the framebuffer. The back end of the processing pipeline remains as fixed functionality because it is easy to implement in nonprogrammable hardware. Making these functions programmable is more complex because read/modify/write operations can introduce significant instruction scheduling issues and pipeline stalls. Most of these fixed functionality operations can be disabled, and alternative operations can be performed within a fragment shader if desired (albeit with possibly lower performance).

2.4 Language Overview

Because of its success as a standard, OpenGL has been the target of our efforts to define an industry-standard, high-level shading language. The shading language that has been defined as a result of the efforts of OpenGL ARB members is called the OpenGL Shading Language. This language has been designed to be forward looking and to eventually support programmability in other areas as well.

This section provides a brief overview of the OpenGL Shading Language. For a complete discussion of the language, see Chapter 3, Chapter 4, and Chapter 5.

2.4.1 Language Design Considerations

In the past few years, semiconductor technology has progressed to the point at which the levels of computation that can be done per vertex or per fragment have gone beyond what is feasible to describe by the traditional OpenGL mechanisms of setting state to influence the action of fixed pipeline stages. A natural way of taming this complexity and the proliferation of OpenGL extensions is to replace parts of the pipeline with user-programmable stages. This has been done in some recent OpenGL extensions, but the programming is done in assembly language. It can be difficult and time-consuming to write shaders in such low-level languages, and maintaining such code can be costly. As programmable graphics hardware evolves, the current crop of shader assembly languages may also prove to be cumbersome and inefficient to support in hardware.

The ideal solution to these issues was to define a forward-looking, hardware-independent, high-level language that would be easy to use and powerful enough to stand the test of time and that would drastically reduce the need for extensions. These desires were tempered by the need for fast implementations within a generation or two of hardware.

The following design goals were fundamental to the design of the OpenGL Shading Language.

Define a language that works well with OpenGL—The OpenGL Shading Language is designed specifically for use within the OpenGL environment. It provides programmable alternatives to certain parts of the fixed functionality of OpenGL. Therefore, the language itself and the programmable processors it defines must have at least as much functionality as what they replace. Furthermore, by design, it is quite easy to refer to existing OpenGL state from within a shader. By design, it is also quite easy to use fixed functionality in one part of the OpenGL processing pipeline and programmable processing in another.

Expose the flexibility of near-future hardware—Graphics hardware has been changing rapidly to a model that allows general programmability for vertex and fragment processing. To expose this programmability, the shading language is high level, with appropriate abstractions for the graphics problem domain. The language includes a rich set of built-in functions that allow expression of operations on vectors as easily as on scalars. Exposing hardware capabilities through a high-level programming language also obviates the need for OpenGL extensions that define small changes to the fixed functionality behavior. Exposing an abstraction that is independent of the actual underlying hardware eliminates the plethora of piecemeal extensions to OpenGL.

Provide hardware independence—As previously mentioned, the first attempts at exposing the programmability of graphics hardware focused on assembly language interfaces. This was a dangerous direction for software developers to take because it results in software that is inherently nonportable. The goal of a high-level shading language is for the abstraction level to be high enough that application developers can code in a portable way and that hardware vendors have plenty of room to provide innovative hardware architectures and compiler technology.

Define a language that exposes the performance of the underlying graphics hardware—Today's graphics hardware is based on programmable processor technology. It is an established fact nowadays that compiler technology can generate extremely high-performance executable code. With the complexity of today's CPUs, it is difficult to manually generate code that can surpass the performance of code generated by a compiler. It is the intent that the object code generated for a shader be independent of other OpenGL state, so that recompiles or managing multiple copies of object code are not necessary.

Define a language that is easy to use—One of the considerations here is that writing shaders should be simple and easy. Since most graphics application programmers are familiar with C and C++, this led us to adopt the salient features of these languages as the basis for the OpenGL Shading Language. We also believed that compilers, not application programmers, should perform difficult tasks. We concluded that a single language (with very minor variations) should be the basis for programming all the programmable processors that we were defining, as well as those we envisioned adding in future versions of OpenGL. This allows application programmers to become familiar with the basic shading language constructs and apply them to all programming tasks involving the programmable processors in OpenGL.

Define a language that will stand the test of time—This design consideration also led us to base the design of the OpenGL Shading Language on previously successful programming languages such as C and RenderMan. Our hope is that programs written when the OpenGL Shading Language was first defined will still be valid in ten years. Longevity also requires standardization of some sort, so we expended a great deal of effort both in making hardware vendors happy with the final language specification and in pushing the specification through the approval process of OpenGL's governing body, the OpenGL Architecture Review Board (ARB).

Don't preclude higher levels of parallel processing—Newer graphics hardware architectures are providing more and more parallelism at both the vertex and the fragment processing levels. So we took great care with the definition of the OpenGL Shading Language to allow for even higher levels of parallel processing. This consideration has shaped the definition of the language in some subtle but important ways.

Don't include unnecessary language features—Some features of C have made implementing optimizing compilers difficult. Some OpenGL Shading Language features address this issue. For example, C allows hidden aliasing of memory by using pointers and passing pointers as function arguments, which may give multiple names to the same memory. These potential aliases handicap the optimizer, leading to complexity or less optimized code. The OpenGL Shading language does not allow pointers, and it calls by value-return to prevent such aliasing. In general, aliasing is disallowed, simplifying the job of the optimizer.

2.4.2 C Basis

As stated previously, the OpenGL Shading Language is based on the syntax of the ANSI C programming language, and at first glance, programs written in this language look very much like C programs. This is intentional, to make the language easier to use for those most likely to be using it, namely, those developing graphics applications in C or C++.

The basic structure of programs written in the OpenGL Shading Language is the same as it is for programs written in C. The entry point of a set of shaders is the function **void main()**; the body of this function is delimited by curly braces. Constants, identifiers, operators, expressions, and statements are basically the same for the OpenGL Shading Language as they are for C. Control flow for looping, if-then-else, and function calls are virtually identical to C.

2.4.3 Additions to C

The OpenGL Shading Language has a number of language features that have been added because of its special-purpose nature as a language for encoding graphics algorithms. Here are some of the main things that have been added to the OpenGL Shading Language that are different from ANSI C.

Vector types are supported for floating-point, integer, and Boolean values. For floating-point values, these vector types are referred to as **vec2** (two floats), **vec3** (three floats), and **vec4** (four floats). Operators work as readily on vector types as they do on scalars. To sum vectors *v1* and *v2*, you simply would say *v1* + *v2*. Individual components of a vector can be accessed either with array syntax or as fields of a structure. Color values can be accessed by appending .r to the name of a vector variable to access the first component, .g to access the second component, .b to access the third, and .a to access the fourth. Position values can be accessed with .x, .y, .z, and .w, and texture values can be accessed with .s, .t, .p, and .q. Multiple components can be selected by specification of multiple names, like .xy.

Floating-point matrix types are also supported as basic types. The data type **mat2** refers to a 2 × 2 matrix of floating-point values, **mat3** refers to a 3 × 3 matrix, **mat4** refers to a 4 × 4 matrix, and **mat*mxn*** refers to an *m* column by *n* row matrix. Matrices are a convenient type for expressing the linear transformations common in 3D graphics. Columns of a matrix can be selected with array syntax, yielding a vector whose components can be accessed as just described.

A set of basic types called SAMPLERS has also been added to create the mechanism by which shaders access texture memory. Samplers are a special type of opaque variable that access a particular texture map. A variable of type **sampler1D** can be used to access a 1D texture map, a variable of type **sampler2D** can be used to access a 2D texture map, and so on. Shadow and cube map textures are also supported through this mechanism.

Qualifiers to global variables have been added to manage the input and output of shaders. The **in**, **uniform**, and **out** qualifiers specify what type of input or output a variable serves. In variables communicate frequently changing values from the application or prior processing stage to a shader, uniform variables communicate infrequently changing values from the application to any shader, and out variables communicate frequently changing values from a shader to a subsequent processing stages.

Shaders written in the OpenGL Shading Language can use built-in variables that begin with the reserved prefix "gl_" in order to access existing OpenGL state and to communicate with the fixed functionality of OpenGL. Both vertex and fragment shaders can access built-in uniform variables that contain state values that are available within the current rendering context. The few built-in uniforms are *gl_DepthRange.near*, *gl_DepthRange.far*, and *gl_DepthRange.diff*. The vertex shader must write the special variable *gl_Position* in order to provide necessary information to the fixed functionality stages between vertex processing and fragment processing, namely, primitive assembly, clipping, culling, and rasterization. A fragment shader may optionally write *gl_FragDepth* to replace the depth produced by rasterization.

A variety of built-in functions is also provided in the OpenGL Shading Language in order to make coding easier and to take advantage of possible hardware acceleration for certain operations. The language defines built-in functions for a variety of operations:

- Trigonometric operations—sine, cosine, tangent, and so on

- Exponential operations—power, exponential, logarithm, square root, and inverse square root

- Common math operations—absolute value, floor, ceiling, fractional part, modulus, and so on

- Geometric operations—length, distance, dot product, cross product, normalization, and so on

- Relational operations based on vectors—component-wise operations such as greater than, less than, equal to, and so on

- Specialized fragment shader functions for computing derivatives and estimating filter widths for antialiasing

- Functions for accessing values in texture memory

- Functions that return noise values for procedural texturing effects

2.4.4 Additions from C++

The OpenGL Shading Language also includes a few notable language features from C++. In particular, it supports function overloading to make it easy to define functions that differ only in the type or number of arguments being passed. This feature is heavily used by the built-in functions. For instance, the dot product function is overloaded to deal with arguments that are types **float**, **vec2**, **vec3**, and **vec4**.

The concept of constructors also comes from C++. Initializers are done only with constructors in the OpenGL Shading Language. Using constructors allows for more than one way of initializing variables.

Another feature borrowed from C++ is that variables can be declared when they are needed; they do not have to be declared at the beginning of a basic block. The basic type **bool** is supported as in C++.

As in C++, functions must be declared before being used. This can be accomplished either with the function's definition (its body) or just with a prototype.

2.4.5 C Features Not Supported

Unlike ANSI C, the OpenGL Shading Language supports limited implicit conversion of data types. Scalar and vector expressions of integer or unsigned integer may be implicitly converted to the equivalent scalar or vector float expression. Otherwise, compiler errors are generated if variables used in an expression are of different types. For instance, an error is generated for the statement `int i = 0.0;` but not for the statement `float f = 0;`. This approach might seem like a bit of a nuisance, but it simplifies the language by eliminating ambiguous circular promotion rules.

The OpenGL Shading Language does not support pointers, strings, or characters, or any operations based on these. It is fundamentally a language for processing numerical data, not for processing character or string data, so there is no need for these features to complicate the language. To lower the implementation burden (both for the compiler and for the graphics hardware), there is no support for byte, short, or long integers.

A few other C language features that were eliminated from consideration in order to simplify the OpenGL Shading Language (or because there was no compelling need for them at the time) are unions, enumerated types, and bit fields in structures. Finally, the language is not file based, so you won't see any **#include** directives or other references to filenames.

2.4.6 Other Differences

There are a few areas in which the OpenGL Shading Language provides the same functionality as C but does so in a different way. One of these is that constructors, rather than type casts, are used for data type conversion. Constructors, not C-style initializers, are also used for variable initialization. There is no support at all for type casting without conversion, so constructors keep the language type safe. Constructors use the syntax of a function call, where the function name is the name of the desired type and the arguments are the values that will be used to construct the desired value.

Constructors allow a much richer set of operations than simple type casts or C-style initializers, and the flexibility that this richness provides comes in quite handy for dealing with vector and matrix data types. In addition to converting from one scalar type to another, constructors can create a larger type out of a smaller type or reduce a larger type to a smaller type. For instance, the constructor `vec3(1.0, 2.0, 3.0)` constructs a **vec3** data type out of three scalar values, and the constructor `vec3` (`myVec4`) strips the fourth component from *myVec4* to create a **vec3** value.

The other area of difference is that, unlike the call-by-value calling convention used by C, the OpenGL Shading Language uses CALL BY VALUE-RETURN. Input parameters are copied into the function at call time, and output parameters are copied back to the caller before the function exits. Because the function deals only with copies of the function parameters, there are no issues regarding aliasing of variables within a function. Function parameters are identified as input parameters with the qualifier **in**, they are identified as output parameters with the qualifier **out**, and they are identified as both input and output parameters with the qualifier **inout**; if no qualifier is present, they are identified as input parameters.

2.5 System Overview

We have already described briefly some of the pieces that provide applications with access to the programmability of underlying graphics hardware. This section briefly describes how these pieces go together in a working system.

2.5.1 Driver Model

A piece of software that controls a piece of hardware and manages shared access to that piece of hardware is commonly called a DRIVER. No matter what environment OpenGL is implemented in, it falls into the driver category because OpenGL manages shared access to the underlying graphics hardware. Some of its tasks must also be coordinated with, or supervised by, facilities in the operating system.

Figure 2.4 illustrates how OpenGL shaders are handled in the execution environment of OpenGL. Applications communicate with OpenGL by calling functions that are part of the OpenGL API. A new OpenGL function, **glCreateShader**, allows applications to allocate within the OpenGL driver the data structures that are necessary for storing an OpenGL shader. These data structures are called SHADER OBJECTS. After a shader object has been created, the application can provide the source code for the shader by calling **glShaderSource**. This command provides to OpenGL the character strings containing the shader source code.

As you can see from Figure 2.4, the compiler for the OpenGL Shading Language is actually part of the OpenGL driver environment. This is one of the

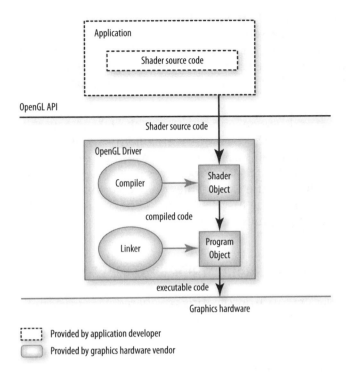

Figure 2.4   Execution model for OpenGL shaders

key differences between the OpenGL Shading Language and other shading
language designs, such as the Stanford Shading Language, High-Level Shader
Language (HLSL) from Microsoft, or Cg from NVIDIA. In these other languages, the high-level shading language compiler sits above the graphics API
and translates the high-level shading language into something that can be
consumed by the underlying graphics API. (See Chapter 17 for more details.)
With the OpenGL Shading Language, the source code for shaders is passed to
the OpenGL driver, and in that environment, the shaders are compiled to the
native machine code as efficiently as possible. After source code for a shader
has been loaded into a shader object in the OpenGL driver environment, it
can be compiled with **glCompileShader**.

A PROGRAM OBJECT is an OpenGL-managed data structure that acts as a container for shader objects. Applications are required to attach shader objects
to a program object by using the command **glAttachShader**. When attached
to a program object, the compiled shader objects can be linked with
glLinkProgram. Support for multiple shader objects (and the subsequent

need for a linker built into OpenGL) is a key difference between the OpenGL Shading Language and assembly-level APIs such as those provided by the OpenGL extensions *ARB_vertex_program* and *ARB_fragment_program*. For more complex shading tasks, separately compiled shader objects are a much more attractive alternative than a single, monolithic block of assembly-level code.

The link step resolves external references between the shaders, checks the compatibility between the vertex shader and the fragment shader, assigns memory locations to uniform variables, and so on. The result is one or more executables that can be installed with **glUseProgram** as part of OpenGL's current state. This command installs the executables on the vertex processor, the fragment processor, or both. The installed executables are responsible for processing all subsequent graphics primitives.

2.5.2 OpenGL Shading Language Compiler/Linker

The source for a single shader is an array of strings of characters, and a single shader is made from the concatenation of these strings. There is no inherent connection between strings and the lines of code in a shader. A shader may be entirely represented by a single string, or each line of shader source code may be contained in a separate string. Each string can contain multiple lines, separated by new-lines. No new-lines need be present in a string; a single line can be formed from multiple strings. No new-lines or other characters are inserted by the OpenGL implementation when it concatenates the strings to form a single shader. It is entirely up to the application programmer to provide shader source code to OpenGL with new-lines between each line of source code.

Diagnostic messages returned from compiling a shader must identify both the line number within a string and the source string to which the diagnostic message applies. Source strings are counted sequentially with the first string counted as string 0. For source code parsing, the current line number is one more than the number of new-lines that have been processed.

The front end of the OpenGL Shading Language compiler has been released as open source by 3Dlabs and can be used by anyone interested in writing his or her own compiler. This publicly available front end performs lexical analysis of OpenGL Shading Language source code to produce a token stream and then performs syntactic and semantic analysis of this token stream to produce a binary, high-level representation of the language. This front end acts as a reference implementation of the OpenGL Shading

Language, and therefore it goes hand-in-hand with the language specification to define the language clearly. Another advantage to using this publicly available front end in an OpenGL Shading Language compiler implementation is that the syntax and semantics for shaders are checked consistently by all implementations that use this front end. More consistency among compiler implementations makes it easier for developers to write shaders that work as intended across a variety of implementations.

It is assumed that the back end of the OpenGL Shading Language compiler will be implemented differently on different platforms. Each implementation must take the high-level representation produced by the publicly available front end and produce optimized machine code for a particular hardware target. This is an area in which individual hardware vendors can add value to their shading language implementation by figuring out ways to map the high-level representation onto the actual machine instructions found in their hardware. Likewise, the linking stage is also highly hardware dependent because it involves operations like assigning variables to actual memory locations in the hardware. A variety of global optimizations may also be performed as part of linking.

The net result of this assumption is that graphics hardware vendors will implement the majority of the OpenGL Shading Language compiler and linker. Along with the OpenGL driver itself, this software will typically be included as part of the graphics driver installation package that is provided by a graphics hardware vendor.

2.5.3 OpenGL Shading Language API

As of OpenGL 2.0, support for the OpenGL Shading Language is available as part of standard OpenGL. The following OpenGL entry points support the OpenGL Shading Language:

- **glAttachShader**—Attach a shader object to a program object

- **glBindAttribLocation**—Specify the generic vertex attribute index to be used for a particular user-defined attribute variable in a vertex shader

- **glCompileShader**—Compile a shader

- **glCreateProgram**—Create a program object

- **glCreateShader**—Create a shader object

- **glDeleteProgram**—Delete a program object

- **glDeleteShader**—Delete a shader object

- **glDetachShader**—Detach a shader object from a program object

- **glDisableVertexAttribArray**—Disable a generic vertex attribute from being sent to OpenGL with vertex arrays

- **glEnableVertexAttribArray**—Enable a generic vertex attribute to be sent to OpenGL with vertex arrays

- **glGetActiveAttrib**—Obtain the name, size, and type of an active attribute variable for a program object

- **glGetActiveUniform**—Obtain the name, size, and type of an active uniform variable for a program object

- **glGetAttachedShaders**—Get the list of shader objects attached to a program object

- **glGetAttribLocation**—Return the generic vertex attribute index that is bound to a specified user-defined attribute variable

- **glGetProgram**—Query one of the parameters of a program object

- **glGetProgramInfoLog**—Obtain the information log for a program object

- **glGetShader**—Query one of the parameters of a shader object

- **glGetShaderInfoLog**—Obtain the information log for a shader object

- **glGetShaderSource**—Get the source code for a specific shader object

- **glGetUniform**—Query the current value of a uniform variable

- **glGetUniformLocation**—Query the location assigned to a uniform variable by the linker

- **glGetVertexAttrib**—Return current state for the specified generic vertex attribute

- **glGetVertexAttribPointer**—Return the vertex array pointer value for the specified generic vertex attribute

- **glIsProgram**—Determine if an object name corresponds to a program object

- **glIsShader**—Determine if an object name corresponds to a shader object

- **glLinkProgram**—Link a program object to create executable code

- **glShaderSource**—Load source code strings into a shader object

- **glUniform**—Set the value of a uniform variable

- **glUseProgram**—Install a program object's executable code as part of current state

- **glValidateProgram**—Return validation information for a program object

- **glVertexAttrib**—Send generic vertex attributes to OpenGL one vertex at a time

- **glVertexAttribPointer**—Specify location and organization of generic vertex attributes to be sent to OpenGL with vertex arrays

These new entry points are all discussed in more detail in Chapter 7. Reference pages for all of the OpenGL Shading Language API entry points defined by these extensions are included in Appendix B at the back of this book.

2.6   Key Benefits

The following key benefits are derived from the choices that were made during the design of the OpenGL Shading Language:

Tight integration with OpenGL—The OpenGL Shading Language was designed for use in OpenGL. It is designed in such a way that an existing, working OpenGL application can easily be modified to take advantage of the capabilities of programmable graphics hardware. Built-in access to existing OpenGL state, reuse of API entry points that are already familiar to application developers, and a close coupling with the existing architecture of OpenGL are all key benefits of using the OpenGL Shading Language for shader development.

Runtime compilation—Source code stays as source code, in its easiest-to-maintain form, for as long as possible. An application passes source code to any conforming OpenGL implementation that supports the OpenGL Shading Language, and it will be compiled and executed properly. There is no need for a multitude of binaries for a multitude of different platforms.[1]

---

1. At the time of this writing, the OpenGL ARB is still considering the need for an API that allows shaders to be specified in a form other than source code. The primary issues are the protection of intellectual property that may be embedded in string-based shader source code and the performance that would be gained by allowing shaders to be at least partially precompiled. When such an API is defined, shader portability may be reduced, but application developers will have the option of getting better code security and better performance.

No reliance on cross-vendor assembly language—Both DirectX and OpenGL have widespread support for assembly language interfaces to graphics programmability. High-level shading languages could be (and have been) built on top of these assembly language interfaces, and such high-level languages can be translated into these assembly language interfaces completely outside the environment of OpenGL or DirectX. This does have some advantages, but relying on an assembly language interface as the primary interface to hardware programmability restricts innovation by graphics hardware designers. Hardware designers have many more choices for acceleration of an expressive high-level language than they do for a restrictive assembly language. It is much too early in the development of programmable graphics hardware technology to establish an assembly language standard for graphics programmability. C, on the other hand, was developed long before any CPU assembly languages that are in existence today, and it is still a viable choice for application development.

Unconstrained opportunities for compiler optimization plus optimal performance on a wider range of hardware—As we've learned through experience with CPUs, compilers are much better at quickly generating efficient code than humans are. By allowing high-level source code to be compiled within OpenGL, rather than outside of OpenGL, individual hardware vendors have the best possible opportunity to deliver optimal performance on their graphics hardware. In fact, compiler improvements can be made with each OpenGL driver release, and the applications won't need to change any application source code, recompile the application, or even relink it. Furthermore, most of the current crop of assembly language interfaces are string based. This makes them inefficient for use as intermediate languages for compilation because two string translations are required. First, the string-based, high-level source must be translated into string-based assembly language, and then that string-based assembly language must be passed to OpenGL and translated from string-based assembly language to machine code.

A truly open, cross-platform standard—No other high-level graphics shading language has been approved as part of an open, multivendor standard. Like OpenGL itself, the OpenGL Shading Language will be implemented by a variety of different vendors for a variety of different environments.

One high-level language for all programmable graphics processing—The OpenGL Shading Language is used to write shaders for both the vertex processor and the fragment processor in OpenGL, with very small differences in the language for the two types of shaders. In the future, it is intended that the OpenGL Shading Language will bring programmability to other areas of OpenGL as well. Areas that have already received some discussion include programmability for packing/unpacking arbitrary image formats and support for programmable tessellation of higher-order surfaces in the graphics hardware.

Support for modular programming—By defining compilation and linking as two separate steps, shader writers have a lot more flexibility in how they choose to implement complex shading algorithms. Rather than implement a complex algorithm as a single, monolithic shader, developers are free to implement it as a collection of shaders that can be independently compiled and attached to a program object. Shaders can be designed with common interfaces so that they are interchangeable, and a link operation joins them to create a program.

No additional libraries or executables—The OpenGL Shading Language and the compiler and linker that support it are defined as part of OpenGL. Applications need not worry about linking against any additional runtime libraries. Compiler improvements are delivered as part of OpenGL driver updates.

2.7 Summary

Here are the key points to understand about how all the pieces fit together at execution time:

- When installed as part of current state, the executable created for the vertex processor is executed once for every vertex provided to OpenGL.

- When installed as part of current state, the executable created for the fragment processor is executed once for every fragment that is produced by rasterization.

- When vertex or fragment shaders are used, the corresponding fixed functionality is disabled. Shaders must implement such functionality themselves if it is desired.

- In variables defined in a vertex shader are per-vertex values that are output from the vertex processor. Rasterization is the process that causes the per-vertex values to be interpolated and per-fragment values to be generated. The per-fragment values become the input to the fragment processor and are accessed in the fragment shader with the same varying variable name as was used in the vertex shader.

- An application can communicate directly with a vertex shader in two ways: by using attribute variables and by using uniform variables.

- Attribute variables are expected to change frequently and may be supplied by the application as often as every vertex.

- Applications can pass arbitrary vertex data to a vertex shader with user-defined attribute variables.

- Applications can pass standard vertex attributes (color, normal, texture coordinates, position, etc.) to a vertex shader with built-in attribute variables.

- An application communicates directly with a fragment shader with uniform variables.

- Uniform variables are expected to change relatively infrequently (at a minimum, they are constant for an entire graphics primitive).

- The compiler and linker for the language are contained within OpenGL, but tools for compiling, linking, and debugging shaders can exist outside of OpenGL as well.

To summarize, the following are the most important points about the OpenGL Shading Language:

- The language is based on the syntax of C.

- Basic structure and many keywords are the same as in C.

- Vectors and matrices are included in the language as basic types.

- Global type qualifiers **in**, **uniform**, and **out** are added to describe variables that manage shader I/O.

  - Variables of type **in** allow the communication of frequently changing values from the application to the vertex shader, or from fixed-function rasterization to the fragment shader.

  - Variables of type **out** allow the communication of frequently changing values to be output from a vertex shader or fragment shader.

  - Variables of type **uniform** allow the application to provide relatively infrequently changing values to both vertex shaders and fragment shaders.

- The data type **sampler** is added for accessing textures.

- Built-in variable names can be used to access standard OpenGL state and to communicate with OpenGL fixed functionality.

- A variety of built-in functions perform common graphics operations.

- Function declarations are required, and overloading based on number and type of arguments is supported as in C++.

- Variables can be declared when needed.

To install and use OpenGL shaders, do the following:

1. Create one or more (empty) shader objects by calling **glCreateShader**.

2. Provide source code for these shaders by calling **glShaderSource**.

3. Compile each of the shaders by calling **glCompileShader**.

4. Create a program object by calling **glCreateProgram**.

5. Attach all the shader objects to the program object by calling **glAttachShader**.

6. Link the program object by calling **glLinkProgram**.

7. Install the executable program as part of OpenGL's current state by calling **glUseProgram**.

After these steps, subsequent graphics primitives will be drawn with the shaders you've provided rather than with OpenGL's defined fixed functionality pipeline.

2.8 Further Information

Just keep reading this book and you'll get to all of the really good stuff! If you really must have more technical details, here are pointers to the official specification documents. The 3Dlabs Web site also has additional material, including slide presentations, demos, example shaders, and source code.

[1] Kessenich, John, Dave Baldwin, and Randi Rost, *The OpenGL Shading Language, Version 1.40*, 3Dlabs/Intel March 2009. www.opengl.org/documentation/specs/

[2] Segal, Mark, and Kurt Akeley, *The OpenGL Graphics System: A Specification (Version 3.1)*, Editor (v1.1): Chris Frazier, (v1.2–3.1): Jon Leech, (v2.0): Jon Leech and Pat Brown, March 2009. www.opengl.org/documentation/spec.html

[3] GLSL Compiler Front-End. Now at http://3dshaders.com.

Chapter 3

Language Definition

by John Kessenich

In this chapter, we present the language features of the OpenGL Shading Language. We start with a simple example of a working pair of vertex and fragment shaders to show their basic structure and interfaces. Each aspect of the language is then discussed in turn.

The OpenGL Shading Language syntax comes from the C family of programming languages. Tokens, identifiers, semicolons, nesting with curly braces, control-flow, and many keywords look like C. Both comment styles, // ... and /* ... */, are accepted. Much is also different, though, and all important differences from C are discussed.

Each shader example is presented as it might appear in a file or onscreen. However, as explained in Chapter 7, the OpenGL API passes shaders as strings, not files, because OpenGL does not consider shaders file based.

3.1 Example Shader Pair

A program typically contains two shaders: one vertex shader and one fragment shader. More than one shader of each type can be present, but there must be exactly one function **main** between all the fragment shaders and exactly one function **main** between all the vertex shaders. Frequently, it's easiest to just have one shader of each type.

The following is a simple vertex and fragment shader pair that can smoothly express a surface temperature with color. The range of temperatures and their colors are parameterized. First, we show the vertex shader. It is executed once for each vertex.

```
#version 140
// Global variables

// uniform qualified variables are changed at most once per primitive
uniform float CoolestTemp;
uniform float TempRange;
uniform mat4  MVPMatrix;

// in qualified variables are typically changed per vertex
in  vec4  mcVertex;
in  float VertexTemp;


// out qualified variables communicate from the vertex shader to
// the fragment shader
out float Temperature;

void main()
{
    // compute a temperature to be interpolated per fragment,
    // in the range [0.0, 1.0]
    Temperature = (VertexTemp - CoolestTemp) /  TempRange;
    gl_Position = MVPMatrix * mcVertex;
}
```

That's it for the vertex shader. Primitive assembly follows the preceding vertex processing, providing the rasterizer with enough information to create fragments. The rasterizer interpolates the *Temperature* values written per vertex to create values per fragment. Each fragment is then delivered to a single execution of the fragment shader, as follows:

```
#version 140
// Global variables

// uniform qualified variables are changed at most once per primitive
// by the application, and vec3 declares a vector of three
// floating-point numbers
uniform vec3 CoolestColor;
uniform vec3 HottestColor;

// Temperature contains the now interpolated per-fragment
// value of temperature set by the vertex shader
in float Temperature;

// out qualified global variables communicate from the fragment shader
// to per-fragment operations (blending) and the framebuffer
out vec4 FragmentColor;
```

```
void main()
{
    // get a color between coolest and hottest colors, using
    // the mix() built-in function
    vec3 color = mix(CoolestColor, HottestColor, Temperature);

    // make a vector of 4 floating-point numbers by appending an
    // alpha of 1.0, and set this fragment's color
    FragmentColor = vec4(color, 1.0);
}
```

Both shaders receive user-defined state from the application through the declared **uniform** qualified variables. The vertex shader gets information associated with each vertex through the **in** qualified variables. Information is passed from the vertex shader's **out** qualified variables to the fragment shader's **in** qualified variables. The **out** declarations in the vertex shader must match the **in** declarations in the fragment shader. The fixed functionality located between the vertex and fragment processors will interpolate the per-vertex values written to each **out** variable. When the fragment shader reads this same **in** variable, it reads the value interpolated for the location of the fragment being processed.

Shaders interact with the fixed functionality OpenGL pipeline by writing built-in variables. OpenGL prefixes built-in variables with "gl_". In the preceding examples, writing to *gl_Position* tells the OpenGL pipeline where the transformed vertices are located.

Shaders may also interact with the fixed functionality by reading or writing user-defined variables. In the preceding examples, mcVertex and VertexTemp read from generic vertex attributes. Writing FragmentColor outputs to the fixed-function per-fragment operations (blending) and, from there, to the framebuffer.

Execution of the preceding shaders occurs multiple times to process a single primitive, once per vertex for the vertex shader and once per fragment for the fragment shader. Many such executions of the same shader can happen in parallel. In general, there is no direct tie or ordering between shader executions. Information can be communicated neither from vertex to vertex nor from fragment to fragment.

3.2 Data Types

We saw vectors of floating-point numbers in the example in the previous section. Many other built-in data types are available to ease the expression of graphical operations. Booleans, integers, matrices, vectors of other types, structures, and arrays are all included. Each is discussed in the following sections. Notably missing are string and character types, since there is little use for them in processing vertex and fragment data.

3.2.1 Scalars

The scalar types available are

float	declares a single floating-point number
int	declares a single integer number
uint	declares a single unsigned integer number
bool	declares a single Boolean number

These declare variables, as is familiar from C/C++.

```
float f;
float g, h = 2.4;
uint NumTextures = 4;
bool skipProcessing;
```

Unlike the original C, the OpenGL Shading Language requires you to provide the type name because there are no default types. As in C++, declarations may appear when needed, not just after an open curly brace ({).

Literal floating-point numbers are also specified as in C, except the only permitted suffixes to specify precision are **f** and **F** since there is only one floating-point type. (Unlike in C, if no suffix is specified, it is implicitly **f**.)

```
3.14159
3.
0.2f
.609F
1.5e10
0.4E-4
etc.
```

In general, floating-point values and operations act as they do in C.

Starting with OpenGL 3.0, integers and unsigned integers are fully supported. Signed ints are 32 bits, including a sign bit, in two's complement form. Unsigned ints must have exactly 32 bits of precision. Arithmetic overflows or underflows will not cause any exception, nor will they saturate; they will simply "wrap," producing the low-order 32 bits of the result.

Bit-wise operations like left-shift (<<) and bit-wise and (&) are supported.

Literal integers can be given as decimal values, octal values, or hexadecimal values, as in C. They may also be suffixed with either **u** or **U**.

```
15u    // a literal decimal unsigned integer
42     // a literal decimal integer
052    // a literal octal integer
0x2A   // a literal hexadecimal integer
```

Boolean variables are as **bool** in C++. They can have only one of two values: true or false. Literal Boolean constants **true** and **false** are provided. Relational operators like less-than (<) and logical operators like logical and (&&) always result in Boolean values. Flow-control constructs like **if-else** accept only Boolean-typed expressions. In these regards, the OpenGL Shading Language is more restrictive than C++.

3.2.2 Vectors

Vectors of **float**, **int**, or **bool** are built-in basic types. They can have two, three, or four components and are named as follows:

vec2	Vector of two floating-point numbers
vec3	Vector of three floating-point numbers
vec4	Vector of four floating-point numbers
ivec2	Vector of two integers
ivec3	Vector of three integers
ivec4	Vector of four integers
uvec2	Vector of two unsigned integers
uvec3	Vector of three unsigned integers
uvec4	Vector of four unsigned integers
bvec2	Vector of two Booleans
bvec3	Vector of three Booleans
bvec4	Vector of four Booleans

Vectors are quite useful. They conveniently store and manipulate colors, positions, texture coordinates, and so on. Built-in variables and built-in functions make heavy use of these types. Also, special operations are supported. Finally, hardware is likely to have vector-processing capabilities that mirror vector expressions in shaders.

Note that the language does not distinguish between a color vector and a position vector or other uses of a floating-point vector. These are all just floating-point vectors from the language's perspective.

Special features of vectors include component access that can be done either through field selection (as with structures) or as array accesses. For example, if *position* is a **vec3**, it can be considered as the vector (x, y, z), and *position.x* will select the first component of the vector.

In all, the following names are available for selecting components of vectors:

x, y, z, w	Treat a vector as a position or direction
r, g, b, a	Treat a vector as a color
s, t, p, q	Treat a vector as a texture coordinate

There is no explicit way of stating that a vector is a color, a position, a coordinate, and so on. Rather, these component selection names are provided simply for readability in a shader. The only compile-time checking done is that the vector is large enough to provide a specified component. Also, if multiple components are selected (swizzling, discussed in Section 3.7.2), all the components are from the same family.

Vectors can also be indexed as a zero-based array to obtain components. For instance, *position[2]* returns the third component of *position*. Variable indices are allowed, making it possible to loop over the components of a vector. Multiplication takes on special meaning when operating on a vector since linear algebraic multiplies with matrices are understood. Swizzling, indexing, and other operations are discussed in detail in Section 3.7.

3.2.3 Matrices

Built-in types are available for matrices of floating-point numbers. There are nonsquare matrices and square matrices up to 4×4 in size.

mat2	2×2 matrix of floating-point numbers
mat3	3×3 matrix of floating-point numbers
mat4	4×4 matrix of floating-point numbers
mat*mxn*	$m \times n$ matrix of floating point numbers (column × row)

These are useful for storing linear transforms or other data. They are treated semantically as matrices, particularly when a vector and a matrix are multiplied together, in which case the proper linear-algebraic computation is performed. When relevant, matrices are organized in column major order, as is the tradition in OpenGL.

You may access a matrix as an array of column vectors—that is, if *transform* is a **mat4**, *transform[2]* is the third column of *transform*. The resulting type of *transform[2]* is **vec4**. Column 0 is the first column. Because *transform[2]* is a vector and you can also treat vectors as arrays, *transform[3][1]* is the second component of the vector forming the fourth column of *transform*. Hence, it ends up looking as if *transform* is a two-dimensional array. Just remember that the first index selects the column, not the row, and the second index selects the row.

3.2.4 Samplers

Texture lookups require some indication as to which texture or texture unit will do the lookup. The OpenGL Shading Language doesn't really care about the underlying implementation of texture units or other forms of organizing texture lookup hardware. Hence, it provides a simple opaque handle to encapsulate what to look up. These handles are called SAMPLERS. The sampler types available are

sampler1D	Accesses a one-dimensional texture
sampler2D	Accesses a two-dimensional texture
sampler3D	Accesses a three-dimensional texture
samplerCube	Accesses a cube-map texture
sampler2DRect	Accesses a two-dimensional rectangle texture
sampler1DShadow	Accesses a one-dimensional depth texture with comparison
sampler2DShadow	Accesses a two-dimensional depth texture with comparison
sampler2DRectShadow	Accesses a two-dimensional rectangle depth texture with comparison
sampler1DArray	Accesses a one-dimensional texture array
sampler2DArray	Accesses a two-dimensional texture array
sampler1DArrayShadow	Accesses a one-dimensional depth texture array with comparison

sampler2DArrayShadow	Accesses a two-dimensional depth texture array with comparison
samplerBuffer	Accesses a texture buffer
isampler1D	Accesses a one-dimensional integer texture
isampler2D	Accesses a two-dimensional integer texture
isampler3D	Accesses a three-dimensional integer texture
isamplerCube	Accesses a cube-map integer texture
isampler2DRect	Accesses a two-dimensional integer rectangle texture
isampler1DArray	Accesses a two-dimensional integer texture array
isampler2DArray	Accesses a two-dimensional integer texture array
isamplerBuffer	Accesses an integer texture buffer
usampler1D	Accesses a one-dimensional unsigned integer texture
usampler2D	Accesses a two-dimensional unsigned integer texture
usampler3D	Accesses a three-dimensional unsigned integer texture
usamplerCube	Accesses a cube-map unsigned integer texture
usampler2DRect	Accesses a two-dimensional unsigned integer rectangle texture
usampler1DArray	Accesses a one-dimensional unsigned integer texture array
usampler2DArray	Accesses a two-dimensional unsigned integer texture array
usamplerBuffer	Accesses an unsigned integer texture buffer

When the application initializes a sampler, the OpenGL implementation stores into it whatever information is needed to communicate which texture to access. Shaders cannot themselves initialize samplers. They can only receive them from the application, through a **uniform** qualified sampler, or pass them on to user-defined or built-in functions. As a function parameter, a sampler cannot be modified, so there is no way for a shader to change a sampler's value.

For example, a sampler could be declared as

```
uniform sampler2D Grass;
```

(Uniform qualifiers are discussed in more detail in Section 3.5.2.)

This variable can then be passed into a corresponding texture lookup function to access a texture:

```
vec4 color = texture(Grass, coord);
```

where *coord* is a **vec2** holding the two-dimensional position used to index the grass texture, and *color* is the result of doing the texture lookup. Together, the compiler and the OpenGL driver validate that *Grass* really references a two-dimensional texture and that *Grass* is passed only into texture lookups.

Shaders may not manipulate sampler values. For example, the expression `Grass + 1` is not allowed. Arrays of samplers are considered archaic and, if used, should be indexed with integral constant expressions. (Arrays of samplers indexed with nonconstant expressions are at best implemented inefficiently by fetching from every sampler that might have been needed in the array.) The new **sampler*n*DArray** types allow for efficient access of sampler arrays, although with the restriction that the texture formats and texture sizes are constant across the sampler array.

3.2.5 Structures

The OpenGL Shading Language provides user-defined structures similar to C. For example,

```
struct light
{
    vec3 position;
    vec3 color;
};
```

As in C++, the name of the structure is the name of this new user-defined type. No **typedef** is needed. In fact, the **typedef** keyword is still reserved because there is not yet a need for it. A variable of type *light* from the preceding example is simply declared as

```
light ceilingLight;
```

Most other aspects of structures mirror C. They can be embedded and nested. Embedded structure type names have the same scope as the structure in which they are declared. However, embedded structures must be named. Structure members can also be arrays. Finally, each level of structure has its own name space for its members' names, as is familiar.

Bit-fields (the capability to declare an integer with a specified number of bits) are not supported.

Currently, structures are the only user-definable type. The keywords **union**, **enum**, and **class** are reserved for possible future use.

3.2.6 Arrays

Arrays of any type can be created. The declaration

```
vec4 points[10];
```

creates an array of ten **vec4** variables, indexed starting with zero. There are no pointers; the only way to declare an array is with square brackets. Declaring an array as a function parameter also requires square brackets and a size because, currently, array arguments are passed as if the whole array is a single object, not as if the argument is a pointer.

Arrays, unless they are function parameters, do not have to be declared with a size. A declaration like

```
vec4 points[];
```

is allowed, as long as *either* of the following two cases is true:

1. Before the array is referenced, it is declared again with a size, with the same type as the first declaration. For example,

```
vec4 points[];    // points is an array of unknown size
vec4 points[10];  // points is now an array of size 10
```

This cannot be followed by another declaration:

```
vec4 points[];    // points is an array of unknown size
vec4 points[10];  // points is now an array of size 10
vec4 points[20];  // this is illegal
vec4 points[];    // this is also illegal
```

2. All indices that statically reference the array are compile-time constants. In this case, the compiler will make the array large enough to hold the largest index it sees used. For example,

```
vec4 points[];         // points is an array of unknown size
points[2] = vec4(1.0); // points is now an array of size 3
points[7] = vec4(2.0); // points is now an array of size 8
```

In this case, at runtime the array has only one size, determined by the largest index the compiler sees. Such automatically sized arrays cannot be passed as function arguments.

Multiple shaders sharing the same array must declare it with the same size. The linker verifies this.

3.2.7 Void

The type **void** declares a function that returns no value. For example, the function **main** returns no value and must be declared as type **void**.

```
void main()
{
    ...
}
```

Other than for functions that return nothing, the **void** type is not useful.

3.2.8 Declarations and Scope

Variables are declared quite similarly to the way they are declared in C++. They can be declared where needed and have scope as in C++. For example,

```
float f;

f = 3.0;

vec4 u, v;

for (int i = 0; i < 10; ++i)
    v = f * u + v;
```

The scope of a variable declared in a **for** statement ends at the end of the loop's substatement. However, variables may not be declared in an

if statement. This simplifies implementation of scoping across the **else** sub-statement, with little practical cost.

As in C, variable names are case sensitive, must start with a letter or underscore (_), and contain only letters, numbers, and underscores (_). User-defined variables cannot start with the string "gl_" because those names are reserved for future use by OpenGL. Names containing consecutive underscores (__) are also reserved.

3.2.9   Type Matching and Promotion

The OpenGL Shading Language is fairly strict with type matching. In general, types being assigned must match, argument types passed into functions must match formal parameter declarations, and types being operated on must match the requirements of the operator.

There are no automatic promotions from one type to another. There are, however, limited implicit conversions. A scalar integer or scalar unsigned integer may be implicitly converted to a scalar float. A vector integer or vector unsigned integer may be implicitly converted to a vector float of the same number of elements.

This fairly strict type matching may occasionally make a shader have an extra explicit conversion. However, it also simplifies the language, preventing some forms of obfuscated code and some classes of defects. For example, there are no ambiguities in which overloaded function should be chosen for a given function call.

3.3   Initializers and Constructors

A shader variable may be initialized when it is declared. As is familiar from C, the following example initializes *b* at declaration time and leaves *a* and *c* undefined:

```
float a, b = 3.0, c;
```

Constant qualified variables must be initialized.

```
const int Size = 4;  // initializer is required
```

Global variables qualified with in or out may not be initialized. Global variables qualified with uniform, however, may be initialized.

```
in float Temperature;          // No initializer allowed
uniform int Size;              // Initializer allowed, but not required
out float density;             // No initializer allowed
```

To initialize aggregate types, at either declaration time or elsewhere, CONSTRUCTORS are used. No initializer uses the brace syntax "{...}" from C. Syntactically, constructors look like function calls that have a type name where the function name would go—for example, to initialize a **vec4** with the values (1.0, 2.0, 3.0, 4.0), use

```
vec4 v = vec4(1.0, 2.0, 3.0, 4.0);
```

Or, because constructor syntax is the same whether it's in an initializer or not, use

```
vec4 v;
v = vec4(1.0, 2.0, 3.0, 4.0);
```

There are constructors for all the built-in types (except samplers) as well as for structures and arrays. Some examples:

```
vec4 v = vec4(1.0, 2.0, 3.0, 4.0);
ivec2 c = ivec2(3, 4);
vec3 color = vec3(0.2, 0.5, 0.8);
vec4 color4 = vec4(color, 1.0)
struct light
{
    vec4 position;
    struct tLightColor
    {
        vec3 color;
        float intensity;
    } lightColor;
} light1 = light(v, tLightColor(color, 0.9));
float a[4] = float[4](1.0, 1.0, 0.0, 1.0 );
```

For matrices, the components are written in column major order. For example,

```
mat2 Matrix0 = mat2( 1.0, 2.0, 3.0, 4.0 );
mat2 Matrix1 = mat2( 1.0, 2.0,
                     3.0, 4.0 ); // Same matrix as above.
```

results in the following matrix:

$$\begin{bmatrix} 1.0 & 3.0 \\ 2.0 & 4.0 \end{bmatrix}$$

So far, we've only shown constructors taking one argument for each component being constructed. Built-in constructors for vectors can also take a single argument, which is replicated into each component.

```
vec3 v = vec3(0.6);
```

is equivalent to

```
vec3 v = vec3(0.6, 0.6, 0.6);
```

This is true only for vectors. Structure constructors must receive one argument per member being constructed.

Matrix constructors also have a single argument form, but in this case it initializes just the diagonal of the matrix. The remaining components are initialized to 0.0.

```
mat2 m = mat2(1.0);   // makes a 2 x 2 identity matrix
```

is equivalent to

```
mat2 m = mat2(1.0, 0.0, 0.0, 1.0);   // makes a 2 x 2 identity matrix
```

Constructors can also have vectors and matrices as arguments. However, constructing matrices from other matrices is reserved for future definition.

```
vec4 v = vec4(1.0);
vec2 u = vec2(v);  // the first two components of v initialize u
mat2 m = mat2(v);
```

Matrix components are read out of arguments in column major order and written in column major order.

Extra components within a single constructor argument are silently ignored. Normally, this is useful for shrinking a value, like eliminating *alpha* from a color or *w* from a position. It is an error to have completely unused arguments passed to a constructor.

```
vec2 t = vec2(1.0, 2.0, 3.0);  // illegal; third argument is unused
```

3.4 Type Conversions

Explicit type conversions are performed with constructors. For example,

```
float f = 2.3;
bool b = bool(f);
```

sets b to **true**. This is useful for flow-control constructs, like **if**, which require Boolean values. Boolean constructors convert nonzero numeric values to **true** and zero numeric values to false.

The OpenGL Shading Language does not provide C-style typecast syntax, which can be ambiguous as to whether a value is converted to a different type or is simply reinterpreted as a different type. In fact, there is no way of reinterpreting a value as a different type in the OpenGL Shading Language. There are no pointers, no type unions, no implicit type changes, and no reinterpret casts. Instead, constructors perform conversions. The arguments to a constructor are converted to the type they are constructing. Hence, the following are allowed:

```
float f = float(3);   // convert integer 3 to floating-point 3.0
float g = float(b);   // convert Boolean b to floating point
vec4 v = vec4(2);     // set all components of v to 2.0
```

For conversion from a Boolean, **true** is converted to 1 or 1.0, and **false** is converted to a zero.

3.5 Qualifiers and Interface to a Shader

Qualifiers prefix both variables and formal function parameters. The qualifiers that modify formal function parameters (**const**, **in**, **out**, and **inout**) are discussed in Section 3.6.2. This section focuses on the other qualifiers, most of which form the interfaces of the shaders to their outside world. The following is the complete list of qualifiers (used outside of formal function parameters):

in	For frequently changing information, from the application to a vertex shader and for interpolated values read in a fragment shader
uniform	For infrequently changing information, from the application to either a vertex shader or a fragment shader
out	For interpolated information passed from a vertex shader to a fragment shader, and for output from a fragment shader
const	For declaring nonwritable, compile-time constant variables, as in C

Getting information into and out of a shader is quite different from more typical programming environments. Information is transferred to and from a shader by reading and writing built-in special variables and user-defined **in**, **uniform**, and **out** global variables. One of the most common built-in special variables was shown in the example at the beginning of this chapter. The special variable *gl_Position* is used for output of the homogeneous coordinates of the vertex position. The complete set of built-in special variables is provided in Chapter 4. Examples of **in**, **uniform**, and **out** qualified variables were seen briefly in the opening example for getting other information into and out of shaders. Each is discussed in this section.

Global variables may be qualified as **in**, **uniform**, or **out**. This is sensible since they are visible outside of shaders in the OpenGL API and, for a single program, they all share a single name space.

Qualifiers are always specified before the type of a variable, and because there is no default type, the form of a qualified variable declaration always includes a type.

```
in float Temperature;
const int NumLights = 3;
uniform vec4 LightPosition[NumLights];
out float LightIntensity;
```

3.5.1 Uniform Qualifiers

Uniform qualified variables (or uniforms) are set only outside a shader and are intended for data that changes less frequently. They can be changed at most once per primitive. All data types and arrays of all data types are supported for uniform qualified variables. All the vertex and fragment shaders forming a single program share a single global name space for uniforms. Hence, uniforms of the same name in a vertex and fragment program will be the same uniform variable.

Uniforms cannot be written to in a shader. This is sensible because an array of processors may be sharing the same resources to hold uniforms and other language semantics break down if uniforms could be modified.

Recall that unless a sampler (e.g., **sampler2D**) is a function parameter, the **uniform** qualifier must be used when it is declared. This is because samplers are opaque, and making them uniforms allows the OpenGL driver to validate that the application initializes a sampler with a texture and texture unit consistent with its use in the shader.

3.5.2 Uniform Blocks

Uniform qualified global variables, except for samplers, may be grouped together into named uniform blocks. The declaration is an optional layout qualifier, the **uniform** keyword, a uniform block name, and a member list similar to a structure definition. Unlike structures, each element in the list directly joins the global namespace. The OpenGL API uses the uniform block name to bind an appropriate uniform buffer object.

The uniform block may also be optionally qualified with a layout qualifier.

The default layout qualifier is **shared**, which prohibits dead-storage elimination of any unused members in the uniform block but otherwise permits the implementation control over the layout. This enables an OpenGL application to share the same uniform buffer object with multiple shader programs.

The **packed** layout qualifier allows dead-storage elimination. It is unlikely that such a buffer can be shared between multiple shader programs, but for large uniform blocks dead-storage elimination might significantly reduce the uniform buffer size.

A standard layout qualifier **std140** prohibits dead-storage elimination and also defines implementation-independent rules for how the elements are to be laid out in the uniform buffer. This may cost some storage space and/or performance but has the advantage of a portable layout across multiple OpenGL implementations.

Finally, matrix layout qualifiers **column_major** (the default) and **row_major** affect *only* the storage of matrices in a buffer object.

Some examples:

```
layout( std140 ) uniform; // provide an alternative default qualifier

uniform xform {
   uniform mat4 MVMatrix;
   uniform mat4 MVPMatrix;
   uniform mat3 NormalMatrix;
};

uniform skinning {
   layout( row_major ) mat4x3 SkinningMatrix[20];
}

layout( packed ) uniform surfaceProperties {
   vec4 BaseColor;
   vec4 RustColor;
};
```

3.5.3 In Qualifiers (Vertex Shader)

The **in** qualifier forms the input interface between the previous stages of the OpenGL pipeline and the shader. For each shader type, they have slightly different properties and limitations.

For vertex shaders, in-qualified global variables form the interface between the OpenGL API's generic vertex attributes and the vertex shader. This enables an application to pass frequently modified data into a vertex shader. They can be changed as often as once per vertex, either directly or indirectly by the application.

Vertex inputs are limited to floating-point scalars, integer scalars, unsigned integer scalars, floating-point vectors, integer vectors, and unsigned integer vectors, and matrices. In-qualified Boolean scalars, Boolean vectors, structures, or arrays are not permitted. This is, in part, a result of encouraging high-performance frequent changing of attributes in hardware implementations of the OpenGL system.

3.5.4 Out Qualifiers (Vertex Shader)

Out-qualified variables are the only way a vertex shader can communicate results through the rasterizer to a fragment shader. The intention is that each vertex in a drawing primitive might have a different value and the rasterizer will create many fragments (perhaps millions) each with unique interpolated values. The vertex shader writes the per-vertex values to be interpolated to an **out** variable.

Vertex shader out variables may be further qualified with interpolation qualifiers.

The default interpolation qualifier is **smooth out**, which interpolates the values of several vertices in a perspective-correct manner. However, there are times when the shader writer does not want perspective-correct interpolation. The interpolation qualifier **noperspective out** provides this control. Finally, it is possible to pass a single value from a single vertex in a primitive (called the PROVOKING VERTEX) to all fragments being rasterized. This is done with the qualifier **flat out**.

Vertex outputs are generally limited to floating-point scalars, floating-point vectors, matrices, and arrays of these. If the output is qualified **flat out**, then integer scalars, unsigned integer scalars, integer vectors, unsigned integer vectors, and arrays of these are also permitted. Structures cannot be output from a vertex shader.

3.5.5 In Qualifiers (Fragment Shader)

In-qualified variables are the way the fragment shader communicates with the rasterizer. Each named in variable must match in type, size, and interpolation qualifier with the out variables of the vertex shader.

3.5.6 Out Qualifiers (Fragment Shader)

Fragment shader out-qualified variables output data to the subsequent per-fragment fixed-function stage. They may not be further qualified. They can apply to floating-point scalars, floating-point vectors, integer scalars, integer vectors, unsigned integer scalars, unsigned integer vectors, and arrays of these. Matrices and structures cannot be output from a fragment shader.

3.5.7 Constant Qualifiers

Variables qualified as **const** (except for formal function parameters) are compile-time constants and are not visible outside the shader that declares them. Both scalar and nonscalar constants are supported. Structure fields may not be qualified with **const**, but structure variables can be declared as **const** and initialized with a structure constructor. Initializers for **const** declarations must be formed from literal values, other **const** qualified variables (not including function call parameters), or expressions of these.

Some examples:

```
const int numIterations = 10;
const float pi = 3.14159;
const vec2 v = vec2(1.0, 2.0);
const vec3 u = vec3(v, pi);
const struct light
{
    vec3 position;
    vec3 color;
} fixedLight = light(vec3(1.0, 0.5, 0.5), vec3(0.8, 0.8, 0.5));
```

All the preceding variables are compile-time constants. The compiler may propagate and fold constants at compile time, using the precision of the processor executing the compiler, and need not allocate any runtime resources to **const** qualified variables.

3.5.8 Absent Qualifier

If no qualifier is specified when a variable (not a function parameter) is declared, the variable can be both read and written by the shader. Nonqualified variables declared at global scope can be shared between shaders of the same type that are linked in the same program. Vertex shaders and fragment shaders each have their own separate global name space for nonqualified globals. However, nonqualified user-defined variables are not visible outside a program.

Unqualified variables have a lifetime limited to a single run of a shader. There is also no concept corresponding to a **static** variable in a C function that would allow a variable to be set to a value and have its shader retain that value from one execution to the next. Implementation of such variables is made difficult by the parallel processing nature of the execution environment, in which multiple instantiations run in parallel, sharing much of the same memory. In general, writable variables must have unique instances per processor executing a shader and therefore cannot be shared.

Because unqualified global variables have a different name space for vertex shaders than that for fragment shaders, it is not possible to share information through such variables between vertex and fragment shaders. Read-only variables can be shared if declared as **uniform**, and variables written by a vertex shader can be read by the fragment shader only through the **in** and **out** mechanism.

3.6 Flow Control

Flow control is very much like that in C++. The entry point into a shader is the function **main**. A program containing both vertex and fragment shaders has two functions named **main**, one for entering a vertex shader to process each vertex and one to enter a fragment shader to process each fragment. Before **main** is entered, any initializers for global variable declarations are executed.

Looping can be done with **for**, **while**, and **do-while**, just as in C++. Variables can be declared in **for** and **while** statements, and their scope lasts until the end of their substatements. The keywords **break** and **continue** also exist and behave as in C.

Selection can be done with **if** and **if-else**, just as in C++, with the exception that a variable cannot be declared in the **if** statement. Selection by means of the selection operator (**?:**) is also available, with the extra constraint that the second and third operands must have exactly the same type.

The type of the expression provided to an **if** statement or a **while** statement, or to terminate a **for** statement, must be a scalar Boolean. As in C, the right-hand operand to logical and (**&&**) is not evaluated (or at least appears not to be evaluated) if the left-hand operand evaluates to false, and the right-hand operand to logical or (**||**) is not evaluated if the left-hand operand evaluates to true. Similarly, only one of the second or third operands in the selection operator (**:?**) will be evaluated. A logical exclusive or (**^^**) is also provided, for which both sides are always evaluated.

A special branch, **discard**, can prevent a fragment from updating the framebuffer. When a fragment shader executes the **discard** keyword, the fragment being processed is marked to be discarded. An implementation might or might not continue executing the shader, but it is guaranteed that there is no effect on the framebuffer.

A **goto** keyword or equivalent is not available, nor are labels. Switching with **switch** is also not provided.

3.6.1 Functions

Function calls operate much as in C++. Function names can be overloaded by parameter type but not solely by return type. Either a function definition (body) or declaration must be in scope before a function is called. Parameter types are always checked. This means an empty parameter list () in a function declaration is not ambiguous, as in C, but rather explicitly means that the function accepts no arguments. Also, parameters must have exact matches since no automatic promotions are done, so selection of overloaded functions is quite straightforward.

Exiting from a function with **return** operates the same as in C++. Functions returning nonvoid types must return values whose type must exactly match the return type of the function.

Functions may not be called recursively, either directly or indirectly.

3.6.2 Calling Conventions

The OpenGL Shading Language uses call by value-return as its calling convention. The call by value part is familiar from C: Parameters qualified as input parameters are copied into the function and not passed as a reference. Because there are no pointers, a function need not worry about its parameters being aliases of some other memory. The return part of call by value-return means parameters qualified as output parameters are returned to the caller by being copied back from the called function to the caller when the function returns.

To specify which parameters are copied when, prefix them with the qualifier keywords **in**, **out**, or **inout**. For something that is just copied into the function but not returned, use **in**. The **in** qualifier is also implied when no qualifiers are specified. To say a parameter is not to be copied in but is to be set and copied back on return, use the qualifier **out**. To say a parameter is copied both in and out, use the qualifier **inout**.

in	Copy in but don't copy back out; still writable within the function
out	Only copy out; readable, but undefined at entry to function
inout	Copy in and copy out

The **const** qualifier can also be applied to function parameters. Here, it does not mean the variable is a compile-time constant, but rather that the function is not allowed to write it. Note that an ordinary, nonqualified input-only parameter can be written to; it just won't be copied back to the caller. Hence, there is a distinction between a parameter qualified as **const in** and one qualified only as **in** (or with no qualifier). Of course, **out** and **inout** parameters cannot be declared as **const**.

Some examples:

```
void ComputeCoord(in vec3 normal,  // Parameter 'normal' is copied in,
                                    // can be written to, but will not be
                                    // copied back out.
                  vec3 tangent,     // Same behavior as if "in" was used.
                  inout vec3 coord)// Copied in and copied back out.
```

Or,

```
vec3 ComputeCoord(const vec3 normal,// normal cannot be written to
                  vec3 tangent,
                  in vec3 coord)    //the function will return the result
```

The following are not legal:

```
void ComputeCoord(const out vec3 normal, //not legal; can't write normal
                  const inout vec3 tang, //not legal; can't write tang
                  in out vec3 coord)     //not legal; use inout
```

Structures and arrays can also be passed as arguments to a function. Keep in mind, though, that these data types are passed by value and there are no references, so it is possible to cause some large copies to occur at function call time. Array parameters must be declared with their size, and only arrays of matching type and size can be passed to an array parameter.

Functions can either return a value or return nothing. If a function returns nothing, it must be declared as type **void**. If a function returns a value, the type can be any type, including struct.

3.6.3 Built-in Functions

A large set of built-in functions is available. Built-in functions are documented in full in Chapter 5.

A shader can override these functions, providing its own definition. To override a function, provide a prototype or definition that is in scope at call time. The compiler or linker then looks for a user-defined version of the function to resolve that call. For example, one of the built-in sine functions is declared as

```
float sin(float x);
```

If you want to experiment with performance or accuracy trade-offs in a sine function or specialize it for a particular domain, you can override the built-in function with your own function.

```
float sin(float x)
{
    return <.. some function of x..>
}

void main()
{
    // call the sin function above, not the built-in sin function
    float s = sin(x);
}
```

This is similar to the typical language linking techniques of using libraries of functions and to having more locally scoped function definitions satisfy references before the library is checked. If the definition is in a different shader, just make sure a prototype is visible before calling the function. Otherwise, the built-in version is used.

3.7 Operations

Table 3.1 includes the operators, in order of precedence, available in the OpenGL Shading Language. The precedence and associativity are consistent with C.

Table 3.1   Operators, in order of precedence

Operator	Description
()	Parenthetical grouping
[ ]	Index
()	Function call and constructor
.	Member selection and swizzle
++ --	Postfix increment/decrement
++ --	Prefix increment/decrement
+ - ~ !	Unary
* / %	Multiplicative
+ −	Additive
<< >>	Bit-wise shift
< > <= >=	Relational
== !=	Equality
&	Bit-wise and
^	Bit-wise exclusive or
|	Bit-wise inclusive or
&&	Logical and

Table 3.1 Operators, in order of precedence, *continued*

Operator	Description
^^	Logical exclusive or
||	Logical inclusive or
?:	Selection
=	Assignment
+= -= *= /= %= <<= >>= &= ^= |=	Arithmetic assignment
,	Sequence

3.7.1 Indexing

Vectors, matrices, and arrays can be indexed with the index operator ([ ]). All indexing is zero based; the first element is at index 0. Indexing an array operates just as in C.

Indexing a vector returns scalar components. This allows giving components numerical names of 0, 1, … and also enables variable selection of vector components, should that be needed. For example,

```
vec4 v = vec4(1.0, 2.0, 3.0, 4.0);
float f = v[2];  // f takes the value 3.0
```

Here, *v[2]* is the floating-point scalar 3.0, which is then assigned into *f*.

Indexing a matrix returns columns of the matrix as vectors. For example,

```
mat4 m = mat4(3.0);  // initializes the diagonal to all 3.0
vec4 v;
v = m[1];    // places the vector (0.0, 3.0, 0.0, 0.0) into v
```

Here, the second column of *m, m[1]* is treated as a vector that is copied into *v*.

Behavior is undefined if an array, vector, or matrix is accessed with an index that is less than zero or greater than or equal to the size of the object.

3.7.2 Swizzling

The normal structure-member selector (.) is also used to SWIZZLE components of a vector—that is, select or rearrange components by listing their names after the swizzle operator (.). Examples:

```
vec4 v4;
v4.rgba;  // is a vec4 and the same as just using v4,
v4.rgb;   // is a vec3,
v4.b;     // is a float,
v4.xy;    // is a vec2,
v4.xgba;  // is illegal - the component names do not come from
          // the same set.
```

The component names can be out of order to rearrange the components, or they can be replicated to duplicate the components.

```
vec4 pos = vec4(1.0, 2.0, 3.0, 4.0);
vec4 swiz = pos.wzyx; // swiz = (4.0, 3.0, 2.0, 1.0)
vec4 dup = pos.xxyy;  // dup = (1.0, 1.0, 2.0, 2.0)
```

At most, four component names can be listed in a swizzle; otherwise, they would result in a nonexistent type. The rules for swizzling are slightly different for R-VALUES (expressions that are read from) and L-VALUES (expressions that say where to write to). R-values can have any combination and repetition of components. L-values must not have any repetition. For example,

```
vec4 pos = vec4(1.0, 2.0, 3.0, 4.0);
pos.xw = vec2(5.0, 6.0); // pos = (5.0, 2.0, 3.0, 6.0)
pos.wx = vec2(7.0, 8.0); // pos = (8.0, 2.0, 3.0, 7.0)
pos.xx = vec2(3.0, 4.0); // illegal - 'x' used twice
```

For R-values, this syntax can be used on any expression whose resultant type is a vector. For example, getting a two-component vector from a texture lookup can be done as

```
vec2 v = texture(sampler, coord).xy;
```

where the built-in function **texture** returns a **vec4**.

3.7.3 Component-wise Operation

With a few important exceptions, when an operator is applied to a vector, it behaves as if it were applied independently to each component of the vector. We refer to this behavior as COMPONENT-WISE for short.

For example,

```
vec3 v, u;
float f;
v = u + f;
```

is equivalent to

```
v.x = u.x + f;
v.y = u.y + f;
v.z = u.z + f;
```

and

```
vec3 v, u, w;
w = v + u;
```

is equivalent to

```
w.x = v.x + u.x;
w.y = v.y + u.y;
w.z = v.z + u.z;
```

If a binary operation operates on a vector and a scalar, the scalar is applied to each component of the vector. If two vectors are operated on, their sizes must match.

Exceptions are multiplication of a vector times a matrix and a matrix times a matrix, which perform standard linear-algebraic multiplies, not component-wise multiplies.

Increment and decrement operators (++ and --) and unary negation (–) behave as in C. When applied to a vector or matrix, they increment or decrement each component. They operate on integer and floating-point-based types.

Arithmetic operators of addition (+), subtraction (–), multiplication (*), and division (/) behave as in C, or component-wise, with the previously described exception of using linear-algebraic multiplication on vectors and matrices.

```
vec4 v, u;
mat4 m;
v * u;  // This is a component-wise multiply
v * m;  // This is a linear-algebraic row-vector times matrix multiply
m * v;  // This is a linear-algebraic matrix times column-vector multiply
m * m;  // This is a linear-algebraic matrix times matrix multiply
```

All other operations are performed component by component.

Logical not (!), logical and (&&), logical or (||), and logical inclusive or (^^) operate only on expressions that are typed as scalar Booleans, and they result in a Boolean. These cannot operate on vectors. A built-in function, **not**, computes the component-wise logical not of a vector of Booleans.

Relational operations (<, >, <=, and >=) operate only on floating-point and integer scalars and result in a scalar Boolean. Certain built-in functions, for instance, **lessThanEqual**, compute a Boolean vector result of component-wise comparisons of two vectors.

The equality operators (== and !=) operate on all types except arrays. They compare every component or structure member across the operands. This results in a scalar Boolean, indicating whether the two operands were equal. For two operands to be equal, their types must match, and each of their components or members must be equal. To compare two vectors in a component-wise fashion, call the built-in functions **equal** and **notEqual**.

Scalar Booleans are produced by the operators equal (==), not equal (!=), relational (<, >, <=, and >=), and logical not (!) because flow-control constructs (**if**, **for**, and so on) require a scalar Boolean. If built-in functions like **equal** are called to compute a vector of Booleans, such a vector can be turned into a scalar Boolean with the built-in functions **any** or **all**. For example, to do something if any component of a vector is less than the corresponding component of another vector, the code would be

```
vec4 u, v;
...
if (any(lessThan(u, v)))
    ...
```

Assignment (=) requires exact type match between the left- and right-hand side. Any type, except for arrays, can be assigned. Other assignment operators (+=, -=, *=, and /=) are similar to C but must make semantic sense when expanded, as in

```
a *= b   ⇒   a = a * b
```

where the expression *a * b* must be semantically valid, and the type of the expression *a * b* must be the same as the type of *a*. The other assignment operators behave similarly.

The ternary selection operator (?:) operates on three expressions: *exp1* ? *exp2* : *exp3*. This operator evaluates the first expression, which must result in a scalar Boolean. If the result is true, the operator selects to evaluate the second expression; otherwise, it selects to evaluate the third expression. Only one of the second and third expressions will appear to be evaluated. The second and third expressions must be the same type, but they can be of any type other than an array. The resulting type is the same as the type of the second and third expressions.

The sequence operator (,) operates on expressions by returning the type and value of the rightmost expression in a comma-separated list of expressions. All expressions are evaluated, in order, from left to right.

3.8 Preprocessor

The preprocessor is much like that in C. Support for

```
#
#define
#undef
#if
#ifdef
#ifndef
#else
#elif
#endif
```

as well as the `defined` and ## operators are exactly as in standard C. This includes macros with arguments and macro expansion. Built-in macros are

```
__LINE__
__FILE__
__VERSION__
```

`__LINE__` substitutes a decimal integer constant that is one more than the number of preceding new-lines in the current source string.

`__FILE__` substitutes a decimal integer constant that says which source string number is currently being processed.

`__VERSION__` substitutes a decimal integer reflecting the version number of the OpenGL Shading Language. The version of the shading language described in this document has `__VERSION__` defined as the decimal integer 140.

Macro names containing two consecutive underscores (__) are reserved for future use as predefined macro names, as are all macro names prefixed with "GL_".

There is also the usual support for

```
#error message
#line
#pragma
```

`#error` puts *message* into the shader's information log. The compiler then proceeds as if a semantic error has been encountered.

`#line` must have, after macro substitution, one of the following two forms:

```
#line line
#line line source-string-number
```

where *line* and *source-string-number* are constant integer expressions. After processing this directive (including its new-line), the implementation behaves as if it were compiling at line number *line+1* and source string number *source-string-number*. Subsequent source strings are numbered sequentially until another `#line` directive overrides that numbering.

`#pragma` is implementation dependent. Tokens following `#pragma` are not subject to preprocessor macro expansion. If an implementation does not recognize the tokens specified by the pragma, the pragma is ignored. However, the following pragmas are defined as part of the language.

```
#pragma STDGL
```

The STDGL pragma reserves pragmas for use by future revisions of the OpenGL Shading Language. No implementation may use a pragma whose first token is STDGL.

Use the optimize pragma

```
#pragma optimize(on)
#pragma optimize(off)
```

to turn optimizations on or off as an aid in developing and debugging shaders. The optimize pragma can occur only outside function definitions. By default, optimization is turned on for all shaders.

The debug pragma

```
#pragma debug(on)
#pragma debug(off)
```

enables compiling and annotating a shader with debug information so that it can be used with a debugger. The debug pragma can occur only outside function definitions. By default, debug is set to off.

Shaders should declare the version of the language to which they are written by using

```
#version number
```

If the targeted version of the language is the version that was approved in conjunction with OpenGL 3.1, then a value of 140 should be used for *number.* Any value less than 110 causes an error to be generated. Any value greater than the latest version of the language supported by the compiler also causes an error to be generated. Version 110 of the language does not require shaders to include this directive, and shaders without this directive are assumed to target version 110 of the OpenGL Shading Language. This directive, when present, must occur in a shader before anything else except comments and white space.

By default, compilers must issue compile-time syntactic, grammatical, and semantic errors for shaders that do not conform to the OpenGL Shading Language specification. Any extended behavior must first be enabled through a preprocessor directive. The behavior of the compiler with respect to extensions is declared with the #extension directive.

```
#extension extension_name : behavior
#extension all : behavior
```

extension_name is the name of an extension. The token `all` means that the specified behavior should apply to all extensions supported by the compiler. The possible values for behavior and their corresponding effects are shown in Table 3.2. A shader could check for the existence of a built-in function named **foo** defined by a language extension named *GL_ARB_foo* in the following way:

```
#ifdef GL_ARB_foo
    #extension GL_ARB_foo : enable
 // use the built-in function fooARB()
#else
    vec4 fooARB(); // provide a fallback for fooARB()
                   // with a user-defined function prototype
#endif
```

Directives that occur later override those that occur earlier. The `all` token sets the behavior for all extensions, overriding all previously issued #extension directives, but only for behaviors `warn` and `disable`.

The initial state of the compiler is as if the directive

```
#extension all : disable
```

were issued, telling the compiler that all error and warning reporting must be done according to the nonextended version of the OpenGL Shading Language that is being targeted (i.e., all extensions are ignored).

Macro expansion is not done on lines containing #extension and #version directives.

Table 3.2   Permitted values for the *behavior* expression in the `#extension` directive

Value of *behavior*	Effect
`require`	Behave as specified by the extension `extension_name`. The compiler reports an error on the `#extension` directive if the specified extension is not supported or if the token `all` is used instead of an extension name.
`enable`	Behave as specified by the extension `extension_name`. The compiler provides a warning on the `#extension` directive if the specified extension is not supported, and it reports an error if the token `all` is used instead of an extension name.
`warn`	Behave as specified by the extension `extension_name`, except cause the compiler to issue warnings on any detectable use of the specified extension, unless such use is supported by other enabled or required extensions. If `all` is specified, then the compiler warns on all detectable uses of any extension used.
`disable`	Behave (including errors and warnings) as if the extension specified by `extension_name` is not part of the language definition. If `all` is specified, then behavior must revert to that of the nonextended version of the language that is being targeted. The compiler warns if the specified extension is not supported.

The number sign (#) on a line by itself is ignored. Any directive not described in this section causes the compiler to generate an error message. The shader is subsequently treated as ill-formed.

3.9 Preprocessor Expressions

Preprocessor expressions can contain the operators listed in Table 3.3.

Preprocessor expressions have precedence, associativity, and behavior matching the standard C preprocessor.

Table 3.3 Preprocessor operators

Operator	Description
+ - ~ ! **defined**	Unary
* / %	Multiplicative
+ -	Additive
<< >>	Bit-wise shift
< > <= >=	Relational
== !=	Equality
& ^ |	Bit-wise
&& ||	Logical

Preprocessor expressions can be executed on the processor running the compiler and not on the graphics processor that executes the shader. Precision is allowed to be this host processor's precision and hence will likely be different from the precision available when expressions are executed in the core language.

As with the core language, string types and operations are not provided. None of the hash-based operators (#, ##, and so on) are provided, nor is a preprocessor **sizeof** operator.

3.10 Error Handling

Compilers accept some ill-formed programs because it is impossible to detect all ill-formed programs. For example, completely accurate detection of usage of an uninitialized variable is not possible. Such ill-formed shaders may execute differently on different platforms. Therefore, the OpenGL Shading Language specification states that portability is ensured only for well-formed programs.

OpenGL Shading Language compilers should detect ill-formed programs and issue diagnostic messages but are not required to do so for all cases. Compilers are required to return messages regarding shaders that are lexically, grammatically, or semantically incorrect. Shaders that generate such error messages cannot be executed. The OpenGL entry points for obtaining any diagnostic messages are discussed in Section 7.6.

3.11 Summary

The OpenGL Shading Language is a high-level procedural language designed specifically for the OpenGL environment. This language allows applications to specify the behavior of programmable, highly parallel graphics hardware. It contains constructs that allow succinct expression of graphics shading algorithms in a way that is natural for programmers experienced in C and C++.

The OpenGL Shading Language includes support for scalar, vector, and matrix types; structures and arrays; sampler types that access textures; data type qualifiers that define shader input and output; constructors for initialization and type conversion; and operators and flow-control statements like those in C and C++.

3.12 Further Information

The OpenGL Shading Language is defined in *The OpenGL Shading Language, Version 1.40*, by Kessenich, Baldwin, and Rost (2009). The grammar for the OpenGL Shading Language is included in its entirety in Appendix A. These two documents can be consulted for additional details about the language itself.

The functionality of the OpenGL Shading Language is augmented by the OpenGL extensions that were designed to support it. Read the specifications for these extensions and the OpenGL specification itself to gain further clarity on the behavior of a system that supports the OpenGL Shading Language. You can also consult the OpenGL books referenced at the conclusion of Chapter 1 for a better overall understanding of OpenGL.

The standard reference for the C programming language is *The C Programming Language* by the designers of the language, Brian Kernighan and Dennis Ritchie (1988). Likewise, the standard for the C++ programming language is *The C++ Programming Language*, written by the designer of C++, Bjarne Stroustrup (2000). Numerous other books on both languages are available.

[1] Kernighan, Brian, and Dennis Ritchie, *The C Programming Language, Second Edition*, Prentice Hall, Englewood Cliffs, New Jersey, 1988.

[2] Kessenich, John, Dave Baldwin, and Randi Rost, *The OpenGL Shading Language, Version 1.40*, 3Dlabs/Intel, March 2009. www.opengl.org/documentation/specs/

[3] Segal, Mark, and Kurt Akeley, *The OpenGL Graphics System: A Specification (Version 3.1)*, Editor (v1.1): Chris Frazier, (v1.2–3.1): Jon Leech, (v2.0): Jon Leech and Pat Brown, March 2009. www.opengl.org/documentation/specs/Stroustrup, Bjarne, *The C++ Programming Language (Special 3rd Edition)*, Addison-Wesley, Reading, Massachusetts, 2000.

Chapter 4

The OpenGL Programmable Pipeline

With contributions by Barthold Lichtenbelt

The OpenGL Shading Language is designed specifically for use with OpenGL. Vertex shader and fragment shader input and output are tied into the standard OpenGL pipeline in a well-defined manner. The basics of how the programmable processors fit into the OpenGL pipeline were covered in Section 2.3. This chapter discusses the details of that integration and the language mechanisms used to achieve it.

Applications can provide data to shaders with user-defined attribute variables and user-defined uniform variables. The OpenGL Shading Language also provides special built-in variables that can communicate between the programmable processors and the surrounding fixed functionality in the following ways:

- Limited OpenGL state is accessible from either vertex shaders or fragment shaders by means of built-in uniform variables.

- Vertex shaders communicate to subsequent processing in OpenGL through the use of special built-in vertex shader output variables and user-defined out variables.

- Fragment shaders obtain the results from the preceding processing through special built-in fragment shader input variables and user-defined in variables.

- Fragment shaders communicate results to subsequent processing stages of OpenGL through special fragment shader output variables and user-defined out variables.

- Built-in constants are accessible from within both types of shaders and define some of the same implementation-dependent constants that are accessible with OpenGL's **glGet** function.

All the built-in identifiers begin with the reserved prefix "gl_" to set them apart.

4.1 The Vertex Processor

The vertex processor executes a vertex shader and replaces the fixed functionality OpenGL per-vertex operations. Specifically, the following fixed functionality operations are removed:

- The transformation of vertex coordinates by the modelview matrix.
- The transformation of the vertex coordinates by the projection matrix.
- The transformation of the texture coordinates by the texture matrices.
- The transformation of normals to eye coordinates.
- Rescaling and normalization of normals.
- Texture coordinate generation.
- Per-vertex lighting computations.
- Color material computations.
- Point size distance attenuation.

The following fixed functionality operations are applied to vertex values that are the result of executing the vertex shader:

- Perspective division on clip coordinates
- Viewport mapping
- Depth range scaling
- View frustum clipping
- Front face determination
- Culling
- Flat-shading
- Associated data clipping
- Final color processing

The basic operation of the vertex processor was discussed in Section 2.3.1. As shown in Figure 2.2, data can come into the vertex shader through user-defined in variables, uniform variables (built in or user defined), or texture maps. Data exits the vertex processor through built-in special variables, user-defined varying variables, and special vertex shader output variables. Built-in constants (described in Section 4.4) are also accessible from within a vertex shader. A vertex shader has no knowledge of the primitive type for the vertex it is working on.

4.1.1 Vertex Attributes

To draw things with OpenGL, applications must provide vertex information such as normal, color, texture coordinates, and so on. These are called generic vertex attributes by the OpenGL API and may be specified outside of draw commands with the OpenGL function **glVertexAttrib**. When set with these function calls, the generic vertex attributes become part of OpenGL's current state.

Geometry can also be drawn with vertex buffers. With this method, applications arrange generic vertex attributes in separate arrays containing positions, normals, colors, texture coordinates, and so on. By calling **glDrawArrays**, applications can send a large number of generic vertex attributes to OpenGL in a single function call.

Generic vertex attributes are connected to the user-defined vertex shader in variables through binding. For example:

```
//
// Vertex Attributes
//
// in qualified global variables are typically changed per vertex
in  vec4  mcVertex;
in  vec3  mcBiNormal;
in  vec3  mcTangentNormal;

in  vec2  mcTexCoord;
in  vec2  mcDetailTexCoord;

in  float PointSize
```

Details on binding generic vertex attributes to a vertex shader through the OpenGL Shading Language API are provided in Section 7.7.

The number of generic vertex attributes a vertex shader can use is limited. This limit is implementation specific and can be queried with **glGet** with the symbolic constant GL_MAX_VERTEX_ATTRIBS. Every OpenGL implementation is required to support at least 16 generic vertex attributes in a vertex shader.

4.1.2 Special Input Variables

There are two special vertex shader inputs, *gl_VertexID* and *gl_InstanceID*. The variable *gl_VertexID* contains the implict vertex index passed by DrawArrays or one of the other drawing commands. The variable *gl_InstanceID* holds the implicit primitive index passed by instanced draw commands.

```
int gl_VertexID;        // may be read
int gl_InstanceID;      // may be read
```

4.1.3 Uniform Variables

Shaders can access limited OpenGL state through built-in uniform variables containing the reserved prefix "gl_". This limited OpenGL state used by the shader is automatically tracked and made available to the shader. This automatic state-tracking mechanism enables the application to use existing OpenGL state commands for state management and have the current values of such state automatically available for use in the shader.

OpenGL state is accessible to both vertex shaders and fragment shaders by means of the built-in uniform variables defined in Section 4.3.

Applications can also define their own uniform variables in a vertex shader and use OpenGL API calls to set their values (see Section 7.8 for a complete description). There is an implementation-dependent limit on the amount of storage allowed for uniform variables in a vertex shader. The limit refers to the storage for the combination of built-in uniform variables and user-defined uniform variables that are actually used in a vertex shader. It is defined in terms of components, where a component is the size of a **float**. Thus, a **vec2** takes up two components, a **vec3** takes three, and so on. This value can be queried with **glGet** with the symbolic constant GL_MAX_VERTEX_UNIFORM_COMPONENTS.

4.1.4 User-Defined Out Variables

Vertex shaders can also define out variables to pass arbitrary values to the fragment shader. Such values are not clamped, but they are subjected to subsequent fixed functionality processing such as clipping and interpolation. The vertex shader may control interpolation with interpolation qualifiers. The **smooth** qualifier will interpolate the output with perspective-correction (the default). The **noperspective** qualifier eliminates the perspective divide during interpolation. The **flat** qualifier selects the value of a provoking vertex. There is an implementation-dependent limit to the number of floating-point values that can be interpolated. This limit can be queried with **glGet** with the symbolic constant GL_MAX_VARYING_FLOATS.

4.1.5 Special Output Variables

Earlier we learned that results from the vertex shader are sent on for additional processing by fixed functionality within OpenGL, including primitive assembly and rasterization. Several special built-in variables are defined as part of the OpenGL Shading Language to allow the vertex shader to pass information to these subsequent processing stages. The built-in variables discussed in this section are available only from within a vertex shader.

The variable *gl_Position* writes the vertex position in clipping coordinates after it has been computed in a vertex shader. Results of primitive assembly and rasterization are undefined if a vertex shader is executed and it does not store a value into *gl_Position.*

The built-in variable *gl_PointSize* writes the size (diameter) of a point primitive. It is measured in pixels. This allows a vertex shader to compute a screen size that is related to the distance to the point, for instance. Results of rasterizing points are undefined if a vertex shader is executed and it does not store a value into *gl_PointSize.* Section 4.5.1 provides more details on using *gl_PointSize.*

If user clipping is enabled, it occurs as a fixed functionality operation after the vertex shader has been executed. For user clipping to function properly in conjunction with the use of a vertex shader, the vertex shader must compute clip distances. These values must then be stored in the built-in variable *gl_ClipDistance.* It is up to the application and shader writer to ensure that the clip distance values are computed in the desired coordinate space. Clip distances work properly in linear (or locally near linear) coordinate spaces. Results of user clipping are undefined if user clipping is enabled and a vertex shader does not store a value into *gl_ClipDistance.* More details on using *gl_ClipDistance* are contained in Section 4.5.2.

These variables each have global scope. They can be written to at any time during the execution of the vertex shader, and they can be read back after they have been written. Reading them before writing them results in undefined behavior. If they are written more than once, the last value written will be the one that is consumed by the subsequent operations.

These variables can be referenced only from within a vertex shader and are intrinsically declared with the following types:

```
vec4  gl_Position;        // may be written to
float gl_PointSize;       // may be written to
float gl_ClipDistances[]; // may be written to
```

4.2 The Fragment Processor

The fragment processor executes a fragment shader and replaces fixed functionality OpenGL fragment operations. Specifically, the following fixed functionality OpenGL operations are removed:

- Texture environments and texture functions
- Texture application
- Color sum
- Fog

The behavior of the following operations does not change:

- Texture image specification
- Alternate texture image specification
- Compressed texture image specification
- Texture parameters that behave as specified even when a texture is accessed from within a fragment shader
- Texture state and proxy state
- Texture object specification
- Texture comparison modes

The basic operation of the fragment processor was discussed in Section 2.3.2. As shown in Figure 2.3, data can come into the fragment shader through user-defined in variables, uniform variables (built in or user defined), special input variables, or texture maps. Data exits the fragment processor through special fragment shader output variables or user-defined output variables Built-in constants (described in Section 4.4) are also accessible from within a fragment shader.

4.2.1 User-Defined In Variables

Fragment shaders can also define in variables to receive arbitrary interpolated values from the vertex shader. The fragment shader may control interpolation with interpolation qualifiers. The *smooth* qualifier will interpolate the output with perspective-correction (the default). The *noperspective* qualifier eliminates the perspective divide during interpolation. The *flat* qualifier selects the value of a provoking vertex. The interpolation qualifiers of a fragment shader must match the interpolation qualifiers of the vertex shader. There is an implementation-dependent limit to the number of floating-point values that can be interpolated. This limit can be queried with **glGet** with the symbolic constant GL_MAX_VARYING_FLOATS.

4.2.2 Special Input Variables

The variable *gl_FragCoord* is available as a variable from within fragment shaders, and it holds the window relative coordinates x, y, z, and $1/w$ for the fragment. This window position value is the result of the fixed functionality that interpolates primitives after vertex processing to generate fragments. The z component contains the depth value as modified by the polygon offset calculation. This built-in variable allows implementation of window position-dependent operations such as screen-door transparency (e.g., use **discard** on any fragment for which *gl_FragCoord.x* is odd or *gl_FragCoord.y* is odd, but not both).

The fragment shader also has access to the built-in variable *gl_FrontFacing* whose value is true if the fragment belongs to a front-facing primitive, and false otherwise. This value can be used to select between two colors calculated by the vertex shader to emulate two-sided lighting, or it can be used to apply completely different shading effects to front and back surfaces. A fragment derives its facing direction from the primitive that generates the fragment. All fragments generated by primitives other than polygons are considered to be front facing. For all other fragments (including fragments resulting from polygons drawn with a polygon mode of GL_POINT or GL_LINE), the determination is made by examination of the sign of the area of the primitive in window coordinates. This sign can possibly be reversed, depending on the last call to **glFrontFace**. If the sign is positive, the fragments are front facing; otherwise, they are back facing.

The special variable *gl_PointCoord* contains a two-dimensional coordinate whose values are in the range 0.0 to 1.0 when a fragment belongs to a point (including fragments resulting from polygons drawn with a polygon mode of GL_POINT); otherwise, the values are undefined.

These special input variables have global scope and can be referenced only from within a fragment shader. They are intrinsically declared with the following types:

```
vec4  gl_FragCoord;
bool  gl_FrontFacing;
vec2  gl_PointCoord;
```

4.2.3 Uniform Variables

As described in Section 4.1.3, OpenGL state is available to both vertex shaders and fragment shaders through built-in uniform variables that begin with the reserved prefix "gl_". The list of uniform variables that can be used to access OpenGL state is provided in Section 4.3.

User-defined uniform variables can be defined and used within fragment shaders in the same manner as they are used within vertex shaders. OpenGL API calls are provided to set their values (see Section 7.8 for complete details).

The implementation-dependent limit that defines the amount of storage available for uniform variables in a fragment shader can be queried with **glGet** with the symbolic constant GL_MAX_FRAGMENT_UNIFORM_COMPONENTS. This limit refers to the storage for the combination of built-in uniform variables and user-defined uniform variables that are actually used in a fragment shader. It is defined in terms of components, where a component is the size of a **float**.

4.2.4 User-Defined Out Variables

The primary purpose of a fragment shader is to compute values that will ultimately be written into the framebuffer. Unless the keyword **discard** is encountered, the output of the fragment shader goes on to be processed by the fixed-function operations at the back end of the OpenGL pipeline.

User-defined out variables in the fragment shader link the fragment outputs to fixed-function per-fragment operations, and from there to the framebuffer. Each output may be a float, an integer, an unsigned integer, vectors, and arrays of that type. They may not be matrices or structures.

Details on binding fragment shader out variables to the fixed-function per-fragment operations through the OpenGL Shading Language API are provided in Section 7.10.

4.2.5 Special Output Variables

Fragment shaders send some of their results on to the back end of the OpenGL pipeline by using the built-in special output variable *gl_FragDepth*. This built-in fragment shader variable has global scope and may be written more than once by a fragment shader. If written more than once, the last value assigned is the one used in the subsequent operations. It can also be read back after it has been written. Reading before writing results in undefined behavior.

If a shader does not write *gl_FragDepth*, the fixed-function value for depth is used as the fragment's depth value. Otherwise, writing to *gl_FragDepth* establishes the depth value for the fragment being processed. As it exits the fragment processor, this value is clamped to the range [0,1] and converted to fixed point with at least as many bits as are in the depth component in the destination framebuffer. Fragment shaders that write to *gl_FragDepth* should take care to write to it for every execution path through the shader. If it is written in one branch of a conditional statement but not the other, the depth value will be undefined for some execution paths.

The *z* component of *gl_FragCoord* contains the depth value resulting from the preceding fixed-function processing. It contains the value that would be used for the fragment's depth if the shader contained no writes to *gl_FragDepth*. This component can be used to achieve an invariant result if a fragment shader conditionally computes *gl_FragDepth* but otherwise wants the fixed functionality fragment depth.

The value *gl_FragDepth* does not need to be clamped within a shader. The fixed functionality pipeline following the fragment processor clamps the value, if needed, to the range required by the buffer into which the fragment will be written.

The fragment shader output variable has global scope, can be referenced only from within a fragment shader, and is intrinsically declared with the following type:

```
float gl_FragDepth;
```

4.3 Built-in Uniform Variables

OpenGL was originally designed as a configurable state machine. It had a large variety of state that could be set. At the time graphics primitives are provided to OpenGL for rendering, the current state settings affect how the graphics primitives are treated and ultimately how they are rendered into the framebuffer.

OpenGL has replaced much of the configurable state machine with programmable processors. The state associated with much of the configurable state machine is deprecated in 3.0. (It had already been removed in OpenGL ES 2.0.)

The built-in uniform variables in Listing 4.1 allow shaders to access limited current OpenGL state. These variables can be accessed from within either vertex shaders or fragment shaders. If an OpenGL state value has not been modified by an application, it contains the default value as defined by OpenGL, and the corresponding built-in uniform variable is also equal to that value.

Listing 4.1   Built-in uniform variables

```
//
// Depth range in window coordinates
//
struct gl_DepthRangeParameters
{
    float near;        // n
    float far;         // f
    float diff;        // f - n
};
uniform gl_DepthRangeParameters gl_DepthRange;
```

4.4 Built-in Constants

The OpenGL Shading Language defines a number of built-in constants. These values can be accessed from within either vertex shaders or fragment shaders. Values for lights, clip planes, and texture units are values that are equivalent to those that would be returned by OpenGL's **glGet** function for the underlying implementation. Implementation-dependent values that are new with the OpenGL Shading Language are the number of floating-point values that could be stored as uniform values accessible by the vertex shader and by the fragment shader, the number of floating-point values that could be defined as varying variables, the number of texture image units that are accessible by the vertex processor and by the fragment processor, the total number of texture image units available to the vertex processor and the fragment processor combined, the number of texture coordinates sets that are supported, and the number of draw buffers that are accessible. All these new implementation-dependent constants can also be obtained in application code with the OpenGL **glGet** function (see Section 7.12).

OpenGL defines minimum values for each implementation-dependent constant. The minimum value informs application writers of the lowest value that is permissible for a conforming OpenGL implementation. The minimum value for each of the built-in constants is shown here:

```
//
// Implementation-dependent constants.  The following values
// are the minimum values allowed for these constants.
//
const int    gl_MaxVertexAttribs           =   16;
const int    gl_MaxVertexUniformComponents = 1024;
const int    gl_MaxVaryingComponents       =   64;
const int    gl_MaxVertexTextureImageUnits =   16;
const int    gl_MaxCombinedTextureImageUnits =   16;
const int    gl_MaxTextureImageUnits       =   16;
const int    gl_MaxFragmentUniformComponents = 1024;
const int    gl_MaxDrawBuffers             =    8;
const int    gl_MaxClipDistances           =    8;
```

4.5 Interaction with OpenGL Fixed Functionality

This section offers a little more detail to programmers who are intimately familiar with OpenGL operations and need to know precisely how the programmable capabilities introduced by the OpenGL Shading Language interact with the rest of the OpenGL pipeline. This section is more suitable for seasoned OpenGL programmers than for OpenGL novices.

4.5.1 Point Size Mode

Vertex shaders can operate in point size mode. A vertex shader can compute a point size in pixels and assign it to the built-in variable *gl_PointSize*. If point size mode is enabled, the point size is taken from this variable and used in the rasterization stage; otherwise, it is taken from the value set with the **glPointSize** command. If *gl_PointSize* is not written while vertex shader point size mode is enabled, the point size used in the rasterization stage is undefined. Vertex shader point size mode is enabled and disabled with **glEnable** or **glDisable** with the symbolic value GL_VERTEX_PROGRAM_POINT_SIZE.

This point size enable is convenient for the majority of applications that do not change the point size within a vertex shader. By default, this mode is disabled, so most vertex shaders for which point size doesn't matter need not write a value to *gl_PointSize*. The value set by calls to **glPointSize** is always used by the rasterization stage.

If the primitive is clipped and vertex shader point size mode is enabled, the point size values are also clipped in a manner analogous to color clipping. The potentially clipped point size is used by the fixed functionality part of the pipeline as the derived point size (the distance attenuated point size). Thus, if the application wants points farther away to be smaller, it should compute some kind of distance attenuation in the vertex shader and scale the point size accordingly. If vertex shader point size mode is disabled, the derived point size is taken directly from the value set with the **glPointSize** command and no distance attenuation is performed. The derived point size is then used, as usual, optionally to alpha-fade the point when multi-sampling is also enabled. Again, see the OpenGL specification for details.

Distance attenuation should be computed in a vertex shader and cannot be left to the fixed functionality distance attenuation algorithm. This fixed functionality algorithm computes distance attenuation as a function of the distance between the eye at (0, 0, 0, 1) and the vertex position, in eye coordinates. However, the vertex position computed in a vertex shader might not have anything to do with locations in eye coordinates. Therefore, when a vertex shader is active, this fixed functionality algorithm is skipped. A point's alpha-fade, on the other hand, can be computed correctly only with the knowledge of the primitive type. That information is not available to a vertex shader, because it executes before primitive assembly. Consider the case of rendering a triangle and having the back polygon mode set to GL_POINT and the front polygon mode to GL_FILL. The vertex shader should fade only the alpha if the vertex belongs to a back facing triangle. But it cannot do that because it does not know the primitive type.

4.5.2 Clipping

User clipping can be used in conjunction with a vertex shader. The vertex shader must provide the clip distances (typically, by taking the dot product of the vertex in eye space with clip planes in eye space). It does that by writing this location to the output variable *gl_ClipDistances*. If *gl_ClipDistances* is not specified and user clipping is enabled, the results are undefined. When a vertex shader that mimics OpenGL's fixed functionality is used, the vertex shader should compute the clip distances of the vertex and store it in *gl_ClipDistance*. For example,

```
in vec4 MCVertex;
uniform mat4 MVMatrix;
uniform vec4 ECClipPlane[6];
// ...
vec4 ECVertex = MVMatrix * MCVertex;
int i;
for (i=0 ; i<6 ; i++ )
{
    gl_ClipDistance[i] = dot( ECVertex, ECClipPlane[i] );

}
```

After user clipping, vertices are clipped against the view volume, as usual. In this operation, the value specified by *gl_Position* (i.e., the homogeneous vertex position in clip space) is evaluated against the view volume.

4.5.3 Position Invariance

For multipass rendering, several vertex shaders may perform one or more passes positional invariance is important. This means that the vertex shaders must compute the exact same vertex position in clip coordinates. Positional invariance can be achieved with the **invariant** qualifier in a vertex shader as follows:

```
invariant gl_Position;
```

The use of the invariant qualifier prevents the compiler optimizer from reordering calculations used in the calculation of *gl_Position*. If each of the shaders in a family of vertex shaders computes *gl_Position* in the same manner, then no matter what other independent operations in the vertex shader differ, those operations cannot directly or indirectly effect the result.

4.5.4 Texturing

One of the major improvements to OpenGL made by the OpenGL Shading Language is in the area of texturing. For one thing, texturing operations can be performed in a vertex shader. But the fragment side of the pipeline has improved as well. The number of texture image units has grown dramatically with fragment shaders. This means that more independent texture lookups can be performed in a single rendering pass. And with programmability, the results of all those texture lookups can be combined in any way the shader writer sees fit.The symbolic constant GL_MAX_TEXTURE_IMAGE_UNITS can be queried with **glGet** to obtain a number of texture image units accessible to shaders.

Three different limits related to texture mapping should be taken into account.

- For a vertex shader, the maximum number of available texture image units is given by GL_MAX_VERTEX_TEXTURE_IMAGE_UNITS.

- For a fragment shader, the maximum number of available texture image units is given by GL_MAX_TEXTURE_IMAGE_UNITS.

- The combined number of texture image units used in the vertex and the fragment processing parts of OpenGL (either a fragment shader or fixed function) cannot exceed the limit GL_MAX_COMBINED_TEXTURE_IMAGE_UNITS. If a vertex shader and the fragment processing part of OpenGL both use the same texture image unit, that counts as two units against this limit. This rule exists because an OpenGL implementation might have only GL_MAX_COMBINED_TEXTURE_IMAGE_UNITS actual texture image units implemented, and it might share those units between the vertex and fragment processing parts of OpenGL.

The somewhat confusing (and often error prone) fixed-function hierarchy of texture-enables (GL_TEXTURE_CUBE_MAP, GL_TEXTURE_3D, GL_TEXTURE_2D, and GL_TEXTURE_1D) is gone. A sampler bound to a texture image unit determines which target will be sampled. (However, samplers of different dimensions may not be bound to the same texture image unit.)

Samplers of type **sampler1DShadow** or **sampler2DShadow** must be used to access depth textures (textures with a base internal format of GL_DEPTH_COMPONENT). The texture comparison mode requires the shader to use one of the variants of the **shadow** built-in functions for accessing the texture (see Section 5.7). If these built-in functions are used to access a texture with a base internal format other than GL_DEPTH_COMPONENT, the result is undefined. Similarly, if a texture access function other than one of the shadow variants is used to access a depth texture, the result is undefined.

If a shader uses a sampler to reference a texture object that is not complete (e.g., one of the textures in a mipmap has a different internal format or border width than the others, see the OpenGL specification for a complete list), the texture image unit returns (R, G, B, A) = (0, 0, 0, 1).

4.6 Summary

Two new programmable units have been added to OpenGL: the vertex processor and the fragment processor. The same language, with minor differences, expresses algorithms intended to run on either processor. The vertex processor replaces the fixed functionality vertex processing of OpenGL, and a shader intended for execution on this processor is called a vertex shader. The vertex shader is executed once for each vertex that is processed by OpenGL. The fragment processor replaces the fixed functionality fragment processing of OpenGL, and a shader that is intended for execution on this processor is called a fragment shader. The fragment shader is executed once for each fragment that arises from rasterization.

Great care was taken to define the interfaces between the programmable stages of OpenGL and the intervening fixed functionality. They also allow a shader to communicate with the preceding and following fixed functionality stages of the graphics-processing pipeline.

4.7 Further Information

The built-in variables defined in this chapter are used in various examples throughout this book. The OpenGL Shading Language specification and the OpenGL specification can be consulted for additional details. The OpenGL books referenced at the conclusion of Chapter 1 can also be consulted for a better understanding of the OpenGL state that is referenced through built-in variables. Parts of the paper *Integrating the OpenGL Shading Language* by Barthold Lichtenbelt have been adapted for inclusion in this book.

[1] Kessenich, John, Dave Baldwin, and Randi Rost, *The OpenGL Shading Language, Version 1.40*, 3Dlabs/Intel, March 2008. www.opengl.org/documentation/specs/

[2] Lichtenbelt, Barthold, *Integrating the OpenGL Shading Language*, 3Dlabs internal white paper, July 2003.

[3] Segal, Mark, and Kurt Akeley, *The OpenGL Graphics System: A Specification (Version 3.1)*, Editor (v1.1): Chris Frazier, (v1.2–3.1): Jon Leech, (v2.0): Jon Leech and Pat Brown, March 2008. www.opengl.org/documentation/specs/

Chapter 5

Built-in Functions

This chapter provides the details of the functions that are defined as part of the OpenGL Shading Language. Feel free to skip ahead to the next chapter if you want to get down to the nitty-gritty of writing your own shaders. This chapter can be useful as a reference after you are well on your way to writing OpenGL shaders for your own application.

The OpenGL Shading Language defines an assortment of built-in convenience functions for scalar and vector operations. The reasons for providing built-in functions for the OpenGL Language include

- Making shaders simpler to develop and easier to understand and maintain.

- Exposing some necessary hardware functionality in a convenient way such as accessing a texture map. The language for these functions cannot be emulated by a shader.

- Representing a trivial operation (clamp, mix, etc.) that is simple for a user to write but that is common and may have direct hardware support. Providing a built-in function makes it much easier for the compiler to map such expressions to complex hardware instructions.

- Representing an operation that graphics hardware is likely to accelerate at some point. The trigonometry functions fall into this category.

Many of the functions are similar to the same named ones in common C libraries, but they support vector input as well as the more traditional scalar input. Because the OpenGL Shading Language supports function overloading, the built-in functions usually have several variants, all with the same name. The difference in the functions is in the type of arguments and the type of the value returned. Quite a few of the built-in functions have four variants: one that takes **float** parameters and returns a **float**, one that takes **vec2** parameters and returns a **vec2**, one that takes **vec3** parameters and returns a **vec3**, and one that takes **vec4** parameters and returns a **vec4**.

Whenever possible, you should use the built-in functions rather than do the equivalent computations in your own shader code. It is expected that the built-in functions will be implemented in an optimal way, perhaps even supported directly in hardware. Almost all the built-in functions can be used in either a vertex shader or a fragment shader, but a few are available only for a specific type of shader. You can write a shader to replace a built-in function with your own code simply by redeclaring and defining the same function name and argument list.

Graphical representations of some of the functions are shown for clear illustration. The functions are generally simple ones, and most readers would have no trouble constructing such diagrams themselves. But as we see in later chapters, many of the built-in functions can be used in unconventional ways to achieve interesting effects in shaders. When you are developing a shader, it is often helpful to draw a simple function diagram to clearly envision the value of a variable at a particular spot in a shader. By seeing a pictorial representation of some of these functions, you may find it easier to draw such diagrams yourself and to gain some insight about how you might use them in procedural shaders. Some common uses for these functions are pointed out along the way, and some are illustrated by shader examples in the later chapters of this book.

5.1 Angle and Trigonometry Functions

Trigonometry functions can be used within either vertex shaders or fragment shaders. Function parameters specified as *angle* are assumed to be in units of radians. In no case do any of these functions result in a divide-by-zero error. If the divisor of a ratio is 0, results are undefined.

These functions all operate component-wise (see Table 5.1). The description column specifies the operation on each component.

In addition to their usefulness as trigonometric functions, **sin** and **cos** can be used in a variety of ways as the basis for a smoothly varying function with no cusps or discontinuities (see Figure 5.1). Such a function can be used to model waves on the surface of an object, to change periodically between two materials, to introduce a rocking motion to an object, or to achieve many other effects.

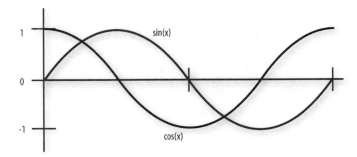

Figure 5.1   The **sin** and **cos** functions

Table 5.1   Angle and trigonometry functions

Syntax	Description
float **radians** (float *degrees*) vec2 **radians** (vec2 *degrees*) vec3 **radians** (vec3 *degrees*) vec4 **radians** (vec4 *degrees*)	Converts *degrees* to radians and returns the result, i.e., result = $\pi/180 \cdot$ *degrees*.
float **degrees** (float *radians*) vec2 **degrees** (vec2 *radians*) vec3 **degrees** (vec3 *radians*) vec4 **degrees** (vec4 *radians*)	Converts *radians* to degrees and returns the result, i.e., result = $180/\pi \cdot$ *radians*.
float **sin** (float *radians*) vec2 **sin** (vec2 *radians*) vec3 **sin** (vec3 *radians*) vec4 **sin** (vec4 *radians*)	The standard trigonometric sine function. The values returned by this function are in the range [–1,1].
float **cos** (float *radians*) vec2 **cos** (vec2 *radians*) vec3 **cos** (vec3 *radians*) vec4 **cos** (vec4 *radians*)	The standard trigonometric cosine function. The values returned by this function are in the range [–1,1].
float **tan** (float *radians*) vec2 **tan** (vec2 *radians*) vec3 **tan** (vec3 *radians*) vec4 **tan** (vec4 *radians*)	The standard trigonometric tangent function.

(continues)

Table 5.1   Angle and trigonometry functions, *continued*

Syntax	Description
float **asin** (float *x*) vec2 **asin** (vec2 *x*) vec3 **asin** (vec3 *x*) vec4 **asin** (vec4 *x*)	Arc sine. Returns an angle whose sine is *x*. The range of values returned by this function is $[-\pi/2, \pi/2]$. Results are undefined if $|x| > 1$.
float **acos** (float *x*) vec2 **acos** (vec2 *x*) vec3 **acos** (vec3 *x*) vec4 **acos** (vec4 *x*)	Arc cosine. Returns an angle whose cosine is *x*. The range of values returned by this function is $[0, \pi]$. Results are undefined if $|x| > 1$.
float **atan** (float *y*, float *x*) vec2 **atan** (vec2 *y*, vec2 *x*) vec3 **atan** (vec3 *y*, vec3 *x*) vec4 **atan** (vec4 *y*, vec4 *x*)	Arc tangent. Returns an angle whose tangent is *y/x*. The signs of *x* and *y* determine what quadrant the angle is in. The range of values returned by this function is $[-\pi, \pi]$. Results are undefined if *x* and *y* are both 0.
float **atan** (float *y_over_x*) vec2 **atan** (vec2 *y_over_x*) vec3 **atan** (vec3 *y_over_x*) vec4 **atan** (vec4 *y_over_x*)	Arc tangent. Returns an angle whose tangent is *y_over_x*. The range of values returned by this function is $[-\pi/2, \pi/2]$.
float **sinh** (float *x*) vec2 **sinh** (vec2 *x*) vec3 **sinh** (vec3 *x*) vec4 **sinh** (vec4 *x*)	Hyperbolic sine. Returns $(e^x - e^{-x})/2$.
float **cosh** (float *x*) vec2 **cosh** (vec2 *x*) vec3 **cosh** (vec3 *x*) vec4 **cosh** (vec4 *x*)	Hyperbolic cosine. Returns $(e^x + e^{-x})/2$.
float **tanh** (float *x*) vec2 **tanh** (vec2 *x*) vec3 **tanh** (vec3 x) vec4 **tanh** (vec4 *x*)	Hyperbolic tangent. Returns $(e^x - e^{-x})/(e^x + e^{-x})$.

Table 5.1 Angle and trigonometry functions, *continued*

Syntax	Description
float **asinh** (float *x*) vec2 **asinh** (vec2 *x*) vec3 **asinh** (vec3 *x*) vec4 **asinh** (vec4 *x*)	Arc hyperbolic sine. Returns the inverse of **sinh**.
float **acosh** (float *x*) vec2 **acosh** (vec2 *x*) vec3 **acosh** (vec3 *x*) vec4 **acosh** (vec4 *x*)	Arc hyperbolic cosine. Returns the non-negative inverse of **cosh**. Results are undefined if $x < 1.0$.
float **atanh** (float *x*) vec2 **atanh** (vec2 *x*) vec3 **atanh** (vec3 *x*) vec4 **atanh** (vec4 *x*)	Arc hyperbolic tangent. Returns the inverse of **tanh**. Results are undefined if $|x| >= 1.0$.

5.2 Exponential Functions

Exponential functions can be used within either vertex shaders or fragment shaders. These all operate component-wise (see Table 5.2). The description column specifies the operation on each component.

Table 5.2 Exponential functions

Syntax	Description
float **pow** (float *x*, float *y*) vec2 **pow** (vec2 *x*, vec2 *y*) vec3 **pow** (vec3 *x*, vec3 *y*) vec4 **pow** (vec4 *x*, vec4 *y*)	Returns *x* raised to the *y* power, i.e., x^y. Results are undefined if $x < 0$. Results are undefined if $x = 0$ and $y = 0$.
float **exp** (float *x*) vec2 **exp** (vec2 *x*) vec3 **exp** (vec3 *x*) vec4 **exp** (vec4 *x*)	Returns the natural exponentiation of *x*, i.e., e^x.

(continues)

Table 5.2 Exponential functions, *continued*

Syntax	Description
float **log** (float *x*) vec2 **log** (vec2 *x*) vec3 **log** (vec3 *x*) vec4 **log** (vec4 *x*)	Returns the natural logarithm of *x*, i.e., returns the value *y*, which satisfies the equation $x = e^y$. Results are undefined if $x <= 0$.
float **exp2** (float *x*) vec2 **exp2** (vec2 *x*) vec3 **exp2** (vec3 *x*) vec4 **exp2** (vec4 *x*)	Returns 2 raised to the *x* power, i.e., 2^x.
float **log2** (float *x*) vec2 **log2** (vec2 *x*) vec3 **log2** (vec3 *x*) vec4 **log2** (vec4 *x*)	Returns the base 2 log of *x*, i.e., returns the value *y*, which satisfies the equation $x = 2^y$. Results are undefined if $x <= 0$.
float **sqrt** (float *x*) vec2 **sqrt** (vec2 *x*) vec3 **sqrt** (vec3 *x*) vec4 **sqrt** (vec4 *x*)	Returns the positive square root of *x*. Results are undefined if $x < 0$.
float **inversesqrt** (float *x*) vec2 **inversesqrt** (vec2 *x*) vec3 **inversesqrt** (vec3 *x*) vec4 **inversesqrt** (vec4 *x*)	Returns the reciprocal of the positive square root of *x*. Results are undefined if $x <= 0$.

5.3 Common Functions

Common functions can be used within either vertex shaders or fragment shaders. These functions all operate in a component-wise fashion (see Table 5.3) The description column specifies the operation on each component.

Table 5.3 Common functions

Syntax	Description
float **abs** (float *x*) vec2 **abs** (vec2 *x*) vec3 **abs** (vec3 *x*) vec4 **abs** (vec4 *x*)	Returns *x* if *x* >= 0; otherwise, it returns –*x*.
int **abs** (int x) ivec2 **abs** (ivec2 x) ivec3 **abs** (ivec3 x) ivec4 **abs** (ivec4 x)	
float **sign** (float *x*) vec2 **sign** (vec2 *x*) vec3 **sign** (vec3 *x*) vec4 **sign** (vec4 *x*)	Returns 1.0 if *x* > 0, 0.0 if *x* = 0, or –1.0 if *x* < 0.
int **sign** (int *x*) ivec2 **sign** (ivec2 *x*) ivec3 **sign** (ivec3 *x*) ivec4 **sign** (ivec4 *x*)	
float **floor** (float *x*) vec2 **floor** (vec2 *x*) vec3 **floor** (vec3 *x*) vec4 **floor** (vec4 *x*)	Returns a value equal to the nearest integer that is less than or equal to *x*.
float **trunc** (float *x*) vec2 **trunc** (vec2 *x*) vec3 **trunc** (vec3 *x*) vec4 **trunc** (vec4 *x*)	Returns a value equal to the nearest integer to *x* whose absolute value is not larger than the absolute value of *x*.
float **round** (float *x*) vec2 **round** (vec2 *x*) vec3 **round** (vec3 *x*) vec4 **round** (vec4 *x*)	Returns a value equal to the nearest integer of *x*. A fractional part of 0.5 will round in an implementation direction.

(continues)

Table 5.3 Common functions, *continued*

Syntax	Description
float **roundEven** (float *x*) vec2 **roundEven** (vec2 *x*) vec3 **roundEven** (vec3 *x*) vec4 **roundEven** (vec4 *x*)	Returns a value equal to the nearest integer to *x*. A fractional part of 0.5 will round toward the nearest even integer. (Example: Both 3.5 and 4.5 for *x* will return 4.0.)
float **ceil** (float *x*) vec2 **ceil** (vec2 *x*) vec3 **ceil** (vec3 *x*) vec4 **ceil** (vec4 *x*)	Returns a value equal to the nearest integer that is greater than or equal to *x*.
float **fract** (float *x*) vec2 **fract** (vec2 *x*) vec3 **fract** (vec3 *x*) vec4 **fract** (vec4 *x*)	Returns *x* – **floor** (*x*).
float **mod** (float *x*, float *y*) vec2 **mod** (vec2 *x*, float *y*) vec3 **mod** (vec3 *x*, float *y*) vec4 **mod** (vec4 *x*, float *y*)	Modulus. Returns *x* – *y* * **floor** (*x*/*y*) for each component in *x* using the floating-point value *y*.
vec2 **mod** (vec2 *x*, vec2 *y*) vec3 **mod** (vec3 *x*, vec3 *y*) vec4 **mod** (vec4 *x*, vec4 *y*)	Modulus. Returns *x* – *y* * **floor** (*x*/*y*) for each component in *x* using the corresponding component of *y*.
float **min** (float *x*, float *y*) vec2 **min** (vec2 *x*, vec2 *y*) vec3 **min** (vec3 *x*, vec3 *y*) vec4 **min** (vec4 *x*, vec4 *y*) int **min** (int *x*, int *y*) ivec2 **min** (ivec2 *x*, ivec2 *y*) ivec3 **min** (ivec3 *x*, ivec3 *y*) ivec4 **min** (ivec4 *x*, ivec4 *y*) uint **min** (uint *x*, uint *y*) uvec2 **min** (uvec2 *x*, uvec2 *y*) uvec3 **min** (uvec3 *x*, uvec3 *y*) uvec4 **min** (uvec4 *x*, uvec4 *y*)	Returns *y* if *y* < *x*; otherwise, it returns *x*.

Table 5.3 Common functions, *continued*

Syntax	Description
vec2 **min** (vec2 *x*, float *y*) vec3 **min** (vec3 *x*, float *y*) vec4 **min** (vec4 *x*, float *y*) ivec2 **min** (ivec2 *x*, int *y*) ivec3 **min** (ivec3 *x*, int *y*) ivec4 **min** (ivec4 *x*, int *y*) uvec2 **min** (uvec2 *x*, uint *y*) uvec3 **min** (uvec3 *x*, uint *y*) uvec4 **min** (uvec4 *x*, uint *y*)	Returns minimum for each component of *x* compared with the scalar value *y*.
float **max** (float *x*, float *y*) vec2 **max** (vec2 *x*, vec2 *y*) vec3 **max** (vec3 *x*, vec3 *y*) vec4 **max** (vec4 *x*, vec4 *y*) int **max** (int *x*, int *y*) ivec2 **max** (ivec2 *x*, ivec2 *y*) ivec3 **max** (ivec3 *x*, ivec3 *y*) ivec4 **max** (ivec4 *x*, ivec4 *y*) uint **max** (uint *x*, uint *y*) uvec2 **max** (uvec2 *x*, uvec2 *y*) uvec3 **max** (uvec3 *x*, uvec3 *y*) uvec4 **max** (uvec4 *x*, uvec4 *y*)	Returns *y* if *x* < *y*; otherwise, it returns *x*.
vec2 **max** (vec2 *x*, float *y*) vec3 **max** (vec3 *x*, float *y*) vec4 **max** (vec4 *x*, float *y*) ivec2 **max** (ivec2 *x*, int *y*) ivec3 **max** (ivec3 *x*, int *y*) ivec4 **max** (ivec4 *x*, int *y*) uvec2 **max** (uvec2 *x*, uint *y*) uvec3 **max** (uvec3 *x*, uint *y*) uvec4 **max** (uvec4 *x*, uint *y*)	Returns maximum for each component of *x* compared with the scalar value *y*.

(continues)

Table 5.3 Common functions, *continued*

Syntax	Description
float **clamp** (float *x*, float *minVal*, float *maxVal*) vec2 **clamp** (vec2 *x*, float *minVal*, float *maxVal*) vec3 **clamp** (vec3 *x*, float *minVal*, float *maxVal*) vec4 **clamp** (vec4 *x*, float *minVal*, float *maxVal*)	Returns **min** (**max** (*x*, *minVal*), *maxVal*) for each component in *x* using the scalar values *minVal* and *maxVal*. Results are undefined if *minVal* > *maxVal*.
int **clamp** (int *x*, int *minVal*, int *maxVal*) ivec2 **clamp** (ivec2 *x*, int *minVal*, int *maxVal*) ivec3 **clamp** (ivec3 *x*, int *minVal*, int *maxVal*) ivec4 **clamp** (ivec4 *x*, int *minVal*, int *maxVal*)	
uint **clamp** (uint *x*, uint *minVal*, uint *maxVal*) uvec2 **clamp** (uvec2 *x*, uint *minVal*, uint *maxVal*) uvec3 **clamp** (uvec3 *x*, uint *minVal*, uint *maxVal*) uvec4 **clamp** (uvec4 *x*, uint *minVal*, uint *maxVal*)	

Table 5.3 Common functions, *continued*

Syntax	Description
vec2 **clamp** (vec2 *x*, vec2 *minVal*, vec2 *maxVal*) vec3 **clamp** (vec3 *x*, vec3 *minVal*, vec3 *maxVal*) vec4 **clamp** (vec4 *x*, vec4 *minVal*, vec4 *maxVal*) ivec2 **clamp** (ivec2 *x*, ivec2 *minVal*, ivec2 *maxVal*) ivec3 **clamp** (ivec3 *x*, ivec3 *minVal*, ivec3 *maxVal*) ivec4 **clamp** (ivec4 *x*, ivec4 *minVal*, ivec4 *maxVal*) uvec2 **clamp** (uvec2 *x*, uvec2 *minVal*, uvec2 *maxVal*) uvec3 **clamp** (uvec3 *x*, uvec3 *minVal*, uvec3 *maxVal*) uvec4 **clamp** (uvec4 *x*, uvec4 *minVal*, uvec4 *maxVal*)	Returns the component-wise result of **min** (**max** (*x*, *minVal*), *maxVal*). Results are undefined if *minVal* > *maxVal*.
float **mix** (float *x*, float *y*, float *a*) vec2 **mix** (vec2 *x*, vec2 *y*, float *a*) vec3 **mix** (vec3 *x*, vec3 *y*, float *a*) vec4 **mix** (vec4 *x*, vec4 *y*, float *a*)	Returns $x * (1.0 - a) + y * a$, i.e., the linear blend of *x* and *y* using the floating-point value *a*. The value for *a* is not restricted to the range [0,1].
vec2 **mix** (vec2 *x*, vec2 *y*, vec2 *a*) vec3 **mix** (vec3 *x*, vec3 *y*, vec3 *a*) vec4 **mix** (vec4 *x*, vec4 *y*, vec4 *a*)	Returns the component-wise result of $x * (1.0 - a) + y * a$, i.e., the linear blend of vectors *x* and *y* using the vector *a*. The value for *a* is not restricted to the range [0,1].
float **step** (float *edge*, float *x*) vec2 **step** (vec2 *edge*, vec2 *x*) vec3 **step** (vec3 *edge*, vec3 *x*) vec4 **step** (vec4 *edge*, vec4 *x*) float **step** (float *edge*, float *x*)	Returns 0.0 if *x* < *edge*; otherwise, it returns 1.0.

(continues)

Table 5.3 Common functions, *continued*

Syntax	Description
vec2 **step** (float *edge*, vec2 *x*) vec3 **step** (float *edge*, vec3 *x*) vec4 **step** (float *edge*, vec4 *x*)	Returns 0.0 for each component in *x* if *x* < the scalar *edge*; otherwise, it returns 1.0.

float **smoothstep** (float *edge0*,
     float *edge1*, float *x*)
vec2 **smoothstep** (vec2 *edge0*,
     vec2 *edge1*, vec2 *x*)
vec3 **smoothstep** (vec3 *edge0*,
     vec3 *edge1*, vec3 *x*)
vec4 **smoothstep** (vec4 *edge0*,
     vec4 *edge1*, vec4 *x*)
	Returns 0.0 if *x* <= *edge0* and 1.0 if *x* >= *edge1* and performs smooth Hermite interpolation between 0.0 and 1.0 when *edge0* < *x* < *edge1*. Results are undefined if *edge0* >= *edge1*.

vec2 **smoothstep** (float *edge0*,
     float *edge1*, vec2 *x*)
vec3 **smoothstep** (float *edge0*,
     float *edge1*, vec3 *x*)
vec4 **smoothstep** (float *edge0*,
     float *edge1*, vec4 *x*)
	Returns 0.0 for each component in *x* if *x* <= the scalar *edge0* and 1.0 if *x* >= the scalar *edge1* and performs smooth Hermite interpolation between 0.0 and 1.0 when *edge0* < *x* < *edge1*. Results are undefined if *edge0* >= *edge1*.

bool **isnan** (float *x*) bvec2 **isnan** (vec2 *x*) bvec3 **isnan** (vec3 *x*) bvec4 **isnan** (vec4 *x*)	Returns **true** if *x* holds a NaN (not a number), **false** otherwise. (Implementations that do not support **NaN** always return **false**.)
bool **isinf** (float *x*) bvec2 **isinf** (vec2 *x*) bvec3 **isinf** (vec3 *x*) bvec4 **isinf** (vec4 *x*)	Returns **true** if *x* holds an **INF** (infinity, positive or negative), **false** otherwise. (Implementations that do not support **INF** always return **false**.)

Aside from their general usefulness as math functions, many of these functions are useful in creating interesting shaders, as we see in subsequent chapters. The **abs** function can ensure that a particular function never produces negative values. It can also introduce a discontinuity in an otherwise smooth function. As we see in Section 15.5, this property of the **abs** function is used to introduce discontinuities in a noise function to produce an effect that looks like turbulence. A graphical representation of the **abs** function is shown in Figure 5.2.

The **sign** function simply maps the incoming value to –1, 0, or 1, depending on its sign. This results in a discontinuous function, as shown in Figure 5.3.

The **floor** function produces a discontinuous stair-step pattern, as shown in Figure 5.4. The fractional part of each incoming value is dropped, so the output value is always the integer value that is closest to but less than or equal to the input value.

The **ceil** function is almost the same as the **floor** function, except that the value returned is always the integer value that is closest to but greater than

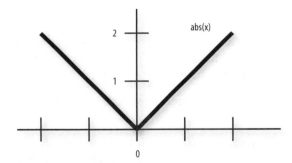

Figure 5.2   The **abs** function

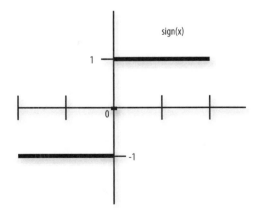

Figure 5.3   The **sign** function

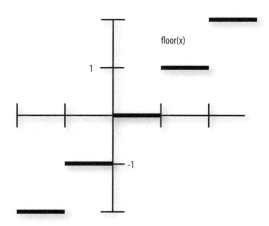

Figure 5.4   The **floor** function

or equal to the input value. This function is shown in Figure 5.5. As you can see, this function looks the same as Figure 5.4 except that the output values are shifted up by one. (Although **ceil** and **floor** always produce integer values, the functions are defined to return floating-point data types.)

The **fract** function produces a discontinuous function where each segment has a slope of 1.0 (see Figure 5.6).

The **mod** function is very similar to **fract**. In fact, if we divide the result of **mod**(*x*, *y*) by *y*, the result is very nearly the same. The only difference is the period of the discontinuous segments (see Figure 5.7).

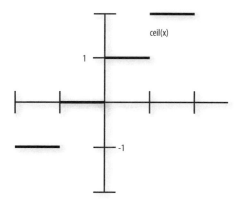

Figure 5.5   The **ceil** function

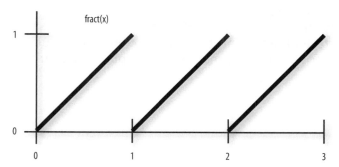

Figure 5.6   The **fract** function

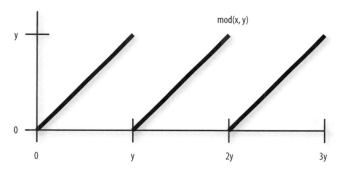

Figure 5.7   The periodic function **mod**(*x, y*)

The **clamp** function is useful for making sure that a value is within a particular range. A common operation is

```
clamp(x, 0.0, 1.0);
```

which clamps the variable x to the range [0,1]. Because two comparisons are necessary for this function, you should use it only when there is a chance that the tested value could be outside either end of the specified range. For the **min** and **max** functions, only one comparison is necessary. If you know a value will not be less than 0, using

```
min(x, 1.0);
```

will likely be faster and may use fewer machine instructions than

```
clamp(x, 0.0, 1.0);
```

because there is no point in testing to see whether the final value is less than 0. Keep in mind that there is no need to clamp the final color and depth values computed by a fragment shader because they are clamped automatically by the back-end fixed functionality processing.

The **min**, **max**, and **clamp** functions are shown in Figure 5.8, Figure 5.9, and Figure 5.10. The **min**(x, y) function has a slope of 1 where x is less than y, and a slope of 0 where x is greater than y. This function is often used to put an upper bound on a value, for instance, to make sure the computed result never exceeds 1.0.

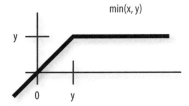

Figure 5.8   The **min** function

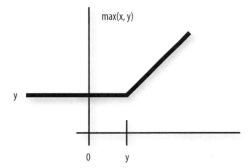

Figure 5.9   The **max** function

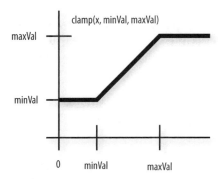

Figure 5.10   The **clamp** function

The **max**(*x*, *y*) function has a slope of 0 where *x* is less than *y*, and a slope of 1 where *x* is greater than *y*. This function is often used to put a lower bound on a value, for instance, to make sure the computed result never goes below 0.

The **clamp**(*x*, *minVal*, *maxVal*) function has a slope of 0 where *x* is less than *minVal* and where *x* is greater than *maxVal*, and it has a slope of 1 in between where *x* is greater than *minVal* and less than *maxVal*. It is functionally equivalent to the expression **min**(**max**(*x*, *minVal*), *maxVal*).

The **step** function creates a discontinuous jump at an arbitrary point (see Figure 5.11). We use this function to create a simple procedural brick shader in Chapter 6.

The **smoothstep** function (see Figure 5.12) is useful in cases where you want a threshold function with a smooth transition. For the case in which *t* is a **float**, this is equivalent to

```
float t;
t = clamp((x - edge0) / (edge1 - edge0), 0.0, 1.0);
return t * t * (3.0 - 2.0 * t);
```

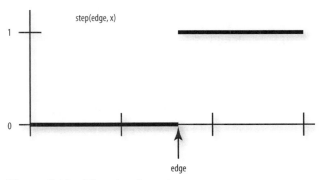

Figure 5.11   The **step** function

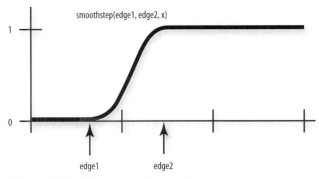

Figure 5.12   The **smoothstep** function

The cases for **vec2**, **vec3**, and **vec4** differ from the preceding example only in the data type used to declare *t*.

5.4 Geometric Functions

Except for **ftransform**, geometric functions can be used within either vertex shaders or fragment shaders. These functions operate on vectors as vectors, not in a component-wise fashion (see Table 5.4).

Table 5.4 Geometric functions

Syntax	Description
float **length** (float *x*) float **length** (vec2 *x*) float **length** (vec3 *x*) float **length** (vec4 *x*)	Returns the length of vector *x*, i.e., **sqrt**($x[0] * x[0] + x[1] * x[1] + ...$).
float **distance** (float *p0*, float *p1*) float **distance** (vec2 *p0*, vec2 *p1*) float **distance** (vec3 *p0*, vec3 *p1*) float **distance** (vec4 *p0*, vec4 *p1*)	Returns the distance between *p0* and *p1*, i.e., **length**($p0 - p1$).
float **dot** (float *x*, float *y*) float **dot** (vec2 *x*, vec2 *y*) float **dot** (vec3 *x*, vec3 *y*) float **dot** (vec4 *x*, vec4 *y*)	Returns the dot product of *x* and *y*, i.e., result = $x[0] * y[0] + x[1] * y[1] + ...$.
vec3 **cross** (vec3 *x*, vec3 *y*)	Returns the cross product of *x* and *y*, i.e., result[0] = $x[1] * y[2] - y[1] * x[2]$ result[1] = $x[2] * y[0] - y[2] * x[0]$ result[2] = $x[0] * y[1] - y[0] * x[1]$
float **normalize** (float *x*) vec2 **normalize** (vec2 *x*) vec3 **normalize** (vec3 *x*) vec4 **normalize** (vec4 *x*)	Returns a vector in the same direction as *x* but with a length of 1.

Table 5.4 Geometric functions, *continued*

Syntax	Description
float **faceforward** (float *N*, float *I*, float *Nref*) vec2 **faceforward** (vec2 *N*, vec2 *I*, vec2 *Nref*) vec3 **faceforward** (vec3 *N*, vec3 *I*, vec3 *Nref*) vec4 **faceforward** (vec4 *N*, vec4 *I*, vec4 *Nref*)	If **dot** (*Nref*, *I*) < 0.0, return *N*; otherwise, return –*N*.
float **reflect** (float *I*, float *N*) vec2 **reflect** (vec2 *I*, vec2 *N*) vec3 **reflect** (vec3 *I*, vec3 *N*) vec4 **reflect** (vec4 *I*, vec4 *N*)	For the incident vector *I* and surface orientation *N*, returns the reflection direction: result = *I* – 2.0 ∗ **dot** (*N*, *I*) ∗ *N* *N* must already be normalized to achieve the desired result. *I* need not be normalized.

float **refract** (float *I*, float *N*, float *eta*)
 	
vec2 **refract** (vec2 *I*, vec2 *N*, float *eta*)
 	
vec3 **refract** (vec3 *I*, vec3 *N*, float *eta*)
 	
vec4 **refract** (vec4 *I*, vec4 *N*, float *eta*)
	For the incident vector *I* and surface normal *N* and the ratio of indices of refraction *eta*, returns the refraction vector. The returned result is computed as
	k = 1.0 – *eta* ∗ *eta* ∗
	    (1.0 – **dot** *(N, I)* ∗ **dot** *(N, I))*
	if (k < 0.0)
	    result = 0.0;
	    // result type is float or vec2/3/4
	else
	    result = *eta* ∗ *I*–
	        (eta ∗ **dot** *(N, I)* ∗ **sqrt** (k)) ∗ *N*
	The input parameters for the incident vector *I* and surface normal *N* must already be normalized to achieve the desired result.

The **float** version of the **distance** function may not seem terribly useful (it's the same as the absolute value of the difference), but the vector forms compute the Euclidean distance between two points. Similarly, the **float** version of **normalize** always returns 1, and the **float** version of **length** always returns the absolute value of the input argument as the result. These scalar forms are useful in that the data type of the argument can be changed without the need to change the code that calls the built-in function.

You can use the **ftransform** function to transform the incoming vertex position:

```
gl_Position = ftransform()
```

It transforms the value of *gl_Vertex* by the current modelview-projection matrix to produce a value for *gl_Position* that is identical to what would have been computed by the fixed functionality pipeline. This function should be used, for example, when an application is rendering the same geometry in separate passes, where one pass uses the fixed functionality path to render and another pass uses the programmable processors.

5.5 Matrix Functions

Matrix functions can be used within either vertex shaders or fragment shaders (see Table 5.5).

Table 5.5 Matrix functions

Syntax	Description
mat2 **matrixCompMult** (mat2 *x*, mat2 *y*) mat3 **matrixCompMult** (mat3 *x*, mat3 *y*) mat4 **matrixCompMult** (mat4 *x*, mat4 *y*)	Multiply matrix *x* by matrix *y* component-wise, i.e., *result*[i][j] is the scalar product of *x*[i][j] and *y*[i][j]. Note: To get linear-algebraic matrix multiplication, use the multiply operator (*****).
mat2 **transpose** (mat2 *m*) mat3 **transpose** (mat3 *m*) mat4 **transpose** (mat4 *m*) mat2x3 **transpose** (mat3x2 *m*) mat3x2 **transpose** (mat2x3 *m*) mat2x4 **transpose** (mat4x2 *m*) mat4x2 **transpose** (mat2x4 *m*) mat3x4 **transpose** (mat4x3 *m*) mat4x3 **transpose** (mat3x4 *m*)	Returns a matrix that is the transpose of *m*. The input matrix is not modified.

Table 5.5 Matrix functions, *continued*

Syntax	Description
mat2 **inverse** (mat2 *m*) mat3 **inverse** (mat3 *m*) mat4 **inverse** (mat4 *m*)	Returns a matrix that is the inverse of *m*. The input matrix is not modified. The values in the returned matrix are undefined if the input matrix is singular or poorly conditioned (nearly singular).
mat2 **outerProduct** (vec2 *c*, vec2 *r*) mat3 **outerProduct** (vec3 *c*, vec3 *r*) mat4 **outerProduct** (vec4 *c*, vec4 *r*) mat2x3 **outerProduct** (vec2 *c*, vec3 *r*) mat3x2 **outerProduct** (vec3 *c*, vec2 *r*) mat2x4 **outerProduct** (vec2 *c*, vec4 *r*) mat4x2 **outerProduct** (vec4 *c*, vec2 *r*) mat3x4 **outerProduct** (vec3 *c*, vec4 *r*) mat4x3 **outerProduct** (vec4 *c*, vec3 *r*)	Returns the outer product. Treats the first parameter as a column vector and the second parameter as a row vector and performs a linear algebra matrix multipy *c**r yielding a matrix.

These functions produce the component-wise multiplication of two matrices. For instance, the result of calling **matrixCompMult** with two 3D matrices *x* and *y* looks like this:

```
mat3 x, y, newmat;
. . .
newmat = matrixCompMult(x, y);
```

$$\begin{bmatrix} x_{00} & x_{01} & x_{02} \\ x_{10} & x_{11} & x_{12} \\ x_{20} & x_{21} & x_{22} \end{bmatrix} \begin{bmatrix} y_{00} & y_{01} & y_{02} \\ y_{10} & y_{11} & y_{12} \\ y_{20} & y_{21} & y_{22} \end{bmatrix} = \begin{bmatrix} x_{00}y_{00} & x_{01}y_{01} & x_{02}y_{02} \\ x_{10}y_{10} & x_{11}y_{11} & x_{12}y_{12} \\ x_{20}y_{20} & x_{21}y_{21} & x_{22}y_{22} \end{bmatrix}$$

This is not usually what you want if you are using matrices to represent transformation steps. In this case, you would use the multiply operator (*****) to perform the linear-algebraic matrix multiplication

```
mat3 x, y, newmat;
. . .
newmat = x * y;
```

which performs the following operation:

$$
\begin{bmatrix} x_{00} & x_{01} & x_{02} \\ x_{10} & x_{11} & x_{12} \\ x_{20} & x_{21} & x_{22} \end{bmatrix}
\begin{bmatrix} y_{00} & y_{01} & y_{02} \\ y_{10} & y_{11} & y_{12} \\ y_{20} & y_{21} & y_{22} \end{bmatrix} =
$$

$$
\begin{bmatrix}
x_{00}y_{00} + x_{01}y_{10} + x_{02}y_{20} & x_{00}y_{01} + x_{01}y_{11} + x_{02}y_{21} & x_{00}y_{02} + x_{01}y_{12} + x_{02}y_{22} \\
x_{10}y_{00} + x_{11}y_{10} + x_{12}y_{20} & x_{10}y_{01} + x_{11}y_{11} + x_{12}y_{21} & x_{10}y_{02} + x_{11}y_{12} + x_{12}y_{22} \\
x_{20}y_{00} + x_{21}y_{10} + x_{22}y_{20} & x_{20}y_{01} + x_{21}y_{11} + x_{22}y_{21} & x_{20}y_{02} + x_{21}y_{12} + x_{22}y_{22}
\end{bmatrix}
$$

5.6 Vector Relational Functions

Relational and equality operators (<, <=, >, >=, ==, !=) are defined to produce scalar Boolean results and can be used within either vertex shaders or fragment shaders. For vector results, use the built-in functions in Table 5.6.

Table 5.6 Vector relational functions

Syntax	Description
bvec2 **lessThan**(vec2 *x*, vec2 *y*) bvec3 **lessThan**(vec3 *x*, vec3 *y*) bvec4 **lessThan**(vec4 *x*, vec4 *y*) bvec2 **lessThan**(ivec2 *x*, ivec2 *y*) bvec3 **lessThan**(ivec3 *x*, ivec3 *y*) bvec4 **lessThan**(ivec4 *x*, ivec4 *y*)	Returns the component-wise compare of *x* < *y*.
bvec2 **lessThanEqual**(vec2 *x*, vec2 *y*) bvec3 **lessThanEqual**(vec3 *x*, vec3 *y*) bvec4 **lessThanEqual**(vec4 *x*, vec4 *y*) bvec2 **lessThanEqual**(ivec2 *x*, ivec2 *y*) bvec3 **lessThanEqual**(ivec3 *x*, ivec3 *y*) bvec4 **lessThanEqual**(ivec4 *x*, ivec4 *y*)	Returns the component-wise compare of *x* <= *y*.

Table 5.6 Vector relational functions, *continued*

Syntax	Description
bvec2 **greaterThan**(vec2 *x*, vec2 *y*) bvec3 **greaterThan**(vec3 *x*, vec3 *y*) bvec4 **greaterThan**(vec4 *x*, vec4 *y*) bvec2 **greaterThan**(ivec2 *x*, ivec2 *y*) bvec3 **greaterThan**(ivec3 *x*, ivec3 *y*) bvec4 **greaterThan**(ivec4 *x*, ivec4 *y*)	Returns the component-wise compare of *x* > *y*.
bvec2 **greaterThanEqual**(vec2 *x*, vec2 *y*) bvec3 **greaterThanEqual**(vec3 *x*, vec3 *y*) bvec4 **greaterThanEqual**(vec4 *x*, vec4 *y*) bvec2 **greaterThanEqual**(ivec2 *x*, ivec2 *y*) bvec3 **greaterThanEqual**(ivec3 *x*, ivec3 *y*) bvec4 **greaterThanEqual**(ivec4 *x*, ivec4 *y*)	Returns the component-wise compare of *x* >= *y*.
bvec2 **equal**(vec2 *x*, vec2 *y*) bvec3 **equal**(vec3 *x*, vec3 *y*) bvec4 **equal**(vec4 *x*, vec4 *y*) bvec2 **equal**(ivec2 *x*, ivec2 *y*) bvec3 **equal**(ivec3 *x*, ivec3 *y*) bvec4 **equal**(ivec4 *x*, ivec4 *y*) bvec2 **equal**(bvec2 *x*, bvec2 *y*) bvec3 **equal**(bvec3 *x*, bvec3 *y*) bvec4 **equal**(bvec4 *x*, bvec4 *y*)	Returns the component-wise compare of *x* == *y*.
bvec2 **notEqual**(vec2 *x*, vec2 *y*) bvec3 **notEqual**(vec3 *x*, vec3 *y*) bvec4 **notEqual**(vec4 *x*, vec4 *y*) bvec2 **notEqual**(ivec2 *x*, ivec2 *y*) bvec3 **notEqual**(ivec3 *x*, ivec3 *y*) bvec4 **notEqual**(ivec4 *x*, ivec4 *y*) bvec2 **notEqual**(bvec2 *x*, bvec2 *y*) bvec3 **notEqual**(bvec3 *x*, bvec3 *y*) bvec4 **notEqual**(bvec4 *x*, bvec4 *y*)	Returns the component-wise compare of *x* != *y*.

(continues)

Table 5.6 Vector relational functions, *continued*

Syntax	Description
bool **any**(bvec2 *x*) bool **any**(bvec3 *x*) bool **any**(bvec4 *x*)	Returns true if any component of *x* is **true**.
bool **all**(bvec2 *x*) bool **all**(bvec3 *x*) bool **all**(bvec4 *x*)	Returns true only if all components of *x* are **true**.
bvec2 **not**(bvec2 *x*) bvec3 **not**(bvec3 *x*) bvec4 **not**(bvec4 *x*)	Returns the component-wise logical complement of *x*.

5.7 Texture Access Functions

Texture access functions are available to both vertex and fragment shaders. Each of these functions takes as its first argument a variable of type **sampler**. If a variable qualified by **sampler1D** is used, then the texture access operation reads from the 1D texture that has previously been associated with that sampler by the application. Similarly, a **sampler2D** variable is used to access a 2D texture, and so on. The texture precedence rules for OpenGL fixed functionality are ignored. It is up to the application to set up texture state before the shader executes in order to get the expected results (see Section 7.9).

The texture access functions obtain texture values from either mipmapped or non-mipmapped textures. However, implicit derivatives and level-of-detail are not computed for vertex shaders since each vertex is processed in isolation and there is no local neighborhood. For fragment shaders, there is limited access to neighboring fragments sufficient to calculate implicit derivatives and level of detail. So, there are some differences in operation between vertex and fragment texture access functions. Texture properties such as size, pixel format, number of dimensions, filtering method, number of mipmap levels, depth comparison, and so on, are also defined by OpenGL API calls. Such properties are taken into account as the texture is accessed through the built-in functions defined in this section.

The built-in functions use suffixes to indicate modifications to the texture function.

The built-in functions suffixed with "Proj" can perform projective texturing. This allows a texture to be projected onto an object in much the same way that a slide projector projects an image onto a surface. Functions suffixed with "Proj" can compute shadow maps for rendering shadows, among other things.

The suffix "Lod" is used to specify an explicit level of detail and may be used in either the vertex or fragment shader.

The suffix "Grad" is used to specify an explicit derivative and may be used in either the vertex or fragment shader.

The suffix "Offset" adds an offset to the *u* and *v* values used to select texels in the texture image. The offset can be useful for computing custom filter kernels on texture images.

The suffixes can be combined together (though only one of "Lod" or "Grad" can be used in any given function) to combine modifications for the texture function.

The *bias* parameter is optional for fragment shaders. The *bias* parameter is not accepted in a vertex shader. For a fragment shader, if *bias* is present, it is added to the calculated level of detail before the texture access operation is performed. If the *bias* parameter is not provided, the implementation automatically selects level of detail. For a texture that is not mipmapped, the texture is used directly. If a mipmap texture is accessed from a fragment shader, the level of detail may be computed by the implementation for use during the texture lookup.

A number of examples in later sections illustrate the use of these functions. With the programmability available with the OpenGL Shading Language, texture memory can store much more than just image data. These texture access functions provide fast, flexible access to such data in order to achieve a wide variety of effects (see Table 5.7).

Texturing results are undefined if

- A texture function that requires an implicit derivative is called in the vertex shader, or
- A texture function that requires an implicit derivative is called inside nonuniform control flow, or
- A **shadow** sampler is not specified for a depth format texture with depth comparisons enabled, or
- A **shadow** sampler is specified for a depth format texture with depth comparisons disabled, or
- A **shadow** sampler is specified for a texture that is not a depth format.

Table 5.7 Texture access functions

Syntax	Description
int **textureSize** (sampler1D *sampler*, int *lod*)	Returns the width of level *lod* of the 1D texture currently specified by *sampler.*
vec4 **texture** (sampler1D *sampler*, float *coord* [, float *bias*]) vec4 **textureProj** (sampler1D *sampler*, vec2 *coord* [, float *bias*]) vec4 **textureProj** (sampler1D *sampler*, vec4 *coord* [, float *bias*]) vec4 **textureLod** (sampler1D *sampler*, float *coord*, float *lod*) vec4 **textureGrad** (sampler1D *sampler*, float *coord*, float *dPdx*, float *dPdy*) vec4 **textureOffset** (sampler1D *sampler*, float *coord*, int *offset*, [, float *bias*])	Use the texture coordinate *coord* to access the 1D texture currently specified by *sampler.* Unsuffixed access the texture (with optional lod *bias*). **Proj** suffix accesses the texture with projection (with optional lod *bias*) **Lod** suffix accesses the texture with explict *lod.* **Grad** suffix accesses the texture with explict partial derivatives *dPdx* and *dPdy.* **Offset** suffix accesses the texture (with optional lod *bias*) with the *offset* added to the *u* texel coordinate before looking up each texel.
vec4 **texelFetch** (sampler1D *sampler*, int *coord*, int *lod*) vec4 **texelFetchOffset** (sampler1D *sampler*, int *coord*, int *lod*, int *offset*)	Use the texel integer *coord* to lookup a single texel of the explicit *lod* to access the 1D texture currently specified by *sampler:* **Offset** suffix accesses the texture (with optional lod *bias*) with the *offset* added to the *u* texel coordinate before looking up each texel.

Table 5.7 Texture access functions, *continued*

Syntax	Description

vec4 **textureProjLod** (sampler1D *sampler*, vec2 *coord* , float *lod*)
vec4 **textureProjLod** (sampler1D *sampler*, vec4 *coord* , float *lod*)
vec4 **textureProjGrad** (sampler1D *sampler*, vec2 *coord*, float *dPdx*,
      float *dPdy*)
vec4 **textureProjGrad** (sampler1D *sampler*, vec4 *coord*, float *dPdx*,
      float *dPdy*)
vec4 **textureProjOffset** (sampler1D *sampler*, vec2 *coord*, int *offset*
      [, float *bias*])
vec4 **textureProjOffset** (sampler1D *sampler*, vec4 *coord*, int *offset*
      [, float *bias*])
vec4 **textureLodOffset** (sampler1D *sampler*, float *coord*, float *lod*, int *offset*)
vec4 **textureGradOffset** (sampler1D *sampler*, float *coord*, float *dPdx*,
      float *dPdy*, int *offset*)
	Use the texture coordinate *coord* to access the 1D texture currently specified by *sampler:*
	Combinations of the suffixes **Proj**, **Lod**, **Grad**, and **Offset** are as described earlier.

vec4 **textureProjLodOffset** (sampler1D *sampler*, vec2 *coord*, float *lod*,
      int *offset*)
vec4 **textureProjLodOffset** (sampler1D *sampler*, vec4 *coord*, float *lod*,
      int *offset*)
vec4 **textureProjGradOffset** (sampler1D *sampler*, vec2 *coord*, float *dPdx*,
      float *dPdy*, int *offset*)
vec4 **textureProjGradOffset** (sampler1D *sampler*, vec4 *coord*, float *dPdx*,
      float *dPdy*, int *offset*)
	Use the texture coordinate *coord* to access the 1D texture currently specified by *sampler:*
	Combinations of the suffixes **Proj**, **Lod**, **Grad**, and **Offset** are as described earlier.

int **textureSize** (isampler1D *sampler*, int *lod*)	Returns the width of level *lod* of the 1D texture currently specified by *sampler.*

(continues)

Table 5.7 Texture access functions, *continued*

Syntax	Description
ivec4 **texture** (isampler1D *sampler*, float *coord* [, float *bias*])	Use the texture coordinate *coord* to access the 1D texture currently specified by *sampler*.
ivec4 **textureProj** (isampler1D *sampler*, vec2 *coord* [, float *bias*])	Unsuffixed access the texture (with optional lod *bias*).
ivec4 **textureProj** (isampler1D *sampler*, vec4 *coord* [, float *bias*])	**Proj** suffix accesses the texture with projection (with optional lod *bias*).
ivec4 **textureLod** (isampler1D *sampler*, float *coord*, float *lod*)	**Lod** suffix accesses the texture with explicit *lod*.
ivec4 **textureGrad** (isampler1D *sampler*, float *coord*, float *dPdx*, float *dPdy*)	**Grad** suffix accesses the texture with explicit partial derivatives *dPdx* and *dPdy*.
ivec4 **textureOffset** (isampler1D *sampler*, float *coord*, int *offset*, [, float *bias*])	**Offset** suffix accesses the texture (with optional lod *bias*) with the *offset* added to the *u* texel coordinate before looking up each texel.
ivec4 **texelFetch** (isampler1D *sampler*, int *coord*, int *lod*)	Use the texel integer *coord* to look up a single texel of the explicit *lod* to access the 1D texture currently specified by *sampler*.
ivec4 **texelFetchOffset** (isampler1D *sampler*, int *coord*, int *lod*, int *offset*)	**Offset** suffix accesses the texture (with optional lod *bias*) with the *offset* added to the *u* texel coordinate before looking up each texel.

Table 5.7 Texture access functions, *continued*

Syntax	Description

ivec4 **textureProjLod** (isampler1D *sampler*, vec2 *coord* , float *lod*)
ivec4 **textureProjLod** (isampler1D *sampler*, vec4 *coord* , float *lod*)
ivec4 **textureProjGrad** (isampler1D *sampler*, vec2 *coord*,
    float *dPdx*, float *dPdy*)
 	
ivec4 **textureProjGrad** (isampler1D *sampler*, vec4 *coord*,
    float *dPdx*, float *dPdy*)
 	
ivec4 **textureProjOffset** (isampler1D *sampler*, vec2 *coord*, int *offset*
    [, float *bias*])
ivec4 **textureProjOffset** (isampler1D *sampler*, vec4 *coord*, int *offset*
    [, float *bias*])
ivec4 **textureLodOffset** (isampler1D *sampler*, float *coord*, float *lod*,
    int *offset*)
 	
ivec4 **textureGradOffset** (isampler1D *sampler*, float *coord*,
    float *dPdx*, float *dPdy*, int *offset*)
	Use the texture coordinate *coord* to access the 1D texture currently specified by *sampler*.
	
	Combinations of the suffixes **Proj**, **Lod**, **Grad**, and **Offset** are as described earlier.

ivec4 **textureProjLodOffset** (isampler1D *sampler*, vec2 *coord*,
    float *lod*, int *offset*)
ivec4 **textureProjLodOffset** (isampler1D *sampler*, vec4 *coord*,
    float *lod*, int *offset*)
ivec4 **textureProjGradOffset** (isampler1D *sampler*, vec2 *coord*, float *dPdx*,
    float *dPdy*, int *offset*)
ivec4 **textureProjGradOffset** (isampler1D *sampler*, vec4 *coord*,
    float *dPdx*, float *dPdy*, int *offset*)
	Use the texture coordinate *coord* to access the 1D texture currently specified by *sampler*.
	
	Combinations of the suffixes **Proj**, **Lod**, **Grad**, and **Offset** are as described earlier.

(continues)

Table 5.7 Texture access functions, *continued*

Syntax	Description
int **textureSize** (usampler1D *sampler*, int *lod*)	Returns the width of level *lod* of the 1D texture currently specified by *sampler*.
uvec4 **texture** (usampler1D *sampler*, float *coord* [, float *bias*])	Use the texture coordinate *coord* to access the 1D texture currently specified by *sampler*.
uvec4 **textureProj** (usampler1D *sampler*, vec2 *coord* [, float *bias*])	Unsuffixed access the texture (with optional lod *bias*).
uvec4 **textureProj** (usampler1D *sampler*, vec4 *coord* [, float *bias*])	**Proj** suffix accesses the texture with projection (with optional lod *bias*).
uvec4 **textureLod** (usampler1D *sampler*, float *coord*, float *lod*)	**Lod** suffix accesses the texture with explicit *lod*.
uvec4 **textureGrad** (usampler1D *sampler*, float *coord*, float *dPdx*, float *dPdy*)	**Grad** suffix accesses the texture with explicit partial derivatives *dPdx* and *dPdy*.
uvec4 **textureOffset** (usampler1D *sampler*, float *coord*, int *offset*, [, float *bias*])	**Offset** suffix accesses the texture (with optional lod *bias*) with the *offset* added to the *u* texel coordinate before looking up each texel.
uvec4 **texelFetch** (usampler1D *sampler*, int *coord*, int *lod*)	Use the texel integer *coord* to look up a single texel of the explicit *lod* to access the 1D texture currently specified by *sampler*.
uvec4 **texelFetchOffset** (usampler1D *sampler*, int *coord*, int *lod*, int *offset*)	**Offset** suffix accesses the texture (with optional lod *bias*) with the *offset* added to the *u* texel coordinate before looking up each texel.

Table 5.7 Texture access functions, *continued*

Syntax	Description
uvec4 **textureProjLod** (usampler1D *sampler*, vec2 *coord* , float *lod*)	Use the texture coordinate *coord* to access the 1D texture currently specified by *sampler:*
uvec4 **textureProjLod** (usampler1D *sampler*, vec4 *coord* , float *lod*)	Combinations of the suffixes **Proj**, **Lod**, **Grad**, and **Offset** are as described earlier.
uvec4 **textureProjGrad** (usampler1D *sampler*, vec2 *coord*, float *dPdx*, float *dPdy*)	
uvec4 **textureProjGrad** (usampler1D *sampler*, vec4 *coord*, float *dPdx*, float *dPdy*)	
uvec4 **textureProjOffset** (usampler1D *sampler*, vec2 *coord*, int *offset* [, float *bias*])	
uvec4 **textureProjOffset** (usampler1D *sampler*, vec4 *coord*, int *offset* [, float *bias*])	
uvec4 **textureLodOffset** (usampler1D *sampler*, float *coord*, float *lod*, int *offset*)	
uvec4 **textureGradOffset** (usampler1D *sampler*, float *coord*, float *dPdx*, float *dPdy*, int *offset*)	
uvec4 **textureProjLodOffset** (usampler1D *sampler*, vec2 *coord*, float *lod*, int *offset*)	Use the texture coordinate *coord* to access the 1D texture currently specified by *sampler:*
uvec4 **textureProjLodOffset** (usampler1D *sampler*, vec4 *coord*, float *lod*, int *offset*)	Combinations of the suffixes **Proj**, **Lod**, **Grad**, and **Offset** are as described earlier.
uvec4 **textureProjGradOffset** (usampler1D *sampler*, vec2 *coord*, float *dPdx*, float *dPdy*, int *offset*)	
uvec4 **textureProjGradOffset** (usampler1D *sampler*, vec4 *coord*, float *dPdx*, float *dPdy*, int *offset*)	

(continues)

Table 5.7 Texture access functions, *continued*

Syntax	Description
ivec2 **textureSize** (sampler2D *sampler*, int *lod*)	Returns the width and height of level *lod* of the 2D texture currently specified by *sampler*.
vec4 **texture**(sampler2D *sampler*, vec2 *coord* [, float *bias*])	Use the texture coordinate *coord* to access the 2D texture currently specified by *sampler*.
vec4 **textureProj** (sampler2D *sampler*, vec3 *coord* [, float *bias*])	Unsuffixed access the texture (with optional lod *bias*).
vec4 **textureProj** (sampler2D *sampler*, vec4 *coord* [, float *bias*])	**Proj** suffix accesses the texture with projection (with optional lod *bias*).
vec4 **textureLod** (sampler2D *sampler*, vec2 *coord*, float *lod*)	**Lod** suffix accesses the texture with explicit *lod*.
vec4 **textureGrad** (sampler2D *sampler*, vec2 *coord*, vec2 *dPdx*, vec2 *dPdy*)	**Grad** suffix accesses the texture with explicit partial derivatives *dPdx* and *dPdy*.
vec4 **textureOffset** (sampler2D *sampler*, vec2 *coord*, ivec2 *offset*, [, float *bias*])	**Offset** suffix accesses the texture (with optional lod *bias*) with the *offset* added to the *u* and *v* texel coordinates before looking up each texel.
vec4 **texelFetch** (sampler2D *sampler*, ivec2 *coord*, int *lod*)	Use the texel integer *coord* to look up a single texel of the explicit *lod* to access the 2D texture currently specified by *sampler*.
vec4 **texelFetchOffset** (sampler2D *sampler*, ivec2 *coord*, int *lod*, ivec2 *offset*)	**Offset** suffix accesses the texture (with optional lod *bias*) with the *offset* added to the *u* and *v* texel coordinate before looking up each texel.

Table 5.7 Texture access functions, *continued*

Syntax	Description
vec4 **textureProjLod** (sampler2D *sampler*, vec3 *coord* , float *lod*)	Use the texture coordinate *coord* to access the 2D texture currently specified by *sampler*.
vec4 **textureProjLod** (sampler2D *sampler*, vec4 *coord* , float *lod*)	Combinations of the suffixes **Proj**, **Lod**, **Grad**, and **Offset** are as described earlier.
vec4 **textureProjGrad** (sampler2D *sampler*, vec3 *coord*, vec2 *dPdx*, vec2 *dPdy*)	
vec4 **textureProjGrad** (sampler2D *sampler*, vec4 *coord*, vec2 *dPdx*, vec2 *dPdy*)	
vec4 **textureProjOffset** (sampler2D *sampler*, vec3 *coord*, ivec2 *offset* [, float *bias*])	
vec4 **textureProjOffset** (sampler2D *sampler*, vec4 *coord*, ivec2 *offset* [, float *bias*])	
vec4 **textureLodOffset** (sampler2D *sampler*, vec2 *coord*, float *lod*, ivec2 *offset*)	
vec4 **textureGradOffset** (sampler2D *sampler*, vec2 *coord*, vec2 *dPdx*, vec2 *dPdy*, ivec2 *offset*)	
vec4 **textureProjLodOffset** (sampler2D *sampler*, vec3 *coord*, float *lod*, ivec2 *offset*)	Use the texture coordinate *coord* to access the 2D texture currently specified by *sampler*.
vec4 **textureProjLodOffset** (sampler2D *sampler*, vec4 *coord*, float *lod*, ivec2 *offset*)	Combinations of the suffixes **Proj**, **Lod**, **Grad**, and **Offset** are as described earlier.
vec4 **textureProjGradOffset** (sampler2D *sampler*, vec3 *coord*, vec2 *dPdx*, vec2 *dPdy*, ivec2 *offset*)	
vec4 **textureProjGradOffset** (sampler2D *sampler*, vec4 *coord*, vec2 *dPdx*, vec2 *dPdy*, ivec2 *offset*)	

(continues)

Table 5.7 Texture access functions, *continued*

Syntax	Description
ivec2 **textureSize** (isampler2D *sampler*, int *lod*)	Returns the width and height of level *lod* of the 2D texture currently specified by *sampler*.
ivec4 **texture** (isampler2D *sampler*, vec2 *coord* [, float *bias*]) ivec4 **textureProj** (isampler2D *sampler*, vec3 *coord* [, float *bias*]) ivec4 **textureProj** (isampler2D *sampler*, vec4 *coord* [, float *bias*]) ivec4 **textureLod** (isampler2D *sampler*, vec2 *coord*, float *lod*) ivec4 **textureGrad** (isampler2D *sampler*, vec2 *coord*,vec2 *coord* dPdx, vec2 dPdy) ivec4 **textureOffset** (isampler2D *sampler*, vec2 *coord*, ivec2 *offset*, [, float *bias*])	Use the texture coordinate *coord* to access the 2D texture currently specified by *sampler*. Unsuffixed access the texture (with optional lod *bias*). **Proj** suffix accesses the texture with projection (with optional lod *bias*). **Lod** suffix accesses the texture with explicit *lod*. **Grad** suffix accesses the texture with explicit partial derivatives *dPdx* and *dPdy*. **Offset** suffix accesses the texture (with optional lod *bias*) with the *offset* added to the *u* and *v* texel coordinates before looking up each texel.
ivec4 **texelFetch** (isampler2D *sampler*, ivec2 *coord*, int *lod*) ivec4 **texelFetchOffset** (isampler2D *sampler*, ivec2 *coord*, int *lod*, ivec2 *offset*)	Use the texel integer *coord* to look up a single texel of the explicit *lod* to access the 2D texture currently specified by *sampler*. **Offset** suffix accesses the texture (with optional lod *bias*) with the *offset* added to the *u* and *v* texel coordinate before looking up each texel.

Table 5.7 Texture access functions, *continued*

Syntax	Description
ivec4 **textureProjLod** (isampler2D *sampler*, vec3 *coord* , float *lod*) ivec4 **textureProjLod** (isampler2D *sampler*, vec4 *coord* , float *lod*)	Use the texture coordinate *coord* to access the 2D texture currently specified by *sampler*.

ivec4 **textureProjGrad** (isampler2D *sampler*, vec3 *coord*,
        vec2 *dPdx*, vec2 *dPdy*)
ivec4 **textureProjGrad** (isampler2D *sampler*, vec4 *coord*,
        vec2 *dPdx*, vec2 *dPdy*)
	Combinations of the suffixes **Proj**, **Lod**, **Grad**, and **Offset** are as described earlier.

ivec4 **textureProjOffset** (isampler2D *sampler*, vec3 *coord*, ivec2 *offset* [, float *bias*])	
ivec4 **textureProjOffset** (isampler2D *sampler*, vec4 *coord*, ivec2 *offset* [, float *bias*])	
ivec4 **textureLodOffset** (isampler2D *sampler*, vec2 *coord*, float *lod*, ivec2 *offset*)	
ivec4 **textureGradOffset** (isampler2D *sampler*, vec2 *coord*, vec2 *dPdx*, vec2 *dPdy*, ivec2 *offset*)	

ivec4 **textureProjLodOffset** (isampler2D *sampler*, vec3 *coord*,
        float *lod*, ivec2 *offset*)
ivec4 **textureProjLodOffset** (isampler2D *sampler*, vec4 *coord*,
        float *lod*, ivec2 *offset*)
	Use the texture coordinate *coord* to access the 2D texture currently specified by *sampler*.

ivec4 **textureProjGradOffset** (isampler2D *sampler*, vec3 *coord*,
        vec2 *dPdx*, vec2 *dPdy*, ivec2 *offset*)
ivec4 **textureProjGradOffset** (isampler2D *sampler*, vec4 *coord*,
        vec2 *dPdx*, vec2 *dPdy*, ivec2 *offset*)
	Combinations of the suffixes **Proj**, **Lod**, **Grad**, and **Offset** are as described earlier.

(continues)

Table 5.7 Texture access functions, *continued*

Syntax	Description
ivec2 **textureSize** (usampler2D *sampler*, int *lod*)	Returns the width and height of level *lod* of the 2D texture currently specified by *sampler*.
uvec4 **texture** (usampler2D *sampler*, vec2 *coord* [, float *bias*])	Use the texture coordinate *coord* to access the 2D texture currently specified by *sampler*.
uvec4 **textureProj** (usampler2D *sampler*, vec3 *coord* [, float *bias*]) uvec4 **textureProj** (usampler2D *sampler*, vec4 *coord* [, float *bias*])	Unsuffixed access the texture (with optional lod *bias*). **Proj** suffix accesses the texture with projection (with optional lod *bias*).
uvec4 **textureLod** (usampler2D *sampler*, vec2 *coord*, float *lod*)	**Lod** suffix accesses the texture with explicit *lod*.
uvec4 **textureGrad** (usampler2D *sampler*, vec2 *coord*, vec2 *dPdx*, vec2 *dPdy*)	**Grad** suffix accesses the texture with explicit partial derivatives *dPdx* and *dPdy*.
uvec4 **textureOffset** (usampler2D *sampler*, vec2 *coord*, ivec2 *offset*, [, float *bias*])	**Offset** suffix accesses the texture (with optional lod *bias*) with the *offset* added to the *u* and *v* texel coordinates before looking up each texel.
uvec4 **texelFetch** (usampler2D *sampler*, ivec2 *coord*, int *lod*) uvec4 **texelFetchOffset** (usampler2D *sampler*, ivec2 *coord*, int *lod*, ivec2 *offset*)	Use the texel integer *coord* to look up a single texel of the explicit *lod* to access the 2D texture currently specified by *sampler*. **Offset** suffix accesses the texture (with optional lod *bias*) with the *offset* added to the *u* and *v* texel coordinate before looking up each texel.

Table 5.7 Texture access functions, *continued*

Syntax	Description
uvec4 **textureProjLod** (usampler2D *sampler*, vec3 *coord* , float *lod*)	Use the texture coordinate *coord* to access the 2D texture currently specified by *sampler.*
uvec4 **textureProjLod** (usampler2D *sampler*, vec4 *coord* , float *lod*)	Combinations of the suffixes **Proj, Lod,**
uvec4 **textureProjGrad** (usampler2D *sampler*, vec3 *coord*, vec2 *dPdx*, vec2 *dPdy*)	**Grad,** and **Offset** are as described earlier.
uvec4 **textureProjGrad** (usampler2D *sampler*, vec4 *coord*, vec2 *dPdx*, vec2 *dPdy*)	
uvec4 **textureProjOffset** (usampler2D *sampler*, vec3 *coord*, ivec2 *offset*[, float *bias*])	
uvec4 **textureProjOffset** (usampler2D *sampler*, vec4 *coord*, ivec2 *offset*[, float *bias*])	
uvec4 **textureLodOffset** (usampler2D *sampler*, vec2 *coord*, float *lod*, ivec2 *offset*)	
uvec4 **textureGradOffset** (usampler2D *sampler*, vec2 *coord*, vec2 *dPdx*, vec2 *dPdy*, ivec2 *offset*)	
uvec4 **textureProjLodOffset** (usampler2D *sampler*, vec3 *coord*, float *lod*, ivec2 *offset*)	Use the texture coordinate *coord* to access the 2D texture currently specified by *sampler.*
uvec4 **textureProjLodOffset** (usampler2D *sampler*, vec4 *coord*, float *lod*, ivec2 *offset*)	Combinations of the suffixes **Proj, Lod,**
uvec4 **textureProjGradOffset** (usampler2D *sampler*, vec3 *coord*, vec2 *dPdx*, vec2 *dPdy*, ivec2 *offset*)	**Grad,** and **Offset** are as described earlier.
uvec4 **textureProjGradOffset** (usampler2D *sampler*, vec4 *coord*, vec2 *dPdx*, vec2 *dPdy*, ivec2 *offset*)	

(continues)

Table 5.7 Texture access functions, *continued*

Syntax	Description
ivec2 **textureSize** (sampler2DRect *sampler*)	Returns the width and height of the rectangle texture currently specified by *sampler*.
vec4 **texture** (sampler2DRect *sampler*, vec2 *coord*) vec4 **textureProj** (sampler2DRect *sampler*, vec3 *coord*) vec4 **textureProj** (sampler2DRect *sampler*, vec4 *coord*) vec4 **textureGrad** (sampler2DRect *sampler*, vec2 *coord*, vec2 *dPdx*, vec2 *dPdy*) vec4 **textureOffset** (sampler2DRect *sampler*, vec2 *coord*, ivec2 *offset*)	Use the unnormalized texture coordinate *coord* to access the rectangle texture currently specified by *sampler*. Unsuffixed access the texture. **Proj** suffix accesses the texture with projection. **Grad** suffix accesses the texture with explicit partial derivatives *dPdx* and *dPdy*. **Offset** suffix accesses the texture with the *offset* added to the *u* and *v* texel coordinates before looking up each texel.
vec4 **texelFetch** (sampler2DRect *sampler*, ivec2 *coord*) vec4 **texelFetchOffset** (sampler2DRect *sampler*, ivec2 *coord*, ivec2 *offset*)	Use the texel integer *coord* to look up a single texel of the rectangle texture currently specified by *sampler*. **Offset** suffix accesses the texture with the *offset* added to the *u* and *v* texel coordinate before looking up each texel.

Table 5.7 Texture access functions, *continued*

Syntax	Description
vec4 **textureProjGrad** (sampler2DRect *sampler*, vec3 *coord*, vec2 *dPdx*, vec2 *dPdy*)	Use the unnormalized texture coordinate *coord* to access the rectangle texture currently specified by *sampler*:
vec4 **textureProjGrad** (sampler2DRect *sampler*, vec4 *coord*, vec2 *dPdx*, vec2 *dPdy*)	Combination of the suffixes **Proj**, **Grad** and **Offset** are as described earlier.
vec4 **textureProjOffset** (sampler2DRect *sampler*, vec3 *coord*, ivec2 *offset*)	
vec4 **textureProjOffset** (sampler2DRect *sampler*, vec4 *coord*, ivec2 *offset*)	
vec4 **textureProjGradOffset** (sampler2DRect *sampler*,vec3 *coord*, vec2 *dPdx*, vec2 *dPdy*, ivec2 *offset*)	
vec4 **textureProjGradOffset** (sampler2DRect *sampler*, vec4 *coord*, vec2 *dPdx*, vec2 *dPdy*, ivec2 *offset*)	
ivec2 **textureSize** (isampler2DRect *sampler*)	Returns the width and height of the rectangle texture currently specified by *sampler.*
ivec4 **texture** (isampler2DRect *sampler*, vec2 *coord*)	Use the unnormalized texture coordinate *coord* to access the rectangle texture currently specified by *sampler:*
ivec4 **textureProj** (isampler2DRect *sampler*, vec3 *coord*)	Unsuffixed access the texture.
ivec4 **textureProj** (isampler2DRect *sampler*, vec4 *coord*)	**Proj** suffix accesses the texture with projection.
ivec4 **textureGrad** (isampler2DRect *sampler*, vec2 *coord*, vec2 *dPdx*, vec2 *dPdy*)	**Grad** suffix accesses the texture with explicit partial derivatives *dPdx* and *dPdy.*
ivec4 **textureOffset** (isampler2DRect *sampler*, vec2 *coord*, ivec2 *offset*)	**Offset** suffix accesses the texture with the *offset* added to the *u* and *v* texel coordinates before looking up each texel.

(continues)

Table 5.7 Texture access functions, *continued*

Syntax	Description
ivec4 **texelFetch** (isampler2DRect *sampler*, ivec2 *coord*) ivec4 **texelFetchOffset** (isampler2DRect *sampler*, ivec2 *coord*, ivec2 *offset*)	Use the texel integer *coord* to look up a single texel of the rectangle texture currently specified by *sampler*: **Offset** suffix accesses the texture with the *offset* added to the *u* and *v* texel coordinate before looking up each texel.
ivec4 **textureProjGrad** (isampler2DRect *sampler*, vec3 *coord*, vec2 *dPdx*, vec2 *dPdy*) ivec4 **textureProjGrad** (isampler2DRect *sampler*, vec4 *coord*, vec2 *dPdx*, vec2 *dPdy*) ivec4 **textureProjOffset** (isampler2DRect *sampler*, vec3 *coord*, ivec2 *offset*) ivec4 **textureProjOffset** (isampler2DRect *sampler*, vec4 *coord*, ivec2 *offset*) ivec4 **textureProjGradOffset** (isampler2DRect *sampler*, vec3 *coord*, vec2 *dPdx*, vec2 *dPdy*, ivec2 *offset*) ivec4 **textureProjGradOffset** (isampler2DRect *sampler*, vec4 *coord*, vec2 *dPdx*, vec2 *dPdy*, ivec2 *offset*)	Use the unnormalized texture coordinate *coord* to access the rectangle texture currently specified by *sampler*: Combination of the suffixes **Proj**, **Grad** and **Offset** are as described earlier.
ivec2 **textureSize** (usampler2DRect *sampler*)	Returns the width and height of the rectangle texture currently specified by *sampler*.

Table 5.7 Texture access functions, *continued*

Syntax	Description
uvec4 **texture** (usampler2DRect *sampler*, vec2 *coord*)	Use the unnormalized texture coordinate *coord* to access the rectangle texture currently specified by *sampler*.
uvec4 **textureProj** (usampler2DRect *sampler*, vec3 *coord*)	Unsuffixed access the texture.
uvec4 **textureProj** (usampler2DRect *sampler*, vec4 *coord*)	
uvec4 **textureGrad** (usampler2DRect *sampler*, vec2 *coord*, vec2 *dPdx*, vec2 *dPdy*)	**Proj** suffix accesses the texture with projection.
	Grad suffix accesses the texture with explicit partial derivatives *dPdx* and *dPdy*.
uvec4 **textureOffset** (usampler2DRect *sampler*, vec2 *coord*, ivec2 *offset*)	**Offset** suffix accesses the texture with the *offset* added to the *u* and *v* texel coordinates before looking up each texel.
uvec4 **texelFetch** (usampler2DRect *sampler*, ivec2 *coord*)	Use the texel integer *coord* to look up a single texel of the rectangle texture currently specified by *sampler*.
uvec4 **texelFetchOffset** (usampler2DRect *sampler*, ivec2 *coord*, ivec2 *offset*)	**Offset** suffix accesses the texture with the *offset* added to the *u* and *v* texel coordinate before looking up each texel.

(continues)

Table 5.7 Texture access functions, *continued*

Syntax	Description
uvec4 **textureProjGrad** (usampler2DRect *sampler*, vec3 *coord*, vec2 *dPdx*, vec2 *dPdy*)	Use the unnormalized texture coordinate *coord* to access the rectangle texture currently specified by *sampler*.
uvec4 **textureProjGrad** (usampler2DRect *sampler*, vec4 *coord*, vec2 *dPdx*, vec2 *dPdy*)	Combination of the suffixes **Proj**, **Grad** and **Offset** are as described earlier.
uvec4 **textureProjOffset** (usampler2DRect *sampler*, vec3 *coord*, ivec2 *offset*)	
uvec4 **textureProjOffset** (usampler2DRect *sampler*, vec4 *coord*, ivec2 *offset*)	
uvec4 **textureProjGradOffset** (usampler2DRect *sampler*, vec3 *coord*, vec2 *dPdx*, vec2 *dPdy*, ivec2 *offset*)	
uvec4 **textureProjGradOffset** (uusampler2DRect *sampler*, vec4 *coord*, vec2 *dPdx*, vec2 *dPdy*, ivec2 *offset*)	
ivec3 **textureSize** (sampler3D *sampler*, int *lod*)	Returns the width, height and depth of level *lod* of the 3D texture currently specified by *sampler*.
vec4 **texture** (sampler3D *sampler*, vec3 *coord* [, float *bias*])	Use the texture coordinate *coord* to access the 3D texture currently specified by *sampler*.
vec4 **textureProj** (sampler3D *sampler*, vec4 *coord* [, float *bias*])	Unsuffixed access the texture (with optional lod *bias*).
vec4 **textureLod** (sampler3D *sampler*, vec3 *coord*, float *lod*)	**Proj** suffix accesses the texture with projection (with optional lod *bias*).
vec4 **textureGrad** (sampler3D *sampler*, vec3 *coord*,vec3 *dPdx*, vec3 *dPdy*)	**Lod** suffix accesses the texture with explict *lod*.
vec4 **textureOffset** (sampler3D *sampler*, vec3 *coord*, ivec3 *offset*, [, float *bias*])	**Grad** suffix accesses the texture with explicit partial derivatives *dPdx* and *dPdy*.
	Offset suffix accesses the texture (with optional lod *bias*) with the *offset* added to the *u*, *v*, and *w* texel coordinates before looking up each texel.

Table 5.7 Texture access functions, *continued*

Syntax	Description
vec4 **texelFetch** (sampler3D *sampler*, ivec3 *coord*, int *lod*) vec4 **texelFetchOffset** (sampler3D *sampler*, ivec3 *coord*, int *lod*, ivec3 *offset*)	Use the texel integer *coord* to look up a single texel of the explicit *lod* to access the 3D texture currently specified by *sampler*. **Offset** suffix accesses the texture (with optional lod *bias*) with the *offset* added to the *u*, *v*, and *w* texel coordinate before looking up each texel.
vec4 **textureProjLod** (sampler3D *sampler*, vec4 *coord* , float *lod*) vec4 **textureProjGrad** (sampler3D *sampler*, vec4 *coord*, vec3 *dPdx*, vec3 *dPdy*) vec4 **textureProjOffset** (sampler3D *sampler*, vec4 *coord*, ivec3 *offset* [, float *bias*]) vec4 **textureLodOffset** (sampler3D *sampler*, vec3 *coord*, float *lod*, ivec3 *offset*) vec4 **textureGradOffset** (sampler3D *sampler*, vec3 *coord*, vec3 *dPdx*, vec3 *dPdy*, ivec3 *offset*)	Use the texture coordinate *coord* to access the 3D texture currently specified by *sampler*. Combinations of the suffixes **Proj**, **Lod**, **Grad**, and **Offset** are as described earlier.
vec4 **textureProjLodOffset** (sampler3D *sampler*, vec4 *coord*, float *lod*, ivec3 *offset*) vec4 **textureProjGradOffset** (sampler3D *sampler*, vec4 *coord*, vec3 *dPdx*, vec3 *dPdy*, ivec3 *offset*)	Use the texture coordinate *coord* to access the 3D texture currently specified by *sampler*. Combinations of the suffixes **Proj**, **Lod**, **Grad**, and **Offset** are as described earlier.
ivec3 **textureSize** (isampler3D *sampler*, int *lod*)	Returns the width, height and depth of level *lod* of the 3D texture currently specified by *sampler*.

(continues)

Table 5.7 Texture access functions, *continued*

Syntax	Description
ivec4 **texture** (isampler3D *sampler*, vec3 *coord*[, float *bias*])	Use the texture coordinate *coord* to access the 3D texture currently specified by *sampler*.
ivec4 **textureProj** (isampler3D *sampler*, vec4 *coord* [, float *bias*])	Unsuffixed access the texture (with optional lod *bias*).
ivec4 **textureLod** (isampler3D *sampler*, vec3 *coord*, float *lod*)	
ivec4 **textureGrad** (isampler3D *sampler*, vec3 *coord*, vec3 *dPdx*, vec3 *dPdy*)	**Proj** suffix accesses the texture with projection (with optional lod *bias*).
ivec4 **textureOffset** (isampler3D *sampler*, vec3 *coord*, ivec3 *offset*, [, float *bias*])	**Lod** suffix accesses the texture with explicit *lod*.
	Grad suffix accesses the texture with explicit partial derivatives *dPdx* and *dPdy*.
	Offset suffix accesses the texture (with optional lod *bias*) with the *offset* added to the *u*, *v*, and *w* texel coordinates before looking up each texel.
ivec4 **texelFetch** (isampler3D *sampler*, ivec3 *coord*, int *lod*)	Use the texel integer *coord* to look up a single texel of the explicit *lod* to access the 3D texture currently specified by *sampler*.
ivec4 **texelFetchOffset** (isampler3D *sampler*, ivec3 *coord*, int *lod*, ivec3 *offset*)	**Offset** suffix accesses the texture (with optional lod *bias*) with the *offset* added to the *u* and *v* texel coordinate before looking up each texel.

5.7   Texture Access Functions   **161**

Table 5.7 Texture access functions, *continued*

Syntax	Description
ivec4 **textureProjLod** (isampler3D *sampler*, vec4 *coord* , float *lod*)	Use the texture coordinate *coord* to access the 3D texture currently specified by *sampler*.
ivec4 **textureProjGrad** (isampler3D *sampler*, vec4 *coord*, vec3 *dPdx*, vec3 *dPdy*)	Combinations of the suffixes **Proj**, **Lod**, **Grad**, and **Offset** are as described earlier.
ivec4 **textureProjOffset** (isampler3D *sampler*, vec4 *coord*, ivec3 *offset* [, float *bias*])	
ivec4 **textureLodOffset** (isampler3D *sampler*, vec3 *coord*, float *lod*, ivec3 *offset*)	
ivec4 **textureGradOffset** (isampler3D *sampler*, vec3 *coord*, vec3 *dPdx*, vec3 *dPdy*, ivec3 *offset*)	
ivec4 **textureProjLodOffset** (isampler3D *sampler*, vec4 *coord*, float *lod*, ivec3 *offset*)	Use the texture coordinate *coord* to access the 3D texture currently specified by *sampler*.
ivec4 **textureProjGradOffset** (isampler3D *sampler*, vec4 *coord*, vec3 *dPdx*, vec3 *dPdy*, ivec3 *offset*)	Combinations of the suffixes **Proj**, **Lod**, **Grad**, and **Offset** are as described earlier.
ivec3 **textureSize** (usampler3D *sampler*, int *lod*)	Returns the width, height and depth of level *lod* of the 3D texture currently specified by *sampler*.

(continues)

Table 5.7 Texture access functions, *continued*

Syntax	Description
uvec4 **texture** (usampler3D *sampler*, vec3 *coord*[, float *bias*])	Use the texture coordinate *coord* to access the 3D texture currently specified by *sampler*.
uvec4 **textureProj** (usampler3D *sampler*, vec4 *coord* [, float *bias*])	Unsuffixed access the texture (with optional lod *bias*).
uvec4 **textureLod** (usampler3D *sampler*, vec3 *coord*, float *lod*)	**Proj** suffix accesses the texture with projection (with optional lod *bias*).
uvec4 **textureGrad** (usampler3D *sampler*, vec3 *coord*, vec3 *dPdx*, vec3 *dPdy*)	**Lod** suffix accesses the texture with explicit *lod*.
uvec4 **textureOffset** (usampler3D *sampler*, vec3 *coord*, ivec3 *offset*, [, float *bias*])	**Grad** suffix accesses the texture with explicit partial derivatives *dPdx* and *dPdy*.
	Offset suffix accesses the texture (with optional lod *bias*) with the *offset* added to the *u* and *v* texel coordinates before looking up each texel.
uvec4 **texelFetch** (usampler3D *sampler*, ivec3 *coord*, int *lod*)	Use the texel integer *coord* to look up a single texel of the explicit *lod* to access the 3D texture currently specified by *sampler*.
uvec4 **texelFetchOffset** (usampler3D *sampler*, ivec3 *coord*, int *lod*, ivec3 *offset*)	**Offset** suffix accesses the texture (with optional lod *bias*) with the *offset* added to the *u*, *v*, and *w* texel coordinate before looking up each texel.

Table 5.7 Texture access functions, *continued*

Syntax	Description

uvec4 **textureProjLod** (usampler3D *sampler*, vec4 *coord* , float *lod*)
uvec4 **textureProjGrad** (usampler3D *sampler*, vec4 *coord*,
      vec3 *dPdx*, vec3 *dPdy*)
uvec4 **textureProjOffset** (usampler3D *sampler*, vec4 *coord*,
      ivec3 *offset*[, float *bias*])
uvec4 **textureLodOffset** (usampler3D *sampler*, vec3 *coord*,
      float *lod*, ivec3 *offset*)
uvec4 **textureGradOffset** (usampler3D *sampler*, vec3 *coord*,
      vec3 *dPdx*, vec3 *dPdy*, ivec3 *offset*)
	Use the texture coordinate *coord* to access the 3D texture currently specified by *sampler*. Combinations of the suffixes **Proj**, **Lod**, **Grad**, and **Offset** are as described earlier.

uvec4 **textureProjLodOffset** (usampler3D *sampler*, vec4 *coord*,
      float *lod*, ivec3 *offset*)
uvec4 **textureProjGradOffset** (usampler3D *sampler*, vec4 *coord*,
      vec3 *dPdx*, vec3 *dPdy*, ivec3 *offset*)
	Use the texture coordinate *coord* to access the 3D texture currently specified by *sampler*. Combinations of the suffixes **Proj**, **Lod**, **Grad**, and **Offset** are as described earlier.

ivec2 **textureSize** (samplerCube *sampler*, int *lod*)	Returns the width and height of level *lod* of the cube map texture currently specified by *sampler*.
vec4 **texture** (samplerCube *sampler*, vec3 *coord* [, float *bias*]) vec4 **textureLod** (samplerCube *sampler*, vec3 *coord*, float *lod*) vec4 **textureGrad** (samplerCube *sampler*, vec3 *coord*, vec3 *dPdx*, vec3 *dPdy*)	Use the texture coordinate *coord* to access the cube map texture currently specified by *sampler*. Unsuffixed access the texture (with optional lod *bias*). **Lod** suffix accesses the texture with explicit *lod*. **Grad** suffix accesses the texture with explicit partial derivatives *dPdx* and *dPdy*.

(continues)

Table 5.7 Texture access functions, *continued*

Syntax	Description
vec4 **texelFetch** (samplerCube *sampler*, ivec3 *coord*, int *lod*)	Use the texel integer *coord* to look up a single texel of the explicit *lod* to access the cube map texture currently specified by *sampler*.
ivec2 **textureSize** (isamplerCube *sampler*, int *lod*)	Returns the width and height of level *lod* of the cube map texture currently specified by *sampler*.
ivec4 **texture** (isamplerCube *sampler*, vec3 *coord* [, float *bias*]) ivec4 **textureLod** (isamplerCube *sampler*, vec3 *coord*, float *lod*) ivec4 **textureGrad** (isamplerCube *sampler*, vec3 *coord*, vec3 *dPdx*, vec3 *dPdy*)	Use the texture coordinate *coord* to access the cube map texture currently specified by *sampler*. Unsuffixed access the texture (with optional lod *bias*). **Lod** suffix accesses the texture with explicit *lod*. **Grad** suffix accesses the texture with explicit partial derivatives *dPdx* and *dPdy*.
ivec4 **texelFetch** (isamplerCube *sampler*, ivec3 *coord*, int *lod*)	Use the texel integer *coord* to look up a single texel of the explicit *lod* to access the cube map texture currently specified by *sampler*.
ivec2 **textureSize** (usamplerCube *sampler*, int *lod*)	Returns the width and height of level *lod* of the cube map texture currently specified by *sampler*.

Table 5.7 Texture access functions, *continued*

Syntax	Description
uvec4 **texture** (usamplerCube *sampler*, vec3 *coord*[, float *bias*]) uvec4 **textureLod** (usamplerCube *sampler*, vec3 *coord*, float *lod*) uvec4 **textureGrad** (usamplerCube *sampler*, vec3 *coord*, vec3 *dPdx*, vec3 *dPdy*)	Use the texture coordinate *coord* to access the cube map texture currently specified by *sampler*. Unsuffixed access the texture (with optional lod *bias*). **Lod** suffix accesses the texture with explicit *lod*. **Grad** suffix accesses the texture with explicit partial derivatives *dPdx* and *dPdy*.
uvec4 **texelFetch** (usamplerCube *sampler*, ivec3 *coord*, int *lod*)	Use the texel integer *coord* to look up a single texel of the explicit *lod* to access the cube map texture currently specified by *sampler*.
int **textureSize** (sampler1DArray *sampler*, int *lod*)	Returns the width of level *lod* of the 1D texture array currently specified by *sampler*.
vec4 **texture** (sampler1DArray *sampler*, vec2 *coord*[, float *bias*]) vec4 **textureLod** (sampler1DArray *sampler*, vec2 *coord*, float *lod*) vec4 **textureGrad** (sampler1DArray *sampler*, vec2 *coord*, float *dPdx*, float *dPdy*) vec4 **textureOffset** (sampler1DArray *sampler*, vec2 *coord*, int *offset*, [, float *bias*])	Use the texture coordinate *coord* to access the 1D texture array currently specified by *sampler*. Unsuffixed access the texture (with optional lod *bias*). **Lod** suffix accesses the texture with explicit *lod*. **Grad** suffix accesses the texture with explicit partial derivatives *dPdx* and *dPdy*. **Offset** suffix accesses the texture (with optional lod *bias*) with the *offset* added to the *u* texel coordinate before looking up each texel.

(continues)

Table 5.7 Texture access functions, *continued*

Syntax	Description
vec4 **texelFetch** (sampler1DArray *sampler*, ivec2 *coord*, int *lod*) vec4 **texelFetchOffset** (sampler1DArray *sampler*, ivec2 *coord*, int *lod*, int *offset*)	Use the texel integer *coord* to look up a single texel of the explicit *lod* to access the 1D texture currently specified by *sampler*. **Offset** suffix accesses the texture (with optional lod *bias*) with the *offset* added to the *u* texel coordinate before looking up each texel.
vec4 **textureLodOffset** (sampler1DArray *sampler*, vec2 *coord*, float *lod*, int *offset*) vec4 **textureGradOffset** (sampler1DArray *sampler*, vec2 *coord*, float *dPdx*, float *dPdy*, int *offset*)	Use the texture coordinate *coord* to access the 1D texture currently specified by *sampler*. Combinations of the suffixes **Lod**, **Grad**, and **Offset** are as described earlier.
int **textureSize** (isampler1DArray *sampler*, int *lod*)	Returns the width of level *lod* of the 1D texture array currently specified by *sampler*.
ivec4 **texture** (isampler1DArray *sampler*, vec2 *coord* [, float *bias*]) ivec4 **textureLod** (isampler1DArray *sampler*, vec2 *coord*, float *lod*) ivec4 **textureGrad** (isampler1DArray *sampler*, vec2 *coord*, float *dPdx*, float *dPdy*) ivec4 **textureOffset** (isampler1DArray *sampler*, vec2 *coord*, int *offset*, [, float *bias*])	Use the texture coordinate *coord* to access the 1D texture array currently specified by *sampler*. Unsuffixed access the texture (with optional lod *bias*). **Lod** suffix accesses the texture with explicit *lod*. **Grad** suffix accesses the texture with explicit partial derivatives *dPdx* and *dPdy*. **Offset** suffix accesses the texture (with optional lod *bias*) with the *offset* added to the *u* texel coordinate before looking up each texel.

Table 5.7 Texture access functions, *continued*

Syntax	Description
ivec4 **texelFetch** (isampler1DArray *sampler*, ivec2 *coord*, int *lod*) ivec4 **texelFetchOffset** (isampler1DArray *sampler*, ivec2 *coord*, int *lod*, int *offset*)	Use the texel integer *coord* to look up a single texel of the explicit *lod* of the 1D texture array currently specified by *sampler*. **Offset** suffix accesses the texture (with optional lod *bias*) with the *offset* added to the *u* texel coordinate before looking up each texel.
ivec4 **textureLodOffset** (isampler1DArray *sampler*, vec2 *coord*, float *lod*, int *offset*) ivec4 **textureGradOffset** (isampler1DArray *sampler*, fvec2 *coord*, float *dPdx*, float *dPdy*, int *offset*)	Use the texture coordinate *coord* to access the 1D texture array currently specified by *sampler*. Combinations of the suffixes **Lod**, **Grad**, and **Offset** are as described earlier.
int **textureSize** (usampler1DArray *sampler*, int *lod*)	Returns the width of level *lod* of the 1D texture array currently specified by *sampler*.
uvec4 **texture** (usampler1DArray *sampler*, vec2 *coord* [, float *bias*]) uvec4 **textureLod** (usampler1DArray *sampler*, vec2 *coord*, float *lod*) uvec4 **textureGrad** (usampler1DArray *sampler*, vec2 *coord*, float *dPdx*, float *dPdy*) uvec4 **textureOffset** (usampler1DArray *sampler*, vec2 *coord*, int *offset*, [, float *bias*])	Use the texture coordinate *coord* to access the 1D texture array currently specified by *sampler*. Unsuffixed access the texture (with optional lod *bias*). **Lod** suffix accesses the texture with explicit *lod*. **Grad** suffix accesses the texture with explicit partial derivatives *dPdx* and *dPdy*. **Offset** suffix accesses the texture (with optional lod *bias*) with the *offset* added to the *u* texel coordinate before looking up each texel.

(continues)

Table 5.7 Texture access functions, *continued*

Syntax	Description
uvec4 **texelFetch** (usampler1DArray *sampler*, ivec2 *coord*, int *lod*) uvec4 **texelFetchOffset** (usampler1DArray *sampler*, ivec2 *coord*, int *lod*, int *offset*)	Use the texel integer *coord* to look up a single texel of the explicit *lod* of the 1D texture array currently specified by *sampler*. **Offset** suffix accesses the texture (with optional lod *bias*) with the *offset* added to the *u* texel coordinate before looking up each texel.
uvec4 **textureLodOffset** (usampler1DArray *sampler*, vec2 *coord*, float *lod*, int *offset*) uvec4 **textureGradOffset** (usampler1DArray *sampler*, vec2 *coord*, float *dPdx*, float *dPdy*, int *offset*)	Use the texture coordinate *coord* to access the 1D texture array currently specified by *sampler*. Combinations of the suffixes **Lod**, **Grad**, and **Offset** are as described earlier.
ivec2 **textureSize** (sampler2DArray *sampler*, int *lod*)	Returns the width and height of level *lod* of the 1D texture array currently specified by *sampler*.
vec4 **texture** (sampler2DArray *sampler*, vec3 *coord*[, float *bias*]) vec4 **textureLod** (sampler2DArray *sampler*, vec3 *coord*, float *lod*) vec4 **textureGrad** (sampler2DArray *sampler*, vec3 *coord*, vec2 *dPdx*, vec2 *dPdy*) vec4 **textureOffset** (sampler2DArray *sampler*, vec3 *coord*, vec2 *offset*, [, float *bias*])	Use the texture coordinate *coord* to access the 1D texture array currently specified by *sampler*. Unsuffixed access the texture (with optional lod *bias*). **Lod** suffix accesses the texture with explicit *lod*. **Grad** suffix accesses the texture with explicit partial derivatives *dPdx* and *dPdy*. **Offset** suffix accesses the texture (with optional lod *bias*) with the *offset* added to the *u* texel coordinate before looking up each texel.

Table 5.7 Texture access functions, *continued*

Syntax	Description
vec4 **texelFetch** (sampler2DArray *sampler*, ivec3 *coord*, int *lod*) vec4 **texelFetchOffset** (sampler2DArray *sampler*, ivec3 *coord*, int *lod*, ivec2 *offset*)	Use the texel integer *coord* to look up a single texel of the explicit *lod* of the 1D texture array currently specified by *sampler*: **Offset** suffix accesses the texture (with optional lod *bias*) with the *offset* added to the *u* texel coordinate before looking up each texel.
vec4 **textureLodOffset** (sampler2DArray *sampler*, vec3 *coord*, float *lod*, int *offset*) vec4 **textureGradOffset** (sampler2DArray *sampler*, vec3 *coord*, vec2 *dPdx*, vec2 *dPdy*, ivec2 *offset*)	Use the texture coordinate *coord* to access the 1D texture array currently specified by *sampler*: Combinations of the suffixes **Lod**, **Grad**, and **Offset** are as described earlier.
ivec2 **textureSize** (isampler2DArray *sampler*, int *lod*)	Returns the width and height of level *lod* of the 1D texture array currently specified by *sampler*.
ivec4 **texture** (isampler2DArray *sampler*, vec3 *coord*[, float *bias*]) ivec4 **textureLod** (isampler2DArray *sampler*, vec3 *coord*, float *lod*) ivec4 **textureGrad** (isampler2DArray *sampler*, vec3 *coord*, vec2 *dPdx*, vec2 *dPdy*) ivec4 **textureOffset** (isampler2DArray *sampler*, vec3 *coord*, vec2 *offset*, [, float *bias*])	Use the texture coordinate *coord* to access the 1D texture array currently specified by *sampler*. Unsuffixed access the texture (with optional lod *bias*). **Lod** suffix accesses the texture with explicit *lod*. **Grad** suffix accesses the texture with explicit partial derivatives *dPdx* and *dPdy*. **Offset** suffix accesses the texture (with optional lod *bias*) with the *offset* added to the *u* texel coordinate before looking up each texel.

(continues)

Table 5.7 Texture access functions, *continued*

Syntax	Description
ivec4 **texelFetch** (isampler2DArray *sampler*, ivec3 *coord*, int *lod*) ivec4 **texelFetchOffset** (isampler2DArray *sampler*, ivec3 *coord*, int *lod*, ivec2 *offset*)	Use the texel integer *coord* to look up a single texel of the explicit *lod* of the 1D texture array currently specified by *sampler*. **Offset** suffix accesses the texture (with optional lod *bias*) with the *offset* added to the *u* texel coordinate before looking up each texel.
ivec4 **textureLodOffset** (isampler2DArray *sampler*, vec3 *coord*, float *lod*, int *offset*) ivec4 **textureGradOffset** (isampler2DArray *sampler*, vec3 *coord*, vec2 *dPdx*, vec2 *dPdy*, ivec2 *offset*)	Use the texture coordinate *coord* to access the 1D texture array currently specified by *sampler*. Combinations of the suffixes **Lod**, **Grad**, and **Offset** are as described earlier.
ivec2 **textureSize** (usampler2DArray *sampler*, int *lod*)	Returns the width and height of level *lod* of the 1D texture array currently specified by *sampler*.
uvec4 **texture** (usampler2DArray *sampler*, vec3 *coord*[, float *bias*]) uvec4 **textureLod** (usampler2DArray *sampler*, vec3 *coord*, float *lod*) uvec4 **textureGrad** (usampler2DArray *sampler*, vec3 *coord*, vec2 *dPdx*, vec2 *dPdy*) uvec4 **textureOffset** (usampler2DArray *sampler*, vec3 *coord*, vec2 *offset*, [, float *bias*])	Use the texture coordinate *coord* to access the 1D texture array currently specified by *sampler*. Unsuffixed access the texture (with optional lod *bias*). **Lod** suffix accesses the texture with explicit *lod*. **Grad** suffix accesses the texture with explicit partial derivatives *dPdx* and *dPdy*. **Offset** suffix accesses the texture (with optional lod *bias*) with the *offset* added to the *u* and *v* texel coordinate before looking up each texel.

Table 5.7 Texture access functions, *continued*

Syntax	Description
uvec4 **texelFetch** (usampler2DArray *sampler*, ivec3 *coord*, int *lod*) uvec4 **texelFetchOffset** (usampler2DArray *sampler*, ivec3 *coord*, int *lod*, ivec2 *offset*)	Use the texel integer *coord* to look up a single texel of the explicit *lod* to access the 1D texture array currently specified by *sampler*. **Offset** suffix accesses the texture (with optional lod *bias*) with the *offset* added to the *u* and *v* texel coordinate before looking up each texel.
uvec4 **textureLodOffset** (usampler2DArray *sampler*, vec3 *coord*, float *lod*, int *offset*)	Use the texture coordinate *coord* to access the 1D texture array currently specified by *sampler*.
uvec4 **textureGradOffset** (usampler2DArray *sampler*, vec3 *coord*, vec2 *dPdx*, vec2 *dPdy*, ivec2 *offset*)	Combinations of the suffixes **Lod**, **Grad**, and **Offset** are as described earlier.
int **textureSize** (samplerBuffer *sampler*)	Returns the size of the buffer texture currently specified by *sampler*.
vec4 **texelFetch** (samplerBuffer *sampler*, int *coord*, int *lod*)	Use the texel integer *coord* to look up a single texel of the buffer texture currently specified by *sampler*.
int **textureSize** (isamplerBuffer *sampler*)	Returns the size of the buffer texture currently specified by *sampler*.
ivec4 **texelFetch** (isamplerBuffer *sampler*, int *coord*, int *lod*)	Use the texel integer *coord* to look up a single texel of the buffer texture currently specified by *sampler*.

(continues)

Table 5.7 Texture access functions, *continued*

Syntax	Description
int **textureSize** (usamplerBuffer *sampler*)	Returns the size of the buffer texture currently specified by *sampler*.
uvec4 **texelFetch** (usamplerBuffer *sampler*, int *coord*, int *lod*)	Use the texel integer *coord* to look up a single texel of the buffer texture currently specified by *sampler*.
int **textureSize** (sampler1DShadow *sampler*, int *lod*)	Returns the width of level *lod* of the 1D shadow texture currently specified by *sampler*.
float **texture** (sampler1DShadow *sampler*, vec3 *coord*[, float *bias*]) float **textureProj** (sampler1DShadow *sampler*, vec4 *coord* [, float *bias*]) float **textureLod** (sampler1DShadow *sampler*, vec3 *coord*, float *lod*) float **textureGrad** (sampler1DShadow *sampler*, vec3 *coord*, float *dPdx*, float *dPdy*) float **textureOffset** (sampler1DShadow *sampler*, vec3 *coord*, int *offset*, [, float *bias*])	Use the texture coordinate *coord* to access the 1D shadow texture currently specified by *sampler*: Unsuffixed access the texture (with optional lod *bias*). **Proj** suffix accesses the texture with projection (with optional lod *bias*). **Lod** suffix accesses the texture with explicit *lod*. **Grad** suffix accesses the texture with explicit partial derivatives *dPdx* and *dPdy*. **Offset** suffix accesses the texture (with optional lod *bias*) with the *offset* added to the *u* texel coordinate before looking up each texel.

Table 5.7 Texture access functions, *continued*

Syntax	Description
float **textureProjLod** (sampler1DShadow *sampler*, vec4 *coord* , float *lod*)	Use the texture coordinate *coord* to access the 1D shadow texture currently specified by *sampler*.
float **textureProjGrad** (sampler1DShadow *sampler*, vec4 *coord*, float *dPdx*, float *dPdy*)	Combinations of the suffixes **Proj, Lod, Grad,** and **Offset** are as described earlier.
float **textureProjOffset** (sampler1DShadow *sampler*, vec4 *coord*, int *offset* [, float *bias*])	
float **textureLodOffset** (sampler1DShadow *sampler*, vec3 *coord*, float *lod*, int *offset*)	
float **textureGradOffset** (sampler1DShadow *sampler*, vec3 *coord*, float *dPdx*, float *dPdy*, int *offset*)	
float **textureProjLodOffset** (sampler1DShadow *sampler*, vec4 *coord*, float *lod*, int *offset*)	Use the texture coordinate *coord* to access the 1D shadow texture currently specified by *sampler*.
float **textureProjGradOffset** (sampler1DShadow *sampler*, vec4 *coord*, float *dPdx*, float *dPdy*, int *offset*)	Combinations of the suffixes **Proj, Lod, Grad,** and **Offset** are as described earlier.
ivec2 **textureSize** (sampler2DShadow *sampler*, int *lod*)	Returns the width and height of level *lod* of the 2D shadow texture currently specified by *sampler*.

(continues)

Table 5.7 Texture access functions, *continued*

Syntax	Description
float **texture** (sampler2DShadow *sampler*, vec3 *coord* [, float *bias*])	Use the texture coordinate *coord* to access the 2D shadow texture currently specified by *sampler*.
float **textureProj** (sampler2DShadow *sampler*, vec4 *coord* [, float *bias*])	Unsuffixed access the texture (with optional lod *bias*).
float **textureLod** (sampler2DShadow *sampler*, vec3 *coord*, float *lod*)	**Proj** suffix accesses the texture with projection (with optional lod *bias*).
float **textureGrad** (sampler2DShadow *sampler*, vec3 *coord*, vec2 *dPdx*, vec2 *dPdy*)	**Lod** suffix accesses the texture with explicit *lod*.
float **textureOffset** (sampler2DShadow *sampler*, vec3 *coord*, ivec2 *offset*, [, float *bias*])	**Grad** suffix accesses the texture with explicit partial derivatives *dPdx* and *dPdy*.
	Offset suffix accesses the texture (with optional lod *bias*) with the *offset* added to the *u* and *v* texel coordinate before looking up each texel.
float **textureProjLod** (sampler2DShadow *sampler*, vec4 *coord* , float *lod*) float **textureProjGrad** (sampler2DShadow *sampler*, vec4 *coord*, vec2 *dPdx*, vec2 *dPdy*)	Use the texture coordinate *coord* to access the 2D shadow texture currently specified by *sampler*.
float **textureProjOffset** (sampler2DShadow *sampler*, vec4 *coord*, ivec2 *offset* [, float *bias*])	Combinations of the suffixes **Proj**, **Lod**, **Grad**, and **Offset** are as described earlier.
float **textureLodOffset** (sampler2DShadow *sampler*, vec3 *coord*, float *lod*, ivec2 *offset*)	
float **textureGradOffset** (sampler2DShadow *sampler*, vec3 *coord*, vec2 *dPdx*, vec2 *dPdy*, ivec2 *offset*)	
float **textureProjLodOffset** (sampler2DShadow *sampler*, vec4 *coord*, float *lod*, ivec2 *offset*) float **textureProjGradOffset** (sampler2DShadow *sampler*, vec4 *coord*, vec2 *dPdx*, vec2 *dPdy*, ivec2 *offset*)	Use the texture coordinate *coord* to access the 2D shadow texture currently specified by *sampler*. Combinations of the suffixes **Proj**, **Lod**, **Grad**, and **Offset** are as described earlier.

Table 5.7 Texture access functions, *continued*

Syntax	Description
ivec2 **textureSize** (sampler2DRectShadow *sampler*, int *lod*)	Returns the width and height of level *lod* of the rect shadow texture currently specified by *sampler*.
float **texture** (sampler2DRectShadow *sampler*, vec3 *coord*) float **textureProj** (sampler2DRectShadow *sampler*, vec4 *coord*) float **textureGrad** (sampler2DRectShadow *sampler*, vec3 *coord*, vec2 *dPdx*, vec2 *dPdy*) float **textureOffset** (sampler2DRectShadow *sampler*, vec3 *coord*, ivec2 *offset*)	Use the texture coordinate *coord* to access the rect shadow texture currently specified by *sampler*: Unsuffixed access the texture. **Proj** suffix accesses the texture with projection. **Grad** suffix accesses the texture with explicit partial derivatives *dPdx* and *dPdy*. **Offset** suffix accesses the texture with the *offset* added to the *u* and *v* texel coordinate before looking up each texel.
float **textureProjGrad** (sampler2DRectShadow *sampler*, vec4 *coord*, vec2 *dPdx*, vec2 *dPdy*) float **textureProjOffset** (sampler2DRectShadow *sampler*, vec4 *coord*, ivec2 *offset*) float **textureGradOffset** (sampler2DRectShadow *sampler*, vec3 *coord*, vec2 *dPdx*, vec2 *dPdy*, ivec2 *offset*)	Use the texture coordinate *coord* to access the rect shadow texture currently specified by *sampler*: Combinations of the suffixes **Proj**, **Grad**, and **Offset** are as described earlier.
float **textureProjGradOffset** (sampler2DShadow *sampler*, vec4 *coord*, vec2 *dPdx*, vec2 *dPdy*, ivec2 *offset*)	Use the texture coordinate *coord* to access the rect shadow texture currently specified by *sampler*: Combinations of the suffixes **Proj**, **Grad**, and **Offset** are as described earlier.

(continues)

5.8 Fragment Processing Functions

Fragment processing functions are available only in shaders intended for use on the fragment processor. Fragment shaders have limited access to neighboring fragments sufficient to calculate derivatives. Two fragment processing functions obtain derivatives, and the other fragment processing estimates the filter width used to antialias procedural textures based on those derivatives.

The derivative functions, **dFdx** and **dFdy**, determine the rate of change of an expression. The function **dFdx**(p) evaluates the derivative of the expression p in the x direction in window coordinates, and the function **dFdy**(p) evaluates the derivative of the expression p in the y direction in window coordinates. These values indicate how fast the expression is changing in window space, and this information can be used to take steps to prevent aliasing. For instance, if texture coordinates are changing rapidly, it may be better to set the resulting color to the average color for the texture in order to avoid aliasing.

It only makes sense to apply these functions to expressions that vary from one fragment to the next. Because the value of a uniform variable does not change from one pixel to the next, its derivative in x and in y is always 0. See Table 5.8.

Table 5.8 Fragment processing functions

Syntax	Description
float **dFdx** (float p) vec2 **dFdx** (vec2 p) vec3 **dFdx** (vec3 p) vec4 **dFdx** (vec4 p)	Returns the derivative in x for the input argument p
float **dFdy** (float p) vec2 **dFdy** (vec2 p) vec3 **dFdy** (vec3 p) vec4 **dFdy** (vec4 p)	Returns the derivative in y for the input argument p
float **fwidth** (float p) vec2 **fwidth** (vec2 p) vec3 **fwidth** (vec3 p) vec4 **fwidth** (vec4 p)	Returns the sum of the absolute derivative in x and y for the input argument p, i.e., return = **abs** (**dFdx** (p)) + **abs** (**dFdy** (p));

5.9 Noise Functions

Noise functions (see Table 5.9) are available to both fragment and vertex shaders. These stochastic functions, first described by Ken Perlin, increase visual complexity. Values returned by the following noise functions give the appearance of randomness, but they are not truly random. A more complete description of and motivation for the noise function can be found in Chapter 15.

Table 5.9 Noise Functions

Syntax	Description
float **noise1** (float x) float **noise1** (vec2 x) float **noise1** (vec3 x) float **noise1** (vec4 x)	Returns a 1D noise value based on the input value x
vec2 **noise2** (float x) vec2 **noise2** (vec2 x) vec2 **noise2** (vec3 x) vec2 **noise2** (vec4 x)	Returns a 2D noise value based on the input value x
vec3 **noise3** (float x) vec3 **noise3** (vec2 x) vec3 **noise3** (vec3 x) vec3 **noise3** (vec4 x)	Returns a 3D noise value based on the input value x
vec4 **noise4** (float x) vec4 **noise4** (vec2 x) vec4 **noise4** (vec3 x) vec4 **noise4** (vec4 x)	Returns a 4D noise value based on the input value x

The built-in noise functions are defined to have the following characteristics:

- The return values are always in the range $[-1,1]$ and cover at least the range $[-0.6,0.6]$ with a Gaussian-like distribution.

- The return values have an overall average of 0.

- The functions are repeatable, in that a particular input value always produces the same return value.

- They are statistically invariant under rotation; that is, no matter how the domain is rotated, it has the same statistical character.

- They have a statistical invariance under translation; that is, no matter how the domain is translated, it has the same statistical character.

- They typically give different results under translation.

- The spatial frequency is narrowly concentrated, centered somewhere between 0.5 and 1.0.

- They are C^1 continuous everywhere; that is the first derivative is continuous.

5.10 Summary

The OpenGL Shading Language contains a rich set of built-in functions. Some of these functions are similar to those found in C and C++, and others are similar to those found in RenderMan. These functions expose hardware functionality (e.g., texture access) or support common operations (e.g., square root, clamp), or they represent operations likely to be accelerated in future generations of graphics hardware (trigonometry functions, noise, etc.).

Function overloading is used extensively because many of these functions operate on either vectors or scalars. Vendors that support the OpenGL Shading Language are expected to provide optimal implementations of these functions, so the built-in functions should be used whenever possible.

The built-in mathematical functions can be used in some unique and perhaps unexpected ways to create procedural textures. Shader examples throughout the rest of this book illustrate this. Visualizing the function needed to achieve a particular effect can be a vital part of the shader development process.

5.11 Further Information

Many of the built-in functions described in this chapter are used in example shaders in the remainder of this book. All you need to do is keep reading to see them in action.

Some additional detail on the built-in functions can be found in the *The OpenGL Shading Language, Version 1.40,* by John Kessenich, Dave Baldwin, and Randi Rost (2008).

Various OpenGL Shading Language built-in functions, including the derivative and filter width functions, were inspired by similar functions in RenderMan. Motivation for some of these functions is discussed in *The RenderMan Companion: A Programmer's Guide to Realistic Computer Graphics* by Steve Upstill (1990) and *Advanced RenderMan: Creating CGI for Motion Pictures* by Anthony A. Apodaca and Larry Gritz (1999). For additional details on noise functions, see the papers by Perlin and the references provided at the end of Chapter 15.

[1] Apodaca, Anthony A., and Larry Gritz, *Advanced RenderMan: Creating CGI for Motion Pictures*, Morgan Kaufmann Publishers, San Francisco, 1999. www.renderman.org/RMR/Books/arman/materials.html

[2] Kessenich, John, Dave Baldwin, and Randi Rost, *The OpenGL Shading Language, Version 1.40*, 3Dlabs/Intel, March 2008. www.opengl.org/documentation/specs/

[3] Perlin, Ken, *An Image Synthesizer*, Computer Graphics (SIGGRAPH '85 Proceedings), pp. 287–296, July 1985.

[4] Perlin, Ken, *Improving Noise*, Computer Graphics (SIGGRAPH 2002 Proceedings), pp. 681–682, July 2002. http://mrl.nyu.edu/perlin/paper445.pdf

[5] Pixar, *The RenderMan Interface Specification*, Version 3.2, Pixar, July 2000. https://renderman.pixar.com/products/rispec/index.htm

[6] Segal, Mark, and Kurt Akeley, *The OpenGL Graphics System: A Specification (Version 3.1)*, Editor (v1.1): Chris Frazier, (v1.2–3.1): Jon Leech, (v2.0): Jon Leech and Pat Brown, March 2008. www.opengl.org/documentation/spec.html

[7] Upstill, Steve, *The RenderMan Companion: A Programmer's Guide to Realistic Computer Graphics*, Addison-Wesley, Reading, Massachusetts, 1990.

[8] Zwillinger, Dan, *CRC Standard Mathematical Tables and Formulas*, 30th Edition, CRC Press, 1995. www.geom.uiuc.edu/docs/reference/CRC-formulas/

Chapter 6

Simple Shading Example

Now that we've described the OpenGL Shading Language, let's look at a simple example. In this example, we apply a brick pattern to an object. The brick pattern is calculated entirely within a fragment shader. If you'd prefer to skip ahead to the next chapter for a more in-depth discussion of the API that allows shaders to be defined and manipulated, feel free to do so.

The shader for rendering a procedural brick pattern was the first interesting shader ever executed by the OpenGL Shading Language on programmable graphics hardware. It ran for the first time in March 2002, on the 3Dlabs Wildcat VP graphics accelerator. Dave Baldwin published the first GLSL brick fragment shader in a white paper that described the language destined to become the OpenGL Shading Language. His GLSL shader was based on a RenderMan shader by Darwyn Peachey that was published in the book *Texturing and Modeling: A Procedural Approach*. Steve Koren and John Kessenich adapted Dave's shader to get it working on real hardware for the first time, and it has subsequently undergone considerable refinement for inclusion in this book.

This example, like most of the others in this book, consists of three essential components: the source code for the vertex shader, the source code for the fragment shader, and the application code that initializes and uses these shaders. This chapter focuses on the vertex and fragment shaders. The application code for using these shaders is discussed in Section 7.13, after the details of the OpenGL Shading Language API have been discussed.

With this first example, we take a little more time discussing the details in order to give you a better grasp of what's going on. In examples later in the book, we focus mostly on the details that differ from previous examples.

6.1 Brick Shader Overview

One approach to writing shaders is to come up with a description of the effect that you're trying to achieve and then decide which parts of the shader need to be implemented in the vertex shader, which need to be implemented in the fragment shader, and how the application will tie everything together.

In this example, we develop a shader that applies a computed brick pattern to all objects that are drawn. We don't attempt the most realistic-looking brick shader, but rather a fairly simple one that illustrates many of the concepts we introduced in the previous chapters. We don't use textures for this brick pattern; the pattern itself is generated algorithmically. We can build a lot of flexibility into this shader by parameterizing the different aspects of our brick algorithm.

Let's first come up with a description of the overall effect we're after. We want

- A single light source

- Diffuse and specular reflection characteristics

- A brick pattern based on the position in modeling coordinates of the object being rendered—where the *x* coordinate is related to the brick horizontal position and the *y* coordinate is related to the brick vertical position

- Alternate rows of bricks offset by one-half the width of a single brick

- Easy-to-modify colors and ratios: brick color, mortar color, brick-to-brick horizontal distance, brick-to-brick vertical distance, brick width fraction (ratio of the width of a brick to the overall horizontal distance between two adjacent bricks), and brick height fraction (ratio of the height of a brick to the overall vertical distance between two adjacent bricks)

The brick geometry parameters that we use to control geometry and color are illustrated in Figure 6.1. Brick size and brick percentage parameters are both stored in user-defined uniform variables of type **vec2**. The horizontal distance between two bricks, including the width of the mortar, is provided by *BrickSize.x*. The vertical distance between two rows of bricks, including the height of the mortar, is provided by *BrickSize.y*. These two values are given in units of modeling coordinates. The fraction of *BrickSize.x* represented by the brick only is provided by *BrickPct.x*. The fraction of *BrickSize.y* represented by the brick only is provided by *BrickPct.y*. These two values are in the range [0,1]. Finally, the brick color and the mortar color are represented by the variables *BrickColor* and *MortarColor*.

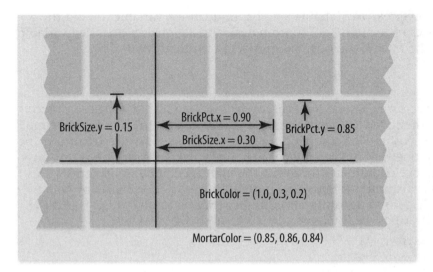

Figure 6.1 Parameters for defining brick

Now that we're armed with a firm grasp of our desired outcome, we'll design our vertex shader, then our fragment shader, and then the application code that will tie it all together.

6.2 Vertex Shader

The vertex shader embodies the operations that occur on each vertex that is provided to OpenGL. To define our vertex shader, we need to answer three questions.

- What data must be passed to the vertex shader for every vertex (i.e., generic attribute variables or in variables)?

- What global state is required by the vertex shader (i.e., uniform variables)?

- What values are computed by the vertex shader (i.e., out variables)?

Let's look at these questions one at a time.

We can't draw any geometry at all without specifying a value for each vertex position. Furthermore, we can't do any lighting unless we have a surface normal for each location for which we want to apply a lighting computation. So at the very least, we need a vertex position and a normal for every incoming vertex. We'll define a global in-qualified variable to hold the MCvertex (vertex in model coordinates), and a global in-qualified variable to hold the MCnormal (normal in model coordinates):

```
in vec4     MCvertex;
in vec3     MCnormal;
```

We need access to several matrices for our brick algorithm. We need to access the current modelview-projection matrix (*MVPMatrix*) in order to transform our vertex position into the clipping coordinate system. We need to access the current modelview matrix (*MVMatrix*) in order to transform the vertex position into eye coordinates for use in the lighting computation. And we also need to transform our incoming normals into eye coordinates by using OpenGL's normal transformation matrix (*NormalMatrix*, which is just the inverse transpose of the upper-left 3×3 subset of *MVMatrix*).

```
uniform mat4 MVMatrix;
uniform mat4 MVPMatrix;
uniform mat3 NormalMatrix;
```

In addition, we need the position of a single light source. We define the light source position as a uniform variable like this:[1]

```
uniform vec3 LightPosition;
```

We also need values for the lighting calculation to represent the contribution from specular reflection and the contribution from diffuse reflection. We could define these as uniform variables so that they could be changed dynamically by the application, but to illustrate some additional features of the language, we define them as constants like this:

```
const float SpecularContribution = 0.3;
const float DiffuseContribution  = 1.0 - SpecularContribution;
```

Finally, we need to define the values that are passed on to the fragment shader. Every vertex shader must compute the homogeneous vertex position and store its value in the standard variable *gl_Position*, so we know that our brick vertex shader must do likewise. On the fly, we compute the brick pattern in the fragment shader as a function of the incoming geometry's *x* and *y* values in modeling coordinates, so we define an out variable called *MCposition* for this purpose. To apply the lighting effect on top of our brick, we do part of the lighting computation in the fragment shader and apply

---

1. The shaders in this book observe the convention of capitalizing the first letter of user-specified uniform, in, out, and nonqualified global variable names to set them apart from local variables.

the final lighting effect after the brick/mortar color has been computed in the fragment shader. We do most of the lighting computation in the vertex shader and simply pass the computed light intensity to the fragment shader in an out variable called *LightIntensity*. These two out variables are defined like this:

```
out float    LightIntensity;
out vec2     MCposition;
```

We're now ready to get to the meat of our brick vertex shader. We begin by declaring a main function for our vertex shader and computing the vertex position in eye coordinates:

```
void main()
{
    vec3 ecPosition = vec3(MVMatrix * MCvertex);;
```

In this first line of code, our vertex shader defines a variable called *ecPosition* to hold the eye coordinate position of the incoming vertex. We compute the eye coordinate position by transforming the vertex position (*MCvertex*) by the current modelview matrix (*MVMatrix*). Because one of the operands is a matrix and the other is a vector, the * operator performs a matrix multiplication operation rather than a component-wise multiplication.

The result of the matrix multiplication is a **vec4**, but *ecPosition* is defined as a **vec3**. There is no automatic conversion between variables of different types in the OpenGL Shading Language, so we convert the result to a **vec3** by using a constructor. This causes the fourth component of the result to be dropped so that the two operands have compatible types. (Constructors provide an operation that is similar to type casting, but it is much more flexible, as discussed in Section 3.3.) As we'll see, the eye coordinate position is used a couple of times in our lighting calculation.

The lighting computation that we perform is a simple one. Some light from the light source is reflected in a diffuse fashion (i.e., in all directions). Where the viewing direction is very nearly the same as the reflection direction from the light source, we see a specular reflection. To compute the diffuse reflection, we need to compute the angle between the incoming light and the surface normal. To compute the specular reflection, we need to compute the angle between the reflection direction and the viewing direction. First, we transform the incoming normal:

```
    vec3 tnorm      = normalize(NormalMatrix * MCnormal);
```

This line defines a new variable called *tnorm* for storing the transformed normal (remember, in the OpenGL Shading Language, variables can be declared when needed). The incoming surface normal (*MCnormal*, a user-defined in variable for accessing the normal value through a generic vertex attribute) is transformed by the current normal transformation matrix (*NormalMatrix*). The resulting vector is normalized (converted to a vector of unit length) by the built-in function **normalize**, and the result is stored in *tnorm*.

Next, we need to compute a vector from the current point on the surface of the three-dimensional object we're rendering to the light source position. Both of these should be in eye coordinates (which means that the value for our uniform variable *LightPosition* must be provided by the application in eye coordinates). The light direction vector is computed as follows:

```
vec3 lightVec  = normalize(LightPosition - ecPosition);
```

The object position in eye coordinates was previously computed and stored in *ecPosition*. To compute the light direction vector, we subtract the object position from the light position. The resulting light direction vector is also normalized and stored in the newly defined local variable *lightVec*.

The calculations we've done so far have set things up almost perfectly to call the built-in function **reflect**. Using our transformed surface normal and the computed incident light vector, we can now compute a reflection vector at the surface of the object; however, **reflect** requires the incident vector (the direction from the light to the surface), and we've computed the direction to the light source. Negating *lightVec* gives us the proper vector:

```
vec3 reflectVec = reflect(-lightVec, tnorm);
```

Because both vectors used in this computation were unit vectors, the resulting vector is a unit vector as well. To complete our lighting calculation, we need one more vector—a unit vector in the direction of the viewing position. Because, by definition, the viewing position is at the origin (i.e., (0,0,0)) in the eye coordinate system, we can simply negate and normalize the computed eye coordinate position, *ecPosition*:

```
vec3 viewVec   = normalize(-ecPosition);
```

With these four vectors, we can perform a per-vertex lighting computation. The relationship of these vectors is shown in Figure 6.2.

The modeling of diffuse reflection is based on the assumption that the incident light is scattered in all directions according to a cosine distribution function. The reflection of light is strongest when the light direction vector and the surface normal are coincident. As the difference between the two angles increases to 90°, the diffuse reflection drops off to zero. Because both vectors have been normalized to produce unit vectors, we can determine the cosine of the angle between *lightVec* and *tnorm* by performing a dot

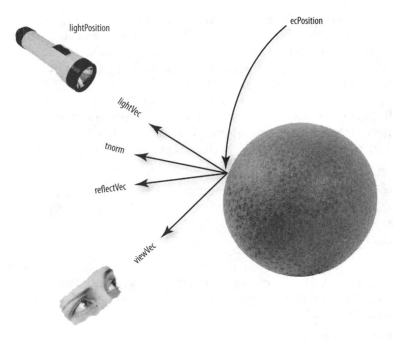

Figure 6.2 Vectors involved in the lighting computation for the brick vertex shader

product operation between those vectors. We want the diffuse contribution to be 0 if the angle between the light and the surface normal is greater than 90° (there should be no diffuse contribution if the light is behind the object), and the **max** function accomplishes this:

```
float diffuse = max(dot(lightVec, tnorm), 0.0);
```

The specular component of the light intensity for this vertex is computed by

```
float spec = 0.0;
if (diffuse > 0.0)
{
    spec = max(dot(reflectVec, viewVec), 0.0);
    spec = pow(spec, 16.0);
}
```

The variable for the specular reflection value is defined and initialized to 0. We compute a specular value other than 0 only if the angle between the light direction vector and the surface normal is less than 90° (i.e., the diffuse value is greater than 0) because we don't want any specular highlights if the light source is behind the object. Because both *reflectVec* and *viewVec* are normalized, computing the dot product of these two vectors gives us the cosine of the angle between them. If the angle is near zero (i.e., the reflection vector and the viewing vector are almost the same), the resulting value is near 1.0. By raising the result to the 16th power in the subsequent line of code, we effectively "sharpen" the highlight, ensuring that we have a specular highlight only in the region where the reflection vector and the view vector are almost the same. The choice of 16 for the exponent value is arbitrary. Higher values produce more concentrated specular highlights, and lower values produce less concentrated highlights. This value could also be passed in as a uniform variable so that it can be easily modified by the end user.

All that remains is to multiply the computed diffuse and specular reflection values by the *diffuseContribution* and *specularContribution* constants and sum the two values:

```
LightIntensity = DiffuseContribution * diffuse +
                 SpecularContribution * spec;
```

This value will be assigned to the out variable *LightIntensity* and interpolated between vertices. We also have one other out variable to compute, and we can do that quite easily.

```
MCposition = MCvertex.xy;
```

When the brick pattern is applied to a geometric object, we want the brick pattern to remain constant with respect to the surface of the object, no matter how the object is moved. We also want the brick pattern to remain constant with respect to the surface of the object, no matter what the viewing position. To generate the brick pattern algorithmically in the fragment shader, we need to provide a value at each fragment that represents a location on the surface. For this example, we provide the modeling coordinate at each vertex by setting our out variable *MCposition* to the same value as our incoming vertex position (which is, by definition, in modeling coordinates).

We don't need the *z* or *w* coordinate in the fragment shader, so we need a way to select just the *x* and *y* components of *MCvertex*. We could have used a constructor here (e.g., **vec2**(*MCvertex*)), but to show off another language feature, we use the component selector **.xy** to select the first two components of *MCvertex* and store them in our out variable *MCposition*.

All that remains to be done is what all vertex shaders must do: compute the homogeneous vertex position. We do this by transforming the incoming vertex value by the current modelview-projection matrix:

```
gl_Position    = MVPMatrix * MCvertex;
}
```

For clarity, the code for our vertex shader is provided in its entirety in
Listing 6.1.

Listing 6.1 Source code for brick vertex shader

```
#version 140

in vec4     MCvertex;
in vec3     MCnormal;

uniform mat4 MVMatrix;
uniform mat4 MVPMatrix;
uniform mat3 NormalMatrix;

uniform vec3 LightPosition;

const float SpecularContribution = 0.3;
const float DiffuseContribution  = 1.0 - SpecularContribution;

out float   LightIntensity;
out vec2    MCposition;

void main()
{
    vec3 ecPosition = vec3(MVMatrix * MCvertex);
    vec3 tnorm      = normalize(NormalMatrix * MCnormal);
    vec3 lightVec   = normalize(LightPosition - ecPosition);
    vec3 reflectVec = reflect(-lightVec, tnorm);
    vec3 viewVec    = normalize(-ecPosition);
    float diffuse   = max(dot(lightVec, tnorm), 0.0);
    float spec      = 0.0;

    if (diffuse > 0.0)
    {
        spec = max(dot(reflectVec, viewVec), 0.0);
        spec = pow(spec, 16.0);
    }

    LightIntensity  = DiffuseContribution * diffuse +
                      SpecularContribution * spec;

    MCposition      = MCvertex.xy;
    gl_Position     = MVPMatrix * MCvertex;
}
```

6.3 Fragment Shader

The typical purpose of a fragment shader is to compute the color to be
applied to a fragment or to compute the depth value for the fragment or

both. In this case (and indeed with most fragment shaders), we're concerned only about the color of the fragment. We're perfectly happy using the depth value that's been computed by the OpenGL rasterization stage. Therefore, the entire purpose of this shader is to compute the color of the current fragment.

Our brick fragment shader starts off by defining a few more uniform variables than did the vertex shader. The brick pattern that will be rendered on our geometry is parameterized to make it easier to modify. The parameters that are constant across an entire primitive can be stored as uniform variables and initialized (and later modified) by the application. This makes it easy to expose these controls to the end user for modification through user interface elements such as sliders and color pickers. The brick fragment shader uses the parameters that are illustrated in Figure 6.1. These are defined as uniform variables as follows:

```
uniform vec3   BrickColor, MortarColor;
uniform vec2   BrickSize;
uniform vec2   BrickPct;
```

We want our brick pattern to be applied consistently to our geometry in order to have the object look the same no matter where it is placed in the scene or how it is rotated. The key to determining the placement of the brick pattern is the modeling coordinate position that is computed by the vertex shader and passed in the in variable *MCposition*:

```
in vec2       MCposition;
```

This variable was computed at each vertex by the vertex shader in the previous section, and it is interpolated across the primitive and made available to the fragment shader at each fragment location. Our fragment shader can use this information to determine where the fragment location is in relation to the algorithmically defined brick pattern. The other in variable that is provided as input to the fragment shader is defined as follows:

```
in float      LightIntensity;
```

This in variable contains the interpolated value for the light intensity that we computed at each vertex in our vertex shader. Note that both of the in variables in our fragment shader are defined with the same type that was used to define them in our vertex shader. A link error would be generated if this were not the case.

The purpose of this fragment shader is to calculate the fragment color. We define an out variable *FragColor*.

```
out vec4      FragColor;
```

With our uniform, in, and out variables defined, we can begin with the actual code for the brick fragment shader.

```
void main()
{
    vec3   color;
    vec2   position, useBrick;
```

In this shader, we do things more like we would in C and define all our local variables before they're used at the beginning of our **main** function. In some cases, this can make the code a little cleaner or easier to read, but it is mostly a matter of personal preference and coding style. The first actual line of code in our brick fragment shader computes values for the local **vec2** variable *position*:

```
    position = MCposition / BrickSize;
```

This statement divides the fragment's *x* position in modeling coordinates by the brick column width and the *y* position in modeling coordinates by the brick row height. This gives us a "brick row number" (*position.y*) and a "brick number" within that row (*position.x*). Keep in mind that these are signed, floating-point values, so it is perfectly reasonable to have negative row and brick numbers as a result of this computation.

Next, we use a conditional to determine whether the fragment is in a row of bricks that is offset (see Figure 6.3):

```
    if (fract(position.y * 0.5) > 0.5)
        position.x += 0.5;
```

The "brick row number" (*position.y*) is multiplied by 0.5, the integer part is dropped by the **fract** function, and the result is compared to 0.5. Half the time (or every other row), this comparison is true, and the "brick number" value (*position.x*) is incremented by 0.5 to offset the entire row by half the width of a brick. This is illustrated by the graph in Figure 6.3.

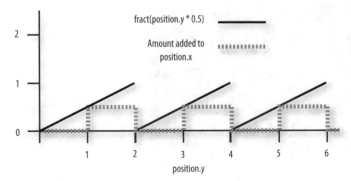

Figure 6.3 A graph of the function **fract**(*position.y* * 0.5) shows how the even/odd row determination is made. The result of this function is compared against 0.5. If the value is greater than 0.5, a value of 0.5 is added to *position.x*; otherwise, nothing is added. The result is that rows whose integer values are 1, 3, 5, …, are shifted half a brick position to the right.

Following this, we compute the fragment's location within the current brick.

```
position = fract(position);
```

This computation gives us the vertical and horizontal position within a single brick. This position serves as the basis for determining whether to use the brick color or the mortar color.

Figure 6.4 shows how we might visualize the results of the fragment shader to this point. If we were to apply this shader to a square with modeling coordinates of (–1.0, –1.0) at the lower-left corner and (1.0, 1.0) at the upper right, our partially completed shader would show the beginnings of the brick pattern we're after. Because the overall width of the square is 2.0 units in modeling coordinates, our division of *MCposition.x* by *BrickSize.x* gives us 2.0 / 0.3, or roughly six and two-thirds bricks across, as we see in Figure 6.4. Similarly, the division of *MCposition.y* by *BrickSize.y* gives us 2.0 / 0.15, or roughly thirteen and two-thirds rows of bricks from top to bottom. For this illustration, we shaded each fragment by summing the fractional part of *position.x* and *position.y*, multiplying the result by 0.5, and then storing this value in the red, green, and blue components of *FragColor*.

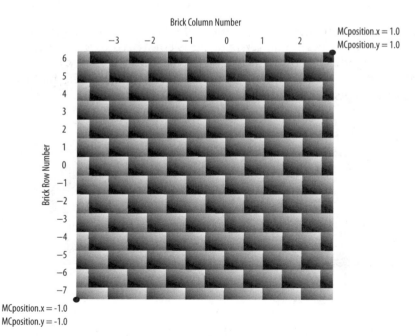

Figure 6.4   Intermediate results of brick fragment shader

To complete our brick shader, we need a function that gives us a value of 1.0 when the brick color should be used and 0 when the mortar color should be used. If we can achieve this, we can end up with a simple way to choose the appropriate color. We know that we're working with a horizontal component of the brick texture function and a vertical component. If we can create the desired function for the horizontal component and the desired function for the vertical component, we can just multiply the two values together to get our final answer. If the result of either of the individual functions is 0 (mortar color), the multiplication causes the final answer to be 0; otherwise, it is 1.0, and the brick color is used.

We use the **step** function to achieve the desired effect. The **step** function takes two arguments, an edge (or threshold) and a parameter to test against that edge. If the value of the parameter to be tested is less than the edge value, the function returns 0; otherwise, it returns 1.0. (Refer to Figure 5.11 for a graph of this function.) In typical use, the **step** function produces a pattern of pulses (i.e., a square wave) whereby the function starts at 0 and rises to 1.0 when the threshold is reached. We can get a function that starts at 1.0 and drops to 0 just by reversing the order of the two arguments provided to this function.

```
useBrick = step(position, BrickPct);
```

In this line of code, we compute two values that tell us whether we are in the brick or in the mortar in the horizontal direction (*useBrick.x*) and in the vertical direction (*useBrick.y*). The built-in function **step** produces a value of 0 when *BrickPct.x < position.x* and a value of 1.0 when *BrickPct.x >= position.x*. Because of the **fract** function, we know that *position.x* varies from (0,1). The variable *BrickPct* is a uniform variable, so its value is constant across the primitive. This means that the value of *useBrick.x* is 1.0 when the brick color should be used and 0 when the mortar color should be used as we move horizontally. The same thing is done in the vertical direction, with *position.y* and *BrickPct.y* computing the value for *useBrick.y*. By multiplying *useBrick.x* by *useBrick.y*, we can get a value of 0 or 1.0 that lets us select the appropriate color for the fragment. The periodic step function for the horizontal component of the brick pattern is illustrated in Figure 6.5.

The values of *BrickPct.x* and *BrickPct.y* can be computed by the application to give a uniform mortar width in both directions based on the ratio of column width to row height, or the values can be chosen arbitrarily to give a mortar appearance that looks right.

All that remains is to compute our final color value and store it in the out variable *FragColor*.

```
color  = mix(MortarColor, BrickColor, useBrick.x * useBrick.y);
color *= LightIntensity;
FragColor = vec4(color, 1.0);
}
```

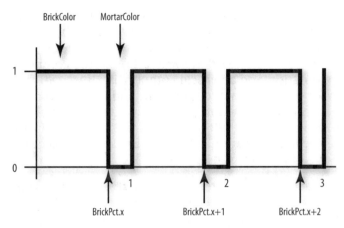

Figure 6.5 The periodic step function that produces the horizontal component of the procedural brick pattern

Here we compute the color of the fragment and store it in the local variable *color*. We use the built-in function **mix** to choose the brick color or the mortar color, depending on the value of *useBrick.x * useBrick.y*. Because *useBrick.x* and *useBrick.y* can have values of only 0 (mortar) or 1.0 (brick), we choose the brick color only if both values are 1.0; otherwise, we choose the mortar color.

The resulting value is then multiplied by the light intensity, and that result is stored in the local variable *color*. This local variable is a **vec3**, and *FragColor* is defined as a **vec4**, so we create our final color value by using a constructor to add a fourth component (alpha) equal to 1.0 and assign the result to the out variable *FragColor*.

The source code for the complete fragment shader is shown in Listing 6.2.

Listing 6.2 Source code for brick fragment shader

```
#version 140

uniform vec3   BrickColor, MortarColor;
uniform vec2   BrickSize;
uniform vec2   BrickPct;

in vec2        MCposition;
in float       LightIntensity;

out vec4       FragColor;

void main()
{
    vec3   color;
    vec2   position, useBrick;
```

```
    position = MCposition / BrickSize;

    if (fract(position.y * 0.5) > 0.5)
        position.x += 0.5;

    position = fract(position);

    useBrick = step(position, BrickPct);
//
    color  = mix(MortarColor, BrickColor, useBrick.x * useBrick.y);
    color *= LightIntensity;
    FragColor = vec4(color, 1.0);
}
```

When comparing this shader to the vertex shader in the previous example, we notice one of the key features of the OpenGL Shading Language, namely, that the language used to write these two shaders is almost identical. Both shaders have a main function, some uniform variables, and some local variables; expressions are the same; built-in functions are called in the same way; constructors are used in the same way; and so on. The only perceptible differences exhibited by these two shaders are (A) the vertex shader accesses generic attribute variables through user-defined in variables, such as *MCvertex* and *MCnormal*, (B) the vertex shader writes to the built-in variable *gl_Position*, whereas the fragment shader writes to the user-defined out variable *FragColor*, and (C) the out variables **LightIntensity** and **MCposition** are written by the vertex shader, and the fragment shader reads the in variables **LightIntensity** and **MCposition**.

The application code to create and use these shaders is shown in Section 7.13, after the OpenGL Shading Language API has been presented. The result of rendering some simple objects with these shaders is shown in Figure 6.6. A color version of the result is shown in Color Plate 34.

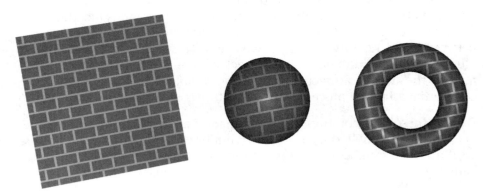

Figure 6.6   A flat polygon, a sphere, and a torus rendered with the brick shaders

6.4 Observations

A couple of problems with our shader make it unfit for anything but the simplest cases. Because the brick pattern is computed with the modeling coordinates of the incoming object, the apparent size of the bricks depends on the size of the object in modeling coordinates. The brick pattern might look fine with some objects, but the bricks may turn out much too small or much too large on other objects. At the very least, we should probably have a uniform variable in the vertex shader to scale the modeling coordinates. The application could allow the end user to adjust the scale factor to make the brick pattern look good on the object being rendered.

Another potential issue is that we've chosen to base the brick pattern on the object's x and y coordinates in modeling space. This can result in some unrealistic-looking effects on objects that aren't as regular as the objects shown in Figure 6.6. By using only the x and y coordinates of the object, we end up modeling bricks that are infinitely deep. The brick pattern looks fine when viewed from the front of the object, but when you look at it from the side, you'll be able to see how the brick extends in depth. To get a truly three-dimensional brick shader, we'd need to add a third dimension to our procedural texture calculation and use the z component of the position in modeling coordinates to determine whether we were in brick or mortar in the z dimension as well (see if you can modify the shaders to do this).

If we look closely at our brick pattern, we also notice aliasing artifacts (jaggies) along the transition from brick color to mortar color. These artifacts are due to the **step** function causing an instantaneous change from 0 to 1.0 (or from 1.0 to 0) when we cross the transition point between brick color and mortar color. Our shader has no alternative but to pick one color or the other for each fragment, and, because we cannot sample at a high enough frequency to represent this instantaneous change at the brick/mortar border, aliasing artifacts occur. Instead of using the **step** function, we could have used the built-in **smoothstep** function. This function is like the **step** function, except that it defines two edges and a smooth interpolation between 0 and 1.0 between those two edges. This would have the effect of blurring the transition between the brick color and the mortar color, thus making the aliasing artifacts much less noticeable. A method for analytically antialiasing the procedural brick texture is described in Section 17.4.5.

Despite these shortcomings, our brick shaders are perfectly good examples of a working OpenGL shader. Together, our brick vertex and fragment shaders illustrate a number of the interesting features of the OpenGL Shading Language.

6.5 Summary

This chapter has applied the language concepts from previous chapters to the development of working shaders that create a procedurally defined brick pattern. The vertex shader is responsible for transforming the vertex position, passing along the modeling coordinate position of the vertex, and computing a light intensity value at each vertex, using a single simulated light source. The fragment shader is responsible for determining whether each fragment should be brick color or mortar color. Once this determination is made, the light intensity value is applied to the chosen color, and the final color value is passed from the fragment shader so that it can ultimately be written in the framebuffer. The source code for these two shaders was discussed line by line to explain clearly how they work. This pair of shaders illustrates many of the features of the OpenGL Shading Language and can be used as a springboard for doing bigger and better things with the language.

6.6 Further Information

This shader and others are available from the 3Dlabs developer Web site. Source code for getting started with OpenGL shaders is also available.

[1] *Former 3Dlabs developer Web site*. Now at http://3dshaders.com.

[2] Baldwin, Dave, *OpenGL 2.0 Shading Language White Paper, Version 1.0*, 3Dlabs, October, 2001.

[3] Ebert, David S., John Hart, Bill Mark, F. Kenton Musgrave, Darwyn Peachey, Ken Perlin, and Steven Worley, *Texturing and Modeling: A Procedural Approach, Third Edition*, Morgan Kaufmann Publishers, San Francisco, 2002. www.texturingandmodeling.com

[4] Kessenich, John, Dave Baldwin, and Randi Rost, *The OpenGL Shading Language, Version 1.40*, 3Dlabs/Intel, March 2008. www.opengl.org/documentation/specs/

[5] Segal, Mark, and Kurt Akeley, *The OpenGL Graphics System: A Specification (Version 3.1)*, Editor (v1.1): Chris Frazier, (v1.2–3.1): Jon Leech, (v2.0): Jon Leech and Pat Brown, March 2008. www.opengl.org/documentation/specs/

Chapter 7

OpenGL Shading Language API

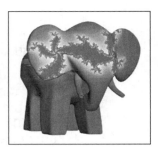

In support of the OpenGL Shading Language, more than 40 entry points were added to OpenGL starting in version 2.0. This set of API calls is referred to throughout this book as the OPENGL SHADING LANGUAGE API. In this chapter, we look at the OpenGL entry points that have been added to create, load, compile, and link shaders, as well as the entry points that have been added for passing generic vertex attributes and uniform variables to shaders. Reference pages for all of the OpenGL Shading Language API entry points are found in Appendix B.

At the end of this chapter, we discuss the application code that is needed to create and use the brick shader presented in Chapter 6. If you just can't wait, go ahead and sneak a peek at Section 7.13, and then come back here to learn the details of the API.

Here is an overview of creating and using OpenGL shaders:

1. Create one or more (empty) shader objects with **glCreateShader**.

2. Provide source code for these shaders with **glShaderSource**.

3. Compile each of the shaders with **glCompileShader**.

4. Create a program object with **glCreateProgram**.

5. Attach all the shader objects to the program object with **glAttachShader**.

6. Link the program object with **glLinkProgram**.

7. Install the executable program as part of OpenGL's current state with **glUseProgram**.

8. If the shaders uses the default uniform block, query the locations of uniform variables with **glGetUniformLocation** and then set their values with **glUniform**.

9. If the shaders use named uniform blocks, query the uniform block information with **glGetUniformBlockIndex** and **glGetActiveUniformBlockiv**. Query the offsets of the uniform variables within the uniform block with **glGetActiveUniformsiv**. The uniform blocks are associated with buffer object binding points with **glUniformBlockBinding**, and buffer objects are bound to those binding points with **glBindBufferRange**.

10. If the vertex shader uses user-defined in variables, the application must provide values for them, using OpenGL API calls that place attribute values in generic, numbered vertex attribute locations. Before such attribute data is passed to the shader, the index of the generic vertex attribute should be associated with an in variable in a vertex shader in one of two ways. Applications can create this association explicitly by calling **glBindAttribLocation** before linking. Alternatively, if no explicit association is made, OpenGL makes these associations automatically during linking. An application can query the assignment that was made with **glGetAttribLocation**. Thereafter, generic vertex attributes can be passed to a vertex shader with **glVertexAttrib** or with **glVertexAttribPointer** and **glEnableVertexArrayPointer** in conjunction with standard OpenGL commands to draw vertex arrays.

11. If the fragment shader uses user-defined out variables, the application may create an association between a user-defined out variable and a fragment data index with **glBindFragDataLocation** before linking. Alternatively, if no explicit association is made, OpenGL makes these associations automatically during linking. An application can query the assignment that was made with **glGetFragDataLocation**.

12. An application may optionally record vertex shader out variables to one or more transform feedback buffers. Before vertex shader out variables are recorded, the vertex shader out variables are associated with feedback buffer binding points with **glTransformFeedbackVarying**, and buffer objects are bound to those binding points with **glBindBufferRange**.

7.1 Obtaining Version Information

With the addition of the OpenGL Shading Language, the OpenGL version number was changed from 1.5 to 2.0. The number before the period is referred to as the MAJOR VERSION NUMBER, and the number after the period is referred to as the MINOR VERSION NUMBER. This did not reflect a change in compatibility, as is often the case when a product's major version number is changed. Instead, the OpenGL ARB believed that inclusion of a high-level shading language was a major addition to OpenGL. To call attention to this important capability, the committee decided that a change to OpenGL's major version number was warranted.

This caused some incompatibility with applications that were written assuming that OpenGL would never have a major version number greater than 1. The OpenGL Shading Language also has a version number since it is expected that it too will have additional features added over time. Both of these values can be queried with the OpenGL function **glGetString**.

To write applications that will work properly in a variety of OpenGL environments and that will stand the test of time, be sure to properly query and parse the OpenGL and OpenGL Shading Language version strings. Both strings are defined as

<version number><space><vendor-specific information>

The version number is defined to be either

majorVersionNumber.minorVersionNumber

or

majorVersionNumber.minorVersionNumber.releaseNumber

where each component contains one or more digits. The vendor specification information and the release number are optional and might not appear in the version string. The version number is not a floating-point number, but a series of integers separated by periods.

To determine the OpenGL version number, call **glGetString** with the symbolic constant GL_VERSION. To determine the OpenGL Shading Language version, call **glGetString** with the symbolic constant GL_SHADING_LANGUAGE_VERSION. The shading language version that was approved at the time OpenGL 2.0 was approved was 1.10.

Listing 7.1 contains code for C functions that query and parse the OpenGL and OpenGL Shading Language version strings. Both functions assume that a valid OpenGL context already exists, and both return 0 for the major and minor number if an error is encountered. Values returned by these functions can be tested to see if the underlying implementation provides the necessary support.

Listing 7.1 C functions to obtain OpenGL and OpenGL Shading Language version information

```
void getGlVersion(int *major, int *minor)
{
    const char *verstr = (const char *) glGetString(GL_VERSION);
    if ((verstr == NULL) || (sscanf(verstr,"%d.%d", major, minor) != 2))
    {
        *major = *minor = 0;
        fprintf(stderr, "Invalid GL_VERSION format!!!\n");
    }
}

void getGlslVersion(int *major, int *minor)
{
    int gl_major, gl_minor;
    getGlVersion(&gl_major, &gl_minor);

    *major = *minor = 0;
    if(gl_major == 1)
    {
        /* GL v1.x can provide GLSL v1.00 only as an extension */
        const char *extstr = (const char *) glGetString(GL_EXTENSIONS);
        if ((extstr != NULL) &&
            (strstr(extstr, "GL_ARB_shading_language_100") != NULL))
        {
            *major = 1;
            *minor = 0;
        }
    }
    else if (gl_major >= 2)
    {
        /* GL v2.0 and greater must parse the version string */
        const char *verstr =
            (const char *) glGetString(GL_SHADING_LANGUAGE_VERSION);

        if((verstr == NULL) ||
            (sscanf(verstr, "%d.%d", major, minor) != 2))
        {
            *major = *minor = 0;
            fprintf(stderr,
                "Invalid GL_SHADING_LANGUAGE_VERSION format!!!\n");
        }
    }
}
```

7.2 Creating Shader Objects

The design of the OpenGL Shading Language API mimics the process of developing a C or C++ application. The first step is to create the source code. The source code must then be compiled, the various compiled modules must be linked, and finally the resulting code can be executed by the target processor.

To support the concept of a high-level shading language within OpenGL, the design must provide storage for source code, compiled code, and executable code. The solution to this problem is to define two new OpenGL-managed data structures, or objects. These objects provide the necessary storage, and operations on these objects have been defined to provide functionality for specifying source code and then compiling, linking, and executing the resulting code. When one of these objects is created, OpenGL returns a unique identifier for it. This identifier can be used to manipulate the object and to set or query the parameters of the object.

The first step toward utilizing programmable graphics hardware is to create a shader object. This creates an OpenGL-managed data structure that can store the shader's source code. The command to create a shader is

---

GLuint **glCreateShader**(GLenum *shaderType*)

Creates an empty shader object and returns a nonzero value by which it can be referenced. A shader object maintains the source code strings that define a shader. *shaderType* specifies the type of shader to be created. Two types of shaders are supported. A shader of type GL_VERTEX_SHADER is a shader that runs on the programmable vertex processor; it replaces the fixed functionality vertex processing in OpenGL. A shader of type GL_FRAGMENT_SHADER is a shader that runs on the programmable fragment processor; it replaces the fixed functionality fragment processing in OpenGL.

When created, a shader object's GL_SHADER_TYPE parameter is set to either GL_VERTEX_SHADER or GL_FRAGMENT_SHADER, depending on the value of *shaderType*.

After a shader object is created, strings that define the shader's source code must be provided. The source code for a shader is provided as an array of strings. The command for defining a shader's source code is

---

void **glShaderSource**(GLuint *shader,*

GLsizei *count,*

const GLchar ****string,*

const GLint **length*)

Sets the source code in *shader* to the source code in the array of strings specified by *string.* Any source code previously stored in the shader object is completely replaced. The number of strings in the array is specified by *count.* If *length* is NULL, then each string is assumed to be null terminated. If *length* is a value other than NULL, it points to an array containing a string length for each of the corresponding elements of *string.* Each element in the *length* array can contain the length of the corresponding string (the null character is not counted as part of the string length) or a value less than 0 to indicate that the string is null terminated. The source code strings are not scanned or parsed at this time; they are simply copied into the specified shader object. An application can modify or free its copy of the source code strings immediately after the function returns.

The multiple strings interface provides a number of benefits, including

- A way to organize common pieces of source code (for instance, the in variable definitions and out variable definitions that are shared between a vertex shader and a fragment shader)

- A way to share prefix strings (analogous to header files) between shaders

- A way to share **#define** values to control the compilation process

- A way to include user-defined or third-party library functions

7.3 Compiling Shader Objects

After the source code strings have been loaded into a shader object, the source code must be compiled to check its validity. The result of compilation remains as part of the shader object until another compilation operation occurs or until the shader object itself is deleted. The command to compile a shader object is

---

void **glCompileShader**(GLuint *shader*)

Compiles the source code strings that have been stored in the shader object specified by *shader*.

The compilation status is stored as part of the shader object's state. This value is set to GL_TRUE if the shader was compiled without errors and is ready for use, and GL_FALSE otherwise. It can be queried by calling **glGetShader** with arguments *shader* and GL_COMPILE_STATUS.

A shader will fail to compile if it is lexically, grammatically, or semantically incorrect. Whether or not the compilation was successful, information about the compilation can be obtained from the shader object's information log with **glGetShaderInfoLog**.

The OpenGL Shading Language has compilation rules that are slightly different depending on the type of shader being compiled, and so the compilation takes into consideration whether the shader is a vertex shader or a fragment shader.

Information about the compile operation can be obtained by calling **glGetShaderInfoLog** (described in Section 7.6) with *shader*, but the information log should not be used as an indication of whether the compilation was successful. If the shader object was compiled successfully, either the information log is an empty string or it contains information about the compile operation. If the shader object was not compiled successfully, the information log contains information about any lexical, grammatical, or semantic errors that occurred, along with warning messages and any other information the compiler deems pertinent.

7.4 Linking and Using Shaders

Each shader object is compiled independently. To create a program, applications need a mechanism for specifying a list of shader objects to be linked. You can specify the list of shaders objects to be linked by creating a program object and attaching to it all the shader objects needed to create the program.

To create a program object, use the following command:

GLuint **glCreateProgram**(void)

Creates an empty program object and returns a nonzero value by which it can be referenced. A program object is an object to which shader objects can be attached. This provides a mechanism to specify the shader objects that will be linked to create a program. It also provides a means for checking the compatibility between shaders that will be used to create a program (for instance, checking the compatibility between a vertex shader and a fragment shader). When no longer needed as part of a program object, shader objects can be detached.

After the program object has been defined, shader objects can be attached to it. Attaching simply means creating a reference to the shader object so that it will be included when an attempt to link a program object is made. This is the application's way of describing the recipe for creating a program. The command to attach a shader object to a program object is

---

void **glAttachShader**(GLuint *program*,
                   GLuint *shader*)

Attaches the shader object specified by *shader* to the program object specified by *program*. This indicates that *shader* will be included in link operations that are performed on *program*.

There is no inherent limit on the number of shader objects that can be attached to a program object. All operations that can be performed on a shader object are valid whether or not the shader object is attached to a program object. It is permissible to attach a shader object to a program object before source code has been loaded into the shader object or before the shader object has been compiled. It is also permissible to attach a shader object to more than one program object. In other words, **glAttachShader** simply specifies the set of shader objects to be linked.

To create a valid program, all the shader objects attached to a program object must be compiled, and the program object itself must be linked. The link operation assigns locations for uniform variables, initializes user-defined uniform variables, resolves references between independently compiled shader objects, and checks to make sure the vertex and fragment shaders are compatible with one another. To link a program object, use the command

---

void **glLinkProgram**(GLuint *program*)

Links the program object specified by *program*. If any shader objects of type GL_VERTEX_SHADER are attached to *program*, they are used to create an executable that will run on the programmable vertex processor. If any shader objects of type GL_FRAGMENT_SHADER are attached to *program*, they are used to create an executable that will run on the programmable fragment processor.

The status of the link operation is stored as part of the program object's state. This value is set to GL_TRUE if the program object was linked without errors and is ready for use and set to GL_FALSE otherwise. It can be queried by calling **glGetProgram** with arguments *program* and GL_LINK_STATUS.

As a result of a successful link operation, all active user-defined uniform variables (see Section 7.8) belonging to *program* are initialized to 0, and each of the program object's active uniform variables is assigned a location that can be queried with **glGetUniformLocation**. Also, any active user-defined attribute variables (see Section 7.7) that have not been bound to a generic vertex attribute index are bound to one at this time.

If *program* contains shader objects of type GL_VERTEX_SHADER but it does not contain shader objects of type GL_FRAGMENT_SHADER, the vertex shader is linked to the implicit interface for fixed functionality fragment processing. Similarly, if *program* contains shader objects of type GL_FRAGMENT_SHADER but it does not contain shader objects of type GL_VERTEX_SHADER, the fragment shader is linked to the implicit interface for fixed functionality vertex processing.

glLinkProgram also installs the generated executables as part of the current rendering state if the link operation was successful and the specified program object is already currently in use as a result of a previous call to **glUseProgram**. If the program object currently in use is relinked unsuccessfully, its link status is set to GL_FALSE, but the previously generated executables and associated state remain part of the current state until a subsequent call to **glUseProgram** removes them. After they are removed, they cannot be made part of current state until the program object has been successfully relinked.

Linking of a program object can fail for a number of reasons.

* The number of active attribute variables supported by the implementation has been exceeded.

* The number of active uniform variables supported by the implementation has been exceeded.

- The **main** function is missing for the vertex shader or the fragment shader.

- An in variable actually used in the fragment shader is not declared as an out variable with the same type (or is not declared at all) in the vertex shader.

- A reference to a function or variable name is unresolved.

- A shared global is declared with two different types or two different initial values.

- One or more of the attached shader objects has not been successfully compiled.

- Binding a generic attribute matrix caused some rows of the matrix to fall outside the allowed maximum of GL_MAX_VERTEX_ATTRIBS.

- Not enough contiguous vertex attribute slots could be found to bind attribute matrices.

The program object's information log is updated at the time of the link operation. If the link operation is successful, a program is generated. It may contain an executable for the vertex processor, an executable for the fragment processor, or both. Whether the link operation succeeds or fails, the information and executables from the previous link operation will be lost. After the link operation, applications are free to modify attached shader objects, compile attached shader objects, detach shader objects, and attach additional shader objects. None of these operations affect the information log or the program that is part of the program object until the next link operation on the program object.

Information about the link operation can be obtained by calling **glGetProgramInfoLog** (described in Section 7.6) with *program*. If the program object was linked successfully, the information log either is an empty string or contains information about the link operation. If the program object was not linked successfully, the information log contains information about any link errors that occurred, along with warning messages and any other information the linker chooses to provide.

When the link operation has completed successfully, the program it contains can be installed as part of the current rendering state. The command to install the program as part of the rendering state is

---

void **glUseProgram**(GLuint *program*)

Installs the program object specified by *program* as part of current rendering state.

A program object contains an executable that will run on the vertex processor if it contains one or more shader objects of type GL_VERTEX_SHADER that have been successfully compiled and linked. Similarly, a program object contains an executable that will run on the fragment processor if it contains one or more shader objects of subtype GL_FRAGMENT_SHADER that have been successfully compiled and linked.

If *program* contains shader objects of type GL_VERTEX_SHADER but it does not contain shader objects of type GL_FRAGMENT_SHADER, an executable is installed on the vertex processor but fixed functionality is used for fragment processing. Similarly, if *program* contains shader objects of type GL_FRAGMENT_SHADER but it does not contain shader objects of type GL_VERTEX_SHADER, an executable is installed on the fragment processor but fixed functionality is used for vertex processing. If *program* is 0, the programmable processors are disabled, and fixed functionality is used for both vertex and fragment processing.

Successfully installing an executable on a programmable processor causes the corresponding fixed functionality of OpenGL to be disabled. Specifically, if an executable is installed on the vertex processor, the OpenGL fixed functionality is disabled as described in Section 4.1. Similarly, if an executable is installed on the fragment processor, the OpenGL fixed functionality is disabled as described in Section 4.2.

While a program object is in use, applications are free to modify attached shader objects, compile attached shader objects, attach additional shader objects, detach shader objects, delete any shader objects attached, or delete the program object itself. None of these operations affect the executables that are part of the current state. However, relinking the program object that is currently in use installs the program as part of the current rendering state if the link operation was successful. While a program object is in use, the state that controls the disabled fixed functionality can also be updated with the normal OpenGL calls.

7.5 Cleaning Up

Objects should be deleted when they are no longer needed, and deletion can be accomplished with the following commands:

---

void **glDeleteShader**(GLuint *shader*)

Frees the memory and invalidates the name associated with the shader object specified by *shader*. This command effectively undoes the effects of a call to **glCreateShader**.

If a shader object to be deleted is attached to a program object, it will be flagged for deletion, but it will not be deleted until it is no longer attached to any program object for any rendering context (i.e., it must be detached from wherever it was attached before it can be deleted). A value of 0 for *shader* is silently ignored.

To determine whether a shader object has been flagged for deletion, call **glGetShader** with arguments *shader* and GL_DELETE_STATUS.

---

void **glDeleteProgram**(GLuint *program*)

Frees the memory and invalidates the name associated with the program object specified by *program*. This command effectively undoes the effects of a call to **glCreateProgram**.

If a program object is in use as part of a current rendering state, it will be flagged for deletion, but it will not be deleted until it is no longer part of current state for any rendering context. If a program object to be deleted has shader objects attached to it, those shader objects are automatically detached but not deleted unless they have already been flagged for deletion by a previous call to **glDeleteShader**.

To determine whether a program object has been flagged for deletion, call **glGetProgram** with arguments *program* and GL_DELETE_STATUS.

When a shader object no longer needs to be attached to a program object, it can be detached with the command

---

void **glDetachShader**(GLuint *program*, GLuint *shader*)

Detaches the shader object specified by *shader* from the program object specified by *program*. This command undoes the effect of the command **glAttachShader.**

If *shader* has already been flagged for deletion by a call to **glDeleteShader** and it is not attached to any other program object, it is deleted after it has been detached.

A programming tip that might be useful in keeping things orderly is to delete shader objects as soon as they have been attached to a program object. They won't be deleted at this time, but they will be flagged for deletion when they are no longer referenced. To clean up later, the application only needs to delete the program object. All the attached shader objects will be automatically detached, and, because they are flagged for deletion, they will be automatically deleted at that time as well.

7.6   Query Functions

The OpenGL Shading Language API contains several functions for querying object state. To obtain information about a shader object, use the following command:

---

void **glGetShaderiv**(GLuint *shader*,

GLenum *pname*,

GLint **params*)

Returns in *params* the value of a parameter for a specific shader object. This function returns information about a shader object. Permitted parameters and their meanings are described in Table 7.1. In this table, the value for *pname* is shown on the left, and the operation performed is shown on the right.

Table 7.1   Queriable shader object parameters

Parameter	Operation
GL_SHADER_TYPE	*params* returns a value of either GL_VERTEX_SHADER or GL_FRAGMENT_SHADER, depending on whether *shader* is the name of a vertex shader object or a fragment shader object.
GL_DELETE_STATUS	*params* returns GL_TRUE if *shader* is currently flagged for deletion, and GL_FALSE otherwise.
GL_COMPILE_STATUS	*params* returns GL_TRUE if the last compile operation on *shader* was successful, and GL_FALSE otherwise.

(continues)

Table 7.1 Queriable shader object parameters, *continued*

Parameter	Operation
GL_INFO_LOG_LENGTH	*params* returns the number of characters in the information log for *shader*, including the null termination character. If the object has no information log, a value of 0 is returned.
GL_SHADER_SOURCE_ LENGTH	*params* returns the length of the concatenation of the source strings that make up the shader source for *shader*, including the null termination character. If no source code exists, 0 is returned.

A similar function is provided for querying the state of a program object: the status of an operation on a program object, the number of attached shader objects, the number of active attributes (see Section 7.7), the number of active uniform variables (see Section 7.8), or the length of any of the strings maintained by a program object. The command to obtain information about a program object is

---

void **glGetProgramiv**(GLuint *program*,

GLenum *pname*,

GLint **params*)

Returns in *params* the value of a parameter for a particular program object. This function returns information about a program object. Permitted parameters and their meanings are described in Table 7.2. In this table, the value for *pname* is shown on the left, and the operation performed is shown on the right.

Table 7.2 Queriable program object parameters

Parameter	Operation
GL_DELETE_STATUS	*params* returns GL_TRUE if *program* is currently flagged for deletion, and GL_FALSE otherwise.
GL_LINK_STATUS	*params* returns GL_TRUE if the last link operation on *program* was successful, and GL_FALSE otherwise.

Table 7.2   Queriable program object parameters, *continued*

Parameter	Operation
GL_VALIDATE_STATUS	*params* returns GL_TRUE if the last validation operation on *program* was successful, and GL_FALSE otherwise.
GL_INFO_LOG_LENGTH	*params* returns the number of characters in the information log for *program*, including the null termination character. If the object has no information log, a value of 0 is returned.
GL_ATTACHED_SHADERS	*params* returns the number of shader objects attached to *program*.
GL_ACTIVE_ATTRIBUTES	*params* returns the number of active attribute variables for *program*.
GL_ACTIVE_ATTRIBUTE_MAX_ LENGTH	*params* returns the length of the longest active attribute variable name for *program*, including the null termination character. If no active attribute variables exist, 0 is returned.
GL_ACTIVE_UNIFORMS	*params* returns the number of active uniform variables for *program*.
GL_ACTIVE_UNIFORM_MAX_ LENGTH	*params* returns the length of the longest active uniform variable name for *program*, including the null termination character. If no active uniform variables exist, 0 is returned.

The command to obtain the current shader string from a shader object is

void **glGetShaderSource**(GLuint *shader*
                    GLsizei *bufSize*,
                    GLsizei **length*,
                    GLchar **source*)

Returns a concatenation of the source code strings from the shader object specified by *shader*. The source code strings for a shader object are the result of a previous call to **glShaderSource**. The string returned by the function is null terminated.

glGetShaderSource returns in *source* as much of the source code string as it can, up to a maximum of *bufSize* characters. The number of characters actually returned, excluding the null termination character, is specified by *length*. If the length of the returned string is not required, a value of NULL can be passed in the *length* argument. The size of the buffer required to store the returned source code string can be obtained by calling **glGetShader** with the value GL_SHADER_SOURCE_LENGTH.

Information about the compilation operation is stored in the information log for a shader object. Similarly, information about the link and validation operations is stored in the information log for a program object. The information log is a string that contains diagnostic messages and warnings. The information log may contain information useful during application development even if the compilation or link operation was successful. The information log is typically useful only during application development, and an application should not expect different OpenGL implementations to produce identical descriptions of error. To obtain the information log for a shader object, call

---

void **glGetShaderInfoLog**(GLuint *shader*,

　　　　　　　　GLsizei *maxLength*,

　　　　　　　　GLsizei **length*,

　　　　　　　　GLchar **infoLog*)

Returns the information log for the specified shader object. The information log for a shader object is modified when the shader is compiled. The string that is returned is null terminated.

glGetShaderInfoLog returns in *infoLog* as much of the information log as it can, up to a maximum of *maxLength* characters. The number of characters actually returned, excluding the null termination character, is specified by *length*. If the length of the returned string is not required, a value of NULL can be passed in the *length* argument. The size of the buffer required to store the returned information log can be obtained by calling **glGetShader** with the value GL_INFO_LOG_LENGTH.

The information log for a shader object is a string that may contain diagnostic messages, warning messages, and other information about the last compile operation. When a shader object is created, its information log is a string of length 0.

To obtain the information log for a program object, call

---

void **glGetProgramInfoLog**(GLuint *program*,

GLsizei *maxLength*,

GLsizei **length*,

GLchar **infoLog*)

Returns the information log for the specified program object. The information log for a program object is modified when the program object is linked or validated. The string that is returned is null terminated.

glGetProgramInfoLog returns in *infoLog* as much of the information log as it can, up to a maximum of *maxLength* characters. The number of characters actually returned, excluding the null termination character, is specified by *length*. If the length of the returned string is not required, a value of NULL can be passed in the *length* argument. The size of the buffer required to store the returned information log can be obtained by calling **glGetProgram** with the value GL_INFO_LOG_LENGTH.

The information log for a program object is an empty string, a string containing information about the last link operation, or a string containing information about the last validation operation. It may contain diagnostic messages, warning messages, and other information. When a program object is created, its information log is a string of length 0.

The way the API is set up, you first need to perform a query to find out the length of the information log (number of characters in the string). After allocating a buffer of the appropriate size, you can call **glGetShaderInfoLog** or **glGetProgramInfoLog** to put the information log string into the allocated buffer. You can then print it if you want to do so. Listing 7.2 shows a C function that does all this for a shader object. The code for obtaining the information log for a program object is almost identical.

Listing 7.2 C function to print the information log for an object

```
void printShaderInfoLog(GLuint shader)
{
    int infologLen = 0;
    int charsWritten = 0;
    GLchar *infoLog;

    glGetShaderiv(shader, GL_INFO_LOG_LENGTH, &infologLen);

    printOpenGLError();   // Check for OpenGL errors

    if (infologLen > 0)
    {
        infoLog = (GLchar*) malloc(infologLen);
        if (infoLog == NULL)
```

```
    {
        printf("ERROR: Could not allocate InfoLog buffer\n");
        exit(1);
    }
    glGetShaderInfoLog(shader, infologLen, &charsWritten, infoLog);
    printf("InfoLog:\n%s\n\n", infoLog);
    free(infoLog);
    }
    printOpenGLError();   // Check for OpenGL errors
}
```

You can obtain the program object that is currently in use by calling **glGet** with the symbolic constant GL_CURRENT_PROGRAM.

The command to query a list of shader objects attached to a particular program object is

---

void **glGetAttachedShaders**(GLuint *program*,

GLsizei *maxCount*,

GLsizei **count*,

GLuint **shaders*)

Returns the handles of the shader objects attached to *program*. It returns in *shaders* as many of the handles of these shader objects as it can, up to a maximum of *maxCount*. The number of handles actually returned is specified by *count*. If the number of handles actually returned is not required (for instance, if it has just been obtained with **glGetProgram**), a value of NULL may be passed for *count*. If no shader objects are attached to *program*, a value of 0 is returned in *count*. The actual number of attached shaders can be obtained by calling **glGetProgram** with the value GL_ATTACHED_SHADERS.

Two new functions have been added to determine whether an object is a shader object or a program object. These functions may be useful if you have to process an object (for instance, to print its information log) without knowing whether it is a valid shader or program object. These two functions are defined as

---

GLboolean **glIsShader**(GLuint *shader*)

Returns GL_TRUE if *shader* is the name of a shader object. If *shader* is zero or a nonzero value that is not the name of a shader object, **glIsShader** returns GL_FALSE.

GLboolean **glIsProgram**(GLuint *program*)

Returns GL_TRUE if *program* is the name of a program object. If *program* is zero or a nonzero value that is not the name of a program object, **glIsProgram** returns GL_FALSE.

7.7 Specifying Vertex Attributes

The brave new world of programmability means that applications no longer need to be limited to the standard vertex attributes like normal or color once defined by OpenGL. There are many per-vertex attributes that applications might like to pass into a vertex shader. It is easy to imagine that, in addition to normal or color, applications will want to specify per-vertex data such as tangents, temperature, pressure, and who knows what else. How do we allow applications to pass nontraditional attributes to OpenGL and operate on them in vertex shaders?

The answer is that OpenGL provides a small number of generic locations, sometimes called CURRENT VERTEX STATE, for passing in vertex attributes. Each location is numbered and has room to store up to four floating-point components (i.e., it is a **vec4**). An implementation that supports 16 attribute locations will have them numbered from 0 to 15. An application can pass a vertex attribute into any of the generic numbered slots by using one of the following functions:

---

void **glVertexAttrib{1|2|3|4}{s|f|d}**(GLuint *index*, *TYPE v*)

void **glVertexAttrib{1|2|3}{s|f|d}v**(GLuint *index*, const *TYPE *v*)

void **glVertexAttrib4{b|s|i|f|d|ub|us|ui}v**(GLuint *index*, const *TYPE *v*)

Sets the generic vertex attribute specified by *index* to the value specified by *v*. This command can have up to three suffixes that differentiate variations of the parameters accepted. The first suffix can be 1, 2, 3, or 4 to specify whether *v* contains 1, 2, 3, or 4 components. If the second and third components are not provided, they are assumed to be 0, and if the fourth component is not provided, it is assumed to be 1. The second suffix indicates the data type of *v* and may specify byte (**b**), short (**s**), int (**i**), float (**f**), double (**d**), unsigned byte (**ub**), unsigned short (**us**), or unsigned int (**ui**). The third suffix is an optional **v** meaning that *v* is a pointer to an array of values of the specified data type.

This set of commands has a certain set of rules for converting data to the floating-point internal representation specified by OpenGL. Floats and doubles are mapped into OpenGL internal floating-point values as you would expect, and integer values are converted to floats by a decimal point added to the right of the value provided. Thus, a value of 27 for a byte, int, short, unsigned byte, unsigned int, or unsigned short becomes a value of 27.0 for computation within OpenGL.

Another set of entry points supports the passing of normalized values as generic vertex attributes:

---

void **glVertexAttrib4Nub**(GLuint *index*, *TYPE v*)

void **glVertexAttrib4N{b|s|i|f|d|ub|us|ui}v**(GLuint *index*, const *TYPE* *v)

Sets the generic vertex attribute specified by *index* to the normalized value specified by *v*. In addition to **N** (to indicate normalized values), this command can have two suffixes that differentiate variations of the parameters accepted. The first suffix indicates the data type of *v* and specifies byte (**b**), short (**s**), int (**i**), float (**f**), double (**d**), unsigned byte (**ub**), unsigned short (**us**), or unsigned int (**ui**). The second suffix is an optional **v** meaning that *v* is a pointer to an array of values of the specified data type.

N in a command name indicates that, for data types other than float or double, the arguments will be linearly mapped to a normalized range in the same way as data provided to the integer variants of **glColor** or **glNormal**— that is, for signed integer variants of the functions, the most positive, representable value maps to 1.0, and the most negative representable value maps to –1.0. For the unsigned integer variants, the largest representable value maps to 1.0, and the smallest representable value maps to 0.

Attribute variables are allowed to be of type **mat2**, **mat3**, or **mat4**. Attributes of these types can be loaded with the **glVertexAttrib** entry points. Matrices must be loaded into successive generic attribute slots in column major order, with one column of the matrix in each generic attribute slot. Thus, to load a **mat4** attribute, you would load the first column in generic attribute slot *i*, the second in slot *i* + 1, the third in slot *i* + 2, and the fourth in slot *i* + 3.

Applications more commonly specify vertices with the vertex array interface instead. This interface allows you to store vertex data in vertex buffers and set offsets to those buffers. Instead of sending one vertex at a time to OpenGL, you can send a whole set of primitives at a time. With vertex buffer objects, it is even possible that vertex data is stored in memory on the graphics board to exact maximum performance.

When a vertex buffer is sent to OpenGL, the vertex data in the vertex buffer is processed one vertex at a time, with each generic vertex attribute copied to an in variable in the vertex shader.

The vertex array API allows generic vertex attributes to be specified as vertex arrays. The following call establishes the vertex array pointer for a generic vertex attribute:

---

void **glVertexAttribPointer**(GLuint *index*,

GLint *size*,

GLenum *type*,

GLboolean *normalized*,

GLsizei *stride*,

const GLvoid *pointer)

Specifies the location and data format of an array of generic vertex attribute values to use when rendering. The generic vertex attribute array to be specified is indicated by *index*. *size* specifies the number of components per attribute and must be 1, 2, 3, or 4. *type* specifies the data type of each component (GL_BYTE, GL_UNSIGNED_BYTE, GL_SHORT, GL_UNSIGNED_SHORT, GL_INT, GL_UNSIGNED_INT, GL_FLOAT, or GL_DOUBLE). *stride* specifies the byte stride from one attribute to the next, allowing attribute values to be intermixed with other attribute values or stored in a separate array. A value of 0 for *stride* means that the values are stored sequentially in memory with no gaps between successive elements. If set to GL_TRUE, *normalize* specifies that values stored in an integer format are to be mapped to the range [–1.0,1.0] (for signed values) or [0.0,1.0] (for unsigned values) when they are accessed and converted to floating point. Otherwise, values are converted to floats directly without normalization. *pointer* is the memory address of the first generic vertex attribute in the vertex array.

After the vertex array information has been specified for a generic vertex attribute array, the array needs to be enabled. When enabled, the generic vertex attribute data in the specified array is provided along with other enabled vertex array data when vertex array drawing commands such as **glDrawArrays** are called. To enable or disable a generic vertex attribute array, use the commands

---

void **glEnableVertexAttribArray**(GLuint *index*)

void **glDisableVertexAttribArray**(GLuint *index*)

Enables or disables the generic vertex attribute array specified by *index*. By default, all client-side capabilities are disabled, including all generic vertex attribute arrays. If enabled, the values in the generic vertex attribute array are accessed and used for rendering when calls are made to vertex array commands such as **glArrayElement**, **glDrawArrays**, **glDrawElements**, **glDrawRangeElements**, **glMultiDrawArrays**, or **glMultiDrawElements**.

This solves the question of how generic vertex data is passed into OpenGL, but how do we access that data from within a vertex shader? We don't want to refer to these numbered locations in our shader, because this approach is not very descriptive and is prone to errors. The OpenGL Shading Language API provides two ways for associating generic vertex indices with vertex shader attribute variables.

The first way is to let the linker assign the bindings automatically. In this case, the application would need to query OpenGL after linking to determine the generic vertex indices that were assigned and then would use these indices when passing the attributes to OpenGL.

The second way is for the application to choose the index value of the generic vertex attribute to be used and explicitly bind it to a specific attribute variable in the vertex shader by using the following function before linking occurs:

---

void **glBindAttribLocation**(GLuint *program*,

GLuint *index*,

const GLchar **name*)

Associates a user-defined attribute variable in the program object specified by *program* with a generic vertex attribute index. The name of the user-defined attribute variable is passed as a null-terminated string in *name*. If *name* was bound previously, that information is lost. Thus, you cannot bind one user-defined attribute variable to multiple indices, but you can bind multiple user-defined attribute variables to the same index. The generic vertex attribute index to be bound to this variable is specified by *index*. When *program* is made part of current state, values provided through the generic vertex attribute *index* modify the value of the user-defined attribute variable specified by *name*.

If *name* refers to a matrix attribute variable, *index* refers to the first column of the matrix. Other matrix columns are then automatically bound to locations *index+1* for a matrix of type **mat2**; *index+1* and *index+2* for a matrix of type **mat3**; and *index+1*, *index+2*, and *index+3* for a matrix of type **mat4**.

Applications are not allowed to bind any of the standard OpenGL vertex attributes with this command because they are bound automatically when needed. Any attribute binding that occurs after the program object has been linked does not take effect until the next time the program object is linked.

glBindAttribLocation can be called before any vertex shader objects are attached to the specified program object. It is also permissible to bind an attribute variable name that is never used in a vertex shader to a generic attribute index.

Applications are allowed to bind more than one vertex shader attribute name to the same generic vertex attribute index. This is called ATTRIBUTE ALIASING, and it is allowed only if just one of the aliased attributes is active in the executable program or if no path through the shader consumes more than one attribute of a set of attributes aliased to the same location. Another way of saying this is that more than one attribute name may be bound to a generic attribute index if, in the end, only one name is used to access the generic attribute in the vertex shader. The compiler and linker are allowed to assume that no aliasing is done and are free to employ optimizations that work only in the absence of aliasing. OpenGL implementations are not required to do error checking to detect attribute aliasing.

The binding between an attribute variable name and a generic attribute index can be specified at any time with **glBindAttribLocation**. Attribute bindings do not go into effect until **glLinkProgram** is called, so any attribute variables that need to be bound explicitly for a particular use of a shader should be bound before the link operation occurs. After a program object has been linked successfully, the index values for attribute variables remain fixed (and their values can be queried) until the next link command occurs. To query the attribute binding for a named vertex shader attribute variable, use **glGetAttribLocation**. It returns the binding that actually went into effect the last time **glLinkProgram** was called for the specified program object. Attribute bindings that have been specified since the last link operation are not returned by **glGetAttribLocation**.

GLint **glGetAttribLocation**(GLuint *program*,
                         const GLchar **name*)

Queries the previously linked program object specified by *program* for the attribute variable specified by *name* and returns the index of the generic vertex attribute that is bound to that attribute variable. If *name* is a matrix attribute variable, the index of the first column of the matrix is returned. If the named attribute variable is not an active attribute in the specified program object or if *name* starts with the reserved prefix "*gl_*", a value of −1 is returned.

Using these functions, we can create a vertex shader that contains a user-defined attribute variable named *Opacity* that is used directly in the lighting calculations. We can decide that we want to pass per-vertex opacity values in generic attribute location 1 and set up the proper binding with the following line of code:

```
glBindAttribLocation(myProgram, 1, "Opacity");
```

Subsequently, we can call **glVertexAttrib** to pass a single opacity value to every vertex:

```
glVertexAttrib1f(1, opacity);
```

Or we can call **glEnableVertexAttribArray** to pass potentially different opacity values to every vertex:

```
glEnableVertexAttribArray(1);
```

The jargon in this section can get a little confusing, so let's look at a diagram to make sure we have things straight. Let's look at the case of generic vertex attributes as illustrated in Figure 7.1. A user-defined in variable must be bound to a generic vertex attribute index. This binding can be done with **glBindAttribLocation**, or it can happen implicitly at link time.

Let's assume we have a vertex shader that uses three user-defined in variables: *Opacity, Binormal,* and *MyData*. These are shown on the right side of Figure 7.1. These user-defined in variables can each be bound to a generic vertex attribute index as follows:

```
glBindAttribLocation(myProgram, 1, "Opacity");
glBindAttribLocation(myProgram, 2, "Binormal");
glBindAttribLocation(myProgram, 3, "MyData");
```

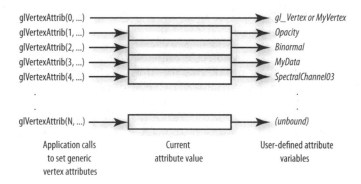

Figure 7.1 Mapping of generic vertex attribute commands to user-defined attribute variables

This sets up the mapping so that values written into generic vertex attribute locations 1, 2, and 3 will modify the values of the in variables *Opacity, Binormal,* and *MyData* in the vertex shader. The diagram shows that generic vertex attribute index *N* is not currently bound to any user-defined in variable.

As mentioned, each of the generic attribute locations has enough room for four floating-point components. Applications are permitted to store 1, 2, 3, or 4 components in each location. A vertex shader may access a single location by using a user-defined in variable that is a **float**, a **vec2**, a **vec3**, or a **vec4**. It may access two consecutive locations by using a user-defined in variable that is a **mat2**, three using a **mat3**, and four using a **mat4**.

The bindings between generic attribute index values and user-defined in variables (i.e., the arrows on the right side of Figure 7.1) are part of the state maintained within a program object, whereas the contents of the attribute array itself is considered current attribute state. The application can provide a different program object and specify different names and mappings for attribute variables in the vertex shader, and if no calls have been made to update the attribute values in the interim, the attribute variables in the new vertex shader get the values left behind by the previous one.

Attribute variables that can be accessed when a vertex shader is executed are called ACTIVE ATTRIBUTES. To obtain information about an active attribute, use the following command:

---

void **glGetActiveAttrib**(GLuint *program,*

GLuint *index,*

GLsizei *bufSize,*

GLsizei **length,*

GLint **size,*

GLenum **type,*

GLchar **name*)

Returns information about an active attribute variable in the program object specified by *program.* The number of active attributes in a program object can be obtained by calling **glGetProgram** with the value GL_ACTIVE_ATTRIBUTES. A value of 0 for *index* causes information about the first active attribute variable to be returned. Permissible values for *index* range from 0 to the number of active attributes minus 1.

A vertex shader can use built-in attribute variables, user-defined attribute variables, or both. Built-in attribute variables have a prefix of "*gl_*" and reference conventional OpenGL vertex attributes (e.g., *gl_Vertex*, *gl_Normal*, etc.; see Section 4.1.1 for a complete list). User-defined attribute variables have arbitrary names and obtain their values through numbered generic vertex attributes. An attribute variable (either built-in or user-defined) is considered active if it is determined during the link operation that it can be accessed during program execution. Therefore, *program* should have previously been the target of a call to **glLinkProgram,** but it is not necessary for it to have been linked successfully.

The size of the character buffer needed to store the longest attribute variable name in *program* can be obtained by calling **glGetProgram** with the value GL_ACTIVE_ATTRIBUTE_MAX_LENGTH. This value should be used to allocate a buffer of sufficient size to store the returned attribute name. The size of this character buffer is passed in *bufSize*, and a pointer to this character buffer is passed in *name*.

glGetActiveAttrib returns the name of the attribute variable indicated by *index*, storing it in the character buffer specified by *name*. The string returned is null terminated. The actual number of characters written into this buffer is returned in *length*, and this count does not include the null termination character. If the length of the returned string is not required, a value of NULL can be passed in the *length* argument.

The *type* argument returns a pointer to the attribute variable's data type. The symbolic constants GL_FLOAT, GL_FLOAT_VEC2, GL_FLOAT_VEC3, GL_FLOAT_VEC4, GL_FLOAT_MAT2, GL_FLOAT_MAT3, and GL_FLOAT_MAT4 may be returned. The *size* argument returns the size of the attribute in units of the type returned in *type*.

The list of active attribute variables may include both built-in attribute variables (which begin with the prefix "*gl_*") as well as user-defined attribute variable names.

This function returns as much information as it can about the specified active attribute variable. If no information is available, *length* is 0 and *name* is an empty string. This situation could occur if this function is called after a link operation that failed. If an error occurs, the return values *length*, *size*, *type*, and *name* are unmodified.

The **glGetActiveAttrib** command can be useful in an environment in which shader development occurs separately from application development. If some attribute-naming conventions are agreed to between the shader writers and the application developers, the latter could query the program object at runtime to determine the attributes that are actually needed and could pass those down. This approach can provide more flexibility in the shader development process.

To query the state of a particular generic vertex attribute, call one of the following commands:

void **glGetVertexAttribfv**(GLuint *index*,

GLenum *pname*,

GLfloat **params*)

void **glGetVertexAttribiv**(GLuint *index*,

GLenum *pname*,

GLint **params*)

void **glGetVertexAttribdv**(GLuint *index*,

GLenum *pname*,

GLdouble **params*)

Returns in *params* the value of a generic vertex attribute parameter. The generic vertex attribute to be queried is specified by *index*, and the parameter to be queried is specified by *pname*. Parameters and return values are summarized in Table 7.3. All the parameters except GL_CURRENT_ VERTEX_ATTRIB represent client-side state.

Table 7.3 Generic vertex attribute parameters

Parameter	Operation
GL_VERTEX_ATTRIB_ ARRAY_ENABLED	*params* returns a single value that is nonzero (true) if the vertex attribute array for *index* is enabled and 0 (false) if it is disabled. The initial value is GL_FALSE.
GL_VERTEX_ATTRIB_ ARRAY_SIZE	*params* returns a single value, the size of the vertex attribute array for *index*. The size is the number of values for each element of the vertex attribute array, and it is 1, 2, 3, or 4. The initial value is 4.
GL_VERTEX_ATTRIB_ ARRAY_STRIDE	*params* returns a single value, the array stride (number of bytes between successive elements) for the vertex attribute array for *index*. A value of 0 indicates that the array elements are stored sequentially in memory. The initial value is 0.
GL_VERTEX_ATTRIB_ ARRAY_TYPE	*params* returns a single value, a symbolic constant indicating the array type for the vertex attribute array for *index*. Possible values are GL_BYTE, GL_UNSIGNED_BYTE, GL_SHORT, GL_UNSIGNED_SHORT, GL_INT, GL_ UNSIGNED_INT, GL_FLOAT, and GL_DOUBLE. The initial value is GL_FLOAT.

(continues)

Table 7.3 Generic vertex attribute parameters, *continued*

Parameter	Operation
GL_VERTEX_ATTRIB_ ARRAY_NORMALIZED	*params* returns a single value that is nonzero (true) if fixed-point data types for the vertex attribute array indicated by *index* are normalized when they are converted to floating point and 0 (false) otherwise. The initial value is GL_FALSE.
GL_CURRENT_VERTEX_ ATTRIB	*params* returns four values that represent the current value for the generic vertex attribute specified by *index*. Generic vertex attribute 0 is unique in that it has no current state, so an error is generated if *index* is 0. The initial value for all other generic vertex attributes is (0, 0, 0, 1).

---

void **glGetVertexAttribPointerv**(GLuint *index*,

GLenum *pname*,

GLvoid ****pointer*)

Returns pointer information. *index* is the generic vertex attribute to be queried, *pname* is a symbolic constant specifying the pointer to be returned, and *params* is a pointer to a location in which to place the returned data. The only accepted value for *pname* is GL_VERTEX_ATTRIB_ARRAY_ POINTER. This causes *params* to return a single value that is a pointer to the vertex attribute array for the generic vertex attribute specified by *index*.

7.8 Specifying Uniform Variables

As described in the previous section, attribute variables provide frequently modified data to the vertex shader. Less frequently changing data can be specified using uniform variables. Uniform variables are declared within a shader and can be loaded directly by the application. This lets applications provide any type of arbitrary data to a shader. Applications can modify these values as often as every primitive in order to modify the behavior of the shader (although performance may suffer if this is done). Typically, uniform variables are used to supply state that stays constant for many primitives.

The basic model for specifying uniform variables is different from the model for specifying attribute variables. As discussed in the preceding section, for attribute variables, the application can specify the attribute location before linking occurs. In contrast, the locations or offsets of uniform variables cannot be specified by the application. Instead, they are always determined by OpenGL at link time. As a result, applications need to query the uniform location or offset after linking occurs.

Uniforms are gathered together into uniform blocks. There are two types of uniform blocks in OpenGL, the default uniform block and named uniform blocks.

7.8.1 Default Uniform Block

The default uniform block contains all the uniform variables that are declared outside of named uniform blocks. Any uniforms may be in the default uniform block, though any uniform of sampler type must be in the default uniform block.

One advantage of the default uniform block is that the uniform storage is associated with the program object, so the default uniform block is best for uniforms closely associated with an individual shader. One disadvantage of the default uniform block is that changing a uniform value is relatively expensive, so uniforms in the default uniform block are best reserved for infrequently changing uniform values.

To update the value of a user-defined uniform variable, an application needs to determine its location and then specify its value. The locations of uniform variables are assigned at link time and do not change until the next link operation occurs. Each time linking occurs, the locations of uniform variables may change, and so the application must query them again before setting them. The locations of the user-defined uniform variables in a program object can be queried with the following command:

GLint **glGetUniformLocation**(GLuint *program*,
const GLchar **name*)

Returns an integer that represents the location of a specific uniform variable within a program object. *name* must be a null-terminated string that contains no white space. *name* must be an active uniform variable name in *program* that is not a structure, an array of structures, or a subcomponent of a vector or a matrix. This function returns –1 if *name* does not correspond to an active uniform variable in *program*, if *name* is associated with a named uniform block, or if *name* starts with the reserved prefix "*gl_*".

Uniform variables that are structures or arrays of structures can be queried with **glGetUniformLocation** for each field within the structure. The array element operator "[]" and the structure field operator "." can be used in *name* to select elements within an array or fields within a structure. The result of using these operators is not allowed to be another structure, an array of structures, or a subcomponent of a vector or a matrix. Except if the last part of *name* indicates a uniform variable array, the location of the first element of an array can be retrieved with the name of the array or with the name appended by "[0]".

The actual locations assigned to uniform variables are not known until the program object is linked successfully. After linking has occurred, the command **glGetUniformLocation** can obtain the location of a uniform variable. This location value can then be passed to **glUniform** to set the value of the uniform variable or to **glGetUniform** in order to query the current value of the uniform variable. After a program object has been linked successfully, the index values for uniform variables remain fixed until the next link command occurs. Uniform variable locations and values can be queried after a link only if the link was successful.

Loading of user-defined uniform values is possible only for the program object that is currently in use. All user-defined uniform variables are initialized when a program object is successfully linked, either to an explicit default or to 0. User-defined uniform values are part of the state of a program object. Their values can be modified only when the program object is part of current rendering state, but the values of uniform variables are preserved as the program object is swapped in and out of current state. The following commands load uniform variables into the program object that is currently in use:

---

void **glUniform{1|2|3|4}{f|i}**(GLint *location*, *TYPE v*)

Sets the user-defined uniform variable or uniform variable array specified by *location* to the value specified by *v*. The suffix **1**, **2**, **3**, or **4** indicates whether *v* contains 1, 2, 3, or 4 components. This value should match the number of components in the data type of the specified uniform variable (e.g., **1** for **float**, **int**, **bool**; **2** for **vec2**, **ivec2**, **bvec2**, etc.). The suffix **f** indicates that floating-point values are being passed, and the suffix **i** indicates that integer values are being passed; this type should also match the data type of the specified uniform variable. The **i** variants of this function should be used to provide values for uniform variables defined as **int**, **ivec2**, **ivec3**, and **ivec4**, or arrays of these. The **f** variants should be used to provide values for uniform variables of type **float**, **vec2**, **vec3**, or **vec4**, or arrays of these. Either the **i** or the **f** variants can be used to provide values for uniform variables of type **bool**, **bvec2**, **bvec3**, and **bvec4** or arrays of these. The uniform variable is set to **false** if the input value is 0 or 0.0f, and it is set to **true** otherwise.

---

void **glUniform{1|2|3|4}{f|i}v**(GLint *location*,

GLuint *count*,

const *TYPE v*)

Sets the user-defined uniform variable or uniform variable array specified by *location* to the values specified by *v*. These commands pass a count and a pointer to the values to be loaded into a uniform variable or a uniform variable array. A count of 1 should be used for modifying the value of a single uniform variable, and a count of 1 or greater can be used to modify an array. The number specified in the name of the command specifies the number of components for each element in *v*, and it should match the number of components in the data type of the specified uniform variable (e.g., **1** for **float**, **int**, **bool**; **2** for **vec2**, **ivec2**, **bvec2**, etc.). The **v** in the command name indicates that a pointer to a vector of values is being passed. The **f** and **i** suffixes are defined in the same way as for the nonvector variants of **glUniform**.

For uniform variable arrays, each element of the array is considered to be of the type indicated in the name of the command (e.g., **glUniform3f** or **glUniform3fv** can be used to load a uniform variable array of type **vec3**). The number of elements of the uniform variable array to be modified is specified by *count*.

---

void **glUniformMatrix{2|3|4}fv**(GLint *location*,

GLuint *count*,

GLboolean *transpose*,

const GLfloat **v*)

Sets the user-defined uniform matrix variable or uniform matrix array variable specified by *location* to the values specified by *v*. The number in the command name is interpreted as the dimensionality of the matrix. The number **2** indicates a 2×2 matrix (i.e., 4 values), the number **3** indicates a 3×3 matrix (i.e., 9 values), and the number **4** indicates a 4×4 matrix (i.e., 16 values). If *transpose* is GL_FALSE, each matrix is assumed to be supplied in column major order. If transpose is GL_TRUE, each matrix is assumed to be supplied in row major order. The *count* argument specifies the number of matrices to be passed. A count of 1 should be used for modifying the value of a single matrix, and a count greater than 1 can be used to modify an array of matrices.

glUniform1i and **glUniform1iv** are the only two functions that can be used to load uniform variables defined as sampler types (see Section 7.9). Attempting to load a sampler with any other function results in an error.

Errors can also be generated by **glUniform** for any of the following reasons:

- If there is no current program object

- If *location* is an invalid uniform variable location for the current program object

- If the number of values specified by *count* would exceed the declared extent of the indicated uniform variable or uniform variable array

- Other than the preceding exceptions noted, if the type and size of the uniform variable as defined in the shader do not match the type and size specified in the name of the command used to load its value

In all of these cases, the indicated uniform variable will not be modified.

When the location of a user-defined uniform variable has been determined, the following command can be used to query its current value:

---

void **glGetUniformfv**(GLuint *program*,

  GLint *location*,

  GLfloat **params*)

void **glGetUniformiv**(GLuint *program*,

  GLint *location*,

  GLint **params*)

Return in *params* the value(s) of the specified uniform variable. The type of the uniform variable specified by *location* determines the number of values returned. If the uniform variable is defined in the shader as a **bool**, **int**, or **float**, a single value is returned. If it is defined as a **vec2**, **ivec2**, or **bvec2**, two values are returned. If it is defined as a **vec3**, **ivec3**, or **bvec3**, three values are returned, and so on. To query values stored in uniform variables declared as arrays, call **glGetUniform** for each element of the array. To query values stored in uniform variables declared as structures, call **glGetUniform** for each field in the structure. The values for uniform variables declared as a matrix are returned in column major order.

The locations assigned to uniform variables are not known until the program object is linked. After linking has occurred, the command **glGetUniformLocation** can obtain the location of a uniform variable. This location value can then be passed to **glGetUniform** to query the current value of the uniform variable. After a program object has been linked successfully, the index values for uniform variables remain fixed until the next link command occurs. The uniform variable values can be queried after a link only if the link was successful.

The location of a uniform variable cannot be used for anything other than specifying or querying that particular uniform variable. Say you declare a uniform variable as a structure that has three fields in succession that are defined as floats. If you call **glGetUniformLocation** to determine that the first of those three floats is at location n, do not assume that the next one is at location $n + 1$. It is possible to query the location of the ith element in an array. That value can then be passed to **glUniform** to load one or more values into the array, starting at the ith element of the array. It is not possible to take i and add an integer N and use the result to try to modify element $i + N$ in the array. The location of array element $i + N$ should be queried specifically before any attempt to set its value. These location values do not necessarily represent real memory locations. Applications that assume otherwise will not work.

For example, consider the following structure defined within a shader:

```
uniform struct
{
    struct
    {
        float a;
        float b[10];
    } c[2];
    vec2 d;
}   e;
```

and consider the following API calls that attempt to determine locations within that structure:

```
loc1 = glGetUniformLocation(progObj, "e.d");        // is valid
loc2 = glGetUniformLocation(progObj, "e.c[0]");     // is not valid
loc3 = glGetUniformLocation(progObj, "e.c[0].b") ;  // is valid
loc4 = glGetUniformLocation(progObj, "e.c[0].b[2]"); // is valid
```

The location *loc2* cannot be retrieved because *e.c[0]* references a structure.

Now consider the following commands to set parts of the uniform variable:

```
glUniform2f(loc1, 1.0f, 2.0f);     // is valid
glUniform2i(loc1, 1, 2);           // is not valid
glUniform1f(loc1, 1.0f);           // is not valid
glUniform1fv(loc3, 10, floatPtr);  // is valid
glUniform1fv(loc4, 10, floatPtr);  // is not valid
glUniform1fv(loc4, 8, floatPtr);   // is valid
```

The second command in the preceding list is invalid because *loc1* references a uniform variable of type **vec2**, not **ivec2**. The third command is invalid because *loc1* references a **vec2**, not a **float**. The fifth command in the preceding list is invalid because it attempts to set values that will exceed the length of the array.

Uniform variables (either built in or user defined) that can be accessed when a shader is executed are called ACTIVE UNIFORMS. You can think of this as though the process of compiling and linking is capable of deactivating uniform variables that are declared but never used. This provides more flexibility in coding style—modular code can define lots of uniform variables, and those that can be determined to be unused are typically optimized away.

To obtain the list of active uniform variables from a program object, use **glGetActiveUniform**. This command can be used by an application to query the uniform variables in a program object and set up user interface elements to allow direct manipulation of all the user-defined uniform values.

---

void **glGetActiveUniform**(GLuint *program,*

GLuint *index,*

GLsizei *bufSize,*

GLsizei **length,*

GLint **size,*

GLenum **type,*

GLchar **name*)

Returns information about an active uniform variable in the program object specified by program. The number of active uniform variables can be obtained by calling **glGetProgram** with the value GL_ACTIVE_UNIFORMS. A value of 0 for *index* selects the first active uniform variable. Permissible values for *index* range from 0 to the number of active uniform variables minus 1.

Shaders may use built-in uniform variables, user-defined uniform variables, or both. Built-in uniform variables have a prefix of *"gl_"* and reference existing OpenGL state or values derived from such state (e.g., *gl_Fog*, *gl_ModelViewMatrix*, etc.; see Section 4.3 for a complete list). User-defined uniform variables have arbitrary names and obtain their values from the application through calls to **glUniform.** A uniform variable (either built in or user defined) is considered active if it is determined during the link operation that it can be accessed during program execution. Therefore, *program* should have previously been the target of a call to **glLinkProgram,** but it is not necessary for it to have been linked successfully.

The size of the character buffer required to store the longest uniform variable name in *program* can be obtained by calling **glGetProgram** with the value GL_ACTIVE_UNIFORM_MAX_LENGTH. This value should be used to allocate a buffer of sufficient size to store the returned uniform variable name. The size of this character buffer is passed in *bufSize*, and a pointer to this character buffer is passed in *name*.

glGetActiveUniform returns the name of the uniform variable indicated by *index*, storing it in the character buffer specified by *name*. The string returned is null terminated. The actual number of characters written into this buffer is returned in *length*, and this count does not include the null termination character. If the length of the returned string is not required, a value of NULL can be passed in the *length* argument.

The *type* argument returns a pointer to the uniform variable's data type. One of the following symbolic constants may be returned: GL_FLOAT, GL_FLOAT_VEC2, GL_FLOAT_VEC3, GL_FLOAT_VEC4, GL_INT, GL_INT_VEC2, GL_INT_VEC3, GL_INT_VEC4, GL_BOOL, GL_BOOL_VEC2, GL_BOOL_VEC3, GL_BOOL_VEC4, GL_FLOAT_MAT2, GL_FLOAT_MAT3, GL_FLOAT_MAT4, GL_SAMPLER_1D, GL_SAMPLER_2D, GL_SAMPLER_3D, GL_SAMPLER_CUBE, GL_SAMPLER_1D_SHADOW, or GL_SAMPLER_2D_SHADOW.

If one or more elements of an array are active, the name of the array is returned in *name*, the type is returned in *type*, and the *size* parameter returns the highest array element index used, plus one, as determined by the compiler and linker. Only one active uniform variable will be reported for a uniform array.

Uniform variables that are declared as structures or arrays of structures are not returned directly by this function. Instead, each of these uniform variables is reduced to its fundamental components containing the "." and "[]" operators such that each of the names is valid as an argument to **glGetUniformLocation.** Each of these reduced uniform variables is counted as one active uniform variable and is assigned an index. A valid name cannot be a structure, an array of structures, or a subcomponent of a vector or matrix.

The size of the uniform variable is returned in *size.* Uniform variables other than arrays have a size of 1. Structures and arrays of structures are reduced as described earlier, such that each of the names returned will be a data type in the earlier list. If this reduction results in an array, the size returned is as described for uniform arrays; otherwise, the size returned is 1.

The list of active uniform variables may include both built-in uniform variables (which begin with the prefix "*gl_*") as well as user-defined uniform variable names.

This function returns as much information as it can about the specified active uniform variable. If no information is available, *length* is 0, and *name* is an empty string. This situation could occur if this function is called after a link operation that failed. If an error occurs, the return values *length*, *size*, *type*, and *name* are unmodified.

Using **glGetActiveUniform**, the application developer can programmatically query the uniform variables actually used in a shader and automatically create a user interface that allows the end user to modify those uniform variables. If among the shader writers there were some convention concerning the names of uniform variables, the user interface could be even more specific. For instance, any uniform variable name that ended with "Color" would be edited with the color selection tool. This function can also be useful when mixing and matching a set of vertex and fragment shaders designed to play well with each other, using a subset of known uniform variables. It can be much safer and less tedious to programmatically determine which uniform variables to send down than to hardcode all the combinations.

7.8.2 Named Uniform Blocks

OpenGL 3.1 adds named uniform blocks and the OpenGL Shading Language API to support them. Named uniform blocks are backed by uniform buffer objects. They can therefore be updated far more efficiently with buffer data commands or by mapping the buffer object. An entire uniform buffer object can also be changed rapidly by changing the buffer object bound to a uniform buffer binding point.

Sets of uniform variables (except uniforms of type sampler) can be grouped into named uniform blocks. For example, consider this named uniform block:

```
uniform MatrixBlock
{
    uniform mat4 MVmatrix;
    uniform mat4 MVPmatrix;
    uniform mat3 NormalMatrix;
};
```

The named uniform block is named **MatrixBlock**. It contains three uniforms added directly to the global namespace, **MVmatrix**, **MVPmatrix**, and **NormalMatrix**.

To update the value of a user-defined uniform variable in a named uniform block, an application needs to determine its offset and then specify its value. The offsets of uniform variables are assigned at link time and do not change until the next link operation occurs. Each time linking occurs, the locations of uniform variables may change, and so the application must query them again before setting them. First, the index of a named uniform block can be queried with the following command:

GLuint **glGetUniformBlockIndex**(GLuint *program*,

const GLchar **name*)

Returns the uniform block index for the uniform block named by *name* of the program object specified by *program*. If *name* does not identify an active uniform block, then GL_INVALID_INDEX is returned.

Information about the named uniform block can also be queried, including the number of active uniforms in the named uniform block, the indices of the active uniforms, and the size of the uniform buffer needed to back the named uniform block.

GLuint **glGetUniformBlockiv**(GLuint *program*,

GLuint *index*,

GLenum *pname*,

GLint **params*)

Returns in *params* the value of a uniform block parameter of the program object specified by *program*. Parameters and return values are summarized in Table 7.4. The uniform block to be queried is specified by *index*, and the parameter to be queried is specified by *pname*.

Table 7.4 Named uniform block parameters

Parameter	Operation
GL_UNIFORM_BLOCK_BINDING	*params* returns a single value that is the index of the uniform buffer binding point. The initial value is 0.
GL_UNIFORM_BLOCK_DATA_SIZE	*params* returns a single value that is the implementation-dependent minimum total buffer size in basic machine units.
GL_UNIFORM_BLOCK_NAME_LENGTH	*params* returns a single value that is the total length (including the null terminator) of the name of the uniform block.
GL_UNIFORM_BLOCK_ACTIVE_UNIFORMS	*params* returns a single value that is the number of active uniforms of the uniform block.
GL_UNIFORM_BLOCK_ACTIVE_UNIFORM_INDICES	*params* returns a list of the active uniform indices for the uniform block.

(continues)

Table 7.4 Named uniform block parameters, *continued*

Parameter	Operation
GL_UNIFORM_BLOCK_REFERENCED_BY_VERTEX_SHADER	*params* returns a single value that is nonzero (true) if the uniform block is referenced by the vertex shader and 0 (false) if it is not.
GL_UNIFORM_BLOCK_REFERENCED_BY_FRAGMENT_SHADER	*params* returns a single value that is nonzero (true) if the uniform block is referenced by the fragment shader and 0 (false) if it is not.

Information about each uniform in the named uniform block can then be queried, including their names and offsets. The application can collect the information needed to update the values of a buffer object.

GLuint **glGetActiveUniformsiv**(GLuint *program,*

GLsizei *count,*

const GLuint **indices,*

GLenum *pname,*

GLint **params*)

Returns in *params* information about the uniforms selected by *indices* of the program object specified by *program*. Parameters and return values are summarized in Table 7.5. The uniforms to be queried is specified by *pname*, and the parameter to be queried is specified by *pname*.

Table 7.5 Queriable active uniform parameters

Parameter	Operation
GL_UNIFORM_TYPE	*params* returns an array identifying the types of the uniforms specified by indices.
GL_UNIFORM_SIZE	*params* returns an array identifying the sizes of the uniforms specified by indices.
GL_UNIFORM_NAME_LENGTH	*params* returns an array identifying the lengths of the uniform names specified by indices.

Table 7.5 Queriable active uniform parameters, *continued*

Parameter	Operation
GL_UNIFORM_BLOCK_ INDEX	*params* returns an array identifying the uniform block index uniforms specified by indices. For uniforms in the default uniform block, –1 is returned.
GL_UNIFORM_OFFSET	*params* returns an array of uniform buffer offsets, in basic machine units, of the uniforms specified by indices. For uniforms in the default uniform block, –1 is returned.
GL_UNIFORM_ARRAY_ STRIDE	*params* returns an array identifying the stride between elements, in basic machine units, of the uniforms specified by indices. For uniforms in the default uniform block, –1 is returned. For uniforms that are not arrays, 0 is returned.
GL_UNIFORM_MATRIX_ STRIDE	*params* returns an array identifying the stride between elements, in basic machine units, of the uniforms specified by indices. For uniforms in the default uniform block, –1 is returned. For uniforms that are not matrices, 0 is returned.
GL_UNIFORM_MATRIX_IS_ ROW_MAJOR	*params* returns an array identifying whether the matrix is a row-major matrix. A value of 1 indicates a row-major matrix. A value of 0 indicates a column-major matrix, a matrix in the default uniform block, or a nonmatrix.

After linking a shader, each named uniform block may be bound to a uniform buffer binding point.

---

void **glUniformBlockBinding**(GLuint *program*,
                               GLuint *index*,
                               GLuint binding)

The binding point *bind* is assigned to the named uniform block selected by *index* of the program object specified by *program*. The *index* must be an active named uniform block of the program object, otherwise INVALID_ VALUE is generated.

7.9 Samplers

glUniform1i and **glUniform1iv** load uniform variables defined as sampler types (i.e., uniform variables of type **sampler1D**, **sampler2D**, **sample3D**, **samplerCube**, **sampler1DShadow**, or **sampler2DShadow**). They may be declared within either vertex shaders or fragment shaders.

The value contained in a sampler is used within a shader to access a particular texture map. The value loaded into the sampler by the application should be the number of the texture unit to be used to access the texture. For vertex shaders, this value should be less than the implementation-dependent constant GL_MAX_VERTEX_TEXTURE_IMAGE_UNITS, which can be queried with **glGet**. For fragment shaders, this value should be less than the implementation-dependent constant GL_MAX_TEXTURE_IMAGE_UNITS.

The suffix on the sampler type indicates the texture type to be accessed: 1D, 2D, 3D, cube map, 1D shadow, or 2D shadow. In OpenGL, a texture object of each of the first four texture types can be bound to a single texture unit, and this suffix allows the desired texture object to be chosen. A 1D shadow sampler is used to access the 1D texture when depth comparisons are enabled, and a 2D shadow sampler is used to access the 2D texture when depth comparisons are enabled. If two uniform variables of different sampler types contain the same value, an error is generated when the next rendering command is issued. Attempting to load a sampler with any command other than **glUniform1i** or **glUniform1iv** results in an error being generated.

From within a shader, samplers should be considered an opaque data type. The current API provides a way of specifying an integer representing the texture image unit to be used. In the future, the API may be extended to allow a sampler to refer directly to a texture object.

Samplers that can be accessed when a program is executed are called ACTIVE SAMPLERS. The link operation fails if it determines that the number of active samplers exceeds the maximum allowable limits. The number of active samplers permitted on the vertex processor is specified by GL_MAX_VERTEX_TEXTURE_IMAGE_UNITS, the number of active samplers permitted on the fragment processor is specified by GL_MAX_TEXTURE_IMAGE_UNITS, and the number of active samplers permitted on both processors combined is GL_COMBINED_TEXTURE_IMAGE_UNITS.

More detail on using samplers within a shader is provided in Section 10.1.

7.10 Multiple Render Targets

Another feature added to OpenGL in version 2.0 was the ability to render into multiple buffers simultaneously. The OpenGL Shading Language makes provisions for this capability with user-defined fragment shader out variables. The number of data buffers that may be written by a fragment shader is implementation dependent but must be at least 4.

With this capability, applications can develop fragment shaders that compute multiple values for each fragment and store them in offscreen memory. These values can be accessed during a future rendering pass. Among other things, this lets applications implement complex multipass algorithms and use the graphics hardware for general-purpose computation.

To set up OpenGL for rendering into multiple target buffers, use

---

void **glDrawBuffers**(GLsizei *n*,

const GLenum **bufs*)

Defines an array of buffers into which fragment color values or fragment data will be written. If a fragment shader is active and it writes values to the user-defined out variables, then those values are written into the buffers specified by *bufs*.

The symbolic constants contained in *bufs* are defined in Table 7.6. Except for GL_NONE, none of the symbolic constants may appear more than once in *bufs*. The maximum number of draw buffers supported is implementation dependent and can be queried by calling **glGet** with the argument GL_MAX_DRAW_BUFFERS.

Table 7.6 Buffer names for use with the **glDrawBuffers** call

Parameter	Operation
GL_NONE	The fragment color/data value is not written into any color buffer.
GL_COLOR_ATTACHMENT*i*	The fragment color/data value is written into the draw buffer specified by GL_COLOR_ATTACHMENT*i*.

An error is generated if **glDrawBuffers** specifies a buffer that does not exist in the current GL context.

User-defined fragment shader out variables may be bound to data buffers with the following command:

---

void **glBindFragDataLocation**(GLuint *program,*

GLuint *index,*

const GLchar **name)*

The user-defined out variable *name* is assigned to the draw buffer selected by *index* of the program object specified by *program.* The *index* must be an active user-defined out variable of the program object, otherwise INVALID_ VALUE is generated.

---

void **glDrawBuffers**(GLsizei *n,*

const GLenum **bufs)*

Defines an array of buffers into which fragment color values or fragment data will be written. If a fragment shader is active and it writes values to the user-defined out variables, then those values are written into the buffers specified by *bufs.*

The symbolic constants contained in *bufs* are defined in Table 7.6. Except for GL_NONE, none of the symbolic constants may appear more than once in *bufs.* The maximum number of draw buffers supported is implementation dependent and can be queried by calling **glGet** with the argument GL_MAX_DRAW_BUFFERS.

7.11 Development Aids

A situation that can be difficult to diagnose is one in which a program may fail to execute because of the value of a sampler variable. These variables can be changed anytime between linking and program execution. To ensure robust behavior, OpenGL implementations must do some runtime checking just before the shader is executed (i.e., when a rendering operation is about to occur). At this point, the only way to report an error is to set the OpenGL error flag, and this is not usually something that applications check at this performance-critical juncture.

To provide more information when these situations occur, the OpenGL Shading Language API defines a new function that can be called to perform this runtime check explicitly and provide diagnostic information.

---

void **glValidateProgram**(GLuint *program*)

Checks whether the executables contained in *program* can execute given the current OpenGL state. The information generated by the validation process is stored in *program*'s information log. The validation information may consist of an empty string, or it may be a string containing information about how the current program object interacts with the rest of current OpenGL state. This function provides a way for OpenGL implementors to convey more information about why the current program is inefficient, suboptimal, failing to execute, and so on.

The status of the validation operation is stored as part of the program object's state. This value is set to GL_TRUE if the validation succeeded and GL_FALSE otherwise. It can be queried by calling **glGetProgram** with arguments *program* and GL_VALIDATE_STATUS. If validation is successful, *program* is guaranteed to execute given the current state. Otherwise, *program* is guaranteed to not execute.

This function is typically useful only during application development. The informational string stored in the information log is completely implementation dependent. Therefore, an application should not expect different OpenGL implementations to produce identical information strings.

Because the operations described in this section can severely hinder performance, they should be used only during application development and removed before shipment of the production version of the application.

7.12 Implementation-Dependent API Values

Some of the features we've described in previous sections have implementation-dependent limits. All of the implementation-dependent values in the OpenGL Shading Language API are defined in the list that follows, and all of them can be queried with **glGet**. Several implementation-dependent values were raised in OpenGL 3.0.

GL_MAX_COMBINED_TEXTURE_IMAGE_UNITS—Defines the total number of hardware units that can be used to access texture maps from the vertex processor and the fragment processor combined. The minimum legal value is 32.

GL_MAX_DRAW_BUFFERS—Defines the maximum number of buffers that can be written into from within a single fragment shader using out variables. The minimum legal value is 8. (The limit prior to OpenGL 3.0 was 1.)

GL_MAX_FRAGMENT_UNIFORM_COMPONENTS—Defines the number of components (i.e., floating-point values) that are available for fragment shader uniform variables. The minimum legal value is 1024 (was 64).

GL_MAX_TEXTURE_IMAGE_UNITS—Defines the total number of hardware units that can be used to access texture maps from the fragment processor. The minimum legal value is 16 (was 2).

GL_MAX_VARYING_COMPONENTS—Defines the number of components available for varying variables, the out variables in the vertex shader, and the matching in variables in the fragment shader. The minimum legal value is 64 (was 32 floating-point values).

GL_MAX_VERTEX_ATTRIBS—Defines the number of active vertex attributes that are available. The minimum legal value is 16.

GL_MAX_VERTEX_TEXTURE_IMAGE_UNITS—Defines the number of hardware units that can be used to access texture maps from the vertex processor. The minimum legal value is 16 (was 0).

GL_MAX_VERTEX_UNIFORM_COMPONENTS—Defines the number of components (i.e., floating-point values) that are available for vertex shader default uniform block. The minimum legal value is 1024 (was 512).

Several implementation-dependent values are new in OpenGL 3.1.

GL_MAX_CLIP_DISTANCES—Defines the number of clip distances that are available per program. The minimum legal value is 8.

GL_MAX_COMBINED_UNIFORM_BLOCKS—Defines the number of uniform blocks that are available per program. The minimum legal value is 24.

GL_MAX_FRAGMENT_UNIFORM_BLOCKS—Defines the number of fragment uniform blocks that are available per program. The minimum legal value is 12.

GL_MAX_VERTEX_UNIFORM_BLOCKS—Defines the number of vertex uniform blocks that are available per program. The minimum legal value is 12.

GL_MAX_UNIFORM_BLOCK_SIZE—Defines the size in basic-machine units (usually bytes) of a uniform block. The minimum legal value is 16384.

7.13 Application Code for Brick Shaders

Each shader is going to be a little bit different. Each vertex shader may use a different set of attribute variables or different uniform variables, attribute variables may be bound to different generic vertex attribute index values, and so on. One of the demo programs whose source code is available for download from the 3Dlabs Web site is called **ogl2brick**. It is a small, clear example of how to create and use a vertex shader and a fragment shader. The code in **ogl2brick** was derived from an earlier demo program called **ogl2demo**, written primarily by Barthold Lichtenbelt with contributions from several others. In **ogl2brick** an "install" function installs the brick shaders that were presented in Chapter 6. We discuss that shader installation function, but first we define a simple function that make it a little easier to set the values of uniform variables.

```
GLint getUniLoc(GLuint program, const GLchar *name)
{
    GLint loc;

    loc = glGetUniformLocation(program, name);

    if (loc == -1)
        printf("No such uniform named \"%s\"\n", name);

    printOpenGLError();  // Check for OpenGL errors
    return loc;
}
```

Shaders are passed to OpenGL as strings. For our shader installation function, we assume that each of the shaders has been defined as a single string, and pointers to those strings are passed to the following function. This function does all the work to load, compile, link, and install our brick shaders. The function definition and local variables for this function are declared as follows:

```
int installBrickShaders(const GLchar *brickVertex,
                        const GLchar *brickFragment)
{
    GLuint brickVS, brickFS, brickProg;   // handles to objects
    GLint  vertCompiled, fragCompiled;    // status values
    GLint  linked;
```

The argument *brickVertex* contains a pointer to the string containing the source code for the brick vertex shader, and the argument *brickFragment* contains a pointer to the source code for the brick fragment shader. Next, we declare variables to refer to three OpenGL objects: a shader object that stores and compiles the brick vertex shader, a second shader object that stores and compiles the brick fragment shader, and a program object to which the shader objects will be attached. Flags to indicate the status of the compile and link operations are defined next.

The first step is to create two empty shader objects, one for the vertex shader and one for the fragment shader.

```
brickVS = glCreateShader(GL_VERTEX_SHADER);
brickFS = glCreateShader(GL_FRAGMENT_SHADER);
```

Source code can be loaded into the shader objects after they have been created. The shader objects are empty, and we have a single null-terminated string containing the source code for each shader, so we can call **glShaderSource** as follows:

```
glShaderSource(brickVS, 1, &brickVertex, NULL);
glShaderSource(brickFS, 1, &brickFragment, NULL);
```

The shaders are now ready to be compiled. For each shader, we call **glCompileShader** and then call **glGetShader** to see what transpired. **glCompileShader** sets the shader object's GL_COMPILE_STATUS parameter to GL_TRUE if it succeeded and GL_FALSE otherwise. Regardless of whether the compilation succeeded or failed, we print the information log for the shader. If the compilation was unsuccessful, this log will have information about the compilation errors. If the compilation was successful, this log may still have useful information that would help us improve the shader in some way. You would typically check the info log only during application development or after running a shader for the first time on a new platform. The function exits if the compilation of either shader fails.

```
glCompileShader(brickVS);
printOpenGLError();  // Check for OpenGL errors
glGetShaderiv(brickVS, GL_COMPILE_STATUS, &vertCompiled);
printShaderInfoLog(brickVS);

glCompileShader(brickFS);
printOpenGLError();  // Check for OpenGL errors
glGetShaderiv(brickFS, GL_COMPILE_STATUS, &fragCompiled);
printShaderInfoLog(brickFS);

if (!vertCompiled || !fragCompiled)
    return 0;
```

This section of code uses the **printShaderInfoLog** function that we defined previously.

At this point, the shaders have been compiled successfully, and we're almost ready to try them out. First, the shader objects need to be attached to a program object so that they can be linked.

```
brickProg = glCreateProgram();
glAttachShader(brickProg, brickVS);
glAttachShader(brickProg, brickFS);
```

The program object is linked with **glLinkProgram**. Again, we look at the information log of the program object regardless of whether the link succeeded or failed. There may be useful information for us if we've never tried this shader before.

```
glLinkProgram(brickProg);
printOpenGLError();  // Check for OpenGL errors
glGetProgramiv(brickProg, GL_LINK_STATUS, &linked);
printProgramInfoLog(brickProg);

if (!linked)
    return 0;
```

If we make it to the end of this code, we have a valid program that can become part of current state simply by calling **glUseProgram**.

```
glUseProgram(brickProg);
```

Before returning from this function, we also want to initialize the values of the uniform variables used in the two shaders. To obtain the location that was assigned by the linker, we query the uniform variable by name, using the **getUniLoc** function defined previously. Then we use that location to immediately set the initial value of the uniform variable.

```
glUniform3f(getUniLoc(brickProg, "BrickColor"), 1.0, 0.3, 0.2);
glUniform3f(getUniLoc(brickProg, "MortarColor"), 0.85, 0.86, 0.84);
glUniform2f(getUniLoc(brickProg, "BrickSize"), 0.30, 0.15);
glUniform2f(getUniLoc(brickProg, "BrickPct"), 0.90, 0.85);
glUniform3f(getUniLoc(brickProg, "LightPosition"), 0.0, 0.0, 4.0);

return 1;
}
```

When this function returns, the application is ready to draw geometry that will be rendered with our brick shaders. The result of rendering some simple objects with this application code and the shaders described in Chapter 6 is shown in Figure 6.6. The complete C function is shown in Listing 7.3.

Listing 7.3 C function for installing brick shaders

```
int installBrickShaders(const GLchar *brickVertex,
                        const GLchar *brickFragment)
{

    GLuint brickVS, brickFS, brickProg;  // handles to objects
    GLint  vertCompiled, fragCompiled;   // status values
    GLint  linked;

    // Create a vertex shader object and a fragment shader object
```

```
brickVS = glCreateShader(GL_VERTEX_SHADER);
brickFS = glCreateShader(GL_FRAGMENT_SHADER);

// Load source code strings into shaders

glShaderSource(brickVS, 1, &brickVertex, NULL);
glShaderSource(brickFS, 1, &brickFragment, NULL);

// Compile the brick vertex shader and print out
// the compiler log file.

glCompileShader(brickVS);
printOpenGLError();  // Check for OpenGL errors
glGetShaderiv(brickVS, GL_COMPILE_STATUS, &vertCompiled);
printShaderInfoLog(brickVS);

// Compile the brick fragment shader and print out
// the compiler log file.

glCompileShader(brickFS);
printOpenGLError();  // Check for OpenGL errors
glGetShaderiv(brickFS, GL_COMPILE_STATUS, &fragCompiled);
printShaderInfoLog(brickFS);

if (!vertCompiled || !fragCompiled)
    return 0;

// Create a program object and attach the two compiled shaders

brickProg = glCreateProgram();
glAttachShader(brickProg, brickVS);
glAttachShader(brickProg, brickFS);

// Bind user-defined in variable to vertex attribute

glBindVertexAttrib( brickProg, 1, "MCvertex");
glBindVertexAttrib( brickProg, 2, "MCnormal");

// Bind user-defined out variable to data buffer

glBindFragData( brickProg, 0, "FragColor");"

// Link the program object and print out the info log

glLinkProgram(brickProg);
printOpenGLError();  // Check for OpenGL errors
glGetProgramiv(brickProg, GL_LINK_STATUS, &linked);
printProgramInfoLog(brickProg);

if (!linked)
    return 0;
```

```
// Install program object as part of current state

glUseProgram(brickProg);

// Set up initial uniform values

glUniform3f(getUniLoc(brickProg, "BrickColor"), 1.0, 0.3, 0.2);
glUniform3f(getUniLoc(brickProg, "MortarColor"), 0.85, 0.86, 0.84);
glUniform2f(getUniLoc(brickProg, "BrickSize"), 0.30, 0.15);
glUniform2f(getUniLoc(brickProg, "BrickPct"), 0.90, 0.85);
glUniform3f(getUniLoc(brickProg, "LightPosition"), 0.0, 0.0, 4.0);

    return 1;
}
```

7.14 Summary

The set of function calls added to OpenGL to create and manipulate shaders is actually quite small. The interface mimics the software development process followed by a C/C++ programmer. To install and use OpenGL shaders, do the following:

1. Create one or more (empty) shader objects with **glCreateShader**.

2. Provide source code for these shaders with **glShaderSource**.

3. Compile each of the shaders with **glCompileShader**.

4. Create a program object with **glCreateProgram**.

5. Attach all the shader objects to the program object with **glAttachShader**.

6. Link the program object with **glLinkProgram**.

7. Install the executable program as part of OpenGL's current state with **glUseProgram**.

8. If the shaders uses the default uniform block, query the locations of uniform variables with **glGetUniformLocation** and then set their values with **glUniform**.

9. If the shaders use named uniform blocks, query the uniform block information with **glGetUniformBlockIndex** and **glGetActiveUniformBlockiv**. Query the offsets of the uniform variables within the uniform block with **glGetActiveUniformsiv**. The uniform blocks are associated with buffer object binding points with **glUniformBlockBinding**, and buffer objects are bound to those binding points with **glBindBufferRange**.

10. If the vertex shader uses user-defined in variables, the application must provide values for them, using OpenGL API calls that place attribute values in generic, numbered vertex attribute locations. Before such attribute data is passed to the shader, the index of the generic vertex attribute should be associated with an in variable in a vertex shader in one of two ways. Applications can create this association explicitly by calling **glBindAttribLocation** before linking. Alternatively, if no explicit association is made, OpenGL makes these associations automatically during linking. An application can query the assignment that was made with **glGetAttribLocation**. Thereafter, generic vertex attributes can be passed to a vertex shader with **glVertexAttrib** or with **glVertexAttribPointer** and **glEnableVertexArrayPointer** in conjunction with standard OpenGL commands to draw vertex arrays.

11. If the fragment shader uses user-defined out variables, the application may create an association between a user-defined out variable and a fragment data index with **glBindFragDataLocation** before linking. Alternatively, if no explicit association is made, OpenGL makes these associations automatically during linking. An application can query the assignment that was made with **glGetFragDataLocation**.

12. An application may optionally record vertex shader out variables to one or more transform feedback buffers. Before vertex shader out variables are recorded, the vertex shader out variables are associated with feedback buffer binding points with **glTransformFeedbackVarying**, and buffer objects are bound to those binding points with **glBindBufferRange**.

A number of query functions obtain information about shader and program objects.

7.15 Further Information

Reference pages for the OpenGL Shading Language API can be found in Appendix B. Source code for the example in this chapter can be found at the 3Dlabs developer Web site. More complex source code examples and a variety of shaders can be found there as well.

[1] *Former 3Dlabs developer Web site.* Now at http://3dshaders.com.

[2] Ebert, David S., John Hart, Bill Mark, F. Kenton Musgrave, Darwyn Peachey, Ken Perlin, and Steven Worley, *Texturing and Modeling: A Procedural Approach, Third Edition*, Morgan Kaufmann Publishers, San Francisco, 2002. www.texturingandmodeling.com

[3] Kessenich, John, Dave Baldwin, and Randi Rost, *The OpenGL Shading Language, Version 1.40*, 3Dlabs/Intel, March 2008. http://www.opengl.org/documentation/specs/

[4] OpenGL Architecture Review Board, *OpenGL Reference Manual, Fourth Edition: The Official Reference to OpenGL, Version 1.4*, Editor: Dave Shreiner, Addison-Wesley, Reading, Massachusetts, 2004.

[5] Segal, Mark, and Kurt Akeley, *The OpenGL Graphics System: A Specification (Version 3.1)*, Editor (v1.1): Chris Frazier, (v1.2–3.1): Jon Leech, (v2.0): Jon Leech and Pat Brown, March 2008. www.opengl.org/documentation/spec.html

[6] Shreiner, Dave, and the Khronos OpenGL ARB Working Group, *OpenGL Programming Guide, Seventh Edition: The Official Guide to Learning OpenGL, Versions 3.0 and 3.1*, Addison-Wesley, Boston, Massachusetts, 2010.

Chapter 8

Shader Development

At the time of this writing, several shader development tools for the OpenGL Shading Language are available. There are some specialized tools for shader development, notably, AMD's RenderMonkey and Apple's GLSLEditorSample. More generalized tools for OpenGL development such as Graphic Remedy's gDEBugger are now adding significant support for debugging shaders. A whole ecosystem of tools for shader development is beginning to arise.

This chapter sets forth some ideas on the shader development process and describes the tools that are currently available. Both general software development techniques and techniques that are unique to shader development are discussed.

8.1 General Principles

Shader development can be thought of as another form of software engineering; therefore, existing software engineering principles and practices should be brought into play when you are developing shaders. Spend some time designing the shader before writing any code. The design should aim to keep things as simple as possible while still getting the job done. If the shader is part of a larger shader development effort, take care to design the shader for reliability and reuse.

In short, you should treat shader development the same as you would any other software development tasks, allocating appropriate amounts of time for design, implementation, testing, and documentation.

Here are a few more useful thoughts for developing shaders. Consider these to be friendly advice and not mandates. There will be situations in which some of these shader development suggestions make sense and others in which they do not.

8.1.1 Understand the Problem

It is worth reminding yourself periodically that you will be most successful at developing shaders if you understand the problem before you write any of the shader code. The first step is to make sure you understand the rendering algorithm you plan on implementing. If your aim is to develop a shader for bump mapping, make sure you understand the necessary mathematics before plunging into coding. It is usually easier to think things through with a pencil and paper and get the details straight in your mind before you begin to write code.

Because the tools for developing shaders are currently less powerful than those for developing code intended to run on the CPU, you might consider implementing a simulation of your algorithm on the CPU before coding it in the OpenGL Shading Language. Doing this will let you use the powerful debugging tools available for typical software development, single-step through source code, set breakpoints, and really watch your code in action.

8.1.2 Add Complexity Progressively

Many shaders depend on a combination of details to achieve the desired effect. Develop your shader in such a way that you implement and test the largest and most important details first and add progressive complexity after the basic shader is working. For instance, you may want to develop a shader that combines effects from noise with values read from several texture maps and then performs some unique lighting effects. You can approach this task in a couple of different ways. One way would be to get your unique lighting effects working first with a simple shading model. After testing this part of the shader, you can add the effects from reading the texture maps and thoroughly test again. After this, you can add the noise effects, again, testing as you proceed.

In this way, you have reduced a large development task into several smaller ones. After a task has been successfully completed and tested, move on to the next task.

8.1.3 Test and Iterate

Sometimes it is impossible to visualize ahead of time the effect a shader will have. This is particularly true when you are dealing with mathematical functions that are complex or hard to visualize, such as noise. In this case, you may want to parameterize your algorithm and modify the parameters systematically. You can take notes as you modify the parameters and observe the effect. These observations will be useful comments in the shader source, providing insight for someone who might come along later and want to tweak the shader in a different direction.

After you have found a set of parameters that gives you the desired effect, you can consider simplifying the shader by removing some of the "tweakable" parameters and replacing them with constants. This may make your shader less flexible, but it may make it easier for someone coming along later to understand.

8.1.4 Strive for Simplicity

There's a lot to be said for simplicity. Simple shaders are easier to understand and easier to maintain. There's often more than one algorithm for achieving the effect you want. Have you chosen the simplest one? There's often more than one way to implement a particular algorithm. Have you chosen the language features that let you express the algorithm in the simplest way possible?

8.1.5 Exploit Modularity

The OpenGL Shading Language and its API support modular shaders, so take advantage of this capability. Use the principle of "divide and conquer" to develop small, simple modules that are designed to work together. Your lighting modules might all be interchangeable and offer support for standard light source types as well as custom lighting modules. You may also have fog modules that offer a variety of fog effects. If you do things right, you can mix and match any of your lighting modules with any of your fog modules. You can apply this principle to other aspects of shader computation, both for vertex shaders and for fragment shaders.

8.2 Performance Considerations

After you have done all the right things from a software engineering stand-point, your shader may or may not have acceptable performance. Here are some ideas for eking out better performance from your carefully crafted shader.

8.2.1 Consider Computational Frequency

Shading computations can occur in three areas: on the CPU, on the vertex processor, and on the fragment processor. It is tempting to put most of your shader computation in the fragment shader because this is executed for every pixel that is drawn, and you will, therefore, get the highest-quality image. But if performance is a concern, you may be able to identify computations that can be done with acceptable quality per vertex instead of per fragment. By moving the computation to the vertex shader, you can make your fragment shader faster. In some cases, there may be no visible difference between doing the computation in the vertex shader versus doing it in the fragment shader. This might be the case with fog computations, for example.

One way to think about the problem is to implement rapidly changing characteristics in the fragment shader and to implement characteristics that don't change as rapidly in the vertex shader. For instance, diffuse lighting effects change slowly over a surface and so can usually be computed with sufficient quality in the vertex shader. Specular lighting effects might need to be implemented in the fragment shader to achieve high quality. If a particular value changes linearly across an object's surface, you can get the same result by computing the value per vertex and interpolating it as you would by computing the value at each fragment. In this case, you may as well have the vertex shader do the computation. Unless you are rendering very small triangles, your fragment shader will execute far more times than your vertex shader will, so it is more efficient to do the computation in the vertex shader.

Similarly, you may be able to find computations that can be done once on the CPU and remain constant for a great many executions of your vertex shader or fragment shader. You can often save shader instruction space or improve shader performance (or both) by precomputing values in your application code and passing them to your shader as uniform variables. Sometimes you can spot these things by analyzing your shader code. If you pass *length* in as a uniform variable and your shader always computes

sqrt(*length*), you're better off doing the computation once on the host CPU and passing that value to your shader rather than computing the value for every execution of your shader. If your shader needs both *length* and **sqrt**(*length*), you can pass both values in as uniform variables.

Deciding where to perform computation also involves knowing where the computational bottleneck occurs for a particular rendering operation. You just need to speed up the slowest part of the system to see an improvement in performance. Conversely, you shouldn't spend time improving the performance of something that isn't a bottleneck, because you won't see the gain in performance anyway.

8.2.2 Analyze Your Algorithm

You can often make your shader more efficient just by understanding the math it uses. For instance, you might want to limit the range of the variable *finalcolor* to [0,1]. But if you know that you are adding values only to compute this variable and the values that you're adding are always positive, there's really no need to check the result against 0. An instruction like **min**(*finalcolor*, 1.0) clamps the result at 1.0, and this instruction likely has higher performance than an instruction like **clamp**(*finalcolor*, 0.0, 1.0) because it needs only to compare values against one number instead of two. If you define the valid range of all the variables in your shader, you can more easily see the boundary conditions that you need to handle.

8.2.3 Use the Built-in Functions

Whenever possible, use the built-in functions to implement the effect that you're trying to achieve. Built-in functions are intended to be implemented in an optimal way by the graphics hardware vendor. If your shader hand-codes the same effect as a built-in function, there's little chance that it will be faster than the built-in function but a good chance that it will be slower.

8.2.4 Use Vectors

The OpenGL Shading Language lets you express vector computations naturally, and underlying graphics hardware is often built to operate simultaneously on a vector of values. Therefore, you should take advantage of this and use vectors for calculations whenever possible. On the other hand, you shouldn't use vectors that are bigger than the computations require. Such use can waste registers, hardware interpolators (in the case of varying variables), processing bandwidth, or memory bandwidth.

8.2.5 Use Textures to Encode Complex Functions

Because fragment processing is now programmable, textures can be used for a lot more than just image data. You might want to consider storing a complex function in a texture and doing a single lookup rather than a complex computation within the fragment shader. This is illustrated in Chapter 15, in which we encode a noise function as a 3D texture. This approach takes advantage of the specialized high-performance hardware that performs texture access, and it can also take advantage of texture filtering hardware to interpolate between values encoded in the texture.

8.2.6 Review the Information Logs

One of the main ways that an OpenGL implementation can provide feedback to an application developer is through the shader object and program object information logs (see Section 7.6). During shader development, you should review the messages in the information logs for compiler and linker errors, but you should also review them to see if they include any performance or functionality warnings or other descriptive messages. These information logs are one of the primary ways for OpenGL implementations to convey implementation-dependent information about performance, resource limitations, and so on.

8.3 Shader Debugging

Shader development tools are in their infancy, so debugging shaders can be a difficult task. Here are a few practical tips that may be helpful as you try to debug your shaders.

8.3.1 Use the Vertex Shader Output

To determine whether vertex shader code is behaving as expected, you can use conditionals to test intermediate values to see if a value is something unexpected. If it is, you can modify one of the shader's output values so that a visually distinct change occurs. For instance, if you think that the value *foo* should never be greater than 5.0, you can set the color values that are being passed to the fragment shader to magenta or neon green if the value of *foo* exceeds 5.0. If that's not distinctive enough and you've already computed the transformed homogeneous position, you can do something like this:

```
if (foo > 5.0)
    gl_Position += 1.0;
```

This code adds 1 to each component of the transformed position for which *foo* was greater than 5. When it is executed, you should see the object shift on the screen. With this approach, you can systematically check your assumptions about the intermediate values being generated by the vertex shader.

8.3.2 Use the Fragment Shader Output

Fragment shaders can produce a fragment color, a fragment depth, or an array of fragment data values. You can use the **discard** keyword to prevent the computed fragment value from updating the framebuffer. The depth value may not be helpful during debugging, but you can either color-code your fragment colors or use the **discard** keyword to discard fragments with certain qualities. These techniques provide you with visual feedback about what's going on within the shader.

For instance, if you're not quite sure if your 2D texture coordinates span the whole range from 0 to 1.0, you could put an **if** test in the shader and discard fragments with certain qualities. You can discard all the fragments for which both *s* and *t* texture coordinates are greater than 0.5 or for which either coordinate is greater than 0.99, and so on. The model will be drawn with "missing" pixels where fragments were discarded. The **discard** keyword is quite useful because it can appear anywhere in a fragment shader. You can put the discard statement near the beginning of a complex fragment shader and gradually move it down in the code as you verify that things are working properly.

Similarly, you can assign values to *FragColor* that convey debugging information. If you have a mathematical function in your shader that is expected to range from [0,1] and average 0.5, you can assign solid green to *FragColor* if the value is less than 0, solid red if it is between 0 and 0.5, solid blue if it is between 0.5 and 1.0, and solid white if it is greater than 1.0. This kind of debugging information can quickly tell you whether a certain computation is going astray.

8.3.3 Use Simple Geometry

For debugging texture computations, it may be useful to render a single large rectangle with identity matrices for the modeling, viewing, and projection matrices and to look carefully at what is occurring. Use a distinct texture image, for example, color bars or a simple color gradient ramp (yellow to blue perhaps), so that you can visually verify that the texturing operation is occurring as you expect it to.

8.4 Shader Development Tools

In coming years, we should see some exciting advances in the area of tools for shader development. This section briefly describes shader development tools available at the time of this writing.

8.4.1 RenderMonkey

As the era of programmable graphics hardware has unfolded, we've learned that there is more to developing shaders than just developing the code for the shaders themselves. Shaders can be highly customized to the point that they may work as intended only on a single model. Shader source code, textures, geometry, and initial values for uniform variables are all important parts of a production-quality shader. Shader development tools must capture all the essential elements of a shader and allow these elements to easily be modified and maintained.

Another factor in shader development is that the person writing the shader is not necessarily the same person developing the application code that deploys the shader. Often, an artist will be employed to design textures and contribute to or even control the shader development process. The collaboration between the artist and programmer is an important one for entertainment-based applications and must be supported by shader development tools.

An integrated development environment (IDE) allows programmers and artists to develop and experiment with shaders outside the environment of the application. This reduces the complexity of the shader development task and encourages rapid prototyping and experimentation. Finished shaders are a form of intellectual property, and maintenance, portability, and easy deployment to a variety of platforms are essential to maximizing the benefit of this type of company asset. The idea behind an IDE is that all the essential elements of the finished shader can be encapsulated, managed, shared, and exported for use in the final application.

ATI first released an IDE called RenderMonkey in 2002. In its initial release, RenderMonkey supported shader development for DirectX vertex shaders and pixel shaders. However, RenderMonkey was architected in such a way that it could easily be extended to support other shader programming languages. In 2004, ATI and 3Dlabs collaborated to produce the first version of RenderMonkey that added support for high-level shader development in OpenGL with the OpenGL Shading Language. In 2006, AMD and ATI merged, and RenderMonkey continues to evolve, adding OpenGL ES Shading Language development. The RenderMonkey IDE is currently available for free from AMD's developer Web site, http://developer.amd.com/.

RenderMonkey was designed for extensibility. At its core is a flexible framework that allows easy incorporation of shading languages. It is an environment that is language agnostic, allowing any high-level shading language to be supported by means of plug-ins. It currently supports the pixel shaders and vertex shaders defined in Microsoft's DirectX 8.1 and 9.0, the High-Level Shader Language (HLSL) defined in DirectX 9.0, the OpenGL Shading Language, and the OpenGL ES Shading Language.

In RenderMonkey, the encapsulation of all the information necessary to re-create a shading effect is called an EFFECT WORKSPACE. An effect workspace consists of effects group nodes, variable nodes, and stream mapping nodes. Each effects group is made up of one or more effect nodes, and each effect node is made up of one or more rendering passes. Each rendering pass may contain rendering state, source code for a vertex shader, source code for a fragment shader, geometry, and textures. All the effect data is organized into a tree hierarchy that is visible in the workspace viewer.

Effects group nodes collect related effects into a single container. This is sometimes handy for taming the complexity of dealing with lots of different effects. You might also use an effects group as a container for several similar effects with different performance characteristics (for instance, "best quality," "fast," and "fastest"). The criteria for grouping things within effects groups is entirely up to you.

Effect nodes encompass all the information needed to implement a real-time visual effect. The effect may be composed of multiple passes. Starting state is inherited from a default effect to provide a known starting state for all effects. The default effect can store effect data that is common to all shading effects.

Pass nodes define a drawing operation (i.e., a rendering pass). Each pass inherits data from previous passes within the effect, and the first pass inherits from the default effect. A typical pass contains a vertex shader and fragment shader pair, a render state block, textures, geometry, and nodes of other types (for example, variable nodes). Different geometry can be used in each pass to render effects like fur.

Variable nodes define the parameters that are available from within a shader. For the OpenGL Shading Language, variable nodes are the mechanisms for defining uniform variables. Intuitive names and types can be assigned to variable nodes, and the contents of a variable node can be manipulated with a GUI widget.

RenderMonkey is built completely out of plug-ins. Source code for some plug-ins is available, and you are encouraged to write your own plug-ins to perform tasks necessary for your workflow or to support importing and exporting your data with proprietary formats. Existing RenderMonkey modules are listed here:

- Shader editors—These are modeled on the interface of Microsoft's Visual Studio to provide an intuitive interface. They support editing of vertex and fragment shaders; syntax coloring; and creation of OpenGL, HLSL, and assembly language shaders.

- Variable editors—Shader parameters can be edited with GUI widgets that "know" the underlying data type for editing; editors exist for colors, vectors, matrices, and scalars; and custom widgets can be created.

- Artist editor—Shader parameters relevant to the art designer can be presented in an artist-friendly fashion so that they can be viewed and modified; programmers can select which parameters are artist-editable; and changes can be seen in real time.

- Previewers—These allow real-time viewing of the shading effect; changes to the shader source code or its parameters are immediately reflected in the preview window; view settings are customizable; views (front, back, side, etc.) are preset; and DirectX 9.0 and OpenGL Shading Language/OpenGL previews are available.

- Exporter—Everything required to re-create a shading effect is encapsulated and written into a single XML file.

- Importer—Everything required to re-create a shading effect is read back from an XML file.

- COLLADA viewer—This is an open source COLLADA effects previewer.

The XML file format was chosen as the basis for encapsulating shader information in RenderMonkey because it is an industry standard, it has a user-readable file format, it is user extensible, and it works with the many free parsers that are available. It is relatively easy to adapt an existing XML parser for your own use or to write a new one. The XML file that encapsulates a shader effect contains all shader source code, all render states, all models, and all texture information. This makes it straightforward to create, manage, and share shader assets.

8.4.2   Apple GLSLEditorSample

This small free gem is included in Apple's developer tools for Mac OS X. This sample application is an Xcode project with complete source code, so it is highly customizable. But even for casual use, it has all the basics for a simple shader developer environment. Like RenderMonkey, it has shader editor windows for vertex and fragment shaders, windows to set uniform variables and other OpenGL state, simple and intuitive texture setup, and diagnostic windows for error messages.

8.4.3   Graphic Remedy gDEBugger

This broad OpenGL debugging environment is available on Windows, Mac OS X, and Linux. At the time of this writing, it already fully supports OpenGL 3.0. Particularly significant for OpenGL 3.0 are the tools it provides to aid in identifying deprecated OpenGL functions. The debugging environment lets you easily view all of the programs and shaders used by an application and adds "edit on the fly" to replace selected shaders during a debugging session.

8.4.4   OpenGL Shading Language Compiler Front End

In June 2003, 3Dlabs released an open source version of its lexical analyzer, parser, and semantic checker (i.e., an OpenGL Shading Language COMPILER

FRONT END). This code reads an OpenGL shader and turns it into a token stream. This process is called LEXICAL ANALYSIS. The token stream is then processed to ensure that the program consists of valid statements. This process is referred to as SYNTACTIC ANALYSIS, or parsing. SEMANTIC ANALYSIS is then performed to determine whether the shader conforms to the semantic rules defined or implied by the OpenGL Shading Language specification. The result of this processing is turned into a high-level representation of the original source code. This high-level intermediate language (HIL) is a binary representation of the original source code that can be further processed by a target-specific back end to provide machine code for a particular type of graphics hardware.

It is anticipated that individual hardware vendors will implement the back end needed for their particular hardware. The compiler back end will typically include intellectual property and hardware-specific information that is proprietary to the graphics hardware vendor. It is not anticipated that 3Dlabs or other hardware vendors will make public the source code for their compiler back ends.

Still, the compiler front end provided by 3Dlabs has been, and will continue to be, a useful tool for the development of the OpenGL Shading Language, and it will be useful for other organizations that want to develop an OpenGL Shading Language compiler or tools for shader development. As the language specification was nearing completion, the compiler front end was being developed. Except for the preprocessor (which was derived from another open source preprocessor), it was implemented from scratch with the publicly available system utilities *flex* and *bison*. It was not derived from existing code. This made it a clean way to double-check the specification and discover language flaws before the specification was released. Indeed, a number of such flaws were discovered through this effort, and, as a result, the specification was improved before its release.

Because of its clean implementation, the OpenGL Shading Language compiler front end also serves as additional technical documentation about the language. The specification should be your first stop, but if you really want to know the details of what's allowed in the language and what's not, studying the compiler front end will provide a definitive answer.

OpenGL implementors that base their compiler on the compiler front end from 3Dlabs will also be doing a big favor to their end users: The semantics of the OpenGL Shading Language will be checked in the same way for all implementations that use this front end. This will benefit developers as they encounter consistent error-checking between different implementations.

Although few readers of this book will likely end up developing an OpenGL Shading Language compiler, this resource is nevertheless a useful one to know about. The source code for the compiler front end is available for download at the former 3Dlabs Web site (now at http://3dshaders.com).

Using the GLSL compiler front end, 3Dlabs has also written a tool called GLSLvalidate. This tool reads a file containing a shader and uses the compiler front end to parse it. Errors are reported in the output window. This tool can be executed on any platform; an OpenGL 2.0 driver is not required. This tool is provided as open source by 3Dlabs.

Another tool from 3Dlabs, GLSLParserTest, determines whether your OpenGL implementation properly supports the OpenGL Shading Language specification. It attempts to compile some 200 shaders and compares the results against the reference compiler. Some shaders should compile, and some should not. Results are printed, and the information log for any shader can be examined. Again, this tool is provided as open source (see the former 3Dlabs developer Web site, now at http://3dshaders.com).

8.5 Scene Graphs

by Mike Weiblen

A SCENE GRAPH is a hierarchical data structure containing a description of a scene to be rendered. Rather than explicitly coding a scene to be rendered as OpenGL API calls, an application builds a scene graph and then calls the scene graph rendering engine to do the actual rendering by traversing the data structure. In this way, a scene graph allows a developer to focus on what to draw, rather than on the details of how to draw. In typical terminology, the term *scene graph* is often used to describe the toolkit for both the data structure itself and the rendering engine that traverses the data structure to render the scene.

Scene graphs make it possible for a developer of visualization applications to leverage the performance of OpenGL without necessarily being an expert in all the details of OpenGL; the scene graph itself encapsulates OpenGL best practices. Because a scene graph is a toolkit layer on top of OpenGL, it raises the programming abstractions closer to the application domain.

As a tree, a scene graph consists of nodes that have one or more children. Since OpenGL state often has a hierarchical nature (such as the modelview matrix stack), that state can easily be mapped to nodes in the tree.

The following are some of the attributes and benefits of scene graphs:

- Encapsulation of best practices for rendering OpenGL, such as optimized GL state control; optimized internal data representations; and minimal geometry sent for rendering based on camera visibility.

- Implementation of sophisticated rendering architectures for performance, for example, pervasive multithreading, multi-CPU, multi-graphics pipe, or synchronized multisystem clustering.

- Definition of the output viewports. For complex display systems such as multiprojector domes, the scene graph can provide support for nonlinear distortion compensation.

- Hierarchical in-memory representation, for example, a tree of nodes with child nodes or a directed acyclic graph (DAG).

- OpenGL state control. By associating GL state with nodes in the graph, the scene graph renderer collects those state requests and applies them efficiently to the OpenGL pipeline. The scene graph can implement a form of lazy state application, by which it avoids forcing state changes down the pipe if no geometry actually requires it for rendering. State can be inherited from parents down to children.

- View culling, by which the spatial position of scene graph nodes are tested against the position of a camera's view volume; only if a node will actually contribute to visible pixels will its geometry be sent to the pipe for rendering. (There is no reason to send vertices to the pipe for geometry that is behind the eyepoint.)

- Instancing of assets. One model of a tire can be referenced four times on a single car; a single car can be instanced many times to create a parking lot full of cars.

The typical application code for a scene graph–based rendering application is conceptually not much more than

```
build the scene graph (loading files from disc at startup, etc.)
do forever
{
    update the camera position
    update other time-varying entities in the scene (such as vehicles
    or particle effects)

    draw the scene
}
```

Although a scene graph allows a visualization developer to focus on what to draw rather than on the details of how to draw it, that does not mean the developer is isolated from direct OpenGL control. In fact, the developer could define custom rendering methods. But for many common rendering tasks, the scene graph renderer already provides a complete solution and acts as a reusable toolkit for leveraging that capability. As expected from a well-designed toolkit, there are no inviolate rules; if you as the developer really need to do something out of the ordinary, the toolkit provides the avenues necessary.

The palette of nodes available for constructing the scene graph provides ways to apply attributes to be inherited by the children of that node. Here are some examples (certainly not an exhaustive list) of scene graph nodes:

- Parent node—Multiple child nodes can be attached.

- Transform nodes—The children are transformed by the parent's transformation matrix.

- Switch nodes—Only one child of the parent will be rendered, governed by a switching condition.

- Level-of-detail node (a specialized switch node)—Only one child is rendered, according to the distance of the node from the camera.

- Billboard node—Its children are automatically oriented toward the camera.

- Light node—Other nodes in the scene are illuminated by lights at the position and with the attributes contained here.

By helping the developer focus on "what" rather than "how," a scene graph can simplify the use of shaders. For example, using the hierarchical nature of a scene graph, a developer can compose a scene that has a shader with default values for uniform variables near the root of the scene graph, so it affects much of the scene. Alternative values for uniform variables attached at lower nodes can specialize the shader for a particular piece of geometry. The scene graph rendering engine can take over the tasks of determining if or when to compile or link the components of the shader and when to actually send updates for uniform variables to the pipeline, depending on visibility.

Several OpenGL scene graph products are currently available. OpenScene-Graph (or OSG, www.openscenegraph.org/) is an open source project that also has recently included support for OpenGL and the OpenGL Shading Language. OpenSG (www.opensg.org) is another open source OpenGL scene graph. Depending on your application, any one of these could save you a great deal of time and application development effort.

8.6 Summary

Writing shaders is similar in many ways to other software engineering tasks. A good dose of common sense can go a long way. Software engineering principles should be applied just as for any other software engineering task. This is especially true in these early generations of programmable graphics hardware. Shader development is more challenging because early OpenGL Shading Language implementations might be incomplete in some ways, compilers will be immature, performance characteristics may differ widely between vendors, and tools to aid shader development are in their infancy. RenderMonkey, GLSLEditorSample and gDEBugger are shader development tools that are available now. Perhaps others will be following.

On the other hand, writing shaders for programmable graphics hardware presents some unique challenges. Good decisions need to be made about how to split the computation between the CPU, the vertex processor, and the fragment processor. It is useful to have a solid foundation in mathematics and computer graphics before attempting to write shaders. Thorough knowledge of how OpenGL works is also a key asset, and having some understanding of the underlying graphics hardware can be helpful. It often pays to collaborate with an artist when developing a shader. This can help you develop a shader that is parameterized in such a way that it can be put to a variety of uses in the final application.

8.7 Further Information

Numerous books describe sound software engineering principles and practices. Two that describe tactics specific to developing shaders are *Texturing and Modeling: A Procedural Approach* by David X. Ebert et al. (2002) and *Advanced RenderMan: Creating CGI for Motion Pictures* by Anthony A. Apodaca and Larry Gritz (1999). Some of the shader development discussion in these books is specific to RenderMan, but many of the principles are also relevant to developing shaders with the OpenGL Shading Language.

For performance tuning, the best advice I have right now is to become good friends with the developer relations staff at your favorite graphics hardware company (or companies). These are the people who can provide you with additional insight or information about the underlying graphics hardware architecture and the relative performance of various aspects of the hardware. Until we go through another generation or two of programmable graphics hardware development (and perhaps even longer), performance differences between various hardware architectures will depend on the trade-offs made by the hardware architects and the driver developers. Scour the Web sites of these companies, attend their presentations at trade shows, and ask lots of questions.

The ATI developer Web site contains a number of presentations on Render-Monkey. The RenderMonkey IDE and documentation can be downloaded from either the ATI Web site or the 3Dlabs Web site. The 3Dlabs Web site contains the open source GLSL compiler front end, the GLSLvalidate tool, and other useful tools and examples.

[1] *3Dlabs developer Web site.* Now at http://3dshaders.com.

[2] Apodaca, Anthony A., and Larry Gritz, *Advanced RenderMan: Creating CGI for Motion Pictures*, Morgan Kaufmann Publishers, San Francisco, 1999. www.renderman.org/RMR/Books/ arman/ materials.html

[3] *AMD developer Web site.* http://developer.amd.com/

[4] *Apple developer Web site.* http://developer.apple.com/

[5] Ebert, David S., John Hart, Bill Mark, F. Kenton Musgrave, Darwyn Peachey, Ken Perlin, and Steven Worley, *Texturing and Modeling: A Procedural Approach, Third Edition*, Morgan Kaufmann Publishers, San Francisco, 2002. www.texturingandmodeling.com/

[6] *Graphic Remedy Web site.* www.gremedy.com/

[7] *NVIDIA developer Web site.* http://developer.nvidia.com/

[8] *OpenSceneGraph Web site.* www.openscenegraph.org/

[9] *OpenSG Web site.* www.opensg.org/

Chapter 9

Emulating OpenGL Fixed Functionality

The programmability of OpenGL opens many new possibilities for never-before-seen rendering effects. Programmable shaders can provide results that are superior to OpenGL fixed functionality, especially in the area of realism. Nevertheless, it can still be instructive to examine how some of OpenGL's fixed functionality rendering steps could be implemented with OpenGL shaders. While simplistic, these code snippets may be useful as stepping stones to bigger and better things.

This chapter describes OpenGL shader code that mimics the behavior of the OpenGL fixed functionality vertex, fragment, and matrix processing. The shader code snippets are derived from the Full OpenGL Pipeline and Pixel Pipeline shaders developed by Dave Baldwin for inclusion in the white paper *OpenGL 2.0 Shading Language*. Further refinement of this shader code occurred for the first edition of this book. These code snippets were then verified and finalized with a tool called **ShaderGen** that takes a description of OpenGL's fixed functionality state and automatically generates the equivalent shaders. **ShaderGen** was implemented by Inderaj Bains and Joshua Doss while at 3Dlabs.

The goal of the shader code in this chapter is to faithfully represent OpenGL fixed functionality. The code examples in this chapter reference OpenGL state wherever possible through user-defined variables. By doing this, these examples are "forward looking." But don't get too enamored with the shaders presented in this chapter. In later chapters of this book, we explore a variety of shaders that provide more flexible or more efficient results than those discussed in this chapter.

We need to provide a small warning, however. Matrix operations, especially matrix concatenation and matrix inversion, are not that cheap. So in Chapter 16, we will show a technique for running these matrix shader functions less often than once a vertex.

9.1 Transformation

The features of the OpenGL Shading Language make it very easy to express transformations between the coordinate spaces defined by OpenGL. We've already seen the transformation that will be used by almost every vertex shader. The incoming vertex position must be transformed into clipping coordinates for use by the fixed functionality stages that occur after vertex processing. This is done in one of two ways, either this:

```
uniform mat4 MVPmatrix; // modelview-projection matrix
// ...

in vec4 MCVertex;
// ...

a(); // A function that does not modify gl_Position, MVP, or MCVertex

// ...
// Transform vertex to clip space
gl_Position = MVP * MCVertex;
```

or this:

```
uniform mat4 MVPmatrix; // modelview-projection matrix
// ...

invariant gl_Position;
in vec4 MCVertex;
// ...

a(); // A function that does not modify gl_Position, MVP or MCVertex

// ...
// Transform vertex to clip space
gl_Position = MVPmatrix * MCVertex;
```

The only difference between these two methods is the **invariant** qualifier modifying **gl_Position**. The first case may or may not compute the transformed positions in exactly the same way no matter what unrelated function or expression is linked to the shader. This can cause problems in rendering if a multipass algorithm is used to render the same geometry more than once. The **invariant** qualifier instructs the compiler and linker to ignore expressions and functions that are not directly related to the computation of the output. The second case must compute the transformed positions in exactly the same way no matter what unrelated function or expression is linked to the shader. For multipass algorithms, the second method is preferred because it produces the same transformed position for a family of shaders.

OpenGL specifies that light positions are transformed by the modelview matrix when they are provided to OpenGL. This means that they are stored in eye coordinates. It is often convenient to perform lighting computations in eye space, so it is often necessary to transform the incoming vertex position into eye coordinates as shown in Listing 9.1.

Listing 9.1 Computation of eye coordinate position

```
uniform mat4 MVMatrix;
// ...

vec4 ecPosition;
vec3 ecPosition3;    // in 3 space
// ...

// Transform vertex to eye coordinates
if (NeedEyePosition)
{
    ecPosition  = MVMatrix * MCVertex;
    ecPosition3 = (vec3(ecPosition)) / ecPosition.w;
}
```

This snippet of code computes the homogeneous point in eye space (a **vec4**) as well as the nonhomogeneous point (a **vec3**). Both values are useful as we shall see.

To perform lighting calculations in eye space, incoming surface normals must also be transformed. A user-defined uniform variable is available to store the normal transformation matrix, as shown in Listing 9.2.

Listing 9.2 Transformation of normal

```
uniform mat3 NormalMatrix;
// ...

in vec3 MCNormal;
// ...

vec3 normal;

normal = NormalMatrix * MCNormal;
```

In many cases, the application may not know anything about the characteristics of the surface normals that are being provided. For the lighting computations to work correctly, each incoming normal must be normalized so that it is unit length. In an OpenGL shader, if normalization is required, we do it as shown in Listing 9.3.

Listing 9.3 Normalization of normal

```
normal = normalize(normal);
```

Sometimes an application will always be sending normals that are unit length and the modelview matrix is always one that does uniform scaling. In this case, rescaling can be used to avoid the possibly expensive square root operation that is a necessary part of normalization. If the rescaling factor is supplied by the application through the OpenGL API, the normal can be rescaled as shown in Listing 9.4.

Listing 9.4 Normal rescaling

```
uniform float NormalScale;
// ...

normal = normal * NormalScale;
```

The rescaling factor is stored as state within OpenGL and can be accessed from within a shader by the user-defined uniform variable *NormalScale*.

Texture coordinates can also be transformed. A texture matrix is defined for each texture coordinate set in OpenGL and can be accessed with the user-defined uniform matrix array variable *TextureMatrix*. Incoming texture coordinates can be transformed in the same manner as vertex positions, as shown in Listing 9.5.

Listing 9.5 Texture coordinate transformation

```
uniform TextureMatrix[MaxTextureCoords];
// ...

in vec4 MultiTexCoord0;
out vec4 TexCoord[MaxTexCoord];

TexCoord[0] = TextureMatrix[0] * MultiTexCoord0;
```

9.2 Light Sources

The lighting computations defined by OpenGL are somewhat involved. Let's start by defining a function for each of the types of light sources defined by OpenGL: directional lights, point lights, and spotlights. We pass in variables that store the total ambient, diffuse, and specular contributions from all light sources. These must be initialized to 0 before any of the light source computation routines are called.

9.2.1 Directional Lights

A directional light is assumed to be at an infinite distance from the objects being lit. According to this assumption, all light rays from the light source are parallel when they reach the scene. Therefore, a single direction vector can be used for every point in the scene. This assumption simplifies the math, so the code to implement a directional light source is simpler and typically runs faster than the code for other types of lights. Because the light source is assumed to be infinitely far away, the direction of maximum highlights is the same for every point in the scene. This direction vector can be computed ahead of time for each light source *i* and stored in *LightSource[i].halfVector*. This type of light source is useful for mimicking the effects of a light source like the sun.

The directional light function shown in Listing 9.6 computes the cosine of the angle between the surface normal and the light direction, as well as the cosine of the angle between the surface normal and the half angle between the light direction and the viewing direction. The former value is multiplied by the light's diffuse color to compute the diffuse component from the light. The latter value is raised to the power indicated by *FrontMaterial.shininess* before being multiplied by the light's specular color.

The only way either a diffuse reflection component or a specular reflection component can be present is if the angle between the light source direction and the surface normal is in the range [–90°,90°]. We determine the angle by examining *nDotVP*. This value is set to the greater of 0 and the cosine of the angle between the light source direction and the surface normal. If this value ends up being 0, the value that determines the amount of specular reflection is set to 0 as well. Our directional light function assumes that the vectors of interest are normalized, so the dot product between two vectors results in the cosine of the angle between them.

Listing 9.6   Directional light source computation

```
void DirectionalLight(const in int   i,
                      const in vec3 normal,
                      inout    vec4 ambient,
                      inout    vec4 diffuse,
                      inout    vec4 specular)
{
    float nDotVP; // normal . light direction
    float nDotHV; // normal . light half vector
    float pf; // power factor

    nDotVP = max(0.0, dot(normal,
                 normalize(vec3(LightSource[i].position))));
    nDotHV = max(0.0, dot(normal, vec3(LightSource[i].halfVector)));

    if (nDotVP == 0.0)
        pf = 0.0;
    else
        pf = pow(nDotHV, FrontMaterial.shininess);

    ambient  += LightSource[i].ambient;
    diffuse  += LightSource[i].diffuse * nDotVP;
    specular += LightSource[i].specular * pf;
}
```

9.2.2   Point Lights

Point lights mimic lights that are near the scene or within the scene, such as lamps or ceiling lights or street lights. There are two main differences between point lights and directional lights. First, with a point light source, the direction of maximum highlights must be computed at each vertex rather than with the precomputed value from *LightSource[i].halfVector.* Second, light received at the surface is expected to decrease as the point light source gets farther and farther away. This is called ATTENUATION. Each light source has constant, linear, and quadratic attenuation factors that are taken into account when the lighting contribution from a point light is computed.

These differences show up in the first few lines of the point light function (see Listing 9.7). The first step is to compute the vector from the surface to the light position. We compute this distance by using the length function. Next, we normalize *VP* so that we can use it in a dot product operation to compute a proper cosine value. We then compute the attenuation factor and the direction of maximum highlights as required. The remaining code is the same as for our directional light function except that the ambient, diffuse, and specular terms are multiplied by the attenuation factor.

One optimization that we could make is to have two point light functions, one that computes the attenuation factor and one that does not. If the values for the constant, linear, and quadratic attenuation factors are (1, 0, 0) (the default values), we could use the function that does not compute attenuation and get better performance.

Listing 9.7 Point light source computation

```
void PointLight(const in int   i,
                const in vec3 eye,
                const in vec3 ecPosition3,
                const in vec3 normal,
                inout     vec4 ambient,
                inout     vec4 diffuse,
                inout     vec4 specular)
{
    float nDotVP;       // normal . light direction
    float nDotHV;       // normal . light half vector
    float pf;           // power factor
    float attenuation;  // computed attenuation factor
    float d;            // distance from surface to light source
    vec3  VP;           // direction from surface to light position
    vec3  halfVector;   // direction of maximum highlights

    // Compute vector from surface to light position
    VP = vec3(LightSource[i].position) - ecPosition3;

    // Compute distance between surface and light position
    d = length(VP);

    // Normalize the vector from surface to light position
    VP = normalize(VP);

    // Compute attenuation

    attenuation = 1.0 / (LightSource[i].constantAttenuation +
                    LightSource[i].linearAttenuation * d +
                    LightSource[i].quadraticAttenuation * d * d);

    halfVector = normalize(VP + eye);

    nDotVP = max(0.0, dot(normal, VP));
    nDotHV = max(0.0, dot(normal, halfVector));

    if (nDotVP == 0.0)
       pf = 0.0;
    else
       pf = pow(nDotHV, FrontMaterial.shininess);

    ambient  += LightSource[i].ambient * attenuation;
    diffuse  += LightSource[i].diffuse * nDotVP * attenuation;
    specular += LightSource[i].specular * pf * attenuation;
}
```

9.2.3 Spotlights

In stage and cinema, spotlights project a strong beam of light that illuminates a well-defined area. The illuminated area can be further shaped through the use of flaps or shutters on the sides of the light. OpenGL includes light attributes that simulate a simple type of spotlight. Whereas point lights are modeled as sending light equally in all directions, OpenGL models spotlights as light sources that are restricted to producing a cone of light in a particular direction.

The first and last parts of our spotlight function (see Listing 9.8) look the same as our point light function (shown earlier in Listing 9.7). The differences occur in the middle of the function. A spotlight has a focus direction (*LightSource[i].spotDirection*), and this direction is dotted with the vector from the light position to the surface (*−VP*). The resulting cosine value is compared to the precomputed cosine cutoff value (*LightSource[i].spotCosCutoff*) to determine whether the position on the surface is inside or outside the spotlight's cone of illumination. If it is outside, the spotlight attenuation is set to 0; otherwise, this value is raised to a power specified by *LightSource[i].spotExponent*. The resulting spotlight attenuation factor is multiplied by the previously computed attenuation factor to give the overall attenuation factor. The remaining lines of code are the same as they were for point lights.

Listing 9.8 Spotlight computation

```
void SpotLight(const in int   i,
               const in vec3 eye,
               const in vec3 ecPosition3,
               const in vec3 normal,
               inout      vec4 ambient,
               inout      vec4 diffuse,
               inout      vec4 specular)
{
    float nDotVP;          // normal . light direction
    float nDotHV;          // normal . light half vector
    float pf;              // power factor
    float spotDot;         // cosine of angle between spotlight
    float spotAttenuation; // spotlight attenuation factor
    float attenuation;     // computed attenuation factor
    float d;               // distance from surface to light source
    vec3 VP;               // direction from surface to light position
    vec3 halfVector;       // direction of maximum highlights

    // Compute vector from surface to light position
    VP = vec3(LightSource[i].position) - ecPosition3;

    // Compute distance between surface and light position
    d = length(VP);
```

```
// Normalize the vector from surface to light position
VP = normalize(VP);

// Compute attenuation
attenuation = 1.0 / (LightSource[i].constantAttenuation +
                     LightSource[i].linearAttenuation * d +
                     LightSource[i].quadraticAttenuation * d * d);

// See if point on surface is inside cone of illumination
spotDot = dot(-VP, normalize(LightSource[i].spotDirection));
if (spotDot < LightSource[i].spotCosCutoff)
    spotAttenuation = 0.0; // light adds no contribution
else
    spotAttenuation = pow(spotDot, LightSource[i].spotExponent);

// Combine the spotlight and distance attenuation.
attenuation *= spotAttenuation;

halfVector = normalize(VP + eye);

nDotVP = max(0.0, dot(normal, VP));
nDotHV = max(0.0, dot(normal, halfVector));

if (nDotVP == 0.0)
    pf = 0.0;
else
    pf = pow(nDotHV, FrontMaterial.shininess);

ambient  += LightSource[i].ambient * attenuation;
diffuse  += LightSource[i].diffuse * nDotVP * attenuation;
specular += LightSource[i].specular * pf * attenuation;
}
```

9.3   Material Properties and Lighting

OpenGL lighting calculations require knowing the viewing direction in the eye coordinate system in order to compute specular reflection terms. By default, the view direction is assumed to be parallel to and in the direction of the $-z$ axis. OpenGL also has a mode that requires the viewing direction to be computed from the origin of the eye coordinate system (local viewer). To compute this, we can transform the incoming vertex into eye space by using the current modelview matrix. The x, y, and z coordinates of this point are divided by the homogeneous coordinate w to get a **vec3** value that can be used directly in the lighting calculations. The computation of this eye coordinate position (*ecPosition3*) was illustrated in Section 9.10. To get a unit vector corresponding to the viewing direction, we normalize and negate the eye space position. Shader code to implement these computations is shown in Listing 9.9.

Listing 9.9 Local viewer computation

```
if (NeedLocalViewer)
    eye = -normalize(ecPosition3);
else
    eye = vec3(0.0, 0.0, 1.0);
```

With the viewing direction calculated, we can initialize the variables that accumulate the ambient, diffuse, and specular lighting contributions from all the light sources in the scene. We can then call the functions defined in the previous section to compute the contributions from each light source. In the code in Listing 9.10, we assume that all lights with an index less than the constant NumEnabledLights are enabled. Directional lights are distinguished by having a position parameter with a homogeneous (*w*) coordinate equal to 0 at the time they were provided to OpenGL. (These positions are transformed by the modelview matrix when the light is specified, so the *w* coordinate remains 0 after transformation if the last column of the modelview matrix is the typical (0 0 0 1)). Point lights are distinguished by having a spotlight cutoff angle equal to 180.

Listing 9.10 Loop to compute contributions from all enabled light sources

```
// Clear the light intensity accumulators
amb  =  vec4(0.0);
diff = vec4(0.0);
spec = vec4(0.0);

// Loop through enabled lights, compute contribution from each
for (int i = 0; i < NumEnabledLights; i++)
{
    if (LightSource[i].position.w == 0.0)
        DirectionalLight(i, normal, amb, diff, spec);
    else if (LightSource[i].spotCutoff == 180.0)
        PointLight(i, eye, ecPosition3, normal, amb, diff, spec);
    else
        SpotLight(i, eye, ecPosition3, normal, amb, diff, spec);
}
```

One of the changes made to OpenGL in version 1.2 was to add functionality to compute the color at a vertex in two parts: a primary color that contains the combination of the emissive, ambient, and diffuse terms as computed by the usual lighting equations; and a secondary color that contains just the specular term as computed by the usual lighting equations. If this mode is not enabled (the default case), the primary color is computed with the combination of emissive, ambient, diffuse, and specular terms.

Computing the specular contribution separately allows specular highlights to be applied after texturing has occurred. The specular value is added to the computed color after texturing has occurred to allow the specular highlights to be the color of the light source rather than the color of the surface. Listing 9.11 shows how to compute the surface color (according to OpenGL rules) with everything but the specular contribution:

Listing 9.11 Surface color computation, omitting the specular contribution

```
FrontLightModelProduct.sceneColor +
        amb  * FrontMaterial.ambient +
        diff * FrontMaterial.diffuse;
```

We use a user-defined uniform variable (*FrontLightModelProduct.sceneColor*) to contain the emissive material property for front-facing surfaces plus the product of the ambient material property for front-facing surfaces and the global ambient light for the scene (i.e., *FrontMaterial.emission* + *FrontMaterial.ambient* * *LightModel.ambient*). We can add this together with the intensity of reflected ambient light and the intensity of reflected diffuse light. Next, we can do the appropriate computations, depending on whether the separate specular color mode is indicated, as shown in Listing 9.12.

Listing 9.12 Final surface color computation

```
if (NeedSeparateSpecular)
    FrontSecondaryColor = vec4( spec.rgb *
                                FrontMaterial.specular.rgb, 1.0);
else
    color += spec * FrontMaterial.specular;

FrontColor = clamp(color, 0.0, 1.0);
```

9.4 Two-Sided Lighting

To mimic OpenGL's two-sided lighting behavior, you need to invert the surface normal and perform the same computations as defined in the preceding section, using the back-facing material properties. You can probably do it more cleverly than this, but it might look like Listing 9.13. The functions **DirectionalLight**, **PointLight**, and **SpotLight** that are referenced in this code segment are identical to the functions described in Section 9.2 except that the value *BackMaterial.shininess* is used in the computations instead of the value *FrontMaterial.shininess*.

Listing 9.13 Two-sided lighting computation

```
normal = -normal;

// Clear the light intensity accumulators
amb =  vec4(0.0);
diff = vec4(0.0);
spec = vec4(0.0);

// Loop through enabled lights, compute contribution from each
for (int i = 0; i < NumEnabledLights; i++)
{
    if (LightSource[i].position.w == 0.0)
        DirectionalLight(i, normal, amb, diff, spec);
    else if (LightSource[i].spotCutoff == 180.0)
        PointLight(i, eye, ecPosition3, normal, amb, diff, spec);
    else
        SpotLight(i, eye, ecPosition3, normal, amb, diff, spec);
}

color = BackLightModelProduct.sceneColor +
        amb  * BackMaterial.ambient +
        diff * BackMaterial.diffuse;

if (NeedSeparateSpecular)
    BackSecondaryColor = vec4( spec.rgb *
                               BackMaterial.specular.rgb, 1.0);
else
    color += spec * BackMaterial.specular;

BackColor = clamp(color, 0.0, 1.0);
```

9.5 No Lighting

If no enabled lights are in the scene, it is a simple matter to pass the per-vertex color and secondary color for further processing with the commands shown in Listing 9.14.

Listing 9.14 Setting final color values with no lighting

```
if (NeedSecondaryColor)
    FrontSecondaryColor = clamp(SecondaryColor, 0.0, 1.0);

FrontColor = clamp(color;, 0.0, 1.0);
```

9.6 Fog

In OpenGL, DEPTH-CUING and fog effects are controlled by fog parameters. A fog factor is computed according to one of three equations, and this fog factor performs a linear blend between the fog color and the computed color for the fragment. The depth value to be used in the fog equation can be either the fog coordinate passed in as a user-defined vertex attribute (*FogCoord*) or the eye-coordinate distance from the eye. In the latter case, it is usually sufficient to approximate the depth value as the absolute value of the *z*-coordinate in eye space (i.e., **abs**(*ecPosition.z*)). When there is a wide angle of view, this approximation may cause a noticeable artifact (too little fog) near the edges. If this is the case, you could compute *z* as the true distance from the eye to the fragment with **length**(*ecPosition*). (This method involves a square root computation, so the code may run slower as a result.) The choice of which depth value to use would normally be done in the vertex shader as follows:

```
in float FogCoord;
out float FogFragCoord;
//...

if (UseFogCoordinate)
    FogFragCoord = FogCoord;
else
    FogFragCoord = abs(ecPosition.z);;
```

A linear computation (which corresponds to the traditional computer graphics operation of depth-cuing) can be selected in OpenGL with the symbolic constant GL_LINEAR. For this case, the fog factor *f* is computed with the following equation:

$$f = \frac{end - z}{end - start}$$

start, *end*, and *z* are all distances in eye coordinates. *start* is the distance to the start of the fog effect, *end* is the distance to the end of the effect, and *z* is the value stored in *FogFragCoord*. We can explicitly provide the start and end positions as uniform variables, or we can access the current values in OpenGL state by using the user-defined uniform variables *Fog.start* and *Fog.end*. The shader code to compute the fog factor with the built-in variables for accessing OpenGL state is shown in Listing 9.15.

Listing 9.15 GL_LINEAR fog computation

```
in float FogFragCoord;
// ...

float fog;
fog = (Fog.end - FogFragCoord) * Fog.scale;
```

Because 1.0 / (*Fog.end* – *Fog.start)* doesn't depend on any per-vertex or per-fragment state, this value is precomputed and stored in the user-defined uniform variable *Fog.scale*.

We can achieve a more realistic fog effect with an exponential function. With a negative exponent value, the exponential function will model the diminishing of the original color as a function of distance. A simple exponential fog function can be selected in OpenGL with the symbolic constant GL_EXP. The formula corresponding to this fog function is

$$f = e^{-(density \cdot z)}$$

The *z* value is computed as described for the previous function, and *density* is a value that represents the density of the fog. The user-defined uniform variable *Fog.density* can be used to store the density. The larger this value becomes, the "thicker" the fog becomes. For this function to work as intended, *density* must be greater than or equal to 0.

The OpenGL Shading Language has a built-in **exp** (base *e*) function that we can use to perform this calculation. Our OpenGL shader code to compute the preceding equation is shown in Listing 9.16.

Listing 9.16 GL_EXP fog computation

```
fog = exp(-Fog.density * FogFragCoord);
```

The final fog function defined by OpenGL is selected with the symbolic constant GL_EXP2 and is defined as

$$f = e^{-(density \cdot z)^2}$$

This function changes the slope of the exponential decay function by squaring the exponent. The OpenGL shader code to implement it is similar to the previous function (see Listing 9.17).

Listing 9.17 GL_EXP2 fog computation

```
fog = exp(-Fog.density * Fog.density *
          FogFragCoord * FogFragCoord);
```

OpenGL also requires the final value for the fog factor to be limited to the range [0,1]. We can accomplish this with the statement in Listing 9.18.

Listing 9.18 Clamping the fog factor

```
fog = clamp(fog, 0.0, 1.0);
```

Any of these three fog functions can be computed in either a vertex shader or a fragment shader. Unless you have very large polygons in your scene, you probably won't see any difference if the fog factor is computed in the vertex shader and passed to the fragment shader as a varying variable. This will probably also give you better performance overall, so it's generally the preferred approach. In the fragment shader, when the (almost) final color is computed, the fog factor can be used to compute a linear blend between the fog color and the (almost) final fragment color. The OpenGL shader code in Listing 9.19 does the trick by using the fog color saved as part of current OpenGL state.

Listing 9.19 Applying fog to compute final color value

```
color = mix(vec3(Fog.color), color, fog);
```

The code presented in this section achieves the same results as OpenGL's fixed functionality. But with programmability, you are free to use a completely different approach to compute fog effects.

9.7 Texture Coordinate Generation

OpenGL can be set up to compute texture coordinates automatically, based only on the incoming vertex positions. Five methods are defined, and each can be useful for certain purposes. The texture generation mode specified by GL_OBJECT_LINEAR is useful for cases in which a texture is to remain fixed to a geometric model, such as in a terrain modeling application. GL_EYE_LINEAR is useful for producing dynamic contour lines on an object. Examples of this usage include a scientist studying isosurfaces or a geologist interpreting seismic data. GL_SPHERE_MAP can generate texture coordinates for simple environment mapping. GL_REFLECTION_MAP and GL_NORMAL_MAP can work in conjunction with cube map textures. GL_REFLECTION_MAP passes the reflection vector as the texture coordinate. GL_NORMAL_MAP simply passes the computed eye space normal as the texture coordinate.

A function that generates sphere map coordinates according to the OpenGL specification is shown in Listing 9.20.

Listing 9.20 GL_SPHERE_MAP computation

```
vec2 SphereMap(const in vec3 ecPosition3,
               const in vec3 normal)
{
    float m;
    vec3 r, u;
    u = normalize(ecPosition3);
    r = reflect(u, normal);
    r.z += 1.0;
    m = 0.5 * inversesqrt( dot(r,r) );
    return r.xy * m + 0.5;
}
```

A function that generates reflection map coordinates according to the OpenGL specification looks almost identical to the function shown in Listing 9.20. The difference is that it returns the reflection vector as its result (see Listing 9.21).

Listing 9.21 GL_REFLECTION_MAP computation

```
vec3 ReflectionMap(const in vec3 ecPosition3,
                   const in vec3 normal)
{
    float NdotU, m;
    vec3 u;
    u = normalize(ecPosition3);
    return (reflect(u, normal));
}
```

Listing 9.22 shows the code for selecting between the five texture generation methods and computing the appropriate texture coordinate values.

Listing 9.22 Texture coordinate generation computation

```
// Compute sphere map coordinates if needed
if (TexGenSphere)
    sphereMap = SphereMap(ecPosition3, normal);

// Compute reflection map coordinates if needed
if (TexGenReflection)
    reflection = ReflectionMap(ecPosition3, normal);

// Compute texture coordinate for each enabled texture unit
for (int i = 0; i < NumEnabledTextureUnits; i++)

{
    if (TexGenObject)
    {
```

```
        TexCoord[i].s = dot(MCvertex, ObjectPlaneS[i]);
        TexCoord[i].t = dot(MCvertex, ObjectPlaneT[i]);
        TexCoord[i].p = dot(MCvertex, ObjectPlaneR[i]);
        TexCoord[i].q = dot(MCvertex, ObjectPlaneQ[i]);
    }

    if (TexGenEye)
    {
        TexCoord[i].s = dot(ecPosition, EyePlaneS[i]);
        TexCoord[i].t = dot(ecPosition, EyePlaneT[i]);
        TexCoord[i].p = dot(ecPosition, EyePlaneR[i]);
        TexCoord[i].q = dot(ecPosition, EyePlaneQ[i]);
    }

    if (TexGenSphere)
        TexCoord[i] = vec4(sphereMap, 0.0, 1.0);

    if (TexGenReflection)
        TexCoord[i] = vec4(reflection, 1.0);

    if (TexGenNormal)
        TexCoord[i] = vec4(normal, 1.0);
}
```

In this code, we assume that each texture unit less than *NumEnabledTexture-Units* is enabled. If this value is 0, the whole loop is skipped. Otherwise, each texture coordinate that is needed is computed in the loop.

Because the sphere map and reflection computations do not depend on any of the texture unit state, they can be performed once, and the result is used for all texture units. For the GL_OBJECT_LINEAR and GL_EYE_LINEAR methods, there is a plane equation for each component of each set of texture coordinates. For the former case, we generate the components of *TexCoord[0]* by multiplying the plane equation coefficients for the specified component by the incoming vertex position. For the latter case, we compute the components of *TexCoord[0]* by multiplying the plane equation coefficients by the eye coordinate position of the vertex. Depending on what type of texture access is done during fragment processing, it may not be necessary to compute the *t*, *p*, or *q* texture component,[1] so these computations could be eliminated.

----

1. For historical reasons, the OpenGL texture coordinate components are named *s*, *t*, *r*, and *q*. Because of the desire to have single-letter, component-selection names in the OpenGL Shading Language, components for textures are named *s*, *t*, *p*, and *q*. This lets us avoid using *r*, which is needed for selecting color components as *r*, *g*, *b*, and *a*.

9.8 User Clipping

To take advantage of OpenGL's user clipping (which remains as fixed functionality between vertex processing and fragment processing in programmable OpenGL), a vertex shader must calculate the distances between clip planes and the vertex. The shader writer can choose to transform either the clip planes or the vertex, or both, to a convenient space. The example shader in Listing 9.23 performs user clipping in eye space.

Listing 9.23 User-clipping computation

```
uniform vec4 ClipPlane[MaxClipPlanes];
// ...

for ( int i=0; i<MaxClipPlanes; i++ )
{
    gl_ClipDistance[i] = dot( ClipPlane[i], ecPosition );
}
```

9.9 Texture Application

The built-in texture functions read values from texture memory. The values read from texture memory are used in a variety of ways. OpenGL fixed functionality includes support for texture application formulas enabled with the symbolic constants GL_REPLACE, GL_MODULATE, GL_DECAL, GL_BLEND, and GL_ADD. These modes operate differently, depending on the format of the texture being accessed. The following code illustrates the case in which an RGBA texture is accessed with the sampler *tex0*. The variable *color* is initialized to be *Color* and then modified as needed so that it contains the color value that results from texture application.

GL_REPLACE is the simplest texture application mode of all. It simply replaces the current fragment color with the value read from texture memory. See Listing 9.24.

Listing 9.24 GL_REPLACE computation

```
color = texture(tex0, TexCoord[0].xy);
```

GL_MODULATE causes the incoming fragment color to be multiplied by the value retrieved from texture memory. This is a good texture function to use if lighting is computed before texturing (e.g., the vertex shader performs the lighting computation, and the fragment shader does the texturing). White can be used as the base color for an object rendered with this technique, and the texture then provides the diffuse color. This technique is illustrated with the OpenGL shader code in Listing 9.25.

Listing 9.25 GL_MODULATE computation

```
color *= texture(tex0, TexCoord[0].xy);
```

GL_DECAL is useful for applying an opaque image to a portion of an object. For instance, you might want to apply a number and company logos to the surfaces of a race car or tattoos to the skin of a character in a game. When an RGBA texture is accessed, the alpha value at each texel linearly interpolates between the incoming fragment's RGB value and the texture's RGB value. The incoming fragment's alpha value is used as is. The code for implementing this mode is in Listing 9.26.

Listing 9.26 GL_DECAL computation

```
vec4 texel = texture(tex0, TexCoord[0].xy);
vec3 col = mix(color.rgb, texel.rgb, texel.a);
color = vec4(col, color.a);
```

GL_BLEND is the only texture application mode that takes the current texture environment color into account. The RGB values read from the texture linearly interpolate between the RGB values of the incoming fragment and the texture environment color. We compute the new alpha value by multiplying the alpha of the incoming fragment by the alpha read from the texture. The OpenGL shader code is shown in Listing 9.27.

Listing 9.27 GL_BLEND computation

```
vec4 texel = texture(tex0, TexCoord[0].xy);
vec3 col = mix(color.rgb, TextureEnvColor[0].rgb, texel.rgb);
color = vec4(col, color.a * texel.a);;
```

GL_ADD computes the sum of the incoming fragment color and the value read from the texture. The two alpha values are multiplied together to compute the new alpha value. This is the only traditional texture application mode for which the resulting values can exceed the range [0,1], so we clamp the final result (see Listing 9.28).

Listing 9.28 GL_ADD computation

```
vec4 texel = texture(tex0, TexCoord[0].xy);
color.rgb += texel.rgb;
color.a   *= texel.a;
color = clamp(color, 0.0, 1.0);
```

The texture-combine environment mode that was added in OpenGL 1.3 and extended in OpenGL 1.4 defines a large number of additional simple ways to perform texture application. A variety of new formulas, source values, and operands were defined. The mapping of these additional modes into OpenGL shader code is straightforward but tiresome, so it is omitted here.

9.10 Matrices

The features of the OpenGL Shading Language make it very easy to build the transformation matrices that were provided by OpenGL matrix commands. We've already seen the transformation matrices will be used by almost every vertex shader. In this section, we'll cover these functions, staring with the basic building blocks of computing matrices.

9.10.1 Identity Matrix

This is very simple (see Listing 9.29), but still surprisingly useful.

Listing 9.29 Identity matrix computation

```
mat4 IdentityMatrix( void )
{
    return mat4( 1.0 );
}
```

9.10.2 Scale

Nearly as simple, the **ScaleMatrix** function in Listing 9.30 computes a matrix that scales each of *x*, *y*, and *z* independently. It is a generalization of **IdentityMatrix**.

Listing 9.30 Scale matrix computation

```
mat4 ScaleMatrix( const in vec3 s )
{
    return mat4( s.x, 0.0, 0.0, 0.0,
                 0.0, s.y, 0.0, 0.0,
                 0.0, 0.0, s.z, 0.0,
                 0.0, 0.0, 0.0, 1.0 );
}
```

9.10.3 Translate

The **TranslateMatrix** function computes a transformation matrix.

One thing we need to remember is that matrices are specified in column major order, as is the tradition in OpenGL. The OpenGL specification and the OpenGL Reference Manual follow the linear algebra convention that vectors are columns. We need to "read" the matrices column by column. The first four elements are the first column, even though they show up in the first row of the constructor. While at first glance it might look like the matrix in Listing 9.31 has been transposed, it has not.

Listing 9.31 Translation matrix computation

```
mat4 TranslateMatrix( const in vec3 t )
{
    return mat4( 1.0, 0.0, 0.0, 0.0,
                 0.0, 1.0, 0.0, 0.0,
                 0.0, 0.0, 1.0, 0.0,
                 t.x, t.y, t.z, 1.0 );
}
```

9.10.4 Rotate

The *Rotate* command in OpenGL takes an angle in degrees and an axis that may be unnormalized. We convert the angle in degrees to radians, and we also normalize the axis in the shader function. One optimization that we could make to the shader in Listing 9.32 is to have multiple rotate functions, versions that convert the angle and normalize the axis, and versions that do not.

Listing 9.32 Rotation matrix computation

```
mat4 RotateMatrix( const in float angle,
                   const in vec3  axis )
{
    vec3 n = normalize( axis );
    float theta = radians( angle );
    float c = cos( theta );
    float s = sin( theta );
    mat3 R;
    R[0] = n.xyz*n.x*(1.0-c) + vec3(      c,  n.z*s, -n.y*s );
    R[1] = n.xyz*n.y*(1.0-c) + vec3( -n.z*s,      c,  n.x*s );
    R[2] = n.xyz*n.z*(1.0-c) + vec3(  n.y*s, -n.x*s,      c );
    return mat4( R[0],          0.0,
                 R[1],          0.0,
                 R[2],          0.0,
                 0.0, 0.0, 0.0, 1.0 );
}
```

9.10.5 Ortho

Orthographic projection is not very photorealistic but has a long tradition in several areas, including mechanical engineering, architecture, and even early "3D" video games. It is also the view of a very powerful telescope looking at objects far, far away.

The OpenGL command Ortho takes the left, right, top and bottom clipping planes and projects them orthogonally along the z axis, with the near and far clipping planes capping the view volume (see Listing 9.33).

Listing 9.33 Orthographic matrix projection

```
mat4 OrthoMatrix( const in float    left, const in float right,
                  const in float bottom, const in float    top,
                  const in float  zNear, const in float   zFar )
{
    vec3 delta = vec3( right,      top,   zFar )
               - vec3(  left, bottom, zNear )
               ;
    vec3 sum   = vec3( right,      top,   zFar )
               + vec3(  left, bottom, zNear );

    vec3 ratio = sum / delta;
    vec3 twoRatio = 2.0 / delta;

    return mat4( twoRatio.x,         0.0,          0.0, 0.0,
                        0.0, twoRatio.y,          0.0, 0.0,
                        0.0,         0.0, -twoRatio.z, 0.0,
                   -ratio.x,    -ratio.y,    -ratio.z, 1.0 );

}
```

9.10.6 Frustum

Perspective projection was rediscovered during the Renaissance. The OpenGL command *Frustum* computes a simple version, an extension of Ortho. Instead of projecting orthogonally along the z axis, the four corners of the front image plane are projected along each direction from the origin (eye) to the corner. The view volume is truncated by the near and far planes, or looks like a truncated pyramid—a frustum. The OpenGL shader code is shown in Listing 9.34.

Listing 9.34 Frustum matrix computation

```
mat4 FrustumMatrix( const in float    left, const in float right,
                    const in float bottom, const in float    top,
                    const in float  zNear, const in float   zFar )
```

```
{
    vec3 delta = vec3( right,    top,   zFar )
               - vec3( left, bottom, zNear );

    vec3 sum   = vec3( right,    top,   zFar )
               + vec3( left, bottom, zNear );

    vec3 ratio = sum / delta;
    vec3 twoRatio = 2.0 * zNear / delta;

    return mat4( twoRatio.x,        0.0,                0.0,  0.0,
                        0.0, twoRatio.y,                0.0,  0.0,
                    ratio.x,    ratio.y,           -ratio.z, -1.0,
                        0.0,        0.0, -zNear*twoRatio.z,  0.0 );

}
```

9.11 Operating on the Current Matrices

We have laid the foundation of the core OpenGL matrix computation functions. But the OpenGL matrix commands operate on a current matrix, selected by MatrixMode. We'll ignore the texture matrices and the rarely used color matrices for now.

In Listing 9.35 we put them together into operations on a current matrix.

Listing 9.35 Matrix operations

```
const int MODELVIEW = 0;
const int PROJECTION =1;

int  CurrentMode = MODELVIEW;
mat4 ModelviewMatrix = mat4( 1.0 );
mat4 ProjectionMatrix = mat4( 1.0 );
mat4 CurrentMatrix = mat4( 1.0 );

void MatrixMode ( const in int mode )
{
    if ( mode != CurrentMode )
    {
        switch (mode)
        {
            case MODELVIEW:
            {
                ProjectionMatrix = CurrentMatrix;
                CurrentMatrix = ModelviewMatrix;
                CurrentMode = MODELVIEW;
                break;
            }
            case PROJECTION:
```

```
                {
                    ModelviewMatrix = CurrentMatrix;          `
                    CurrentMatrix = ProjectionMatrix;
                    CurrentMode = PROJECTION;
                    break;
                }
                default:
                {
                    break;
                }
            }
        }
        return;
}

void LoadIdentity( void )
{
    CurrentMatrix = IdentityMatrix();
}
void LoadMatrix( const in mat4 m )
{
    CurrentMatrix = m;
}
void MultMatrix( const in mat4 m )
{
    CurrentMatrix = m
                * CurrentMatrix;
}
void Scale( const in vec3 s )
{
    CurrentMatrix = ScaleMatrix( s )
                * CurrentMatrix;
}
void Translate( const in vec3 t )
{
    CurrentMatrix = TranslateMatrix( t )
                * CurrentMatrix;
}


void Rotate( const in float angle,
            const in vec3  axis )
{
    CurrentMatrix = RotateMatrix( angle, axis )
                * CurrentMatrix;
}
void Ortho( const in float   left, const in float right,
            const in float bottom, const in float   top,
            const in float  zNear, const in float  zFar )
{
    CurrentMatrix = OrthoMatrix( left, right, bottom, top,
                                    zNear, zFar )
                * CurrentMatrix;
}
```

```
void Frustum( const in float    left, const in float right,
              const in float bottom, const in float    top,
              const in float  zNear, const in float   zFar )
{
    CurrentMatrix = FrustumMatrix( left, right, bottom, top,
                                   zNear, zFar )
                * CurrentMatrix;
}
```

9.11.1 A Simple Matrix Transformation Example

We can now "port" a transformation sequence from OpenGL to the
OpenGL Shading Language. This simple example in Listing 9.36 will
scale, rotate, and translate a model from model coordinates into world
coordinates.

We need to provide the warning again. Matrix operations, especially matrix
concatentations, are not that cheap. There are more efficient ways to
accomplish this in a vertex shader.

Listing 9.36 Simple matrix transformation

```
// Shading Language Equivalent  // Original OpenGL code
uniform float MCscale;          // float MCscale;
uniform float MCangle;          // float MCangle;
uniform vec3  MCaxis;           // float MCaxis[3];
uniform vec3  WCtranslate;      // float WCtranslate[3];


// ...

void ModelCoordinates2WorldCoordinates( void )
{
    MatrixMode( MODELVIEW );    // glMatrixMode( GL_MODELVIEW );
    LoadIdentity();             // glLoadIdentity;
    Scale( vec3(MCscale) );     // glScalef( MCscale,
                                //           MCscale,
                                //           MCscale );
    Rotate( MCangle, MCaxis );  // glRotatef( MCangle,
                                //            MCaxis[0],
                                //            MCaxis[1],
                                //            MCaxis[2] );
    Translate( WCtranslate );   // glTranslatef( WCtranslate[0],
                                //               WCtranslate[1],
                                //               WCtranslate[2] );
// ...
}
```

9.12 Summary

The rendering formulas specified by OpenGL have been reasonable ones to implement in fixed functionality hardware for the past decade or so, but they are not necessarily the best ones to use in your shaders. We look at better-performing and more realistic shaders in subsequent chapters. Still, it can be instructive to see how these formulas can be expressed in shaders written in the OpenGL Shading Language. The shader examples presented in this chapter demonstrate the expression of these fixed functionality transformation formulas, but they should not be considered optimal implementations. Take the ideas and the shading code illustrated in this chapter and adapt them to your own needs.

9.13 Further Information

The *OpenGL Programming Guide, Seventh Edition* (2010) by Dave Shreiner and the Khronos OpenGL ARB Working Group, contains more complete descriptions of the various formulas presented in this chapter. The functionality is defined in the OpenGL specification, *The OpenGL Graphics System: A Specification Version 3.0*, by Mark Segal and Kurt Akeley, edited by Jon Leech and Pat Brown (2008). Basic graphics concepts like transformation, lighting, fog, and texturing are also covered in standard graphics texts such as *Introduction to Computer Graphics* by J.D. Foley et al. (1994). *Real-Time Rendering* by Tomas Akenine-Möller and E. Haines (2002) also contains good descriptions of these basic topics.

[1] Akenine-Möller, Tomas, E. Haines, *Real-Time Rendering, Second Edition*, A K Peters, Ltd., Natick, Massachusetts, 2002. www.realtimerendering.com

[2] Baldwin, Dave, *OpenGL 2.0 Shading Language White Paper, Version 1.0*, 3Dlabs, October, 2001.

[3] Foley, J.D., A. van Dam, S.K. Feiner, J.H. Hughes, and R.L. Philips, *Introduction to Computer Graphics*, Addison-Wesley, Reading, Massachusetts, 1994.

[4] Foley, J.D., A. van Dam, S.K. Feiner, and J.H. Hughes, *Computer Graphics: Principles and Practice, Second Edition in C, Second Edition*, Addison-Wesley, Reading, Massachusetts, 1996.

[5] OpenGL Architecture Review Board, *OpenGL Reference Manual, Fourth Edition: The Official Reference to OpenGL, Version 1.4*, Editor: Dave Shreiner, Addison-Wesley, Reading, Massachusetts, 2004.

[6] Segal, Mark, and Kurt Akeley, *The OpenGL Graphics System: A Specification (Version 3.1)*, Editor (v1.1): Chris Frazier, (v1.2–3.1): Jon Leech, (v2.0): Jon Leech and Pat Brown, March 2009. www.opengl.org/documentation/specs/

[7] Shreiner, Dave, and the Khronos OpenGL ARB Working Group, *OpenGL Programming Guide, Seventh Edition: The Official Guide to Learning OpenGL, Versions 3.0 and 3.1*, Addison-Wesley, Boston, Massachusetts, 2010.

Chapter 10

Stored Texture Shaders

Texture mapping is a powerful mechanism built into OpenGL. At the time OpenGL was initially defined (1992), texture-mapping hardware was just starting to be available on commercial products. Nowadays, texture mapping is available on graphics hardware at all price points, even entry-level consumer graphics boards.

When OpenGL 1.0 was defined, texture mapping had a fairly narrow definition. It was simply a way to apply an image to the surface of an object. Since then, hardware has become capable of doing much more in this area, and researchers have come up with a lot of interesting things to do with textures other than just plastering images on surfaces. The scope of texture mapping has also been extended in OpenGL. Texture objects were one of the key additions in OpenGL 1.1. Three-dimensional textures were made part of the standard in OpenGL 1.2. The capability of hardware to access two or more textures simultaneously was exposed in OpenGL 1.3, along with cube map textures and a framework for supporting compressed textures formats. OpenGL 1.4 added support for depth textures and shadows, automatic mipmap generation, and another texture wrap mode (mirrored repeat). If you need a quick review of how texturing works in OpenGL, refer to Section 1.10.

The programmability introduced with the OpenGL Shading Language allows for a much broader definition of texture mapping. With programmable shaders, an application can read values from any number of textures and use them in any way that makes sense. This includes supporting sophisticated algorithms that use the results of one texture access to define the parameters of another texture access. Textures can also store intermediate rendering results; they can serve as lookup tables for complex functions;

they can store normals, normal perturbation factors, gloss values, visibility information, and polynomial coefficients; and they can do many other things. These things could not be done nearly as easily, if at all, in unextended OpenGL, and this flexibility means that texture maps are coming closer to being general-purpose memory that can be used for arbitrary purposes. (Filtering and wrapping behavior still differentiate texture-map access from normal memory access operations.)

This chapter describes several shaders that, at their core, rely on looking up values in texture memory and using those values to achieve interesting effects. We start by talking a little bit about how textures are accessed from within a shader, and then we look at several examples of shaders that access texture memory for various purposes other than just the straightforward application of an image to the surface of a 3D object.

10.1 Access to Texture Maps from a Shader

Applications are required to set up and initialize texturing state properly before executing a shader that accesses texture memory. An application must perform the following steps to set up a texture for use within a shader:

1. Select a specific texture unit, and make it active by calling **glActiveTexture**.

2. Create a texture object, and bind it to the active texture unit by calling **glBindTexture**.

3. Set various parameters (wrapping, filtering, etc.) of the texture object by calling **glTexParameter**.

4. Define the texture by calling **glTexImage**.

It is quite straightforward to access textures from within a shader after texture state has been set up properly by the application. The OpenGL Shading Language has built-in data types (see Section 3.2.4) and built-in functions (see Section 5.7) to accomplish this task.

A uniform variable of type **sampler** must be used to access a texture from within a shader. Within a shader, a sampler is considered an opaque data type containing a value that can access a particular texture. The shader is responsible for declaring such a uniform variable for each texture that it wants to access. The application must provide a value for the sampler before execution of the shader, as described in Section 7.9.

The type of the sampler indicates the type of texture that is to be accessed. A variable of type **sampler1D** accesses a 1D texture; a variable of type

sampler2D accesses a 2D texture; a variable of type **sampler3D** accesses a 3D texture; a variable of type **samplerCube** accesses a cube map texture; and variables of type **samplerShadow1D** and **samplerShadow2D** access 1D and 2D depth textures. For instance, if the application intends to use texture unit 4 to store a 2D texture, the shader must declare a uniform variable of type **sampler2D**, and the application must load a value of 4 into this variable before executing the shader.

The built-in function **texture** performs texture access within a shader. The first argument in each of these built-in functions is a sampler.

The built-in texture-access function also takes a texture coordinate as an argument. Hardware uses this texture coordinate to determine which locations in the texture map are to be accessed. A 1D texture is accessed with a single floating-point texture coordinate. A 2D texture is accessed with a **vec2**, and a 3D texture is accessed with a **vec3**. A projective version of the texture access function, **textureProj**, is also provided. In this function, the individual components of the texture coordinate are divided by the last component of the texture coordinate, and the result is used in the texture access operation.

There are some differences between accessing a texture from a vertex shader and accessing a texture from a fragment shader (the OpenGL Shading Language allows both). The level of detail to be used for accessing a mipmap texture is calculated with implicit derivatives. Derivatives are available in the fragment shader but not in the vertex shader. For this reason, the OpenGL Shading Language includes a built-in texture function that can be used to allow the level of detail to be expressed directly as a function argument, **textureLOD**, and a built-in texture function that allows explicit derivatives as function arguments, **textureGrad**. These may be used in either the vertex or the fragment shader. The OpenGL Shading Language also includes built-in functions that can be used only in a fragment shader that allows a level-of-detail bias to be passed in. This bias value is added to the mechanically computed level-of-detail value. In this way, a shader writer can add a little extra sharpness or blurriness to the texture mapping function, depending on the situation. If any of these functions is used with a texture that is not a mipmap texture, the level-of-detail bias value is ignored.

The built-in functions to access cube maps operate in the same way as defined for fixed functionality. The texture coordinate that is provided is treated as a direction vector that emanates from the center of a cube. This value selects one of the cube map's 2D textures, based on the coordinate with the largest magnitude. The other two coordinates are divided by the absolute value of this coordinate and scaled and biased to calculate a 2D coordinate that will be used to access the chosen face of the cube map.

The built-in functions to access depth textures also operate in the same way as defined for fixed functionality. The texture accessed by one of these functions must have a base internal format of GL_DEPTH_COMPONENT. The value that is returned when this type of texture is accessed depends on the texture-comparison mode, the texture-comparison function, and the depth texture mode. Each of these values can be set with **glTexParameter**.

The built-in texture access functions operate according to the current state of the texture unit that is being accessed and according to the parameters of the texture object that is bound to that texture unit. In other words, the value returned by the built-in texture access functions take into consideration the texturing state that has already been established for the texture unit and the texture object, including wrap mode, minification filter, magnification filter, border color, minimum/maximum level of detail, texture comparison mode, and so on.

10.2 Simple Texturing Example

With these built-in functions for accessing textures, it's easy to write a simple shader that does texture mapping. Our goal is to create a texture-mapped sphere by using a realistic texture of the earth's surface. Application code described in this chapter came from **ogl2demo**, written primarily by Barthold Lichtenbelt. Similar code is available in **GLSLdemo**, written by Philip Rideout.

To achieve good results, it helps to start with excellent textures. Color Plate 3 shows an example of a two-dimensional texture map, a cylindrical projection of the earth's surface, including clouds. This image, and other images in this section, were obtained from the NASA Web site and were created by Reto Stöckli of the NASA/Goddard Space Flight Center. These images of Earth are part of a series of consistently processed data sets (land, sea ice, and clouds) from NASA's remote sensing satellite, the Moderate Resolution Imaging Spectroradiometer, or MODIS. Data from this satellite was combined with other related data sets (topography, land cover, and city lights), all at 1 kilometer resolution. The resulting series of images is extremely high resolution (43200 × 21600 pixels). For our purposes, we can get by with a much smaller texture, so we use versions that have been sampled down to 2048 × 1024.

10.2.1 Application Setup

We assume that the image data has been read into our application and that the image width, image height, a pointer to the image data, and a texture name generated by OpenGL can be passed to our texture initialization function.

```
init2DTexture(GLint texName, GLint texWidth,
              GLint texHeight, GLubyte *texPtr)
{
    glBindTexture(GL_TEXTURE_2D, texName);
    glTexParameteri(GL_TEXTURE_2D, GL_TEXTURE_WRAP_S, GL_REPEAT);
    glTexParameteri(GL_TEXTURE_2D, GL_TEXTURE_WRAP_T, GL_REPEAT);
    glTexParameteri(GL_TEXTURE_2D, GL_TEXTURE_MAG_FILTER, GL_LINEAR);
    glTexParameteri(GL_TEXTURE_2D, GL_TEXTURE_MIN_FILTER, GL_LINEAR);
    glTexImage2D(GL_TEXTURE_2D, 0, GL_RGB, texWidth, texHeight, 0,
                 GL_RGB, GL_UNSIGNED_BYTE, texPtr);
}
```

This initialization function creates a texture object named *texName*. Calls to **glTexParameter** set the wrapping behavior and filtering modes. We've chosen to use repeat as our wrapping behavior and to do linear filtering. We specify the data for the texture by calling **glTexImage2D** (the values passed to this function depend on how the image data has been stored in memory).

When we're ready to use this texture, we can use the following OpenGL calls:

```
glActiveTexture(GL_TEXTURE0);
glBindTexture(GL_TEXTURE_2D, earthTexName);
```

This sequence of calls sets the active texture unit to texture unit 0, binds our earth texture to this texture unit, and makes it active. We need to provide the values for two uniform variables. The vertex shader needs to know the light position, and the fragment shader needs to know the texture unit that is to be accessed. We define the light position as a **vec3** in the vertex shader named *lightPosition* and the texture unit as a **sampler2D** in the fragment shader named *EarthTexture*. Our application code needs to determine the location of these uniform variables and then provide appropriate values. We assume that our shaders have been compiled, linked using a program object whose handle is *programObj*, and installed as part of current state. We can make the following calls to initialize the uniform variables:

```
lightLoc = glGetUniformLocation(programObj, "LightPosition");
glUniform3f(lightLoc, 0.0, 0.0, 4.0);
texLoc   = glGetUniformLocation(programObj, "EarthTexture");
glUniform1i(texLoc, 0);
```

The light source position is set to a point right in front of the object along the viewing axis. We plan to use texture unit 0 for our earth texture, so that is the value loaded into our sampler variable.

The application can now make appropriate OpenGL calls to draw a sphere, and the earth texture will be applied. A surface normal, a 2D texture coordinate, and a vertex position must be specified for each vertex.

10.2.2 Vertex Shader

The vertex shader for our simple texturing example is similar to the simple brick vertex shader described in Section 6.2. The main difference is that a texture coordinate is passed in as a vertex attribute, and it is passed on as a user-defined out variable name *TexCoord* (see Listing 10.1).

Listing 10.1 Vertex shader for simple texturing

```
#version 140
in   vec4   MCVertex;
in   vec3   MCNormal;
out  vec2   TexCoord;

out float LightIntensity;
out vec4  TexCoord;

uniform mat4 MVMatrix;
uniform mat4 MVPMatrix;
uniform mat3 NormalMatrix;

uniform vec3 LightPosition;

const float specularContribution = 0.1;
const float diffuseContribution  = 1.0 - specularContribution;

void main()
{
    vec3 ecPosition = vec3(MVMatrix * MCVertex);
    vec3 tnorm      = normalize(NormalMatrix * MCNormal);
    vec3 lightVec   = normalize(LightPosition - ecPosition);
    vec3 reflectVec = reflect(-lightVec, tnorm);
    vec3 viewVec    = normalize(-ecPosition);

    float spec      = clamp(dot(reflectVec, viewVec), 0.0, 1.0);
    spec            = pow(spec, 16.0);

    LightIntensity  = diffuseContribution
                      * max(dot(lightVec, tnorm), 0.0)
                      + specularContribution * spec;

    TexCoord        = TexCoord0.st;
    gl_Position     = MVPMatrix * MCVertex;
}
```

10.2.3 Fragment Shader

The fragment shader shown in Listing 10.2 applies the earth texture to the incoming geometry. So, for instance, if we define a sphere where the s texture coordinates are related to longitude (e.g., 0° longitude is $s = 0$, and 360° longitude is $s = 1.0$) and t texture coordinates are related to latitude (90° south latitude is $t = 0.0$, and 90° north latitude is $t = 1.0$), then we can apply the texture map to the sphere's geometry as shown in Color Plate 6.

In the following fragment shader, the incoming s and t texture coordinate values (part of the user-defined in variable *TexCoord*) are used to look up a value from the texture currently bound to texture unit 0. The resulting value is multiplied by the light intensity computed by the vertex shader and passed as an in variable. The color is then clamped, and an alpha value of 1.0 is added to create the final fragment color, which is sent on for further processing, including depth testing. The resulting image as mapped onto a sphere is shown in Color Plate 6.

Listing 10.2 Fragment shader for simple texture mapping example

```
#version 140
in float LightIntensity;
in vec2  TexCoord;

out vec4 FragColor;

uniform sampler2D EarthTexture;

void main()
{
    vec3 lightColor = vec3(texture(EarthTexture, TexCoord));
    FragColor    = vec4(lightColor * LightIntensity, 1.0);
}
```

10.3 Multitexturing Example

The resulting image looks pretty good, but with a little more effort we can get it looking even better. For one thing, we know that there are lots of man-made lights on our planet, so when it's nighttime, major towns and cities can be seen as specks of light, even from space. So we use the angle between the light direction and the normal at each surface location to determine whether that location is in "daytime" or "nighttime." For points that are in daytime, we access the texture map that contains daylight colors and do an appropriate lighting calculation. For points in the nighttime region of the planet, we do no lighting and access a texture that shows the earth as illuminated at night. The daytime and nighttime textures are shown in Color Plate 4 and Color Plate 5.

Another somewhat unrealistic aspect to our simple approach is the reflection of sunlight off the surface of oceans and large lakes. Water is a very good reflective surface, and when our viewpoint is nearly the same as the reflection angle for the light source, we should see a specular reflection. But we know that desert, grass, and trees don't have this same kind of reflective property, so how can we get a nice specular highlight on the water but not on the land?

The answer is a technique called a GLOSS MAP. We make a single channel (i.e., grayscale) version of our original texture and assign values of 1.0 for areas that represent water and 0 for everything else. At each fragment, we read this gloss texture and multiply its value by the specular illumination portion of our lighting equation. It's fairly simple to create the gloss map in an image-editing program. The easiest way to do this is by editing the red channel of the cloudless daytime image. In this channel, all the water areas appear black or nearly black because they contain very little red information. We use a selection tool to select all the black (water) areas and then fill the selected area (water regions) with white. We invert the selection and fill the land areas with black. The result is a texture that contains a value of 1.0 (white) for areas in which we want a specular highlight, and a value of 0 (black) for areas in which we don't. We use this "gloss" value as a multiplier in our specular reflection calculation, so areas that represent water include a specular reflection term, and areas that represent land don't. Our gloss map is shown in Figure 10.1.

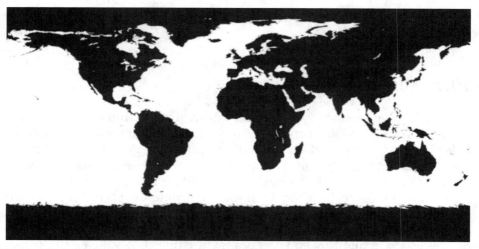

Figure 10.1   Gloss map used to create specular reflections from water surfaces

As you saw in Color Plate 4 and Color Plate 5, our daytime and nighttime textures no longer include cloud cover. So we store our cloud texture as a single channel (i.e., grayscale) texture as shown in Figure 10.2. By doing this, we have more flexibility about how we combine the cloud image with the images of the Earth's surface. For daytime views, we want the clouds to have diffuse reflection but no specular reflection. Furthermore, clouds obscure the surface, so a value of 1.0 for the cloud cover indicates that the earth's surface at that location is completely obscured by clouds. For nighttime views, we don't want any light reflecting from the clouds, but we do want them to obscure the surface below. For convenience, we've stored our single channel cloud image into the red channel of an RGB texture, and we've stored our gloss map as the green channel. The blue channel is unused. (Another choice would be to store the gloss map as the alpha channel for our daytime image and the cloud texture as the alpha channel in our nighttime image.)

10.3.1 Application Setup

The setup required for multitexturing is about the same as it was for the simple texturing example, except that we need to set up three textures instead of one. We can call the **init2Dtexture** function described in Section 10.2.1 three times, once each for the daytime earth texture, the nighttime earth texture,

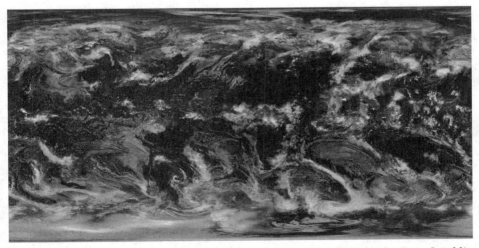

Figure 10.2 Texture map showing cloud cover (Blue Marble image by Reto Stöckli, NASA Goddard Space Flight Center)

and the cloud/gloss texture. We can activate these textures with the following OpenGL calls:

```
glActiveTexture(GL_TEXTURE0);
glBindTexture(GL_TEXTURE_2D, earthDayTexName);

glActiveTexture(GL_TEXTURE1);
glBindTexture(GL_TEXTURE_2D, earthNightTexName);

glActiveTexture(GL_TEXTURE2);
glBindTexture(GL_TEXTURE_2D, earthCloudsTexName);
```

The necessary uniform variables can be initialized as follows:

```
lightLoc = glGetUniformLocation(programObj, "LightPosition");
glUniform3f(lightLoc, 0.0, 0.0, 4.0);
texLoc   = glGetUniformLocation(programObj, "EarthDay");
glUniform1i(texLoc, 0);
texLoc   = glGetUniformLocation(programObj, "EarthNight");
glUniform1i(texLoc, 1);
texLoc   = glGetUniformLocation(programObj, "EarthCloudGloss");
glUniform1i(texLoc, 2);
```

The application can now make appropriate OpenGL calls to draw a sphere. A surface normal, a 2D texture coordinate, and a vertex position must be specified for each vertex.

10.3.2 Vertex Shader

The vertex shader for this multitexturing example is similar to the one described for the simple texturing example in Section 10.2.2, except that the diffuse and specular factors are computed by the vertex shader and passed as separate out variables to the fragment shader. The computed specular value is multiplied by the constant vector (1.0, 0.941, 0.898) to approximate the color of sunlight (see Listing 10.3).

Listing 10.3 Vertex shader for multitexturing

```
#version 140
in  vec4  MCVertex;
in  vec3  MCNormal;
in  vec4  TexCoord0;

out float Diffuse;
out vec3  Specular;
out vec2  TexCoord;

uniform vec3 LightPosition;
```

```
uniform mat4 MVMatrix;
uniform mat4 MVPMatrix;
uniform mat3 NormalMatrix;

void main()
{
    vec3 ecPosition = vec3(MVMatrix * MCVertex);
    vec3 tnorm      = normalize(NormalMatrix * MCNormal);
    vec3 lightVec   = normalize(LightPosition - ecPosition);
    vec3 reflectVec = reflect(-lightVec, tnorm);
    vec3 viewVec    = normalize(-ecPosition);

    float spec      = clamp(dot(reflectVec, viewVec), 0.0, 1.0);
    spec            = pow(spec, 8.0);
    Specular        = spec * vec3(1.0, 0.941, 0.898) * 0.3;

    Diffuse         = max(dot(lightVec, tnorm), 0.0);

    TexCoord        = TexCoord0.st;
    gl_Position     = MVPMatrix * MCVertex;
}
```

10.3.3 Fragment Shader

The fragment shader that performs the desired multitexturing is shown in Listing 10.4. The application has loaded the daytime texture in the texture unit specified by *EarthDay*, the nighttime texture into the texture unit specified by *EarthNight*, and the cloud/gloss texture into the texture unit specified by *EarthCloudGloss*. The lighting computation is done in a vertex shader that computes diffuse and specular reflection factors and passes them to the fragment shader independently. The texture coordinates supplied by the application are also passed to the fragment shader and form the basis of our texture lookup operation.

In our fragment shader, the first thing we do is access our cloud/gloss texture because its values will be used in the computations that follow. Next, we look up the value from our daytime texture, multiply it by our diffuse lighting factor, and add to it the specular lighting factor multiplied by the gloss value. If the fragment is unobscured by clouds, our computation gives us the desired effect of diffuse lighting over the whole surface of the earth with specular highlights from water surfaces. This value is multiplied by 1.0 minus the cloudiness factor. Finally, we add the cloud effect by multiplying our cloudiness factor by the diffuse lighting value and adding this to our previous result.

The nighttime calculation is simpler. Here, we just look up the value from our nighttime texture and multiply that result by 1.0 minus the cloudiness factor. Because this fragment will be in shadow, the diffuse and specular components are not used.

With these values computed, we can determine the value to be used for each fragment. The key is our diffuse lighting factor, which is greater than zero for areas in sunlight, equal to zero for areas in shadow, and near zero for areas near the terminator. The color value ends up being the computed *daytime* value in the sunlit areas, the computed *nighttime* value in the areas in shadow, and a mix of the two values to make a gradual transition near the terminator.

An alpha value of 1.0 is added to produce our final fragment color. Several views from the final shader are shown in Color Plate 7. You can see the nice specular highlight off the Gulf of Mexico in the first image. If you look closely at the third (nighttime) image, you can see the clouds obscuring the central part of the east coast of the United States and the northwestern part of Brazil.

It is worth pointing out that this shader should not be considered a general-purpose shader because it has some built-in assumptions about the type of geometry that will be drawn. It will look "right" only when used with a sphere with proper texture coordinates. More can be done to make the shader even more realistic. The color of the atmosphere actually varies, depending on the viewing position and the position of the sun. It is redder when near the shadow boundary, a fact that we often notice near sunrise and sunset. See the references at the end of the chapter for more information about achieving realistic effects such as Rayleigh scattering.

Listing 10.4   "As the world turns" fragment shader

```
uniform sampler2D EarthDay;
uniform sampler2D EarthNight;
uniform sampler2D EarthCloudGloss;

in float Diffuse;
in vec3  Specular;
in vec2  TexCoord;

out vec4 FragColor;

void main()
{
    // Monochrome cloud cover value will be in clouds.r
    // Gloss value will be in clouds.g
    // clouds.b will be unused
```

```
    vec2 clouds    = texture(EarthCloudGloss, TexCoord).rg;
    vec3 daytime   = (texture(EarthDay, TexCoord).rgb * Diffuse +
                      Specular * clouds.g) * (1.0 - clouds.r) +
                      clouds.r * Diffuse;
    vec3 nighttime = texture(EarthNight, TexCoord).rgb *
                      (1.0 - clouds.r) * 2.0;

    vec3 color = daytime;

    if (Diffuse < 0.1)
        color = mix(nighttime, daytime, (Diffuse + 0.1) * 5.0);

    FragColor = vec4(color, 1.0);
}
```

10.4 Cube Mapping Example

A technique called ENVIRONMENT MAPPING models reflections in a complex environment without resorting to ray-tracing. In this technique, one or more texture maps simulate the environment's reflections. This technique is best used for rendering objects that have some mirrorlike qualities.

The fundamental idea behind environment mapping is that we use the reflection vector from the surface of an object to look up the reflection color from an "environment" that is stored in a texture map. If environment mapping is done properly, the result looks as if the object being rendered is shiny and is reflecting its environment.

There are several ways to do environment mapping, including SPHERE MAPPING and CUBE MAPPING, both of which are supported in standard OpenGL. An example cube map is shown in Color Plate 10.

In this section, we describe OpenGL shaders that use a cube map to perform environment mapping on an object. The object is assumed to have an underlying layer that acts as a diffuse reflector. The result from the diffuse portion is combined with the environment reflection to produce a final value at each pixel.

A cube map is a texture that has six 2D textures that are organized to represent the faces of a cube. Cube maps are accessed with three texture coordinates that are treated as a direction vector emanating from the center of the cube. The cube map faces are differentiated by the sign along each of the three major axis directions. Think of the faces this way: The positive and negative *x* faces are the right and left sides of the cube; positive and negative *y* faces are the top and bottom sides of the cube; and positive and negative *z* faces are the back and front sides of the cube. Graphics hardware can use the three texture coordinates as a direction vector and automatically select the proper face and return a texel value where the direction vector intersects that face of the cube map.

10.4.1 Application Setup

The application needs to do very little to set up this shader. We use a simple lighting model, so the only lighting state that we need to pass in is a single light source position. We access the cube map through texture unit 4. *baseColor* defines the color of the diffuse underlayer of our object, and *mixRatio* sets the ratio of base color to environment map reflection. Here are the definitions for the uniform variables that we use:

```
LightPosition   0.0, 0.0, 4.0
BaseColor       0.4, 0.4, 1.0
MixRatio        0.8
EnvMap          4
```

After the shaders have been installed and the uniform variables have been provided, the application is expected to send a normal and the vertex position for each vertex that is to be drawn. The current values for the model-view matrix, the modelview-projection matrix, and the normal matrix are all accessed from within the vertex shader.

10.4.2 Vertex Shader

Listing 10.5 comprises the vertex shader that is used to do environment mapping with a cube map.

Listing 10.5 Vertex shader used for environment mapping with a cube map

```
#version 140

in   vec4   MCVertex;
in   vec3   MCNormal;

out float LightIntensity;
out vec3   ReflectDir;

uniform vec3 LightPosition;

uniform mat4 MVMatrix;
uniform mat4 MVPMatrix;
uniform mat3 NormalMatrix;
```

```
void main()
{
    gl_Position      = MVPMatrix * MCVertex;
    vec3 normal      = normalize(NormalMatrix * MCNormal);
    vec4 pos         = MVMatrix * MCVertex;
    vec3 eyeDir      = pos.xyz;
    ReflectDir       = reflect(eyeDir, normal);
    vec3 lightDir    = normalize(LightPosition - eyeDir);
    LightIntensity   = max(dot(lightDir, normal),0.0);
}
```

The goal of this vertex shader is to produce two values that will be interpolated across each primitive: a diffuse lighting value and a reflection direction. The reflection direction is used as the texture coordinate for accessing the cube map in the fragment shader.

We compute the transformed position of the vertex in the first line of the program in the usual way. We transform and normalize the incoming normal, and then we compute the eye direction, based on the current model-view matrix and the incoming vertex value. We pass these two values to the built-in function **reflect** to compute the reflection direction vector. Finally, we compute a diffuse lighting value in the same manner that we've done in previous examples.

10.4.3 Fragment Shader

Listing 10.6 contains the fragment shader that performs environment mapping with a cube map.

Listing 10.6 Fragment shader for doing environment mapping with a cube map

```
#version 140

uniform vec3  BaseColor;
uniform float MixRatio;

uniform samplerCube EnvMap;

in vec3  ReflectDir;
in float LightIntensity;

out vec4 FragColor;

void main()
{
    // Look up environment map value in cube map

    vec3 envColor = vec3(texture(EnvMap, ReflectDir));
```

```
// Add lighting to base color and mix

vec3 base = LightIntensity * BaseColor;
envColor   = mix(envColor, base, MixRatio);

FragColor = vec4(envColor, 1.0);
}
```

The fragment shader for cube map environment mapping does three things. First, the computed and interpolated in variable *ReflectDir* is used to access our cube map texture and return the texel value that is used to simulate the reflection from a shiny surface. Second, the base color of the object is modulated by the interpolated light intensity value. Finally, these two values are combined in the ratio defined by the uniform variable *MixRatio*. This uniform variable can be modified by the user to make the object vary between completely shiny and completely diffuse.

10.5 Another Environment Mapping Example

Another option for environment mapping is to use photographic methods to create a single 2D texture map, called an EQUIRECTANGULAR TEXTURE MAP or a LAT-LONG TEXTURE MAP. This type of texture can be obtained from a real-world environment by photography techniques, or it can be created to represent a synthetic environment. An example is shown in Color Plate 9.

Whatever means are used to obtain an image, the result is a single image that spans 360° horizontally and 180° vertically. The image is also distorted as you move up or down from the center of the image. This distortion is done deliberately so that you will see a reasonable representation of the environment if you "shrink-wrap" this texture around the object that you're rendering.

The key to using an equirectangular texture as the environment map is to produce a pair of angles that index into the texture. We compute an altitude angle by determining the angle between the reflection direction and the *XZ* plane. This altitude angle varies from 90° (reflection is straight up) to –90° (reflection is straight down). The sine of this angle varies from 1.0 to –1.0, and we use this fact to get a texture coordinate in the range of [0,1].

We determine an azimuth angle by projecting the reflection direction onto the *XZ* plane. The azimuth angle varies from 0° to 360°, and this gives us the key to get a second texture coordinate in the range of [0,1].

The following OpenGL shaders work together to perform environment mapping on an object by using an equirectangular texture map. These shaders are derived from a "bumpy/shiner" shader pair that was developed with John Kessenich and presented at SIGGRAPH 2002. The altitude and azimuth angles are computed to determine *s* and *t* values for indexing into our 2D environment texture. This texture's wrapping behavior is set so that it wraps in both *s* and *t*. (This supports a little trick that we do in the fragment shader.) Otherwise, the initial conditions are the same as described for the cube map environment mapping example.

10.5.1 Vertex Shader

Listing 10.7 comprises the vertex shader that does environment mapping with an equirectangular texture map. The only real difference between this shader and the one described in Section 10.4.2 is that this one computes *Normal* and *EyeDir* and passes them to the fragment shader as in variables so that the reflection vector can be computed in the fragment shader.

Listing 10.7   Vertex shader used for environment mapping

```
#version 140

in  vec4  MCVertex;
in  vec3  MCNormal;

out vec3  Normal;
out vec3  EyeDir;
out float LightIntensity;

uniform vec3 LightPosition;

uniform mat4 MVMatrix;
uniform mat4 MVPMatrix;
uniform mat3 NormalMatrix;

void main()
{
    gl_Position    = MVPMatrix * MCVertex;
    Normal         = normalize(NormalMatrix * MCNormal);
    vec4 pos       = MVMatrix * MCVertex;
    EyeDir         = pos.xyz;
    vec3 LightDir  = normalize(LightPosition - EyeDir);
    LightIntensity = max(dot(LightDir, Normal), 0.0);
}
```

10.5.2 Fragment Shader

Listing 10.8 contains the fragment shader that does environment mapping by using an equirectangular texture map.

Listing 10.8 Fragment shader for doing environment mapping with an equirectangular texture map

```
#version 140

const vec3 Xunitvec = vec3(1.0, 0.0, 0.0);
const vec3 Yunitvec = vec3(0.0, 1.0, 0.0);

uniform vec3  BaseColor;
uniform float MixRatio;

uniform sampler2D EnvMap;  // = 4

in vec3  Normal;
in vec3  EyeDir;
in float LightIntensity;

out vec4 FragColor;

void main()
{
    // Compute reflection vector

    vec3 reflectDir = reflect(EyeDir, Normal);

    // Compute altitude and azimuth angles

    vec2 index;

    index.t = dot(normalize(reflectDir), Yunitvec);
    reflectDir.y = 0.0;
    index.s = dot(normalize(reflectDir), Xunitvec) * 0.5;

    // Calculate gradiants before discontinuous changes to index

    vec2 dPdx = dFdx( index );
    vec2 dPdy = dFdy( index );

    // Translate index values into proper range

    if (reflectDir.z >= 0.0)
        index = (index + 1.0) * 0.5;
    else
    {
```

```
        index.t = (index.t + 1.0) * 0.5;
        index.s = (-index.s) * 0.5 + 1.0;
    }

    // if reflectDir.z >= 0.0, s will go from 0.25 to 0.75
    // if reflectDir.z <  0.0, s will go from 0.75 to 1.25, and
    // that's OK, because we've set the texture to wrap.

    // Do a lookup into the environment map.

    vec3 envColor = vec3(textureGrad(EnvMap, index, dPdx, dPdy)););

    // Add lighting to base color and mix

    vec3 base = LightIntensity * BaseColor;
    envColor = mix(envColor, base, MixRatio);

    FragColor = vec4(envColor, 1.0);
}
```

The in variables *Normal* and *EyeDir* are the values generated by the vertex shader and then interpolated across the primitive. To get truly precise results, these values should be normalized again in the fragment shader. However, for this shader, skipping the normalization gives us a little better performance, and the quality is acceptable for certain objects.

The constants *Xunitvec* and *Yunitvec* have been set up with the proper values for computing our altitude and azimuth angles. First, we compute our altitude angle by normalizing the *reflectionDir* vector and performing a dot product with the *Yunitvec* constant. Because both vectors are unit vectors, this dot product computation gives us a cosine value for the desired angle that ranges from [–1,1]. Setting the y component of our reflection vector to 0 causes it to be projected onto the *XZ* plane. We normalize this new vector to get the cosine of our azimuth angle. Again, this value ranges from [–1,1]. Because the horizontal direction of our environment texture spans 360°, we multiply by 0.5 so that we get a value that maps into half of our environment map. Then we need to do a little more work to determine which half this is.

If the z portion of our reflection direction is positive, we know that the reflection direction is "toward the front" and we use the computed texture map indices directly. The index values are scaled and biased so that when we access the environment map texture, we get s values that range from [0.25,0.75] and t values that range from [0,1].

If z is negative, we do our calculations a little differently. The t value is still computed the same way, but the s value is scaled and biased so that it ranges from [0.75,1.25]. We can use these values directly because we've set our texture wrap modes to GL_REPEAT. *s* values between 1.0 and 1.25 will map to *s* values from 0 to 0.25 in our actual texture (the trick alluded to earlier). In this way, we can properly access the entire environment texture, depending on the reflection direction. We could compare *s* to 1.0 and subtract 1.0 if its value is greater than 1.0, but this would end up requiring additional instructions in the machine code, and hence the performance would be reduced. By using the repeat mode trick, we get the hardware to take care of this for free.

With our index values set, all we need to do is look up the value in the texture map. We compute a diffusely lit base color value by multiplying our incoming light intensity by *BaseColor*. We mix this value with our environment map value to create a ceramic effect. We then create a **vec4** by adding an alpha value of 1.0 and send the final fragment color on for further processing. The final result is shown in Color Plate 11A. You can see the branches from the tree in the environment on the back and rear of the triceratops. For this example, we used a color of (0.4, 0.4, 1.0) (i.e., light blue) and a mix ratio of 0.8 (i.e., 80% diffuse color, 20% environment map value).

An example of environment mapping that assumes a mirrorlike surface and adds procedural bumps is shown in Color Plate 11B.

10.6 Glyph Bombing

In this section, we develop a shader that demonstrates a couple of different uses for textures. In *Texturing and Modeling: A Procedural Approach*, Darwyn Peachy described a process called TEXTURE BOMBING that creates an irregular texture pattern. The idea is to divide a surface into a grid and then draw a decorative element or image (e.g., a star, a polka dot, or some other shape) within each cell. By applying some randomness to the placement, scaling, or rotation of each texture element, you can easily create an interesting pattern that is suitable for objects such as wallpaper, gift wrap, clothing, and the like. Peachey described a RenderMan shader to perform texture bombing, and in *GPU Gems*, Steve Glanville described a method for texture bombing in Cg.

The basic concept of texture bombing can be taken a bit further. Joshua Doss developed a GLSL shader that randomly selects from several collections of related character glyphs. Two textures are used for the so-called GLYPH BOMBING shader—a single texture that stores character glyphs and a texture that stores random values. Let's examine how this shader works.

10.6.1 Application Setup

The first step is to create a 2D texture that contains the glyphs that will be used. To set this up, you just need to carefully draw characters on a 10×10 grid, using a 2D image-editing program like Photoshop. Each row should have a common theme like the image shown in Figure 10.3. A single uniform variable (*ColAdjust*) is used to select the row to be accessed. Within this row, a glyph is chosen at random, and when it is drawn, it can also be optionally scaled and rotated. Thus, we can easily choose a pattern from a collection snowflakes, musical symbols, animal silhouettes, flower dingbats, and so on. Applying a random color and placing the glyph randomly within the cell add even more irregularity and interest to the final result.

The second texture that this shader uses contains random values in the range of [0,1.0] for each component. We access this texture to obtain a **vec4** containing random numbers and use these values to apply randomness to several computations within the fragment shader.

Figure 10.3 Texture map showing a collection of character glyphs that are used with the glyph bombing shader

Just like the brick shader discussed in Chapter 6, this shader needs a frame of reference for creating the cells in which we draw our glyphs. In this case, we use the object's texture coordinates to establish the reference frame. We can scale the texture coordinates with a uniform variable (*ScaleFactor*) to make the cells larger or smaller. Our glyph texture map contains only levels of gray. We use the value obtained from the glyph texture map to linearly interpolate between a default object color (*ModelColor*) and a random color that is generated when a glyph is drawn.

Because we are allowing random offsets and random rotation, we need to take care of some complications in our shader. Each of these effects can cause the object we are drawing to extend into neighboring cells.

Let's first consider the case of random offsets. When each glyph is drawn, our shader offsets the glyph by adding a value in the range [0,1.0] for each of *x* and *y*. This means that the glyph can be shifted over and up by some amount, possibly contributing to the contents of pixel locations in three neighboring cells to the right and above. Figure 10.4 illustrates the possibilities.

Consequently, as we consider how to compute the value at one particular pixel location, we must consider the possibility that the glyphs to be drawn

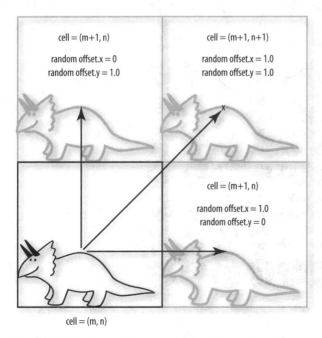

cell = (m+1, n)

random offset.x = 0
random offset.y = 1.0

cell = (m+1, n+1)

random offset.x = 1.0
random offset.y = 1.0

cell = (m+1, n)

random offset.x = 1.0
random offset.y = 0

cell = (m, n)

Figure 10.4   Depending on the random offset for a particular cell, a glyph may contribute to any one of four cells.

in cells to the left and below the current cell may be contributing to the fragment. For instance, the spot marked by the × in Figure 10.4 might actually have contributions from the glyphs in cells (m, n), $(m+1, n)$, $(m, n+1)$ in addition to the glyph contained in the cell $(m+1, n+1)$.

Things get even more interesting when we allow for a random angle of rotation. Now the offset combined with rotation can cause our glyph to extend into any of nine cells, as shown in Figure 10.5. For this case, as we render fragments we must consider all eight surrounding cells in addition to the cell containing the fragment being rendered. We use a Boolean uniform variable, *RandomRotate*, to determine whether we need to loop over four cells or nine.

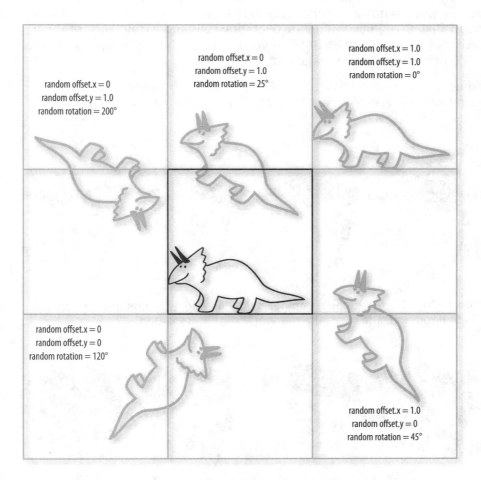

random offset.x = 0
random offset.y = 1.0
random rotation = 200°

random offset.x = 0
random offset.y = 1.0
random rotation = 25°

random offset.x = 1.0
random offset.y = 1.0
random rotation = 0°

random offset.x = 0
random offset.y = 0
random rotation = 120°

random offset.x = 1.0
random offset.y = 0
random rotation = 45°

Figure 10.5 Depending on a random offset and a random angle of rotation, a glyph may contribute to fragments in any of nine adjacent cells.

We use a few additional uniform variables to offer more control over the number of glyphs and their placement and to give an even greater appearance of randomness to the final pattern. *RandomScale* is a Boolean value that causes the size of the glyph to be scaled in both x and y by random values in the range [0,1.0]. (This has no effect on the cells that are affected, because the glyph can only be made smaller by this operation.) Another uniform variable, *Percentage*, indicates the probability that a glyph will be drawn in each cell. Lowering this value increases the number of empty cells in the final image.

We can even include a loop in the shader so that we can apply more than one glyph per cell. The number of glyphs drawn per cell is set with *SamplesPerCell*. Setting this value to increasingly higher values will bring any graphics hardware to its knees. If random rotation is enabled, the fragment shader will need to iterate over nine cells and within each of these cells loop *SamplesPerCell* times in order to draw all the glyphs. This is a lot of computation at every fragment!

Some images that demonstrate different values for *RandomRotate*, *RandomScale*, and *SamplesPerCell* are shown in Figure 10.6, Figure 10.7, and Color Plate 8.

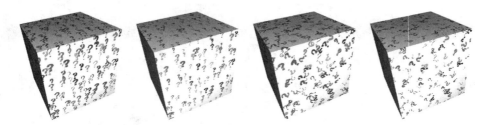

Figure 10.6   Normal glyph bombing, glyph bombing with random scaling, with random rotation, and with both random scaling and rotation

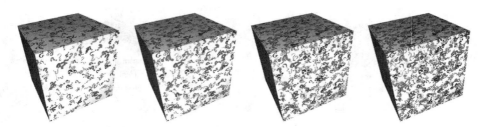

Figure 10.7   Glyph bombing with 2, 3, 4, and 5 glyphs per cell

The uniform variables for this shader and their initial values are

SpecularContribution	`0.2`
LightPosition	`4.0, 14.0, 4.0`
ScaleFactor	`10.0`
ModelColor	`1.0, 1.0, 1.0, 1.0`
GlyphTex	`0`
RandomTex	`1`
ColAdjust	`0.75`
Percentage	`1.0`
SamplesPerCell	`1.0`
R01	`0.29`
RandomScale	`false`
RandomRotate	`false`

10.6.2 Vertex Shader

Listing 10.9 contains the vertex shader for glyph bombing. The only differences between this shader and the vertex shader for bricks discussed in Chapter 6 are that the diffuse factor is multiplied by a somewhat arbitrary factor of two and that the scaled texture coordinates are passed to the fragment shader to form the frame of reference for defining the cells into which glyphs will be drawn.

Listing 10.9 Vertex shader for doing glyph bombing

```
#version 140

in  vec4  MCVertex;
in  vec3  MCNormal;

out vec3  Normal;
out vec2  TexCoord;
out float LightIntensity;

uniform float  SpecularContribution;
uniform vec3   LightPosition;
uniform float  ScaleFactor;

uniform mat4 MVMatrix;
uniform mat4 MVPMatrix;
uniform mat3 NormalMatrix;

void main()
{
    vec3  ecPosition = vec3(MVMatrix * MCVertex);
    vec3  tnorm      = normalize(NormalMatrix * MCNormal);
    vec3  lightVec   = normalize(LightPosition - ecPosition);
    vec3  reflectVec = reflect(-lightVec, tnorm);
    vec3  viewVec    = normalize(-ecPosition);
```

```
float diffuse     = max(dot(lightVec, tnorm), 0.0);
float spec        = 0.0;

if(diffuse > 0.0)
    {
        spec = max(dot(reflectVec, viewVec), 0.0);
        spec = pow(spec, 16.0);
    }

float diffusecontribution  = 1.0 - SpecularContribution;
LightIntensity = diffusecontribution * diffuse * 2.0 +
                     SpecularContribution * spec;

TexCoord = TexCoord0.st * ScaleFactor;

gl_Position = MVPMatrix * MCVertex;
}
```

10.6.3 Fragment Shader

Listing 10.10 contains the fragment shader for glyph bombing. As you can see, this shader makes heavy use of looping. The first step is to assign the base color for the fragment and then compute the fragment's cell and position within the cell. As we iterate through the loops, the value for color accumulates the color for the current fragment, which may be covered by multiple glyphs of different colors. A double for-next loop lets us iterate across four cells if *RandomRotate* is false (0) and across nine cells if it is true (1). This double loop determines whether any of the neighboring cells contain a glyph that contributes to the fragment currently being computed.

For each iteration of the inner loop, we need to determine whether the glyph in the neighboring cell affects the fragment that is being rendered. This requires that we compute the cell number for each neighboring cell as well the offset from the lower-left corner of the neighboring cell to the current fragment.

We use the cell value to compute the initial index value used to access our random number texture. This provides the beginning of a repeatable sequence of random numbers used for the calculations within that cell. This means that whenever we consider the contents of this cell, we always compute the same random glyph, the same random offset, and so on.

To start the random number sequence in a different location for each of the cells, during each loop iteration we compute the index into our random texture by multiplying the current cell value by a uniform variable (*RO1*) that a user can adjust to achieve pleasing results.

At this point, we enter yet another loop. This loop iterates over the number of samples per cell. Within this loop, the first thing we do is access our random number texture to obtain four random numbers in the range [0,1.0]. The result of this operation is a variable (*random*) that we use in performing a number of computations that require an element of randomness. To avoid using the same random number for each iteration of this loop, we add the third and fourth components of the random number to our random texture index. We use this value to access the texture in the next iteration of the loop. Now we get to the heart of the glyph bombing algorithm.

If the first component of the random number we've obtained is greater than or equal to *Percentage*, we exit the loop, use the color value computed thus far as the value for the fragment, and are done with the computation concerning this particular cell. Otherwise, we must generate a value that can index into our glyph texture. The first steps are to use *ColAdjust* to select the row of our glyph texture (*index.t*) and then select a random glyph within that row (*index.s*). Multiplying by 10 and using the floor function divides the texture into 10 sections in each direction. This gives us access to the 100 separate glyphs.

The next thing we need to do is compute a value that can access the proper texel in the glyph for this particular cell (*glyphIndex*). Here the offset, rotation, and scaling factors come into play. If *RandomRotate* is true, we generate a random angle of rotation, compute the corresponding rotation matrix, and use this matrix to transform the texture coordinates for accessing the glyph. This value is then combined with the random offset for the glyph. If we're not doing rotation, we just apply the random offset.

(Interestingly, the fragment shader for drawing glyphs never actually has to add the random offsets for drawing glyphs. Instead, the fragment shader assumes that the random offsets have been added and computes whether a glyph in a neighboring cell contributes to the current fragment by subtracting the random offset and then doing a texture lookup for the glyph in the neighboring cell. This is an example of the type of logic that is sometimes needed to convert a rendering algorithm into a fragment shader.)

The next step is to apply random scaling to the texture coordinates. *random.r* is a value in the range [0, 1.0]. If we divide our glyph index by this value, the glyph index values (i.e., the coordinates used to access the glyph) get larger. And if the coordinates used to access the glyph get larger, the apparent size of the glyph that is drawn gets smaller. By multiplying *random.r* by 0.5 and adding 0.5, we constrain the random scaling to be between 50% and 100% of the original size.

The resulting texture coordinates are clamped to the range [0,1.0], added to the index of the glyph that is rendered, divided by 10, and then used to

access the glyph texture. All the glyphs in our glyph texture have at least
one pixel of white along each edge. By clamping the values to the range
[0,1.0], we effectively say "no contribution for this glyph" whenever the
glyph index values exceed the range [0,1.0]. If the glyph value obtained
is a color other than white, we use the resulting texture value to linearly
interpolate between the color value computed thus far and a random color.
Because the glyph texture contains only levels of gray, the comparison
is only true for texels other than pure white. The **mix** function gives us a
smoothly antialiased edge when the glyph is drawn, and it allows us to
properly layer multiple glyphs of different colors, one on top of the other.

Listing 10.10 Fragment shader for doing glyph bombing

```
#version 140

#define TWO_PI 6.28318

uniform vec4        ModelColor;

uniform sampler2D GlyphTex;
uniform sampler2D RandomTex;

uniform float       ColAdjust;
uniform float       ScaleFactor;
uniform float       Percentage;
uniform float       SamplesPerCell;
uniform float       RO1;

uniform bool        RandomScale;
uniform bool        RandomRotate;

in vec2       TexCoord;
in float      LightIntensity;

out vec4      FragColor;

void main()
{
    vec4 color  = ModelColor;
    vec2 cell   = floor(TexCoord);
    vec2 offset = fract(TexCoord);

    vec2 dPdx = dFdx( TexCoord )/ScaleFactor;
    vec2 dPdy = dFdy( TexCoord )/ScaleFactor;

    for (int i = -1; i <= int (RandomRotate); i++)
{
        for (int j = -1; j <= int (RandomRotate); j++)
        {
            vec2 currentCell   = cell + vec2(float(i), float(j));
            vec2 currentOffset = offset - vec2(float(i), float(j));
```

```
            vec2 randomUV = currentCell * vec2(RO1);

            for (int k = 0; k < int (SamplesPerCell); k++)
            {
                vec4 random = textureGrad(RandomTex, randomUV,
                                          dPdx, dPdy);
                randomUV    += random.ba;

                if (random.r < Percentage)
                {
                    vec2 glyphIndex;
                    mat2 rotator;
                    vec2 index;
                    float rotationAngle, cosRot, sinRot;

                    index.s = floor(random.b * 10.0);
                    index.t = floor(ColAdjust * 10.0);

                    if (RandomRotate)
                    {
                        rotationAngle = TWO_PI * random.g;
                         cosRot = cos(rotationAngle);
                         sinRot = sin(rotationAngle);
                         rotator[0] = vec2(cosRot, sinRot);
                         rotator[1] = vec2(-sinRot, cosRot);
                         glyphIndex = -rotator *
                             (currentOffset - random.rg);
                    }
                    else
                    {
                        glyphIndex = currentOffset - random.rg;
                    }

                    if (RandomScale)
                        glyphIndex /= vec2(0.5 * random.r + 0.5);

                    glyphIndex =
                        (clamp(glyphIndex, 0.0, 1.0) + index) * 0.1;

                    vec4 image = textureGrad(GlyphTex, glyphIndex,
                                             dPdx, dPdy);

                    if (image.r != 1.0)
                        color.rgb = mix(random.rgb * 0.7, color.rgb,
                                        image.r);
                }
            }
        }
    }
    FragColor  = color * LightIntensity;
}
```

This particular shader was designed for flexibility in operation, not performance. Consequently, there are enormous opportunities for making it run faster. There are two texture accesses per iteration of the innermost loop, so enabling rotation and having five samples per cell implies 90 texture accesses per fragment. Still, there are times when some of the techniques demonstrated by this shader come in handy.

10.7 Summary

This chapter discussed several shaders that rely on information stored in texture maps. The programmability of OpenGL opens up all sorts of new uses for texture memory. In the first example, we used two typical color images as texture maps, and we also used one texture as an opacity map and another as a gloss map. In the second example, we accessed a cube map from within a shader. In the third example, we used a typical color image as a texture, but the shader accessed it in a unique manner. In the final example, we used one texture to store small images for rendering and another texture to store random numbers that added irregularity and interest to the final result.

In examples later in this book, you'll see how textures can be used to store normal maps, noise functions, and polynomial coefficients. There is really no end to the possibilities for creating unique effects with stored textures when your mind is free to think of texture memory as storage for things other than color images.

10.8 Further Information

The basics of OpenGL texture mapping are explained in much more detail in *OpenGL Programming Guide, Seventh Edition* (2010), by Dave Shreiner et al. from Addison-Wesley.

More information about the earth images used in Section 10.2 can be found at the NASA Web site at http://earthobservatory.nasa.gov/Newsroom/ BlueMarble.

Papers regarding the realistic rendering of planets include Jim Blinn's 1982 SIGGRAPH paper *Light Reflection Functions for Simulation of Clouds and Dusty Surfaces,* the 1993 SIGGRAPH paper *Display of the Earth Taking into Account Atmospheric Scattering* by Tomoyuki Nishita et al., and the 2002 paper

Physically-based Simulation: A Survey of the Modelling and Rendering of the Earth's Atmosphere by Jaroslav Sloup.

Mipmapping was first described by Lance Williams in his classic 1983 paper *Pyramidal Parametrics*. A good overview of environment mapping techniques is available in the paper *Environment Maps and Their Applications* by Wolfgang Heidrich. This paper was part of the course notes for SIGGRAPH 2000 Course 27, entitled *Procedural Shading on Graphics Hardware*. This material, and a thorough treatment of reflectance and lighting models, can be found in the book *Real-Time Shading*, by Marc Olano et al. (2002).

Texture bombing is described by Darwyn Peachey in *Texturing and Modeling: A Procedural Approach, Third Edition*. The book *GPU Gems* also has a chapter by Steve Glanville on this topic.

[1] Blinn, James, *Light Reflection Functions for Simulation of Clouds and Dusty Surfaces*, Computer Graphics (SIGGRAPH '82 Proceedings), pp. 21–29, July 1982.

[2] Ebert, David S., John Hart, Bill Mark, F. Kenton Musgrave, Darwyn Peachey, Ken Perlin, and Steven Worley, *Texturing and Modeling: A Procedural Approach, Third Edition*, Morgan Kaufmann Publishers, San Francisco, 2002. www.texturingandmodeling.com

[3] Glanville, Steve, *Texture Bombing*, in *GPU Gems: Programming Techniques, Tips, and Tricks for Real-Time Graphics*, Editor: Randima Fernando, Addison-Wesley, Reading, Massachusetts, 2004. http://developer.nvidia.com/object/gpu_gems_home.html

[4] Heidrich, Wolfgang, and Hans-Peter Seidel, *View-Independent Environment Maps*, ACM SIGGRAPH/Eurographics Workshop on Graphics Hardware, pp. 39–45, August 1998.

[5] Heidrich, Wolfgang, *Environment Maps and Their Applications*, SIGGRAPH 2000, Course 27, course notes. www.csee.umbc.edu/~olano/s2000c27/envmap.pdf

[6] NASA, *Earth Observatory*, Web site. http://earthobservatory.nasa.gov/Newsroom/BlueMarble

[7] Nishita, Tomoyuki, Takao Sirai, Katsumi Tadamura, and Eihachiro Nakamae, *Display of the Earth Taking Into Account Atmospheric Scattering*, Computer Graphics (SIGGRAPH '93 Proceedings), pp. 175–182, August 1993. http://nis-lab.is.s.u-tokyo.ac.jp/~nis/abs_sig.html#sig93

[8] OpenGL Architecture Review Board, *OpenGL Reference Manual, Fourth Edition: The Official Reference to OpenGL, Version 1.4*, Editor: Dave Shreiner, Addison-Wesley, Reading, Massachusetts, 2004.

[9] Rost, Randi J., *The OpenGL Shading Language*, SIGGRAPH 2002, Course 17, course notes. http://3dshaders.com/pubs

[10] Shreiner, Dave, and the Khronos OpenGL ARB Working Group, *OpenGL Programming Guide, Seventh Edition: The Official Guide to Learning OpenGL, Versions 3.0 and 3.1*, Addison-Wesley, Boston, Massachusetts, 2010.

[11] Sloup, Jaroslav, *Physically-based Simulation: A Survey of the Modeling and Rendering of the Earth's Atmosphere*, Proceedings of the 18th Spring Conference on Computer Graphics, pp. 141–150, April 2002. http://sgi.felk.cvut.cz/~sloup/html/research/project

[12] Williams, Lance, *Pyramidal Parametrics*, Computer Graphics (SIGGRAPH '83 Proceedings), pp. 1–11, July 1983.

Chapter 11

Procedural Texture Shaders

The fact that we have a full-featured, high-level programming language to express the processing at each fragment means that we can algorithmically compute a pattern on an object's surface. We can use this new freedom to create a wide variety of rendering effects that wouldn't be possible otherwise.

In the previous chapter, we discussed shaders that achieve their primary effect by reading values from texture memory. This chapter focuses on shaders that do interesting things primarily by means of an algorithm defined by the shader. The results from such a shader are synthesized according to the algorithm rather than being based primarily on precomputed values such as a digitized painting or photograph. This type of shader is sometimes called a PROCEDURAL TEXTURE SHADER, and the process of applying such a shader is called PROCEDURAL TEXTURING. Often the texture coordinate or the object coordinate position at each point on the object is the only piece of information needed to shade the object with a shader that is entirely procedural.

In principle, procedural texture shaders can accomplish many of the same tasks as shaders that access stored textures. In practice, there are times when it is more convenient or feasible to use a procedural texture shader and times when it is more convenient or feasible to use a stored texture shader. When deciding whether to write a procedural texture shader or one that uses stored textures, keep in mind some of the main advantages of procedural texture shaders.

- Textures generated procedurally have very low memory requirements compared with stored textures. The only representation of the texture is in the algorithm defined by the code in the procedural texture shader. This representation is extremely compact compared with the size of stored 2D textures. Typically, it is a couple of orders of magnitude smaller (e.g., a few kilobytes for the code in a procedural shader versus a few hundred kilobytes or more for a high-quality 2D texture). This means procedural texture shaders require far less memory on the graphics accelerator. Procedural texture shaders have an even greater advantage when the desire is to have a 3D (solid) texture applied to an object (a few kilobytes versus tens of megabytes or more for a stored 3D texture).

- Textures generated by procedural texture shaders have no fixed area or resolution. They can be applied to objects of any scale with precise results because they are defined algorithmically rather than with sampled data, as in the case of stored textures. There are no decisions to be made about how to map a 2D image onto a 3D surface patch that is larger or smaller than the texture, and there are no seams or unwanted replication. As your viewpoint gets closer and closer to a surface rendered with a procedural texture shader, you won't see reduced detail or sampling artifacts like you might with a shader that uses a stored texture.

- Procedural texture shaders can be written to parameterize key aspects of the algorithm. These parameters can easily be changed, allowing a single shader to produce an interesting variety of effects. Very little can be done to alter the effect from a stored texture after it has been created.

Some of the disadvantages of using procedural shaders rather than stored textures are as follows:

- Procedural texture shaders require the algorithm to be encoded in a program. Not everyone has the technical skills needed to write such a program, whereas it is fairly straightforward to create a 2D or 3D texture with limited technical skills.

- Performing the algorithm embodied by a procedural texture shader at each location on an object can be a lot slower than accessing a stored texture.

- Procedural texture shaders can have serious aliasing artifacts that can be difficult to overcome. Today's graphics hardware has built-in capabilities for antialiasing stored textures (e.g., filtering methods and mipmaps).

- Because of differences in arithmetic precision and differences in implementations of built-in functions such as **noise**, procedural texture shaders could produce somewhat different results on different platforms.

The ultimate choice of whether to use a procedural shader or a stored texture shader should be made pragmatically. Things that would be artwork in the real world (paintings, billboards, anything with writing, etc.) are good candidates for rendering with stored textures. Objects that are extremely important to the final "look" of the image (character faces, costumes, important props) can also be rendered with stored textures because this presents the easiest route for an artist to be involved. Things that are relatively unimportant to the final image and yet cover a lot of area are good candidates for rendering with a procedural shader (walls, floors, ground).

Often, a hybrid approach is the right answer. A golf ball might be rendered with a base color, a hand-painted texture map that contains scuff marks, a texture map containing a logo, and a procedurally generated dimple pattern. Stored textures can also control or constrain procedural effects. If our golf ball needs grass stains on certain parts of its surface and it is important to achieve and reproduce just the right look, an artist could paint a grayscale map that would direct the shader to locations where grass smudges should be applied on the surface (for instance, black portions of the grayscale map) and where they should not be applied (white portions of the grayscale map). The shader can read this CONTROL TEXTURE and use it to blend between a grass-smudged representation of the surface and a pristine surface.

All that said, let's turn our attention to a few examples of shaders that are entirely procedural.

11.1 Regular Patterns

In Chapter 6, we examined a procedural shader for rendering bricks. Our first example in this chapter is another simple one. We try to construct a shader that renders stripes on an object. A variety of man-made objects can be rendered with such a shader: children's toys, wallpaper, wrapping paper, flags, fabrics, and so on.

The object in Figure 11.1 is a partial torus rendered with a stripe shader. The stripe shader and the application in which it is shown were both developed in 2002 by LightWork Design, a company that develops software to provide photorealistic views of objects created with commercial CAD/CAM packages. The application developed by LightWork Design contains a graphical user interface that allows the user to interactively modify the shader's parameters. The various shaders that are available are accessible on the upper-right portion of the user interface, and the modifiable parameters for the current shader are accessible in the lower-right portion of the user interface. In this case, you can see that the parameters for the stripe shader include the stripe color (blue), the background color (orange), the stripe scale (how many stripes there will be), and the stripe width (the ratio of stripe to background; in this case, it is 0.5 to make blue and orange stripes of equal width).

For our stripe shader to work properly, the application needs to send down only the geometry (vertex values) and the texture coordinate at each vertex. The key to drawing the stripe color or the background color is the t texture coordinate at each fragment (the s texture coordinate is not used at all). The application must also supply values that the vertex shader uses to perform a lighting computation. And the aforementioned stripe color, background color, scale, and stripe width must be passed to the fragment shader so that our procedural stripe computation can be performed at each fragment.

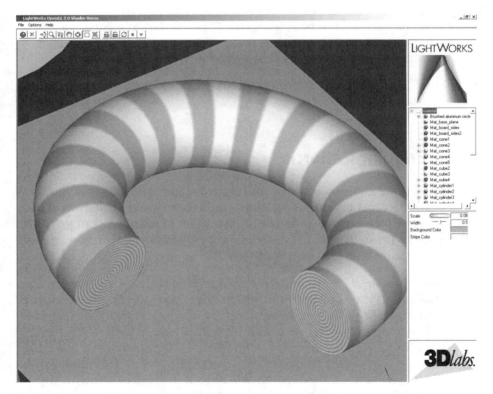

Figure 11.1   Close-up of a partial torus rendered with the stripe shader described in Section 11.1 (courtesy of LightWork Design)

11.1.1 Stripes Vertex Shader

The vertex shader for our stripe effect is shown in Listing 11.1.

Listing 11.1 Vertex shader for drawing stripes

```
#version 140

uniform vec3  LightPosition;
uniform vec3  LightColor;
uniform vec3  EyePosition;
uniform vec3  Specular;
uniform vec3  Ambient;
uniform float Kd;

uniform mat4 MVMatrix;
uniform mat4 MVPMatrix;
uniform mat3 NormalMatrix;

in  vec4  MCVertex;
in  vec3  MCNormal;
in  vec2  TexCoord0;

out vec3  DiffuseColor;
out vec3  SpecularColor;
out float TexCoord;

void main()
{
    vec3 ecPosition = vec3(MVMatrix * MCVertex);
    vec3 tnorm      = normalize(NormalMatrix * MCNormal);
    vec3 lightVec   = normalize(LightPosition - ecPosition);
    vec3 viewVec    = normalize(EyePosition - ecPosition);
    vec3 hvec       = normalize(viewVec + lightVec);

    float spec = clamp(dot(hvec, tnorm), 0.0, 1.0);
    spec = pow(spec, 16.0);

    DiffuseColor    = LightColor * vec3(Kd * dot(lightVec, tnorm));
    DiffuseColor    = clamp(Ambient + DiffuseColor, 0.0, 1.0);
    SpecularColor   = clamp((LightColor * Specular * spec), 0.0, 1.0);

    TexCoord  = TexCoord0.t;
    gl_Position     = MVPMatrix * MCVertex;
}
```

There are some nice features to this particular shader. Nothing in it really makes it specific to drawing stripes. It provides a good example of how we might do the lighting calculation in a general way that would be compatible with a variety of fragment shaders.

As we mentioned, the values for doing the lighting computation (*LightPosition, LightColor, EyePosition, Specular, Ambient,* and *Kd*) are all passed in by the application as uniform variables. The purpose of this shader is to compute *DiffuseColor* and *SpecularColor,* two out variables that will be interpolated across each primitive and made available to the fragment shader at each fragment location. These values are computed in the typical way. A small optimization is that *Ambient* is added to the value computed for the diffuse reflection so that we send one less value to the fragment shader as an out variable. The incoming texture coordinate is passed down to the fragment shader as the out variable *TexCoord,* and the vertex position is transformed in the usual way.

11.1.2 Stripes Fragment Shader

The fragment shader contains the algorithm for drawing procedural stripes. It is shown in Listing 11.2.

Listing 11.2 Fragment shader for drawing stripes

```
#version 140

uniform vec3  StripeColor;
uniform vec3  BackColor;
uniform float Width;
uniform float Fuzz;
uniform float Scale;

in vec3  DiffuseColor;
in vec3  SpecularColor;
in float TexCoord;

out vec4 FragColor;

void main()
{
    float scaledT = fract(TexCoord * Scale);

    float frac1 = clamp(scaledT / Fuzz, 0.0, 1.0);
    float frac2 = clamp((scaledT - Width) / Fuzz, 0.0, 1.0);

    frac1 = frac1 * (1.0 - frac2);
    frac1 = frac1 * frac1 * (3.0 - (2.0 * frac1));

    vec3 finalColor = mix(BackColor, StripeColor, frac1);
    finalColor = finalColor * DiffuseColor + SpecularColor;

    FragColor = vec4(finalColor, 1.0);
}
```

The application provides one other uniform variable, called *Fuzz*. This value controls the smooth transitions (i.e., antialiasing) between stripe color and background color. With a *Scale* value of 10.0, a reasonable value for *Fuzz* is 0.1. It can be adjusted as the object changes size to prevent excessive blurriness at high magnification levels. It shouldn't really be set to a value higher than 0.5 (maximum blurriness of stripe edges).

The first step in this shader is to multiply the incoming *t* texture coordinate by the stripe scale factor and take the fractional part. This computation gives the position of the fragment within the stripe pattern. The larger the value of *Scale*, the more stripes we have as a result of this calculation. The resulting value for the local variable *scaledT* is in the range from [0,1].

We'd like to have nicely antialiased transitions between the stripe colors. One way to do this would be to use **smoothstep** in the transition from *StripeColor* to *BackColor* and use it again in the transition from *BackColor* to *StripeColor*. But this shader uses the fact that these transitions are symmetric to combine the two transitions into one.

So, to get our desired transition, we use *scaledT* to compute two other values, *frac1* and *frac2*. These two values tell us where we are in relation to the two transitions between *BackColor* and *StripeColor*. For *frac1*, if *scaledT/Fuzz* is greater than 1, that indicates that this point is not in the transition zone, so we clamp the value to 1. If *scaledT* is less than *Fuzz*, *scaledT/Fuzz* specifies the fragment's relative distance into the transition zone for one side of the stripe. We compute a similar value for the other edge of the stripe by subtracting *Width* from *scaledT*, dividing by *Fuzz*, clamping the result, and storing it in *frac2*.

These values represent the amount of fuzz (blurriness) to be applied. At one edge of the stripe, *frac2* is 0 and *frac1* is the relative distance into the transition zone. At the other edge of the stripe, *frac1* is 1 and *frac2* is the relative distance into the transition zone. Our next line of code (*frac1 = frac1 ** (1.0 – *frac2*)) produces a value that can be used to do a proper linear blend between *BackColor* and *StripeColor*. But we'd actually like to perform a transition that is smoother than a linear blend. The next line of code performs a Hermite interpolation in the same way as the **smoothstep** function. The final value for *frac1* performs the blend between *BackColor* and *StripeColor*.

The result of this effort is a smoothly "fuzzed" boundary in the transition region between the stripe colors. Without this fuzzing effect, we would have abrupt transitions between the stripe colors that would flash and pop as the object is moved on the screen. The fuzzing of the transition region eliminates those artifacts. A close-up view of the fuzzed boundary is shown in Figure 11.2. (More information about antialiasing procedural shaders can be found in Chapter 17.)

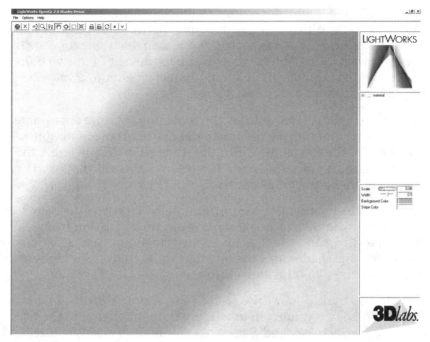

Figure 11.2 Extreme close-up view of one of the stripes that shows the effect of the "fuzz" calculation from the stripe shader (courtesy of LightWork Design)

Now all that remains to be done is to apply the diffuse and specular lighting effects computed by the vertex shader and supply an alpha value of 1.0 to produce our final fragment color. By modifying the five basic parameters of our fragment shader, we can create a fairly interesting number of variations of our stripe pattern, using the exact same shader.

11.2 Toy Ball

Programmability is the key to procedurally defining all sorts of texture patterns. This next shader takes things a bit further by shading a sphere with a procedurally defined star pattern and a procedurally defined stripe. This shader was inspired by the ball in one of Pixar's early short animations, *Luxo Jr.* This shader is quite specialized. It shades any surface as long as it's a sphere. The reason is that the fragment shader exploits the following property of the sphere: The surface normal for any point on the surface points in the same direction as the vector from the center of the sphere to that point on the surface. This property is used to analytically compute the surface normal used in the shading calculations within the fragment shader.

The key to this shader is that the star pattern is defined by the coefficients for five half-spaces that define the star shape. These coefficients were chosen to make the star pattern an appropriate size for the ball. Points on the sphere are classified as "in" or "out," relative to each half space. Locations in the very center of the star pattern are "in" with respect to all five half-spaces. Locations in the points of the star are "in" with respect to four of the five half-spaces. All other locations are "in" with respect to three or fewer half-spaces.

Fragments that are in the stripe pattern are simpler to compute. After we have classified each location on the surface as "star," "stripe," or "other," we can color each fragment appropriately. The color computations are applied in an order that ensures a reasonable result even if the ball is viewed from far away. A surface normal is calculated analytically (i.e., exactly) within the fragment shader. A lighting computation that includes a specular highlight calculation is also applied at every fragment.

11.2.1 Application Setup

The application needs only to provide vertex positions for this shader to work properly. Both colors and normals are computed algorithmically in the fragment shader. The only catch is that for this shader to work properly, the vertices must define a sphere. The sphere can be of arbitrary size because the fragment shader performs all the necessary computations, based on the known geometry of a sphere.

A number of parameters to this shader are specified with uniform variables. The values that produce the images shown in the remainder of this section are summarized in Listing 11.3.

Listing 11.3 Values for uniform variables used by the toy ball shader

```
HalfSpace[0]      1.0,            0.0,           0.0, 0.2
HalfSpace[1]      0.309016994,    0.951056516,   0.0, 0.2
HalfSpace[2]     -0.809016994,    0.587785252,   0.0, 0.2
HalfSpace[3]     -0.809016994,   -0.587785252,   0.0, 0.2
HalfSpace[4]      0.309016994,   -0.951056516,   0.0, 0.2

StripeWidth       0.3

InOrOutInit      -3.0
FWidth            0.005

StarColor         0.6, 0.0, 0.0, 1.0
StripeColor       0.0, 0.3, 0.6, 1.0
BaseColor         0.6, 0.5, 0.0, 1.0

BallCenter        0.0, 0.0, 0.0, 1.0
```

```
LightDir              0.57735, 0.57735, 0.57735, 0.0
HVector               0.32506, 0.32506, 0.88808, 0.0

SpecularColor         1.0, 1.0, 1.0, 1.0
SpecularExponent 200.0

Ka                    0.3
Kd                    0.7
Ks                    0.4
```

11.2.2 Vertex Shader

The fragment shader is the workhorse for this shader duo, so the vertex shader needs only to compute the ball's center position in eye coordinates, the eye-coordinate position of the vertex, and the clip space position at each vertex. The application could provide the ball's center position in eye coordinates, but our vertex shader doesn't have much to do, and doing it this way means the application doesn't have to keep track of the modelview matrix. This value could easily be computed in the fragment shader, but the fragment shader will likely have a little better performance if we leave the computation in the vertex shader and pass the result as a flat interpolated out variable (see Listing 11.4).

Listing 11.4 Vertex shader for drawing a toy ball

```
#version 140
uniform vec4 MCBallCenter;

uniform mat4 MVMatrix;
uniform mat4 MVPMatrix;
uniform mat3 NormalMatrix;

in vec4 MCVertex;

    out vec3 OCPosition;
    out vec4 ECPosition;
flat out vec4 ECBallCenter;

void main (void)
{

    OCPosition = MCVertex.xyz;
    ECPosition = MVMatrix * MCVertex;
    ECBallCenter = MVMatrix * MCBallCenter;

    gl_Position = MVPMatrix * MCVertex;
}
```

11.2.3 Fragment Shader

The toy ball fragment shader is a little bit longer than some of the previous examples, so we build it up a few lines of code at a time and illustrate some intermediate results. Here are the definitions for the local variables that are used in the toy ball fragment shader:

```
vec3  normal;          // Analytically computed normal
vec4  pShade;          // Point in shader space
vec4  surfColor;       // Computed color of the surface
float intensity;       // Computed light intensity
vec4  distance;        // Computed distance values
float inorout;         // Counter for classifying star pattern
```

The first thing we do is turn the surface location that we're shading into a point on a sphere with a radius of 1.0. We can do this with the **normalize** function:

```
pShade.xyz  = normalize(OCPosition.xyz);
pShade.w    = 1.0;
```

We don't want to include the *w* coordinate in the computation, so we use the component selector **.xyz** to select the first three components of *OCposition.* This normalized vector is stored in the first three components of *pShade*. With this computation, *pShade* represents a point on the sphere with radius 1, so all three components of *pShade* are in the range [–1,1]. The *w* coordinate isn't really pertinent to our computations at this point, but to make subsequent calculations work properly, we initialize it to a value of 1.0.

We are always going to be shading spheres with this fragment shader, so we analytically calculate the surface normal of the sphere:

```
normal      = normalize(ECPosition.xyz-ECBallCenter.xyz);
```

Next, we perform our half-space computations. We initialize a counter called *inorout* to a value of –3.0. We increment the counter each time the surface location is "in" with respect to a half-space. Because five half-spaces are defined, the final counter value will be in the range [–3,2]. Values of 1 or 2 signify that the fragment is within the star pattern. Values of 0 or less signify that the fragment is outside the star pattern.

```
inorout = InOrOutInit;       // initialize inorout to -3
```

We have defined the half-spaces as an array of five **vec4** values, done our "in" or "out" computations, and stored the results in an array of five **float** values. But we can take a little better advantage of the parallel nature of the underlying graphics hardware if we do things a bit differently. You'll see how in a minute. First, we compute the distance between *pShade* and the first four half-spaces by using the built-in dot product function:

```
distance[0] = dot(p, HalfSpace[0]);
distance[1] = dot(p, HalfSpace[1]);
distance[2] = dot(p, HalfSpace[2]);
distance[3] = dot(p, HalfSpace[3]);
```

The results of these half-space distance calculations are visualized in (A)–(D) of Figure 11.3. Surface locations that are "in" with respect to the half-space are shaded in gray, and points that are "out" are shaded in black.

You may have been wondering why our counter was defined as a **float** instead of an **int**. We're going to use the counter value as the basis for a smoothly antialiased transition between the color of the star pattern and the color of the rest of the ball's surface. To this end, we use the **smoothstep** function to set the distance to 0 if the computed distance is less than *–FWidth*, to 1 if the computed distance is greater than *FWidth*, and to a smoothly interpolated value between 0 and 1 if the computed distance is in between those two values. By defining *distance* as a **vec4**, we can perform the smooth step computation on four values in parallel. **smoothstep** implies a divide operation, and because *FWidth* is a float, only one divide operation is necessary. This makes it all very efficient.

```
distance    = smoothstep(-FWidth, FWidth, distance);
```

Now we can quickly add the values in *distance* by performing a dot product between *distance* and a **vec4** containing all 1s:

```
inorout     += dot(distance, vec4(1.0));
```

Because we initialized *inorout* to –3, we add the result of the dot product to the previous value of *inorout*. This variable now contains a value in the range [–3,1], and we have one more half-space distance to compute. We compute the distance to the fifth half-space, and we do the computation

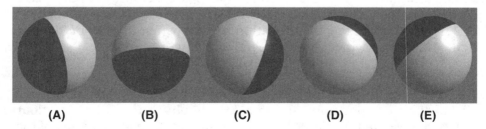

(A)   (B)   (C)   (D)   (E)

Figure 11.3 Visualizing the results of the half-space distance calculations (courtesy of AMD)

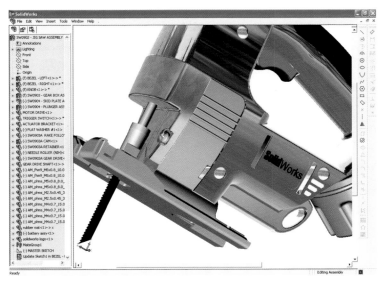

Color Plate 1 Screen shot of the SolidWorks application, showing a jigsaw rendered with OpenGL shaders to simulate a chrome body, galvanized steel housing, and cast iron blade. (Courtesy of Solid-Works Corporation)

Color Plate 2 Screen shots illustrating realistic material shaders developed by LightWork Design. Upper-left and lower-left images use complex OpenGL shaders for accurately visualizing real-world GE Plastics materials. Upper-right image illustrates the real-world visualization of Milliken carpets using the LightWorks Archive (LWA) format. Lower-right image illustrates high-quality lighting created using materials in the LWA format. LightWork Design provides the shaders, materials, and information about the LWA format at http://www.lightworks-user.com. (Created using the LightWorks rendering engine. Copyright LightWork Design)

Color Plate 3
A full-color image of Earth that is used as a texture map for the shader discussed in Section 10.2. (Blue Marble image by Reto Stöckli, NASA Goddard Space Flight Center)

Color Plate 4
"Daytime" texture map used in the fragment shader described in Section 10.3. (Blue Marble images by Reto Stöckli, NASA Goddard Space Flight Center)

Color Plate 5
"Nighttime" texture map used in the fragment shader described in Section 10.3. (Blue Marble images by Reto Stöckli, NASA Goddard Space Flight Center)

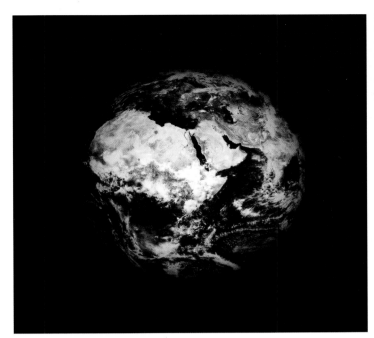

Color Plate 6 Earth image texture mapped onto a sphere using the fragment shader described in Section 10.2. (3Dlabs, Inc./Blue Marble image by Reto Stöckli, NASA Goddard Space Flight Center)

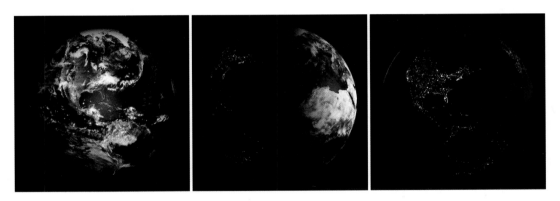

Color Plate 7 As the world turns—daytime, dawn, and nighttime views of Earth, rendered by the shaders discussed in Section 10.3. (3Dlabs, Inc./Blue Marble image by Reto Stöckli, NASA Goddard Space Flight Center)

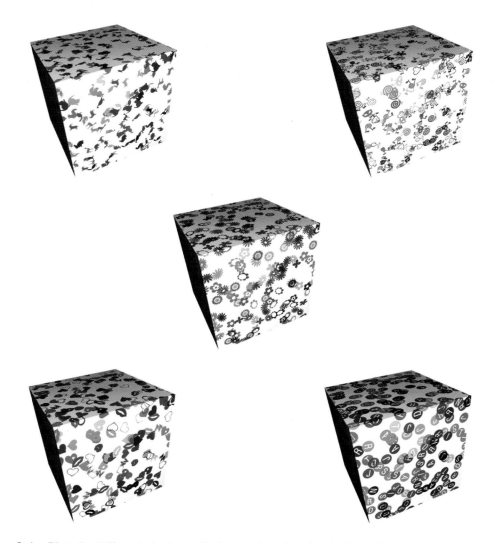

Color Plate 8 Different glyphs applied to a cube using the glyph bombing shader described in Section 10.6. (3Dlabs, Inc.)

Color Plate 9 An equirectangular (or latlong) texture map of Old Town Square, Fort Collins, Colorado. This image is used as the environment map for the shader presented in Section 10.5. (3Dlabs, Inc.)

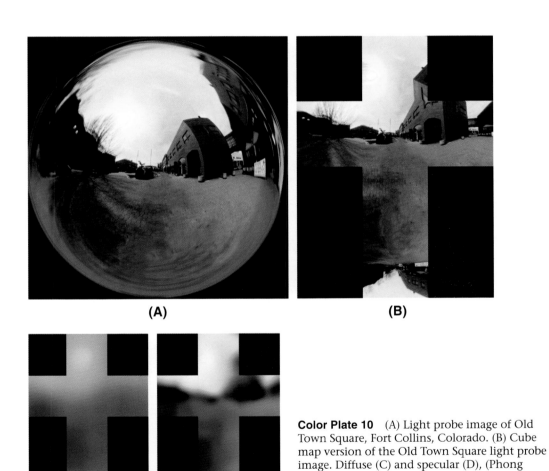

(A)

(B)

(C)

(D)

Color Plate 10 (A) Light probe image of Old Town Square, Fort Collins, Colorado. (B) Cube map version of the Old Town Square light probe image. Diffuse (C) and specular (D), (Phong exponent = 50) environment maps created with HDRshop. (3Dlabs, Inc.)

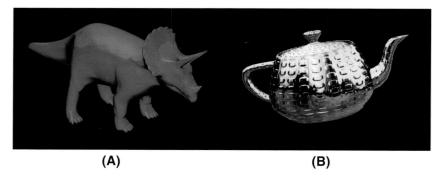

(A)   (B)

Color Plate 11   Environment mapped shader examples. (A) The cube map shown in Color Plate 10 is used together with the environment mapping shaders discussed in Section 10.4. (B) Environment mapping a mirror-like surface with procedural bumps using the environment map shown in Color Plate 9. The bumps are applied using the technique described in Section 11.4. (3Dlabs, Inc.)

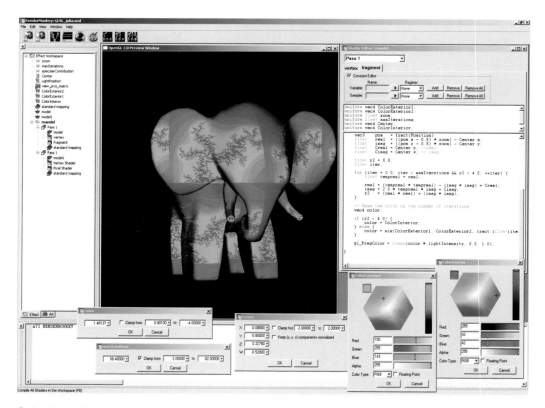

Color Plate 12   Screen shot of the RenderMonkey IDE user interface. The shader that is procedurally generating a Julia set on the surface of the elephant is shown in the source code window. Color selection tools and user interface elements for manipulating user-defined uniform variables are also shown.

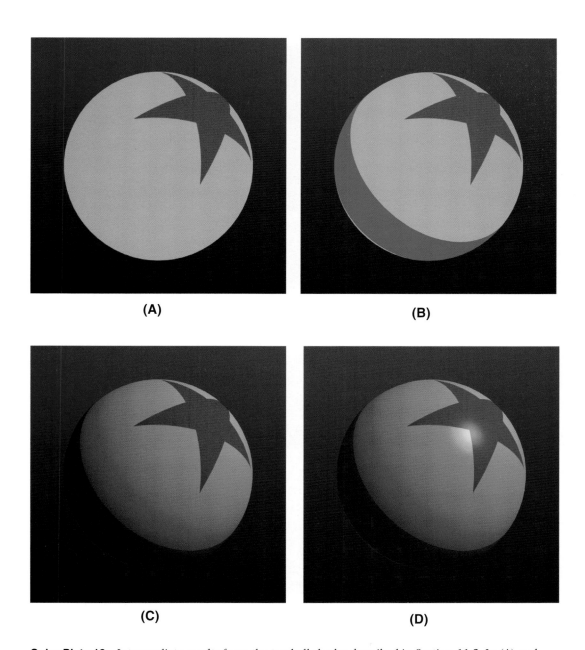

Color Plate 13 Intermediate results from the toy ball shader described in Section 11.2. In (A), red is applied to the procedurally defined star pattern and yellow to the rest of the sphere. In (B), the blue stripe is added. In (C), diffuse lighting is applied. In (D), the analytically defined normal is used to apply a specular highlight. (Courtesy of ATI Research, Inc.)

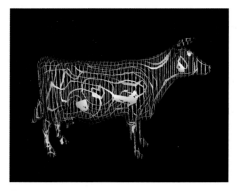

Color Plate 14   The lattice shader presented in Section 11.3 is applied to the cow model. (3Dlabs, Inc.)

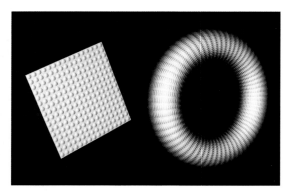

Color Plate 15   A simple box and a torus that have been bump-mapped using the procedural method described in Section 11.4. (3Dlabs, Inc.)

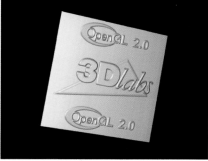
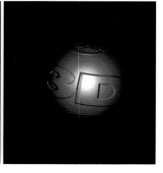

Color Plate 16   A normal map (left) and the rendered result on a simple box and a sphere using the techniques described in Section 11.4.4. (3Dlabs, Inc.)

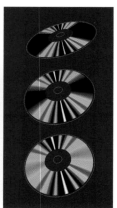

Color Plate 17   The reflection/refraction shader from Section 14.1 used to render a model with chromatic aberration (middle) and without (left). On the middle image, notice the color fringing on the knees, chest, and tops of the arms. On the right, three orientations of an object rendered with the diffraction shader from Section 14.2. (3Dlabs, Inc.)

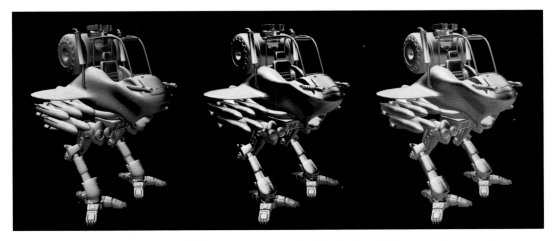

Color Plate 18 The image-based lighting shader described in Section 12.2 can produce a variety of effects using the Old Town Square diffuse and specular environment maps shown in Color Plate 9. Left: *BaseColor* set to (1.0, 1.0, 1.0), *SpecularPercent* is 0, and *DiffusePercent* is 1.0. Middle: *BaseColor* is set to (0, 0, 0), *SpecularPercent* is set to 1.0, and *DiffusePercent* is set to 0. Right: *BaseColor* is set to (0.35, 0.29, 0.09), *SpecularPercent* is set to 0.75, and *DiffusePercent* is set to 0.5. (3Dlabs, Inc.)

Color Plate 19 The spherical harmonics lighting shader described in Section 12.3 is used as the sole lighting for a model with a base color of white (RGB=1.0, 1.0, 1.0). The coefficients from Table 12.1 that are used to create these images are from left: Old Town Square, Grace Cathedral, Galileo's Tomb, Campus Sunset, and St. Peter's Basilica. Ambient occlusion factors are also applied (see Section 13.1). (3Dlabs, Inc.)

 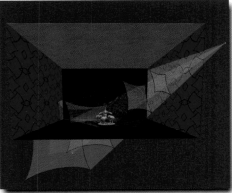

Color Plate 20 Effects of the überlight shader (see Section 12.4) and a user interface for manipulating its controls. (3Dlabs, Inc.)

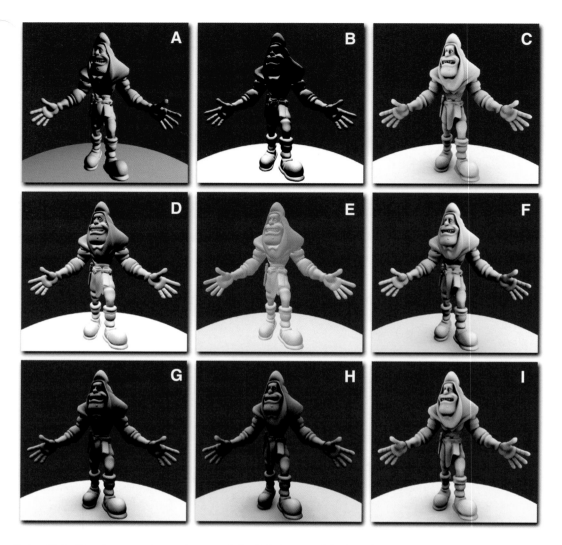

Color Plate 21 A comparison of some of the lighting models described in Chapter 12 and Chapter 13. The model uses a base color of white (RGB=1.0, 1.0, 1.0) to emphasize areas of light and shadow. (A) uses fixed functionality lighting with a light above and to the right of the model. (B) uses fixed functionality with a light directly above the model. These two images illustrate the difficulties with the traditional lighting model. Detail is lost in areas of shadow. (C) multiplies the ambient occlusion value by the model color to achieve quite pleasing results. (D) illustrates hemisphere lighting while (G) illustrates hemisphere lighting plus ambient occlusion. (E) illustrates spherical harmonic lighting using the Old Town Square coefficients, while (H) uses spherical harmonic lighting plus ambient occlusion. (F) is simple diffuse lighting attenuated by the ambient occlusion factor. (I) uses ambient occlusion and the bent normal to access the Old Town Square environment map to determine the color of the light reaching the surface. (3Dlabs, Inc.)

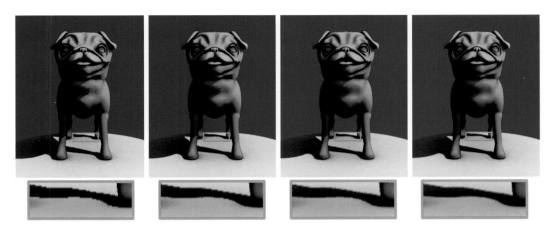

Color Plate 22 Comparing the shadow-generation techniques described in Section 13.2. From left, accessing the shadow map with one sample per pixel, with four samples per pixel, with four dithered samples per pixel, and with 16 samples per pixel. (3Dlabs, Inc.)

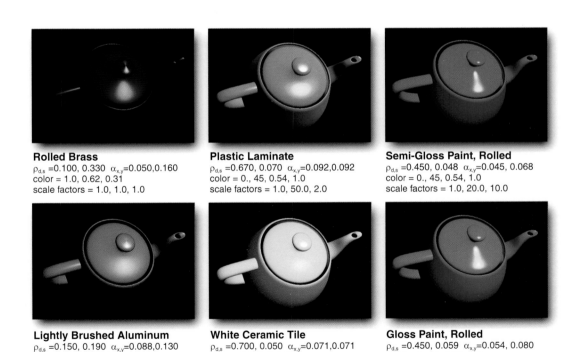

Rolled Brass
$\rho_{d,s}$ =0.100, 0.330 $\alpha_{x,y}$=0.050,0.160
color = 1.0, 0.62, 0.31
scale factors = 1.0, 1.0, 1.0

Plastic Laminate
$\rho_{d,s}$ =0.670, 0.070 $\alpha_{x,y}$=0.092,0.092
color = 0., 45, 0.54, 1.0
scale factors = 1.0, 50.0, 2.0

Semi-Gloss Paint, Rolled
$\rho_{d,s}$ =0.450, 0.048 $\alpha_{x,y}$=0.045, 0.068
color = 0., 45, 0.54, 1.0
scale factors = 1.0, 20.0, 10.0

Lightly Brushed Aluminum
$\rho_{d,s}$ =0.150, 0.190 $\alpha_{x,y}$=0.088,0.130
color = 1.0, 0.99, 1.0
scale factors = 2.0, 2.0, 2.0

White Ceramic Tile
$\rho_{d,s}$ =0.700, 0.050 $\alpha_{x,y}$=0.071,0.071
color = 1.0, 1.0, 1.0
scale factors = 1.0, 10.0, 10.0

Gloss Paint, Rolled
$\rho_{d,s}$ =0.450, 0.059 $\alpha_{x,y}$=0.054, 0.080
color = 0., 45, 0.54, 1.0
scale factors = 1.0, 20.0, 10.0

Color Plate 23 A variety of materials rendered with Ward's BRDF model (see Section 14.3) and his measured/fitted material parameters. Note the difference in the shapes of the specular highlights, particularly on the knob of the teapot. The metals and paints exhibit anisotropic reflection while the plastic and tile materials are isotropic. (3Dlabs, Inc.)

Color Plate 24 Teapots rendered with noise shaders, as described in Chapter 15. Clockwise from upper left: a cloud shader that sums four octaves of noise and uses a blue-to-white color gradient to code the result; a sun surface shader that uses the absolute value function to introduce discontinuities (turbulence); a granite shader that uses a single high-frequency noise value to modulate between white and black; a marble shader that uses noise to modulate a sine function to produce alternating "veins" of color. (3Dlabs, Inc.)

Color Plate 25 A bust of Beethoven rendered with the wood shader described in Section 15.7. (3Dlabs, Inc.)

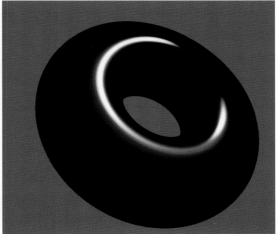

Color Plate 26 Left: The difference between a conventional texture map (lower left) and a polynomial texture map (PTM) (upper right). The conventional texture looks flat and unrealistic as the light source is moved, while the PTM faithfully reproduces changing specular highlights and self-shadowing. Right: A torus rendered using the BRDF PTM shaders described in Section 14.4. Although the paint is basically black, note the change in the highlight color (from bluish-purple in the back to reddish-brown in the front) as the reflection angle changes. (© Copyright 2003 Hewlett-Packard Development Company, L.P., Reproduced with Permission)

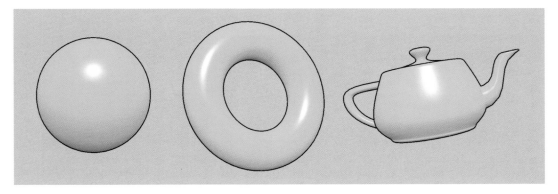

Color Plate 27 Gooch shading applied to three objects (see Section 18.2). Background color (gray), warm color (yellow), and cool color (blue) are chosen in order so that they do not impede the clarity of the outline color (black) or highlight color (white). Details are still visible in this rendering that would be lost in shadow using traditional shading. (3Dlabs, Inc.)

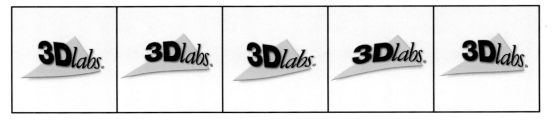

Color Plate 28 Several frames from the animated sequence produced by the wobble shader described in Section 16.8. (3Dlabs, Inc.)

Color Plate 29   Results of the image brightness shader discussed in Section 19.5.1 with *alpha* equal to 0.4, 0.6, 0.8, 1.0, and 1.2 from left to right. The image with *alpha* = 1.0 is the same as the unmodified source image.

Color Plate 30   Results of the image contrast shader discussed in Section 19.5.2 with *alpha* equal to 0.4, 0.6, 0.8, 1.0, and 1.2 from left to right. The image with *alpha* = 1.0 is the same as the unmodified source image.

Color Plate 31   Results of the image saturation shader discussed in Section 19.5.3 with *alpha* equal to 0.0, 0.5, 0.75, 1.0, and 1.25 from left to right. The image with *alpha* = 0.0 is the same as the unmodified target image. The image with *alpha* = 1.0 is the same as the unmodified source image.

Color Plate 32   Results of the image sharpness shader discussed in Section 19.5.4 with *alpha* equal to 0.0, 0.5, 1.0, 1.5, and 2.0 from left to right. The image with *alpha* = 0.0 is the same as the unmodified target image. The image with *alpha* = 1.0 is the same as the unmodified source image.

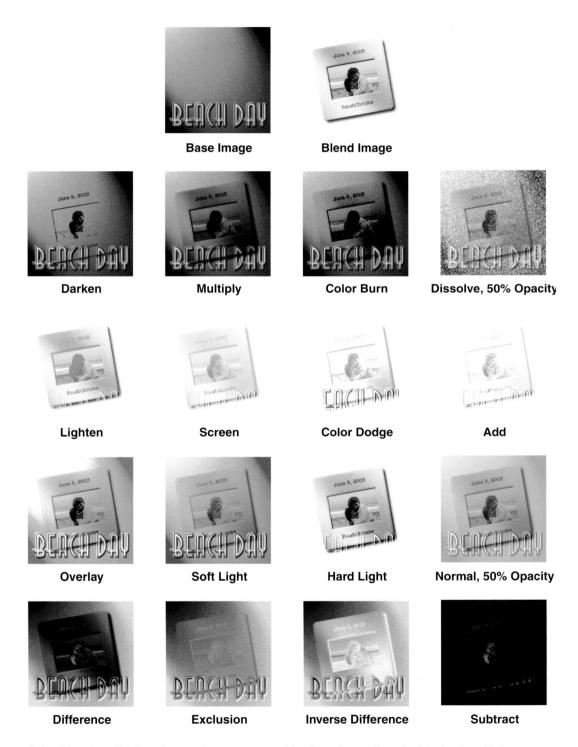

Base Image

Blend Image

Darken

Multiply

Color Burn

Dissolve, 50% Opacity

Lighten

Screen

Color Dodge

Add

Overlay

Soft Light

Hard Light

Normal, 50% Opacity

Difference

Exclusion

Inverse Difference

Subtract

Color Plate 33 Shaders that implement various blend modes, as described in Section 19.6.

Color Plate 34 Brick shader with and without antialiasing. On the left, the results of the brick shader presented in Chapter 6. On the right, results of antialiasing by analytic integration using the brick shader described in Section 17.4.5. (3Dlabs, Inc.)

to determine whether we're "in" or "out" of the stripe around the ball. We call the **smoothstep** function to do the same operation on these two values as was performed on the previous four half-space distances. We update the *inorout* counter by adding the result from the distance computation with the final half-space. The distance computation with respect to the fifth half-space is illustrated in (E) of Figure 11.3.

```
distance.x  = dot(pShade, HalfSpace[4]);
distance.y  = StripeWidth - abs(pShade.z);
distance.xy = smoothstep(-FWidth, FWidth, distance.xy);
inorout     += distance.x;
```

(In this case, we're performing a smooth step operation only on the *x* and *y* components.)

The value for *inorout* is now in the range [–3,2]. This intermediate result is illustrated in Figure 11.4 (A). By clamping the value of *inorout* to the range [0,1], we obtain the result shown in Figure 11.4 (B).

```
inorout     = clamp(inorout, 0.0, 1.0);
```

At this point, we can compute the surface color for the fragment. We use the computed value of *inorout* to perform a linear blend between yellow and red to define the star pattern. If we were to stop here, the result would look like Color Plate 13A. If we take the results of this calculation and do a linear blend with the color of the stripe, we get the result shown in Color Plate 13B. Because we used **smoothstep**, the values of *inorout* and *distance.y* provide a nicely antialiased edge at the border between colors.

```
surfColor   = mix(BaseColor, StarColor, inorout);
surfColor   = mix(surfColor, StripeColor, distance.y);
```

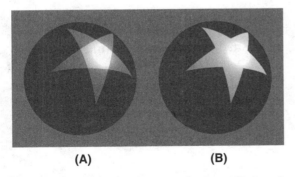

(A)   (B)

Figure 11.4 Intermediate results from "in" or "out" computation. Surface points that are "in" with respect to all five half-planes are shown in white, and points that are "in" with respect to four half-planes are shown in gray (A). The value of *inorout* is clamped to the range [0,1] to produce the result shown in (B). (Courtesy of AMD.)

The result at this stage is flat and unrealistic. Performing a lighting calculation will fix this. The first step is to analytically compute the normal for this fragment, which we can do because we know the eye-coordinate position of the center of the ball (it's provided in the in variable *ECballCenter*) and we know the eye-coordinate position of the fragment (it's passed in the in variable *ECposition*). (This approach could have been used with the earth shader discussed in Section 10.2 to avoid passing the surface normal as an in variable and using the interpolated results.)

```
// Calculate analytic normal of a sphere
normal       = normalize(ECPosition.xyz - ECBallCenter.xyz);
```

The diffuse part of the lighting equation is computed with these three lines of code:

```
// Per-fragment diffuse lighting
intensity  = Ka; // ambient
intensity += Kd * clamp(dot(LightDir.xyz, normal), 0.0, 1.0);
surfColor *= intensity;
```

The result of diffuse-only lighting is shown in Color Plate 13C. The final step is to add a specular contribution with these three lines of code:

```
// Per-fragment specular lighting
intensity  = clamp(dot(HVector.xyz, normal), 0.0, 1.0);
intensity  = Ks * pow(intensity, SpecularExponent);
surfColor.rgb += SpecularColor.rgb * intensity;
```

Notice in Color Plate 13D that the specular highlight is perfect! Because the surface normal at each fragment is computed exactly, there is no misshapen specular highlight caused by tesselation facets like we're used to seeing. The resulting value is written to *gl_FragColor* and sent on for final processing before ultimately being written into the framebuffer.

```
FragColor = surfColor;
```

Voila! Your very own toy ball, created completely out of thin air! The complete listing of the toy ball fragment shader is shown in Listing 11.5.

Listing 11.5 Fragment shader for drawing a toy ball

```
#version 140
uniform vec4   HalfSpace[5]; // half-spaces used to define star pattern
uniform float  StripeWidth;

uniform float  InOrOutInit;  // -3.0
uniform float  FWidth;       // = 0.005

uniform vec4   StarColor;
uniform vec4   StripeColor;
uniform vec4   BaseColor;
```

```
uniform vec4  LightDir;      // light direction, should be normalized
uniform vec4  HVector;       // reflection vector for infinite light


uniform vec4  SpecularColor;
uniform float SpecularExponent;
uniform float Ka;
uniform float Kd;
uniform float Ks;

     in vec4  ECPosition;    // surface position in eye coordinates
     in vec3  OCPosition;    // surface position in object coordinates
flat in vec4  ECBallCenter;  // ball center in eye coordinates

out vec4 FragColor;

void main()
{
    vec3  normal;         // Analytically computed normal
    vec4  pShade;         // Point in shader space
    vec4  surfColor;      // Computed color of the surface
    float intensity;      // Computed light intensity
    vec4  distance;       // Computed distance values
    float inorout;        // Counter for classifying star pattern

    pShade.xyz = normalize(OCPosition.xyz);
    pShade.w   = 1.0;

    inorout    = InOrOutInit;    // initialize inorout to -3.0

    distance[0] = dot(pShade, HalfSpace[0]);
    distance[1] = dot(pShade, HalfSpace[1]);
    distance[2] = dot(pShade, HalfSpace[2]);
    distance[3] = dot(pShade, HalfSpace[3]);

    //float FWidth = fwidth(pShade);
    distance    = smoothstep(-FWidth, FWidth, distance);

    inorout    += dot(distance, vec4(1.0));

    distance.x  = dot(pShade, HalfSpace[4]);
    distance.y  = StripeWidth - abs(pShade.z);
    distance.xy = smoothstep(-FWidth, FWidth, distance.xy);
    inorout    += distance.x;

    inorout    = clamp(inorout, 0.0, 1.0);

    surfColor   = mix(BaseColor, StarColor, inorout);
    surfColor   = mix(surfColor, StripeColor, distance.y);

    // Calculate analytic normal of a sphere
    normal      = normalize(ECPosition.xyz-ECBallCenter.xyz);
```

```
    // Per-fragment diffuse lighting
    intensity  = Ka; // ambient
    intensity += Kd * clamp(dot(LightDir.xyz, normal), 0.0, 1.0);
    surfColor *= intensity;

    // Per-fragment specular lighting
    intensity  = clamp(dot(HVector.xyz, normal), 0.0, 1.0);
    intensity  = Ks * pow(intensity, SpecularExponent);
    surfColor.rgb += SpecularColor.rgb * intensity;

    FragColor = surfColor;
}
```

11.3 Lattice

Here's a little bit of a gimmick. In this example, we show how *not* to draw
the object procedurally.

In this example, we look at how the **discard** command can be used in a
fragment shader to achieve some interesting effects. The **discard** command
causes fragments to be discarded rather than used to update the framebuffer. We use this to draw geometry with "holes." The vertex shader is the
exact same vertex shader used for stripes (Section 11.1.1). The fragment
shader is shown in Listing 11.6.

Listing 11.6 Fragment shader for procedurally discarding part of an object

```
in vec3  DiffuseColor;
in vec3  SpecularColor;
in vec2  TexCoord

out vec3 FragColor;

uniform vec2  Scale;
uniform vec2  Threshold;
uniform vec3  SurfaceColor;

void main()
{
    float ss = fract(TexCoord.s * Scale.s);
    float tt = fract(TexCoord.t * Scale.t);

    if ((ss > Threshold.s) && (tt > Threshold.t)) discard;

    vec3 finalColor = SurfaceColor * DiffuseColor + SpecularColor;
    FragColor = vec4(finalColor, 1.0);
}
```

The part of the object to be discarded is determined by the values of the *s* and *t* texture coordinates. A scale factor is applied to adjust the frequency of the lattice. The fractional part of this scaled texture-coordinate value is computed to provide a number in the range [0,1]. These values are compared with the threshold values that have been provided. If both values exceed the threshold, the fragment is discarded. Otherwise, we do a simple lighting calculation and render the fragment.

In Color Plate 14, the threshold values were both set to 0.13. This means that more than three-quarters of the fragments were being discarded! And that's what I call a "holy cow!"

11.4 Bump Mapping

We have already seen procedural shaders that modified color (*brick*, *stripes*) and opacity (*lattice*). Another whole class of interesting effects can be applied to a surface with a technique called BUMP MAPPING. Bump mapping involves modulating the surface normal before lighting is applied. We can perform the modulation algorithmically to apply a regular pattern, we can add noise to the components of a normal, or we can look up a perturbation value in a texture map. Bump mapping has proved to be an effective way of increasing the apparent realism of an object without increasing the geometric complexity. It can be used to simulate surface detail or surface irregularities.

The technique does not truly alter the surface being shaded; it merely "tricks" the lighting calculations. Therefore, the "bumping" does not show up on the silhouette edges of an object. Imagine modeling a planet as a sphere and shading it with a bump map so that it appears to have mountains that are quite large relative to the diameter of the planet. Because nothing has been done to change the underlying geometry, which is perfectly round, the silhouette of the sphere always appears perfectly round, even if the mountains (bumps) go right up to the silhouette edge. In real life, you would expect the mountains on the silhouette edges to prevent the silhouette from looking perfectly round. For this reason, it is a good idea to use bump mapping to apply only "small" effects to a surface (at least relative to the size of the surface). Wrinkles on an orange, embossed logos, and pitted bricks are all good examples of things that can be successfully bump-mapped.

Bump mapping adds apparent geometric complexity during fragment processing, so once again the key to the process is our fragment shader. This implies that the lighting operation must be performed by our fragment shader instead of by the vertex shader where it is often handled. Again, this points out one of the advantages of the programmability that is available through the OpenGL Shading Language. We are free to perform whatever operations are necessary, in either the vertex shader or the fragment shader. We don't need to be bound to the fixed functionality ideas of where things like lighting are performed.

The key to bump mapping is that we need a valid surface normal at each fragment location, and we also need a light source and viewing direction vectors. If we have access to all these values in the fragment shader, we can procedurally perturb the normal prior to the light source calculation to produce the appearance of "bumps." In this case, we really are attempting to produce bumps or small spherical nodules on the surface being rendered.

The light source computation is typically performed with dot products. For the result to have meaning, all the components of the light source calculation must be defined in the same coordinate space. So if we used the vertex shader to perform lighting, we would typically define light source positions or directions in eye coordinates and would transform incoming normals and vertex values into this space to do the calculation.

However, the eye-coordinate system isn't necessarily the best choice for doing lighting in the fragment shader. We could normalize the direction to the light and the surface normal after transforming them to eye space and then pass them to the fragment shader as out variables. However, the light direction vector would need to be renormalized after interpolation to get accurate results. Moreover, whatever method we use to compute the perturbation normal, it would need to be transformed into eye space and added to the surface normal; that vector would also need to be normalized. Without renormalization, the lighting artifacts would be quite noticeable. Performing these operations at every fragment might be reasonably costly in terms of performance. There is a better way.

Let us look at another coordinate space called the SURFACE-LOCAL COORDINATE SPACE. This coordinate system varies over a rendered object, and it assumes that each point is at (0, 0, 0) and that the unperturbed surface normal at each point is (0, 0, 1). This would be a pretty convenient coordinate system in which to do our bump mapping calculations. But, to do our lighting computation, we need to make sure that our light direction, viewing direction, and the computed perturbed normal are all defined in the same coordinate system. If our perturbed normal is defined in surface-local coordinates, that means we need to transform our light direction and viewing direction into surface-local space as well. How is that accomplished?

What we need is a transformation matrix that transforms each incoming vertex into surface-local coordinates (i.e., incoming vertex (x, y, z) is transformed to $(0, 0, 0)$). We need to construct this transformation matrix at each vertex. Then, at each vertex, we use the surface-local transformation matrix to transform both the light direction and the viewing direction. In this way, the surface local coordinates of the light direction and the viewing direction are computed at each vertex and interpolated across the primitive. At each fragment, we can use these values to perform our lighting calculation with the perturbed normal that we calculate.

But we still haven't answered the real question. How do we create the transformation matrix that transforms from object coordinates to surface-local coordinates? An infinite number of transforms will transform a particular vertex to $(0, 0, 0)$. To transform incoming vertex values, we need a way that gives consistent results as we interpolate between them.

The solution is to require the application to send down one more attribute value for each vertex, a tangent value. Furthermore, we require the application to send us tangents that are consistently defined across the surface of the object. By definition, this tangent vector is in the plane of the surface being rendered and perpendicular to the incoming surface normal. If defined consistently across the object, it serves to orient consistently the coordinate system that we derive. If we perform a cross-product between the tangent vector and the surface normal, we get a third vector that is perpendicular to the other two. This third vector is called the BINORMAL, and it's something that we can compute in our vertex shader. Together, these three vectors form an orthonormal basis, which is what we need to define the transformation from object coordinates into surface-local coordinates. Because this particular surface-local coordinate system is defined with a tangent vector as one of the basis vectors, this coordinate system is sometimes referred to as TANGENT SPACE.

The transformation from object space to surface-local space is shown in Figure 11.5. We transform the object space vector (O_x, O_y, O_z) into surface-local space by multiplying it by a matrix that contains the tangent vector

$$\begin{bmatrix} S_x \\ S_y \\ S_z \end{bmatrix} = \begin{bmatrix} T_x & T_y & T_z \\ B_x & B_y & B_z \\ N_x & N_y & N_z \end{bmatrix} \begin{bmatrix} O_x \\ O_y \\ O_z \end{bmatrix}$$

Figure 11.5 Transformation from object space to surface-local space

(T_x, T_y, T_z) in the first row, the binormal vector (B_x, B_y, B_z) in the second row, and the surface normal (N_x, N_y, N_z) in the third row. We can use this process to transform both the light direction vector and the viewing direction vector into surface-local coordinates. The transformed vectors are interpolated across the primitive, and the interpolated vectors are used in the fragment shader to compute the reflection with the procedurally perturbed normal.

11.4.1 Application Setup

For our procedural bump map shader to work properly, the application must send a vertex position, a surface normal, and a tangent vector in the plane of the surface being rendered. The application passes the tangent vector as a generic vertex attribute and binds the index of the generic attribute to be used to the vertex shader variable *tangent* by calling **glBindAttribLocation**. The application is also responsible for providing values for the uniform variables *LightPosition*, *SurfaceColor*, *BumpDensity*, *BumpSize*, and *SpecularFactor*.

You must be careful to orient the tangent vectors consistently between vertices; otherwise, the transformation into surface-local coordinates will be inconsistent, and the lighting computation will yield unpredictable results. Consistent tangents can be computed algorithmically for mathematically defined surfaces. Consistent tangents for polygonal objects can be computed with neighboring vertices and by application of a consistent ordering with respect to the object's texture coordinates.

The problem with inconsistently defined normals is illustrated in Figure 11.6. This diagram shows two triangles, one with consistently defined tangents and one with inconsistently defined tangents. The gray arrowheads indicate the tangent and binormal vectors (the surface normal is pointing straight out of the page). The white arrowheads indicate the direction toward the light source (in this case, a directional light source is illustrated).

When we transform vertex 1 to surface-local coordinates, we get the same initial result in both cases. When we transform vertex 2, we get a large difference because the tangent vectors are very different between the two vertices. If tangents were defined consistently, this situation would not occur unless the surface had a high degree of curvature across this polygon. And if that were the case, we would really want to tessellate the geometry further to prevent this from happening.

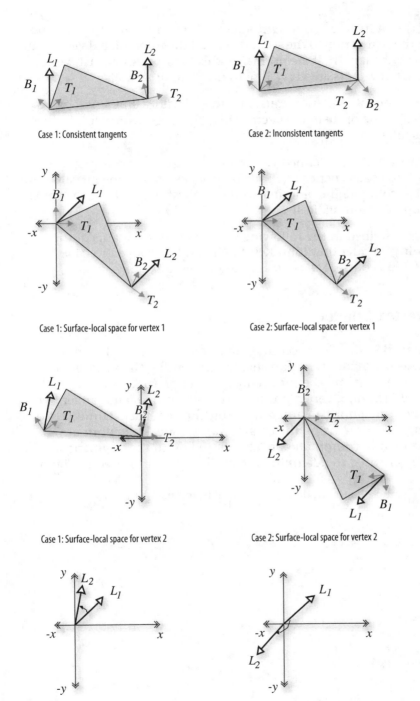

Figure 11.6 Inconsistently defined tangents can lead to large lighting errors.

The result is that in case 1, our light direction vector is smoothly interpolated from the first vertex to the second, and all the interpolated vectors are roughly the same length. If we normalize this light vector at each vertex, the interpolated vectors are very close to unit length as well.

But in case 2, the interpolation causes vectors of wildly different lengths to be generated, some of them near zero. This causes severe artifacts in the lighting calculation.

OpenGL does not have a defined vertex attribute for a tangent vector. The best choice is to use a generic vertex attribute to pass in the tangent value. We don't need to compute the binormal in the application; we have the vertex shader compute it automatically.

The shaders described in the following section are descendants of the "bumpy/shiny" shader that John Kessenich and I developed for the SIGGRAPH 2002 course, *State of the Art in Hardware Shading*.

11.4.2 Vertex Shader

The vertex shader for our procedural bump map shader is shown in Listing 11.7. This shader is responsible for computing the surface-local direction to the light and the surface-local direction to the eye. To do this, it accepts the incoming vertex position, surface normal, and tangent vector; computes the binormal; and transforms the eye space light direction and viewing direction, using the created surface-local transformation matrix. The texture coordinates are also passed on to the fragment shader because they are used to determine the position of our procedural bumps.

Listing 11.7 Vertex shader for doing procedural bump mapping

```
#version 140

uniform vec3 LightPosition;

uniform mat4 MVMatrix;
uniform mat4 MVPMatrix;
uniform mat3 NormalMatrix;

in  vec4 MCVertex;
in  vec3 MCNormal;
in  vec3 MCTangent;
in  vec2 TexCoord0;

out vec3 LightDir;
out vec3 EyeDir;
out vec2 TexCoord;
```

```
void main()
{
    gl_Position     = MVPMatrix * MCVertex;

    EyeDir          = vec3(MVMatrix * MCVertex);
    TexCoord        = TexCoord0.st;

    vec3 n = normalize(NormalMatrix * MCNormal);
    vec3 t = normalize(NormalMatrix * MCTangent);
    vec3 b = cross(n, t);

    vec3 v;
    v.x = dot(LightPosition, t);
    v.y = dot(LightPosition, b);
    v.z = dot(LightPosition, n);
    LightDir = normalize(v);

    v.x = dot(EyeDir, t);
    v.y = dot(EyeDir, b);
    v.z = dot(EyeDir, n);
    EyeDir = normalize(v);
}
```

11.4.3 Fragment Shader

The fragment shader for doing procedural bump mapping is shown in Listing 11.8. A couple of the characteristics of the bump pattern are parameterized by being declared as uniform variables, namely, *BumpDensity* (how many bumps per unit area) and *BumpSize* (how wide each bump will be). Two of the general characteristics of the overall surface are also defined as uniform variables: *SurfaceColor* (base color of the surface) and *SpecularFactor* (specular reflectance property).

The bumps that we compute are round. Because the texture coordinate is used to determine the positioning of the bumps, the first thing we do is multiply the incoming texture coordinate by the *density* value. This controls whether we see more or fewer bumps on the surface. Using the resulting grid, we compute a bump located in the center of each grid square. The components of the perturbation vector *p* are computed as the distance from the center of the bump in the *x* direction and the distance from the center of the bump in the *y* direction. (We only perturb the normal in the *x* and *y* directions. The *z* value for our perturbation normal is always 1.0.) We compute a "pseudodistance" *d* by squaring the components of *p* and summing them. (The real distance could be computed at the cost of doing another square root, but it's not really necessary if we consider *BumpSize* to be a relative value rather than an absolute value.)

To perform a proper reflection calculation later on, we really need to normalize the perturbation normal. This normal must be a unit vector so that we can perform dot products and get accurate cosine values for use in the lighting computation. We normalize a vector by multiplying each component of the normal by 1.0 / $\mathbf{sqrt}(x^2 + y^2 + z^2)$. Because of our computation for d, we've already computed part of what we need (i.e., $x^2 + y^2$). Furthermore, because we're not perturbing z at all, we know that z^2 will always be 1.0. To minimize the computation, we just finish computing our normalization factor at this point in the shader by computing 1.0 / $\mathbf{sqrt}(d + 1.0)$.

Next, we compare d to *BumpSize* to see if we're in a bump or not. If we're not, we set our perturbation vector to 0 and our normalization factor to 1.0. The lighting computation happens in the next few lines. We compute our normalized perturbation vector by multiplying through with the normalization factor *f*. The diffuse and specular reflection values are computed in the usual way, except that the interpolated surface-local coordinate light and view direction vectors are used. We get decent results without normalizing these two vectors as long as we don't have large differences in their values between vertices.

Listing 11.8 Fragment shader for procedural bump mapping

```
#version 140

uniform vec4  SurfaceColor;    // = (0.7, 0.6, 0.18, 1.0)
uniform float BumpDensity;     // = 16.0
uniform float BumpSize;        // = 0.15
uniform float SpecularFactor;  // = 0.5

in  vec3 LightDir;
in  vec3 EyeDir;
in  vec2 TexCoord;

out vec4 FragColor;

void main()
{
    vec3 litColor;
    vec2 c = BumpDensity * TexCoord.st;
    vec2 p = fract(c) - vec2(0.5);

    float d, f;
    d = dot(p,p);
    f = inversesqrt(d + 1.0);

    if (d >= BumpSize)
        { p = vec2(0.0); f = 1.0; }
```

```
    vec3 normDelta = vec3(p.x, p.y, 1.0) * f;
    litColor = SurfaceColor.rgb * max(dot(normDelta, LightDir), 0.0);
    vec3 reflectDir = reflect(LightDir, normDelta);

    float spec = max(dot(EyeDir, reflectDir), 0.0);
    spec = pow(spec, 6.0);
    spec *= SpecularFactor;
    litColor = min(litColor + spec, vec3(1.0));

    FragColor = vec4(litColor, SurfaceColor.a);
}
```

The results from the procedural bump map shader are shown applied to two objects, a simple box and a torus, in Color Plate 15. The texture coordinates are used as the basis for positioning the bumps, and because the texture coordinates go from 0.0 to 1.0 four times around the diameter of the torus, the bumps look much closer together on that object.

11.4.4 Normal Maps

It is easy to modify our shader so that it obtains the normal perturbation values from a texture rather generating them procedurally. A texture that contains normal perturbation values for the purpose of bump mapping is called a BUMP MAP or a NORMAL MAP.

An example of a normal map and the results applied to our simple box object are shown in Color Plate 16. Individual components for the normals can be in the range [–1,1]. To be encoded into an RGB texture with 8 bits per component, they must be mapped into the range [0,1]. The normal map appears chalk blue because the default perturbation vector of (0,0,1) is encoded in the normal map as (0.5,0.5,1.0). The normal map could be stored in a floating-point texture. Today's graphics hardware supports textures with 16-bit floating-point values per color component and textures with 32-bit floating-point values per color component. If you use a floating-point texture format for storing normals, your image quality tends to increase (for instance, reducing banding effects in specular highlights). Of course, textures that are 16 bits per component require twice as much texture memory as 8-bit per component textures, and performance might be reduced.

The vertex program is identical to the one described in Section 11.4.2. The fragment shader is almost the same, except that instead of computing the perturbed normal procedurally, the fragment shader obtains it from a normal map stored in texture memory.

11.5 Summary

A master magician can make it look like something is created out of thin air. With procedural textures, you, as a shader writer, can express algorithms that turn flat gray surfaces into colorful, patterned, bumpy, or reflective ones. The trick is to come up with an algorithm that expresses the texture you envision. By coding this algorithm as an OpenGL shader, you too can create something out of thin air.

In this chapter, we only scratched the surface of what's possible. We created a stripe shader, but grids and checkerboards and polka dots are no more difficult. We created a toy ball with a star, but we could have created a beach ball with snowflakes. Shaders can be written to procedurally include or exclude geometry or to add bumps or grooves. Additional procedural texturing effects are illustrated later in this book. Chapter 15 shows how an irregular function (noise) can achieve a wide range of procedural texturing effects. Shaders for generating procedural textures with a more complex mathematical function (the Mandelbrot and Julia sets) and for creating non-photorealistic effects are also described later in the book.

Procedural textures are mathematically precise, are easy to parameterize, and don't require large amounts of texture memory. The end goal of a vertex shader/fragment shader pair is to produce a color value (and possibly a depth value) that will be written into the framebuffer. Because the OpenGL Shading Language is a procedural programming language, the only limit to this computation is your imagination.

11.6 Further Information

The book *Texturing and Modeling: A Procedural Approach, Third Edition*, by David S. Ebert et al. (2002) is entirely devoted to creating images procedurally. This book contains a wealth of information and inspires a ton of ideas for the creation and use of procedural models and textures.

The shaders written in the RenderMan Shading Language are often procedural in nature, and *The RenderMan Companion* by Steve Upstill (1990) and *Advanced RenderMan: Creating CGI for Motion Pictures* by Anthony A. Apodaca and Larry Gritz (1999) contain some notable examples.

Bump mapping was invented by Jim Blinn and described in his 1978 SIGGRAPH paper, *Simulation of Wrinkled Surfaces*. A very good overview of bump mapping techniques can be found in a paper titled *A Practical and Robust Bump-mapping Technique for Today's GPUs* by Mark Kilgard (2000).

A Photoshop plug-in for creating a normal map from an image is available at NVIDIA's developer Web site at http://developer.nvidia.com/object/ photoshop_dds_plugins.html.

[1] *AMD developer Web site.* http://developer.amd.com/

[2] Apodaca, Anthony A., and Larry Gritz, *Advanced RenderMan: Creating CGI for Motion Pictures*, Morgan Kaufmann Publishers, San Francisco, 1999. www.renderman.org/RMR/Books/arman/materials.html

[3] Blinn, James, *Simulation of Wrinkled Surfaces*, Computer Graphics (SIGGRAPH '78 Proceedings), pp. 286–292, August 1978.

[4] Ebert, David S., John Hart, Bill Mark, F. Kenton Musgrave, Darwyn Peachey, Ken Perlin, and Steven Worley, *Texturing and Modeling: · A Procedural Approach, Third Edition*, Morgan Kaufmann Publishers, San Francisco, 2002. www.texturingandmodeling.com

[5] Kilgard, Mark J., *A Practical and Robust Bump-mapping Technique for Today's GPUs*, Game Developers Conference, NVIDIA White Paper, 2000. http://developer.nvidia.com/object/Practical_ Bumpmapping_Tech.html

[6] *NVIDIA developer Web site.* http://developer.nvidia.com

[7] Rost, Randi J., *The OpenGL Shading Language*, SIGGRAPH 2002, Course 17, course notes. http://3dshaders.com/pubs

[8] Upstill, Steve, *The RenderMan Companion: A Programmer's Guide to Realistic Computer Graphics*, Addison-Wesley, Reading, Massachusetts, 1990.

Chapter 12

Lighting

In the real world, we see things because they reflect light from a light source or because they are light sources themselves. In computer graphics, just as in real life, we won't be able to see an object unless it is illuminated or emits light. To generate more realistic images, we need to have more realistic models for illumination, shadows, and reflection than those we've discussed so far.

In this chapter and the next two, we explore how the OpenGL Shading Language can help us implement such models so that they can execute at interactive rates on programmable graphics hardware. In this chapter, we look at some lighting models that provide more flexibility and give more realistic results than those built into OpenGL's fixed functionality rendering pipeline. Much has been written on the topic of lighting in computer graphics. We examine only a few methods in this chapter. Ideally, you'll be inspired to try implementing some others on your own.

12.1 Hemisphere Lighting

In Chapter 9, we looked carefully at the fixed functionality lighting model built into OpenGL and developed shader code to mimic the fixed functionality behavior. However, this model has a number of flaws, and these flaws become more apparent as we strive for more realistic rendering effects. One problem is that objects in a scene do not typically receive all their illumination from a small number of specific light sources. Interreflections between objects often have noticeable and important contributions to objects in the scene. The traditional computer graphics illumination model attempts to account for this phenomena through an ambient light term. However, this ambient light term is usually applied equally across an object or an entire scene. The result is a flat and unrealistic look for areas of the scene that are not affected by direct illumination.

Another problem with the traditional illumination model is that light sources in real scenes are not point lights or even spotlights—they are area lights. Consider the indirect light coming in from the window and illuminating the floor and the long fluorescent light bulbs behind a rectangular translucent panel. For an even more common case, consider the illumination outdoors on a cloudy day. In this case, the entire visible hemisphere is acting like an area light source. In several presentations and tutorials, Chas Boyd, Dan Baker, and Philip Taylor of Microsoft described this situation as HEMISPHERE LIGHTING and discussed how to implement it in DirectX. Let's look at how we might create an OpenGL shader to simulate this type of lighting environment.

The idea behind hemisphere lighting is that we model the illumination as two hemispheres. The upper hemisphere represents the sky, and the lower hemisphere represents the ground. A location on an object with a surface normal that points straight up gets all of its illumination from the upper hemisphere, and a location with a surface normal pointing straight down gets all of its illumination from the lower hemisphere (see Figure 12.1). By picking appropriate colors for the two hemispheres, we can make the sphere look as though locations with normals pointing up are illuminated and those with surface normals pointing down are in shadow.

To compute the illumination at any point on the surface, we must compute the integral of the illumination received at that point:

$$Color \, = \, a \cdot SkyColor + (1 - a) \cdot GroundColor$$

where

$$a \, = \, 1.0 - (0.5 \cdot \sin(\theta)) \quad \text{for } \theta \leq 90°$$
$$a \, = \, 0.5 \cdot \sin(\theta) \quad \text{for } \theta > 90°$$
$$\theta \, = \, \text{angle between surface normal and north pole direction}$$

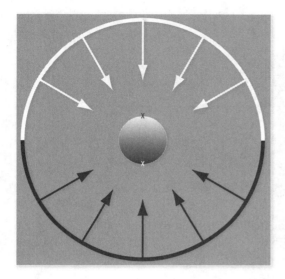

Figure 12.1   A sphere illuminated using the hemisphere lighting model. A point on the top of the sphere (the black "x") receives illumination only from the upper hemisphere (i.e., the sky color). A point on the bottom of the sphere (the white "x") receives illumination only from the lower hemisphere (i.e., the ground color). A point right on the equator would receive half of its illumination from the upper hemisphere and half from the lower hemisphere (e.g., 50% sky color and 50% ground color).

But we can actually calculate a in another way that is simpler but roughly equivalent:

$$a = 0.5 + (0.5 \cdot \cos(\theta))$$

This approach eliminates the need for a conditional. Furthermore, we can easily compute the cosine of the angle between two unit vectors by taking the dot product of the two vectors. This is an example of what Jim Blinn likes to call "the ancient Chinese art of *chi ting*." In computer graphics, if it looks good enough, it is good enough. It doesn't really matter whether your calculations are physically correct or a colossal cheat. The difference between the two functions is shown in Figure 12.2. The shape of the two curves is similar. One is the mirror of the other, but the area under the curves is the same. This general equivalency is good enough for the effect we're after, and the shader is simpler and will likely execute faster as well.

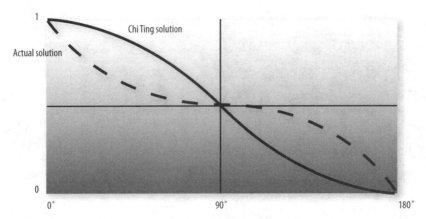

Figure 12.2   Comparing the actual analytic function for hemisphere lighting to a similar but higher-performance function

For the hemisphere shader, we need to pass in uniform variables for the sky color and the ground color. We can also consider the "north pole" to be our light position. If we pass this in as a uniform variable, we can light the model from different directions.

Listing 12.1 shows a vertex shader that implements hemisphere lighting. As you can see, the shader is quite simple. The main purpose of the shader is to compute the diffuse color value and pass it on to fixed functionality fragment processing so that it can be written into the framebuffer. We accomplish this purpose by storing the computed color value in the user-defined out variable *Color*. Results for this shader are shown in Color Plate 21D and G. Compare this to the results of shading with a single directional light source shown in Color Plate 21A and B. Not only is the hemisphere shader simpler and more efficient, it produces a much more realistic lighting effect too! This lighting model can be utilized for tasks like model preview, where it is important to examine all the details of a model. It can also be used in conjunction with the traditional computer graphics illumination model. Point, directional, or spot lights can be added on top of the hemisphere lighting model to provide more illumination to important parts of the scene.

Listing 12.1   Vertex shader for hemisphere lighting

```
#version 140

uniform vec3 LightPosition;
uniform vec3 SkyColor;
uniform vec3 GroundColor;
```

```
uniform mat4 MVMatrix;
uniform mat4 MVPMatrix;
uniform mat3 NormalMatrix;

in vec4     MCVertex;
in vec3     MCNormal;

out vec3    Color;

void main()
{
    vec3 ecPosition = vec3(MVMatrix * MCVertex);
    vec3 tnorm = normalize(NormalMatrix * MCNormal);
    vec3 lightVec = normalize(LightPosition - ecPosition);
    float costheta = dot(tnorm, lightVec);
    float a = costheta * 0.5 + 0.5;
    Color = mix(GroundColor, SkyColor, a);
    gl_Position = MVPMatrix * MCvertex;
}
```

One of the issues with this model is that it doesn't account for self-occlusion. Regions that should really be in shadow because of the geometry of the model appear too bright. We remedy this in Chapter 13.

12.2 Image-Based Lighting

Back in Chapter 10 we looked at shaders to perform environment mapping. If we're trying to achieve realistic lighting in a computer graphics scene, why not just use an environment map for the lighting? This approach to illumination is called IMAGE-BASED LIGHTING; it has been popularized in recent years by researcher Paul Debevec at the University of Southern California. Churches and auditoriums may have dozens of light sources on the ceiling. Rooms with many windows also have complex lighting environments. It is often easier and much more efficient to sample the lighting in such environments and store the results in one or more environment maps than it is to simulate numerous individual light sources.

The steps involved in image-based lighting are

1. Use a LIGHT PROBE (e.g., a reflective sphere) to capture (e.g., photograph) the illumination that occurs in a real-world scene. The captured omnidirectional, high-dynamic range image is called a LIGHT PROBE IMAGE.

2. Use the light probe image to create a representation of the environment (e.g., an environment map).

3.   Place the synthetic objects to be rendered inside the environment.

4.   Render the synthetic objects by using the representation of the environment created in step 2.

On his Web site (www.debevec.org), Debevec offers a number of useful things to developers. For one, he has made available a number of images that can be used as high-quality environment maps to provide realistic lighting in a scene. These images are high dynamic range (HDR) images that represent each color component with a 32-bit floating-point value. Such images can represent a much greater range of intensity values than can 8-bit-per-component images. For another, he makes available a tool called HDRShop that manipulates and transforms these environment maps. Through links to his various publications and tutorials, he also provides step-by-step instructions on creating your own environment maps and using them to add realistic lighting effects to computer graphics scenes.

Following Debevec's guidance, I purchased a 2-inch chrome steel ball from McMaster-Carr Supply Company (www.mcmaster.com). We used this ball to capture a light probe image from the center of the square outside our office building in downtown Fort Collins, Colorado (Color Plate 10A). We then used HDRShop to create a lat-long environment map (Color Plate 9) and a cube map (Color Plate 10B) of the same scene. The cube map and lat-long map can be used to perform environment mapping as described in Chapter 10. That shader simulated a surface with an underlying base color and diffuse reflection characteristics that was covered by a transparent mirror-like layer that reflected the environment flawlessly.

We can simulate other types of objects if we modify the environment maps before they are used. A point on the surface that reflects light in a diffuse fashion reflects light from all the light sources that are in the hemisphere in the direction of the surface normal at that point. We can't really afford to access the environment map a large number of times in our shader. What we can do instead is similar to what we discussed for hemisphere lighting. Starting from our light probe image, we can construct an environment map for diffuse lighting. Each texel in this environment map will contain the weighted average (i.e., the convolution) of other texels in the visible hemisphere as defined by the surface normal that would be used to access that texel in the environment.

Again, HDRShop has exactly what we need. We can use HDRShop to create a lat-long image from our original light probe image. We can then use a command built into HDRShop that performs the necessary convolution. This operation can be time-consuming, because at each texel in the image, the contributions from half of the other texels in the image must be considered. Luckily, we don't need a very large image for this purpose. The effect is essentially the same as creating a very blurry image of the original light probe image. Since there is no high-frequency content in the computed image, a cube map with faces that are 64×64 or 128×128 works just fine. An example of a diffuse environment map is shown in Color Plate 10C.

A single texture access into this diffuse environment map provides us with the value needed for our diffuse reflection calculation. What about the specular contribution? A surface that is very shiny will reflect the illumination from a light source just like a mirror. This is what we saw in the environment mapping shader from Chapter 10. A single point on the surface reflects a single point in the environment. For surfaces that are rougher, the highlight defocuses and spreads out. In this case, a single point on the surface reflects several points in the environment, though not the whole visible hemisphere like a diffuse surface. HDRShop lets us blur an environment map by providing a Phong exponent—a degree of shininess. A value of 1.0 convolves the environment map to simulate diffuse reflection, and a value of 50 or more convolves the environment map to simulate a somewhat shiny surface. An example of the Old Town Square environment map that has been convolved with a Phong exponent value of 50 is shown in Color Plate 10D.

The shaders that implement these concepts end up being quite simple and quite fast. In the vertex shader, all that is needed is to compute the reflection direction at each vertex. This value and the surface normal are sent to the fragment shader as out variables. They are interpolated across each polygon, and the interpolated values are used in the fragment shader to access the two environment maps in order to obtain the diffuse and the specular components. The values obtained from the environment maps are combined with the object's base color to arrive at the final color for the fragment. The shaders are shown in Listing 12.2 and Listing 12.3. Examples of images created with this technique are shown in Color Plate 18.

Listing 12.2   Vertex shader for image-based lighting

```
#version 140

uniform mat4 MVMatrix;
uniform mat4 MVPMatrix;
uniform mat3 NormalMatrix;

in  vec4  MCVertex;
in  vec3  MCNormal;
```

```
out vec3  ReflectDir;
out vec3  Normal;

void main()
{
    gl_Position = MVPMatrix * MCVertex;
    Normal = normalize(NormalMatrix * MCNormal);
    vec4 pos = MVMatrix * MCvertex;
    vec3 eyeDir = pos.xyz;
    ReflectDir = reflect(eyeDir, Normal);
}
```

Listing 12.3 Fragment shader for image-based lighting

```
#version 140

uniform vec3  BaseColor;
uniform float SpecularPercent;
uniform float DiffusePercent;

uniform samplerCube SpecularEnvMap;
uniform samplerCube DiffuseEnvMap;

in  vec3  ReflectDir;
in  vec3  Normal;

out vec4  FragColor;

void main()
{
    // Look up environment map values in cube maps
    vec3 diffuseColor =
        vec3(texture(DiffuseEnvMap, normalize(Normal)));

    vec3 specularColor =
        vec3(texture(SpecularEnvMap, normalize(ReflectDir)));

    // Add lighting to base color and mix

    vec3 color = mix(BaseColor, diffuseColor*BaseColor, DiffusePercent);
    color = mix(color, specularColor + color, SpecularPercent);

    FragColor = vec4(color, 1.0);
}
```

The environment maps that are used can reproduce the light from the whole scene. Of course, objects with different specular reflection properties require different specular environment maps. And producing these environment maps requires some manual effort and lengthy preprocessing. But the resulting quality and performance make image-based lighting a great choice in many situations.

12.3 Lighting with Spherical Harmonics

In 2001, Ravi Ramamoorthi and Pat Hanrahan presented a method that uses spherical harmonics for computing the diffuse lighting term. This method reproduces accurate diffuse reflection, based on the content of a light probe image, without accessing the light probe image at runtime. The light probe image is preprocessed to produce coefficients that are used in a mathematical representation of the image at runtime. The mathematics behind this approach is beyond the scope of this book (see the references at the end of this chapter if you want all the details). Instead, we lay the necessary groundwork for this shader by describing the underlying mathematics in an intuitive fashion. The result is remarkably simple, accurate, and realistic, and it can easily be codified in an OpenGL shader. This technique has already been used successfully to provide real-time illumination for games and has applications in computer vision and other areas as well.

Spherical harmonics provides a frequency space representation of an image over a sphere. It is analogous to the Fourier transform on the line or circle. This representation of the image is continuous and rotationally invariant. Using this representation for a light probe image, Ramamoorthi and Hanrahan showed that you could accurately reproduce the diffuse reflection from a surface with just nine spherical harmonic basis functions. These nine spherical harmonics are obtained with constant, linear, and quadratic polynomials of the normalized surface normal.

Intuitively, we can see that it is plausible to accurately simulate the diffuse reflection with a small number of basis functions in frequency space since diffuse reflection varies slowly across a surface. With just nine terms used, the average error over all surface orientations is less than 3 percent for any physical input lighting distribution. With Debevec's light probe images, the average error was shown to be less than 1 percent, and the maximum error for any pixel was less than 5 percent.

Each spherical harmonic basis function has a coefficient that depends on the light probe image being used. The coefficients are different for each color channel, so you can think of each coefficient as an RGB value. A preprocessing step is required to compute the nine RGB coefficients for the light probe image to be used. Ramamoorthi makes the code for this preprocessing step available for free on his Web site. I used this program to compute the coefficients for all the light probe images in Debevec's light probe gallery as well as the Old Town Square light probe image and summarized the results in Table 12.1.

Table 12.1 Spherical harmonic coefficients for light probe images

Coefficient	Old Town Square			Grace Cathedral			Eucalyptus Grove			St. Peter's Basilica			Uffizi Gallery		
L00	.87	.88	.86	.79	.44	.54	.38	.43	.45	.36	.26	.23	.32	.31	.35
L1m1	.18	.25	.31	.39	.35	.60	.29	.36	.41	.18	.14	.13	.37	.37	.43
L10	.03	.04	.04	-.34	-.18	-.27	.04	.03	.01	-.02	-.01	.00	.00	.00	.00
L11	-.00	-.03	-.05	-.29	-.06	.01	-.10	-.10	-.09	.03	.02	.00	-.01	-.01	-.01
L2m2	-.12	-.12	-.12	-.11	-.05	-.12	-.06	-.06	-.04	.02	.01	.00	-.02	-.02	-.03
L2m1	.00,	.00	.01	-.26	-.22	-.47	.01	-.01	-.05	-.05	-.03	-.01	-.01	-.01	-.01
L20	-.03	-.02	-.02	-.16	-.09	-.15	-.09	-.13	-.15	-.09	-.08	-.07	-.28	-.28	-.32
L21	-.08	-.09	-.09	.56	.21	.14	-.06	-.05	-.04	.01	.00	.00	.00	.00	.00
L22	-.16	-.19	-.22	.21	-.05	-.30	.02	.00	-.05	-.08	-.03	.00	-.24	-.24	-.28

Coefficient	Galileo's Tomb			Vine Street Kitchen			Breezeway			Campus Sunset			Funston Beach Sunset		
L00	1.04	.76	.71	.64	.67	.73	.32	.36	.38	.79	.94	.98	.68	.69	.70
L1m1	.44	.34	.34	.28	.32	.33	.37	.41	.45	.44	.56	.70	.32	.37	.44
L10	-.22	-.18	-.17	.42	.60	.77	-.01	-.01	-.01	-.10	-.18	-.27	-.17	-.17	-.17
L11	.71	.54	.56	-.05	-.04	-.02	-.10	-.12	-.12	.45	.38	.20	-.45	-.42	-.34
L2m2	.64	.50	.52	-.10	-.08	-.05	-.13	-.15	-.17	.18	.14	.05	-.17	-.17	-.15
L2m1	-.12	-.09	-.08	.25	.39	.53	-.01	-.02	.02	-.14	-.22	-.31	-.08	-.09	-.10
L20	-.37	-.28	-.29	.38	.54	.71	-.07	-.08	-.09	-.39	-.40	-.36	-.03	-.02	-.01
L21	-.17	-.13	-.13	.06	.01	-.02	.02	.03	0.03	.09	.07	.04	.16	.14	.10
L22	.55	.42	.42	-.03	-.02	-.03	-.29	-.32	-.36	.67	.67	.52	.37	.31	.20

The equation for diffuse reflection using spherical harmonics is

$$Diffuse = c_1 L_{22}(x^2 - y^2) + c_3 L_{20} z^2 + c_4 L_{20} - c_5 L_{20} + \\ 2c_1(L_{2-2}xy + L_{21}xz + L_{2-1}yz) + 2c_2(L_{11}x + L_{1-1}y + L_{10}z)$$

The constants *c1–c5* result from the derivation of this formula and are shown in the vertex shader code in Listing 12.4. The *L* coefficients are the nine basis function coefficients computed for a specific light probe image in the preprocessing phase. The *x*, *y*, and *z* values are the coordinates of the normalized surface normal at the point that is to be shaded. Unlike low dynamic range images (e.g., 8 bits per color component) that have an implicit minimum value of 0 and an implicit maximum value of 255, high dynamic range images represented with a floating-point value for each color component don't contain well-defined minimum and maximum values. The minimum and maximum values for two HDR images may be quite different from each other, unless the same calibration or creation process was used to create both images. It is even possible to have an HDR image that contains negative values. For this reason, the vertex shader contains an overall scaling factor to make the final effect look right.

The vertex shader that encodes the formula for the nine spherical harmonic basis functions is actually quite simple. When the compiler gets hold of it, it becomes simpler still. An optimizing compiler typically reduces all the operations involving constants. The resulting code is quite efficient because it contains a relatively small number of addition and multiplication operations that involve the components of the surface normal.

Listing 12.4 Vertex shader for spherical harmonics lighting

```
#version 140

uniform mat4 MVMatrix;
uniform mat4 MVPMatrix;
uniform mat3 NormalMatrix;

uniform float ScaleFactor;

const float C1 = 0.429043;
const float C2 = 0.511664;
const float C3 = 0.743125;
const float C4 = 0.886227;
const float C5 = 0.247708;

// Constants for Old Town Square lighting
const vec3 L00  = vec3( 0.871297,  0.875222,  0.864470);
const vec3 L1m1 = vec3( 0.175058,  0.245335,  0.312891);
const vec3 L10  = vec3( 0.034675,  0.036107,  0.037362);
const vec3 L11  = vec3(-0.004629, -0.029448, -0.048028);
const vec3 L2m2 = vec3(-0.120535, -0.121160, -0.117507);
const vec3 L2m1 = vec3( 0.003242,  0.003624,  0.007511);
const vec3 L20  = vec3(-0.028667, -0.024926, -0.020998);
const vec3 L21  = vec3(-0.077539, -0.086325, -0.091591);
const vec3 L22  = vec3(-0.161784, -0.191783, -0.219152);
```

```
in  vec4  MCVertex;
in  vec3  MCNormal;

out vec3  DiffuseColor;

void main()
{
   vec3 tnorm   = normalize(NormalMatrix * MCNormal);

   DiffuseColor = C1 * L22 * (tnorm.x * tnorm.x - tnorm.y * tnorm.y) +
                  C3 * L20 *  tnorm.z * tnorm.z +
                  C4 * L00 -
                  C5 * L20 +
                  2.0 * C1 * L2m2 * tnorm.x * tnorm.y +
                  2.0 * C1 * L21  * tnorm.x * tnorm.z +
                  2.0 * C1 * L2m1 * tnorm.y * tnorm.z +
                  2.0 * C2 * L11  * tnorm.x +
                  2.0 * C2 * L1m1 * tnorm.y +
                  2.0 * C2 * L10  * tnorm.z;

   DiffuseColor *= ScaleFactor;

   gl_Position = MVPMatrix * MCVertex;
```

Listing 12.5 Fragment shader for spherical harmonics lighting

```
#version 140

in vec3      DiffuseColor;

out vec4     FragColor;

void main()
{
    FragColor = vec4(DiffuseColor, 1.0);
}
```

Our fragment shader, shown in Listing 12.5, has very little work to do. Because the diffuse reflection typically changes slowly, for scenes without large polygons we can reasonably compute it in the vertex shader and interpolate it during rasterization. As with hemispherical lighting, we can add procedurally defined point, directional, or spotlights on top of the spherical harmonics lighting to provide more illumination to important parts of the scene. Results of the spherical harmonics shader are shown in Color Plate 19. Compare Color Plate 19A with the Old Town Square environment map in Color Plate 9. Note that the top of the dog's head has a bluish cast, while there is a brownish cast on his chin and chest. Coefficients for some of Paul Debevec's light probe images provide even greater color variations. We could make the diffuse lighting from the spherical harmonics computation more subtle by blending it with the object's base color.

The trade-offs in using image-based lighting versus procedurally defined lights are similar to the trade-offs between using stored textures versus procedural textures, as discussed in Chapter 11. Image-based lighting techniques can capture and re-create complex lighting environments relatively easily. It would be exceedingly difficult to simulate such an environment with a large number of procedural light sources. On the other hand, procedurally defined light sources do not use up texture memory and can easily be modified and animated.

12.4 The Überlight Shader

So far in this chapter we've discussed lighting algorithms that simulate the effect of global illumination for more realistic lighting effects. Traditional point, directional, and spotlights can be used in conjunction with these global illumination effects. However, the traditional light sources leave a lot to be desired in terms of their flexibility and ease of use.

Ronen Barzel of Pixar Animation Studios wrote a paper in 1997 that described a much more versatile lighting model specifically tailored for the creation of computer-generated films. This lighting model has so many features and controls compared to the traditional graphics hardware light source types that its RenderMan implementation became known as the "überlight" shader (i.e., the lighting shader that has everything in it except the proverbial kitchen sink). Larry Gritz wrote a public domain version of this shader that was published in *Advanced RenderMan: Creating CGI for Motion Pictures*, which he coauthored with Anthony A. Apodaca. A Cg version of this shader was published by Fabio Pellacini and Kiril Vidimice of Pixar in the book *GPU Gems*, edited by Randima Fernando. The full-blown überlight shader has been used successfully in a variety of computer-generated films, including *Toy Story*, *Monsters, Inc.*, and *Finding Nemo*. Because of the proven usefulness of the überlight shader, this section looks at how to implement its essential features in the OpenGL Shading Language.

12.4.1 Überlight Controls

In movies, lighting helps to tell the story in several different ways. Sharon Calahan gives a good overview of this process in the book *Advanced RenderMan: Creating CGI for Motion Pictures*. This description includes five important fundamentals of good lighting design that were derived from the book *Matters of Light & Depth* by Ross Lowell:

- Directing the viewer's eye
- Creating depth
- Conveying time of day and season
- Enhancing mood, atmosphere, and drama
- Revealing character personality and situation

Because of the importance of lighting to the final product, movies have dedicated lighting designers. To light computer graphics scenes, lighting designers must have an intuitive and versatile lighting model to use.

For the best results in lighting a scene, it is crucial to make proper decisions about the shape and placement of the lights. For the überlight lighting model, lights are assigned a position in world coordinates. The überlight shader uses a pair of superellipses to determine the shape of the light. A SUPERELLIPSE is a function that varies its shape from an ellipse to a rectangle, based on the value of a roundness parameter. By varying the roundness parameter, we can shape the beam of illumination in a variety of ways (see Figure 12.3 for some examples). The superellipse function is defined as

$$\left(\frac{x}{a}\right)^{\frac{2}{d}} + \left(\frac{y}{b}\right)^{\frac{2}{d}} = 1$$

As the value for d nears 0, this function becomes the equation for a rectangle, and when d is equal to 1, the function becomes the equation for an ellipse. Values in between create shapes in between a rectangle and an ellipse, and these shapes are also useful for lighting. This is referred to in the shader as BARN SHAPING since devices used in the theater for shaping light beams are referred to as BARN DOORS.

It is also desirable to have a soft edge to the light, in other words, a gradual drop-off from full intensity to zero intensity. We accomplish this by defining a pair of nested superellipses. Inside the innermost superellipse, the light has full intensity. Outside the outermost superellipse, the light has zero intensity. In between, we can apply a gradual transition by using the **smoothstep** function. See Figure 12.3 for examples of lights with and without such soft edges.

Two more controls that add to the versatility of this lighting model are the near and far distance parameters, also known as the CUTON and CUTOFF

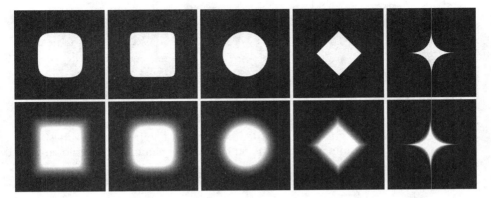

Figure 12.3 A variety of light beam shapes produced with the überlight shader. We enabled barn shaping and varied the roundness and edge width parameters of the superellipse shaping function. The top row uses edge widths of 0, and the bottom row uses 0.3. From left to right, the roundness parameter is set to 0.2, 0.5, 1.0, 2.0, and 4.0.

values. These define the region of the beam that actually provides illumination (see Figure 12.4). Again, smooth transition zones are desired so that the lighting designer can control the transition. Of course, this particular control has no real-world analogy, but it has proved to be useful for softening the lighting in a scene and preventing the light from reaching areas where no light is desired. See Figure 12.5 for an example of the effect of modifying these parameters.

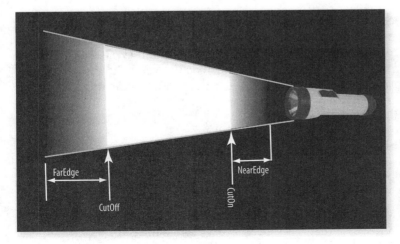

Figure 12.4 Effects of the near and far distance parameters for the überlight shader

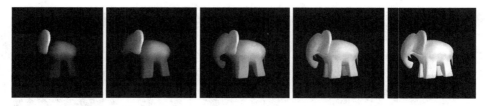

Figure 12.5   Dramatic lighting effects achieved by alteration of the depth cutoff parameters of the überlight shader. In the first frame, the light barely reaches the elephant model. By simply adjusting the far depth edge value, we can gradually bathe our model in light.

12.4.2 Vertex Shader

Listing 12.6 shows the code for the vertex shader for the überlight model. The main purpose of the vertex shader is to transform vertex positions, surface normals, and the viewing (camera) position into the lighting coordinate system. In this coordinate system the light is at the origin, and the *z* axis is pointed toward the origin of the world coordinate system. This allows us to more easily perform the lighting computations in the fragment shader. The computed values are passed to the fragment shader in the form of the out variables *LCpos*, *LCnorm*, and *LCcamera*.

To perform these calculations, the application must provide *ViewPosition*, the position of the camera in world space, and *WCLightPos*, the position of the light source in world coordinates.

To do the necessary transformations, we need matrices that transform points from modeling coordinates to world coordinates (*MCtoWC*) and from world coordinates to the light coordinate system (*WCtoLC*). The corresponding matrices for transforming normals between the same coordinate systems are the inverse transpose matrices (*MCtoWCit* and *WCtoLCit*).

Listing 12.6 Überlight vertex shader

```
#version 140

uniform mat4 MVMatrix;
uniform mat4 MVPMatrix;
uniform mat3 NormalMatrix;

uniform vec3 WCLightPos;      // Position of light in world coordinates
uniform vec4 ViewPosition;    // Position of camera in world space
uniform mat4 WCtoLC;          // World to light coordinate transform
uniform mat4 WCtoLCit;        // World to light inverse transpose
```

```
uniform mat4 MCtoWC;        // Model to world coordinate transform
uniform mat4 MCtoWCit;      // Model to world inverse transpose

in  vec4  MCVertex;
in  vec3  MCNormal;

out vec3  LCpos;            // Vertex position in light coordinates
out vec3  LCnorm;           // Normal in light coordinates
out vec3  LCcamera;         // Camera position in light coordinates

void main()
{
    gl_Position = MVPMatrix * MCVertex;

    // Compute world space position and normal
    vec4 wcPos  = MCtoWC * MCVertex;
    vec3 wcNorm = (MCtoWCit * vec4(MCNormal, 0.0)).xyz;

    // Compute light coordinate system camera position,
    // vertex position and normal
    LCcamera = (WCtoLC * ViewPosition).xyz;
    LCpos    = (WCtoLC * wcPos).xyz;
    LCnorm   = (WCtoLCit * vec4(wcNorm, 0.0)).xyz;
}
```

12.4.3 Fragment Shader

With the key values transformed into the lighting coordinate system for the specified light source, the fragment shader (Listing 12.7) can perform the necessary lighting computations. One subroutine in this shader (**superEllipseShape**) computes the attenuation factor of the light across the cross section of the beam. This value is 1.0 for fragments within the inner superellipse, 0 for fragments outside the outer superellipse, and a value between 0 and 1.0 for fragments between the two superellipses. Another subroutine (**distanceShape**) computes a similar attenuation factor along the direction of the light beam. These two values are multiplied together to give us the illumination factor for the fragment.

The computation of the light reflection is done in a manner similar to shaders we've examined in previous chapters. Because the computed normals may become denormalized by linear interpolation, we must renormalize them in the fragment shader to obtain more accurate results. After the attenuation factors are computed, we perform a simple reflection computation that gives a plastic appearance. You could certainly modify these computations to simulate the reflection from some other type of material.

Listing 12.7   Überlight fragment shader

```
#version 140

uniform vec3 SurfaceColor;

// Light parameters
uniform vec3  LightColor;
uniform vec3  LightWeights;

// Surface parameters
uniform vec3  SurfaceWeights;
uniform float SurfaceRoughness;
uniform bool  AmbientClamping;

// Super ellipse shaping parameters
uniform bool  BarnShaping;
uniform float SeWidth;
uniform float SeHeight;
uniform float SeWidthEdge;
uniform float SeHeightEdge;
uniform float SeRoundness;

// Distance shaping parameters
uniform float DsNear;
uniform float DsFar;
uniform float DsNearEdge;
uniform float DsFarEdge;

in  vec3 LCpos;     // Vertex position in light coordinates
in  vec3 LCnorm;    // Normal in light coordinates
in  vec3 LCcamera;  // Camera position in light coordinates

out vec4 FragColor;

float superEllipseShape(vec3 pos)
{
   if (!BarnShaping)
      return 1.0;
   else
   {
      // Project the point onto the z = 1.0 plane
      vec2 ppos = pos.xy / pos.z;
      vec2 abspos = abs(ppos);

      float w = SeWidth;
      float W = SeWidth + SeWidthEdge;
      float h = SeHeight;
      float H = SeHeight + SeHeightEdge;

      float exp1 = 2.0 / SeRoundness;
      float exp2 = -SeRoundness / 2.0;
```

```
      float inner = w * h * pow(pow(h * abspos.x, exp1) +
                                pow(w * abspos.y, exp1), exp2);

      float outer = W * H * pow(pow(H * abspos.x, exp1) +
                                pow(W * abspos.y, exp1), exp2);

      return 1.0 - smoothstep(inner, outer, 1.0);
   }
}

float distanceShape(vec3 pos)
{
   float depth;

   depth = abs(pos.z);

   float dist = smoothstep(DsNear - DsNearEdge, DsNear, depth) *
                (1.0 - smoothstep(DsFar, DsFar + DsFarEdge, depth));
   return dist;
}

void main()
{
   vec3 tmpLightColor = LightColor;

   vec3 N = normalize(LCnorm);
   vec3 L = -normalize(LCpos);
   vec3 V = normalize(LCcamera-LCpos);
   vec3 H = normalize(L + V);

   vec3 tmpColor = tmpLightColor;

   float attenuation = 1.0;
   attenuation *= superEllipseShape(LCpos);
   attenuation *= distanceShape(LCpos);

   float ndotl = dot(N, L);
   float ndoth = dot(N, H);

   vec3 litResult;
   litResult[0] = AmbientClamping ? max(ndotl, 0.0) : 1.0;
   litResult[1] = max(ndotl, 0.0);
   litResult[2] = litResult[1] * max(ndoth, 0.0) * SurfaceRoughness;
   litResult *= SurfaceWeights * LightWeights;

   vec3 ambient = tmpLightColor * SurfaceColor * litResult[0];
   vec3 diffuse = tmpColor * SurfaceColor * litResult[1];
   vec3 specular = tmpColor * litResult[2];
   FragColor = vec4(attenuation *
                    (ambient + diffuse + specular), 1.0);
}
```

An example of using this shader is shown in Color Plate 20, along with a screenshot of a user interface designed by Philip Rideout for manipulating its controls. The überlight shader as described by Barzel and Gritz actually has several additional features. It can support multiple lights, but our example shader showed just one for simplicity. The key parameters can be defined as arrays, and a loop can be executed to perform the necessary computations for each light source. In the following chapter, we show how to add shadows to this shader.

12.5 Summary

The summary of this chapter is "Just say no!" to the traditional computer graphics lighting model." Now that programmable graphics hardware has freed us from the shackles of the traditional hardware lighting equations, we are free to implement and experiment with a variety of new techniques. Some of the techniques we explored are both faster and more realistic than the traditional methods.

Hemisphere lighting is a simple way to approximate global illumination in a scene. Environment maps are very useful tools for simulating complex lighting environments. It is neither expensive nor difficult to capture images of real-world lighting conditions. Such light probe images can be preprocessed and used to perform image-based lighting directly, or they can be preprocessed to compute spherical harmonic basis function coefficients that can be used for simple and high-performance lighting.

We've also seen that the traditional OpenGL fixed functionality lighting model leaves a lot to be desired in terms of flexibility and ease of use. Lighting models such as the one defined by the überlight shader are much more versatile and easier for artists to use.

12.6 Further Information

Hemisphere lighting has been popularized by Microsoft and is described in several presentations on DirectX. An online article, *Per-Pixel Lighting*, by Microsoft's Phil Taylor describes this technique. Material in this article was derived from a talk given by Dan Baker and Chas Boyd at Meltdown 2001.

Image-based lighting builds on the foundations of texture mapping and reflection mapping first discussed by Jim Blinn and Martin Newell in 1976.

Paul Debevec has recently popularized this area and maintains a Web site (www.debevec.org) with lots of useful information on this topic, including a gallery of light probe images, the history of reflection mapping, electronic versions of his publications, and much more. A related Web site is www.hdrshop.com from which you can download the free (for personal and educational use) version of HDRShop or obtain the commercial version. There are also tutorials that helped me create the light probe images and environment maps described in this chapter.

Spherical harmonic lighting was described by Ravi Ramamoorthi and Pat Hanrahan in their 2001 SIGGRAPH paper. A lengthy and more tractable discussion of the details of this approach is available in a white paper by Robin Green of Sony.

The überlight shader for RenderMan is discussed in the book *Advanced RenderMan: Creating CGI for Motion Pictures* by Apodaca and Gritz. A Cg version of this shader is described by Fabio Pellacini and Kiril Vidimice in the book *GPU Gems*, edited by Randima Fernando.

[1] Apodaca, Anthony A., and Larry Gritz, *Advanced RenderMan: Creating CGI for Motion Pictures*, Morgan Kaufmann Publishers, San Francisco, 1999. www.renderman.org/RMR/Books/arman/materials.html

[2] Baker, Dan, and C. Boyd, *Advanced Shading and Lighting*, Microsoft Corp. Meltdown 2001 Presentation. www.microsoft.com/mscorp/corpevents/meltdown2001/ppt/DXGLighting.ppt

[3] Barzel, Ronen, *Lighting Controls for Computer Cinematography*, Journal of Graphics Tools, 2(1), 1997, pp. 1–20.

[4] Blinn, James, and M.E. Newell, *Texture and Reflection in Computer Generated Images*, Communications of the ACM, vol. 19, no. 10, pp. 542–547, October 1976.

[5] Debevec, Paul, Image-Based Lighting, IEEE Computer Graphics and Applications, vol. 22, no 2, pp. 26-34. www.debevec.org/CGAIBL2/ibl-tutorial-cga2002.pdf

[6] Debevec, Paul, personal Web site. www.debevec.org

[7] Debevec, Paul, and J. Malik, *Recovering High Dynamic Range Radiance Maps from Photographs*, Computer Graphics (SIGGRAPH '97 Proceedings), pp. 369–378. www.debevec.org/Research/HDR/

[8] Debevec, Paul, Rendering Synthetic Objects into Real Scenes: Bridging Traditional and Image-Based Graphics with Global Illumination and High Dynamic Range Photography, Computer Graphics (SIGGRAPH '98 Proceedings), pp. 189–198. http://athens.ict.usc.edu/Research/IBL/

[9] *GPU Gems: Programming Techniques, Tips, and Tricks for Real-Time Graphics*, Editor: Randima Fernando, Addison-Wesley, Reading, Massachusetts, 2004. http://developer.nvidia.com/object/gpu_gems_home.html

[10] Green, Robin, *Spherical Harmonic Lighting: The Gritty Details*, GDC 2003 Presentation. www.research.scea.com/gdc2003/spherical-harmonic-lighting.html

[11] Lowell, Ross, *Matters of Light & Depth*, Lowel-Light Manufacturing, 1992.

[12] Ramamoorthi, Ravi, and P. Hanrahan, *An Efficient Representation for Irradiance Environment Maps*, Computer Graphics (SIGGRAPH 2001 Proceedings), pp. 497–500. http://www1.cs.columbia.edu/~ravir/papers/envmap/index.html

[13] Taylor, Philip, *Per-Pixel Lighting*, Microsoft Corp., Nov. 2001.

Chapter 13

Shadows

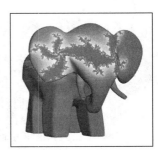

*I have a little shadow that goes in and out with me
And what can be the use of him is more than I can see.*

—From *My Shadow* by Robert Louis Stevenson

Like Robert Louis Stevenson, have you ever wondered what shadows are good for? The previous chapter discussed lighting models, and wherever there is light, there are also shadows. Well, maybe this is true in the real world, but it is not always true in computer graphics. We have talked a lot about illumination already and have developed a variety of shaders that simulate light sources. But so far we have not described any shaders that generate shadows. This lack of shadows is part of the classic computer graphics "look" and is one obvious clue that a scene is synthetic rather than real.

What are shadows good for? Shadows help define the spatial relationships between objects in a scene. Shadows tell us when a character's feet make contact with the floor as he is running. The shape and movement of a bouncing ball's shadow gives us a great deal of information about the ball's location at any point in time. Shadows on objects help reveal shape and form. In film and theater, shadows play a vital role in establishing mood. And in computer graphics, shadows help enhance the apparent realism of the scene.

Although computing shadows adds complexity and slows performance, the increase in comprehension and realism is often worth it. In this chapter, we explore some relatively simple techniques that produce shadows and shadow effects.

13.1   Ambient Occlusion

The lighting model built into OpenGL that we explored in Chapter 9 has a simple assumption for ambient light, namely, that it is constant over the entire scene. But if you look around your current location, you will probably see that this is almost always a bad assumption as far as generating a realistic image is concerned. Look underneath the table, and you will see an area that is darker than other areas. Look at the stack of books on the table, and you will see that there are dark areas between the books and probably a darker area near the base of the books. Almost every scene in real life contains a variety of complex shadows.

The alternative lighting models described in the previous chapter are an improvement over OpenGL's fixed-function lighting model, but they still fall short. If you look carefully at Color Plate 21D, you can see that the lighting still does not look completely realistic. The area under the chin, the junctions of the legs and the boots, and the creases in the clothing are brightly lit. If this were a real scene, we know that these areas would be darker because they would be obscured by nearby parts of the model. Hence, this object looks fake.

A relatively simple way to add realism to computer-generated imagery is a technique called AMBIENT OCCLUSION. This technique uses a precomputed occlusion (or accessibility) factor to scale the calculated direct diffuse illumination factor. It can be used with a variety of illumination methods, including hemisphere lighting and image-based lighting, as discussed in the preceding chapter. It results in soft shadows that darken parts of the object that are only partially accessible to the overall illumination in a scene.

The basic idea with ambient occlusion is to determine, for each point on an object, how much of the potentially visible hemisphere is actually visible and how much is obstructed by nearby parts of the object. The hemisphere that is considered at each point on the surface is in the direction of the surface normal at that point. For instance, consider the venerable teapot in Figure 13.1. The top of the knob on the teapot's lid receives illumination from the entire visible hemisphere. But a point partway down inside the teapot's spout receives illumination only from a very small percentage of the visible hemisphere, in the direction of the small opening at the end of the spout.

For a specific model we can precompute these occlusion factors and save them as per-vertex attribute values. Alternatively, we can create a texture map that stores these values for each point on the surface. One method for computing occlusion factors is to cast a large number of rays from each vertex and keep track of how many intersect another part of the object and how many do not. The percentage of such rays that are unblocked is the

Figure 13.1 A 2D representation of the process of computing occlusion (accessibility) factors. A point on the top of the knob on the teapot's lid has nothing in the way of the visible hemisphere (accessibility = 1.0), while a point inside the spout has its visible hemisphere mostly obscured (accessibility nearer to 0).

accessibility factor. The top of the lid on the teapot has a value of 1 since no other part of the model blocks its view of the visible hemisphere. A point partway down the spout has an accessibility value near 0, because its visible hemisphere is almost completely obscured.

We then multiply the computed accessibility (or occlusion) factor by our computed diffuse reflection value. This has the effect of darkening areas that are obscured by other parts of the model. It is simple enough to use this value in conjunction with our other lighting models. For instance, the hemisphere lighting vertex shader that we developed in Section 12.1 can incorporate ambient occlusion with a few simple changes, as shown in Listing 13.1.

Listing 13.1 Vertex shader for hemisphere lighting with ambient occlusion

```
#version 140

uniform mat4 MVMatrix;
uniform mat4 MVPMatrix;
uniform mat3 NormalMatrix;

uniform vec3 LightPosition;
uniform vec3 SkyColor;
uniform vec3 GroundColor;

in vec4  MCVertex;
in vec3  MCNormal;
in float Accessibility;
```

```
out vec3  DiffuseColor;

void main()
{
    vec3 ecPosition = vec3(MVMatrix  * MCVertex);
    vec3 tnorm      = normalize(NormalMatrix * MCNormal);
    vec3 lightVec   = normalize(LightPosition - ecPosition);
    float costheta  = dot(tnorm, lightVec);
    float a         = 0.5 + 0.5 * costheta;

    DiffuseColor = mix(GroundColor, SkyColor, a) * Accessibility;

    gl_Position     = MVPMatrix * MCVertex;
}
```

The only change made to this shader is to pass in the accessibility factor as an in variable and use this to attenuate the computed diffuse color value. The results are quite a bit more realistic, as you can see by comparing Color Plate 21D and G. The overall appearance is too dark, but this can be remedied by choosing a mid-gray for the ground color rather than black. Color Plate 21F shows ambient occlusion with a simple diffuse lighting model.

The same thing can be done to the image-based lighting shader that we developed in Section 12.2 (see Listing 13.2) and to the spherical harmonic lighting shader that we developed in Section 12.3 (see Listing 13.3). In the former case, the lighting is done in the fragment shader, so the per-vertex accessibility factor must be passed to the fragment shader as an out variable. (Alternatively, the accessibility values could be stored in a texture that could be accessed in the fragment shader.)

Listing 13.2 Fragment shader for image-based lighting

```
#version 140

uniform vec3  BaseColor;
uniform float SpecularPercent;
uniform float DiffusePercent;

uniform samplerCube SpecularEnvMap;
uniform samplerCube DiffuseEnvMap;

in  vec3  ReflectDir;
in  vec3  Normal;
in  float Accessibility;

out vec4  FragColor;

void main()
{
```

```
    // Look up environment map values in cube maps

    vec3 diffuseColor  =
        vec3(texture(DiffuseEnvMap,  normalize(Normal)));

    vec3 specularColor =
        vec3(texture(SpecularEnvMap, normalize(ReflectDir)));

    // Add lighting to base color and mix

    vec3 color = mix(BaseColor, diffuseColor*BaseColor, DiffusePercent);
    color      *= Accessibility;
    color       = mix(color, specularColor + color, SpecularPercent);

    FragColor = vec4(color, 1.0);
}
```

Listing 13.3 Vertex shader for spherical harmonic lighting

```
#version 140

uniform mat4 MVMatrix;
uniform mat4 MVPMatrix;
uniform mat3 NormalMatrix;

uniform float ScaleFactor;

const float C1 = 0.429043;
const float C2 = 0.511664;
const float C3 = 0.743125;
const float C4 = 0.886227;
const float C5 = 0.247708;

// Constants for Old Town Square lighting
const vec3 L00  = vec3( 0.871297,  0.875222,  0.864470);
const vec3 L1m1 = vec3( 0.175058,  0.245335,  0.312891);
const vec3 L10  = vec3( 0.034675,  0.036107,  0.037362);
const vec3 L11  = vec3(-0.004629, -0.029448, -0.048028);
const vec3 L2m2 = vec3(-0.120535, -0.121160, -0.117507);
const vec3 L2m1 = vec3( 0.003242,  0.003624,  0.007511);
const vec3 L20  = vec3(-0.028667, -0.024926, -0.020998);
const vec3 L21  = vec3(-0.077539, -0.086325, -0.091591);
const vec3 L22  = vec3(-0.161784, -0.191783, -0.219152);

in  vec4  MCVertex;
in  vec3  MCNormal;
in  float Accessibility;

out vec3  DiffuseColor;

void main()
{
```

```
foo();
vec3 tnorm    = normalize(NormalMatrix * MCNormal);

DiffuseColor = C1 * L22 * (tnorm.x * tnorm.x - tnorm.y * tnorm.y) +
               C3 * L20 *  tnorm.z * tnorm.z +
               C4 * L00 -
               C5 * L20 +
               2.0 * C1 * L2m2 * tnorm.x * tnorm.y +
               2.0 * C1 * L21  * tnorm.x * tnorm.z +
               2.0 * C1 * L2m1 * tnorm.y * tnorm.z +
               2.0 * C2 * L11  * tnorm.x +
               2.0 * C2 * L1m1 * tnorm.y +
               2.0 * C2 * L10  * tnorm.z;

DiffuseColor *= ScaleFactor;
DiffuseColor *= Accessibility;

gl_Position = MVPMatrix * MCVertex;
}
```

Results for ambient occlusion shaders are shown in Color Plate 21 C, F, G, H, and I. These images come from a GLSL demo program called **deLight**, written by Philip Rideout. Philip also wrote the ray-tracer that generated per-vertex accessibility information for a number of different models.

Ambient occlusion is a view-independent technique, but the computation of the occlusion factors assumes that the object is rigid. If the object has moving parts, the occlusion factors would need to be recomputed for each position. Work has been done recently on methods for computing the occlusion factors in real time (see *Dynamic Ambient Occlusion and Indirect Lighting* by Michael Bunnell in the book *GPU Gems 2*).

During the preprocessing stage, we can also compute an attribute called a BENT NORMAL. We obtain this value by averaging all the nonoccluded rays from a point on a surface. It represents the average direction of the available light arriving at that particular point on the surface. Instead of using the surface normal to access an environment map, we use the bent normal to obtain the color of the light from the appropriate portion of the environment map. We can simulate a soft fill light with a standard point or spotlight by using the bent normal instead of the surface normal and then multiplying the result by the occlusion factor.

Occlusion factors are not only useful for lighting but are also useful for reducing reflections from the environment in areas that are occluded. Hayden Landis of Industrial Light & Magic has described how similar techniques have been used to control reflections in films such as *Pearl Harbor* and *Jurassic Park III*. The technique is modified still further to take into account the type of surface that is reflecting the environment. Additional rays used along the main reflection vector provide an average (blurred) reflection. For diffuse surfaces (e.g., rubber), the additional rays are spread out more widely from the main reflection vector so that the reflection appears more diffuse. For more specular surfaces, the additional rays are nearer the main reflection vector, so the reflection is more mirrorlike.

13.2 Shadow Maps

Ambient occlusion is quite useful for improving the realism of rigid objects under diffuse lighting conditions, but often a scene will need to incorporate lighting from one or more well-defined light sources. In the real world, we know that strong light sources cause objects to cast well-defined shadows. Producing similar shadows in our computer-generated scenes will make them seem more realistic. How can we accomplish this?

The amount of computer graphics literature that discusses generation of shadows is vast. This is partly because no single shadowing algorithm is optimal for all cases. There are numerous trade-offs in performance, quality, and simplicity. Some algorithms work well for only certain types of shadow-casting objects or shadow-receiving objects. Some algorithms work for certain types of light sources or lighting conditions. Some experimentation and adaptation may be needed to develop a shadow-generation technique that is optimal for a specific set of conditions.

OpenGL and the OpenGL Shading Language include facilities for a generally useful shadowing algorithm called SHADOW MAPPING. In this algorithm, the scene is rendered multiple times—once for each light source that is capable of causing shadows and once to generate the final scene, including shadows. Each of the per-light passes is rendered from the point of view of the light source. The results are stored in a texture that is called a SHADOW MAP or a DEPTH MAP. This texture is essentially a visible surface representation from the point of view of the light source. Surfaces that are visible from the point of view of this light source are fully illuminated by the light source. Surfaces that are not visible from the point of view of this light source are in shadow. Each of the textures so generated is accessed during the final rendering pass to create the final scene with shadows from one or more light sources. During the final rendering pass, the distance from the fragment to each light is computed and compared to the depth value in the shadow map for that light. If the distance from the fragment to the light is greater than the depth value in the shadow map, the fragment receives no contribution from that light source (i.e., it is in shadow);

otherwise, the fragment is subjected to the lighting computation for that particular light source.

Because this algorithm involves an extra rendering pass for each light source, performance is a concern if a large number of shadow-casting lights are in the scene. But for interactive applications, it is quite often the case that shadows from one or two lights add sufficiently to the realism and comprehensibility of a scene. More than that and you may be adding needless complexity. And, just like other algorithms that use textures, shadow mapping is prone to severe aliasing artifacts unless proper care is taken.

The depth comparison can also lead to problems. Since the values being compared were generated in different passes with different transformation matrices, it is possible to have a small difference in the values. Therefore, you must use a small epsilon value in the comparison. You can use the **glPolygonOffset** command to bias depth values as the shadow map is being created. You must be careful, though, because too much bias can cause a shadow to become detached from the object casting the shadow.

A way to avoid depth precision problems with illuminated faces is to draw backfaces when you are building the shadow map. This avoids precision problems with illuminated faces because the depth value for these surfaces is usually quite different from the shadow map depth, so there is no possibility of precision problems incorrectly darkening the surface.

Precision problems are still possible on surfaces facing away from the light. You can avoid these problems by testing the surface normal—if it points away from the light, then the surface is in shadow. There will still be problems when the back and front faces have similar depth values, such as at the edge of the shadow. A carefully weighted combination of normal test plus depth test can provide artifact-free shadows even on gently rounded objects. However, this approach does not handle occluders that aren't simple closed geometry.

Despite its drawbacks, shadow mapping is still a popular and effective means of generating shadows. A big advantage is that it can be used with arbitrarily complex geometry. It is supported in RenderMan and has been used to generate images for numerous movies and interactive games. OpenGL supports shadow maps (they are called DEPTH COMPONENT TEXTURES in OpenGL) and a full range of depth comparison modes that can be used with them. Shadow mapping can be performed in OpenGL with either fixed functionality or the programmable processing units. The OpenGL Shading Language contains corresponding functions for accessing shadow maps from within a shader (**texture**, **textureProj**, and the like).

13.2.1 Application Setup

As mentioned, the application must create a shadow map for each light source by rendering the scene from the point of view of the light source. For objects that are visible from the light's point of view, the resulting texture map contains depth values representing the distance to the light. (The source code for the example program deLight available from the 3dshaders.org Web site illustrates specifically how this is done.)

For the final pass of shadow mapping to work properly, the application must create a matrix that transforms incoming vertex positions into projective texture coordinates for each light source. The vertex shader is responsible for performing this transformation, and the fragment shader uses the interpolated projective coordinates to access the shadow map for each light source. To keep things simple, we look at shaders that deal with just a single light source. (You can use arrays and loops to extend the basic algorithm to support multiple light sources.)

We construct the necessary matrix by concatenating

- The modeling matrix (M) that transforms modeling coordinates into world coordinates

- A view matrix (V_{light}) that rotates and translates world coordinates into a coordinate system that has the light source at the origin and is looking at the point (0, 0, 0) in world coordinates

- A projection matrix (P_{light}) that defines the frustum for the view from the light source (i.e., field of view, aspect ratio, near and far clipping planes)

- A scale and bias matrix that takes the clip space coordinates (i.e., values in the range [–1,1]) from the previous step into values in the range [0,1] so that they can be used directly as the index for accessing the shadow map.

The equation for the complete transformation looks like this:

$$\begin{bmatrix} 0.5 & 0 & 0 & 0.5 \\ 0 & 0.5 & 0 & 0.5 \\ 0 & 0 & 0.5 & 0.5 \\ 0 & 0 & 0 & 1 \end{bmatrix} MV_{light}P_{light} \begin{bmatrix} x \\ y \\ z \\ w \end{bmatrix} = \begin{bmatrix} s \\ t \\ r \\ q \end{bmatrix}$$

By performing this transformation in a vertex shader, we can have shadows and can add any desired programmable functionality as well. Let's see how this is done in a vertex shader. Philip Rideout developed some shaders for the deLight demo that use shadow mapping. They have been adapted slightly for inclusion in this book.

13.2.2 Vertex Shader

The vertex shader in Listing 13.4 shows how this is done. We use ambient occlusion in this shader, so these values are passed in as vertex attributes through the attribute variable *Accessibility*. These values attenuate the incoming per-vertex color values after a simple diffuse lighting model has been applied. The alpha value is left unmodified by this process. The matrix that transforms modeling coordinates to light source coordinates is stored in *MCtoLightMatrix*. This matrix transforms the incoming vertex and writes to the out variable *ShadowCoord*.

Listing 13.4 Vertex shader for generating shadows

```
#version 140

uniform mat4 MVMatrix;
uniform mat4 MVPMatrix;
uniform mat3 NormalMatrix;
uniform mat4 MCtoLightMatrix;

uniform vec3 LightPosition;

// Ambient and diffuse scale factors.
const float As = 1.0 / 1.5;
const float Ds = 1.0 / 3.0;

in  float Accessibility;
in  vec4  MCVertex;
in  vec4  MCNormal;
in  vec4  MColor;

out vec4  ShadowCoord;
out vec4  Color;


void main()
{
    vec4 ecPosition = MVMatrix * MCVertex;
    vec3 ecPosition3 = (vec3(ecPosition)) / ecPosition.w;
    vec3 VP = LightPosition - ecPosition3;
    VP = normalize(VP);
    vec3 normal = normalize(NormalMatrix * MCNormal);
    float diffuse = max(0.0, dot(normal, VP));
```

```
    float scale = min(1.0, Accessibility * As + diffuse * Ds);

    vec4 texCoord = MCtoLightMatrix * MCVertex;
    ShadowCoord   = texCoord;

    Color   = vec4(scale * MColor.rgb, MColor.a);
    gl_Position   = MVPMatrix * MCVertex;
}
```

13.2.3 Fragment Shader

A simple fragment shader for generating shadows is shown in Listing 13.5. When **textureProj** is used to access a texture of a shadow sampler, the third component of the texture index (i.e., *ShadowCoord.p*) is compared with the depth value stored in the shadow map. The comparison function is the one specified for the texture object indicated by *ShadowMap*. For nearest filtering, if the comparison results in a value of true, **textureProj** returns 1.0; otherwise, it returns 0.0. For linear filtering, more than one texel is compared to *ShadowCoord.p* (probably four texels). If all comparisons are true, **textureProj** returns 1.0; if all comparisons are false, it returns 0.0; otherwise, it returns a value between 0.0 and 1.0. (OpenGL gives a lot of flexibility here. It may return a weighted average of the results, so the value can be any value between 0.0 and 1.0. It may return a strict percent closer filter [PCF] value resulting in values of 0.0, 0.25, 0.5, 0.75, and 1.0 if there were four comparisons.) We scale and bias this result so that the result ranges from 0.75 (fully shadowed) to 1.0 (fully illuminated). (This shader instruction emulates the ARB_shadow_ambient extension.) Fragments that are fully illuminated are unchanged, fragments that are fully shadowed are multiplied by a factor of 0.75 to make them darker, and fragments that are partially shadowed are multiplied by a value between 0.75 and 1.0.

Listing 13.5 Fragment shader for generating shadows

```
#version 140

uniform sampler2DShadow ShadowMap;

in  vec4 ShadowCoord;
in  vec4 Color;
out vec4 FragColor;

void main()
{
    float shadeFactor = textureProj(ShadowMap, ShadowCoord);
    shadeFactor = shadeFactor * 0.25 + 0.75;
    FragColor = vec4(shadeFactor * Color.rgb, Color.a);
}
```

Chances are that as soon as you execute this shader, you will be disappointed by the aliasing artifacts that appear along the edges of the shadows. This is because there is either only one depth comparison (for nearest filtering) to four depth comparisons (for linear filtering). We can do something about this, and we can customize the shader for a specific viewing situation to get a more pleasing result. Michael Bunnell and Fabio Pellacini describe a method for doing this in an article called *Shadow Map Antialiasing* in the book *GPU Gems*. Philip Rideout implemented this technique in GLSL, as shown in Listing 13.6 and Listing 13.7.

The shader in Listing 13.6 adds a couple of things. The first thing is an additional flat in variable, ShadowScaleBias. The vertex shader essentially distinguishes between two types of shadows—those that are generated by the object itself and those that are generated by another object in the scene. The self-shadows are made a little lighter than other cast shadows for aesthetic reasons. The result is that where the object shadows itself, the shadows are relatively light. And where the object's shadow falls on the floor, the shadows are darker. (See Color Plate 22.)

The second difference is that the shadow map is sampled 16 times (for linear sampling). The purpose of sampling multiple times is to try to do better at determining the shadow boundary. This lets us apply a smoother transition between shadowed and unshadowed regions, thus reducing the jagged edges of the shadow.

Listing 13.6 Fragment shader for generating shadows with antialiased edges, using sixteen samples per fragment (four texture fetches with four depth comparisons each)

```
#version 140

uniform sampler2DShadow ShadowMap;

flat in  vec2  ShadowScaleBias;
     in  vec4  ShadowCoord;
     in  vec4  Color;

     out vec4  FragColor;

void main()
{
    float sum;

    sum  = textureProjOffset(ShadowMap, ShadowCoord, ivec2(-1, -1));
    sum += textureProjOffset(ShadowMap, ShadowCoord, ivec2( 1, -1));
    sum += textureProjOffset(ShadowMap, ShadowCoord, ivec2(-1,  1));
    sum += textureProjOffset(ShadowMap, ShadowCoord, ivec2( 1,  1));
```

```
    sum = sum * ShadowScaleBias.x + ShadowScaleBias.y;

    FragColor = vec4(sum * 0.25 * Color.rgb, Color.a);
}
```

This shader can be extended in the obvious way to perform even more samples per fragment and thus improve the quality of the shadow boundaries even more. However, the more texture lookups that we perform in our shader, the slower it will run.

Using a method akin to dithering, we can actually use four texture fetches that are spread somewhat farther apart to achieve a quality of antialiasing that is similar to that of using quite a few more than four texture fetches per fragment. In Listing 13.7 we include code for computing offsets in x and y from the current fragment location. These offsets form a regular dither pattern that is used to access the shadow map. The results of using four dithered texture fetches per fragment trades off a noisy sampling of a larger area.

Listing 13.7 Fragment shader for generating shadows, using four dithered texture fetches (sixteen depth comparisons for linear filtering)

```
#version 140

uniform sampler2DShadow ShadowMap;

        in   vec4   ShadowCoord;
        in   vec4   Color;
flat in   vec2   ShadowScaleBias;

        out  vec4   FragColor;

void main()
{

    float sum;

    // use modulo to vary the sample pattern
    ivec2 o = ivec2(mod(floor(gl_FragCoord.xy), 2.0));

    sum  = textureProjOffset(ShadowMap, ShadowCoord, ivec2(-1, -1)+o);
    sum += textureProjOffset(ShadowMap, ShadowCoord, ivec2( 1, -1)+o);
    sum += textureProjOffset(ShadowMap, ShadowCoord, ivec2(-1,  1)+o);
    sum += textureProjOffset(ShadowMap, ShadowCoord, ivec2( 1,  1)+o);

    sum = sum * ShadowScaleBias.x + ShadowScaleBias.y;

    FragColor = vec4(sum * 0.25 * Color.rgb, Color.a);
}
```

Sample images using these shaders are shown in Color Plate 22. A small area of the shadow has been enlarged by 400 percent to show the differences in quality at the edge of the shadow.

13.3 Deferred Shading for Volume Shadows

With contributions by Hugh Malan and Mike Weiblen

One of the disadvantages of shadow mapping as discussed in the previous section is that the performance depends on the number of lights in the scene that are capable of casting shadows. With shadow mapping, a rendering pass must be performed for each of these light sources. These shadow maps are utilized in a final rendering pass. All these rendering passes can reduce performance, particularly if a great many polygons are to be rendered.

It is possible to do higher-performance shadow generation with a rendering technique that is part of a general class of techniques known as DEFERRED SHADING. With deferred shading, the idea is to first quickly determine the surfaces that will be visible in the final scene and apply complex and time-consuming shader effects only to the pixels that make up those visible surfaces. In this sense, the shading operations are deferred until it can be established just which pixels contribute to the final image. A very simple and fast shader can render the scene into an offscreen buffer with depth buffering enabled. During this initial pass, the shader stores whatever information is needed to perform the necessary rendering operations in subsequent passes. Subsequent rendering operations are applied only to pixels that are determined to be visible in the high-performance initial pass. This technique ensures that no hardware cycles are wasted performing shading calculations on pixels that will ultimately be hidden.

To render soft shadows with this technique, we need to make two passes. In the first pass, we perform the following two tasks:

1. We use a shader to render the geometry of the scene without shadows or lighting into the framebuffer.

2. We use the same shader to store a normalized camera depth value for each pixel in a separate buffer. (This separate buffer is accessed as a texture in the second pass for the shadow computations.)

In the second pass, the shadows are composited with the existing contents of the framebuffer. To do this compositing operation, we render the shadow volume (i.e., the region in which the light source is occluded) for each shadow casting object. In the case of a sphere, computing the shadow volume is relatively easy. The sphere's shadow is in the shape of a truncated cone, where the apex of the cone is at the light source. One end of the truncated cone is at the center of the sphere (see Figure 13.2). (It is somewhat more complex to compute the shadow volume for an object defined by polygons, but the same principle applies.)

We composite shadows with the existing geometry by rendering the polygons that define the shadow volume. This allows our second pass shader to be applied only to regions of the image that might be in shadow.

To draw a shadow, we use the texture map shown in Figure 13.3. This texture map expresses how much a visible surface point is in shadow relative to a shadow-casting object (i.e., how much its value is attenuated) based on a function of two values: 1) the squared distance from the visible surface point to the central axis of the shadow volume, and 2) the distance from the visible surface point to the center of the shadow-casting object. The first value is used as the s coordinate for accessing the shadow texture, and the second value is used as the t coordinate. The net result is that shadows are

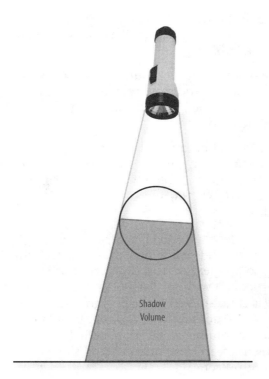

Figure 13.2   The shadow volume for a sphere

relatively sharp when the shadow-casting object is very close to the fragment being tested and the edges become softer as the distance increases.

In the second pass of the algorithm, we do the following:

1. Draw the polygons that define the shadow volume. Only the fragments that could possibly be in shadow are accessed during this rendering operation.

2. For each fragment rendered,

   a. Look up the camera depth value for the fragment as computed in the first pass.

   b. Calculate the coordinates of the visible surface point in the local space of the shadow volume. In this space, the z axis is the axis of the shadow volume, and the origin is at the center of the shadow-casting object. The x component of this coordinate corresponds to the distance from the center of the shadow-casting object and is used directly as the second coordinate for the shadow texture lookup.

   c. Compute the squared distance between the visible surface point and the z axis of the shadow volume. This value becomes the first coordinate for the texture lookup.

   d. Access the shadow texture by using the computed index values to retrieve the light attenuation factor and store this in the output fragment's alpha value. The red, green, and blue components of the output fragment color are each set to 0.

   e. Compute for the fragment the light attenuation factor that will properly darken the existing framebuffer value. For the computation, enable fixed functionality blending, set the blend mode source function to GL_SRC_ALPHA, and set the blend destination function to GL_ONE.

Because the shadow (second pass) shader is effectively a 2D compositing operation, the texel it reads from the depth texture must exactly match the pixel in the framebuffer it affects. So, the texture coordinate and other quantities must be bilinearly interpolated without perspective correction. We interpolate by ensuring that w is constant across the polygon—dividing x, y, and z by w and then setting w to 1.0 does the job. Another issue is that when the viewer is inside the shadow volume, all faces are culled. We handle this special case by drawing a screen-sized quadrilateral since the shadow volume would cover the entire scene.

Figure 13.3   A texture map used to generate soft shadows

13.3.1 Shaders for First Pass

The shaders for the first pass of the volume shadow algorithm are shown in Listings 13.8 and 13.9. In the vertex shader, to accomplish the standard rendering of the geometry (which in this specific case is all texture mapped), we just transform the vertex and pass along the texture coordinate. The other lines of code compute the normalized value for the depth from the vertex to the camera plane. The computed value, *CameraDepth*, is stored in an out variable so that it can be interpolated and made available to the fragment shader.

To render into two buffers by using a fragment shader, the application must call **glDrawBuffers** and pass it a pointer to an array containing symbolic constants that define the two buffers to be written. With framebuffer objects we can bind *FragData[0]* to one renderable color format texture and *FragData[1]* to another renderable depth format texture. Thus, the fragment shader for the first pass of our algorithm contains just two lines of code (Listing 13.9).

Listing 13.8   Vertex shader for first pass of soft volume shadow algorithm

```
#version 140

uniform mat4 MVPMatrix;

uniform vec3  CameraPos;
uniform vec3  CameraDir;
uniform float DepthNear;
uniform float DepthFar;
```

```
in  vec4  MCVertex;
in  vec2  TexCoord0;

out float CameraDepth;  // normalized camera depth
out vec2  TexCoord;

void main()
{
    // offset = vector to vertex from camera's position
    vec3 offset = (MCVertex.xyz / MCVertex.w) - CameraPos;

    // z = distance from vertex to camera plane
    float z = -dot(offset, CameraDir);

    // Depth from vertex to camera, mapped to [0,1]
    CameraDepth = (z - DepthNear) / (DepthFar - DepthNear);

    // typical interpolated coordinate for texture lookup
    TexCoord = TexCoord0;

    gl_Position = MVPMatrix * MCVertex;
}
```

Listing 13.9 Fragment shader for first pass of soft volume shadow algorithm

```
#version 140;

uniform sampler2D TextureMap;

in  float CameraDepth;
in  vec2  TexCoord;

out vec4  FragData[2];

void main()
{
    // draw the typical textured output to visual framebuffer
    FragData[0] = texture(TextureMap, TexCoord);

    // write "normalized vertex depth" to the depth map's alpha.
    FragData[1] = vec4(vec3(0.0), CameraDepth);
}
```

13.3.2 Shaders for Second Pass

The second pass of our shadow algorithm is responsible for compositing shadow information on top of what has already been rendered. After the first pass has been completed, the application must arrange for the depth information rendered into the depth format renderable texture to be made accessible for use as a texture by binding the texture object to the appropriate texture unit.

In the second pass, the only polygons rendered are the ones that define the shadow volumes for the various objects in the scene. We enable blending by calling **glEnable** with the symbolic constant GL_BLEND, and we set the blend function by calling **glBlendFunc** with a source factor of GL_ONE and a destination factor of GL_SRC_ALPHA. The fragment shader outputs the shadow color and an alpha value obtained from a texture lookup operation. This alpha value blends the shadow color value into the framebuffer.

The vertex shader for the second pass (see Listing 13.10) is responsible for computing the coordinates for accessing the depth values that were computed in the first pass. We accomplish the computation by transforming the incoming vertex position, dividing the x, y, and z components by the w component, and then scaling and biasing the x and y components to transform them from the range [–1,1] into the range [0,1]. Values for *ShadowNear* and *ShadowDir* are also computed. These are used in the fragment shader to compute the position of the fragment relative to the shadow-casting object.

Listing 13.10 Vertex shader for second pass of soft volume shadow algorithm

```
#version 140

uniform mat4 MVPMatrix;
uniform mat3 WorldToShadow;
uniform vec3 SphereOrigin;

uniform vec3 CameraPos;
uniform vec3 CameraDir;
uniform float DepthNear;
uniform float DepthFar;

in  vec4  MCVertex;

noperspective out vec2  DepthTexCoord;
noperspective out vec3  ShadowNear;
noperspective out vec3  ShadowDir;

void main()
{
    gl_Position = MVPMatrix * MCVertex;

    // Grab the transformed vertex's XY components as a texcoord
    // for sampling from the depth texture from pass 1.
    // Normalize them from [0,0] to [1,1]
```

```
    DepthTexCoord = gl_Position.xy * 0.5 + 0.5;

    // offset = vector to vertex from camera's position
    vec3 offset = (MCVertex.xyz / MCVertex.w) - CameraPos;

    // z = distance from vertex to camera plane
    float z = -dot(offset, CameraDir);

    vec3 shadowOffsetNear = offset * DepthNear / z;
    vec3 shadowOffsetFar  = offset * DepthFar / z;

    vec3 worldPositionNear = CameraPos + shadowOffsetNear;
    vec3 worldPositionFar  = CameraPos + shadowOffsetFar;

    vec3 shadowFar  = WorldToShadow * (worldPositionFar - SphereOrigin);
    ShadowNear = WorldToShadow * (worldPositionNear - SphereOrigin);
    ShadowDir  = shadowFar - ShadowNear;
}
```

The fragment shader for the second pass is shown in Listing 13.11. In this shader, we access the *cameraDepth* value computed by the first pass by performing a texture lookup. We then map the fragment's position into the local space of the shadow volume. The mapping from world to shadow space is set up so that the center of the occluding sphere maps to the origin, and the circle of points on the sphere at the terminator between light and shadow maps to a circle in the *YZ* plane.

The variables d and l are, respectively, the distance along the shadow axis and the squared distance from it. These values are used as texture coordinates for the lookup into the texture map defining the shape of the shadow.

With the mapping described earlier, points on the terminator map to a circle in the *YZ* plane. The texture map has been painted with the transition from light to shadow occurring at $s=0.5$; to match this, the mapping from world to shadow is set up so that the terminator circle maps to a radius of **sqrt**(0.5).

Finally, the value retrieved from the shadow texture is used as the alpha value for blending the shadow color with the geometry that has already been rendered into the framebuffer.

Listing 13.11 Fragment shader for second pass of soft volume shadow algorithm

```
#version 140

uniform sampler2D DepthTexture;
uniform sampler2D ShadowTexture;
```

```
noperspective in vec2 DepthTexCoord;
noperspective in vec3 ShadowNear;
noperspective in vec3 ShadowDir;

out vec4 FragColor;

const vec3 shadowColor = vec3(0.0);

void main()
{
    // read from DepthTexture
    // (depth is stored in texture's alpha component)
    float cameraDepth = texture(DepthTexture, DepthTexCoord).a;

    vec3 shadowPos = (cameraDepth * ShadowDir) + ShadowNear;
    float l = dot(shadowPos.yz, shadowPos.yz);
    float d = shadowPos.x;

    // k = shadow density: 0=opaque, 1=transparent
    // (use texture's red component as the density)
    float k = texture(ShadowTexture, vec2(l, d)).r;

    FragColor = vec4(shadowColor, k);
}
```

Figure 13.4 shows the result of this multipass shading algorithm in a scene with several spheres. Note how the shadows for the four small spheres get progressively softer edges as the spheres increase in distance from the checkered floor. The large sphere that is farthest from the floor casts an especially soft shadow.

The interesting part of this deferred shading approach is that the volumetric effects are implemented by rendering geometry that bounds the volume of the effect. This almost certainly means processing fewer vertices and fewer fragments. The shaders required are relatively simple and quite fast. Instead of rendering the geometry once for each light source, the geometry is rendered just once, and all the shadow volumes due to all light sources can be rendered in a single compositing pass. Localized effects such as shadow maps, decals, and projective textures can be accomplished easily. Instead of having to write tricky code to figure out the subset of the geometry to which the effect applies, you write a shader that is applied to each pixel and use that shader to render geometry that bounds the effect. This technique can be extended to render a variety of different effects—volumetric fog, lighting, and improved caustics, to name a few.

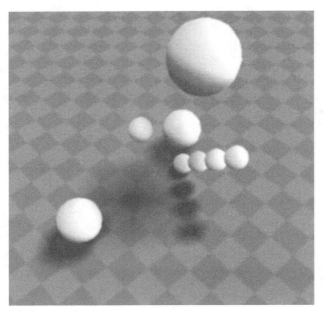

Figure 13.4   Screenshot of the volume shadows shader in action. Notice that spheres that are farther from the surface have shadows with softer edges.

13.4 Summary

There are a number of techniques for generating shadows, and this chapter described several that particularly lend themselves to real-time usage. Ambient occlusion is a technique that complements the global illumination techniques described in Chapter 12 by adding soft shadows that would naturally appear in the corners and crevices of objects in a scene. Shadow mapping is a technique that is well suited to implementation with OpenGL shaders on today's graphics hardware. A number of variations to shadow mapping can be used to improve its quality. We looked at a couple of methods that produce antialiased shadow edges. Finally, we also looked at a method that uses a deferred shading approach to render shadow volumes in order to produce soft shadows.

13.5 Further Information

The SIGGRAPH 2002 course notes are contained the article *Production-Ready Global Illumination* by Hayden Landis. This document describes ambient environments, reflection occlusion, and ambient occlusion, and it explains how they are used in the ILM computer graphics production environment. The article *Ambient Occlusion* by Matt Pharr and Simon Green provides further details about the preprocessing step and gives example shaders written in Cg. The *GPU Gems 2* book contains an article by Michael Bunnell that describes efforts to compute occlusion factors in real time.

Frank Crow pioneered the development of shadow algorithms for computer graphics. Mark Segal and others described the basics of using texture mapping hardware to generate shadows in a 1992 SIGGRAPH paper. Randima Fernando and Mark Kilgard discuss a Cg implementation of these techniques in the book *The Cg Tutorial*. Eric Haines wrote a survey of real-time shadow algorithms and presented this information at GDC in 2001. Some of this material is also in the book *Real-Time Rendering* by Tomas Akenine-Möller and E. Haines.

Deferred shading has recently been a hot topic in computer games development. In the book *GPU Gems 2*, Oles Shishkovtsov discusses how this approach was used for the computer game *S.T.A.L.K.E.R.* His article also mentions presentations from the 2004 Game Developer's Conference.

[1] Akenine-Möller, Tomas, and E. Haines, *Real-Time Rendering, Second Edition*, AK Peters, Ltd., Natick, Massachusetts, 2002. www.realtimerendering.com

[2] Bunnell, Michael, *Dynamic Ambient Occlusion and Indirect Lighting*, in *GPU Gems 2: Programming Techniques for High-Performance Graphics and General-Purpose Computation*, Editor: Matt Pharr, Addison-Wesley, Reading, Massachusetts, 2005. http://download.nvidia.com/developer/GPU_Gems_2/GPU_Gems2_ch14.pdf

[3] Bunnell, Michael, and Fabio Pellacini, *Shadow Map Antialiasing*, in *GPU Gems: Programming Techniques, Tips, and Tricks for Real-Time Graphics*, Editor: Randima Fernando, Addison-Wesley, Reading, Massachusetts, 2004. http://developer.nvidia.com/object/gpu_gems_home.html

[4] Crow, Franklin C., *Shadow Algorithms for Computer Graphics*, Computer Graphics (SIGGRAPH '77 Proceedings), vol. 11, no. 2, pp. 242–248, July 1977.

[5] Fernando, Randima, and Mark J. Kilgard, *The Cg Tutorial: The Definitive Guide to Programmable Real-Time Graphics*, Addison-Wesley, Boston, Massachusetts, 2003.

[6] Haines, Eric, *Real-Time Shadows*, GDC 2001 Presentation. www.gdconf.com/archives/2001/haines.pdf

[7] Landis, Hayden, *Production-Ready Global Illumination*, SIGGRAPH 2002 Course Notes, course 16, RenderMan In Production. www.debevec.org/HDRI2004/landis-S2002-course16-prodreadyGI.pdf

[8] Pharr, Matt and Simon Green, *Ambient Occlusion,* in *GPU Gems: Programming Techniques, Tips, and Tricks for Real-Time Graphics*, Editor: Randima Fernando, Addison-Wesley, Reading, Massachusetts, 2004. http://developer.nvidia.com/object/gpu_gems_home.html

[9] Reeves, William T., David H. Salesin, and Robert L. Cook, *Rendering Antialiased Shadows with Depth Maps*, Computer Graphics (SIGGRAPH '87 Proceedings), vol. 21, no. 4, pp. 283–291, July 1987.

[10] Segal, Mark, C. Korobkin, R. van Widenfelt, J. Foran, and P. Haeberli, *Fast Shadows and Lighting Effects Using Texture Mapping*, Computer Graphics (SIGGRAPH '92 Proceedings), vol. 26, no. 2, pp. 249–252, July 1992.

[11] Shishkovtsov, Oles, *Deferred Shading in S.T.A.L.K.E.R.*, in *GPU Gems 2: Programming Techniques for High-Performance Graphics and General-Purpose Computation*, Editor: Matt Pharr, Addison-Wesley, Reading, Massachusetts, 2005. http://developer.nvidia.com/object/gpu_gems_2_home.html

[12] Woo, Andrew, P. Poulin, and A. Fournier, *A Survey of Shadow Algorithms*, IEEE Computer Graphics and Applications, vol. 10, no. 6, pp.13–32, November 1990.

[13] Zhukov, Sergei, A. Iones, G. Kronin, *An Ambient Light Illumination Model*, Proceedings of Eurographics Rendering Workshop '98.

Chapter 14

Surface Characteristics

Up to this point, we have primarily been modeling surface reflection in a simplistic way. The traditional reflection model is simple enough to compute and gives reasonable results, but it reproduces the appearance of only a small number of materials. In the real world, there is enormous variety in the way objects interact with light. To simulate the interaction of light with materials such as water, metals, metallic car paints, CDs, human skin, butterfly wings, and peacock feathers, we need to go beyond the basics.

One way to achieve greater degrees of realism in modeling the interaction between light and surfaces is to use models that are more firmly based on the physics of light reflection, absorption, and transmission. Such models have been the pursuit of graphics researchers since the 1970s. With the programmable graphics hardware of today, we are now at a point where such models can be used in real-time graphics applications to achieve unprecedented realism. A performance optimization that is often employed is to precompute these functions and store the results in textures that can be accessed from within a shader. A second way to achieve greater degrees of realism is to measure or photograph the characteristics of real materials and use these measurements in our shading algorithms. In this chapter, we look at shaders based on both approaches.

In addition, we have not yet looked at any shaders that allow for the transmission of light through a surface. This is our first example as we look at several shaders that model materials with differing surface characteristics.

14.1 Refraction

Refraction is the bending of light as it passes through a boundary between surfaces with different optical densities. You can easily see this effect by looking through the side of an aquarium or at a straw in a glass of water. Light bends by different amounts as it passes from one material to another, depending on the materials that are transmitting light. This effect is caused by light traveling at different speeds in different types of materials. This characteristic of a material is called its INDEX OF REFRACTION, and this value has been determined for many common materials that transmit light. It is easy to model refraction in our shaders with the built-in function **refract**. The key parameter that is required is the ratio of the index of refraction for the two materials forming a boundary where refraction occurs. The application can compute this ratio and provide it to the OpenGL shader as a uniform variable. Given a surface normal, an angle of incidence, and the aforementioned ratio, the **refract** function applies Snell's law to compute the refracted vector. We can use the refracted vector in a fragment shader to access a cube map to determine the surface color for a transparent object.

Once again, our goal is to produce results that are "good enough." In other words, we're after a refraction effect that looks plausible, rather than a physically accurate simulation. One simplification that we make is that we model the refraction effect at only one surface boundary. When light goes from air through glass, it is refracted once at the air-glass boundary, transmitted through the glass, and refracted again at the glass-air boundary on the other side. We satisfy ourselves with simulating the first refraction effect. The results of refraction are complex enough that most people would not be able to tell the difference in the final image.

If we go ahead and write a shader that performs refraction, we will likely be somewhat disappointed in the results. It turns out that most transparent objects exhibit both reflection and refraction. The surface of a lake reflects the mountains in the distance if you are looking at the lake from one side. But if you get into your boat and go out into the lake and look straight down, you may see fish swimming around underneath the surface. This is known as the FRESNEL EFFECT. The Fresnel equations describe the reflection and refraction that occur at a material boundary as a function of the angle of incidence, the polarization and wavelength of the light, and the indices of refraction of the materials involved. It turns out that many materials exhibit a higher degree of reflectivity at extremely shallow (grazing) angles. Even a material such as nonglossy paper exhibits this phenomenon. For instance, hold a sheet of paper (or a book) so that you are looking at a page at a grazing angle and looking toward a light source. You will see a specular (mirrorlike) reflection from the paper, something you wouldn't see at steeper angles.

Because the Fresnel equations are relatively complex, we make the simplifying assumptions that (A) the light in our scene is not polarized, (B) all light is of the same wavelength (but we loosen this assumption later in this section), and (C) it is sufficient to use an approximation to the Fresnel equations rather than the exact equations themselves. An approximation for the ratio between reflected light and refracted light created by Christophe Schlick is

$$F = f + (1 - f)(1 - V \bullet N)^5$$

In this equation, V is the direction of view, N is the surface normal, and f is the reflectance of the material when θ is 0 given by

$$f = \frac{\left(1.0 - \frac{n_1}{n_2}\right)^2}{\left(1.0 + \frac{n_1}{n_2}\right)^2}$$

where n_1 and n_2 are the indices of refraction for materials 1 and 2.

Let's put this together in a shader. Figure 14.1 shows the relevant parameters in two dimensions. For the direction of view V, we want to compute a reflected ray and a refracted ray. We use each of these to access a texture in a cube map. We linearly blend the two values with a ratio we compute using the Fresnel approximations described earlier.

In *The Cg Tutorial*, Randima Fernando and Mark Kilgard describe Cg shaders for refraction that can easily be implemented in GLSL. The code for our vertex shader is shown in Listing 14.1. The ratio of indices of refraction for the two materials is precomputed and stored in the constant *Eta*. A value of 0.66 represents a boundary between air (index of refraction 1.000293) and glass (index of refraction 1.52). We can allow the user to control the amount of reflectivity at grazing angles by using a variable for the Fresnel power. Lower values provide higher degrees of reflectivity at grazing angles, whereas

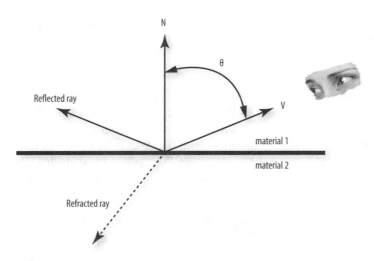

Figure 14.1 The geometry of refraction

higher values reduce this effect. The value for *f* in the previous equations is also stored as a constant. (We could have the application provide *Eta* and *FresnelPower* as uniform variables. This would then require the application to compute and pass *F* as well.)

The vertex shader uses the viewing position and the surface normal to compute a reflected ray and a refracted ray. The vertex position is transformed into eye coordinates. The **reflect** and **refract** functions both require an incident vector. This is just the vector going in the direction opposite of *V* in Figure 14.1. We compute this vector (*i*) by subtracting the viewing position (which is defined as being at (0, 0, 0) in the eye coordinate system) from the eye coordinate position and normalizing the result. We also transform the surface normal into the eye coordinate system and normalize it (*n*).

To compute the angle θ, we really need the vector *V* as shown in Figure 14.1 instead of *i* so that we can perform a dot product operation. We get this vector by negating *i*. We plug the values into the Fresnel approximation equation to get the ratio between the reflective and refractive components.

The values for *i* and *n* are sent to the built-in functions **reflect** and **refract** to compute a reflected vector and a refracted vector. These are used in the fragment shader to access the environment map. The application that uses these shaders allows the environment map to be rotated independently of the geometry. This transformation is stored in one of OpenGL's texture matrices. The resulting rays must be transformed with this matrix to access the proper location in the rotated environment.

Listing 14.1 Vertex shader for Fresnel reflection/refraction effect

```
#version 140

in vec4      MCvertex;
in vec3      MCnormal;

uniform mat4 MVMatrix;
uniform mat4 MVPMatrix;
uniform mat3 NormalMatrix;
uniform mat4 TextureMatrix;

const float Eta = 0.66; // Ratio of indices of refraction
const float FresnelPower = 5.0;

const float F = ((1.0-Eta) * (1.0-Eta)) / ((1.0+Eta) * (1.0+Eta));

out vec3  Reflect;
out vec3  Refract;
out float Ratio;

void main()
{
    vec4 ecPosition  = MVMatrix * MCvertex;
    vec3 ecPosition3 = ecPosition.xyz / ecPosition.w;

    vec3 i = normalize(ecPosition3);
    vec3 n = normalize(NormalMatrix * MCnormal);

    Ratio   = F + (1.0 - F) * pow((1.0 - dot(-i, n)), FresnelPower);

    Refract = refract(i, n, Eta);
    Refract = vec3(TextureMatrix * vec4(Refract, 1.0));

    Reflect = reflect(i, n);
    Reflect = vec3(TextureMatrix * vec4(Reflect, 1.0));

    gl_Position = MVPMatrix * MCvertex;
}
```

The corresponding fragment shader is shown in Listing 14.2. All the hard work has been done in the vertex shader. All that remains for the fragment shader is to perform the two environment map lookups and to use the computed ratio to blend the two values.

Listing 14.2 Fragment shader for Fresnel reflection/refraction effect

```
#version 140

uniform samplerCube Cubemap;

in vec3  Reflect;
in vec3  Refract;
in float Ratio;

out vec4 FragColor;

void main()
{
    vec3 refractColor = vec3(texture(Cubemap, Refract));
    vec3 reflectColor = vec3(texture(Cubemap, Reflect));

    vec3 color = mix(refractColor, reflectColor, Ratio);

    FragColor = vec4(color, 1.0);
}
```

With a small modification, we can get our reflection/refraction shader to perform another cool effect, although we stray a bit further from realistic physics. As stated earlier, the refraction of light is wavelength dependent. We made the simplifying assumption that all our light was a single wavelength, and this allowed us to compute a single refracted ray. In reality, there would be a continuum of refracted rays, one for each constituent wavelength of the light source. The breaking up of a light source into its constituent components, for example, with a prism, is called CHROMATIC DISPERSION. In camera lenses, this effect is undesirable and is called CHROMATIC ABERRATION.

We can model our light as though it contains three wavelengths of light: red, green, and blue. By providing a slightly different index of refraction for each of red, green, and blue, we can compute three slightly different refraction rays (see Listing 14.3). These three rays are passed to the fragment shader, where they perform three environment map accesses. The *RefractR* ray obtains just the red component of the final refracted color, and *RefractG* and *RefractB* obtain the green and blue components similarly. The result is used as the refracted color value. The remainder of the fragment shader is the same (see Listing 14.4).

Listing 14.3 Vertex shader for chromatic aberration effect

```
#version 140

uniform mat4 MVMatrix;
uniform mat4 MVPMatrix;
uniform mat3 NormalMatrix;
uniform mat4 TextureMatrix;

in vec4      MCVertex;
in vec3      MCNormal;

const float EtaR = 0.65;
const float EtaG = 0.67; // Ratio of indices of refraction
const float EtaB = 0.69;
const float FresnelPower = 5.0;

const float F = ((1.0-EtaG) * (1.0-EtaG)) / ((1.0+EtaG) * (1.0+EtaG));

out vec3 Reflect;
out vec3 RefractR;
out vec3 RefractG;
out vec3 RefractB;
out float Ratio;

void main()
{
    vec4 ecPosition  = MVMatrix * MCVertex;
    vec3 ecPosition3 = ecPosition.xyz / ecPosition.w;

    vec3 i = normalize(ecPosition3);
    vec3 n = normalize(NormalMatrix * MCNormal);

    Ratio    = F + (1.0 - F) * pow((1.0 - dot(-i, n)), FresnelPower);

    RefractR = refract(i, n, EtaR);
    RefractR = vec3(TextureMatrix * vec4(RefractR, 1.0));

    RefractG = refract(i, n, EtaG);
    RefractG = vec3(TextureMatrix * vec4(RefractG, 1.0));

    RefractB = refract(i, n, EtaB);
    RefractB = vec3(TextureMatrix * vec4(RefractB, 1.0));

    Reflect  = reflect(i, n);
    Reflect  = vec3(TextureMatrix * vec4(Reflect, 1.0));

    gl_Position = MVPMatrix * MCVertex;
}
```

Listing 14.4   Fragment shader for chromatic aberration effect

```
#version 140

uniform samplerCube Cubemap;

in vec3  Reflect;
in vec3  RefractR;
in vec3  RefractG;
in vec3  RefractB;
in float Ratio;

out vec4 FragColor;

void main()
{
   vec3 refractColor, reflectColor;

   refractColor.r = vec3(texture(Cubemap, RefractR)).r;
   refractColor.g = vec3(texture(Cubemap, RefractG)).g;
   refractColor.b = vec3(texture(Cubemap, RefractB)).b;

   reflectColor = vec3(texture(Cubemap, Reflect));

   vec3 color = mix(refractColor, reflectColor, Ratio);

   FragColor = vec4(color, 1.0);
}
```

Results of these shaders are shown in Color Plate 17. Notice the color fringes that occur on the character's knee and chest and on the top of his arm.

14.2 Diffraction

by Mike Weiblen

DIFFRACTION is the effect of light bending around a sharp edge. A device called a DIFFRACTION GRATING leverages that effect to efficiently split white light into the rainbow of its constituent colors. Jos Stam described how to approximate this effect, first with assembly language shaders (in a SIGGRAPH '99 paper) and then with Cg (in an article in the book *GPU Gems*). Let's see how we can approximate the behavior of a diffraction grating with an OpenGL shader.

First, let's quickly review the wave theory of light and diffraction gratings. One way of describing the behavior of visible light is as waves of electromagnetic radiation. The distance between crests of those waves is called the WAVELENGTH, usually represented by the Greek letter lambda (λ).

The wavelength is what determines the color we perceive when the light hits the sensing cells on the retina of the eye. The human eye is sensitive to the range of wavelengths beginning from about 400 nanometers (nm) for deep violet up to about 700nm for dark red. Within that range are what humans perceive as all the colors of the rainbow.

A diffraction grating is a tool for separating light based on its wavelength, similar in effect to a prism but using diffraction rather than refraction. Diffraction gratings typically are very closely spaced parallel lines in an opaque or reflective material. They were originally made with a mechanical engine that precisely scribed parallel lines onto the surface of a mirror. Modern gratings are usually created with photographic processes.

The lines of a grating have a spacing roughly on the order of the wavelengths of visible light. Because of the difference in path length when white light is reflected from adjacent mirrored lines, the different wavelengths of reflected light interfere and reinforce or cancel, depending on whether the waves constructively or destructively interfere.

For a given wavelength, if the path length of light reflecting from two adjacent lines differs by an integer number of wavelengths (meaning that the crests of the waves reflected from each line coincide), that color of light constructively interferes and reinforces in intensity. If the path difference is an integer number of wavelengths plus half a wavelength (meaning that crests of waves from one line coincide with troughs from the other line), those waves destructively interfere and extinguish at that wavelength. That interference condition varies according to the wavelength of the light, the spacing of the grating lines, and the angle of the light's path (both incident and reflected) with respect to the grating surface. Because of that interference, white light breaks into its component colors as the light source and eyepoint move with respect to the diffracting surface.

Everyday examples of diffraction gratings include compact discs, novelty "holographic" gift-wrapping papers, and the rainbow logos on modern credit cards used to discourage counterfeiting.

To demonstrate this shader, we use the everyday compact disc as a familiar example; extending this shader for other applications is straightforward.

While everyone is familiar with the overall physical appearance of a CD, let's look at the microscopic characteristics that make it a functional diffraction grating. A CD consists of one long spiral of microscopic pits embossed onto one side of a sheet of mirrored plastic. The dimensions of those pits is on the order of several hundred nanometers or the same order of magnitude as the wavelengths of visible light. The track pitch of the spiral of pits (i.e., the spacing between each winding of the spiral) is nominally 1600 nanometers. The range of those dimensions, being so close to visible wavelengths, is what gives a CD its rainbow light-splitting qualities.

Our diffraction shader computes two independent output color components per vertex:

• An anisotropic glint that reflects the color of the light source

• A color based on accumulation of the wavelengths that constructively interfere for the given light source and eyepoint locations

We can do this computation just by using a vertex shader. The vertex shader writes to the out variable *Color* and the special output variable *gl_Position*, and no programmable fragment processing is necessary. The fragment shader simply passes the in variable *Color* to the out variable *FragColor.*

The code for the diffraction vertex shader is shown in Listing 14.5. To render the diffraction effect, the shader requires the application to send a normal and tangent for each vertex. For this shader, the tangent is defined to be parallel to the orientation of the simulated grating lines. In the case of a compact disc (which has a spiral of pits on its mirrored surface), the close spacing of that spiral creates a diffraction grating of basically concentric circles, so the tangent is tangent to those circles.

Since the shader uses wavelength to compute the constructive interference, we need to convert wavelength to OpenGL's RGB representation of color. We use the function **lambda2rgb**, which approximates the conversion of wavelength to RGB by using a bump function. We begin the conversion by mapping the range of visible wavelengths to a normalized 0.0 to 1.0 range. From that normalized wavelength, we create a **vec3** by subtracting an offset for each of the red/green/blue bands. Then for each color component, we compute the contribution with the bump expression $1 - cx^2$ clamped to the range of [0,1]. The *c* term controls the width of the bump and is selected for best appearance by allowing the bumps to overlap somewhat, approximating a relatively smooth rainbow spread. This bump function is quick and easy to implement, but we could use another approach to the wavelength-to-RGB conversion, for example, using the normalized wavelength to index into a lookup table or using a 1D texture, which would be tuned for enhanced spectral qualities.

More than one wavelength can satisfy the constructive interference condition at a vertex for a given set of lighting and viewing conditions, so the shader must accumulate the contribution from each of those wavelengths. Using the condition that constructive interference occurs at path differences of integer wavelength, the shader iterates over those integers to determine the reinforced wavelength. That wavelength is converted to an RGB value by the **lambda2rgb** function and accumulated in *diffColor*.

A specular glint of *HighlightColor* is reflected from the grating lines in the region where diffractive interference does not occur. The *SurfaceRoughness* term controls the width of that highlight to approximate the scattering of light from the microscopic pits.

The final steps of the shader consist of the typical vertex transformation to compute *gl_Position* and the summing of the lighting contributions to determine *Color*. The *diffAtten* term attenuates the diffraction color slightly to prevent the colors from being too intensely garish.

A simplification we made in this shader is this: Rather than attempt to represent the spectral composition of the *HighlightColor* light source, we assume the incident light source is a flat spectrum of white light.

Being solely a vertex shader, the coloring is computed only at vertices. Since diffraction gratings can produce dramatic changes in color for a small displacement, there is an opportunity for artifacts caused by insufficient tessellation. Depending on the choice of performance trade-offs, this shader could easily be ported to a fragment shader if per-pixel shading is preferred.

Results from the diffraction shader are shown in Figure 14.2 and Color Plate 17.

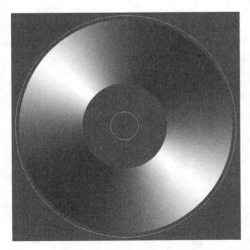

Figure 14.2 The diffraction shader simulates the look of a vinyl phonograph record (3Dlabs, Inc.).

Listing 14.5 Vertex shader for diffraction effect

```
#version 140


uniform mat4 MVMatrix;
uniform mat4 MVPMatrix;
uniform mat3 NormalMatrix;

uniform vec3  LightPosition;
uniform float GratingSpacing;
uniform float SurfaceRoughness;
uniform vec4  HighlightColor;

in   vec4  MCVertex;
in   vec3  MCNormal;
in   vec3  MCTangent; // parallel to grating lines at each vertex

out vec4  Color;

// map a visible wavelength [nm] to OpenGL's RGB representation

vec3 lambda2rgb(float lambda)
{
    const float ultraviolet = 400.0;
    const float infrared    = 700.0;

    // map visible wavelength range to 0.0 -> 1.0
    float a = (lambda-ultraviolet) / (infrared-ultraviolet);

    // bump function for a quick/simple rainbow map
    const float C = 7.0;            // controls width of bump
    vec3 b = vec3(a) - vec3(0.75, 0.5, 0.25);
    return max((1.0 - C * b * b), 0.0);
}

void main()
{
    // extract positions from input uniforms
    vec3 lightPosition = LightPosition.xyz;
    vec3 eyePosition   = -MVMatrix[3].xyz / MVMatrix[3].w;

    // H = halfway vector between light and viewer from vertex
    vec3 P = vec3(MVMatrix * MCVertex);
    vec3 L = normalize(lightPosition - P);
    vec3 V = normalize(eyePosition - P);
    vec3 H = L + V;

    // accumulate contributions from constructive interference
    // over several spectral orders.
    vec3  T = NormalMatrix * MCTangent;
    float u = abs(dot(T, H));
```

```
vec3 diffColor = vec3(0.0);

const int numSpectralOrders = 3;
for (int m = 1; m <= numSpectralOrders; ++m)
{
    float lambda = GratingSpacing * u / float(m);
    diffColor += lambda2rgb(lambda);
}

// compute anisotropic highlight for zero-order (m = 0) reflection.
vec3  N = NormalMatrix * MCNormal;
float w = dot(N, H);
float e = SurfaceRoughness * u / w;
vec3 hilight = exp(-e * e) * HighlightColor.rgb;

// write the values required for fixed-function fragment processing
const float diffAtten = 0.8; // attenuation of the diffraction color
Color = vec4(diffAtten * diffColor + hilight, 1.0);
gl_Position = MVPMatrix * MCVertex;
}
```

14.3 BRDF Models

The traditional OpenGL reflectance model and the one that we have been using for most of the previous shader examples in this book (see, for example, Section 6.2) consists of three components: ambient, diffuse, and specular. The ambient component is assumed to provide a certain level of illumination to everything in the scene and is reflected equally in all directions by everything in the scene. The diffuse and specular components are directional in nature and are due to illumination from a particular light source. The diffuse component models reflection from a surface that is scattered in all directions. The diffuse reflection is strongest where the surface normal points directly at the light source, and it drops to zero where the surface normal is pointing 90° or more away from the light source. Specular reflection models the highlights caused by reflection from surfaces that are mirrorlike or nearly so. Specular highlights are concentrated on the mirror direction.

But relatively few materials have perfectly specular (mirrorlike) or diffuse (Lambertian) reflection characteristics. To model more physically realistic surfaces, we must go beyond the simplistic lighting/reflection model that is built into OpenGL. This model was developed empirically and is not physically accurate. Furthermore, it can realistically simulate the reflection from only a relatively small class of materials.

For more than two decades, computer graphics researchers have been rendering images with more realistic reflection models called BIDIRECTIONAL REFLECTANCE DISTRIBUTION FUNCTIONS, or BRDFs. A BRDF model for computing the reflection from a surface takes into account the input direction of incoming light and the outgoing direction of reflected light. The elevation and azimuth angles of these direction vectors are used to compute the relative amount of light reflected in the outgoing direction (the fixed functionality OpenGL model uses only the elevation angle). A BRDF model renders surfaces with ANISOTROPIC reflection properties (i.e., surfaces that are not rotationally invariant in their surface reflection properties). Instruments have been developed to measure the BRDF of real materials. In some cases, the measured data has been used to create a function with a few parameters that can be modified to model the reflective characteristics of a variety of materials. In other cases, the measured data has been sampled to produce texture maps that reconstruct the BRDF function at runtime. A variety of different measuring, sampling, and reconstruction methods have been devised to use BRDFs in computer graphics, and this is still an area of active research.

Generally speaking, the amount of light that is reflected to a particular viewing position depends on the position of the light, the position of the viewer, and the surface normal and tangent. If any of these changes, the amount of light reflected to the viewer may also change. The surface characteristics also play a role because different wavelengths of light may be reflected, transmitted, or absorbed, depending on the physical properties of the material. Shiny materials have concentrated, near-mirrorlike specular highlights. Rough materials have specular highlights that are more spread out. Metals have specular highlights that are the color of the metal rather than the color of the light source. The color of reflected light may change as the reflection approaches a grazing angle with the surface. Materials with small brush marks or grooves reflect light differently as they are rotated, and the shapes of their specular highlights also change. These are the types of effects that BRDF models are intended to accurately reproduce.

A BRDF is a function of two pairs of angles as well as the wavelength and polarization of the incoming light. The angles are the altitude and azimuth of the incident light vector (θ_i, ϕ_i) and the altitude and azimuth of the reflected light vector (θ_r, ϕ_r). Both sets of angles are given with respect to a given tangent vector. For simplicity, some BRDF models omit polarization effects and assume that the function is the same for all wavelengths. Because the incident and reflected light vectors are measured against a fixed tangent vector in the plane of a surface, BRDF models can reproduce the reflective characteristics of anisotropic materials such as brushed or rolled metals. And because both the incident and reflected light vectors are considered, BRDF models can also reproduce the changes in specular highlight shapes or colors that occur when an object is illuminated by a light source at a grazing angle.

BRDF models can be either theoretical or empirical. Theoretical models attempt to model the physics of light and materials in order to reproduce the observed reflectance properties. In contrast, an empirical model is a function with adjustable parameters that is designed to fit measured reflectance data for a certain class of materials. The volume of measured data typically prohibits its direct use in a computer graphics environment, and this data is often imperfect or incomplete. Somehow, the measured data must be boiled down to a few useful values that can be plugged into a formula or used to create textures that can be accessed during rendering. A variety of methods for reducing the measured data have been developed.

One such model was described by Greg Ward in a 1992 SIGGRAPH paper. He and his colleagues at Lawrence Berkeley Laboratory built a device that was relatively efficient in collecting reflectance data from a variety of materials. The measurements were the basis for creating a mathematical reflectance model that provided a reasonable approximation to the measured data. Ward's goal was to produce a simple empirical formula that was physically valid and fit the measured reflectance data for a variety of different materials. Ward measured the reflectivity of various materials to determine a few key values with physical meaning and plugged those values into the formula he developed to replicate the measured data in a computer graphics environment.

To understand Ward's model, we should first review the geometry involved, as shown in Figure 14.3. This diagram shows a point on a surface and the relevant direction vectors that are used in the reflection computation:

- N is the unit surface normal.
- L is the unit vector in the direction of the simulated light source.
- V is the unit vector in the direction of the viewer.
- R is the unit vector in the direction of reflection from the simulated light source.
- H is the unit angular bisector of V and L (sometimes called the halfway vector).
- T is a unit vector in the plane of the surface that is perpendicular to N (i.e., the tangent).
- B is a unit vector in the plane of the surface that is perpendicular to both N and T (i.e., the binormal).

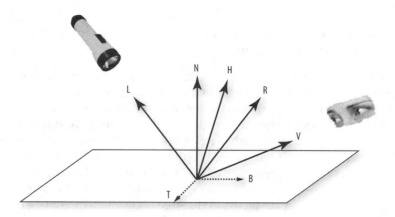

Figure 14.3 The geometry of reflection

The formula developed by Ward is based on a Gaussian reflectance model. The key parameters of the formula are the diffuse reflectivity of the surface (ρ_d), the specular reflectivity of the surface (ρ_s), and the standard deviation of the surface slope (α). The final parameter is a measure of the roughness of a surface. The assumption is that a surface is made up of tiny microfacets that reflect in a specular fashion. For a mirrorlike surface, all the microfacets line up with the surface. For a rougher surface, some random orientation of these microfacets causes the specular highlight to spread out more. The fraction of facets that are oriented in the direction of *H* is called the FACET SLOPE DISTRIBUTION FUNCTION, or the SURFACE SLOPE. Several possibilities for this function have been suggested.

With but a single value for the surface slope, the mathematical model is limited in its ability to reproduce materials exhibiting anisotropic reflection. To deal with this, Ward's model includes two α values, one for the standard deviation of the surface slope in the *x* direction (i.e., in the direction of the surface tangent vector *T*) and one for the standard deviation of the surface slope in the *y* direction (i.e., in the direction of the surface binormal value *B*). The formula used by Ward to fit his measured reflectance data and the key parameters derived from that data is

$$\rho_{bd}(\theta_i, \phi_i, \theta_r, \phi_r) = \frac{\rho_d}{\pi} + \rho_s \cdot \frac{1}{\sqrt{\cos\theta_i \cos\theta_r}} \cdot \frac{1}{4\pi\alpha_x\alpha_y} \cdot \exp\left[-2\frac{\left[\frac{H \bullet T}{\alpha_x}\right]^2 + \left[\frac{H \bullet B}{\alpha_y}\right]^2}{1 + H \bullet N}\right]$$

This formula looks a bit onerous, but Ward has supplied values for ρ_d, ρ_s, α_x, and α_y for several materials, and all we need to do is code the formula in the OpenGL Shading Language. The result of this BRDF is plugged into the overall equation for illumination, which looks like this:

$$L(\theta_r, \phi_r) = I\frac{\rho_d}{\pi} + L_s\rho_s + \sum_{i=1}^{N} L_i\omega_i\cos\theta_i\rho_{bd}(\theta_i, \phi_i, \theta_r, \phi_r)$$

This formula basically states that the reflected radiance is the sum of a general indirect radiance contribution, plus an indirect semispecular contribution, plus the radiance from each of N light sources in the scene. I is the indirect radiance, L_s is the radiance from the indirect semispecular contribution, and L_i is the radiance from light source i. For the remaining terms, ω_i is the solid angle in steradians of light source i, and ρ_{bd} is the BRDF defined in the previous equation.

This all translates quite easily into OpenGL Shading Language code. To get higher-quality results, we compute all the vectors in the vertex shader, interpolate them, and then perform the reflection computations in the fragment shader.

The application is expected to provide four attributes for every vertex. The four attributes are a vertex coordinate, a normal, a tangent vector, and a binormal vector, which the application computes. These four attributes should be provided to OpenGL with a generic vertex array. The location to be used for these generic attributes can be bound to the appropriate attribute in our vertex shader with **glBindAttribLocation**. For instance, if we choose to pass the vertex values in vertex attribute location 1, the normal in vertex attribute location 2, the tangent values in vertex attribute location 3, and the binormal values in vertex attribute location 4, we would set up the binding with these lines of code:

```
glBindAttribLocation(programObj, 1, "MCvertex");
glBindAttribLocation(programObj, 2, "MCNormal");
glBindAttribLocation(programObj, 3, "MCTangent");
glBindAttribLocation(programObj, 4, "MCBinormal");
```

Listing 14.6 contains the vertex shader. Its primary job is to compute and normalize the vectors shown in Figure 14.3, namely, the unit vectors *N*, *L*, *V*, *H*, *R*, *T*, and *B*. We compute the values for *N*, *T*, and *B* by transforming the application-supplied normal, tangent, and binormal into eye coordinates. We compute the reflection vector *R* by using the built-in function **reflect**.

We determine *L* by normalizing the direction to the light source. Because the viewing position is defined to be at the origin in eye coordinates, we compute *V* by transforming the viewing position into eye coordinates and subtracting the surface position in eye coordinates. *H* is the normalized sum of *L* and *V*. All seven of these values are stored in out variables that will be interpolated and made available to the fragment shader.

Listing 14.6   Vertex shader for rendering with Ward's BRDF model

```
#version 140

uniform mat4 MVMatrix;
uniform mat4 MVPMatrix;
uniform mat3 NormalMatrix;

uniform vec3 LightDir; // Light direction in eye coordinates
uniform vec4 ViewPosition;

in  vec4  MCvertex;
in  vec3  MCnormal;
in  vec3  MCTangent;
in  vec3  MCBinormal;
*/
out vec3  N, L, H, R, T, B;

void main()
{
   vec3 V, eyeDir;
   vec4 pos;

   pos     = MVPMatrix * MCVertex;
   eyeDir = pos.xyz;

   N = normalize(NormalMatrix * MCNormal);
   L = normalize(LightDir);
   V = normalize((MVMatrix * ViewPosition).xyz - pos.xyz);
   H = normalize(L + V);
   R = normalize(reflect(eyeDir, N));
   T = normalize(NormalMatrix * MCTangent);
   B = normalize(NormalMatrix * MCBinormal);

   gl_Position = MVPMatrix * MCVertex;
}
```

It is then up to the fragment shader to implement the equations defined previously. The values that parameterize a material (ρ_d, ρ_s, α_x, α_y) are passed as the uniform variables *P* and *A*. We can use the values from the table published in Ward's paper or try some values of our own. The base color of the surface is also passed as a uniform variable (Ward's measurements did not include color for any of the materials). Instead of dealing with the radiance and solid angles of light sources, we just use a uniform variable to supply coefficients that manipulate these terms directly.

The vectors passed as out variables become denormalized during interpolation, but if the polygons in the scene are all relatively small, this effect is hard to notice. For this reason, we can usually skip the step of renormalizing these values in the fragment shader. The first three lines of code in the fragment shader (Listing 14.7) compute the expression in the *exp* function from Ward's BRDF. The next two lines obtain the necessary cosine values by computing the dot product of the appropriate vectors. We then use these values to compute the value for *brdf*, which is the same as ρ_{bd} in the earlier equations. The next equation puts it all together into an intensity value that attenuates the base color for the surface. The attenuated value becomes the final color for the fragment.

Listing 14.7 Fragment shader for rendering with Ward's BRDF model

```
#version 140

const float PI = 3.14159;
const float ONE_OVER_PI = 1.0 / PI;

uniform vec4 SurfaceColor; // Base color of surface
uniform vec2 P; // Diffuse (x) and specular reflectance (y)
uniform vec2 A; // Slope distribution in x and y
uniform vec3 Scale; // Scale factors for intensity computation

in   vec3  N, L, H, R, T, B;

out vec4  FragColor;

void main()
{
    float e1, e2, E, cosThetaI, cosThetaR, brdf, intensity;

    e1 = dot(H, T) / A.x;
    e2 = dot(H, B) / A.y;
    E = -2.0 * ((e1 * e1 + e2 * e2) / (1.0 + dot(H, N)));

    cosThetaI = dot(N, L);
    cosThetaR = dot(N, R);

    brdf = P.x * ONE_OVER_PI +
           P.y * (1.0 / sqrt(cosThetaI * cosThetaR)) *
           (1.0 / (4.0 * PI * A.x * A.y)) * exp(E);
```

```
    intensity = Scale[0] * P.x * ONE_OVER_PI +
                Scale[1] * P.y * cosThetaI * brdf +
                Scale[2] * dot(H, N) * P.y;

    vec3 color = intensity * SurfaceColor.rgb;

    FragColor = vec4(color, 1.0);
}
```

Some results from this shader are shown in Color Plate 23. It certainly would be possible to extend the formula and surface parameterization values to operate on three channels instead of just one. The resulting shader could be used to simulate materials whose specular highlight changes color depending on the viewing angle.

14.4 Polynomial Texture Mapping with BRDF Data

This section describes the OpenGL Shading Language BRDF shaders that use the Polynomial Texture Mapping technique developed by Hewlett-Packard. The shaders presented are courtesy of Brad Ritter, Hewlett-Packard. The BRDF data is from Cornell University. It was obtained by measurement of reflections from several types of automotive paints that were supplied by Ford Motor Co.

One reason this type of rendering is important is that it achieves realistic rendering of materials whose reflection characteristics vary as a function of view angle and light direction. Such is the case with these automotive paints. To a car designer, it is extremely important to be able to visualize the final "look" of the car, even when it is painted with a material whose reflection characteristics vary as a function of view angle and light direction. One of the paint samples tested by Cornell, Mystique Lacquer, has the peculiar property that the color of its specular highlight color changes as a function of viewing angle. This material cannot be adequately rendered if only conventional texture-mapping techniques are used.

The textures used in this example are called POLYNOMIAL TEXTURE MAPS, or PTMs. PTMs are essentially light-dependent texture maps; PTMs are described in a 2001 SIGGRAPH paper by Malzbender, Gelb, and Wolters. PTMs reconstruct the color of a surface under varying lighting conditions. When a surface is rendered with a PTM, it takes on different illumination characteristics depending on the direction of the light source. As with bump mapping, this behavior helps viewers by providing perceptual clues about the surface geometry. But PTMs go beyond bump maps in that they capture surface variations resulting from self-shadowing and interreflections. PTMs are generated from real materials and preserve the visual characteristics of the actual materials. Polynomial texture mapping is an image-based technique that does not require bump maps or the modeling of complex geometry.

The image in Color Plate 26 (left) shows two triangles from a PTM demo developed by Hewlett-Packard. The triangle on the upper right has been rendered with a polynomial texture map, and the triangle on the lower left has been rendered with a conventional 2D texture map. The objects that were used in the construction of the texture maps were a metallic bezel with the Hewlett-Packard logo on it and a brushed metal notebook cover with an embossed 3Dlabs logo. As you move the simulated light source in the demo, the conventional texture looks flat and somewhat unrealistic, whereas the PTM texture faithfully reproduces the highlights and surface shadowing that occur on the real-life objects. In the image captured here, the light source is a bit in front and above the two triangles. The PTM shows realistic reflections, but the conventional texture can reproduce the lighting effect only from a single lighting angle (in this case, as if the light were directly in front of the object).

The PTM technique developed by HP requires as input a set of images of the desired object, with the object illuminated by a light source of a different known direction for each image, all captured from the same viewpoint. For each texel of the PTM, these source images are sampled and a least-squares biquadric curve fit is performed to obtain a polynomial that approximates the lighting function for that texel. This part of the process is partly science and partly art (a bit of manual intervention can improve the end results). The biquadric equation generated in this manner allows runtime reconstruction of the lighting function for the source material. The coefficients stored in the PTM are A, B, C, D, E, and F, as shown in this equation:

$$Au^2 + Bv^2 + Cuv + Du + Ev + F$$

One use of PTMs is for representing materials with surface properties that vary spatially across the surface. Materials such as brushed metal, woven fabric, wood, and stone all reflect light differently depending on the viewing angle and light source direction. They may also have interreflections and self-shadowing. The PTM technique captures these details and reproduces them at runtime. There are two variants for PTMs: luminance (LRGB) and RGB. An LRGB PTM uses the biquadric polynomials to determine the brightness of each rendered pixel. Because each texel in an LRGB PTM has its own biquadric polynomial function, the luminance or brightness characteristics of each texel can be unique. An RGB PTM uses a separate biquadric polynomial for each of the three colors: red, green, and blue. This allows objects rendered with an RGB PTM to vary in color as the light position shifts. Thus, color-shifting materials such as holograms can be accurately reconstructed with an RGB PTM.

The key to creating a PTM for these types of spatially varying materials is to capture images of them as lit from a variety of light source directions. Engineers at Hewlett-Packard have developed an instrument—a dome with multiple light sources and a camera mounted at the top—to do just that. This device can automatically capture 50 images of the source material from a single fixed camera position as illuminated by light sources in different positions. A photograph of this picture-taking device is shown in Figure 14.4.

The image data collected with this device is the basis for creating a PTM for the real-world texture of a material (e.g., automobile paints). These types of PTMs have four degrees of freedom. Two of these represent the spatially varying characteristics of the material. These two degrees of freedom are controlled by the 2D texture coordinates. The remaining two degrees of freedom represent the light direction. These are the two independent variables in the biquadric polynomial.

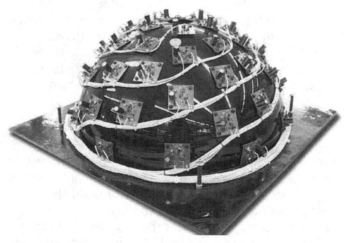

Figure 14.4   A device for capturing images for the creation of polynomial texture maps (Copyright © 2003, Hewlett-Packard Development Company, L.P., reproduced with permission)

A BRDF PTM is slightly different from a spatially varying PTM. BRDF PTMs model homogeneous materials—that is, they do not vary spatially. BRDF PTMs use two degrees of freedom to represent the light direction, and the remaining two degrees of freedom represent the view direction. The parameterized light direction (Lu, Lv) is used for the independent variables of the biquadric polynomial, and the parameterized view direction (Vu, Vv) is used as the 2D texture coordinate.

No single parameterization works well for all BRDF materials. A further refinement to enhance quality for BRDF PTMs for the materials we are trying to reproduce is to reparameterize the light and view vectors as half angle and difference vectors (Hu, Hv) and (Du, Dv). In the BRDF PTM shaders discussed in the next section, Hu and Hv are the independent variables of the biquadric polynomial, and (Du, Dv) is the 2D texture coordinate. A large part of the vertex shader's function is to calculate (Hu, Hv) and (Du, Dv).

BRDF PTMs can be created as either LRGB or RGB PTMs. The upcoming example shows how an RGB BRDF PTM is rendered with OpenGL shaders. RGBA textures with 8 bits per component are used because the PTM file format and tools developed by HP are based on this format.

14.4.1 Application Setup

To render BRDF surfaces using the following shaders, the application must set up a few uniform variables. The vertex shader must be provided with values for uniform variables that describe the eye direction (i.e., an infinite viewer) and the position of a single light source (i.e., a point light source). The fragment shader requires the application to provide values for scaling and biasing the six polynomial coefficients. (These values were prescaled when the PTM was created to preserve precision, and they must be rescaled with the scale and bias factors that are specific to that PTM.)

The application is expected to provide the surface normal, vertex position, tangent, and binormal in exactly the same way as the BRDF shader discussed in the previous section. Before rendering, the application should also set up seven texture maps: three 2D texture maps to hold the A, B, and C coefficients for red, green, and blue components of the PTM; three 2D texture maps to hold the D, E, and F coefficients for red, green, and blue components of the PTM; and a 1D texture map to hold a lighting function.

This last texture is set up by the application whenever the lighting state is changed. The light factor texture solves four problems:

- The light factor texture is indexed with *LdotN*, which is positive for front-facing vertices and negative for back-facing vertices. As a first level of complexity, the light texture can solve the front-facing/back-facing discrimination problem by being 1.0 for positive index values and 0.0 for back-facing values.

- We'd like to be able to light BRDF PTM shaded objects with colored lights. As a second level of complexity, the light texture (which has three channels, R, G, and B) uses a light color instead of 1.0 for positive index values.

- An abrupt transition from front-facing to back-facing looks awkward and unrealistic on rendered images. As a third level of complexity, we apply a gradual transition in the light texture values from 0 to 1.0. We use a sine or cosine curve to determine these gradual texture values.

- There is no concept of ambient light for PTM rendering. It can look very unrealistic to render back-facing pixels as (0,0,0). Instead of using 0 values for negative indices, we use values such as 0.1.

14.4.2 Vertex Shader

The BRDF PTM vertex shader is shown in Listing 14.8. This shader produces five out values:

- *gl_Position*, as required by every vertex shader

- *TexCoord*, which is used to access our texture maps to get the two sets of polynomial coefficients

- *Du*, a float that contains the cosine of the angle between the light direction and the tangent vector

- *Dv*, a float that contains the cosine of the angle between the light direction and the binormal vector

- *LdotN*, a float that contains the cosine of the angle between the incoming surface normal and the light direction

The shader assumes a viewer at infinity and one point light source.

Listing 14.8 Vertex shader for rendering BRDF-based polynomial texture maps

```glsl
#version 140
//
// PTM vertex shader by Brad Ritter, Hewlett-Packard
// and Randi Rost, 3Dlabs.
//
// © Copyright 2003 3Dlabs, Inc., and
// Hewlett-Packard Development Company, L.P.,
// Reproduced with Permission
//

uniform mat4 MVPMatrix;

uniform vec3 LightPos;
uniform vec3 EyeDir;

in  vec4  MCvertex;
in  vec3  MCnormal;
in  vec3  MCTangent;
in  vec3  MCBinormal;

out float Du;
out float Dv;
out float LdotN;
out vec2  TexCoord;

void main()
{
    vec3 lightTemp;
    vec3 halfAngleTemp;
    vec3 tPrime;
    vec3 bPrime;

    // Transform vertex
    gl_Position = MVPMatrix * MCVertex;
    lightTemp = normalize(LightPos - MCVertex.xyz);

    // Calculate the Half Angle vector
    halfAngleTemp = normalize(EyeDir + lightTemp);

    // Calculate T' and B'
    // T' = |T - (T.H)H|
    tPrime = MCTangent - (halfAngleTemp * dot(MCTangent, halfAngleTemp));
    tPrime = normalize(tPrime);

    // B' = H x T'
    bPrime = cross(halfAngleTemp, tPrime);
    Du = dot(lightTemp, tPrime);
    Dv = dot(lightTemp, bPrime);
```

```
    // Multiply the Half Angle vector by NOISE_FACTOR
    // to avoid noisy BRDF data
    halfAngleTemp = halfAngleTemp * 0.9;

    // Hu = Dot(HalfAngle, T)
    // Hv = Dot(HalfAngle, B)
    // Remap [-1.0..1.0] to [0.0..1.0]
    TexCoord.s = dot(MCTangent, halfAngleTemp) * 0.5 + 0.5;
    TexCoord.t = dot(MCBinormal, halfAngleTemp) * 0.5 + 0.5;

    // "S" Text Coord3: Dot(Light, Normal);
    LdotN = dot(lightTemp, MCNormal) * 0.5 + 0.5;
}
```

The light source position and eye direction are passed in as uniform variables by the application. In addition to the standard OpenGL vertex and normal vertex attributes, the application is expected to pass in a tangent and a binormal per vertex, as described in the previous section. These two generic attributes are defined with appropriate names in our vertex shader.

The first line of the vertex shader transforms the incoming vertex value by the current modelview-projection matrix. The next line computes the light source direction for our positional light source by subtracting the vertex position from the light position. Because *LightPos* is defined as a **vec3** and the user defined in variable *MCVertex* is defined as a **vec4**, we must use the **.xyz** component selector to obtain the first three elements of *MCVertex* before doing the vector subtraction operation. The result of the vector subtraction is then normalized and stored as our light direction.

The following line of code computes the half angle by summing the eye direction vector and the light direction vector and normalizing the result.

The next few lines of code compute the 2D parameterization of our half angle and difference vector. The goal here is to compute values for *u* (*Du*) and *v* (*Dv*) that can be plugged into the biquadric equation in our fragment shader. The technique we use is called Gram-Schmidt orthonormalization. *H* (half angle), *T'*, and *B'* are the orthogonal axes of a coordinate system. *T'* and *B'* maintain a general alignment with the original *T* (tangent) and *B* (binormal) vectors. Where *T* and *B* lie in the plane of the triangle being rendered, *T'* and *B'* are in a plane perpendicular to the half angle vector. More details on the reasons for choosing *H*, *T'*, and *B'* to define the coordinate system are available in the paper *Interactive Rendering with Arbitrary BRDFs Using Separable Approximations* by Jan Kautz and Michael McCool (1999).

BRDF data often has noisy data values for extremely large incidence angles (i.e., close to 180°), so in the next line of code, we avoid the noisy data in a somewhat unscientific manner by applying a scale factor to the half angle. This effectively causes these values to be ignored.

Our vertex shader code then computes values for *Hu* and *Hv* and places them in the out variable *TexCoord*. These are plugged into our biquadric equation in the fragment shader as the *u* and *v* values. These values hold our parameterized difference vector and are used to look up the required polynomial coefficients from the texture maps, so they are mapped into the range [0,1].

Finally, we compute a value that applies the lighting effect. This value is simply the cosine of the angle between the surface normal and the light direction. It is also mapped into the range [0,1] because it is the texture coordinate for accessing a 1D texture to obtain the lighting factor that is used.

14.4.3 Fragment Shader

The fragment shader for our BRDF PTM surface rendering is shown in Listing 14.9.

Listing 14.9 Fragment shader for rendering BRDF-based polynomial texture maps

```
#version 140
//
// PTM fragment shader by Brad Ritter, Hewlett-Packard
// and Randi Rost, 3Dlabs.
//
// © Copyright 2003 3Dlabs, Inc., and
// Hewlett-Packard Development Company, L.P.,
// Reproduced with Permission
//
uniform sampler2D ABCred;        // = 0
uniform sampler2D DEFred;        // = 1
uniform sampler2D ABCgrn;        // = 2
uniform sampler2D DEFgrn;        // = 3
uniform sampler2D ABCblu;        // = 4
uniform sampler2D DEFblu;        // = 5
uniform sampler1D Lighttexture;  // = 6

uniform vec3 ABCscale, ABCbias;
uniform vec3 DEFscale, DEFbias;

in  float Du;        // passes the computed L*tPrime value
in  float Dv;        // passes the computed L*bPrime value
in  float LdotN;     // passes the computed L*Normal value
in  vec2  TexCoord;  // passes s, t, texture coords
```

```
out vec4  FragColor;

void main()
{
   vec3 ABCcoef, DEFcoef;
   vec3 ptvec;

   // Read coefficient values for red and apply scale and bias factors
   ABCcoef = (texture(ABCred, TexCoord).rgb - ABCbias) * ABCscale;
   DEFcoef = (texture(DEFred, TexCoord).rgb - DEFbias) * DEFscale;

   // Compute red polynomial
   ptvec.r = ABCcoef[0] * Du * Du +
             ABCcoef[1] * Dv * Dv +
             ABCcoef[2] * Du * Dv +
             DEFcoef[0] * Du +
             DEFcoef[1] * Dv +
             DEFcoef[2];

   // Read coefficient values for green and apply scale and bias factors
   ABCcoef = (texture(ABCgrn, TexCoord).rgb - ABCbias) * ABCscale;
   DEFcoef = (texture(DEFgrn, TexCoord).rgb - DEFbias) * DEFscale;

   // Compute green polynomial
   ptvec.g = ABCcoef[0] * Du * Du +
             ABCcoef[1] * Dv * Dv +
             ABCcoef[2] * Du * Dv +
             DEFcoef[0] * Du +
             DEFcoef[1] * Dv +
             DEFcoef[2];

   // Read coefficient values for blue and apply scale and bias factors
   ABCcoef = (texture(ABCblu, TexCoord).rgb - ABCbias) * ABCscale;
   DEFcoef = (texture(DEFblu, TexCoord).rgb - DEFbias) * DEFscale;

   // Compute blue polynomial
   ptvec.b = ABCcoef[0] * Du * Du +
             ABCcoef[1] * Dv * Dv +
             ABCcoef[2] * Du * Dv +
             DEFcoef[0] * Du +
             DEFcoef[1] * Dv +
             DEFcoef[2];

   // Multiply result * light factor
   ptvec *= texture(Lighttexture, LdotN).rgb;

   // Assign result to FragColor
   FragColor = vec4(ptvec, 1.0);
}
```

This shader is relatively straightforward if you've digested the information in the previous three sections. The values in the *s* and *t* components of

TexCoord hold a 2D parameterization of the difference vector. *TexCoord* indexes into each of our coefficient textures and retrieves the values for the A, B, C, D, E, and F coefficients. The BRDF PTMs are stored as mipmap textures, and, because we're not providing a *bias* argument, the computed level-of-detail bias is just used directly. Using vector operations, we scale and bias the six coefficients by using values passed from the application through uniform variables.

We then use these scaled, biased coefficient values together with our parameterized half angle (*Du* and *Dv*) in the biquadric polynomial to compute the red value for the surface. We repeat the process to compute the green and blue values as well. We compute the lighting factor by accessing the 1D light texture, using the cosine of the angle between the light direction and the surface normal. Finally, we multiply the lighting factor by our polynomial vector and use an alpha value of 1.0 to produce the final fragment color.

The image in Color Plate 26 (right) shows our BRDF PTM shaders rendering a torus with the BRDF PTM created for the Mystique Lacquer automotive paint. The basic color of this paint is black, but, in the orientation captured for the still image, the specular highlight shows up as mostly white with a reddish-brown tinge on one side of the highlight and a bluish tinge on the other. As the object is moved around or as the light is moved around, our BRDF PTM shaders properly render the shifting highlight color.

14.5 Summary

This chapter looked at how shaders model the properties of light that arrives at a particular point on a surface. Light can be transmitted, reflected, or absorbed. We developed shaders that model the reflection and refraction of light based on an approximation to the Fresnel equations, a shader that simulates diffraction, and shaders that implement a bidirectional reflectance distribution function. Finally, we studied a shader that uses image-based methods to reproduce varying lighting conditions and self-shadowing for a variety of materials.

Pardon the pun, but the shaders presented in this chapter (as well as in the preceding two chapters) only begin to scratch the surface of the realistic rendering effects that are possible with the OpenGL Shading Language. The hope is that by developing shaders to implement a few examples of lighting, shadows, and reflection, you will be equipped to survey the literature and implement a variety of similar techniques. The shaders we've developed can be further streamlined and optimized for specific purposes.

14.6 Further Information

A thorough treatment of reflectance and lighting models can be found in the book *Real-Time Shading* by Marc Olano et al. (2002). *Real-Time Rendering* by Tomas Akenine-Möller and E. Haines also contains discussions of Fresnel reflection and the theory and implementation of BRDFs. The paper discussing the Fresnel approximation we've discussed was published by Christophe Schlick as part of Eurographics '94. Cg shaders that utilize this approximation are described in the *Cg Tutorial* and *GPU Gems* books. The diffraction shader is based on work presented by Jos Stam in a 1999 SIGGRAPH paper called *Diffraction Shaders*. Stam later developed a diffraction shader in Cg and discussed it in the book *GPU Gems*.

The specific paper that was drawn upon heavily for the BRDF reflection section was Gregory Ward's *Measuring and Modeling Anisotropic Reflection*, which appeared in the 1992 SIGGRAPH conference proceedings. A classic early paper that set the stage for this work was the 1981 SIGGRAPH paper, *A Reflectance Model for Computer Graphics* by Robert L. Cook and Kenneth E. Torrance.

The SIGGRAPH 2001 proceedings contain the paper *Polynomial Texture Maps* by Tom Malzbender, Dan Gelb, and Hans Wolters. Additional information is available at the Hewlett-Packard Laboratories Web site, www.hpl.hp.com/ptm/. At this site, you can find example data files, a PTM viewing program, the PTM file format specification, and utilities to assist in creating PTMs.

The book *Physically-Based Rendering: From Theory to Implementation* by Matt Pharr and Greg Humphreys is a thorough treatment of techniques for achieving realism in computer graphics.

[1] Akenine-Möller, Tomas, and E. Haines, *Real-Time Rendering, Second Edition*, AK Peters, Ltd., Natick, Massachusetts, 2002. www.realtimerendering.com

[2] Cook, Robert L., and Kenneth E. Torrance, *A Reflectance Model for Computer Graphics*, Computer Graphics (SIGGRAPH '81 Proceedings), pp. 307–316, July 1981.

[3] Fernando, Randima, and Mark J. Kilgard, *The Cg Tutorial: The Definitive Guide to Programmable Real-Time Graphics*, Addison-Wesley, Boston, Massachusetts, 2003.

[4] Hewlett-Packard, *Polynomial Texture Mapping*, Web site. www.hpl.hp.com/ptm

[5] Kautz, Jan, and Michael D. McCool, *Interactive Rendering with Arbitrary BRDFs Using Separable Approximations*, 10th Eurographics Workshop on Rendering, pp. 281–292, June 1999. www.mpi-sb.mpg.de/~jnkautz/publications

[6] Malzbender, Tom, Dan Gelb, and Hans Wolters, *Polynomial Texture Maps*, Computer Graphics (SIGGRAPH 2001 Proceedings), pp. 519–528, August 2001. www.hpl.hp.com/research/ptm/papers/ptm.pdf

[7] Olano, Marc, John Hart, Wolfgang Heidrich, and Michael McCool, *Real-Time Shading*, AK Peters, Ltd., Natick, Massachusetts, 2002.

[8] Pharr, Matt, and Greg Humphreys, *Physically Based Rendering: From Theory to Implementation*, Morgan Kaufmann, San Francisco, 2004. http://pbrt.org/

[9] Schlick, Christophe, *An Inexpensive BRDF Model for Physically Based Rendering*, Eurographics '94, published in Computer Graphics Forum, vol. 13., no. 3, pp. 149–162, September, 1994.

[10] Stam, Jos, *Diffraction Shaders*, Computer Graphics (SIGGRAPH '99 Proceedings, pp. 101–110, August 1999. www.dgp.toronto.edu/people/stam/reality/Research/pdf/diff.pdf

[11] Stam, Jos, *Simulating Diffraction*, in *GPU Gems: Programming Techniques, Tips, and Tricks for Real-Time Graphics*, Editor: Randima Fernando, Addison-Wesley, Reading, Massachusetts, 2004. http://developer.nvidia.com/object/gpu_gems_home.html

[12] Ward, Gregory, *Measuring and Modeling Anisotropic Reflection*, Computer Graphics (SIGGRAPH '92 Proceedings), pp. 265–272, July 1992. http://radsite.lbl.gov/radiance/papers/sg92/paper.html

Chapter 15

Noise

In computer graphics, it's easy to make things look good. By definition, geometry is drawn and rendered precisely. However, when realism is a goal, perfection isn't always such a good thing. Real-world objects have dents and dings and scuffs. They show wear and tear. Computer graphics artists have to work hard to make a perfectly defined bowling pin look like it has been used and abused for 20 years in a bowling alley or to make a space ship that seems a little worse for wear after many years of galactic travel.

This was the problem that Ken Perlin was trying to solve when he worked for a company called Magi in the early 1980s. Magi was working with Disney on a feature film called *Tron* that was the most ambitious film in its use of computer graphics until that time. Perlin recognized the "imperfection" of the perfectly rendered objects in that film, and he resolved to do something about it.

In a seminal paper published in 1985, Perlin described a renderer that he had written that used a technique he called NOISE. His definition of noise was a little different from the everyday definition of noise. Normally, when we refer to noise, we're referring to something like a random pattern of pixels on a television channel with no signal (also called SNOW) or to static on the radio on a frequency that doesn't have any nearby station broadcasting.

But a truly random function like this isn't that useful for computer graphics. For computer graphics, we need a function that is repeatable so that an object can be drawn from different view angles. We also need the ability to draw the object the same way, frame after frame, in an animation. Truly random functions do not depend on any input values, so an object rendered with such a function would look different each time it was drawn.

The visual artifacts caused by this type of rendering would look horrible as the object was moved around the screen. What is needed is a function that produces the same output value for a given input value every time and yet gives the appearance of randomness. This function also needs to be continuous at all levels of detail.

Perlin was the first to come up with a usable function for that purpose. Since then, a variety of similar noise functions have been defined and used in combinations to produce interesting rendering effects such as

- Rendering natural phenomena (clouds, fire, smoke, wind effects, etc.)

- Rendering natural materials (marble, granite, wood, mountains, etc.)

- Rendering man-made materials (stucco, asphalt, cement, etc.)

- Adding imperfections to perfect models (rust, dirt, smudges, dents, etc.)

- Adding imperfections to perfect patterns (wiggles, bumps, color variations, etc.)

- Adding imperfections to time periods (time between blinks, amount of change between successive frames, etc.)

- Adding imperfections to motion (wobbles, jitters, bumps, etc.)

Actually, the list is endless. Today, most rendering libraries include support for Perlin noise or something nearly equivalent. It is a staple of realistic rendering, and it's been heavily used in the generation of computer graphics images for the movie industry. For his groundbreaking work in this area, Perlin was presented with an Academy Award for technical achievement in 1997.

Because noise is such an important technique, it is included as a built-in function in the OpenGL Shading Language. There are several ways to make use of noise within a fragment shader. After laying the groundwork for noise, we take a look at several shader examples that depend on noise to achieve an interesting effect.

15.1 Noise Defined

The purpose of this section is not to explain the mathematical underpinnings of noise but to provide enough of an intuitive feel that you can grasp the noise-based OpenGL shaders presented in the chapter and then use the OpenGL Shading Language to create additional noise-based effects. For a deeper understanding of noise functions, consult the references listed at the end of this chapter, especially *Texturing and Modeling: A Procedural Approach, Third Edition* by David S. Ebert et al., which contains several significant discussions of noise, including a description by Perlin of his original noise function. In that book, Darwyn Peachey also provides a taxonomy of noise functions called *Making Noises*. The application of different noise functions and combinations of noise functions are discussed by Ken Musgrave in his section on building procedural planets.

As Perlin describes it, you can think of noise as "seasoning" for graphics. It often helps to add a little noise, but noise all by itself isn't all that appealing. A perfect model looks a little less perfect and, therefore, a little more realistic if some subtle noise effects are applied.

The ideal noise function has some important qualities.

- It is a continuous function that gives the appearance of randomness.

- It is a function that is repeatable (i.e., it generates the same value each time it is presented with the same input).

- It has a well-defined range of output values (usually the range is $[-1,1]$ or $[0,1]$).

- It results in values that do not show obvious regular patterns or periods.

- It is a function whose small-scale form is roughly independent of large-scale position.

- It is a function that is isotropic (i.e., its statistical character is rotationally invariant).

- It can be defined for 1, 2, 3, 4, or even more dimensions.

This definition of noise provides an irregular primitive that adds variety or an apparent element of "randomness" to a regular pattern or period. It can be used as part of modeling, rendering, or animation. Its characteristics make it a valuable tool for creating a variety of interesting effects. Algorithms for creating noise functions make various trade-offs in quality and performance, so they meet the preceding criteria with varying degrees of success.

We can construct a simple noise function (called VALUE NOISE by Peachey) by first assigning a pseudorandom number in the range $[-1,1]$ to each integer value along the x axis, as shown in Figure 15.1, and then smoothly interpolating between these points, as shown in Figure 15.2. The function is repeatable in that, for a given input value, it always returns the same output value.

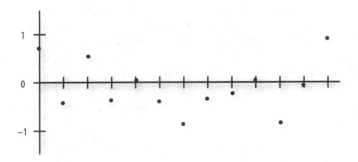

Figure 15.1   A discrete 1D noise function

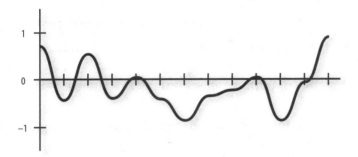

Figure 15.2   A continuous 1D noise function

A key choice to be made in this type of noise function is the method used to interpolate between successive points. Linear interpolation is not good enough, because the resulting noise pattern shows obvious artifacts. A cubic interpolation method is usually used to produce smooth-looking results.

By varying the frequency and the amplitude, you can get a variety of noise functions (see Figure 15.3).

As you can see, the "features" in these functions get smaller and closer together as the frequency increases and the amplitude decreases. When two frequencies are related by a ratio of 2:1, it's called an OCTAVE. Figure 15.3 illustrates five octaves of the 1D noise function. These images of noise don't look all that useful, but by themselves they can provide some interesting characteristics to shaders. If we add the functions at different frequencies (see Figure 15.4), we start to see something that looks even more interesting.

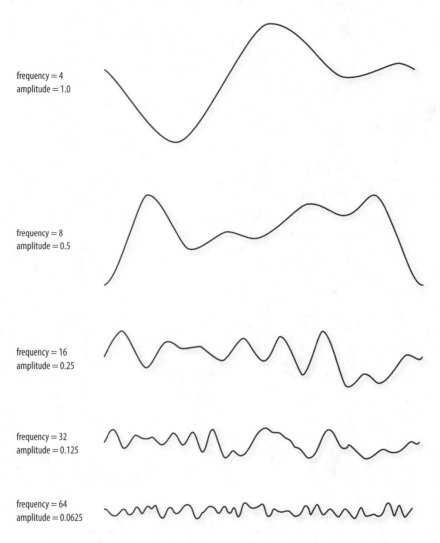

frequency = 4
amplitude = 1.0

frequency = 8
amplitude = 0.5

frequency = 16
amplitude = 0.25

frequency = 32
amplitude = 0.125

frequency = 64
amplitude = 0.0625

Figure 15.3 Varying the frequency and the amplitude of the noise function

The result is a function that contains features of various sizes. The larger bumps from the lower-frequency functions provide the overall shape, whereas the smaller bumps from the higher-frequency functions provide detail and interest at a smaller scale. The function that results from summing the noise of consecutive octaves, each at half the amplitude of the previous octave, was called 1/f noise by Perlin, but the terms "fractional Brownian motion" and "fBm" are used more commonly today.

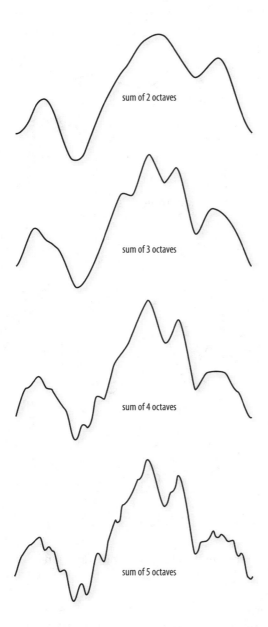

Figure 15.4   Result of summing noise functions of different amplitude and frequency

If you sum octaves of noise in a procedural shader, at some point you will begin to add frequencies that cause aliasing artifacts. Algorithms for anti-aliasing noise functions typically stop adding detail (higher-frequency noise) before this occurs. This is another key aspect of the noise function— it can be faded to the average value at the point at which aliasing artifacts would begin to occur.

The noise function defined by Perlin (PERLIN NOISE) is sometimes called GRADIENT NOISE. It is defined as a function whose value is 0 at each integer input value, and its shape is created by defining a pseudorandom gradient vector for the function at each of these points. The characteristics of this noise function make it a somewhat better choice, in general, for the effects we're after (see Ebert et al. [2002] for details). It is used for the implementation of the noise function in RenderMan, and it is also intended to be used for implementations of the **noise** function built into the OpenGL Shading Language.

Lots of other noise functions have been defined, and there are many ways to vary the basic ideas. The examples of Perlin noise shown previously have a frequency multiplier of 2, but it can be useful to use a frequency multiplier, such as 2.21, that is not an integer value. This frequency multiplier is called the LACUNARITY of the function. The word comes from the Latin word *lacuna*, which means *gap*. Using a value larger than 2 allows us to build up more "variety" more quickly (e.g., by summing fewer octaves to achieve the same apparent visual complexity). Similarly, it is not necessary to divide the amplitude of each successive octave by 2.

Summed noise functions are the basis for the terrain and features found in the planet-building software package *MojoWorld* from Pandromeda. In *Texturing and Modeling: A Procedural Approach*, Ken Musgrave defines a fractal as "a geometrically complex object, the complexity of which arises through the repetition of a given form over a range of scales." The relationship between the change in frequency and the change in amplitude determines the fractal dimension of the resulting function. If we use a noise function as the basis for generating a terrain model, we can take steps to make it behave differently at different locations. For instance, natural terrain has plains, rolling hills, foothills, and mountains. Varying the fractal dimension based on location can create a similar appearance—such a function is called a MULTIFRACTAL.

You can achieve interesting effects by using different noise functions for different situations or by combining noise functions of different types. It's not that easy to visualize in advance the results of calculations that depend on noise values, so varied experience will be a key ally as you try to achieve the effect you're after.

15.1.1 2D Noise

Armed with a basic idea of what the noise function looks like in one dimension, we can take a look at two-dimensional noise. Figure 15.5 contains images of 2D Perlin noise at various frequencies mapped into the range [0,1] and displayed as a grayscale image. Each successive image is twice the frequency of the previous one. In each image, the contrast has been enhanced to make the peaks brighter and the valleys darker. In actual use, each subsequent image has an average that is half the previous one and an amplitude that is half the previous one. If we were to print images of the actual values, the images would be much grayer, and it would be harder to see what 2D noise really looks like.

As in the 1D case, adding the different frequency functions provides more interesting results (Figure 15.6).

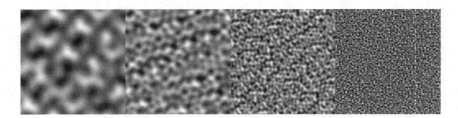

Figure 15.5   Basic 2D noise, at frequencies 4, 8, 16, and 32 (contrast enhanced)

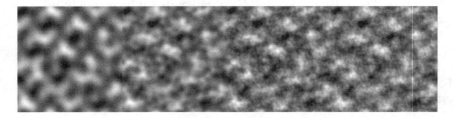

Figure 15.6   Summed noise, at 1, 2, 3, and 4 octaves (contrast enhanced)

The first image in Figure 15.6 is exactly the same as the first image in Figure 15.5. The second image in Figure 15.6 is the sum of the first image in Figure 15.6 plus half of the second image in Figure 15.5 shifted so that its average intensity value is 0. This causes intensity to be increased in some areas and decreased in others. The third image in Figure 15.6 adds the third octave of noise to the first two, and the fourth image in Figure 15.6 adds the fourth octave. The fourth picture is starting to look a little bit like clouds in the sky.

15.1.2 Higher Dimensions of Noise

3D and 4D noise functions are obvious extensions of the 1D and 2D functions. It's a little hard to generate pictures of 3D noise, but the images in Figure 15.5 can be thought of as 2D slices out of a 3D noise function. Neighboring slices have continuity between them.

Often, a higher dimension of noise is used to control the time aspect of the next lower-dimension noise function. For instance, 1D noise can add some wiggle to otherwise straight lines in a drawing. If you have a 2D noise function, one dimension can control the wiggle, and the second dimension can animate the effect (i.e., make the wiggles move in successive frames). Similarly, a 2D noise function can create a 2D cloud pattern, whereas a 3D noise function can generate the 2D cloud pattern and animate it in a realistic way. With a 4D noise function, you can create a 3D object like a planet and use the fourth dimension to watch it evolve in "fits and starts."

15.1.3 Using Noise in OpenGL Shaders

You include noise in an OpenGL shader in three ways:

1. Use the OpenGL Shading Language built-in **noise** functions.

2. Write your own noise function in the OpenGL Shading Language.

3. Use a texture map to store a previously computed noise function.

With today's graphics hardware, option 3 typically gives the best performance, so in this chapter, we look at some shaders based on this approach. In the next chapter, we look at a shader that uses the built-in **noise** functions to animate geometry. The important thing is to realize the usefulness of noise in computer-generated imagery.

15.2 Noise Textures

The programmability offered by the OpenGL Shading Language lets us use values stored in texture memory in new and unique ways. We can pre-compute a noise function and save it in a 1D, 2D, or 3D texture map. We can then access this texture map (or texture maps) from within a shader. Because textures can contain up to four components, we can use a single texture map to store four octaves of noise or four completely separate noise functions.

Listing 15.1 shows a C function that generates a 3D noise texture. This function creates an RGBA texture with the first octave of noise stored in the red texture component, the second octave stored in the green texture component, the third octave stored in the blue component, and the fourth octave stored in the alpha component. Each octave has twice the frequency and half the amplitude as the previous one.

This function assumes the existence of a **noise3** function that can generate 3D noise values in the range [–1,1]. If you want, you can start with Perlin's C implementation (available from www.texturingandmodeling.com/ CODE/PERLIN/PERLIN.C). John Kessenich made some small changes to this code (adding a **setNoiseFrequency** function) to produce noise values that wrap smoothly from one edge of the array to the other. This means we can use the texture with the wrapping mode set to GL_REPEAT, and we won't see any discontinuities in the function when it wraps. The revised version of the code is in a program from 3Dlabs called **GLSLdemo**, and the source code for this example program can be downloaded from the 3Dlabs Web site at http://developer.3dlabs.com.

Listing 15.1 C function to generate a 3D noise texture

```
int noise3DTexSize = 128;
GLuint noise3DTexName = 0;
GLubyte *noise3DTexPtr;

void make3DNoiseTexture(void)
{
    int f, i, j, k, inc;
    int startFrequency = 4;
    int numOctaves = 4;
    double ni[3];
    double inci, incj, inck;
    int frequency = startFrequency;
    GLubyte *ptr;
    double amp = 0.5;
```

```
if ((noise3DTexPtr = (GLubyte *) malloc(noise3DTexSize *
                                        noise3DTexSize *
                                        noise3DTexSize * 4)) == NULL)
{
    fprintf(stderr,"ERROR: Could not allocate 3D noise texture\n");
    exit(1);
}

for (f = 0, inc = 0; f < numOctaves;
      ++f, frequency *= 2, ++inc, amp *= 0.5)
{
    setNoiseFrequency(frequency);
    ptr = noise3DTexPtr;
    ni[0] = ni[1] = ni[2] = 0;

    inci = 1.0 / (noise3DTexSize / frequency);
    for (i = 0; i < noise3DTexSize; ++i, ni[0] += inci)
    {
        incj = 1.0 / (noise3DTexSize / frequency);
        for (j = 0; j < noise3DTexSize; ++j, ni[1] += incj)
        {
            inck = 1.0 / (noise3DTexSize / frequency);
            for (k = 0; k < noise3DTexSize; ++k, ni[2] += inck, ptr+= 4)
            {
                *(ptr+inc) = (GLubyte)(((noise3(ni)+1.0) * amp)*128.0);
            }
        }
    }
}
}
```

This function computes noise values for four octaves of noise and stores them in a 3D RGBA texture of size $128 \times 128 \times 128$. This code also assumes that each component of the texture is stored as an 8-bit integer value. The first octave has a frequency of 4 and an amplitude of 0.5. In the innermost part of the loop, we call the **noise3** function to generate a noise value based on the current value of *ni*. The **noise3** function returns a value in the range [–1,1], so by adding 1, we end up with a noise value in the range [0,2]. Multiplying by our amplitude value of 0.5 gives a value in the range [0,1]. Finally, we multiply by 128 to give us an integer value in the range [0,128] that can be stored in the red component of a texture. (When accessed from within a shader, the value is a floating-point value in the range [0,0.5].)

The amplitude value is cut in half and the frequency is doubled in each pass through the loop. The result is that integer values in the range [0,64] are stored in the green component of the noise texture, integer values in the range [0,32] are stored in the blue component of the noise texture, and

integer values in the range [0,16] are stored in the alpha component of the
texture. We generated the images in Figure 15.5 by looking at each of these
channels independently after scaling the values by a constant value that
allowed them to span the maximum intensity range (i.e., integer values in
the range [0,255] or floating-point values in the range [0,1]).

After the values for the noise texture are computed, the texture can be provided to the graphics hardware with the code in Listing 15.2. First, we pick
a texture unit and bind to it the 3D texture we've created. We set up its
wrapping parameters so that the texture wraps in all three dimensions.
This way, we always get a valid result for our noise function no matter what
input values are used. We still have to be somewhat careful to avoid using
the texture in a way that makes obvious repeating patterns. The next two
lines set the texture filtering modes to linear because the default is mipmap
linear and we're not using mipmap textures here. (Using a mipmap texture
might be appropriate in some circumstances, but we are controlling the
scaling factors from within our noise shaders, so a single texture is sufficient.) When all the parameters are set up, we can download the noise
texture to the hardware by using the **glTexImage3D** function.

Listing 15.2   A function for activating the 3D noise texture

```
void init3DNoiseTexture()
{
    glGenTextures(1, &noise3DTexName);

    glActiveTexture(GL_TEXTURE6);
    glBindTexture(GL_TEXTURE_3D, noise3DTexName);
    glTexParameterf(GL_TEXTURE_3D, GL_TEXTURE_WRAP_S, GL_REPEAT);
    glTexParameterf(GL_TEXTURE_3D, GL_TEXTURE_WRAP_T, GL_REPEAT);
    glTexParameterf(GL_TEXTURE_3D, GL_TEXTURE_WRAP_R, GL_REPEAT);
    glTexParameterf(GL_TEXTURE_3D, GL_TEXTURE_MAG_FILTER, GL_LINEAR);
    glTexParameterf(GL_TEXTURE_3D, GL_TEXTURE_MIN_FILTER, GL_LINEAR);

    glTexImage3D(GL_TEXTURE_3D, 0, GL_RGBA, noise3DTexSize,
                 noise3DTexSize, noise3DTexSize, 0, GL_RGBA,
                 GL_UNSIGNED_BYTE, noise3DTexPtr);
}
```

This is an excellent approach if the period of repeatability can be avoided
in the final rendering. One way to avoid it is to make sure that no texture
value is accessed more than once when the target object is rendered. For
instance, if a $128 \times 128 \times 128$ texture is being used and the position on the
object is used as the input to the noise function, the repeatability won't be
visible if the entire object fits within the texture.

15.3 Trade-offs

As previously mentioned, three methods can be used to generate noise values in a shader. How do you know which is the best choice for your application? A lot depends on the underlying implementation, but generally speaking, if we assume a hardware computation of noise that does not use texturing, the points favoring usage of the OpenGL Shading Language built-in **noise** function are the following:

- It doesn't consume any texture memory (a $128 \times 128 \times 128$ texture map stored as RGBA with 8 bits per component uses 8MB of texture memory).

- It doesn't use a texture unit.

- It is a continuous function rather than a discrete one, so it does not look "pixelated" no matter what the scaling is.

- The repeatability of the function should be undetectable, especially for 2D and 3D noise (but it depends on the hardware implementation).

- Shaders written with the built-in **noise** function don't depend on the application to set up appropriate textures.

The advantages of using a texture map to implement the noise function are as follows:

- Because the noise function is computed by the application, the application has total control of this function and can ensure matching behavior on every hardware platform.

- You can store four noise values (i.e., one each for the R, G, B, and A values of the texture) at each texture location. This lets you precompute four octaves of noise, for instance, and retrieve all four values with a single texture access.

- Accessing a texture map may be faster than calling the built-in **noise** function.

User-defined functions can implement noise functions that provide a different appearance from that of the built-in **noise** functions. A user-defined function can also provide matching behavior on every platform, whereas the built-in **noise** functions cannot (at least not until all graphics hardware developers support the **noise** function in exactly the same way). But hardware developers will optimize the built-in **noise** function, perhaps accelerating it with special hardware, so it is apt to be faster than user-defined noise functions.

In the long run, using the built-in **noise** function or user-defined noise functions will be the way to go for most applications. This will result in noise that doesn't show a repetitive pattern, has greater numerical precision, and doesn't use up any texture resources. Applications that want full control over the noise function and can live within the constraints of a fixed-size noise function can be successful using textures for their noise. With current generation hardware, noise textures may also provide better performance and require fewer instructions in the shader.

15.4 A Simple Noise Shader

Now we put all these ideas into some OpenGL shaders that do some interesting rendering for us. The first shader we look at uses noise in a simple way to produce a cloud effect.

15.4.1 Application Setup

Very little needs to be passed to the noise shaders discussed in this section and in Section 15.5 and Section 15.6. The vertex position must be passed in as always, and the surface normal is needed for performing lighting computations. Colors and scale factors are parameterized as uniform variables for the various shaders.

15.4.2 Vertex Shader

The code shown in Listing 15.3 is the vertex shader that we use for the four noise fragment shaders that follow. It is fairly simple because it really only needs to accomplish three things.

- As in all vertex shaders, our vertex shader transforms the incoming vertex value and stores it in the built-in special variable *gl_Position*.

- Using the incoming normal and the uniform variable *LightPos*, the vertex shader computes the light intensity from a single white light source and applies a scale factor of 1.5 to increase the amount of illumination.

- The vertex shader scales the incoming vertex value and stores it in the out variable *MCposition*. This value is available to us in our fragment shader as the modeling coordinate position of the object at every fragment. It is an ideal value to use as the input for our 3D texture lookup.

No matter how the object is drawn, fragments always produce the same position values (or very close to them); therefore, the noise value obtained for each point on the surface is also the same (or very close to it). The application can set a uniform variable called *Scale* to optimally scale the object in relationship to the size of the noise texture.

Listing 15.3   Cloud vertex shader

```
#version 140

uniform mat4 MVMatrix;
uniform mat4 MVPMatrix;
uniform mat3 NormalMatrix;

uniform vec3 LightPos;
uniform float Scale;

in  vec4  MCvertex;
in  vec3  MCnormal;

out float LightIntensity;
out vec3  MCposition;

void main()
{
   vec3 ECposition = vec3(MVMatrix * MCVertex);
   MCposition      = vec3(MCVertex) * Scale;
   vec3 tnorm      = normalize(vec3(NormalMatrix * MCNormal));
   LightIntensity  = dot(normalize(LightPos - ECposition), tnorm);
   LightIntensity *= 1.5;
   gl_Position     = MVPMatrix * MCVertex;
}
```

15.4.3 Fragment Shader

After we've computed a noise texture and used OpenGL calls to download it to the graphics card, we can use a fairly simple fragment shader together with the vertex shader described in the previous section to make an interesting "cloudy sky" effect (see Listing 15.4). This shader results in something that looks like the sky on a mostly cloudy day. You can experiment with the color values to get a result that is visually pleasing.

This fragment shader receives as input the two in variables—*LightIntensity* and *MCposition*—that were computed by the vertex shader shown in the previous section. These values were computed at each vertex by the vertex shader and then interpolated across the primitive by the rasterization hardware. Here, in our fragment shader, we have access to the interpolated value of each of these variables at every fragment.

The first line of code in the shader performs a 3D texture lookup on our 3D noise texture to produce a four-component result. We compute the value of *intensity* by summing the four components of our noise texture. This value is then scaled by 1.5 and used to perform a linear blend between two colors: white and sky blue. The four channels in our noise texture have mean values of 0.25, 0.125, 0.0625, and 0.03125. An additional 0.03125 term is added to account for the average values of all the octaves at higher frequencies. You can think of this as fading to the average values of all the higher frequency octaves that aren't being included in the calculation, as described earlier in Section 15.1. Scaling the sum by 1.5 stretches the resulting value to use up more of the range from [0,1].

The computed color is then scaled by *LightIntensity* value to simulate a diffuse surface lit by a single light source. The result is assigned to the out variable *FragColor* with an alpha value of 1.0 to produce the color value that is used by the remainder of the OpenGL pipeline. An object rendered with this shader is shown in Color Plate 24. Notice that the texture on the teapot looks a lot like the final image in Figure 15.6.

Listing 15.4   Fragment shader for cloudy sky effect

```
#version 140

uniform sampler3D Noise;
uniform vec3 SkyColor;      // (0.0, 0.0, 0.8)
uniform vec3 CloudColor;    // (0.8, 0.8, 0.8)

in  float LightIntensity;
in  vec3  MCposition;

out vec4  FragColor;

void main()
{
    vec4 noisevec = texture(Noise, MCposition);

    float intensity = (noisevec[0] + noisevec[1] +
                       noisevec[2] + noisevec[3] + 0.03125) * 1.5;

    vec3 color = mix(SkyColor, CloudColor, intensity) * LightIntensity;
    FragColor = vec4(color, 1.0);
}
```

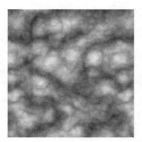

Figure 15.7 Absolute value noise or "turbulence"

15.5 Turbulence

We can obtain some additional interesting effects by taking the absolute value of the noise function. This technique introduces a discontinuity of the derivative because the function folds on itself when it reaches 0 (see Figure 5.2 for an illustration of the absolute value function). When this folding is done to noise functions at several frequencies and the results are summed, the result is cusps or creases in the texture at various scales. Perlin started referring to this type of noise as TURBULENCE because it is reminiscent of turbulent flow. It shows up in a variety of places in nature, so this type of noise can be used to simulate various things like flames or lava. The two-dimensional appearance of this type of noise is shown in Figure 15.7.

15.5.1 Sun Surface Shader

We can achieve an effect that looks like a pit of hot molten lava or the surface of the sun by using the same vertex shader as the cloud shader and a slightly different fragment shader. The main difference is that we scale each noise value and shift it over so that it is centered at 0; then we take its absolute value. After summing the values, we scale the result again to occupy nearly the full range of [0,1]. We clamp this value and use it to mix between yellow and red to get the result shown in Color Plate 24 (see Listing 15.5). (In Chapter 16, we examine some ways of animating these textures to make them more interesting.)

Listing 15.5 Sun surface fragment shader

```
#version 140

in float LightIntensity;
in vec3 MCposition;
```

```
uniform sampler3D Noise;
uniform vec3  Color1;       // (0.8, 0.7, 0.0)
uniform vec3  Color2;       // (0.6, 0.1, 0.0)
uniform float NoiseScale;   // 1.2

out vec4 FragColor;

void main()
{
    vec4 noisevec = texture(Noise, MCposition * NoiseScale);

    float intensity = abs(noisevec[0] - 0.25) +
                      abs(noisevec[1] - 0.125) +
                      abs(noisevec[2] - 0.0625) +
                      abs(noisevec[3] - 0.03125);

    intensity = clamp(intensity * 6.0, 0.0, 1.0);
    vec3 color = mix(Color1, Color2, intensity) * LightIntensity;
    FragColor = vec4(color, 1.0);
}
```

15.5.2 Marble

Yet another variation on the noise function is to use it as part of a periodic function such as sine. By adding noise to the input value for the sine function, we get a "noisy" oscillating function. We use this to create a look similar to the alternating color veins of some types of marble. Listing 15.6 shows the fragment shader to do it. Again, we use the same vertex shader. Results of this shader are also shown in Color Plate 24.

Listing 15.6   Fragment shader for marble

```
#version 140

uniform sampler3D Noise;

uniform vec3 MarbleColor;
uniform vec3 VeinColor;

in float LightIntensity;
in vec3  MCposition;

out vec4 FragColor;

void main()
{
    vec4 noisevec = texture(Noise, MCposition);
```

```
      float intensity = abs(noisevec[0] - 0.25) +
                        abs(noisevec[1] - 0.125) +
                        abs(noisevec[2] - 0.0625) +
                        abs(noisevec[3] - 0.03125);

      float sineval = sin(MCposition.y * 6.0 + intensity * 12.0) * 0.5
                        + 0.5;
      vec3 color     = mix(VeinColor, MarbleColor, sineval)
                        * LightIntensity;
      FragColor      = vec4(color, 1.0);
}
```

15.6 Granite

With noise, it's also easy just to try to make stuff up. In this example,
I wanted to simulate a grayish rocky material with small black specks. To
generate a relatively high-frequency noise texture, I used only the fourth
component (the highest frequency one). I scaled it by an arbitrary amount
to provide an appropriate intensity level and then used this value for each
of the red, green, and blue components. The shader in Listing 15.7 generates an appearance similar to granite, as shown in Color Plate 24.

Listing 15.7 Granite fragment shader

```
#version 140

uniform sampler3D Noise;

uniform float NoiseScale;

in float LightIntensity;
in vec3  MCposition;

out vec4 FragColor;

void main()
{
    vec4 noisevec   = texture(Noise, NoiseScale * MCposition);
    float intensity = min(1.0, noisevec[3] * 18.0);
    vec3 color      = vec3(intensity * LightIntensity);
    FragColor       = vec4(color, 1.0);
}
```

15.7 Wood

We can do a fair approximation of wood with this approach as well. In *Advanced Renderman*, Anthony A. Apodaca and Larry Gritz describe a model for simulating the appearance of wood. We can adapt their approach to create wood shaders in the OpenGL Shading Language. Here are the basic ideas behind the wood fragment shader shown in Listing 15.8:

- The wood is composed of light and dark areas alternating in concentric cylinders surrounding a central axis.

- Noise is added to warp the cylinders to create a more natural-looking pattern.

- The center of the "tree" is taken to be the y axis.

- Throughout the wood, a high-frequency grain pattern gives the appearance of wood that has been sawed, exposing the open grain nature of the wood.

The wood shader uses the same vertex shader as the other noise-based shaders discussed in this chapter.

15.7.1 Application Setup

The wood shaders don't require too much from the application. The application is expected to pass in a vertex position and a normal per vertex, using the usual OpenGL entry points. In addition, the vertex shader takes a light position and a scale factor that are passed in as uniform variables. The fragment shader takes a number of uniform variables that parameterize the appearance of the wood.

The uniform variables needed for the wood shaders are initialized as follows:

```
LightPos          0.0, 0.0, 4.0
Scale             2.0
LightWood         0.6, 0.3, 0.1
DarkWood          0.4, 0.2, 0.07
RingFreq          4.0
LightGrains       1.0
DarkGrains        0.0
GrainThreshold    0.5
NoiseScale        0.5, 0.1, 0.1
Noisiness         3.0
GrainScale        27.0
```

15.7.2 Fragment Shader

Listing 15.8 shows the fragment shader for procedurally generated wood.

Listing 15.8 Fragment shader for wood

```
#version 140

uniform sampler3D Noise;

uniform vec3 LightWood;
uniform vec3 DarkWood;
uniform float RingFreq;
uniform float LightGrains;
uniform float DarkGrains;
uniform float GrainThreshold;
uniform vec3 NoiseScale;
uniform float Noisiness;
uniform float GrainScale;

in  float LightIntensity;
in  vec3  MCposition;

out vec4  FragColor;

void main()
{
    vec3 noisevec = vec3(texture(Noise, MCposition * NoiseScale) *
                                            Noisiness);
    vec3 location = MCposition + noisevec;

    float dist = sqrt(location.x * location.x + location.z * location.z);
    dist *= RingFreq;

    float r = fract(dist + noisevec[0] + noisevec[1] + noisevec[2])
            * 2.0;

    if (r > 1.0)
        r = 2.0 - r;

    vec3 color = mix(LightWood, DarkWood, r);

    r = fract((MCposition.x + MCposition.z) * GrainScale + 0.5);
    noisevec[2] *= r;
    if (r < GrainThreshold)
        color += LightWood * LightGrains * noisevec[2];
    else
        color -= LightWood * DarkGrains * noisevec[2];

    color *= LightIntensity;
    FragColor = vec4(color, 1.0);
}
```

As you can see, we've parameterized quite a bit of this shader through the use of uniform variables to make it easy to manipulate through the application's user interface. As in many procedural shaders, the object position is the basis for computing the procedural texture. In this case, the object position is multiplied by *NoiseScale* (a **vec3** that allows us to scale the noise independently in the *x*, *y*, and *z* directions), and the computed value is used as the index into our 3D noise texture. The noise values obtained from the texture are scaled by the value *Noisiness*, which allows us to increase or decrease the contribution of the noise.

Our tree is assumed to be a series of concentric rings of alternating light wood and dark wood. To give some interest to our grain pattern, we add the noise vector to our object position. This has the effect of adding our low frequency (first octave) noise to the *x* coordinate of the position and the third octave noise to the *z* coordinate (the *y* coordinate won't be used). The result is rings that are still relatively circular but have some variation in width and distance from the center of the tree.

To compute where we are in relation to the center of the tree, we square the *x* and *z* components and take the square root of the result. This gives us the distance from the center of the tree. The distance is multiplied by *RingFreq*, a scale factor that gives the wood pattern more rings or fewer rings.

Following this, we attempt to create a function that goes from 0 up to 1.0 and then back down to 0. We add three octaves of noise to the distance value to give more interest to the wood grain pattern. We could compute different noise values here, but the ones we've already obtained will do just fine. Taking the fractional part of the resulting value gives us a function in the range [0.0, 1.0). Multiplying this value by 2.0 gives us a function in the range [0.0, 2.0). And finally, by subtracting 1.0 from values that are greater than 1.0, we get our desired function that varies from 0 to 1.0 and back to 0.

We use this "triangle" function to compute the basic color for the fragment, using the built-in **mix** function. The **mix** function linearly blends *LightWood* and *DarkWood* according to our computed value *r*.

At this point, we would have a pretty nice result for our wood function, but we attempt to make it a little better by adding a subtle effect to simulate the look of open-grain wood that has been sawed. (You may not be able to see this effect on the object shown in Color Plate 25.)

Our desire is to produce streaks that are roughly parallel to the *y* axis. So we add the *x* and *z* coordinates, multiply by the *GrainScale* factor (another uniform variable that we can adjust to change the frequency of this effect), add 0.5, and take the fractional part of the result. Again, this gives us a function that varies from [0.0, 1.0), but for the default values for *GrainScale* (27.0) and *RingFreq* (4.0), this function for *r* goes from 0 to 1.0 much more often than our previous function for *r*.

We could just make our "grains" go linearly from light to dark, but we try something a little more subtle. We multiply the value of *r* by our third octave noise value to produce a value that increases nonlinearly. Finally, we compare our value of *r* to the *GrainThreshold* value (the default is 0.5). If the value of *r* is less than *GrainThreshold*, we modify our current color by adding to it a value we computed by multiplying the *LightWood* color, the *LightGrains* color, and our modified noise value. Conversely, if the value of *r* is greater than *GrainThreshold*, we modify our current color by subtracting from it a value we computed by multiplying the *DarkWood* color, the *DarkGrains* color, and our modified noise value. (By default, the value of *LightGrains* is 1.0, and the value of *DarkGrains* is 0, so we don't actually see any change if *r* is greater than *GrainThreshold*.)

You can play around with this effect and see if it really does help the appearance. It seemed to me that it added to the effect of the wood texture for the default settings I've chosen, but there probably is a way to achieve a better effect more simply.

With our final color computed, all that remains is to multiply the color by the interpolated diffuse lighting factor and add an alpha value of 1.0 to produce our final fragment value. The results of our shader are applied to a bust of Beethoven in Color Plate 25.

15.8 Summary

This chapter introduced noise, an incredibly useful function for adding irregularity to procedural shaders. After a brief description of the mathematical definition of this function, we used it as the basis for shaders that simulated clouds, turbulent flow, marble, granite, and wood. The noise function is available as a built-in function in the OpenGL Shading Language. Noise functions can also be created with user-defined shader functions or textures. However it is implemented, noise can increase the apparent realism of an image or an animation by adding imperfections, complexity, and an element of apparent randomness.

15.9 Further Information

Ken Perlin has a tutorial and history of the noise function as well as a recent reference implementation in the Java programming language at his Web site (www.noisemachine.com). A lot of other interesting things are available on Ken's home page at NYU (http://mrl.nyu.edu/~perlin). His paper, *An Image Synthesizer*, appeared in the 1985 SIGGRAPH proceedings, and his improvements to the original algorithm were published in the paper *Improving Noise* as part of SIGGRAPH 2002. He also described a clever method for combining two small 3D textures to get a large 3D Perlin-like noise function in the article *Implementing Improved Perlin Noise* in the book *GPU Gems*.

The book *Texturing & Modeling: A Procedural Approach, Third Edition*, by David S. Ebert et al. (2000) contains several excellent discussions on noise, and that book's Web site, www.texturingandmodeling.com contains C source code for a variety of noise functions that appear in the book, including Perlin's original noise function. Perlin has written a chapter for that book that provides more depth on his noise algorithm, and Ken Musgrave explores breathtakingly beautiful mathematical worlds based on a variety of noise functions. Planet-building software built on these ideas is available from Musgrave's company, Pandromeda, at www.pandromeda.com. In Chapter 2 of that book, Darwyn Peachey describes a variety of noise functions, and in Chapter 7, David Ebert describes an approach similar to the 3D texturing approach described previously. *Advanced RenderMan: Creating CGI for Motion Pictures* by Anthony A. Apodaca and Larry Gritz (1999) also contains a discussion of noise and presents some excellent noise-based RenderMan shaders.

[1] Apodaca, Anthony A., and Larry Gritz, *Advanced RenderMan: Creating CGI for Motion Pictures*, Morgan Kaufmann Publishers, San Francisco, 1999. www.renderman.org/RMR/Books/arman/materials.html

[2] Ebert, David S., John Hart, Bill Mark, F. Kenton Musgrave, Darwyn Peachey, Ken Perlin, and Steven Worley, *Texturing and Modeling: A Procedural Approach, Third Edition*, Morgan Kaufmann Publishers, San Francisco, 2002. www.texturingandmodeling.com

[3] Hart, John C., *Perlin Noise Pixel Shaders*, ACM SIGGRAPH/Eurographics Workshop on Graphics Hardware, pp. 87–94, August 2001. http://graphics.cs.uiuc.edu/~jch/papers/pixelnoise.pdf

[4] Perlin, Ken, *An Image Synthesizer*, Computer Graphics (SIGGRAPH '85 Proceedings), pp. 287–296, July 1985.

[5] Perlin, Ken, *Implementing Improved Perlin Noise* in *GPU Gems:*
     Programming Techniques, Tips, and Tricks for Real-Time Graphics,
     Editor: Randima Fernando, Addison-Wesley, Reading,
     Massachusetts, 2004. http://developer.nvidia.com/object/
     gpu_gems_home.html

[6] Perlin, Ken, *Improving Noise*, Computer Graphics (SIGGRAPH 2002
     Proceedings), pp. 681–682, July 2002.
     http://mrl.nyu.edu/perlin/paper445.pdf

[7] Perlin, Ken, personal Web site. www.noisemachine.com

[8] Perlin, Ken, personal Web site. http://mrl.nyu.edu/~perlin

Chapter 16

Animation

> *Animation can explain whatever the mind of man can conceive. This facility makes it the most versatile and explicit means of communication yet devised for quick mass appreciation.*
>
> —Walt Disney

As Walt Disney noted, animation is largely about explanation. Rotating an object provides information about shape and form. Doing a simulated walk-through of a building gives a sense of how it would feel to be inside the building. Watching a character's facial expressions provides insight into the emotions the character is feeling.

With the latest graphics hardware and the OpenGL Shading Language, we can do even more realistic rendering in real time on low-cost graphics hardware. I was somewhat surprised when I found out how easy it was to animate programmable shaders. By developing shaders that modify their behavior over time, we can turn over even more of the rendering task to the graphics hardware.

This chapter describes how a shader can be written to produce an animation effect. Typically, the animation effect is controlled by one or more uniform variables that convey an application's sense of time. These variables pass a frame count, an elapsed time value, or some other value that can be used as the basis for chronology. If there are multiple objects in a scene and they are expected to animate in different ways, each object is rendered with its own unique shader. If objects have identical characteristics other than the animation effect, the source code for each of the shaders can be the same except for the portion that defines the animation effect.

A shader can be written to behave differently depending on these control values, and so, if they are updated at each frame, the scene is drawn slightly differently in each frame to produce the animation effect. Discontinuities in cyclical motion can be avoided by design, with a smooth overlap whereby the end of the cycle wraps back to the beginning. By controlling the animation effect in an OpenGL shader, the application need not perform any complex computations to achieve this motion. All it needs to do is update the control value(s) of each frame and redraw the object. However, the application can perform animation computations in addition to the animation effects built into a shader to produce extremely interesting effects.

Interesting animation effects can be created with stored textures, procedural textures, noise, and other mechanisms. In this chapter, we describe simple animation effects and discuss shaders for modifying the shape and position of an object and for simulating an oscillating motion.

16.1 On/Off

Suppose you have an object in the scene that must be drawn two different ways, such as a neon restaurant sign saying "OPEN" that repeatedly flashes on and off. It would certainly be possible to write two different shaders for rendering this object, one for when the sign is "on" and one for when the sign is "off." However, in a situation like this, it may actually be easier to write a single shader that takes a control variable specifying whether the object is to be drawn as on or off. The shader can be written to render one way if the control variable is on and another way if it is off.

To do this, the application would set up a uniform variable that indicates the on/off state. The application would update this variable as needed. To achieve a sequence of three seconds on and one second off, the application would write the variable with the value for on, update the value to off three seconds later, update the value to on one second later, and repeat this sequence. In the interim, the application just continually redraws the geometry every frame. The decoupling of the rendering from the animation effect might make the application a little simpler and a little more maintainable as a result.

16.2 Threshold

An improvement to the "on/off" animation is to have the application pass the shader one or more values that are tested against one or more threshold values within the shader. Using one control value and two threshold values, you could write a shader with three behaviors: one for when the control value is less than the first threshold value, one for when the control value is between the two threshold values, and one for when the control value is greater than the second threshold value.

In the case just described, you actually may have a transition period when the neon light is warming up to full brightness or dissipating to its off condition. This type of transition helps to "soften" the change between two states so that the transition appears more natural. The **smoothstep** function is handy for calculating such a transition.

16.3 Translation

We can achieve a simple animation effect for stored textures or procedural textures just by adding an offset to the texture access calculation. For instance, if we wanted to have procedural clouds that drift slowly across the sky, we could make a simple change to the cloud shader that we discussed in Section 15.4. Instead of using the object position as the index into our 3D noise texture, we add an offset value. The offset is defined as a uniform variable and can be updated by the application at each frame. If we want the clouds to drift slowly from left to right, we just subtract a small amount from the *x* component of this uniform variable each frame. If we want the clouds to move rapidly from bottom to top, we just subtract a larger amount from the *y* component of this value. To achieve a more complex effect, we might modify all three coordinates each frame. We could use a noise function in computing this offset to make the motion more natural and less like a scrolling effect.

The cloud shader as modified so as to be animatable is shown in Listing 16.1.

Listing 16.1   Animatable fragment shader for cloudy sky effect

```
#version 140

uniform sampler3D Noise;
uniform vec3 SkyColor;      // (0.0, 0.0, 0.8)
uniform vec3 CloudColor;    // (0.8, 0.8, 0.8)
```

```
uniform vec3 Offset;         // updated each frame by the application

in   float LightIntensity;
in   vec3  MCPosition;
out vec4  FragColor;

void main()
{
    vec4   noisevec  = texture(Noise, MCPosition + Offset);

    float intensity = (noisevec[0] + noisevec[1] +
                        noisevec[2] + noisevec[3]) * 0.33;

    vec3 color = mix(SkyColor, CloudColor, intensity) * LightIntensity;
    FragColor = vec4(color, 1.0);
}
```

16.4 Morphing

Another cool animation effect, called MORPHING, gradually blends between two things. This could be used to mix two effects over a sequence of frames. A complete animation sequence can be created by performing KEY-FRAME INTERPOLATION. Important frames of the animation are identified, and the frames in between them can be generated with substantially less effort. Instead of the application doing complex calculations to determine the proper way to render the "in between" object or effect, it can all be done automatically within the shader.

You can blend between the geometry of two objects to create a TWEENED (INBETWEEN) version or do a linear blend between two colors, two textures, two procedural patterns, and so on. All it takes is a shader that uses a control value that is the ratio of the two items being blended and that is updated each frame by the application. In some cases, a linear blend is sufficient. For an oscillating effect, you'll probably want to have the application compute the interpolation factor by using a spline function to avoid jarring discontinuities in the animation. (You could have the shader compute the interpolation value, but it's better to have the application compute it once per frame rather than have the vertex shader compute it once per vertex or have the fragment shader compute it needlessly at every fragment.)

For instance, using generic vertex attributes, you can actually pass the geometry for two objects at a time. The geometry for the first object would be passed through a second of generic vertex attributes 0, 2, 4. A second set of vertex information can be passed by means of generic vertex attributes 1, 3, 5, etc. The application can provide a blending factor through a uniform variable, and the vertex shader can use this blending factor to do a weighted average of the two sets of vertex data. The tweened vertex position is the one that actually gets transformed, the tweened normal is the one actually used for lighting calculations, and so on.

To animate a character realistically, you need to choose the right number of key frames as well as the proper number of inbetweens to use. In their classic book, *Disney Animation—The Illusion of Life,* Frank Thomas and Ollie Johnston (1995, pp. 64–65) describe this concept as "Timing" and explain it in the following way:

> *Just two drawings of a head, the first showing it leaning toward the right shoulder and the second with it over on the left and its chin slightly raised, can be made to communicate a multitude of ideas, depending entirely on the Timing used. Each inbetween drawing added between these two "extremes" gives a new meaning to the action.*

No inbetweens	*The character has been hit by a tremendous force. His head is nearly snapped off.*
One inbetween	*. . . has been hit by a brick, rolling pin, frying pan.*
Two inbetweens	*. . . has a nervous tic, a muscle spasm, an uncontrollable twitch.*
Three inbetweens	*. . . is dodging the brick, rolling pin, frying pan.*
Four inbetweens	*. . . is giving a crisp order, "Get going!" "Move it!"*
Five inbetweens	*. . . is more friendly, "Over here." "Come on—hurry!"*
Six inbetweens	*. . . sees a good-looking girl, or the sports car he has always wanted.*
Seven inbetweens	*. . . tries to get a better look at something.*
Eight inbetweens	*. . . searches for the peanut butter on the kitchen shelf.*
Nine inbetweens	*. . . appraises, considering thoughtfully.*
Ten inbetweens	*. . . stretches a sore muscle.*

16.4.1   Sphere Morph Vertex Shader

The shader in Listing 16.2, developed by Philip Rideout, morphs between two objects—a square that is generated by the application and a sphere that is procedurally generated in the vertex shader. The sphere is defined entirely by a single value—its radius—provided by the application through a uniform variable. The application passes the geometry defining the square to the vertex shader with the user-defined in variables *MCNormal* and *MCVertex*. The vertex shader computes the corresponding vertex and normal on the sphere with a subroutine called **sphere**. The application provides a time-varying variable (*Blend*) for morphing between these two objects. Because we are using the two input vertex values to compute a third, in-between, value, we cannot use the **ftransform** function. We'll transform the computed vertex directly within the vertex shader.

Listing 16.2   Vertex shader for morphing between a plane and a sphere

```
#version 140

uniform mat4 MVPMatrix;
uniform mat4 MVMatrix;
uniform mat3 NormalMatrix;

uniform vec3 LightPosition;
uniform vec3 SurfaceColor;

uniform float Radius;
uniform float Blend;

const float PI = 3.14159;
const float TWO_PI = PI * 2.0;

in   vec4   MCVertex;
in   vec4   MCNormal;

out vec4   Color;

vec3 sphere(vec2 domain)
{
    vec3 range;
    range.x = Radius * cos(domain.y) * sin(domain.x);
    range.y = Radius * sin(domain.y) * sin(domain.x);
    range.z = Radius * cos(domain.x);
    return range;
}

void main()
{
```

```
        vec2 p0 = MCVertex.xy * TWO_PI;
        vec3 normal = sphere(p0);;
        vec3 r0 = Radius * normal;
        vec3 vertex = r0;

        normal = mix(MCNormal, normal, abs(Blend));
        vertex = mix(MCVertex.xyz, vertex, abs(Blend));

        normal = normalize(NormalMatrix * normal);
        vec3 position = vec3(MVMatrix * vec4(vertex, 1.0));

        vec3 lightVec = normalize(LightPosition - position);
        float diffuse = max(dot(lightVec, normal), 0.0);

        if (diffuse < 0.125)
            diffuse = 0.125;

        Color = vec4(SurfaceColor * diffuse, 1.0);
        gl_Position = MVPMatrix * vec4(vertex,1.0);
}
```

In this shader, a simple lighting model is used. The color value that is generated by the vertex shader is simply passed through the fragment shader to be used as our final fragment color.

The sphere is somewhat unique in that it can be procedurally generated. Another way to morph between two objects is to specify the geometry for one object and to specify the geometry for the second object, using generic vertex attributes. The shader then just has to blend between the two sets of geometry in the same manner as described for the sphere morph shader.

16.5   Other Blending Effects

Another blending effect gradually causes an object to disappear over a sequence of frames. The control value could be used as the alpha value to cause the object to be drawn totally opaque (alpha is 1.0), totally invisible (alpha is 0), or partially visible (alpha is between 0 and 1.0).

You can also fade something in or out by using the **discard** keyword. The lattice shader described in Section 11.3 discards a specific percentage of pixels in the object each time it is drawn. You could vary this percentage from 0 to 1.0 to make the object appear, or vary from 1.0 to 0 to make the object disappear. Alternatively, you could evaluate a noise function at each location on the surface and compare with this value instead. In this way, you can cause an object to erode or rust away over time.

16.6 Vertex Noise

In the previous chapter, we talked about some of the interesting and useful things that can be done with noise. Listing 16.3 shows a vertex shader by Philip Rideout that calls the built-in **noise3** function in the vertex shader and uses it to modify the shape of the object over time. The result is that the object changes its shape irregularly.

Listing 16.3   Vertex shader using noise to modify and animate an object's shape

```
#version 140

uniform vec3  LightPosition;
uniform vec3  SurfaceColor;
uniform vec3  Offset;
uniform float ScaleIn;
uniform float ScaleOut;

uniform mat4  MVMatrix;
uniform mat4  MVPMatrix;
uniform mat3  NormalMatrix;

in  vec4  MCVertex;
in  vec3  MCNormal;

out vec4  Color;

void main()
{
    vec3 normal = MCNormal;
    vec3 vertex = MCVertex.xyz
                + noise3(Offset + MCVertex.xyz * ScaleIn) * ScaleOut;

    normal = normalize(NormalMatrix * normal);
    vec3 position = vec3(MVMatrix * vec4(vertex,1.0));
    vec3 lightVec = normalize(LightPosition - position);
    float diffuse = max(dot(lightVec, normal), 0.0);

    if (diffuse < 0.125)
        diffuse = 0.125;

    Color = vec4(SurfaceColor * diffuse, 1.0);
    gl_Position = MVPMatrix * vec4(vertex,1.0);
}
```

The key to this shader is the call to **noise3** with a value (*Offset*) that changes over time. The vertex itself is also used as input to the **noise3** function so that the effect is repeatable. The *ScaleIn* and *ScaleOut* factors control the amplitude of the effect. The result of this computation is added to the incoming vertex position to compute a new vertex position.

16.7 Particle Systems

A new type of rendering primitive was invented by Bill Reeves and his colleagues at Lucasfilm in the early 1980s as they struggled to come up with a way to animate the fire sequence called "The Genesis Demo" in the motion picture *Star Trek II: The Wrath of Khan*. Traditional rendering methods were more suitable for rendering smooth, well-defined surfaces. What Reeves was after was a way to render a class of objects he called "fuzzy"—things like fire, smoke, liquid spray, comet tails, fireworks, and other natural phenomena. These things are fuzzy because none of them has a well-defined boundary and the components typically change over time.

The technique that Reeves invented to solve this problem was described in the 1983 paper *Particle Systems—A Technique for Modeling a Class of Fuzzy Objects*. PARTICLE SYSTEMS had been used in rendering before, but Reeves realized that he could get the particles to behave the way he wanted them to by giving each particle its own set of initial conditions and by establishing a set of probabilistic rules that governed how particles would change over time.

There are three main differences between particle systems and traditional surface-based rendering techniques. First, rather than an object being defined with polygons or curved surfaces, it is represented by a cloud of primitive particles that define its volume. Second, the object is considered dynamic rather than static. The constituent particles come into existence, evolve, and then die. During their lifetime, they can change position and form. Finally, objects defined in this manner are not completely specified. A set of initial conditions are specified, along with rules for birth, death, and evolution. Stochastic processes are used to influence all three stages, so the shape and appearance of the object is nondeterministic.

Some assumptions are usually made to simplify the rendering of particle systems, among them,

- Particles do not collide with other particles.

- Particles do not reflect light; they emit light.

- Particles do not cast shadows on other particles.

Particle attributes often include position, color, transparency, velocity, size, shape, and lifetime. For rendering a particle system, each particle's attributes are used along with certain global parameters to update its position and appearance at each frame. Each particle's position might be updated on the basis of the initial velocity vector and the effects from gravity, wind, friction, and other global factors. Each particle's color (including transparency), size, and shape can be modified as a function of global time, the age of the particle, its height, its speed, or any other parameter that can be calculated.

What are the benefits of using particle systems as a rendering technique? For one thing, complex systems can be created with little human effort. For another, the complexity can easily be adjusted. And as Reeves says in his 1983 paper, "The most important thing about particle systems is that they move: good dynamics are quite often the key to making things look real."

16.7.1 Application Setup

For this shader, my goal was to produce a shader that acted like a "confetti cannon"—something that spews out a large quantity of small, brightly colored pieces of paper. They don't come out all at once, but they come out in a steady stream until none are left. Initial velocities are somewhat random, but there is a general direction that points up and away from the origin. Gravity influences these particles and eventually brings them back to earth.

The code in Listing 16.4 shows the C subroutine that I used to create the initial values for my particle system. To accomplish the look I was after, I decided that for each particle I needed its initial position, a randomly generated color, a randomly generated initial velocity (with some constraints), and a randomly generated start time.

The subroutine **createPoints** lets you create an arbitrary-sized, two-dimensional grid of points for the particle system. There's no reason for a two-dimensional grid, but I was interested in seeing the effect of particles "popping off the grid" like pieces of popcorn. It would be even easier to define the particle system as a 1D array, and all of the vertex positions could have exactly the same initial value (for instance (0,0,0)).

But I set it up as a 2D array, and so you can pass in a width and height to define the number of particles to be created. After the memory for the arrays is allocated, a nested loop computes the values for each of the particle attributes at each grid location. Each vertex position has a y-coordinate value of 0, and the x and z coordinates vary across the grid. Each color component is assigned a random number in the range [0.5,1.0] so that mostly bright pastel colors are used. The velocity vectors are assigned random numbers to which I gave a strong upward bias by multiplying the y coordinate by 10. The general direction of the particles is aimed away from the origin by the addition of 3 to both the x and the z coordinates. Finally, each particle is given a start-time value in the range [0,10].

Listing 16.4   C subroutine to create vertex data for particles

```c
static GLint arrayWidth, arrayHeight;
static GLfloat *verts = NULL;
static GLfloat *colors = NULL;
static GLfloat *velocities = NULL;
static GLfloat *startTimes = NULL;

void createPoints(GLint w, GLint h)
{
    GLfloat *vptr, *cptr, *velptr, *stptr;
    GLfloat i, j;

    if (verts != NULL)
        free(verts);

    verts  = malloc(w * h * 3 * sizeof(float));
    colors = malloc(w * h * 3 * sizeof(float));
    velocities = malloc(w * h * 3 * sizeof(float));
    startTimes = malloc(w * h * sizeof(float));

    vptr = verts;
    cptr = colors;
    velptr = velocities;
    stptr  = startTimes;

    for (i = 0.5 / w - 0.5; i < 0.5; i = i + 1.0/w)
        for (j = 0.5 / h - 0.5; j < 0.5; j = j + 1.0/h)
        {
            *vptr       = i;
            *(vptr + 1) = 0.0;
            *(vptr + 2) = j;
            vptr += 3;

            *cptr       = ((float) rand() / RAND_MAX) * 0.5 + 0.5;
            *(cptr + 1) = ((float) rand() / RAND_MAX) * 0.5 + 0.5;
            *(cptr + 2) = ((float) rand() / RAND_MAX) * 0.5 + 0.5;
            cptr += 3;

            *velptr       = (((float) rand() / RAND_MAX)) + 3.0;
            *(velptr + 1) =  ((float) rand() / RAND_MAX) * 10.0;
            *(velptr + 2) = (((float) rand() / RAND_MAX)) + 3.0;
            velptr += 3;

            *stptr = ((float) rand() / RAND_MAX) * 10.0;
            stptr++;
        }

    arrayWidth  = w;
    arrayHeight = h;
}
```

We need to use generic vertex attributes to specify the particle's position, color, initial velocity, and start time. Let's pick indices 3 and 4 and define the necessary constants:

```
#define VERTEX_ARRAY 1
#define COLOR_ARRAY 2
#define VELOCITY_ARRAY 3
#define START_TIME_ARRAY 4
```

After we have created a program object, we can bind a generic vertex attribute index to a vertex shader attribute variable name. (We can do this even before the vertex shader is attached to the program object.) These bindings are checked and go into effect at the time **glLinkProgram** is called. To bind the generic vertex attribute index to a vertex shader variable name, we do the following:

```
glBindAttribLocation(ProgramObject, VERTEX_ARRAY, "MCVertex");
glBindAttribLocation(ProgramObject, COLOR_ARRAY, "MColor");
glBindAttribLocation(ProgramObject, VELOCITY_ARRAY, "Velocity");
glBindAttribLocation(ProgramObject, START_TIME_ARRAY, "StartTime");
```

After the shaders are compiled, attached to the program object, and linked, we're ready to draw the particle system. All we need to do is call the **drawPoints** function shown in Listing 16.5. In this function, we set the point size to 2 to render somewhat larger points. The next four lines of code set up pointers to the vertex arrays that we're using. In this case, we have four: one for vertex positions (i.e., initial particle position), one for particle color, one for initial velocity, and one for the particle's start time (i.e., birth). After that, we enable the arrays for drawing by making calls to **glEnableVertexAttribArray** for the generic vertex attributes. Next we call **glDrawArrays** to render the points, and finally, we clean up by disabling each of the enabled vertex arrays.

Listing 16.5   C subroutine to draw particles as points

```
void drawPoints()
{

    glPointSize(2.0);

    glVertexAttribPointer(VERTEX_ARRAY,      3, GL_FLOAT,
                          GL_FALSE,  0, verts);
    glVertexAttribPointer(COLOR_ARRAY,       3, GL_FLOAT,
                          GL_FALSE,  0, colors);
    glVertexAttribPointer(VELOCITY_ARRAY,    3, GL_FLOAT,
                          GL_FALSE,  0, velocities);
```

```
glVertexAttribPointer(START_TIME_ARRAY, 1, GL_FLOAT,
                      GL_FALSE,  0, startTimes);

glEnableVertexAttribArray(VERTEX_ARRAY);
glEnableVertexAttribArray(COLOR_ARRAY);
glEnableVertexAttribArray(VELOCITY_ARRAY);
glEnableVertexAttribArray(START_TIME_ARRAY);

glDrawArrays(GL_POINTS, 0, arrayWidth * arrayHeight);

glDisableVertexAttribArray(VERTEX_ARRAY);
glDisableVertexAttribArray(COLOR_ARRAY);
glDisableVertexAttribArray(VELOCITY_ARRAY);
glDisableVertexAttribArray(START_TIME_ARRAY);
}
```

To achieve the animation effect, the application must communicate its notion of time to the vertex shader, as shown in Listing 16.6. Here, the variable *ParticleTime* is incremented once each frame and loaded into the uniform variable *Time*. This allows the vertex shader to perform computations that vary (animate) over time.

Listing 16.6   C code snippet to update the time variable each frame

```
if (DoingParticles)
{
    location = glGetUniformLocation(ProgramObject, "Time");
    ParticleTime += 0.001f;
    glUniform1f(location, ParticleTime);
    CheckOglError();
}
```

16.7.2 Confetti Cannon Vertex Shader

The vertex shader (see Listing 16.7) is the key to this example of particle system rendering. Instead of simply transforming the incoming vertex, we use it as the initial position to compute a new position based on a computation involving the uniform variable *Time*. It is this newly computed position that is actually transformed and rendered.

This vertex shader defines the in variables *MCVertex*, *MColor*, *Velocity*, and *StartTime*. In the previous section, we saw how generic vertex attribute arrays were defined and bound to these vertex shader attribute variables. As a result of this, each vertex has an updated value for the in variables *MCVertex*, *MColor*, *Velocity*, and *StartTime*.

The vertex shader starts by computing the age of the particle. If this value is less than zero, the particle has not yet been born. In this case, the particle is just assigned the color provided through the uniform variable *Background*. (If you actually want to see the grid of yet-to-be-born particles, you could provide a color value other than the background color. And if you want to be a bit more clever, you could pass the value *t* as a varying variable to the fragment shader and let it discard fragments for which *t* is less than zero. For our purposes, this wasn't necessary.)

If a particle's start time is less than the current time, the following kinematic equation is used to determine its current position:

$$P = P_i + vt + \frac{1}{2}at^2$$

In this equation P_i represents the initial position of the particle, *v* represents the initial velocity, *t* represents the elapsed time, *a* represents the acceleration, and *P* represents the final computed position. For acceleration, we use the value of acceleration due to gravity on Earth, which is 9.8 meters per second^2. In our simplistic model, we assume that gravity affects only the particle's height (*y* coordinate) and that the acceleration is negative (i.e., the particle is slowing down and falling back to the ground). The coefficient for the t^2 term in the preceding equation therefore appears in our code as the constant −4.9, and it is applied only to *vert.y*.

After this, all that remains is to transform the computed vertex and store the result in *gl_Position*.

Listing 16.7   Confetti cannon (particle system) vertex shader

```
#version 140

uniform float Time;           // updated each frame by the application
uniform vec4  Background;     // constant color equal to background

uniform mat4  MVPMatrix;

in   vec4  MCVertex;
in   vec4  MColor;

in   vec3  Velocity;      // initial velocity
in   float StartTime;     // time at which particle is activated

out  vec4  Color;
```

```
void main()
{
    vec4  vert;
    float t = Time - StartTime;

    if (t >= 0.0)
    {
        vert      = MCVertex + vec4(Velocity * t, 0.0);
        vert.y -= 4.9 * t * t;
        Color    = MColor;
    }
    else
    {
        vert  = MCVertex;        // Initial position
        Color = Background;      // "pre-birth" color
    }

    gl_Position  = MVPMatrix * vert;
}
```

The value computed by the vertex shader is simply passed through the fragment shader to become the final color of the fragment to be rendered. Some frames from the confetti cannon animation sequence are shown in Figure 16.1.

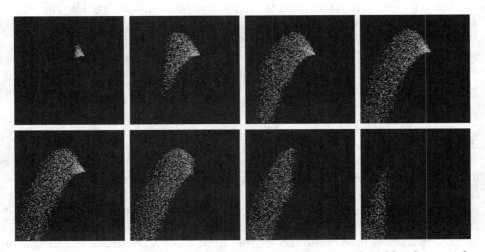

Figure 16.1   Several frames from the animated sequence produced by the particle system shader. In this animation, the particle system contains 10,000 points with randomly assigned initial velocities and start times. The position of the particle at each frame is computed entirely in the vertex shader according to a formula that simulates the effects of gravity. (3Dlabs, Inc.)

16.7.3 Further Enhancements

There's a lot that you can do to make this shader more interesting. You might pass the *t* value from the vertex shader to the fragment shader as suggested earlier and make the color of the particle change over time. For instance, you could make the color change from yellow to red to black to simulate an explosion. You could reduce the alpha value over time to make the particle fade out. You might also provide a "time of death" and extinguish the particle completely at a certain time or when a certain distance from the origin is reached. Instead of drawing the particles as points, you might draw them as short lines so that you could blur the motion of each particle. You could also vary the size of the point (or line) over time to create particles that grow or shrink. You can make the physics model a lot more sophisticated than the one illustrated. To make the particles look better, you could render them as point sprites. A point sprite is a point that is rendered as a textured quadrilateral that always faces the viewer.

The real beauty in doing particle systems within a shader is that the computation is done completely in graphics hardware rather than on the host CPU. If the particle system data is stored in a vertex buffer object, there's a good chance that it will be stored in the on-board memory of the graphics hardware, so you won't even be using up any I/O bus bandwidth as you render the particle system each frame. With the OpenGL Shading Language, the equation for updating each particle can be arbitrarily complex. And, because the particle system is rendered like any other 3D object, you can rotate it around and view it from any angle while it is animating. There's really no end to the effects (and the fun!) that you can have with particle systems.

16.8 Wobble

The previous three examples discussed animating the geometry of an object and used the vertex processor to achieve this animation (because the geometry of an object cannot be modified by the fragment processor). The fragment processor can also create animation effects. The main purpose of most fragment shaders is to compute the fragment color, and any of the factors that affect this computation can be varied over time. In this section, we look at a shader that perturbs the texture coordinates in a time-varying way to achieve an oscillating or wobbling effect. With the right texture, this effect can make it very simple to produce an animated effect to simulate a gelatinous surface or a "dancing" logo.

This shader was developed to mimic the wobbly 2D effects demonstrated in some of the real-time graphics demos that are available on the Web (see www.scene.org for some examples). Its author, Antonio Tejada, wanted to use the OpenGL Shading Language to create a similar effect.

The central premise of the shader is that a sine function is used in the fragment shader to perturb the texture coordinates before the texture lookup operation. The amount and frequency of the perturbation can be controlled through uniform variables sent by the application. Because the goal of the shader was to produce an effect that looked good, the accuracy of the sine computation was not critical. For this reason and because the sine function had not been implemented at the time he wrote this shader, Antonio chose to approximate the sine value by using the first two terms of the Taylor series for sine. The fragment shader would have been simpler if the built-in **sin** function had been used, but this approach demonstrates that numerical methods can be used as needed within a shader. (As to whether using two terms of the Taylor series would result in better performance than using the built-in **sin** function, it's hard to say. It probably varies from one graphics hardware vendor to the next, depending on how the **sin** function is implemented.)

For this shader to work properly, the application must provide the frequency and amplitude of the wobbles, as well as a light position. In addition, the application increments a uniform variable called *StartRad* at each frame. This value is used as the basis for the perturbation calculation in the fragment shader. By incrementing the value at each frame, we animate the wobble effect. The application must provide the vertex position, the surface normal, and the texture coordinate at each vertex of the object to be rendered.

The vertex shader for the wobble effect is responsible for a simple lighting computation based on the surface normal and the light position provided by the application. It passes along the texture coordinate without modification. This is exactly the same as the functionality of the earth vertex shader described in Section 10.2.2, so we can simply use that vertex shader.

The fragment shader to achieve the wobbling effect is shown in Listing 16.8. It receives as input the varying variable *LightIntensity* as computed by the vertex shader. This variable is used at the very end to apply a lighting effect to the fragment. The uniform variable *StartRad* provides the starting point for the perturbation computation in radians, and it is incremented by the application at each frame to animate the wobble effect. We can make the wobble effect go faster by using a larger increment value, and we can make it go slower by using a smaller increment amount. We found that an increment value of about 1° gave visually pleasing results.

The frequency and amplitude of the wobbles can be adjusted by the application with the uniform variables *Freq* and *Amplitude*. These are defined as **vec2** variables so that the *x* and *y* components can be adjusted independently. The final uniform variable defined by this fragment shader is *WobbleTex*, which specifies the texture unit to be used for accessing the 2D texture that is to be wobbled.

For the Taylor series approximation for sine to give more precise results, it is necessary to ensure that the value for which sine is computed is in the range [–π/2,π/2]. The constants C_PI (π), C_2PI (2π), C_2PI_I (1/2π), and C_PI_2 (π/2) are defined to assist in this process.

The first half of the fragment shader computes a perturbation factor for the *x* direction. We want to end up with a perturbation factor that depends on both the *s* and the *t* components of the texture coordinate. To this end, the local variable *rad* is computed as a linear function of the *s* and *t* values of the texture coordinate. (A similar but different expression computes the *y* perturbation factor in the second half of the shader.) The current value of *StartRad* is added. Finally, the *x* component of *Freq* is used to scale the result.

The value for *rad* increases as the value for *StartRad* increases. As the scaling factor *Freq.x* increases, the frequency of the wobbles also increases. The scaling factor should be increased as the size of the texture increases on the screen to keep the apparent frequency of the wobbles the same at different scales. You can think of the *Freq* uniform variable as the Richter scale for wobbles. A value of 0 results in no wobbles whatsoever. A value of 1.0 results in gentle rocking, a value of 2.0 causes jiggling, a value of 4.0 results in wobbling, and a value of 8.0 results in magnitude 8.0 earthquakelike effects.

The next seven lines of the shader bring the value of *rad* into the range [–π/2,π/2]. When this is accomplished, we can compute **sin**(*rad*) by using the first two terms of the Taylor series for sine, which is just $x - x^3/3$! The result of this computation is multiplied by the *x* component of *Amplitude*. The value for the computed sine value will be in the range [–1,1]. If we just add this value to the texture coordinate as the perturbation factor, it will *really* perturb the texture coordinate. We want a wobble, not an explosion! Multiplying the computed sine value by a value of 0.05 results in reasonably sized wobbles. Increasing this scale factor makes the wobbles bigger, and decreasing it makes them smaller. You can think of this as how far the texture coordinate is stretched from its original value. Using a value of

0.05 means that the perturbation alters the original texture coordinate by no more than ±0.05. A value of 0.5 means that the perturbation alters the original texture coordinate by no more than ±0.5.

With the *x* perturbation factor computed, the whole process is repeated to compute the *y* perturbation factor. This computation is also based on a linear function of the *s* and *t* texture coordinate values, but it differs from that used for the *x* perturbation factor. Computing the *y* perturbation value differently avoids symmetries between the *x* and *y* perturbation factors in the final wobbling effect, which doesn't look as good when animated.

With the perturbation factors computed, we can finally do our (perturbed) texture access. The color value that is retrieved from the texture map is multiplied by *LightIntensity* to compute the final color value for the fragment. Several frames from the animation produced by this shader are shown in Color Plate 28. These frames show the shader applied to a logo to illustrate the perturbation effects more clearly in static images. But the animation effect is also quite striking when the texture used looks like the surface of water, lava, slime, or even animal/monster skin.

Listing 16.8   Fragment shader for wobble effect

```
#version 140

// Constants
const float C_PI    = 3.1415;
const float C_2PI   = 2.0 * C_PI;
const float C_2PI_I = 1.0 / (2.0 * C_PI);
const float C_PI_2  = C_PI / 2.0;

uniform float StartRad;
uniform vec2  Freq;
uniform vec2  Amplitude;

uniform sampler2D WobbleTex;

in  float LightIntensity;
in  vec2  TexCoord;

out vec4  FragColor;

void main()
{
    vec2  perturb;
    float rad;
    vec3  color;
```

```
// Compute a perturbation factor for the x direction
rad = (TexCoord.s + TexCoord.t - 1.0 + StartRad) * Freq.x;

// Wrap to -2.0*PI, 2*PI
rad = rad * C_2PI_I;
rad = fract(rad);
rad = rad * C_2PI;

// Center in -PI, PI
if (rad >  C_PI) rad = rad - C_2PI;
if (rad < -C_PI) rad = rad + C_2PI;

// Center in -PI/2, PI/2
if (rad >  C_PI_2) rad =  C_PI - rad;
if (rad < -C_PI_2) rad = -C_PI - rad;

perturb.x  = (rad - (rad * rad * rad / 6.0)) * Amplitude.x;

// Now compute a perturbation factor for the y direction
rad = (TexCoord.s - TexCoord.t + StartRad) * Freq.y;

// Wrap to -2*PI, 2*PI
rad = rad * C_2PI_I;
rad = fract(rad);
rad = rad * C_2PI;

// Center in -PI, PI
if (rad >  C_PI) rad = rad - C_2PI;
if (rad < -C_PI) rad = rad + C_2PI;

// Center in -PI/2, PI/2
if (rad >  C_PI_2) rad =  C_PI - rad;
if (rad < -C_PI_2) rad = -C_PI - rad;

perturb.y  = (rad - (rad * rad * rad / 6.0)) * Amplitude.y;

color = vec3(texture(WobbleTex, perturb + TexCoord.st));

FragColor = vec4(color * LightIntensity, 1.0);
}
```

16.9 Animating Once per Frame

If you are mulling over what it means to combine animation in shaders, such as the confetti cannon, with some of the effects we covered earlier, such as shadowing, you might begin to worry about what such combinations imply. We would have to animate the confetti for each cannon, for each of several lights, and then finally from the eye view. Suddenly it seems that doing animation in vertex shaders can be fairly expensive. It can be so expensive in some cases that perhaps it is better to keep the animation with the application on the host CPU.

The answer to this dilemma is fairly simple. Animate only once per frame. OpenGL 3.0 introduces Transform Feedback, which allows the application to capture vertex shader out variables in buffer objects. The vertex animation pass can be done once per frame to capture the transformed vertices and attributes in buffer objects. The buffer objects can then be used in subsequent light and eye passes. Brilliant!

We can make some very small changes in the confetti cannon vertex shader in Listing 16.7:

```
out vec4 Position;
// ...
// gl_Position  = MVPMatrix * vert;
Position = MCtoWorldMatrix * vert;
```

The vertex shader no longer must write the special out variable *gl_Position*. And instead of transforming the position to clip space, which is specific to a specific view and projection, the vertex shader transforms the position to world coordinates.

16.9.1 Application Setup

There are four simple steps to enable transform feedback. First, the application must specify what out variables to record in the transform feedback buffer. In this example, we will be recording *Position* and *Color* into separate feedback buffers:

```
GLchar outStrings[2] = { "Position", "Color" };
glTransformFeedbackVaryings(ProgramObject, 2,
                    outStrings, GL_SEPARATE_ATTRIBS )
```

These bindings are checked and go into effect at the time **glLinkProgram** is called.

Next, the application must bind buffer objects of the appropriate size to the transform feedback buffer binding points:

```
glBindBufferBase(GL_TRANSFORM_FEEDBACK_BUFFER, 0, BufferObjectPosition);
glBindBufferBase(GL_TRANSFORM_FEEDBACK_BUFFER, 1, BufferObjectColor);
```

A small modification to the original draw call is all that is needed to record the vertex out variables to the transform feedback buffer:

```
glBeginTransformFeedback(GL_POINTS);
glDrawArrays(GL_POINTS, 0, arrayWidth * arrayHeight);
glEndTransformFeedback();
```

Finally, unbind the buffer objects from the transform feedback binding points, and bind them to vertex array binding points. But to avoid undefined behavior, be careful not to leave buffer objects bound to both transform feedback binding points and vertex array binding points.

16.9.2 Updating Matrices Once per Frame

Related to animating models, animating the camera and lights involves updating several common matrices. These need to be updated only once per frame, yet with user-defined uniforms they need to be updated for each and every program.

OpenGL 3.1 adds named uniform blocks. These named uniform blocks are backed by buffer objects. We can use a transform feedback buffer to record the output of a vertex shader. This vertex shader is designed to output to a single transform feedback buffer (with the buffer mode GL_INTERLEAVED_ ATTRIBUTES). The recording rules for output to a transform feedback buffer coincidently match the layout rule "std140" for named uniform blocks. (For details of the layout rule "std140," see the OpenGL Shading Language specification.)

We can render a single point to record to a transform feedback buffer and then bind that buffer object to a uniform buffer. All shaders that use that named uniform buffer are updated only once per frame.

This simple example takes two uniform matrices, *MVMatrix* and *PMatrix* as inputs, and it outputs the original *MVMatrix* as well as the derived matrices *MVPMatrix* and *NormalMatrix*:

```
#version 140

uniform mat4 MVMatrix;
uniform mat4 PMatrix;

out mat4    MV;
out mat4    MVP;
out mat3x4  N;

//
```

```
// Vertex shader that records transform feedback buffer
// that can be used with this named uniform block:
//
// layout (std140,column_major) uniform TransformBlock
// {
//      uniform mat4 MVMatrix;
//      uniform mat4 MVPmatrix;
//      uniform mat3 NormalMatrix;
// }
//
void main()
{
   MV = MVMatrix;
   MVP = PMatrix*MV;
   mat4 MVI = inverse(MV);
   mat4 MVIT = transpose(MVI);
   N = mat3x4(MVIT); // the last element of each column is a pad
}
```

This simple example can be readily extended. Many of the transformation functions in Chapter 9 can be combined in useful ways here.

16.10 Summary

With the fixed functionality in previous versions of OpenGL, animation effects were strictly in the domain of the application and had to be computed on the host CPU. With programmability, it has become easy to specify animation effects within a shader and let the graphics hardware do this work. Just about any aspect of a shader—position, shape, color, texture coordinates, and lighting, to name just a few—can be varied according to a global definition of current time.

When you develop a shader for an object that will be in motion, you should also consider how much of the animation effect you can encode within the shader. Encoding animation effects within a shader can offload the CPU and simplify the code in the application. This chapter described some simple ways for doing this. On and off, scrolling, and threshold effects are quite easy to do within a shader. Key-frame interpolation can be supported in a simple way through the power of programmability. Particles can be animated, including their position, color, velocity, and any other important attributes. Objects and textures can be made to oscillate, move, grow, or change based on mathematical expressions. "Cameras" and "lights" can move in ways natural for the application and derive the matrices necessary for efficient operation.

Animation is a powerful tool for conveying information, and the OpenGL Shading Language provides another avenue for expressing animation effects.

16.11 Further Information

If you're serious about animated effects, you really should read *Disney Animation: The Illusion of Life* by two of the "Nine Old Men" of Disney animation fame, Frank Thomas and Ollie Johnston (1981). This book is loaded with color images and insight into the development of the animation art form at Disney Studios. It contains several decades worth of information about making great animated films. If you can, try to find a used copy of the original printing from Abbeville Press rather than the reprint by Hyperion. A softcover version was also printed by Abbeville, but this version eliminates much of the history of Disney Studios. A brief encapsulation of some of the material in this book can be found in the 1987 SIGGRAPH paper *Principles of Traditional Animation Applied to 3D Computer Animation* by John Lasseter.

Rick Parent's 2001 book, *Computer Animation: Algorithms and Techniques*, contains descriptions of a variety of algorithms for computer animation. The book *Game Programming Gems*, edited by Mark DeLoura (2000), also has several pertinent sections on animation.

Particle systems were first described by Bill Reeves in his 1983 SIGGRAPH paper, *Particle Systems—A Technique for Modeling a Class of Fuzzy Objects*. In 1998, Jeff Lander wrote an easy-to-follow description of particle systems, titled "The Ocean Spray in Your Face," in his column for *Game Developer Magazine*. He also made source code available for a simple OpenGL-based particle system demonstration program that he wrote.

[1] DeLoura, Mark, ed., *Game Programming Gems*, Charles River Media, Hingham, Massachusetts, 2000.

[2] Lander, Jeff, *The Ocean Spray in Your Face*, Game Developer Magazine, vol. 5, no. 7, pp. 13–19, July 1998.
www.darwin3d.com/gdm1998.htm

[3] Lasseter, John, *Principles of Traditional Animation Applied to 3D Computer Animation*, Computer Graphics, (SIGGRAPH '87 Proceedings), pp. 35–44, July 1987.

[4] Parent, Rick, *Computer Animation: Algorithms and Techniques*, Morgan Kaufmann Publishers, San Francisco, 2001.

[5] Reeves, William T., *Particle Systems—A Technique for Modeling a Class of Fuzzy Objects*, ACM Transactions on Graphics, vol. 2, no. 2, pp. 91–108, April 1983.

[6] Reeves, William T., and Ricki Blau, *Approximate and Probabilistic Algorithms for Shading and Rendering Structured Particle Systems*, Computer Graphics (SIGGRAPH '85 Proceedings), pp. 313–322, July 1985.

[7] Thomas, Frank, and Ollie Johnston, *Disney Animation—The Illusion of Life*, Abbeville Press, New York, 1981.

[8] Thomas, Frank, and Ollie Johnston, *The Illusion of Life—Disney Animation, Revised Edition*, Hyperion, 1995.

[9] Watt, Alan H., and Mark Watt, *Advanced Animation and Rendering Techniques: Theory and Practice*, Addison-Wesley, Reading, Massachusetts, 1992.

Chapter 17

Antialiasing
Procedural Textures

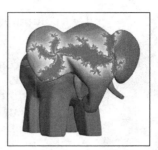

Jaggies, popping, sparkling, stair steps, strobing, and marching ants. They're all names used to describe the anathema of computer graphics—ALIASING. Anyone who has used a computer has seen it. For still images, it's not always that noticeable or objectionable. But as soon as you put an object in motion, the movement of the jagged edges catches your eye and distracts you. From the early days of computer graphics, the fight to eliminate these nasty artifacts has been called ANTIALIASING.

This chapter does not contain a thorough description of the causes of aliasing, nor the methods used to combat it. But it does introduce the reasons the problem occurs and the facilities within the OpenGL Shading Language for antialiasing. Armed with this knowledge, you should be well on your way to fighting the jaggies in your own shaders.

17.1 Sources of Aliasing

The human eye is extremely good at noticing edges. This is how we comprehend shape and form and how we recognize letters and words. Our eye is naturally good at it, and we spend our whole lives practicing it, so naturally it is something we do very, very well.

A computer display is limited in its capability to present an image. The display is made up of a finite number of discrete elements called PIXELS. At a given time, each pixel can produce only one color. This makes it impossible for a computer display to accurately represent detail that is smaller than one pixel in screen space, such as an edge.

When you combine these two things, the human eye's ability to discern edges and the computer graphics display's limitations in replicating them, you have a problem, and this problem is known as aliasing. In a nutshell, aliasing occurs when we try to reproduce a signal with an insufficient sampling frequency. With a computer graphics display, we'll always have a fixed number of samples (pixels) with which to reconstruct our image, and this will always be insufficient to provide adequate sampling, so we will always have aliasing. We can reduce it to the point that it's not noticeable, or we can transform it into some other problem that is less objectionable, like blurriness or noise.

The problem is illustrated in Figure 17.1. In this diagram, we show the results of trying to draw a gray object. The intended shape is shown in Figure 17.1 (A). The computer graphics display limits us to a discrete sampling grid. If we choose only one location within each grid square (usually the center) and determine the color to be used by sampling the desired image at that point, we see some apparent artifacts. This is called POINT SAMPLING and is illustrated in Figure 17.1 (B). The result is ugly aliasing artifacts for edges that don't line up naturally with the sampling grid (see Figure 17.1 (C)). (The drawing is idealized because pixels on a standard CRT do not produce light in the shape of a square, but the artifacts are obvious even when the sampled points are reconstructed as overlapping circles on the computer display.)

Aliasing takes on other forms as well. If you are developing a sequence of images for an animation and you don't properly sample objects that are in

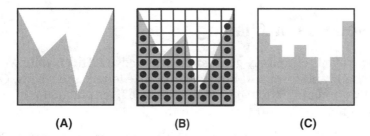

(A)   **(B)**   **(C)**

Figure 17.1   Aliasing artifacts caused by point sampling. The gray region represents the shape of the object to be rendered (A). The computer graphics display presents us with a limited sampling grid (B). The result of choosing to draw or not draw gray at each pixel results in jaggies, or aliasing artifacts (C).

motion, you might notice TEMPORAL ALIASING. This is caused by objects that are moving too rapidly for the sampling frequency being used. Objects may appear to stutter as they move or blink on and off. The classic example of temporal aliasing comes from the movies: A vehicle (car, truck, or covered wagon) in motion is going forward, but the spokes of its wheels appear to be rotating backwards. This effect is caused when the sampling rate (movie frames per second) is too low relative to the motion of the wheel spokes. In reality, the wheel may be rotating two- and three-quarter revolutions per frame, but on film it looks like it's rotating one-quarter revolution *backwards* each frame.

To render images that look truly realistic rather than computer generated, we need to develop techniques for overcoming the inherent limitations of the graphics display.

17.2   Avoiding Aliasing

One way to achieve good results without aliasing is to avoid situations in which aliasing occurs.

For instance, if you know that a particular object will always be a certain size in the final rendered image, you can design a shader that looks good while rendering that object at that size. This is the assumption behind some of the shaders presented previously in this book. The **smoothstep**, **mix**, and **clamp** functions are handy functions to use to avoid sharp transitions and to make a procedural texture look good at a particular scale.

Aliasing is often a problem when you are rendering an object at different sizes. Mipmap textures address this very issue, and you can do something similar with shaders. If you know that a particular object must appear at different sizes in the final rendering, you can design a shader for each different size. Each of these shaders would provide an appropriate level of detail and avoid aliasing for an object of that size. For this to work, the application must determine the approximate size of the final rendered object before it is drawn and then install the appropriate shader. In addition, if a continuous zoom (in or out) is applied to a single object, some "popping" will occur when the level of detail changes.

You can avoid aliasing in some situations by using a texture instead of computing something procedurally. This lets you take advantage of the FILTERING (i.e., antialiasing) support that is built into the texture-mapping hardware. However, there are issues with using stored textures as opposed to doing things procedurally, as discussed in Chapter 11.

17.3 Increasing Resolution

The effects of aliasing can be reduced through a brute force method called SUPERSAMPLING that performs sampling at several locations within a pixel and averages the result of those samples. This is exactly the approach supported in today's graphics hardware with the multisample buffer. This method of antialiasing replaces a single point sampling operation with several, so it doesn't actually eliminate aliasing, but it can reduce aliasing to the point that it is no longer objectionable. You may be able to ignore the issue of aliasing if your shaders will always be used in conjunction with a multisample buffer.

But this approach does use up hardware resources (graphics board memory for storing the multisample buffer), and even with hardware acceleration, it still may be slower than performing the antialiasing as part of the procedural texture-generation algorithm. And, because this approach doesn't eliminate aliasing, your texture is still apt to exhibit signs of aliasing, albeit at a higher frequency than before.

Supersampling is illustrated in Figure 17.2. Each of the pixels is rendered by sampling at four locations rather than at one. The average of the four samples is used as the value for the pixel. This averaging provides a better result, but it is not sufficient to eliminate aliasing because high-frequency components can still be misrepresented.

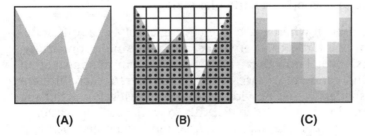

(A)   (B)   (C)

Figure 17.2 Supersampling with four samples per pixel yields a better result, but aliasing artifacts are still present. The shape of the object to be rendered is shown in (A). Sampling occurs at four locations within each pixel as shown in (B). The results are averaged to produce the final pixel value as shown in (C). Some samples that are almost half covered were sampled with just one supersample point instead of two, and one pixel contains image data that was missed entirely, even with supersampling.

Supersampling can also be implemented within a fragment shader. The code that is used to produce the fragment color can be constructed as a function, and this function can be called several times from within the main function of the fragment shader to sample the function at several discrete locations. The returned values can be averaged to create the final value for the fragment. Results are improved if the sample positions are varied stochastically rather than spaced on a regular grid. Supersampling within a fragment shader has the obvious downside of requiring N times as much processing per fragment, where N is the number of samples computed at each fragment.

There will be times when aliasing is unavoidable and supersampling is infeasible. If you want to perform procedural texturing and you want a single shader that is useful at a variety of scales, there's little choice but to address the aliasing issue and take steps to counteract aliasing in your shaders.

17.4 Antialiased Stripe Example

Aliasing does not occur until we attempt to represent a continuous image in screen space. This conversion occurs during rasterization; therefore, our attempts to mitigate its effects always occur in the fragment shader. The OpenGL Shading Language has several functions for this purpose that are available only to fragment shaders. To help explain the motivation for some of the language facilities for filter estimation, we develop a "worst case" scenario—alternating black and white stripes drawn on a sphere. Developing a fragment shader that performs antialiasing enables us to further illustrate the aliasing problem and the methods for reducing aliasing artifacts. Bert Freudenberg developed the first version of the GLSL shaders discussed in this section during the process of creating the antialiased hatching shader described in Section 18.1.

17.4.1 Generating Stripes

The antialiasing fragment shader determines whether each fragment is to be drawn as white or black to create lines on the surface of an object. The first step is to determine the method to be used for drawing lines. We use a single parameter as the basis for our stripe pattern. For illustration, let's assume that the parameter is the *s* coordinate of the object's texture coordinate. We have the vertex shader pass this value to us as a floating-point out variable named *V*, eventually giving us a method for creating vertical stripes on a sphere. Figure 17.3 (A) shows the result of using the *s* texture coordinate directly as the intensity (grayscale) value on the surface of the sphere. The viewing position is slightly above the sphere, so we are looking down at the "north pole." The *s* texture coordinate starts off at 0 (black) and increases to 1 (white) as it goes around the sphere. The edge where black meets white can be seen at the pole, and it runs down the back side of the sphere. The front side of the sphere looks mostly gray but increases from left to right.

We create a sawtooth wave by multiplying the *s* texture coordinate by 16 and taking the fractional part (see Figure 17.3 (B)). This causes the intensity value to start at 0, rise quickly to 1, and then drop back down to 0. (To get a feel for what a sawtooth wave looks like, see the illustrations for the built-in functions **fract** (refer to Figure 5.6) and **mod** (refer to Figure 5.7).) This sequence is repeated 16 times. The OpenGL shader code to implement this is

```
float sawtooth = fract(V * 16.0);
```

This isn't quite the stripe pattern we're after. To get closer, we employ the absolute value function (see Figure 17.3 (C)). By multiplying the value of *sawtooth* by 2 and subtracting 1, we get a function that varies in the range [–1,1]. Taking the absolute value of this function results in a function that

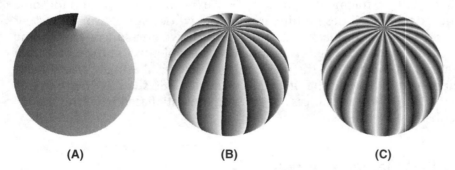

| (A) | (B) | (C) |

Figure 17.3 Using the *s* texture coordinate to create stripes on a sphere. In (A), the *s* texture coordinate is used directly as the intensity (gray) value. In (B), a modulus function creates a sawtooth function. In (C), the absolute value function turns the sawtooth function into a triangle function. (Courtesy of Bert Freudenberg, University of Magdeburg, 2002.)

goes from 1 down to 0 and then back to 1 (i.e., a *triangle* wave). The line of code to do this is

```
float triangle = abs(2.0 * sawtooth - 1.0);
```

A stripe pattern is starting to appear, but it's either too blurry or our glasses need adjustment. We make the stripes pure black and white by using the **step** function. When we compare our triangle variable to 0.5, this function returns 0 whenever *triangle* is less than or equal to 0.5, and 1 whenever *triangle* is greater than 0.5. This could be written as

```
float square = step(0.5, triangle);
```

This effectively produces a square wave, and the result is illustrated in Figure 17.4 (A). We can modify the relative size of the alternating stripes by adjusting the threshold value provided in the **step** function.

17.4.2 Analytic Prefiltering

In Figure 17.4 (A), we see that the stripes are now distinct, but aliasing has reared its ugly head. The **step** function returns values that are either 0 or 1, with nothing in between, so the jagged edges in the transitions between white and black are easy to spot. They will not go away if we increase the resolution of the image; they'll just be smaller. The problem is caused by the fact that the **step** function introduced an immediate transition from white to black or an edge with infinite frequency (see Figure 5.11). There is no way to sample this transition at a high enough frequency to eliminate the aliasing artifacts. To get good results, we need to take steps within our shader to remove such high frequencies.

A variety of antialiasing techniques rely on eliminating extremely high frequencies before sampling. This is called LOW-PASS FILTERING because low frequencies are passed through unmodified, whereas high frequencies are eliminated. The visual effect of low-pass filtering is that the resulting image is blurred.

To eliminate the high frequencies from the stripe pattern, we use the **smoothstep** function. We know that this function produces a smooth transition between white and black. It requires that we specify two edges, and a smooth transition occurs between those two edges. Figure 17.4 (B) illustrates the result from the following line of code:

```
float square = smoothstep(0.4, 0.6, triangle);
```

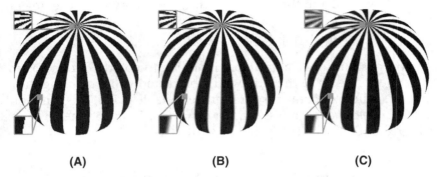

(A)   **(B)**   **(C)**

Figure 17.4   Antialiasing the stripe pattern. We can see that the square wave produced by the **step** function produces aliasing artifacts (A). The **smoothstep** function with a fixed-width filter produces too much blurring near the equator but not enough at the pole (B). An adaptive approach provides reasonable antialiasing in both regions (C). (Courtesy of Bert Freudenberg, University of Magdeburg, 2002.)

17.4.3 Adaptive Analytic Prefiltering

Analytic prefiltering produces acceptable results in some regions of the sphere but not in others. The size of the smoothing filter (0.2) is defined in parameter space. But the parameter does not vary at a constant rate in screen space. In this case, the s texture coordinate varies quite rapidly in screen space near the poles and less rapidly at the equator. Our fixed-width filter produces blurring across several pixels at the equator and very little effect at the poles. What we need is a way to determine the size of the smoothing filter adaptively so that transition can be appropriate at all scales in screen space. This requires a measurement of how rapidly the function we're interested in is changing at a particular position in screen space.

Fortunately, the OpenGL Shading Language provides a built-in function that can give us the rate of change (derivative) of any parameter in screen space. The function **dFdx** gives the rate of change in screen coordinates in the x direction, and **dFdy** gives the rate of change in the y direction. Because these functions deal with screen space, they are available only in a fragment shader. These two functions can provide the information needed to compute a GRADIENT VECTOR for the position of interest.

Given a function $f(x,y)$, the gradient of f at the position (x, y) is defined as the vector

$$G[f(x, y)] = \begin{bmatrix} \dfrac{\partial f}{\partial x} \\ \dfrac{\partial f}{\partial y} \end{bmatrix}$$

In English, the gradient vector comprises the partial derivative of function f with respect to x (i.e., the measure of how rapidly f is changing in the x direction) and the partial derivative of the function f with respect to y (i.e., the measure of how rapidly f is changing in the y direction). The important properties of the gradient vector are that it points in the direction of the maximum rate of increase of the function $f(x,y)$ (the gradient direction) and that the magnitude of this vector equals the maximum rate of increase of $f(x,y)$ in the gradient direction. (These properties are useful for image processing too, as we see later.) The built-in functions **dFdx** and **dFdy** give us exactly what we need to define the gradient vector for functions used in fragment shaders.

The magnitude of the gradient vector for the function $f(x,y)$ is commonly called the GRADIENT of the function $f(x,y)$. It is defined as

$$\mathbf{mag}[G[f(x, y)]] = \mathbf{sqrt}((\partial f/\partial x)^2 + (\partial f/\partial y)^2)$$

In practice, it is not always necessary to perform the (possibly costly) square root operation. The gradient can be approximated with absolute values:

$$\mathbf{mag}[G[f(x, y)]] \cong \mathbf{abs}(f(x, y) - f(x + 1, y)) + \mathbf{abs}(f(x, y) - f(x, y + 1))$$

This is exactly what is returned by the built-in function **fwidth**. The sum of the absolute values is an upper bound on the width of the sampling filter needed to eliminate aliasing. If it is too large, the resulting image looks somewhat blurrier than it should, but this is usually acceptable.

The two methods of computing the gradient are compared in Figure 17.5. As you can see, there is little visible difference. Because the value of the gradient was quite small for the function being evaluated on this object, the values were scaled so that they would be visible.

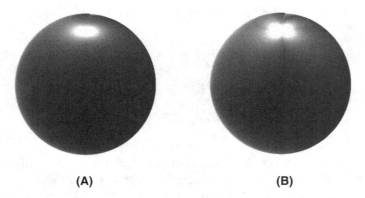

(A)   (B)

Figure 17.5 Visualizing the gradient. In (A), the magnitude of the gradient vector is used as the intensity (gray) value. In (B), the gradient is approximated with absolute values. (Actual gradient values are scaled for visualization.) (Courtesy of Bert Freudenberg, University of Magdeburg, 2002.)

To compute the actual gradient for the in variable *V* within a fragment shader, we use

```
float width = length(vec2(dFdx(V), dFdy(V)));
```

To approximate it, we use the potentially higher-performance calculation.

```
float width = fwidth(V);
```

We then use the filter width within our call to **smoothstep** as follows:

```
float edge = dp * Frequency * 2.0;
float square = smoothstep(0.5 - edge, 0.5 + edge, triangle);
```

If we put this all together in a fragment shader, we get Listing 17.1.

Listing 17.1 Fragment shader for adaptive analytic antialiasing

```
#version 140

uniform float Frequency;        // Stripe frequency = 6
uniform vec3  Color0;
uniform vec3  Color1;

in  float V;                    // generic varying
in  float LightIntensity;

out vec4 FragColor;
```

```
void main()
{
    float sawtooth = fract(V * Frequency);
    float triangle = abs(2.0 * sawtooth - 1.0);
    float dp = length(vec2(dFdx(V), dFdy(V)));
    float edge = dp * Frequency * 2.0;
    float square = smoothstep(0.5 - edge, 0.5 + edge, triangle);
    vec3  color = mix(Color0, Color1, square);
    FragColor = vec4(color, 1.0);
    FragColor.rgb *= LightIntensity;
}
```

If we scale the frequency of our texture, we must also increase the filter width accordingly. After the value of the function is computed, it is replicated across the red, green, and blue components of a **vec3** and used as the color of the fragment. The results of this adaptive antialiasing approach are shown in Figure 17.4 (C). The results are much more consistent across the surface of the sphere. A simple lighting computation is added, and the resulting shader is applied to the teapot in Figure 17.6.

This approach to antialiasing works well until the filter width gets larger than the frequency. This is the situation that occurs at the north pole of the sphere. The stripes very close to the pole are much thinner than one pixel, so no step function will produce the correct gray value here. In such regions, you need to switch to integration or frequency clamping, both of which are discussed in subsequent sections.

Figure 17.6 Effect of adaptive analytical antialiasing on striped teapots. On the left, the teapot is drawn with no antialiasing. On the right, the adaptive antialiasing shader is used. A small portion of the striped surface is magnified 200 percent to make it easier to see the difference.

17.4.4 Analytic Integration

The weighted average of a function over a specified interval is called a CONVOLUTION. The values that do the weighting are called the CONVOLUTION KERNEL or the CONVOLUTION FILTER. In some cases, we can reduce or eliminate aliasing by determining the convolution of a function ahead of time and then sampling the convolved function rather than the original function. The convolution can be performed over a fixed interval in a computation that is equivalent to convolving the input function with a box filter. A box filter is far from ideal, but it is simple and easy to compute and often good enough.

This method corresponds to the notion of antialiasing by AREA SAMPLING. It is different from point sampling or supersampling in that we attempt to calculate the area of the object being rendered relative to the sampling region. Referring to Figure 17.2, if we used an area sampling technique, we would get more accurate values for each of the pixels, and we wouldn't miss that pixel that just had a sliver of coverage.

In *Advanced RenderMan: Creating CGI for Motion Pictures*, Apodaca and Gritz (1999) explain how to perform analytic antialiasing of a periodic step function, sometimes called a PULSE TRAIN. Darwyn Peachey described how to apply this method to his procedural brick RenderMan shader in *Texturing and Modeling: A Procedural Approach*, and Dave Baldwin published a GLSL version of this shader in the original paper on the OpenGL Shading Language. We use this technique to analytically antialias the procedural brick GLSL shader we described back in Chapter 6. Recall that the simple brick example used the **step** function to produce the periodic brick pattern. The function that creates the brick pattern in the horizontal direction is illustrated in Figure 17.7. From 0 to *BrickPct.x* (the brick width fraction), the function is 1.0. At the value of *BrickPct.x*, there is an edge with infinite slope as the function drops to 0. At the value 1, the function jumps back up to 1.0, and the process is repeated for the next brick.

The key to antialiasing this function is to compute its integral, or accumulated, value. We have to consider the possibility that, in areas of high complexity, the filter width that is computed by **fwidth** will cover several of these pulses. By sampling the integral rather than the function itself, we get a properly weighted average and avoid the high frequencies caused by point sampling that would produce aliasing artifacts.

So what is the integral of this function? It is illustrated in Figure 17.8. From 0 to *BrickPct.x*, the function value is 1, so the integral increases with a slope of 1. From *BrickPct.x* to 1.0, the function has a value of 0, so the integral stays constant in this region. At 1, the function jumps back to 1.0, so the integral increases until the function reaches *BrickPct.x* + 1. At this point, the integral changes to a slope of 0 again, and this pattern of ramps and plateaus continues.

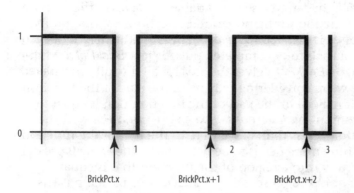

Figure 17.7 The periodic step function, or pulse train, that defines the horizontal component of the procedural brick texture

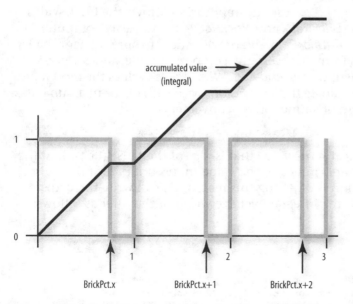

Figure 17.8 Periodic step function (pulse train) and its integral

We perform antialiasing by determining the value of the integral over the area of the filter, and we do that by evaluating the integral at the edges of the filter and subtracting the two values. The integral for this function consists of two parts: the sum of the area for all the pulses that have been fully completed before the edge we are considering and the area of the possibly partially completed pulse for the edge we are considering.

For our procedural brick shader, we use the variable *position.x* as the basis for generating the pulse function in the horizontal direction. So, the number of fully completed pulses is just **floor**(*position.x*). Because the height of each pulse is 1.0, the area of each fully completed pulse is just *BrickPct.x*. Multiplying **floor**(*position.x*) by *BrickPct.x* gives the area for all the fully completed pulses. The edge that we're considering may be in the part of the function that is equal to 0, or it may be in the part of the function that is equal to 1. We can find out by computing **fract**(*position.x*) – (1.0 – *BrickPct.x*). If the result of this subtraction is less than 0, we were in the part of the function that returns 0, so nothing more needs to be done. But if the value is greater than zero, we are partway into a region of the function that is equal to 1. Because the height of the pulse is 1, the area of this partial pulse is **fract**(*position.x*) – (1.0 – *BrickPct.x*). Therefore, the second part of our integral is the expression **max**(**fract**(*position.x*) – (1.0 – *BrickPct.x*), 0.0).

We use this integral for both the horizontal and vertical components of our procedural brick pattern. Because the application knows the brick width and height fractions (*BrickPct.x* and *BrickPct.y*), it can easily compute 1.0 – *BrickPct.x* and 1.0 – *BrickPct.y* and provide them to our fragment shader as well. This keeps us from unnecessarily computing these values several times for every fragment that is rendered. We call these values the mortar percentage. Because we evaluate this expression twice with different arguments, we define it as a macro or a function for convenience.

```
#define Integral(x, p, notp) ((floor(x)*(p)) + max(fract(x)-(notp), 0.0))
```

The parameter *p* indicates the value that is part of the pulse (i.e., when the function is 1.0), and *notp* indicates the value that is not part of the pulse (i.e., when the function is 0). Using this macro, we can write the code to compute the value of the integral over the width of the filter as follows:

```
vec2 fw, useBrick;

fw = fwidth(position);

useBrick = (Integral(position + fw, BrickPct, MortarPct) -
            Integral(position, BrickPct, MortarPct)) / fw;
```

The result is divided by the area of the filter (a box filter is assumed in this case) to obtain the average value for the function in the selected interval.

17.4.5 Antialiased Brick Fragment Shader

Now we can put all this to work to build better bricks. We replace the simple point sampling technique used in the example in Chapter 6 with analytic integration. The resulting shader is shown in Listing 17.2. The difference between the aliased and antialiased brick shaders is shown in Color Plate 34.

Listing 17.2 Source code for an antialiased brick fragment shader

```
#version 140

uniform vec3  BrickColor, MortarColor;
uniform vec2  BrickSize;
uniform vec2  BrickPct;
uniform vec2  MortarPct;

in  vec2  MCPosition;
in  float LightIntensity;

out vec4  FragColor;

#define Integral(x, p, notp) ((floor(x)*(p)) + max(fract(x)-(notp), 0.0))

void main()
{
    vec2 position, fw, useBrick;
    vec3 color;

    // Determine position within the brick pattern
    position = MCPosition / BrickSize;

    // Adjust every other row by an offset of half a brick
    if (fract(position.y * 0.5) > 0.5)
        position.x += 0.5;

    // Calculate filter size
    fw = fwidth(position);

    // Perform filtering by integrating the 2D pulse made by the
    // brick pattern over the filter width and height
    useBrick = (Integral(position + fw, BrickPct, MortarPct) -
                Integral(position, BrickPct, MortarPct)) / fw;

    // Determine final color
    color  = mix(MortarColor, BrickColor, useBrick.x * useBrick.y);
    color *= LightIntensity;
    FragColor = vec4(color, 1.0);
}
```

17.5 Frequency Clamping

Certain functions do not have an analytic solution, or they are just too difficult to solve. If this is the case, you might try a technique called FREQUENCY CLAMPING. In this technique, the average value of the function replaces the actual value of the function when the filter width is too large. This is convenient for functions such as sine and noise whose average is known.

17.5.1 Antialiased Checkerboard Fragment Shader

The checkerboard pattern is the standard measure of the quality of an antialiasing technique (see Figure 17.9). Larry Gritz wrote a checkerboard

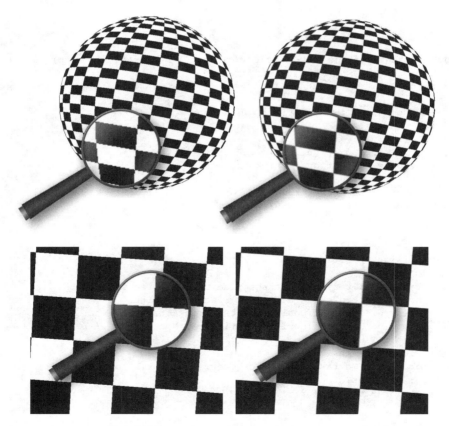

Figure 17.9   Checkerboard pattern rendered with the antialiased checkerboard shader. On the left, the filter width is set to 0, so aliasing occurs. On the right, the filter width is computed using the **fwidth** function.

RenderMan shader that performs antialiasing by frequency sampling, and Dave Baldwin translated this shader to GLSL. Listing 17.3 shows a fragment shader that produces a procedurally generated, antialiased checkerboard pattern. The vertex shader transforms the vertex position and passes along the texture coordinate, nothing more. The application provides values for the two colors of the checkerboard pattern, the average of these two colors (the application can compute this and provide it through a uniform variable, rather than having the fragment shader compute it for every fragment), and the frequency of the checkerboard pattern.

The fragment shader computes the appropriate size of the filter and uses it to perform smooth interpolation between adjoining checkerboard squares. If the filter is too wide (i.e., the in variable is changing too quickly for proper filtering), the average color is substituted. Even though this fragment shader uses a conditional statement, care is taken to avoid aliasing. In the transition zone between the **if** clause and the **else** clause, a smooth interpolation is performed between the computed color and the average color.

Listing 17.3 Source code for an antialiased checkerboard fragment shader

```
#version 140

uniform vec3  Color0;
uniform vec3  Color1;
uniform vec3  AvgColor;
uniform float Frequency;

in  vec2 TexCoord;
out vec4 FragColor;

void main()
{
    vec3 color;

    // Determine the width of the projection of one pixel into s-t space
    vec2 fw = fwidth(TexCoord);

    // Determine the amount of fuzziness
    vec2 fuzz = fw * Frequency * 2.0;

    float fuzzMax = max(fuzz.s, fuzz.t);

    // Determine the position in the checkerboard pattern
    vec2 checkPos = fract(TexCoord * Frequency);

    if (fuzzMax < 0.5)
    {
        // If the filter width is small enough,
        // compute the pattern color
```

```
            vec2 p = smoothstep(vec2(0.5), fuzz + vec2(0.5), checkPos) +
                     (1.0 - smoothstep(vec2(0.0), fuzz, checkPos));

            color = mix(Color0, Color1,
                        p.x * p.y + (1.0 - p.x) * (1.0 - p.y));

            // Fade in the average color when we get close to the limit
            color = mix(color, AvgColor, smoothstep(0.125, 0.5, fuzzMax));
        }
        else
        {
            // Otherwise, use only the average color
            color = AvgColor;
        }

        FragColor = vec4(color, 1.0);
    }
```

17.6 Summary

With increased freedom comes increased responsibility. The OpenGL Shading Language permits the computation of procedural textures without restriction. It is quite easy to write a shader that exhibits unsightly aliasing artifacts (using a conditional or a step function is all it takes), and it can be difficult to eliminate these artifacts. After describing the aliasing problem in general terms, this chapter explored several options for antialiasing procedural textures. Facilities in the language, such as the built-in functions for smooth interpolation (**smoothstep**), for determining derivatives in screen space (**dFdx**, **dFdy**), and for estimating filter width (**fwidth**) can assist in the fight against jaggies. These functions were fundamental components of shaders that were presented to perform antialiasing by prefiltering, adaptive prefiltering, integration, and frequency clamping.

17.7 Further Information

Most signal processing and image processing books contain a discussion of the concepts of sampling, reconstruction, and aliasing. Books by Glassner, Wolberg, and Gonzalez and Woods can be consulted for additional information on these topics. Technical memos by Alvy Ray Smith address the issues of aliasing in computer graphics directly.

The book *Advanced RenderMan: Creating CGI for Motion Pictures* by Anthony A. Apodaca and Larry Gritz (1999) contains a chapter that describes shader antialiasing in terms of the RenderMan shading language, and much of the discussion is germane to the OpenGL Shading Language as well. Darwyn Peachey has a similar discussion in *Texturing & Modeling: A Procedural Approach, Third Edition*, by David Ebert et al. (2002).

Bert Freudenberg developed an OpenGL shader to do adaptive antialiasing and presented this work at the SIGGRAPH 2002 in San Antonio, Texas. In this chapter, I've re-created the images Bert used in his talk, but he deserves the credit for originally developing the images and the shaders to illustrate some of the topics I've covered. This subject is also covered in his Ph.D. thesis, *Real-Time Stroke-based Halftoning*.

[1] *Former 3Dlabs developer Web site*. Now at http://3dshaders.com/.

[2] Apodaca, Anthony A., and Larry Gritz, *Advanced RenderMan: Creating CGI for Motion Pictures*, Morgan Kaufmann Publishers, San Francisco, 1999. www.renderman.org/RMR/Books/arman/materials.html

[3] Baldwin, Dave, *OpenGL 2.0 Shading Language White Paper, Version 1.0*, 3Dlabs, October, 2001.

[4] Cook, Robert L., *Stochastic Sampling in Computer Graphics*, ACM Transactions on Graphics, vol. 5, no. 1, pp. 51–72, January 1986.

[5] Crow, Franklin C., *The Aliasing Problem in Computer-Generated Shaded Images*, Communications of the ACM, 20(11), pp. 799–805, November 1977.

[6] Crow, Franklin C., *Summed-Area Tables for Texture Mapping*, Computer Graphics (SIGGRAPH '84 Proceedings), pp. 207–212, July 1984.

[7] Dippé, Mark A. Z., and Erling Henry Wold, *Antialiasing Through Stochastic Sampling*, Computer Graphics (SIGGRAPH '85 Proceedings), pp. 69–78, July 1985.

[8] Ebert, David S., John Hart, Bill Mark, F. Kenton Musgrave, Darwyn Peachey, Ken Perlin, and Steven Worley, *Texturing and Modeling: A Procedural Approach, Third Edition*, Morgan Kaufmann Publishers, San Francisco, 2002. www.texturingandmodeling.com

[9] Freudenberg, Bert, *A Non-Photorealistic Fragment Shader in OpenGL 2.0*, Presented at the SIGGRAPH 2002 Exhibition in San Antonio, July 2002. http://isgwww.cs.uni-magdeburg.de/~bert/publications

[10] Freudenberg, Bert, *Real-Time Stroke-based Halftoning*, Ph.D. thesis, University of Magdeburg, submitted in 2003.

[11] Glassner, Andrew S., *Principles of Digital Image Synthesis*, Vol. 1, Morgan Kaufmann Publishers, San Francisco, 1995.

[12] Glassner, Andrew S., *Principles of Digital Image Synthesis*, Vol. 2, Morgan Kaufmann Publishers, San Francisco, 1995.

[13] Gonzalez, Rafael C., and Richard E. Woods, *Digital Image Processing,
      Second Edition*, Prentice Hall, Upper Saddle River, New Jersey, 2002.

[14] Gritz, Larry, *LGAntialiasedChecks.sl*, RenderMan Repository Web site.
      www.renderman.org/RMR/Shaders/LGShaders/index.html

[15] Smith, Alvy Ray, *Digital Filtering Tutorial for Computer Graphics*,
      Lucasfilm Technical Memo 27, revised March 1983.
      www.alvyray.com/memos/default.htm

[16] Smith, Alvy Ray, *Digital Filtering Tutorial, Part II*, Lucasfilm Technical
      Memo 27, revised March 1983. www.alvyray.com/memos/
      default.htm

[17] Smith, Alvy Ray, *A Pixel Is Not a Little Square, a Pixel Is Not a Little
      Square, a Pixel Is Not a Little Square! (And a Voxel Is Not a Little Cube)*,
      Technical Memo 6, Microsoft Research, July 1995.
      www.alvyray.com/memos/default.htm

[18] Wolberg, George, *Digital Image Warping*, Wiley-IEEE Press, 2002.

Chapter 18

Non-photorealistic Shaders

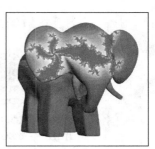

A significant amount of computer graphics research has been aimed at achieving more and more realistic renditions of synthetic scenes. A long-time goal has been to render a scene so perfectly that it is indistinguishable from a photograph of the real scene, a goal called PHOTOREALISM. With the latest graphics hardware, some photorealistic effects are becoming possible in real-time rendering.

This quest for realism is also reflected in graphics APIs such as OpenGL. The OpenGL specification defines specific formulas for calculating effects such as illumination from light sources, material properties, and fog. These formulas attempt to define effects as realistically as possible while remaining relatively easy to implement in hardware, and they have duly been cast into silicon by intrepid graphics hardware designers.

But the collection of human art and literature shows us that photorealism is not the only important style for creating images. The availability of low-cost programmable graphics hardware has sparked the growth of an area called NON-PHOTOREALISTIC RENDERING, or NPR. Researchers and practitioners in this field are attempting to use computer graphics to produce a wide range of artistic effects other than photorealism. In this chapter, we look at a few examples of shaders whose main focus is something other than generating results that are as realistic as possible.

18.1 Hatching Example

Bert Freudenberg of the University of Magdeburg in Germany was one of the first people outside 3Dlabs to come up with a unique OpenGL shader. His area of research has been to use programmable hardware to produce real-time NPR effects such as hatching and half-toning. He experimented with a prototype implementation of the OpenGL Shading Language in the summer of 2002 and produced a hatching shader that he agreed to share with us for this book.

This shader has a few unique features, and the steps involved in designing this shader are described in Bert's Ph.D. thesis, *Real-Time Stroke-based Half-toning* (2003). Bert's hatching shader is based on a woodblock printing shader by Scott Johnston that is discussed in *Advanced RenderMan: Creating CGI for Motion Pictures* by Anthony A. Apodaca and Larry Gritz (1999).

The goal in a hatching shader is to render an object in a way that makes it look hand-drawn, for instance with strokes that look like they may have been drawn with pen and ink. Each stroke contributes to the viewer's ability to comprehend the tone, texture, and shape of the object being viewed. The effect being sought in this shader is that of a woodcut print. In a woodcut, a wooden block carved with small grooves is covered with ink and pressed onto a surface. The image left on the surface is the mirror image of the image carved into the wood block. No ink is left where the grooves are cut, only where the wood is left uncut. Lighting is simulated by varying the width of the grooves according to light intensity.

We face a number of challenges in developing a shader that simulates the look of a woodcut print. The first thing we need is a way of generating stripes that defines the tone and texture of the object. Alternating white and black lines provides the highest-contrast edges and thus represents a worst-case scenario for aliasing artifacts; thus, antialiasing is a prime consideration. We also want our lines to "stay put" on the object so that we can use the object in an animation sequence. Finally, the lines in a woodcut print are not always perfectly straight and uniform as though they were drawn by a computer. They are cut into the wood by a human artist, so they have some character. We'd like the lines that our shader generates to have some character as well.

18.1.1 Application Setup

The application needs to send vertex positions, normals, and a single set of texture coordinates to the hatching shader. The normals are used in a simple lighting formula, and the texture coordinates are used as the base for procedurally defining the hatching pattern. The light position is passed in as a uniform variable, and the application also updates the value of the *Time* uniform variable at each frame so that the behavior of the shader can be modified slightly each frame. What do you suppose we use to give our lines some character? You guessed it—the noise function. In this case, we have the application generate the noise values that are needed and store the results in a 3D texture. For this reason, the value for a uniform variable of type **sampler3D** is provided by the application to inform the fragment shader which texture unit should be accessed to obtain the noise values.

18.1.2 Vertex Shader

The hatch vertex shader is shown in Listing 18.1. The first line is the only line that looks different from shaders we've discussed previously. The out variable *ObjPos* is the basis for our hatching stroke computation in the fragment shader. To animate the wiggle of the lines, the vertex shader adds the uniform variable *Time* to the z coordinate of the incoming vertex position. This makes it appear as though the wiggles are "flowing" along the z axis. A scaling value is also used to make the hatching strokes match the scale of the object being rendered. (To accommodate a variety of objects, we should probably replace this value with a uniform variable.) The remainder of the vertex shader performs a simple diffuse lighting equation, copies the t coordinate of the incoming texture coordinate into the out variable *V*, and computes the value of the built-in variable *gl_Position*.

Listing 18.1   Vertex shader for hatching

```
#version 140

uniform mat4 MVMatrix;
uniform mat4 MVPMatrix;
uniform mat3 NormalMatrix;

uniform vec3  LightPosition;
uniform float Time;

in  vec4  MCVertex;
in  vec3  MCNormal;
in  vec2  TexCoord0;

out vec3  ObjPos;
out float V;
out float LightIntensity;

void main()
{
    ObjPos          = (vec3(MCVertex) + vec3(0.0, 0.0, Time)) * 0.2;
```

```
vec3 pos        = vec3(MVMatrix * MCVertex);
vec3 tnorm      = normalize(NormalMatrix * MCNormal);
vec3 lightVec   = normalize(LightPosition - pos);

LightIntensity  = max(dot(lightVec, tnorm), 0.0);

V = TexCoord0.t;  // try .s for vertical stripes

gl_Position = MVPMatrix * MCVertex;
}
```

18.1.3 Generating Hatching Strokes

The purpose of our fragment shader is to determine whether each fragment is to be drawn as white or black in order to create lines on the surface of the object. As we mentioned, there are some challenges along the way. To prepare for the full-blown hatching shader, we develop some of the techniques we need and illustrate them on a simple object: a sphere.

We start with the same code that was presented in Section 17.4.1 for generating vertical stripes, namely,

```
float sawtooth = fract(V * 16.0);
float triangle = abs(2.0 * sawtooth - 1.0);
float square = step(0.5, triangle);
```

Recall that V was an out variable passed from the vertex shader. It was equal to the s texture coordinate if we wanted to generate vertical stripes and equal to the t texture coordinate if we wanted to generate horizontal stripes. We chose the number 16 to give us 16 white stripes and 16 black stripes. The result of this code is illustrated in Figure 18.1. We can modify the relative

Figure 18.1   A sphere with a stripe pattern generated procedurally based on the s texture coordinate (courtesy of Bert Freudenberg, University of Magdeburg, 2002)

size of the white and black stripes by adjusting the threshold value provided in the **step** function.

18.1.4 Obtaining Uniform Line Density

We now have reasonable-looking stripes, but they aren't of uniform width. They appear fatter along the equator and pinched in at the pole. We'd like to end up with lines that are of roughly equal width in screen space. This requires the use of the **dFdx** and **dFdy** functions:

```
float dp = length(vec2(dFdx(V), dFdy(V)));
```

As we learned in Section 17.4.3, this computation provides us with the gradient (i.e., how rapidly V is changing at this point on the surface). We can use this value to adjust the density of lines in screen space.

Computing the actual gradient with the **length** function involves a potentially costly square root operation. Why not use the approximation to the gradient discussed in Section 17.4.3? In this case we must compute the actual gradient because the approximation to the gradient isn't quite good enough for our purposes. We're not using this value to estimate the filter width for antialiasing; instead, we're using it to compute the stripe frequency. This computation needs to be rotationally invariant so that our stripes don't jump around just because we rotate the object. For this reason, we need to compute the actual length of the gradient vector, not just the sum of the absolute values of the two components of the gradient vector.

So, we use the base 2 logarithm of this value (shown applied to the sphere in Figure 18.2 (A)) to adjust the density in discrete steps—each time *dp* doubles, the number of lines doubles unless we do something about it. The stripes get too thin and too dense if doubling occurs. To counteract this effect (because we are interested in getting a constant line density in screen space), we decrease the number of stripes when the density gets too high. We do this by negating the logarithm.

```
float logdp     = -log2(dp);
float ilogdp    = floor(logdp);
float frequency = exp2(ilogdp);
float sawtooth  = fract(V * frequency * stripes);
```

A sphere with a higher stripe frequency is shown in Figure 18.2 (B). As you can see, the lines look reasonable in the lower part of the sphere, but there are too many at the pole. By applying the stripe frequency adjustment, we

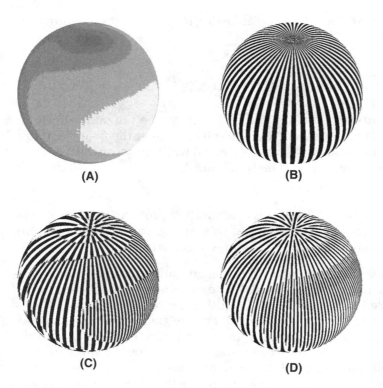

Figure 18.2 Adjusting the stripe frequency. The integer part of the logarithm of the gradient (A) is the basis for determining stripe frequency. First, the sphere is shown with a higher frequency of stripes (B). The integer part of the logarithm then adjusts the stripe frequency in (C), and the effect of tapering the ends is shown in (D). (Courtesy of Bert Freudenberg, University of Magdeburg, 2002.)

end up with stripes of roughly equal width across the sphere (see Figure 18.2 (C)). Notice the correlation between Figure 18.2 (A) and Figure 18.2 (C).

The next issue to address is the abrupt changes that occur as we jump from one stroke frequency to the next. Our eyes detect a distinct edge along these transitions, and we need to take steps to soften this edge so that it is less distracting. We can accomplish this by using the fractional part of *logdp* to do a smooth blend between two frequencies of the triangle wave. This value is 0 at the start of one frequency, and it increases to 1.0 at the point where the jump to the next frequency occurs.

```
float transition = logdp - ilogdp;
```

As we saw earlier, we can generate a triangle wave with frequency double that of a triangle wave with frequency *t* by taking **abs**(2.0 * *t* − 1.0). We can use the value of *transition* to linearly interpolate between *t* and **abs**(2.0 * *t* − 1.0) by computing (1.0 − *transition*) * *t* + *transition* * **abs**(2.0 * *t* − 1.0). This is exactly the same as if we did **mix**(**abs**(2.0 * *t* − 1.0), *t*, *transition*). But instead of using **mix**, we note that this is equivalent to **abs**((1.0 − *transition*) * *t* − *transition*). Using the previously computed value for our base frequency (*triangle*), we end up with the following code:

```
triangle = abs((1.0 - transition) * triangle - transition);
```

The result of drawing the sphere with uniform stripe density and tapered ends is shown in Figure 18.2 (D).

18.1.5 Simulating Lighting

To simulate the effect of lighting, we'd like to make the dark stripes more prominent in regions that are in shadow and the white stripes more prominent in regions that are lit. We can do this by using the computed light intensity to modify the threshold value used in the **step** function. In regions that are lit, the threshold value is decreased so that black stripes get thinner. In regions that are in shadow, the threshold value is increased so that the black stripes get wider.

```
const float edgew = 0.2;            // width of smooth step

float edge0  = clamp(LightIntensity - edgew, 0.0, 1.0);
float edge1  = clamp(LightIntensity, 0.0, 1.0);
float square = 1.0 - smoothstep(edge0, edge1, triangle);
```

Once again, we use the **smoothstep** function to antialias the transition. Because our stripe pattern is a (roughly) constant width in screen space, we can use a constant filter width rather than an adaptive one. The results of the lighting effect can be seen in Figure 18.3.

18.1.6 Adding Character

If a woodcut block is made by a human artist and not by a machine, the cuts in the wood aren't perfect in thickness and spacing. How do we add some imperfections into our mathematically perfect description of hatching lines? With noise (see Chapter 15). For this shader, we don't need anything fancy; we just want to add some "wiggle" to our otherwise perfect lines or

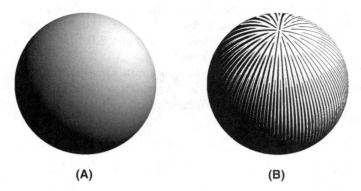

(A)   (B)

Figure 18.3   Applying lighting to the sphere. In (A), the sphere is lit with a simple lighting model and no stripes. In (B), the light intensity modulates the width of the stripes to simulate the effect of lighting. (Courtesy of Bert Freudenberg, University of Magdeburg, 2002.)

perhaps some "patchiness" to our simple lighting equation. We can use a tileable 3D texture containing Perlin noise in the same way for this shader as for the shaders in Chapter 15.

To add wiggle to our lines, we modify the sawtooth generation function.

```
float sawtooth = fract((V + noise * 0.1) * frequency * stripes);
```

The result of noise added to our stripe pattern is illustrated in Figure 18.4.

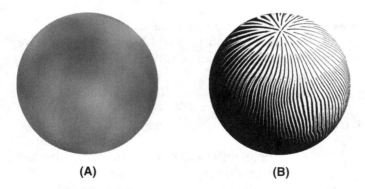

(A)   (B)

Figure 18.4   Adding noise to the hatching algorithm. In (A), the Perlin noise function is applied directly to the sphere's surface. In (B), it modulates the parameter that defines the frequency of the hatching strokes. (Courtesy of Bert Freudenberg, University of Magdeburg, 2002.)

Figure 18.5   Woodcut-style teapot rendered with the hatching shader (courtesy of Bert Freudenberg, University of Magdeburg, 2002)

18.1.7 Hatching Fragment Shader

The pieces described in the preceding sections are put together in the general-purpose hatching shader shown in Listing 18.2. It bases its hatching stroke computation on the *t* texture coordinate, so the result is horizontal stripes rather than vertical ones. The results of applying this shader to the teapot model are shown in Figure 18.5.

Listing 18.2   Fragment shader for woodcut-style rendering

```
#version 140

uniform sampler3D Noise;                // value of Noise = 3;

const float frequency = 1.0;

in  vec3  ObjPos;               // object space coord (noisy)
in  float V;                    // generic varying
in  float LightIntensity;

out vec4  FragColor;


void main()
{
    float dp       = length(vec2(dFdx(V), dFdy(V)));
    float logdp    = -log2(dp * 8.0);
```

```
float ilogdp    = floor(logdp);
float stripes   = exp2(ilogdp);

float noise     = texture(Noise, ObjPos).x;

float sawtooth = fract((V + noise * 0.1) * frequency * stripes);
float triangle = abs(2.0 * sawtooth - 1.0);

// adjust line width
float transition = logdp - ilogdp;

// taper ends
triangle = abs((1.0 + transition) * triangle - transition);

const float edgew = 0.3;              // width of smooth step

float edge0  = clamp(LightIntensity - edgew, 0.0, 1.0);
float edge1  = clamp(LightIntensity, 0.0, 1.0);
float square = 1.0 - smoothstep(edge0, edge1, triangle);

FragColor = vec4(vec3(square), 1.0);
}
```

18.2 Technical Illustration Example

Pick up just about any instruction manual, technical book, or encyclopedia and you will see a variety of illustrations other than photographs or photo-realistic graphics. Technical illustrators have learned various techniques over the years to convey relevant information as simply and as clearly as possible. Details that do not contribute to understanding are omitted, and details that are crucial to understanding are clear and straightforward. This style of illustration differs from mainstream computer graphics for which an enormous amount of detail may be presented in an image to make it look more realistic. The effort to convey information as succinctly as possible in a technical illustration is summed up by a strategy referred to by Edward Tufte (1997) as "the smallest effective difference." In his book *Visual Explanations*, Tufte says, "Make all visual distinctions as subtle as possible, but still clear and effective."

Various NPR practitioners are attempting to develop algorithms to create technical illustrations. The goal is to simplify or even automate the task of creating high-quality technical illustrations according to time-honored illustration techniques. Much of our comprehension about an object's shape comes from lighting. Yet the traditional lighting equation is deficient at conveying shape information in areas that are not lit directly, because these areas appear flat. The only lighting in these areas comes from the ambient term, which is constant. Technical illustrations also highlight important edges in black so that they are distinct and clearly convey the shape of the object. If a small ambient term is used in the traditional lighting model, black edge highlights typically are indistinguishable from unlit regions of the object, which are also very near black.

In 1998, Bruce and Amy Gooch, Peter Shirley, and Elaine Cohen surveyed illustrations and came up with a list of common characteristics for color illustrations done with airbrush and pen.

- Surface boundaries, silhouette edges, and discontinuities in the surface of an object are usually drawn with black curves.

- A single light source is used, and it produces a white highlight on objects.

- The light source is usually positioned above the object so that the diffuse reflection term varies in the range [0,1] across the visible portion of the object.

- Effects that add complexity (realism) such as shadows, reflections, and multiple light sources are not shown.

- Matte objects are shaded with intensities far from white and black so as to be clearly distinct from (black) edges and (white) highlights.

- The warmth or coolness of the color indicates the surface normal (and hence the curvature of the surface).

These characteristics were incorporated into a "low dynamic range artistic tone algorithm" that we now refer to as GOOCH SHADING.

One of the important aspects of Gooch shading is the generation of black curves that represent important edges. There are a number of techniques for rendering such edges. Perhaps the best method is to have them identified during the modeling process by the person designing the model. In this case, the edges can be rendered as antialiased black lines that are drawn on top of the object itself, that is, in a second rendering pass that draws the edges after the objects in the scene have been completely rendered.

If important edges have not been identified during the modeling process, several methods can generate them automatically. Quality of results varies according to the method used and the characteristics of the objects in the scene. Interior boundary or crease edges should also be identified, and these are sometimes critical to comprehension. A technique that identifies boundary or crease edges as well as silhouette edges involves using vertex and fragment shaders to write world-space normals and depth values into the framebuffer. The result is stored as a texture, and a subsequent rendering pass with different vertex and fragment shaders can use an edge detection algorithm on this "image" to detect discontinuities (i.e., edges) in the scene (Jason Mitchell (2002)).

A technique for drawing silhouette edges for simple objects, described by Jeff Lander (2000) in *Under the Shade of the Rendering Tree*, requires drawing the geometry twice. First, we draw just the front-facing polygons using filled polygons and the depth comparison mode set to GL_LESS. The Gooch shaders are active when we do this. Then, we draw the back-facing polygons as lines with the depth comparison mode set to GL_LEQUAL. This has the effect of drawing lines such that a front-facing polygon shares an edge with a back-facing polygon. We draw these lines with a trivial fragment shader that outputs black FragColor with polygon mode set so that back-facing polygons are drawn as lines. The OpenGL calls to do this are shown in Listing 18.3.

Listing 18.3   C code for drawing silhouette edges on simple objects

```
// Enable culling
glEnable(GL_CULL_FACE);

// Draw front-facing polygons as filled using the Gooch shader
glPolygonMode(GL_FRONT_AND_BACK, GL_FILL);
glDepthFunc(GL_LESS);
glCullFace(GL_BACK);
glUseProgram(ProgramGooch);
drawSphere(0.6f, 64);

// Draw back-facing polygons as black lines using standard OpenGL
glLineWidth(5.0);
glPolygonMode(GL_BACK_AND_BACK, GL_LINE);
glDepthFunc(GL_LEQUAL);
glCullFace(GL_FRONT);
glUseProgram(ProgramBlackFragment);
drawSphere(0.6f, 64);
```

A second aspect of Gooch shading is that specular highlights are computed with the exponential specular term of the Phong lighting model and are rendered in white. Highlights convey information about the curvature of the surface, and choosing white as the highlight color ensures that highlights are distinct from edges (which are black) and from the colors shading the object (which are chosen to be visually distinct from white or black).

A third aspect of the algorithm is that a limited range of luminance values is used to convey information about the curvature of the surfaces that are being rendered. This part of the shading uses the color of the object, which is typically chosen to be an intermediate value that doesn't interfere visually with white or black.

Because the range of luminance values is limited, a warm-to-cool color gradient is also added to convey more information about the object's surface. Artists use "warm" colors (yellow, red, and orange) and "cool" colors (blue, violet, and green) to communicate a sense of depth. Warm colors, which appear to advance, indicate objects that are closer. Cool colors, which appear to recede, indicate objects that are farther away.

The actual shading of the object depends on two factors. The diffuse reflection factor generates luminance values in a limited range to provide one part of the shading. A color ramp that blends between two colors provides the other part of the shading. One of the two colors is chosen to be a cool (recessive) color, such as blue, to indicate surfaces that are angled away from the light source. The other color is chosen to be a warm (advancing) color, such as yellow, to indicate surfaces facing toward the light source. The blue-to-yellow ramp provides an undertone that ensures a cool-to-warm transition regardless of the diffuse object color that is chosen.

The formulas used to compute the colors used for Gooch shading are as follows:

$$k_{cool} = k_{blue} + \alpha k_{diffuse}$$

$$k_{warm} = k_{yellow} + \beta k_{diffuse}$$

$$k_{final} = \left(\frac{1 + N \cdot L}{2}\right) k_{cool} + \left(1 - \frac{1 + N \cdot L}{2}\right) k_{warm}$$

k_{cool} is the color for the areas that are not illuminated by the light source. We compute this value by adding the blue undertone color and the diffuse color of the object, $k_{diffuse}$. The value α is a variable that defines how much of the object's diffuse color will be added to the blue undertone color. k_{warm} is the color for the areas that are fully illuminated by the light source. This value is computed as the sum of the yellow undertone color and the object's diffuse color multiplied by a scale factor, β.

The final color is just a linear blend between the colors k_{cool} and k_{warm} based on the diffuse reflection term $N \cdot L$, where N is the normalized surface normal and L is the unit vector in the direction of the light source. Since $N \cdot L$ can vary from $[-1,1]$, we add 1 and divide the result by 2 to get a value in the range $[0,1]$. This value determines the ratio of k_{cool} and k_{warm} to produce the final color value.

18.2.1 Application Setup

We implement this shading algorithm in two passes (i.e., we draw the geometry twice). We use the Lander technique to render silhouette edges in black. In the first pass, we cull back-facing polygons and render the front-facing polygons with the Gooch shader. In the second pass, we cull all the front-facing polygons and use a trivial fragment shader to render the edges of the back-facing polygons in black. We draw the edges with a line width greater than one pixel so that they can be seen outside the object. For this shader to work properly, only vertex positions and normals need to be passed to the vertex shader.

18.2.2 Vertex Shader

The goals of the Gooch vertex shader are to produce a value for the $(1 + N \cdot L) / 2$ term in the previous equations and to pass on the reflection vector and the view vector so that the specular reflection can be computed in the fragment shader (see Listing 18.4). Other elements of the shader are identical to shaders discussed earlier.

Listing 18.4   Vertex shader for Gooch matte shading

```
#version 140

uniform mat4 MVMatrix;
uniform mat4 MVPMatrix;
uniform mat3 NormalMatrix;

uniform vec3  LightPosition;  // (0.0, 10.0, 4.0)

in  vec4  MCVertex;
in  vec3  MCNormal;
in  vec2  TexCoord0;

out float NdotL;
out vec3  ReflectVec;
out vec3  ViewVec;

void main()
{
    vec3 ecPos      = vec3(MVMatrix * MCVertex);
    vec3 tnorm      = normalize(NormalMatrix * MCNormal);
    vec3 lightVec   = normalize(LightPosition - ecPos);
    ReflectVec      = normalize(reflect(-lightVec, tnorm));
    ViewVec         = normalize(-ecPos);
    NdotL           = dot(lightVec, tnorm) * 0.5 + 0.5;
    gl_Position     = MVPMatrix * MCVertex;
}
```

18.2.3 Fragment Shader

The fragment shader implements the tone-based shading portion of the
Gooch shading algorithm and adds the specular reflection component
(see Listing 18.5). The colors and ratios are defined as uniform variables so
that they can be easily modified by the application. The reflection and view
vectors are normalized in the fragment shader because interpolation may
have caused them to have a length other than 1.0. The result of rendering
with the Gooch shader and the silhouette edge algorithm described by
Lander is shown in Color Plate 27.

Listing 18.5 Fragment shader for Gooch matte shading

```
#version 140

uniform vec3  SurfaceColor;  // (0.75, 0.75, 0.75)
uniform vec3  WarmColor;     // (0.6, 0.6, 0.0)
uniform vec3  CoolColor;     // (0.0, 0.0, 0.6)
uniform float DiffuseWarm;   // 0.45
uniform float DiffuseCool;   // 0.45

in  float NdotL;
in  vec3  ReflectVec;
in  vec3  ViewVec;

out vec4 FragColor;

void main()
{
    vec3 kcool    = min(CoolColor + DiffuseCool * SurfaceColor, 1.0);
    vec3 kwarm    = min(WarmColor + DiffuseWarm * SurfaceColor, 1.0);
    vec3 kfinal   = mix(kcool, kwarm, NdotL);

    vec3 nreflect = normalize(ReflectVec);
    vec3 nview    = normalize(ViewVec);

    float spec    = max(dot(nreflect, nview), 0.0);
    spec          = pow(spec, 32.0);

    FragColor = vec4(min(kfinal + spec, 1.0), 1.0);
}
```

18.3 Mandelbrot Example

C'mon, now, what kind of a book on graphics programming would this be
without an example of drawing the Mandelbrot set?

Our last shader of the chapter doesn't fall into the category of attempting to achieve an artistic or painterly effect, but it's an example of performing a type of general-purpose computation on the graphics hardware for scientific visualization. In this case, the graphics hardware enables us to do real-time exploration of a famous mathematical function that computes the Mandelbrot set. In 1998, Michael Rivero created a RenderMan shader that creates the Mandelbrot set as a texture. Subsequently, Dave Baldwin adapted this shader for GLSL, Steve Koren then made some modifications to it to get it working on programmable hardware for the first time, and I've adapted this shader further for inclusion in this book.

The point of including this shader is to emphasize the fact that with the OpenGL Shading Language, computations that were previously possible only in the realm of the CPU can now be executed on the graphics hardware. Performing the computations completely on the graphics hardware is a big performance win because the computations can be carried out on many pixels in parallel. Visualization of a complex mathematical function such as the Mandelbrot set barely begins to tap the potential for using programmable shader technology for scientific visualization.

18.3.1 About the Mandelbrot Set

To understand the Mandelbrot set, we must first recall a few things from our high school mathematics days. No real number, when multiplied by itself, yields a negative value. But the imaginary number called i is defined to be equal to the square root of –1. With i, the square root of any negative number can easily be described. For instance, $3i$ squared is –9, and conversely the square root of –9 is $3i$.

Numbers that consist of a real number and an imaginary number, such as $6 + 4i$, are called COMPLEX NUMBERS. Arithmetic operations can be performed on complex numbers just as on real numbers. The result of multiplying two complex numbers is as follows:

$$x = a + bi$$

$$y = c + di$$

$$xy = ac + adi + cbi - bd$$

$$= (ac - bd) + (ad + bc)i$$

Because complex numbers contain two parts, the set of complex numbers is two-dimensional. Complex numbers can be plotted on the complex number plane, which uses the horizontal axis to represent the real part and the vertical axis to represent the imaginary part (see Figure 18.6).

In Figure 18.6, we see three symbols plotted on the complex number plane. A small square is plotted at the complex number $2 + i$, a small circle is plotted at $-1 + 2i$, and a triangle is plotted at $-1.5 - 0.5i$.

With the assistance of 1970s computer technology (quite inferior by today's consumer PC standards), a mathematician named Benoit Mandelbrot began studying a recursive function involving complex numbers.

$$Z_0 = c$$

$$Z_{n+1} = Z_n^2 + c$$

In this function, the value of Z is initialized to c, the value of the complex number being tested. For each iteration, the value of Z is squared and added to c to determine a new value for Z. This amazingly simple iterative formula produces what has been called the most complex object in mathematics, and perhaps the most complex structure ever seen!

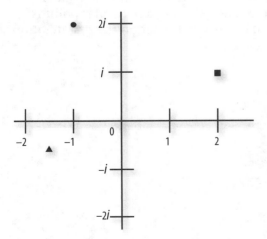

Figure 18.6   A portion of the complex number plane

It turns out that for some values of c, the function eventually approaches infinity, and for other values it does not. Quite simply, values of c that go off to infinity are not part of the Mandelbrot set, and the rest are. If we use a computer (or an OpenGL Shading Language–capable graphics accelerator!) to test thousands of points on the complex number plane and assign a gray level to those that go off to infinity and black to those that don't, we see the following familiar cardioid/prickly pear shape start to appear (see Figure 18.7).

How exactly do we test whether these values go off to infinity? Well, Mandelbrot helped us out a bit here. He showed that if the magnitude of Z (its distance from the origin) was greater than 2, the value of the function would go to infinity. To encode this function in a programming language, all we need to do is stop iterating when the magnitude of Z surpasses 2. Even easier, because we're always dealing with Z^2, we can simply check to see if Z^2 is greater than 4.

The values inside the black region of Figure 18.7 do not go off to infinity in any reasonable number of iterations. How do we deal with these? To prevent our computer or graphics hardware from locking up in an infinite loop, we need to decide on the maximum number of iterations to allow before we give up and assume the point is inside the Mandelbrot set. With these two exit criteria, we can write a simple loop that computes the Mandelbrot set.

The beauty of the Mandelbrot set can be enhanced if we color code the number of iterations needed to determine whether a particular point is inside the set. Values determined to be outside the set on the first iteration

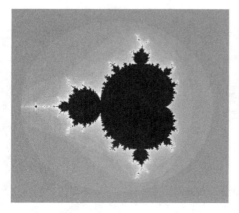

Figure 18.7   Simple plot of the Mandelbrot set

are given one color value, values determined to be outside the set on the second iteration are given another color value, and so on. In Figure 18.7, I've used gray levels to indicate the number of iterations. The medium gray on the outside represents values that are identified as outside the Mandelbrot set on the very first iteration. Values in white along the edge took 20 iterations to be identified as being outside the Mandelbrot set.

The edges of the Mandelbrot set hold an infinite amount of self-similar variety. By continuing to zoom in on the edge detail, you can find complex numbers whose magnitude stayed below 2 for hundreds or even thousands of iterations of the function before finally exceeding the threshold and zooming off to infinity.

Here are a few other deep thoughts that you can use to amaze and amuse your friends:

- The length of the border for the Mandelbrot set is infinite.

- All the regions inside the Mandelbrot set (i.e., the black regions) are connected.

- There is exactly one band surrounding the Mandelbrot set for each iteration value (e.g., a band that exceeded the threshold on the first iteration, a band that exceeded on the second iteration, and so on). The iteration bands go completely around the Mandelbrot set, do not break, and do not cross each other. When you've zoomed in to explore an edge region with amazing complexity, this is pretty astonishing.

- There are an infinite number of "mini-Mandelbrots" (regions that look like warped or transformed versions of the full Mandelbrot set) within the original.

18.3.2 Vertex Shader

The vertex shader for the Mandelbrot set (see Listing 18.6) is almost exactly the same as the vertex shader for the simple brick example that was described in Section 6.2. The only difference is that we assume that texture coordinates will be provided in the range of [0,1] for both s and t, and we map these values into the range [–2.5, 2.5] and store the result into an out variable named *Position*. This enables the fragment shader to plot values directly onto a coordinate system that is just the right size for plotting the Mandelbrot set, and it has the point (0,0) in the middle. If the application draws a single polygon that is a screen-aligned square and has texture coordinate (0,0) in the lower-left corner and (1,1) in the upper right, the result is a standard representation of the Mandelbrot set. Of course, with our OpenGL Mandelbrot shader, the Mandelbrot set can be "textured" onto any geometry, and we even apply a simple lighting model as an added bonus.

Listing 18.6   Vertex shader for drawing the Mandelbrot set

```
#version 140

uniform mat4 MVMatrix;
uniform mat4 MVPMatrix;
uniform mat3 NormalMatrix;

uniform vec3  LightPosition;
uniform float SpecularContribution;
uniform float DiffuseContribution;
uniform float Shininess;

in  vec4  MCVertex;
in  vec3  MCNormal;
in  vec3  TexCoord0;

out float LightIntensity;
out vec3  Position;

void main()
{
    vec3 ecPosition = vec3(MVMatrix * MCVertex);
    vec3 tnorm      = normalize(NormalMatrix * MCNormal);
    vec3 lightVec   = normalize(LightPosition - ecPosition);
    vec3 reflectVec = reflect(-lightVec, tnorm);
    vec3 viewVec    = normalize(-ecPosition);
    float spec      = max(dot(reflectVec, viewVec), 0.0);
    spec            = pow(spec, Shininess);
    LightIntensity  = DiffuseContribution *
                      max(dot(lightVec, tnorm), 0.0) +
                      SpecularContribution * spec;
    Position        = TexCoord0 * 5.0 - 2.5;
    gl_Position     = MVPMatrix * MCVertex;
}
```

18.3.3 Fragment Shader

The fragment shader implements the algorithm described in the previous section. Uniform variables establish the maximum number of iterations and the starting point for viewing the Mandelbrot set (center value and zoom factor). The application is given artistic license to use uniform variables to set one color for points inside the set and two colors to use for points outside the set. For values outside the set, the color gradient from *OuterColor1* to *OuterColor2* is broken into 20 separate bands, and the cycle is repeated if the number of iterations goes past 20. It is repeated again if the number of iterations goes past 40, and so on.

This shader maps the *x* coordinate of the computed position in the complex number plane (i.e., the value in *Position.x*) to the real number in the iterative function, and the *y* coordinate to the imaginary number. After the initial conditions have been established, the shader enters a loop with two exit criteria—if we reach the maximum number of iterations allowed or if the point proves to be outside the set. Within the loop, the function $Z^2 + c$ is computed for use in the next iteration. After the loop is exited, we compute the color of the fragment. If we're inside the set, we use the inside color. If we're on the edge or outside, we blend the edge color and the outer color, depending on the number of iterations that have occurred.

The complete fragment shader is shown in Listing 18.7.

Listing 18.7   Fragment shader for computing the Mandelbrot set

```
#version 140

uniform float MaxIterations;
uniform float Zoom;
uniform float Xcenter;
uniform float Ycenter;
uniform vec3  InnerColor;
uniform vec3  OuterColor1;
uniform vec3  OuterColor2;

in  vec3  Position;
in  float LightIntensity;
out vec4  FragColor;

void main()
{
    float   real = Position.x * Zoom + Xcenter;
    float   imag = Position.y * Zoom + Ycenter;
    float   Creal = real;   // Change this line...
    float   Cimag = imag;   // ...and this one to get a Julia set

    float r2 = 0.0;
    float iter;

    for (iter = 0.0; iter < MaxIterations && r2 < 4.0; ++iter)
    {
        float tempreal = real;
```

```
        real = (tempreal * tempreal) - (imag * imag) + Creal;
        imag = 2.0 * tempreal * imag + Cimag;
        r2   = (real * real) + (imag * imag);
    }

    // Base the color on the number of iterations

    vec3 color;

    if (r2 < 4.0)
        color = InnerColor;
    else
        color = mix(OuterColor1, OuterColor2, fract(iter * 0.05));

    color *= LightIntensity;

    FragColor = vec4(color, 1.0);
}
```

There is obviously room for improvement in this shader. One thing you might do is improve the color selection algorithm. One possibility is to use a 1D texture to store a color lookup table. The number of iterations could be used to index into this table to obtain the color for drawing the fragment.

After you've invented a pleasing coloring scheme, you can explore some of the popular Mandelbrot "tourist locations." Various books and Web sites have published the coordinates of interesting locations in the Mandelbrot set, and these shaders are set up so that you can plug those coordinates in directly and zoom in and see for yourself. Figure 18.8 shows a few that I explored.

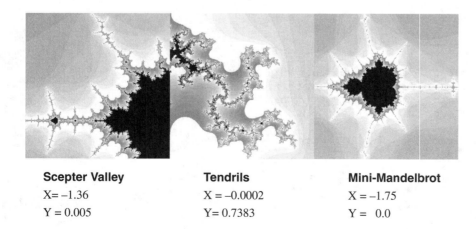

Scepter Valley
X= –1.36
Y = 0.005

Tendrils
X = –0.0002
Y= 0.7383

Mini-Mandelbrot
X = –1.75
Y = 0.0

Figure 18.8   Results from the Mandelbrot shader

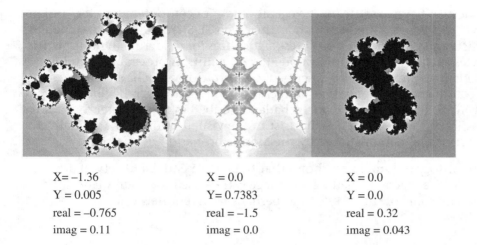

X= −1.36	X = 0.0	X = 0.0
Y = 0.005	Y= 0.7383	Y = 0.0
real = −0.765	real = −1.5	real = 0.32
imag = 0.11	imag = 0.0	imag = 0.043

Figure 18.9 Some Julia sets rendered with the Mandelbrot shader

18.3.4 Julia Sets

Julia sets are related to the Mandelbrot set. Each point in the Mandelbrot set can be used to generate a Julia set, and these are just as much fun to explore as the Mandelbrot set. The only difference is that the constant c in the equation term $Z^2 + c$ is initialized to the value of a point in the Mandelbrot set other than the one currently being plotted. To change the Mandelbrot shader into a fragment shader for doing Julia sets, change the two lines of code that initialize the value of c.

```
float   Creal = -1.36;   // Now we'll see an interesting Julia set
float   Cimag = 0.11;
```

Figure 18.9 shows a few examples of the Julia sets that can be rendered with this shader. You might want to change this shader so that the values for *Creal* and *Cimag* can be passed in as uniform variables when you want to draw a Julia set. The numbers are no longer imaginary. Now we can do real-time exploration of the mathematical universe through the OpenGL Shading Language!

18.4 Summary

Realism is no longer the goal for all applications of interactive computer graphics. Because of the flexibility of programmable graphics hardware, we no longer have to settle for the classic "look" of computer graphics. A high-level procedural language such as the OpenGL Shading Language enables artists and practitioners to express algorithms for rendering in more artistic styles such as pen-and-ink, woodcut, and paints. A procedural hatching shader was presented and described to illustrate how such rendering can be accomplished. Various styles of technical illustration can be done interactively, as shown by the Gooch shader described in this chapter. It is also possible to write shaders that assist in the visualization of mathematical functions, as demonstrated by the Mandelbrot and Julia set shaders.

The history of human art shows that there is an endless variety of artistic styles. The OpenGL Shading Language can be used to create shaders that emulate some of these styles and perhaps to invent new ones.

18.5 Further Information

Books devoted to the topic of non-photorealistic rendering include *Non-Photorealistic Rendering* by Amy Gooch and Bruce Gooch (2001) and *Non-Photorealistic Computer Graphics* by Thomas Strothotte and Stefan Schlechtweg (2002).

The Gooch shading algorithm is defined and described in the SIGGRAPH 1998 paper, *A Non-Photorealistic Lighting Model for Automatic Technical Illustration*, by Amy Gooch, Bruce Gooch, Peter Shirley, and Elaine Cohen. This paper draws on concepts presented by Edward Tufte in *Visual Explanations* (1997). A short discussion of NPR can be found in *Real-Time Rendering, Second Edition*, by Tomas Akenine-Möller and Eric Haines (2002). I've also included a lot of references to NPR resources in the main bibliography at the end of this book.

The classic text on fractals and the Mandelbrot set is, of course, *The Fractal Geometry of Nature, Updated and Augmented,* by Benoit Mandelbrot (1983). In 1986, Heinz-Otto Peitgen and Peter Richter wrote *The Beauty of Fractals,* another book you can enjoy looking at as well as reading. Peitgen and Dietmer Saupe (1988) edited a book called *The Science of Fractal Images*, which contains numerous examples and algorithms and additional material by Mandelbrot, Richard Voss, and others. A couple of the Mandelbrot "tourist destinations" that I've listed were described by Paul Derbyshire on the now defunct Web site, *PGD's Quick Guide to the Mandelbrot Set.*

[1] Akenine-Möller, Tomas, E. Haines, *Real-Time Rendering, Second Edition*, AK Peters, Ltd., Natick, Massachusetts, 2002. www.realtimerendering.com

[2] Baldwin, Dave, *OpenGL 2.0 Shading Language White Paper, Version 1.0*,
     3Dlabs, October, 2001.

[3] Derbyshire, Paul, *PGD's Quick Guide to the Mandelbrot Set*, personal Web
     site. www.globalserve.net/~derbyshire/manguide.html (defunct)

[4] Freudenberg, Bert, Maic Masuch, and Thomas Strothotte, *Walk-Through
     Illustrations: Frame-Coherent Pen-and-Ink Style in a Game Engine*,
     Computer Graphics Forum, Volume 20 (2001), Number 3,
     Manchester, U.K. http://isgwww.cs.uni-magdeburg.de/~bert/
     publications

[5] Freudenberg, Bert, Maic Masuch, and Thomas Strothotte, *Real-Time
     Halftoning: A Primitive For Non-Photorealistic Shading*, Rendering
     Techniques 2002, Proceedings 13th Eurographics Workshop,
     pp. 227–231, 2002. http://isgwww.cs.uni-magdeburg.de/~bert/
     publications

[6] Freudenberg, Bert, and Maic Masuch, *Non-Photorealistic Shading in an
     Educational Game Engine*, SIGGRAPH and Eurographics Campfire,
     Snowbird, Utah, June 1–June 4, 2002.
     http://isgwww.cs.uni-magdeburg.de/~bert/publications

[7] Freudenberg, Bert, *Real-Time Stroke-based Halftoning*, Ph.D. thesis,
     University of Magdeburg, submitted in 2003.

[8] Gooch, Amy, *Interactive Non-Photorealistic Technical Illustration*, Master's
     thesis, University of Utah, December 1998.
     www.cs.utah.edu/~gooch/publication.html

[9] Gooch, Amy, Bruce Gooch, Peter Shirley, and Elaine Cohen, *A Non-
     Photorealistic Lighting Model for Automatic Technical Illustration*,
     Computer Graphics (SIGGRAPH '98 Proceedings), pp. 447–452,
     July 1998. www.cs.utah.edu/~gooch/publication.html

[10] Gooch, Bruce, Peter-Pike J. Sloan, Amy Gooch, Peter Shirley, and
     Richard Riesenfeld, *Interactive Technical Illustration*, Proceedings
     1999 Symposium on Interactive 3D Graphics, pp. 31–38, April
     1999. www.cs.utah.edu/~gooch/publication.html

[11] Gooch, Bruce, and Amy Gooch, *Non-Photorealistic Rendering*, AK Peters
     Ltd., Natick, Massachusetts, 2001.
     www.cs.utah.edu/~gooch/book.html

[12] Lander, Jeff, *Under the Shade of the Rendering Tree*, Game Developer
     Magazine, vol. 7, no. 2, pp. 17–21, Feb. 2000.
     www.darwin3d.com/gdm2000.htm

[13] Mandelbrot, Benoit B., *The Fractal Geometry of Nature, Updated and
     Augmented*, W. H. Freeman and Company, New York, 1983.

[14] Mitchell, Jason L., *Image Processing with Pixel Shaders in Direct3D*, in
     Engel, Wolfgang, ed., ShaderX, Wordware, May 2002.
     www.pixelmaven.com/jason

[15] Peitgen, Heinz-Otto, and P. H. Richter, *The Beauty of Fractals, Images of Complex Dynamical Systems,* Springer Verlag, Berlin Heidelberg, 1986.

[16] Peitgen, Heinz-Otto, D. Saupe, M. F. Barnsley, R. L. Devaney, B. B. Mandelbrot, R. F. Voss, *The Science of Fractal Images,* Springer Verlag, New York, 1988.

[17] Strothotte, Thomas, and S. Schlectweg, *Non-Photorealistic Computer Graphics, Modeling, Rendering, and Animation,* Morgan Kaufmann Publishers, San Francisco, 2002.

[18] Tufte, Edward, *Visual Explanations*, Graphics Press, Cheshire, Connecticut, 1997.

Chapter 19

Shaders for Imaging

In this chapter, we describe shaders whose primary function is to operate on two-dimensional images rather than on three-dimensional geometric primitives.

A fragment shader can be used to process texture values read from a texture map. We can divide imaging operations into two broad categories: those that require access to a single pixel at a time and those that require access to multiple pixels at a time. With the OpenGL Shading Language, you can easily implement in a fragment shader the imaging operations that require access to only a single pixel at a time. Operations that require access to multiple pixels at a time require that the image first be stored in texture memory. You can then access the image multiple times from within a fragment shader to achieve the desired result.

An OpenGL shader typically can perform imaging operations much faster on the graphics hardware than on the CPU because of the highly parallel nature of the graphics hardware. So, we let the fragment shader handle the task. This approach also frees the CPU to perform other useful tasks. If the image to be modified is stored as a texture on the graphics accelerator, the user can interact with it in real time to correct color, remove noise, sharpen an image, and do other such operations, and all the work can be done on the graphics board, with very little traffic on the I/O bus.

19.1   Geometric Image Transforms

If you want to rotate an image, the traditional response has always been "Load the image into texture memory, use it to draw a textured rectangle, and transform the rectangle." Although this approach does require an extra read and write of the image within the graphics system—the image must be written into texture memory and then read as the rectangle is drawn—the speed and bandwidth of today's graphics accelerators make this an acceptable approach for all but the most demanding applications. With the OpenGL Shading Language, you can even provide the same rectangle coordinates every time you draw the image and let the vertex shader do the scaling, translation, or rotation of the rectangle. You can perform image warping by texturing a polygon mesh instead of a single rectangle. Hardware support for texture filtering can produce high-quality results for any of these operations.

19.2   Mathematical Mappings

A common imaging operation supported by OpenGL fixed functionality is scale-and-bias. In this operation, each incoming color component is multiplied by a scale factor, and a bias value is added. You can use the result to map color values from one linear range to another. This is straightforward in the OpenGL Shading Language with the use of the standard math operators. You can do more complex mathematical mappings on pixel values with built-in functions such as **pow**, **exp2**, and **log2**.

The built-in dot product function (**dot**) can produce a single intensity value from a color value. The following code computes a CIE luminance value from linear RGB values defined according to *ITU-R Recommendation BT.709* (the HDTV color standard):

```
float luminance = dot(vec3(0.2125, 0.7154, 0.0721), rgbColor);
```

This luminance mapping function is the standard used in manufacturing contemporary monitors, and it defines a linear RGB color space. The coefficients 0.299, 0.587, and 0.114 are often used to convert an RGB value to a luminance value. However, these values were established with the inception of the NTSC standard in 1953 to compute luminance for the monitors of that time, and they are used to convert nonlinear RGB values to luminance values. They do not accurately calculate luminance for today's CRT monitors, but they are still appropriate for computing nonlinear video luma from nonlinear RGB input values as follows:

```
float luma = dot(vec3(0.299, 0.587, 0.114), rgbColor);
```

19.3   Lookup Table Operations

OpenGL defines a number of lookup tables as part of its fixed functionality. Several are defined as part of the imaging subset. Lookup tables are simply a way of mapping an input value to one or more output values. This operation provides a level of indirection that is often useful for processing color information. The fact that OpenGL has programmable processors means that you can compute the input values as part of a shader and use the output value as part of further computation within the shader. This creates a lot of new possibilities for lookup tables.

A flexible and efficient way to perform lookup table operations with an OpenGL shader is to use a 1D texture map. The lookup table can be an arbitrary size (thus overcoming a common gripe about OpenGL lookup tables often being limited by implementations to 256 entries). You can use the lookup table to map a single input value to a single output value or to a two-, three-, or four-component value. If you want the values returned to be discrete values, set the 1D texture's filtering modes to GL_NEAREST. If you want interpolation to occur between neighboring lookup table values, use GL_LINEAR.

You can use an intensity value in the range [0,1] as the texture coordinate for a 1D texture access. The built-in texture functions always return an RGBA value. If a texture with a single channel has been bound to the texture unit specified by the sampler, the value of that texture is contained in each of the red, green, and blue channels, so you can pick any of them.

```
float color = texture(lut, intensity).r; // GL_PIXEL_MAP_I_TO_I
```

You can perform an intensity-to-RGBA lookup with a single texture access.

```
vec4  color = texture(lut, intensity);    // GL_PIXEL_MAP_I_TO_R,G,B,A
```

An RGBA-to-RGBA lookup operation requires four texture accesses.

```
vec4 colorOut;
colorOut.r = texture(lut, colorIn.r).r;   // GL_PIXEL_MAP_R_TO_R
colorOut.g = texture(lut, colorIn.g).g;   // GL_PIXEL_MAP_G_TO_G
colorOut.b = texture(lut, colorIn.b).b;   // GL_PIXEL_MAP_B_TO_B
colorOut.a = texture(lut, colorIn.a).a;   // GL_PIXEL_MAP_A_TO_A
```

However, if you don't need alpha and you are willing to use a 3D texture to store the color table, you can do an RGB-to-RGB lookup with a single texture access.

```
colorOut.rgb = texture(lut, colorIn.rgb).rgb;
```

In this case, the variable *lut* must be defined as a **sampler3d**, whereas in the previous cases it needed to be defined as a **sampler1d**.

19.4 Color Space Conversions

A variety of color space conversions can be implemented in OpenGL shaders. In this section, we look at converting CIE colors to RGB, and vice versa. Conversions between other color spaces can be done similarly.

The CIE system was defined in 1931 by the Committee Internationale de L'Èclairage (CIE). It defines a device-independent color space based on the characteristics of human color perception. The CIE set up a hypothetical set of primaries, XYZ, that correspond to the way the eye's retina behaves. After experiments based on color matching by human observers, the CIE defined the primaries so that all visible light maps into a positive mixture of X, Y, and Z and so that Y correlates approximately to the apparent lightness of a color. The CIE system precisely defines any color. With this as a standard reference, colors can be transformed from the native (device-dependent) color space of one device to the native color space of another device.

A matrix formulation is convenient for performing such conversions. The HDTV standard as defined in *ITU-R Recommendation BT.709* (1990) has the following CIE XYZ primaries and uses the D_{65} (natural sunlight) white point:

	R	G	B	white
x	0.640	0.300	0.150	0.3127
y	0.330	0.600	0.060	0.3290
z	0.030	0.100	0.790	0.3582

Listing 19.1 shows the OpenGL shader code that transforms CIE color values to HDTV standard RGB values by using the D_{65} white point, and Listing 19.2 shows the reverse transformation. The matrices look like they are transposed compared to the colorimetry literature because in the OpenGL Shading Language matrix values are provided in column major order.

Listing 19.1   OpenGL shader code to transform CIE values to RGB

```
const mat3 CIEtoRGBmat = mat3(3.240479, -0.969256,  0.055648,
                             -1.537150,  1.875992, -0.204043,
                             -0.498535,  0.041556,  1.057311);

vec3 rgbColor = cieColor * CIEtoRGBmat;
```

Listing 19.2   OpenGL shader code to transform RGB values to CIE

```
const mat3 RGBtoCIEmat = mat3(0.412453, 0.212671, 0.019334,
                              0.357580, 0.715160, 0.119193,
                              0.180423, 0.072169, 0.950227);

vec3 cieColor = rgbColor * RGBtoCIEmat;
```

19.5 Image Interpolation and Extrapolation

In 1994, Paul Haeberli and Douglas Voorhies published an interesting paper that described imaging operations that could be performed with interpolation and extrapolation operations. These operations could actually be programmed on the high-end graphics systems of that time; today, thanks to the OpenGL Shading Language, they can be done quite easily on consumer graphics hardware.

The technique is quite simple. The idea is to determine a target image that can be used together with the source image to perform interpolation and extrapolation. The equation is set up as a simple linear interpolation that blends two images:

$$Image_{out} = (1 - \alpha) \cdot Image_{target} + \alpha \cdot Image_{source}$$

The target image is actually an image that you want to interpolate or extrapolate away from. Values of *alpha* between 0 and 1 interpolate between the two images, and values greater than 1 extrapolate between the two images. For instance, to adjust brightness, the target image is one in which every pixel is black. When *alpha* is 1, the result is the source image. When *alpha* is 0, the result is that all pixels are black. When *alpha* is between 0 and 1, the result is a linear blend of the source image and the black image, effectively darkening the image. When *alpha* is greater than 1, the image is brightened.

Such operations can be applied to images (pixel rectangles in OpenGL jargon) with a fragment shader as they are being sent to the display. In cases in which a target image is really needed (in many cases, it is not needed, as we shall see), it can be stored in a texture and accessed by the fragment shader. If the source and target images are downloaded into memory on the graphics card (i.e., stored as textures), these operations can be blazingly fast, limited only by the memory speed and the fill rate of the graphics hardware. This should be much faster than performing the same operations on the CPU and downloading the image across the I/O bus every time it's modified.

19.5.1 Brightness

Brightness is the easiest example. The target image is composed entirely of black pixels (e.g., pixel values (0,0,0)). Therefore, the first half of the interpolation equation goes to zero, and the equation reduces to a simple scaling of the source pixel values. This is implemented with the fragment shader in

Listing 19.3, and the results for several values of *alpha* are shown in Color Plate 29.

Listing 19.3   Fragment shader for adjusting brightness uniform float Alpha;

```
#version 140

uniform float Alpha;

in  vec4 Color;
out vec4 FragColor;

void main(void)
{
    FragColor = Color * Alpha;
}
```

19.5.2 Contrast

A somewhat more interesting example is contrast (see Listing 19.4). Here the target image is chosen to be a constant gray image with each pixel containing a value equal to the average luminance of the image. This value and the *alpha* value are assumed to be computed by the application and sent to the shader as uniform variables. The results of the contrast shader are shown in Color Plate 30.

Listing 19.4   Fragment shader for adjusting contrast

```
#version 140

uniform vec3  AvgLuminance;
uniform float Alpha;

in  vec3  Color;
out vec4  FragColor;

void main()
{
    vec3 color  = mix(AvgLuminance, Color, Alpha);
    FragColor   = vec4(color, 1.0);
}
```

19.5.3 Saturation

The target image for a saturation adjustment is an image containing only luminance information (i.e., a grayscale version of the source image). This image can be computed pixel-by-pixel by extraction of the luminance value from each RGB value. The proper computation depends on knowing the color space in which the RGB values are specified. For RGB values specified according to the HDTV color standard, you could use the coefficients shown in the shader in Listing 19.5. Results of this shader are shown in Color Plate 31. As you can see, extrapolation can provide useful results for values that are much greater than 1.0.

Listing 19.5 Fragment shader for adjusting saturation

```
#version 140

const   vec3   lumCoeff = vec3(0.2125, 0.7154, 0.0721);
uniform float Alpha;

in  vec4 Color;
out vec4 FragColor;

void main()
{
    vec3 intensity = vec3(dot(Color.rgb, lumCoeff));
    vec3 color     = mix(intensity, Color.rgb, Alpha);
    FragColor      = vec4(color, 1.0);
}
```

19.5.4 Sharpness

Remarkably, this technique also lends itself to adjusting any image convolution operation (see Listing 19.6). For instance, you can construct a target image by blurring the original image. Interpolation from the source image to the blurred image reduces high frequencies, and extrapolation (*alpha* greater than 1) increases them. The result is image sharpening through UNSHARP MASKING. The results of the sharpness fragment shader are shown in Color Plate 32.

Listing 19.6 Fragment shader for adjusting sharpness

```
#version 140

uniform sampler2D Blurry;
uniform float Alpha;

in  vec2  TexCoord;
in  vec4  Color;
out vec4  FragColor;

void main()
{
    vec3 blurred  = vec3(texture(Blurry, TexCoord.st));
    vec3 color    = Color.rgb * Alpha + blurred * (1.0 - Alpha);
    FragColor     = vec4(color, 1.0);
}
```

These examples showed the simple case in which the entire image is modified with a single *alpha* value. More complex processing is possible. The *alpha* value could be a function of other variables. A control texture could define a complex shape that indicates the portion of the image to be modified. A brush pattern could apply the operation selectively to small regions of the image. The operation could be applied selectively to pixels with a certain luminance range (e.g., shadows, highlights, or midtones).

Fragment shaders can also interpolate between more than two images, and the interpolation need not be linear. Interpolation can be done along several axes simultaneously with a single target image. A blurry, desaturated version of the source image can be used with the source image to produce a sharpened, saturated version in a single operation.

19.6 Blend Modes

With the expressiveness of a high-level language, it is easy to combine, or blend, two images in a variety of ways. Both images can be stored in texture memory, or one can be in texture memory and one can be downloaded by the application with **glDrawPixels**. For example, here's a fragment shader that adds together two images:

```
#version 140

uniform sampler2D BaseImage;
uniform sampler2D BlendImage;
uniform float Opacity;

in  vec2 TexCoord;
out vec4 FragColor;

void main (void)
{
    vec4 base  = texture(BaseImage, TexCoord.xy);
    vec4 blend = texture(BlendImage, TexCoord.xy);

    vec4 result = blend + base;
        result = clamp(result, 0.0, 1.0);

    FragColor = mix(base, result, Opacity);
}
```

The following sections contain snippets of OpenGL shader code that perform pixel-by-pixel blending for some of the common blend modes. In each case,

- *base* is a **vec4** containing the RGBA color value from the base (original) image.

- *blend* is a **vec4** containing the RGBA color value from the image that is being blended into the base image.

- *result* is a **vec4** containing the RGBA color that results from the blending operation.

- If it's needed in the computation, *white* is a **vec4** containing (1.0, 1.0, 1.0, 1.0).

- If it's needed in the computation, *lumCoeff* is a **vec4** containing (0.2125, 0.7154, 0.0721, 1.0).

- As a final step, *base* and *result* are combined by use of a floating-point value called *Opacity*, which determines the contribution of each.

There is no guarantee that the results of the code snippets provided here will produce results identical to those of your favorite image editing program, but the effects should be similar. The OpenGL shader code for the various blend modes is based on information published by Jens Gruschel in his article *Blend Modes*, available at www.pegtop.net/delphi/blendmodes. Unless otherwise noted, the blend operations are not commutative (you will get different results if you swap the base and blend images).

Results of the blend mode shaders are shown in Color Plate 33.

19.6.1 Normal

NORMAL is often used as the default blending mode. The blend image is placed over the base image. The resulting image equals the blend image when the opacity is 1.0 (i.e., the base image is completely covered). For opacities other than 1.0, the result is a linear blend of the two images based on *Opacity*.

```
result = blend;
```

19.6.2 Average

The AVERAGE blend mode adds the two images and divides by two. The result is the same as NORMAL when the opacity is set to 0.5. This operation is commutative.

```
result = (base + blend) * 0.5;
```

19.6.3 Dissolve

In the DISSOLVE mode, either *blend* or *base* is chosen randomly at every pixel. The value of *Opacity* is used as a probability factor for choosing the *blend* value. Thus, as the opacity gets closer to 1.0, the *blend* value is more likely to be chosen than the *base* value. If we draw the image as a texture on a rectangular polygon, we can use the texture coordinate values as the argument to **noise1D** to provide a value with which we can select in a pseudo-random, but repeatable, way. We can apply a scale factor to the texture coordinates to obtain noise of a higher frequency and give the appearance of randomness. The value returned by the noise function is in the range [–1,1] so we add 1 and multiply by 0.5 to get it in the range [0,1].

```
float noise = (noise1(vec2(TexCoord * noiseScale)) + 1.0) * 0.5;
result = (noise < Opacity) ? blend : base;
```

19.6.4 Behind

BEHIND chooses the *blend* value only where the base image is completely transparent (i.e., *base.a* = 0.0). You can think of the base image as a piece of clear acetate, and the effect of this mode is as if you were painting the blend image on the back of the acetate—only the areas painted behind transparent pixels are visible.

```
result = (base.a == 0.0) ? blend : base;
```

19.6.5 Clear

CLEAR always uses the *blend* value, and the alpha value of *result* is set to 0 (transparent). This blend mode is more apt to be used with drawing tools than on complete images.

```
result.rgb = blend.rgb;
result.a   = 0.0;
```

19.6.6 Darken

In DARKEN mode, the two values are compared, and the minimum value is chosen for each component. This operation makes images darker because the blend image can do nothing except make the base image darker. A blend image that is completely white (RGB = 1.0, 1.0, 1.0) does not alter the base image. Regions of black (0, 0, 0) in either image cause the result to be black.

It is commutative—the result is the same if the blend image and the base image are swapped.

```
result = min(blend, base);
```

19.6.7 Lighten

LIGHTEN can be considered the opposite of DARKEN. Instead of taking the minimum of each component, we take the maximum. The blend image can therefore never do anything but make the result lighter. A blend image that is completely black (RGB = 0, 0, 0) does not alter the base image. Regions of white (1.0, 1.0, 1.0) in either image cause the result to be white. The operation is commutative because swapping the two images does not change the result.

```
result = max(blend, base);
```

19.6.8 Multiply

In MULTIPLY mode, the two values are multiplied together. This produces a darker result in all areas in which neither image is completely white. White is effectively an identity (or transparency) operator because any color multiplied by white will be the original color. Regions of black (0, 0, 0) in either image cause the result to be black. The result is similar to the effect of stacking two color transparencies on an overhead projector. This operation is commutative.

```
result = blend * base;
```

19.6.9 Screen

SCREEN can be thought of as the opposite of MULTIPLY because it multiplies the inverse of the two input values. The result of this multiplication is then inverted to produce the final result. Black is effectively an identity (or transparency) operator because any color multiplied by the inverse of black (i.e., white) will be the original color. This blend mode is commutative.

```
result = white - ((white - blend) * (white - base));
```

19.6.10 Color Burn

COLOR BURN darkens the base color as indicated by the blend color by decreasing luminance. There is no effect if the *blend* value is white. This computation can result in some values less than 0, so truncation may occur when the resulting color is clamped.

```
result = white - (white - base) / blend;
```

19.6.11 Color Dodge

COLOR DODGE brightens the base color as indicated by the blend color by increasing luminance. There is no effect if the *blend* value is black. This computation can result in some values greater than 1, so truncation may occur when the result is clamped.

```
result = base / (white - blend);
```

19.6.12 Overlay

OVERLAY first computes the luminance of the base value. If the luminance value is less than 0.5, the *blend* and *base* values are multiplied together. If the luminance value is greater than 0.5, a screen operation is performed. The effect is that the *base* value is mixed with the *blend* value, rather than being replaced. This allows patterns and colors to overlay the base image, but shadows and highlights in the base image are preserved. A discontinuity occurs where luminance = 0.5. To provide a smooth transition, we actually do a linear blend of the two equations for luminance in the range [0.45,0.55].

```
float luminance = dot(base, lumCoeff);
if (luminance < 0.45)
    result = 2.0 * blend * base;
else if (luminance > 0.55)
    result = white - 2.0 * (white - blend) * (white - base);
else
{
    vec4 result1 = 2.0 * blend * base;
    vec4 result2 = white - 2.0 * (white - blend) * (white - base);
    result = mix(result1, result2, (luminance - 0.45) * 10.0);
}
```

19.6.13 Soft Light

SOFT LIGHT produces an effect similar to a soft (diffuse) light shining through the blend image and onto the base image. The resulting image is essentially a muted combination of the two images.

```
result = 2.0 * base * blend + base * base - 2.0 * base * base * blend;
```

19.6.14 Hard Light

HARD LIGHT mode is identical to OVERLAY mode, except that the luminance value is computed with the *blend* value rather than the *base* value. The effect is similar to shining a harsh light through the blend image and onto the base image. Pixels in the blend image with a luminance of 0.5 have no effect on the base image. This mode is often used to produce embossing effects. The **mix** function provides a linear blend between the two functions for luminance in the range [0.45,0.55].

```
float luminance = dot(blend, lumCoeff);
if (luminance < 0.45)
    result = 2.0 * blend * base;
else if (luminance > 0.55)
    result = white - 2.0 * (white - blend) * (white - base);
else
{
    vec4 result1 = 2.0 * blend * base;
    vec4 result2 = white - 2.0 * (white - blend) * (white - base);
    result = mix(result1, result2, (luminance - 0.45) * 10.0);
}
```

19.6.15 Add

In the ADD mode, the result is the sum of the blend image and the base image. Truncation may occur because resulting values can exceed 1.0. The blend and base images can be swapped, and the result will be the same.

```
result = blend + base;
```

19.6.16 Subtract

SUBTRACT subtracts the blend image from the base image. Truncation may occur because resulting values may be less than 0.

```
result = base - blend;
```

19.6.17 Difference

In the DIFFERENCE mode, the result is the absolute value of the difference between the *blend* value and the *base* value. A result of black means the two initial values were equal. A result of white means they were opposite. This mode can be useful for comparing images because identical images produce a completely black result. An all-white blend image can be used to invert the base image. Blending with black produces no change. Because of the absolute value operation, this blend mode is commutative.

```
result = abs(blend - base);
```

19.6.18 Inverse Difference

The INVERSE DIFFERENCE blend mode performs the "opposite" of DIFFERENCE. Blend values of white and black produce the same results as for DIFFERENCE (white inverts and black has no effect), but colors in between white and black become lighter instead of darker. This operation is commutative.

```
result = white - abs(white - base - blend);
```

19.6.19 Exclusion

EXCLUSION is similar to DIFFERENCE, but it produces an effect that is lower in contrast (softer). The effect for this mode is in between the effects of the DIFFERENCE and INVERSE DIFFERENCE modes. Blending with white inverts the base image, blending with black has no effect, and colors in between become gray. This is also a commutative blend mode.

```
result = base + blend - (2.0 * base * blend);
```

19.6.20 Opacity

In OPACITY mode, an opacity value in the range [0,1] can also specify the relative contribution of the base image and the computed result. The *result* value from any of the preceding formulas can be further modified to compute the effect of the *opacity* value as follows:

```
finalColor = mix(base, result, Opacity);
```

19.7 Convolution

CONVOLUTION is a common image processing operation that filters an image by computing the sum of products between the source image and a smaller image called the CONVOLUTION KERNEL or the CONVOLUTION FILTER. Depending on the choice of values in the convolution kernel, a convolution operation can perform blurring, sharpening, noise reduction, edge detection, and other useful imaging operations.

Mathematically, the discrete 2D convolution operation is defined as

$$H(x, y) = \sum_{j=0}^{height-1} \sum_{i=0}^{width-1} F(x+i, y+j) \cdot G(i, j)$$

In this equation, the function F represents the base image, and G represents the convolution kernel. The double summation is based on the width and height of the convolution kernel. We compute the value for a particular pixel in the output image by aligning the center of the convolution kernel with the pixel at the same position in the base image, multiplying the values of the base image pixels covered by the convolution kernel by the values in the corresponding locations in the convolution kernel, and then summing the results.

The flexibility of the OpenGL Shading Language enables convolution operations with arbitrary-sized kernels and full floating-point precision. Furthermore, the convolution operation can be written in an OpenGL shader such that the minimum number of multiplication operations is actually performed (i.e., kernel values equal to 0 do not need to be stored or used in the convolution computation).

But there are a couple of hurdles to overcome. First, this operation seems naturally suited to implementation as a fragment shader, but the fragment shader is not allowed to access the values of any neighboring fragments. How can we perform a neighborhood operation such as convolution without access to the "neighborhood"?

The answer to this dilemma is that we store the base image in texture memory and access it as a texture. We can draw a screen-aligned rectangle that's the same size on the screen as the base image and enable texturing to render the image perfectly. We can introduce a fragment shader into this process, and instead of sampling the image just once during the texturing process, we can access each of the values under the convolution kernel and compute the convolution result at every pixel.

A second hurdle is that, although the OpenGL Shading Language supports loops, even nested loops, it does not currently support two-dimensional arrays. We can easily overcome this by "unrolling" the convolution kernel and storing it as a one-dimensional array. Each location in this array stores an x- and y-offset from the center of the convolution kernel and the value of the convolution kernel at that position. In the fragment shader, we process this array in a single loop, adding the specified offsets to the current texture location, accessing the base image, and multiplying the retrieved pixel value by the convolution kernel value. Storing the convolution kernel this way means that we can store the values in row major order, column major order, backwards, or all mixed up. We don't even need to include convolution kernel values that are zero, because they do not contribute to the convolved image.

The interesting work for performing convolution is done with fragment shaders. The vertex shader is required to perform an identity mapping of the input geometry (a screen-aligned rectangle that is the size of the base image), and it is required to pass on texture coordinates. The texture coordinate (0,0) should be assigned to the lower-left corner of the rectangle, and the texture coordinate (1,1) should be assigned to the upper-right corner of the rectangle.

One additional issue with convolution operations is deciding what to do when the convolution kernel extends beyond the edges of the base image. A convenient side effect of using OpenGL texture operations to perform the convolution is that the texture-wrapping modes defined by OpenGL map nicely to the common methods of treating convolution borders. Thus,

- To achieve the same effect as the GL_CONSTANT_BORDER, set the GL_TEXTURE_WRAP_S and GL_TEXTURE_WRAP_T parameters of the texture containing the base image to GL_CLAMP_TO_BORDER. This method uses the border color when the convolution kernel extends past the image boundary.

- If the desired behavior is the same as GL_REPLICATE_BORDER, set the GL_TEXTURE_WRAP_S and GL_TEXTURE_WRAP_T parameters of the texture containing the base image to GL_CLAMP_TO_EDGE. This method uses the pixel value at the edge of the image when the convolution kernel extends past the image boundary.

- If you want to mimic the GL_REDUCE convolution border mode, draw a rectangle that is smaller than the image to be convolved. For a 3×3 convolution kernel, the rectangle should be smaller by two pixels in *width* and two pixels in *height*. In this case, the texture coordinate of the lower-left corner is $(1/width, 1/height)$, and the texture coordinate of the upper-right corner is $(1 - 1/width, 1 - 1/height)$.

The texture filtering modes should be set to GL_NEAREST to avoid unintended interpolation.

19.7.1 Smoothing

Image smoothing operations can attenuate high frequencies in an image. A common image smoothing operation is known as NEIGHBORHOOD AVERAGING. This method uses a convolution kernel that contains a weighting of 1.0 in each location. The final sum is divided by a value equal to the number of locations in the convolution kernel. For instance, a 3×3 neighborhood averaging convolution filter would look like this:

1	1	1
1	1	1
1	1	1

The resulting sum would be divided by 9 (or multiplied by 1/9). Neighborhood averaging, as the name implies, has the effect of averaging all the pixels in a region with equal weighting. It effectively smears the value of each pixel to its neighbors, resulting in a blurry version of the original image.

Because all the elements of the convolution kernel are equal to 1, we can write a simplified fragment shader to implement neighborhood averaging (see Listing 19.7). This shader can be used for neighborhood averaging for any kernel size where *width * height* is less than or equal to 25 (i.e., up to 5×5). The results of this operation are shown in Figure 19.1 (B).

Listing 19.7 Fragment shader for the neighborhood averaging convolution operation

```
#version 140

// maximum size supported by this shader
const int MaxKernelSize = 25;

// array of offsets for accessing the base image
uniform vec2 Offset[MaxKernelSize];

// size of kernel (width * height) for this execution
uniform int KernelSize;

// final scaling value
uniform vec4 ScaleFactor;
```

```
// image to be convolved
uniform sampler2D BaseImage;

// texture coordinate output from vertex shader
in vec2 TexCoord;

// fragment shader output
out vec4 FragColor;

void main()
{
    int i;
    vec4 sum = vec4(0.0);

    for (i = 0; i < KernelSize; i++)
        sum += texture(BaseImage, TexCoord.st + Offset[i]);

    FragColor = sum * ScaleFactor;
}
```

Image smoothing by means of convolution is often used to reduce noise. This works well in regions of solid color or intensity, but it has the side effect of blurring high frequencies (edges). A convolution filter that applies higher weights to values nearer the center can do a better job of eliminating noise while preserving edge detail. Such a filter is the Gaussian filter, which can be encoded in a convolution kernel as follows:

1/273	4/273	7/273	4/273	1/273
4/273	16/273	26/273	16/273	4/273
7/273	26/273	41/273	26/273	7/273
4/273	16/273	26/273	16/273	4/273
1/273	4/273	7/273	4/273	1/273

Listing 19.8 contains the code for a more general convolution shader. This shader can handle convolution kernels containing up to 25 entries. In this shader, each convolution kernel entry is expected to have been multiplied by the final scale factor, so there is no need to scale the final sum.

Listing 19.8 Fragment shader general convolution computation

```
#version 140

// maximum size supported by this shader
const int MaxKernelSize = 25;
```

```
// array of offsets for accessing the base image
uniform vec2 Offset[MaxKernelSize];

// size of kernel (width * height) for this execution
uniform int KernelSize;

// value for each location in the convolution kernel
uniform vec4 KernelValue[MaxKernelSize];

// image to be convolved
uniform sampler2D BaseImage;

// texture coordinate output from vertex shader
in vec2 TexCoord;

// fragment shader output
out vec4 FragColor;

void main()
{
    int i;
    vec4 sum = vec4(0.0);

    for (i = 0; i < KernelSize; i++)
    {
        vec4 tmp = texture(BaseImage, TexCoord.st + Offset[i]);
        sum += tmp * KernelValue[i];
    }

    FragColor = sum;
}
```

The original image in Figure 19.1 (A) has had uniform noise added to it to create the image in Figure 19.1 (C). The Gaussian smoothing filter is then applied to this image to remove noise, and the result is shown in Figure 19.1 (D). Notice in particular that the noise has been significantly reduced in areas of nearly constant intensity.

As the size of the convolution kernel goes up, the number of texture reads that is required increases as the square of the kernel size. For larger kernels, this can become the limiting factor for performance. Some kernels, including the Gaussian kernel just described, are said to be separable because the convolution operation with a *width* × *height* kernel can be performed as two passes, with one-dimensional convolutions of size *width* × 1 and 1 × *height*. With this approach, there is an extra write for each pixel (the result of the first pass), but the number of texture reads is reduced from *width* × *height* to *width* + *height*.

(A) Original 512 × 512 grayscale image

(B) 5 × 5 neighborhood averaging

(C) Original with noise added

(D) Noise reduction with Gaussian filter

Figure 19.1   Results of various convolution operations

19.7.2 Edge Detection

Another common use for the convolution operation is edge detection. This operation is useful for detecting meaningful discontinuities in intensity level. The resulting image can aid in image comprehension or can enhance the image in other ways.

One method for detecting edges involves the Laplacian operator.

0	1	0
1	−4	1
0	1	0

We can plug the Laplacian convolution kernel into the fragment shader shown in Listing 19.8. This results in the image shown in Figure 19.2.

Figure 19.2 Edge detection with the Laplacian convolution kernel (image scaled for display)

19.7.3 Sharpening

A common method of image sharpening is to add the results of an edge detection filter back onto the original image. To control the degree of sharpening, a scaling factor scales the edge image as it is added.

One way to sharpen an image is with the negative Laplacian operator. This convolution filter is defined as

0	−1	0
−1	4	−1
0	−1	0

The fragment shader that implements image sharpening in this fashion is almost identical to the general convolution shader shown in the previous section (see Listing 19.9). The only difference is that the result of the convolution operation is added to the original image. Before it is added, the convolution result is scaled by a scale factor provided by the application through a uniform variable. The results of unsharp masking are shown in Figure 19.3 and Figure 19.4.

Listing 19.9 Fragment shader for unsharp masking

```
#version 140

// maximum size supported by this shader
const int MaxKernelSize = 25;

// array of offsets for accessing the base image
uniform vec2 Offset[MaxKernelSize];
```

```
// size of kernel (width * height) for this execution
uniform int KernelSize;

// value for each location in the convolution kernel
uniform vec4 KernelValue[MaxKernelSize];

// scaling factor for edge image
uniform vec4 ScaleFactor;

// image to be convolved
uniform sampler2D BaseImage;

// texture coordinate output from vertex shader
in vec2 TexCoord;

// fragment shader output
out vec4 FragColor;


void main()
{
    int i;
    vec4 sum = vec4(0.0);

    for (i = 0; i < KernelSize; i++)
    {
        vec4 tmp = texture(BaseImage, TexCoord.st + Offset[i]);
        sum += tmp * KernelValue[i];
    }

    vec4 baseColor = texture(BaseImage, vec2(TexCoord));
    FragColor = ScaleFactor * sum + baseColor;
}
```

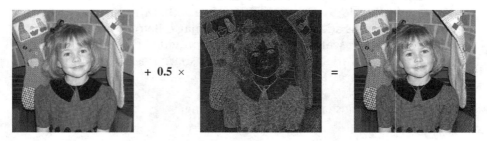

Figure 19.3   Results of the unsharp masking shader. (Laplacian image in center is scaled for display.) Zoomed views of the original and resulting images are shown in Figure 19.4.

Figure 19.4   Results of the unsharp masking shader. Original image is on the left, sharpened image on the right.

19.8   Summary

In addition to support for rendering 3D geometry, OpenGL also contains a great deal of support for rendering images. The OpenGL Shading Language allows fully programmable processing of images. With this programmability and the parallel processing nature of the underlying graphics hardware, image processing operations can be performed orders-of-magnitude faster on the graphics accelerator than on the CPU. This programmability can be used to implement traditional image processing operations such as image blurring, sharpening, and noise removal; high-quality color correction; brightness, saturation, and contrast adjustment; geometric transformations such as rotation and warping; blending; and many other image processing operations. Furthermore, applications no longer need to be constrained to manipulating monochrome or color images. Multispectral processing and analysis are also possible.

The world of digital imagery is exploding as a result of the rapid development and acceptance of consumer products for digital photography and digital video. The OpenGL Shading Language will undoubtedly be at the heart of many tools that support this revolution in the future.

19.9   Further Information

The OpenGL literature doesn't always do justice to the imaging capabilities of OpenGL. In 1996, I wrote a paper called *Using OpenGL for Imaging* that attempted to describe and highlight clearly the fixed functionality imaging capabilities of OpenGL, including the capabilities of several pertinent imaging extensions. This paper was published as part of the SPIE Medical Imaging '96 Image Display Conference in Newport Beach, CA, and is available on this book's companion Web site at http://3dshaders.com/pubs. Another good resource for understanding how to use OpenGL for imaging is the course notes for the SIGGRAPH '99 course *Advanced Graphics Programming Techniques Using OpenGL* by Tom McReynolds and David Blythe. These can be found online at www.opengl.org/resources/tutorials/sig99/advanced99/notes/notes.html. This material has also been published in a recent book by Morgan Kaufmann.

Charles Poynton (1997) is one of the luminaries (pun intended) of the color technology field, and his *Frequently Asked Questions about Color* and *Frequently Asked Questions about Gamma* are informative and approachable treatments of a variety of topics relating to color and imaging. I found these on the Web on Charles's home page at www.poynton.com/Poynton-color.html.

The CIE color system is defined in Publication CIE 17.4–1987, *International Lighting Vocabulary*, Vienna, Austria, Central Bureau of the Committee Internationale de L'Èclairage, currently in its fourth edition. The HDTV color standard is defined in *ITU-R BT.709-2–Parameter Values for the HDTV Standards for Production and International Programme Exchange*, Geneva: ITU, 1990.

The paper *Image Processing by Interpolation and Extrapolation* by Paul Haeberli and Douglas Voorhies appeared in IRIS Universe Magazine in1994. A slightly shorter version of this paper is available online at www.graficaobscura.com/interp/.

A classic textbook on image processing is *Digital Image Processing, Second Edition*, by Rafael C. Gonzalez and Richard E. Woods, Addison-Wesley, 2002. An amazing little book (literally amazing, and literally little) is the *Pocket Handbook of Image Processing Algorithms in C* by Harley Myler and Arthur Weeks (1993).

[1] Gonzalez, Rafael C., and Richard E. Woods, *Digital Image Processing, Second Edition*, Prentice Hall, Upper Saddle River, New Jersey, 2002.

[2] Gruschel, Jens, *Blend Modes,* Pegtop Software Web site.
      www.pegtop.net/delphi/blendmodes

[3] Haeberli, Paul, and Douglas Voorhies, *Image Processing by Interpolation and Extrapolation*, IRIS Universe Magazine No. 28, Silicon Graphics, August, 1994. www.graficaobscura.com/interp/

[4] Hall, Roy, *Illumination and Color in Computer Generated Imagery*, Springer-Verlag, New York, 1989.

[5] *International Lighting Vocabulary*, Publication CIE No. 17.4, Joint
     publication IEC (International Electrotechnical Commission) and
     CIE (Committee Internationale de L'Èclairage), Geneva, 1987.
     www.cie.co.at/framepublications.html

[6] ITU-R Recommendation BT.709, *Basic Parameter Values for the HDTV
     Standard for the Studio and for International Programme Exchange*,
     [formerly CCIR Rec. 709], Geneva, ITU, 1990.

[7] Lindbloom, Bruce J., *Accurate Color Reproduction for Computer Graphics
     Applications*, Computer Graphics (SIGGRAPH '89 Proceedings),
     pp. 117–126, July 1989.

[8] Lindbloom, Bruce J., personal Web site, 2003.
     www.brucelindbloom.com/

[9] McReynolds, Tom, David Blythe, Brad Grantham, and Scott Nelson,
     Advanced Graphics Programming Techniques Using OpenGL,
     SIGGRAPH '99 course notes, 1999. www.opengl.org/
     resources/tutorials/sig99/advanced99/notes/notes.html

[10] McReynolds, Tom, and David Blythe, *Advanced Graphics Programming
     Techniques Using OpenGL*, Morgan Kaufmann, 2005.

[11] Myler, Harley R., and Arthur R. Weeks, *The Pocket Handbook of Image
     Processing Algorithms in C*, Prentice Hall, Upper Saddle River, NJ,
     1993.

[12] Poynton, Charles A., *A Technical Introduction to Digital Video*,
     John Wiley & Sons, New York, 1996.

[13] Poynton, Charles A., *Frequently Asked Questions about Color*, 1997.
     www.poynton.com/Poynton-color.html

[14] Rost, Randi, *Using OpenGL for Imaging*, SPIE Medical Imaging '96
     Image Display Conference, February 1996.
     http://3dshaders.com/pubs

[15] Wolberg, George, *Digital Image Warping*, Wiley-IEEE Press, 2002.

Chapter 20

Language Comparison

The OpenGL Shading Language is by no means the first graphics shading language ever defined. Here are a few other notable shading languages and a little about how each one compares to the OpenGL Shading Language. Compare the diagrams in this chapter with the OpenGL Shading Language execution model in Figure 2.4 for a visual summary.

20.1 Chronology of Shading Languages

Rob Cook and Ken Perlin are usually credited with being the first to develop languages to describe shading calculations. Both of these efforts targeted offline (noninteractive) rendering systems. Perlin's work included the definition of the noise function and the introduction of control constructs. Cook's work on shade trees at Lucasfilm (later Pixar) introduced the classification of shaders as surface shaders, light shaders, atmosphere shaders, and so on, and the ability to describe the operation of each through an expression. This work evolved into the effort to develop a full-featured language for describing shading calculations, which was taken up by Pat Hanrahan and culminated in the 1988 release of the first version of the *RenderMan Interface Specification* by Pixar. Subsequently, RenderMan became the de facto industry-standard shading language for offline rendering systems for the entertainment industry. It remains in widespread use today.

The first interactive shading language was demonstrated at the University of North Carolina on a massively parallel graphics architecture called PixelFlow that was developed over the decade of the 1990s. The shading language used on PixelFlow could render scenes with procedural shading at 30 frames per second or more. The shading language component of this system was described by Marc Olano in 1998.

After leaving UNC, Olano joined a team at SGI that was defining and implementing an interactive shading language that would run on top of OpenGL and use multipass rendering methods to execute the shaders. This work culminated in the release in 2000 of a product from SGI called OpenGL Shader, the first commercially available real-time, high-level shading language.

In June 1999, the Computer Graphics Laboratory at Stanford embarked on an effort to define a real-time shading language that could be accelerated by existing consumer graphics hardware. This language was called the Stanford Real-Time Shading Language. Results of this system were demonstrated in 2001.

The OpenGL Shading Language, Microsoft's HLSL, and NVIDIA's Cg are all efforts to define a commercially viable, real-time, high-level shading language. The white paper that first described the shading language that would become the OpenGL Shading Language was published in October 2001 by Dave Baldwin of 3Dlabs. NVIDIA's Cg specification was published in June of 2002, and Microsoft's HLSL specification was published in November 2002 as part of the beta release of the DirectX 9.0 Software Development Kit. Some cross-pollination of ideas occurred among these three efforts because of the interrelationships of the companies involved.

In subsequent sections, we compare the OpenGL Shading Language with other commercially available high-level shading languages.

20.2 RenderMan

In 1988, after several years of development, Pixar published the *RenderMan Interface Specification*. This was an interface intended to define the communications protocol between modeling programs and rendering programs aimed at producing images of photorealistic quality, as shown in Figure 20.1. The original target audience for this interface was animation production, and the interface has proved to be very successful for this market. It has been used as the interface for producing computer graphics special effects for films such as *Jurassic Park*, *Star Wars Episode 1: The Phantom Menace*, *The Lord of the Rings: The Two Towers*, and others. It has also been used for films that have been done entirely with computer graphics such as *Finding Nemo*, *Toy Story*, *A Bug's Life*, and *Monsters, Inc.*

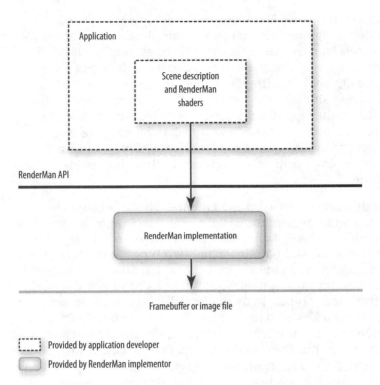

Figure 20.1 RenderMan execution environment

One of the main differences between the OpenGL Shading Language and RenderMan is that RenderMan attempts to define the entire interface between modeling programs and rendering programs. It provides an entire graphics processing pipeline of its own that has no relationship to OpenGL. Although a hardware implementation was envisioned at the time Render-Man was first defined, it was primarily designed as a high-quality, realistic rendering interface; therefore, it provides no compromises for interactivity or direct hardware implementation on today's graphics hardware. Render-Man includes support for describing geometric primitives, hierarchical modeling, stacking geometric transformations, camera attributes, shading attributes, and constructive solid geometry. OpenGL already provides many of these capabilities; therefore, they need not be addressed in the OpenGL Shading Language.

Of particular interest, however, is the portion of RenderMan called the RenderMan Shading Language. This language completely describes arbitrary shaders that can be passed to a renderer through the RenderMan interface. This language was also based on C, and as such, it bears some resemblance to the OpenGL Shading Language. In a general way, the RenderMan interface is similar to OpenGL, and the RenderMan Shading Language is similar to the OpenGL Shading Language. The RenderMan interface and OpenGL both let you define the characteristics of a scene (viewing parameters, primitives to be rendered, etc.). Both shading languages compute the color, position, opacity, and other characteristics of a point in the scene.

One of the main differences between the OpenGL Shading Language and the RenderMan Shading Language is in the abstraction of the shading problem. The OpenGL Shading Language closely maps onto today's commercial graphics hardware and has abstracted two types of shaders so far: vertex shaders and fragment shaders. The RenderMan Shading Language has always had uncompromising image quality as its fundamental goal, and it abstracts five shader types: light shaders, displacement shaders, surface shaders, volume shaders, and imager shaders. The RenderMan shader types lend themselves to the implementation of high-quality software rendering implementations, but they do not match up as well with hardware that has been designed to support interactive rendering with OpenGL. As a result, RenderMan implementations have typically been software based, but attempts to accelerate RenderMan shaders in hardware have been made (read *Interactive Multi-Pass Programmable Shading* by Peercy, Olano, Airey, and Ungar, 2000). The OpenGL Shading Language was designed from the beginning for acceleration by commodity graphics hardware.

There are some differences in the data types supported by the two languages. RenderMan supports native types that represent colors, points, and normals, whereas the OpenGL Shading Language includes the more generic vectors of 1, 2, 3, or 4 floating-point values that can support any of those. RenderMan goes a bit further in making the language graphics-specific by including built-in support for coordinate spaces named *object*, *world*, *camera*, *NDC*, *raster*, and *screen*.

RenderMan supports a number of predefined surface shader variables, light source variables, volume shader variables, displacement shader variables, and imager shader variables. The OpenGL Shading Language contains built-in variables that are specific to OpenGL state values, some of which are similar to the RenderMan predefined variables. Because it is aimed at producing animation, RenderMan also has built-in variables to represent time. The

OpenGL Shading Language does not, but such values can be passed to shaders through uniform variables to accomplish the same thing.

On the other hand, the two languages have much in common. In a very real sense, the OpenGL Shading Language can be thought of as a descendant of the RenderMan Shading Language. The data type qualifiers **uniform** and **varying** were invented in RenderMan and have been carried forward to mean the same things in the OpenGL Shading Language. Expressions and precedence of operators in both languages are very much like C. Keywords such as **if, else, while, for, break,** and **return** are the same in both languages. The list of built-in math functions for the OpenGL Shading Language is largely similar to the list of built-in math functions for the RenderMan Shading Language.

20.3   OpenGL Shader (ISL)

OpenGL Shader was a software package developed by SGI and released in 2000. It was available as a commercial product for several years, but is no longer available. OpenGL Shader defined both a shading language (Interactive Shading Language, or ISL) and a set of API calls that defined shaders and used them in the rendering process.

The fundamental premise of OpenGL Shader was that the OpenGL API could be used as an assembly language for executing programmable shaders (see Figure 20.2). Hardware with more features (e.g., multitexture and fragment programmability) could be viewed as having a more powerful assembly language. A sequence of statements in an ISL shader could end up being translated into one or more rendering passes. Each pass could be a geometry pass (geometry is drawn to use vertex, rasterization, and fragment operations), a copy pass (a region of the framebuffer is copied back into the same place in the framebuffer to use pixel, rasterization, and fragment operations), or a copy texture pass (a region of the framebuffer is copied to a texture to use pixel operations). Compiler optimization technology determined the type of pass required to execute a sequence of source code instructions and, if possible, to reduce the number of passes needed overall. The final version of OpenGL Shader was optimized for multiple hardware back ends and could exploit the features exposed on a particular platform to reduce the number of passes required.

Like every other shading language worth its salt, ISL is based on C. However, because of its fundamental premise, ISL shaders end up looking quite

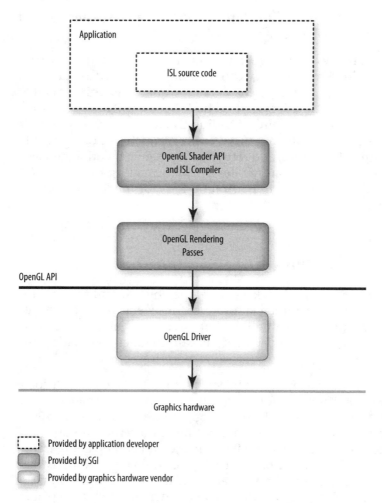

Figure 20.2   OpenGL Shader (ISL) execution environment

different from OpenGL shaders. Many of the instructions in an ISL shader end up look like directives to perform a rendering pass. For example, consider the following ISL source code:

```
varying color b;
FB  = diffuse();
FB *= color(.5, .2, 0, 1);
b   = FB;
FB  = specular(30.0);
FB += b;
```

The identifier *FB* specifies a result to be stored in the framebuffer. This sequence of operations first calls a subshader that executes a light shader to compute a diffuse color for the geometry being rendered. This value is multiplied by the color value (.5, .2, 0, 1), and the result is then stored in a region of texture memory called *b*. A specular reflection calculation is performed next, and finally the diffuse component and specular components are added together. Although it has the appearance of requiring multiple passes, this sequence of instructions can actually be executed in a single pass on a number of different graphics accelerators.

ISL supports surface and light shaders, which are merged and compiled. In this regard, it is more similar to the RenderMan way of doing things than it is to the OpenGL distinction of vertex and fragment shaders.

Another difference between the OpenGL Shading Language and ISL is that ISL was designed to provide portability for interactive shading by means of the OpenGL capabilities of both past and current hardware, whereas the OpenGL Shading Language was designed to expose the programmability of current and future hardware. The OpenGL Shading Language is not intended for hardware without a significant degree of programmability, but ISL executes shaders with the identical visual effect on a variety of hardware, including hardware with little or no explicit support for programmability.

Yet another difference between ISL and the OpenGL Shading Language is that ISL was designed with the constraints of using the OpenGL API as an assembly language, without requiring any changes in the underlying hardware. The OpenGL Shading Language was designed to define new capabilities for the underlying hardware, and so it supports a more natural syntax for expressing graphics algorithms. The high-level language defined by the OpenGL Shading Language can be translated into the machine code native to the graphics hardware with an optimizing compiler written by the graphics hardware vendor.

20.4   HLSL

HLSL stands for High-Level Shader Language, and it was defined by Microsoft and introduced with DirectX 9 in 2002. In terms of its syntax and functionality, HLSL is much closer to the OpenGL Shading Language than either RenderMan or ISL. HLSL supports the paradigm of programmability at the vertex level and at the fragment level just as in the OpenGL Shading Language. An HLSL vertex shader corresponds to an OpenGL vertex shader, and an HLSL pixel shader corresponds to an OpenGL fragment shader.

One of the main differences between the OpenGL Shading Language and HLSL is in the execution environment (see Figure 20.3). The HLSL compiler is really a translator that lives outside DirectX in the sense that HLSL programs are never sent directly to the DirectX 9 or DirectX 10 API for execution. Instead, the HLSL compiler translates HLSL source into assembly-level source or binary programs called VERTEX SHADERS and PIXEL SHADERS (in Microsoft DirectX parlance). Various levels of functionality have been defined for these assembly level shaders, and they are differentiated by

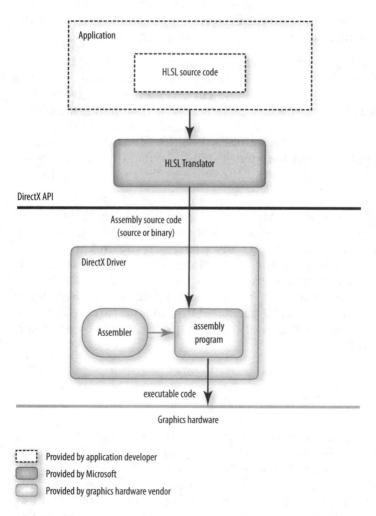

Figure 20.3   Execution environment for Microsoft's HLSL

a version number (e.g., Vertex Shader 1.0, 2.0, 3.0, 4.0; Pixel Shader 1.1, 1.4, 2.0, 3.0, 4.0).

One advantage of this approach is that HLSL programs can be translated offline, or long before the application is actually executed. However, the translation is done to a binary representation of assembly code. This binary representation may still need to be translated to native machine code at execution time. This is in contrast to the OpenGL Shading Language model, in which the compiler is part of the driver, and the graphics hardware vendor writes the compiler. Giving the graphics hardware vendor the responsibility of translating from high-level shading language source to machine code grants these vendors a lot of room for shader optimization and architectural innovation.

HLSL is designed to make it easier for application developers to deal with the various levels of functionality found in these assembly-level shaders. Using HLSL and the support environment that has been built around it, application developers can write shaders in a high-level shading language and be reasonably confident that their shaders will run on hardware with widely varying capabilities.

However, because HLSL is more expressive than the capabilities of graphics hardware that exists today and much more expressive than hardware shipped in the past, HLSL shaders are not guaranteed to run on every platform. Shader writers have two choices: They can write their shader for the lowest common denominator (i.e., hardware with very little programmability), or they can target their shader at a certain class of hardware by using a language feature called PROFILES. Microsoft provides supporting software called the DirectX Effects Framework to help developers organize and deploy a set of shaders that do the same thing for hardware with differing capabilities.

The fundamental data types in HLSL are the same as those in the OpenGL Shading Language except for slight naming differences. HLSL also supports half- and double-precision floats. Like the OpenGL Shading Language, HLSL accommodates vectors, matrices, structures, and arrays. Expressions in HLSL are as in C/C++. User-defined functions and conditionals are supported in the same manner as in the OpenGL Shading Language. Looping constructs (**for, do**, and **while**) are defined in HLSL, but the current documentation states that they are not yet implemented. HLSL has a longer list of built-in functions than does the OpenGL Shading Language, but those that are in both languages are very similar or identical.

One area of difference is the way in which values are passed between vertex shaders and pixel (HLSL) or fragment (OpenGL Shading Language) shaders. HLSL defines both input semantics and output semantics (annotations that identify data usage) for both vertex shaders and pixel shaders. This provides the same functionality as the OpenGL Shading Language varying and built-in variables. You are allowed to pass arbitrary data into and out of vertex and pixel shaders, but you must do so in named locations such as *POSITION*, *COLOR[i]*, *TEXCOORD[i]*, and so on. This requirement means that you may have to pass your light direction variable *lightdir* in a semantic slot named *TEXCOORD[i]*, for instance—a curious feature for a high-level language. The OpenGL Shading Language lets you use arbitrary names for passing values between vertex shaders and fragment shaders.

Another obvious difference between HLSL and the OpenGL Shading Language is that HLSL was designed for DirectX, Microsoft's proprietary graphics API, and the OpenGL Shading Language was designed for OpenGL. Microsoft can add to and change DirectX, whereas OpenGL is an open, cross-platform standard that changes more slowly but retains compatibility with previous versions.

20.5 Cg

Cg is a high-level shading language that is similar to HLSL. Cg has been defined, implemented, and supported by NVIDIA. Comparing Cg to the OpenGL Shading Language is virtually the same as comparing HLSL to the OpenGL Shading Language. There are a few minor differences between Cg and HLSL (for instance, HLSL has a double data type but Cg does not), but Cg and HLSL were developed by Microsoft and NVIDIA working together, so their resulting products are very similar.

One advantage that Cg has over both HLSL and the OpenGL Shading Language is that the Cg translator can generate either DirectX vertex shader/pixel shader assembly code or OpenGL vertex/fragment program (assembly-level) code. This provides the potential for using Cg shaders in either the DirectX environment or the OpenGL environment (see Figure 20.4). However, it also requires the application to make calls to a library provided by NVIDIA that sits between the application and the underlying graphics API (either OpenGL or DirectX). This library is called the Cg Runtime library. For simple applications, it can help cover up the limitations of the underlying driver (for instance, it can cover up the fact that a DirectX driver supports multiple versions of vertex and pixel shaders and automatically selects the most appropriate version to use). But this intervening layer can also complicate things for more complicated applications because it covers up details of shader management.

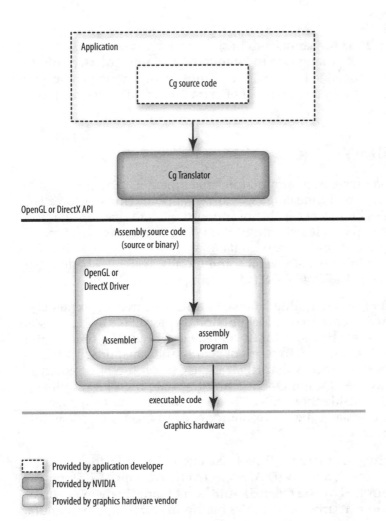

Figure 20.4   The Cg execution environment

NVIDIA has its own version of the framework that surrounds the shading language. CgFX is a shader specification and interchange format whose file format is the same as that supported by the .fx Effect format for DirectX 9. The CgFX runtime library, like the Cg runtime library, supports both OpenGL and DirectX, so in this way the Microsoft and NVIDIA products differ.

Because it is so similar to HLSL, the advantages and disadvantages of Cg with respect to the OpenGL Shading Language are also similar: proprietary versus standard (thus earlier to market), support for less capable hardware at the cost of hardware dependencies in shader source code, translation from high-level shading language to "standard" assembly interface offline versus a compiler embedded in the driver, a more complete shader development system but with the requirement of extra runtime libraries, and so on.

20.6 Summary

Shading languages have been around for some time now. The first shading languages were non-real-time languages aimed at producing photorealistic imagery. Graphics hardware capable of supporting an interactive shading language showed up in research labs in the 1990s, and today, this type of programmable graphics hardware is available at consumer price points. This has led to the development of several commercially available shading languages, notably, ISL, the OpenGL Shading Language, HLSL, and Cg.

In the spectrum of programming languages, the last three are extremely similar. Each was designed to provide functionality available in RenderMan by the use of C/C++ as the basis for the language syntax. The result is that all three languages are similar in terms of syntax and capability. The single biggest technical difference is that HLSL and Cg sit on top of standard interfaces such as DirectX and OpenGL and translate high-level source code to assembly outside those APIs. The OpenGL Shading Language, on the other hand, translates high-level source code to machine code within the OpenGL driver.

As far as nontechnical differences, the HLSL and CG specifications are controlled by Microsoft and NVIDIA, respectively. The OpenGL Shading Language is controlled by the OpenGL ARB, a standards body made up of representatives from a variety of graphics hardware and computer manufacturers. HLSL is designed for use in Microsoft's DirectX environment, and the OpenGL Shading Language is designed for use with OpenGL in a variety of operating environments. Cg is designed to be used in either DirectX or OpenGL environments.

20.7 Further Information

The RenderMan Shading Language is specified in Pixar's *The RenderMan Interface Specification* (2000), and its use is described in the books *The RenderMan Companion: A Programmer's Guide to Realistic Computer Graphics*

(Upstill 1990) and *Advanced RenderMan: Creating CGI for Motion Pictures* (Apodaca and Gritz 1999).

OpenGL Shader and ISL are described in the SIGGRAPH 2000 paper *Interactive Multi-Pass Programmable Shading*. The book *Real-Time Shading* by Olano, Hart, Heidrich, and McCool (2002) contains chapters describing various shading languages, including RenderMan, ISL, and shading languages defined and implemented by researchers at the University of North Carolina, Stanford, and the University of Waterloo.

The Stanford Real-Time Shading Language is described in the SIGGRAPH 2001 paper, *A Real-Time Procedural Shading System for Programmable Graphics Hardware*, and in the course notes for *Real-Time Shading*, Course 24, SIGGRAPH 2001.

There are sure to be books out that describe Microsoft's HLSL, but at the time of this writing, the only documentation I could find is available from Microsoft on the DirectX 9 page of its Web site, www.microsoft.com/directx. A good starting point is *Introduction to the DirectX 9 High-Level Shader Language* by Craig Peeper and Jason Mitchell. This paper also appears as a chapter in the book *ShaderX2: Shader Programming Tips and Tricks with DirectX 9.0* by Wolfgang Engel.

Cg is described in documentation from NVIDIA in the book *The Cg Tutorial: The Definitive Guide to Programmable Real-Time Graphics* by Fernando and Kilgard (2003) and in the SIGGRAPH 2003 paper *Cg: A System for Programming Graphics Hardware in a C-like Language*.

The bibliography at the end of this book contains references to other notable noncommercial shading languages.

[1] Apodaca, Anthony A., and Larry Gritz, *Advanced RenderMan: Creating CGI for Motion Pictures*, Morgan Kaufmann Publishers, San Francisco, 1999. www.renderman.org/RMR/Books/arman/materials.html

[2] Baldwin, Dave, *OpenGL 2.0 Shading Language White Paper*, Version 1.0, 3Dlabs, October, 2001.

[3] Cook, Robert L., *Shade Trees*, Computer Graphics (SIGGRAPH '84 Proceedings), pp. 223–231, July 1984.

[4] Fernando, Randima, and Mark Kilgard, *The Cg Tutorial, the Definitive Guide to Programmable Real-Time Graphics*, Addison-Wesley, Boston, Massachusetts, 2003.

[5] Kessenich, John, Dave Baldwin, and Randi Rost, *The OpenGL Shading Language, Version 1.10*, 3Dlabs, April 2004. www.opengl.org/documentation/spec.html

[6]   Mark, William R., *Real-Time Shading: Stanford Real-Time Procedural Shading System*, SIGGRAPH 2001, Course 24, course notes, 2001. http://graphics.stanford.edu/projects/shading/pubs/sigcourse2001.pdf

[7]   Mark, William R., R. Steven Glanville, Kurt Akeley, and Mark Kilgard, *Cg: A System for Programming Graphics Hardware in a C-like Language*, Computer Graphics (SIGGRAPH 2003 Proceedings), pp. 896–907, July 2003. www.cs.utexas.edu/users/billmark/papers/Cg

[8]   Microsoft, *DirectX 10.0 SDK*, 2007. http://msdn.microsoft.com/directx

[9]   NVIDIA Corporation, Cg Toolkit, Release 1.4, software and documentation. http://developer.nvidia.com/object/cg_toolkit.html

[10] Olano, Marc, and Anselmo Lastra, *A Shading Language on Graphics Hardware: The PixelFlow Shading System*, Computer Graphics (SIGGRAPH '98 Proceedings), pp. 159–168, July 1998. www.csee.umbc.edu/~olano/papers

[11] Olano, Marc, John Hart, Wolfgang Heidrich, and Michael McCool, *Real-Time Shading*, AK Peters, Ltd., Natick, Massachusetts, 2002.

[12] Peeper, Craig, and Jason Mitchell, *Introduction to the DirectX 9 High-Level Shader Language*, in *ShaderX2 : Shader Programming Tips and Tricks with DirectX 9.0*, Editor: Wolfgang Engel, Wordware Publishing, 2003. www.ati.com/developer/ShaderX2_IntroductionToHLSL.pdf

[13] Peercy, Mark S., Marc Olano, John Airey, and P. Jeffrey Ungar, *Interactive Multi-Pass Programmable Shading*, Computer Graphics (SIGGRAPH 2000 Proceedings), pp. 425–432, July 2000. www.csee.umbc.edu/~olano/papers

[14] Perlin, Ken, *An Image Synthesizer*, Computer Graphics (SIGGRAPH '85 Proceedings), pp. 287–296, July 1985.

[15] Pixar, *The RenderMan Interface Specification*, Version 3.2, Pixar, July 2000. https://renderman.pixar.com/products/rispec/index.htm

[16] Proudfoot, Kekoa, William R. Mark, Svetoslav Tzvetkov, and Pat Hanrahan, *A Real-Time Procedural Shading System for Programmable Graphics Hardware*, Computer Graphics (SIGGRAPH 2001 Proceedings), pp. 159–170, August 2001. http://graphics.stanford.edu/projects/shading/pubs/sig2001

[17] *SGI OpenGL Shader Web site*. www.sgi.com/software/shader (defunct)

[18] *ShaderX2 : Shader Programming Tips and Tricks with DirectX 9.0*, Editor: Wolfgang Engel, Wordware Publishing, 2003. www.shaderx2.com

[19] Upstill, Steve, *The RenderMan Companion: A Programmer's Guide to Realistic Computer Graphics*, Addison-Wesley, Reading, Massachusetts, 1990.

Language Grammar

The grammar is fed from the output of lexical analysis. The tokens returned from lexical analysis are

```
ATTRIBUTE CONST BOOL FLOAT INT UINT
BREAK CONTINUE DO ELSE FOR IF DISCARD RETURN SWITCH CASE DEFAULT
BVEC2 BVEC3 BVEC4 IVEC2 IVEC3 IVEC4 UVEC2 UVEC3 UVEC4 VEC2 VEC3 VEC4
MAT2 MAT3 MAT4 CENTROID IN OUT INOUT UNIFORM VARYING

NOPERSPECTIVE FLAT SMOOTH LAYOUT
MAT2X2 MAT2X3 MAT2X4
MAT3X2 MAT3X3 MAT3X4
MAT4X2 MAT4X3 MAT4X4
SAMPLER1D SAMPLER2D SAMPLER3D SAMPLERCUBE SAMPLER1DSHADOW
SAMPLER2DSHADOW
SAMPLERCUBESHADOW SAMPLER1DARRAY SAMPLER2DARRAY SAMPLER1DARRAYSHADOW
SAMPLER2DARRAYSHADOW ISAMPLER1D ISAMPLER2D ISAMPLER3D ISAMPLERCUBE
ISAMPLER1DARRAY ISAMPLER2DARRAY USAMPLER1D USAMPLER2D USAMPLER3D
USAMPLERCUBE USAMPLER1DARRAY USAMPLER2DARRAY
STRUCT VOID WHILE

IDENTIFIER TYPE_NAME FLOATCONSTANT INTCONSTANT UINTCONSTANT BOOLCONSTANT
FIELD_SELECTION
LEFT_OP RIGHT_OP
INC_OP DEC_OP LE_OP GE_OP EQ_OP NE_OP
AND_OP OR_OP XOR_OP MUL_ASSIGN DIV_ASSIGN ADD_ASSIGN
MOD_ASSIGN LEFT_ASSIGN RIGHT_ASSIGN AND_ASSIGN XOR_ASSIGN OR_ASSIGN
SUB_ASSIGN

LEFT_PAREN RIGHT_PAREN LEFT_BRACKET RIGHT_BRACKET LEFT_BRACE RIGHT_BRACE
DOT COMMA COLON EQUAL SEMICOLON BANG DASH TILDE PLUS STAR SLASH PERCENT
LEFT_ANGLE RIGHT_ANGLE VERTICAL_BAR CARET AMPERSAND QUESTION

INVARIANT
HIGH_PRECISION MEDIUM_PRECISION LOW_PRECISION PRECISION
```

The following describes the grammar for the OpenGL Shading Language in terms of the preceding tokens:

variable_identifier:
    IDENTIFIER

primary_expression:
    variable_identifier
    INTCONSTANT
    UINTCONSTANT
    FLOATCONSTANT
    BOOLCONSTANT
    LEFT_PAREN expression RIGHT_PAREN

postfix_expression:
    primary_expression
    postfix_expression LEFT_BRACKET integer_expression
      RIGHT_BRACKET
    function_call
    postfix_expression DOT FIELD_SELECTION
    postfix_expression INC_OP
    postfix_expression DEC_OP

integer_expression:
    expression

function_call:
    function_call_or_method

function_call_or_method:
    function_call_generic
    postfix_expression DOT function_call_generic

function_call_generic:
>   *function_call_header_with_parameters RIGHT_PAREN*
>   *function_call_header_no_parameters RIGHT_PAREN*

function_call_header_no_parameters:
>   *function_call_header VOID*
>   *function_call_header*

function_call_header_with_parameters:
>   *function_call_header assignment_expression*
>   *function_call_header_with_parameters COMMA*
>   *assignment_expression*

function_call_header:
>   *function_identifier LEFT_PAREN*

// Grammar Note: Constructors look like functions,
// but lexical analysis recognized most of them as keywords.
// They are now recognized through "type_specifier".

function_identifier:
>   *type_specifier*
>   *IDENTIFIER*
>   *FIELD_SELECTION*

unary_expression:
>   *postfix_expression*
>   *INC_OP unary_expression*
>   *DEC_OP unary_expression*
>   *unary_operator unary_expression*

// Grammar Note: No traditional style type casts.

unary_operator:
    PLUS
    DASH
    BANG
    TILDE

// Grammar Note: No '*' or '&' unary ops. Pointers are not
    supported.

multiplicative_expression:
    unary_expression
    multiplicative_expression STAR unary_expression
    multiplicative_expression SLASH unary_expression
    multiplicative_expression PERCENT unary_expression

additive_expression:
    multiplicative_expression
    additive_expression PLUS multiplicative_expression
    additive_expression DASH multiplicative_expression

shift_expression:
    additive_expression
    shift_expression LEFT_OP additive_expression
    shift_expression RIGHT_OP additive_expression

relational_expression:
    shift_expression
    relational_expression LEFT_ANGLE shift_expression
    relational_expression RIGHT_ANGLE shift_expression
    relational_expression LE_OP shift_expression
    relational_expression GE_OP shift_expression

equality_expression:

    relational_expression

    equality_expression EQ_OP relational_expression

    equality_expression NE_OP relational_expression

and_expression:

    equality_expression

    and_expression AMPERSAND equality_expression

exclusive_or_expression:

    and_expression

    exclusive_or_expression CARET and_expression

inclusive_or_expression:

    exclusive_or_expression

    inclusive_or_expression VERTICAL_BAR
      exclusive_or_expression

logical_and_expression:

    inclusive_or_expression

    logical_and_expression AND_OP inclusive_or_expression

logical_xor_expression:

    logical_and_expression

    logical_xor_expression XOR_OP logical_and_expression

logical_or_expression:

    logical_xor_expression

    logical_or_expression OR_OP logical_xor_expression

conditional_expression:

    logical_or_expression

    logical_or_expression QUESTION expression COLON
      assignment_expression

assignment_expression:

 conditional_expression

 unary_expression assignment_operator assignment_expression

assignment_operator:

 EQUAL

 MUL_ASSIGN

 DIV_ASSIGN

 MOD_ASSIGN

 ADD_ASSIGN

 SUB_ASSIGN

 LEFT_ASSIGN

 RIGHT_ASSIGN

 AND_ASSIGN

 XOR_ASSIGN

 OR_ASSIGN

expression:

 assignment_expression

 expression COMMA assignment_expression

constant_expression:

 conditional_expression

declaration:

 function_prototype SEMICOLON

 init_declarator_list SEMICOLON

 PRECISION precision_qualifier type_specifier_no_prec
  SEMICOLON

 type_qualifier IDENTIFIER LEFT_BRACE
  struct_declaration_list RIGHT_BRACE SEMICOLON

 type_qualifier SEMICOLON

function_prototype:

> *function_declarator RIGHT_PAREN*

function_declarator:

> *function_header*
>
> *function_header_with_parameters*

function_header_with_parameters:

> *function_header parameter_declaration*
>
> *function_header_with_parameters COMMA*
>   *parameter_declaration*

function_header:

> *fully_specified_type IDENTIFIER LEFT_PAREN*

parameter_declarator:

> *type_specifier IDENTIFIER*
>
> *type_specifier IDENTIFIER LEFT_BRACKET*
>   *constant_expression RIGHT_BRACKET*

parameter_declaration:

> *parameter_type_qualifier parameter_qualifier*
>   *parameter_declarator*
>
> *parameter_qualifier parameter_declarator*
>
> *parameter_type_qualifier parameter_qualifier*
>   *parameter_type_specifier*
>
> *parameter_qualifier parameter_type_specifier*

parameter_qualifier:

> */* empty */*
>
> *IN*
>
> *OUT*
>
> *INOUT*

parameter_type_specifier:

    type_specifier

init_declarator_list:

    single_declaration

    init_declarator_list COMMA IDENTIFIER

    init_declarator_list COMMA IDENTIFIER LEFT_BRACKET RIGHT_BRACKET

    init_declarator_list COMMA IDENTIFIER LEFT_BRACKET constant_expression RIGHT_BRACKET

    init_declarator_list COMMA IDENTIFIER LEFT_BRACKET RIGHT_BRACKET EQUAL initializer

    init_declarator_list COMMA IDENTIFIER LEFT_BRACKET constant_expression RIGHT_BRACKET EQUAL initializer

    init_declarator_list COMMA IDENTIFIER EQUAL initializer

single_declaration:

    fully_specified_type

    fully_specified_type IDENTIFIER

    fully_specified_type IDENTIFIER LEFT_BRACKET RIGHT_BRACKET

    fully_specified_type IDENTIFIER LEFT_BRACKET constant_expression RIGHT_BRACKET

    fully_specified_type IDENTIFIER LEFT_BRACKET RIGHT_BRACKET EQUAL initializer

    fully_specified_type IDENTIFIER LEFT_BRACKET constant_expression RIGHT_BRACKET EQUAL initializer

    fully_specified_type IDENTIFIER EQUAL initializer

    INVARIANT IDENTIFIER   // Vertex only.

// Grammar Note: No 'enum' or 'typedef'.

fully_specified_type:

    type_specifier

    type_qualifier type_specifier

invariant_qualifier:
>   *INVARIANT*

interpolation_qualifier:
>   *SMOOTH*
>   *FLAT*
>   *NOPERSPECTIVE*

layout_qualifier:
>   *LAYOUT LEFT_PAREN layout_list RIGHT_PAREN*

layout_list:
>   *IDENTIFIER*
>   *layout_list COMMA IDENTIFIER*

parameter_type_qualifier:
>   *CONST*

type_qualifier:
>   *storage_qualifier*
>   *layout_qualifier*
>   *layout_qualifier storage_qualifier*
>   *interpolation_qualifier type_qualifier*
>   *invariant_qualifier type_qualifier*
>   *invariant_qualifier interpolation_qualifier type_qualifier*

storage_qualifier:
>   *CONST*
>   *ATTRIBUTE   // Vertex only.*
>   *VARYING*
>   *CENTROID VARYING*
>   *IN*
>   *OUT*
>   *CENTROID IN*
>   *CENTROID OUT*
>   *UNIFORM*

type_specifier:

>   *type_specifier_no_prec*
>
>   *precision_qualifier type_specifier_no_prec*

type_specifier_no_prec:

>   *type_specifier_nonarray*
>
>   *type_specifier_nonarray LEFT_BRACKET RIGHT_BRACKET*
>
>   *type_specifier_nonarray LEFT_BRACKET constant_expression RIGHT_BRACKET*

type_specifier_nonarray:

>   *VOID*
>
>   *FLOAT*
>
>   *INT*
>
>   *UINT*
>
>   *BOOL*
>
>   *VEC2*
>
>   *VEC3*
>
>   *VEC4*
>
>   *BVEC2*
>
>   *BVEC3*
>
>   *BVEC4*
>
>   *IVEC2*
>
>   *IVEC3*
>
>   *IVEC4*
>
>   *UVEC2*
>
>   *UVEC3*
>
>   *UVEC4*
>
>   *MAT2*
>
>   *MAT3*
>
>   *MAT4*
>
>   *MAT2X2*

MAT2X3

MAT2X4

MAT3X2

MAT3X3

MAT3X4

MAT4X2

MAT4X3

MAT4X4

SAMPLER1D

SAMPLER2D

SAMPLER3D

SAMPLERCUBE

SAMPLER1DSHADOW

SAMPLER2DSHADOW

SAMPLERCUBESHADOW

SAMPLER1DARRAY

SAMPLER2DARRAY

SAMPLER1DARRAYSHADOW

SAMPLER2DARRAYSHADOW

ISAMPLER1D

ISAMPLER2D

ISAMPLER3D

ISAMPLERCUBE

ISAMPLER1DARRAY

ISAMPLER2DARRAY

USAMPLER1D

USAMPLER2D

USAMPLER3D

USAMPLERCUBE

USAMPLER1DARRAY

USAMPLER2DARRAY

struct_specifier:
> TYPE_NAME

precision_qualifier:
> HIGH_PRECISION
> MEDIUM_PRECISION
> LOW_PRECISION

struct_specifier:
> STRUCT IDENTIFIER LEFT_BRACE struct_declaration_list
>   RIGHT_BRACE
> STRUCT LEFT_BRACE struct_declaration_list RIGHT_
>   BRACE

struct_declaration_list:
> *struct_declaration*
> *struct_declaration_list struct_declaration*

struct_declaration:
> *type_specifier struct_declarator_list* SEMICOLON
> *type_qualifier type_specifier struct_declarator_list*
>   SEMICOLON

struct_declarator_list:
> *struct_declarator*
> *struct_declarator_list* COMMA *struct_declarator*

struct_declarator:
> IDENTIFIER
> IDENTIFIER LEFT_BRACKET *constant_expression*
>   RIGHT_BRACKET

initializer:
> *assignment_expression*

declaration_statement:
> *declaration*

statement:
> *compound_statement*
> *simple_statement*

// Grammar Note: labeled statements for SWITCH only;
// 'goto' is not supported.

simple_statement:
> *declaration_statement*
> *expression_statement*
> *selection_statement*
> *switch_statement*
> *case_label*
> *iteration_statement*
> *jump_statement*

compound_statement:
> *LEFT_BRACE RIGHT_BRACE*
> *LEFT_BRACE statement_list RIGHT_BRACE*

statement_no_new_scope:
> *compound_statement_no_new_scope*
> *simple_statement*

compound_statement_no_new_scope:
> *LEFT_BRACE RIGHT_BRACE*
> *LEFT_BRACE statement_list RIGHT_BRACE*

statement_list:
> *statement*
> *statement_list statement*

expression_statement:

    SEMICOLON

    expression SEMICOLON

selection_statement:

    IF LEFT_PAREN expression RIGHT_PAREN
       selection_rest_statement

selection_rest_statement:

    statement ELSE statement

    statement

condition:

    expression

    fully_specified_type IDENTIFIER EQUAL initializer

switch_statement:

    SWITCH LEFT_PAREN expression RIGHT_PAREN
       LEFT_BRACE switch_statement_list RIGHT_BRACE

switch_statement_list:

    /* nothing */

    statement_list

case_label:

    CASE expression COLON

    DEFAULT COLON

iteration_statement:

    WHILE LEFT_PAREN condition RIGHT_PAREN
       statement_no_new_scope

    DO statement WHILE LEFT_PAREN expression
       RIGHT_PAREN SEMICOLON

    FOR LEFT_PAREN for_init_statement for_rest_statement
       RIGHT_PAREN statement_no_new_scope

for_init_statement:

    expression_statement

    declaration_statement

conditionopt:

    condition

    / empty */*

for_rest_statement:

    conditionopt SEMICOLON

    conditionopt SEMICOLON expression

jump_statement:

    CONTINUE SEMICOLON

    BREAK SEMICOLON

    RETURN SEMICOLON

    RETURN expression SEMICOLON

    DISCARD SEMICOLON   // Fragment shader only.

// Grammar Note: No 'goto'. Gotos are not supported.

translation_unit:

    external_declaration

    translation_unit external_declaration

external_declaration:

    function_definition

    declaration

function_definition:

    function_prototype compound_statement_no_new_scope

API Function Reference

This section contains detailed information on the OpenGL commands that support the creation, compilation, linking, and usage of shaders written in the OpenGL Shading Language, as well as the OpenGL commands added to provide generic vertex attributes and user-defined uniform variables to such shaders.

Implementation-Dependent API Values for GLSL

A number of new implementation-dependent values have been defined in OpenGL 3.1 to support the requirements of the OpenGL Shading Language. Each value can be queried with one of the variants of **glGet**.

GL_MAX_COMBINED_TEXTURE_IMAGE_UNITS
> Defines the total number of hardware units that can access texture maps from the vertex processor and the fragment processor combined. The minimum legal value is 32.

GL_MAX_DRAW_BUFFERS
> Defines the maximum number of buffers that can be simultaneously written into from within a fragment shader using the special output variable array *gl_FragData*. This constant effectively defines the size of the *gl_FragData* array.

GL_MAX_FRAGMENT_UNIFORM_COMPONENTS
> Defines the number of components (i.e., floating-point values) that are available for fragment shader uniform variables. The minimum legal value is 1024.

GL_MAX_TEXTURE_IMAGE_UNITS
> Defines the total number of hardware units that can access texture maps from the fragment processor. The minimum legal value is 16.

GL_MAX_VARYING_COMPONENTS
> Defines the number of floating-point variables available for varying variables. The minimum legal value is 64.

GL_MAX_VERTEX_ATTRIBS
> Defines the number of active vertex attributes that are available. The minimum legal value is 16.

GL_MAX_VERTEX_TEXTURE_IMAGE_UNITS
> Defines the number of hardware units that can access texture maps from the vertex processor. The minimum legal value is 16.

GL_MAX_VERTEX_UNIFORM_COMPONENTS
> Defines the number of components (i.e., floating-point values) that are available for vertex shader uniform variables. The minimum legal value is 1024.

Other Queriable Values for GLSL

GL_CURRENT_PROGRAM

Contains the name of the program object that is currently installed as part of current state. If no program object is active, this value is 0. This value can be obtained with one of the variants of **glGet**.

GL_SHADING_LANGUAGE_VERSION

Contains the OpenGL Shading Language version that is supported by the implementation. It is organized as a dot-delimited sequence of multidigit integers. This value can be obtained with **glGetString**.

glAttachShader

NAME

glAttachShader—Attaches a shader object to a program object

C SPECIFICATION

```
void glAttachShader(GLuint program,
                    GLuint shader)
```

PARAMETERS

program   Specifies the program object to which a shader object will be attached

shader   Specifies the shader object that is to be attached

DESCRIPTION

For an executable to be created, there must be a way to specify the list of things that will be linked. Program objects provide this mechanism. Shaders that are to be linked in a program object must first be attached to that program object. **glAttachShader** attaches the shader object specified by *shader* to the program object specified by *program*. This signifies that *shader* will be included in link operations that will be performed on *program*.

All operations that can be performed on a shader object are valid whether or not the shader object is attached to a program object. It is permissible to attach a shader object to a program object before source code has been loaded into the shader object or before the shader object has been compiled. It is permissible to attach multiple shader objects of the same type because each may contain a portion of the complete shader. It is also permissible to attach a shader object to more than one program object. If a shader object is deleted while it is attached to a program object, it is flagged for deletion, and deletion does not occur until **glDetachShader** is called to detach it from all program objects to which it is attached.

NOTES

glAttachShader is available only if the GL version is 2.0 or greater.

ERRORS

GL_INVALID_VALUE is generated if either *program* or *shader* is not a value generated by OpenGL.

GL_INVALID_OPERATION is generated if *program* is not of type GL_PROGRAM_OBJECT.

GL_INVALID_OPERATION is generated if *shader* is not of type GL_SHADER_OBJECT.

GL_INVALID_OPERATION is generated if *shader* is already attached to *program*.

GL_INVALID_OPERATION is generated if **glAttachShader** is executed between the execution of **glBegin** and the corresponding execution of **glEnd**.

ASSOCIATED GETS

glGetAttachedShaders with the handle of a valid program object

glIsProgram

glIsShader

SEE ALSO

glCompileShader, glDetachShader, glLinkProgram, glShaderSource

glBindAttribLocation

NAME

glBindAttribLocation—Associates a generic vertex attribute index with a named attribute variable

C SPECIFICATION

```
void glBindAttribLocation(GLuint program,
                          GLuint index,
                          const GLchar *name)
```

PARAMETERS

program   Specifies the handle of the program object in which the association is to be made

index   Specifies the index of the generic vertex attribute to be bound

name   Specifies a null-terminated string containing the name of the vertex shader attribute variable to which *index* is to be bound

DESCRIPTION

glBindAttribLocation associates a user-defined attribute variable in the program object specified by *program* with a generic vertex attribute index. The name of the user-defined attribute variable is passed as a null-terminated string in *name*. The generic vertex attribute index to be bound to this variable is specified by *index*. When *program* is made part of current state, values provided through the generic vertex attribute *index* modify the value of the user-defined attribute variable specified by *name*.

If *name* refers to a matrix attribute variable, *index* refers to the first column of the matrix. Other matrix columns are then automatically bound to locations *index+1* for a matrix of type mat2; *index+1* and *index+2* for a matrix of type mat3; and *index+1*, *index+2*, and *index+3* for a matrix of type mat4.

This command makes it possible for vertex shaders to use descriptive names for attribute variables rather than generic variables that are numbered from 0 to GL_MAX_VERTEX_ATTRIBS–1. The values sent to each generic attribute index are part of current state, just like standard vertex attributes such as color, normal, and vertex position. If a different program object is made current by calling **glUseProgram**, the generic vertex attributes are tracked in such a way that the same values will be observed by attributes in the new program object that are also bound to *index*.

Attribute variable name-to-generic attribute index bindings for a program object can be explicitly assigned at any time with **glBindAttribLocation**. Attribute bindings do not go into effect until **glLinkProgram** is called. After a program object has been linked successfully, the index values for generic attributes remain fixed (and their values can be queried) until the next link command occurs.

Applications are not allowed to bind any of the standard OpenGL vertex attributes with this command, because they are bound automatically when needed. Any attribute binding that occurs after the program object has been linked does not take effect until the next time the program object is linked.

NOTES

glBindAttribLocation is available only if the GL version is 2.0 or greater.

glBindAttribLocation can be called before any vertex shader objects are bound to the specified program object. It is also permissible to bind a generic attribute index to an attribute variable name that is never used in a vertex shader.

If *name* was bound previously, that information is lost. Thus, you cannot bind one user-defined attribute variable to multiple indices, but you can bind multiple user-defined attribute variables to the same index.

Applications are allowed to bind more than one user-defined attribute variable to the same generic vertex attribute index. This is called *aliasing*, and it is allowed only if just one of the aliased attributes is active in the executable program or if no path through the shader consumes more than one attribute of a set of attributes aliased to the same location. The compiler and linker are allowed to assume that no aliasing is done and are free to employ optimizations that work only in the absence of aliasing. OpenGL implementations are not required to do error checking to detect aliasing. Because there is no way to bind standard attributes, it is not possible to alias generic attributes with conventional ones (except for generic attribute 0).

Active attributes that are not explicitly bound are bound by the linker when **glLinkProgram** is called. The locations assigned can be queried with **glGetAttribLocation**.

OpenGL copies the *name* string when **glBindAttribLocation** is called, so an application can free its copy of the *name* string immediately after the function returns.

ERRORS

GL_INVALID_VALUE is generated if *index* is greater than or equal to GL_MAX_VERTEX_ATTRIBS.

GL_INVALID_OPERATION is generated if *name* starts with the reserved prefix "gl_".

GL_INVALID_VALUE is generated if *program* is not a value generated by OpenGL.

GL_INVALID_OPERATION is generated if *program* is not of type GL_PROGRAM_OBJECT.

GL_INVALID_OPERATION is generated if **glBindAttribLocation** is executed between the execution of **glBegin** and the corresponding execution of **glEnd**.

ASSOCIATED GETS

glGet with argument GL_MAX_VERTEX_ATTRIBS

glGetActiveAttrib with argument *program*

glGetAttribLocation with arguments *program* and *name*

glIsProgram

SEE ALSO

glDisableVertexAttribArray, glEnableVertexAttribArray, glUseProgram, glVertexAttrib, glVertexAttribPointer

glCompileShader

NAME

glCompileShader—Compiles a shader object

C SPECIFICATION
```
void glCompileShader(GLuint shader)
```

PARAMETERS

shader   Specifies the shader object to be compiled

DESCRIPTION

glCompileShader compiles the source code strings that have been stored in the shader object specified by *shader.*

The compilation status is stored as part of the shader object's state. This value is set to GL_TRUE if the shader was compiled without errors and is ready for use, and GL_FALSE otherwise. It can be queried by calling **glGetShader** with arguments *shader* and GL_COMPILE_STATUS.

Compilation of a shader can fail for a number of reasons, as specified by the *OpenGL Shading Language Specification.* Whether or not the compilation was successful, information about the compilation can be obtained from the shader object's information log by calling **glGetShaderInfoLog**.

NOTES

glCompileShader is available only if the GL version is 2.0 or greater.

ERRORS

GL_INVALID_VALUE is generated if *shader* is not a value generated by OpenGL.

GL_INVALID_OPERATION is generated if *shader* is not of type GL_SHADER_OBJECT.

GL_INVALID_OPERATION is generated if **glCompileShader** is executed between the execution of **glBegin** and the corresponding execution of **glEnd**.

ASSOCIATED GETS

glGetShaderInfoLog with argument *shader*

glGetShader with arguments *shader* and GL_COMPILE_STATUS

glIsShader

SEE ALSO

glCreateShader, **glLinkProgram**, **glShaderSource**

glCreateProgram

NAME

glCreateProgram—Creates a program object

C SPECIFICATION

```
GLuint glCreateProgram(void)
```

DESCRIPTION

glCreateProgram creates an empty program object and returns a nonzero value by which it can be referenced. A program object is an object to which shader objects can be attached. This provides a mechanism to specify the shader objects that will be linked to create a program. It also provides a means for checking the compatibility of the shaders that will be used to create a program (for instance, checking the compatibility between a vertex shader and a fragment shader). When no longer needed as part of a program object, shader objects can be detached.

One or more executables are created in a program object by these actions: successfully attaching shader objects to the program object with **glAttachShader**, successfully compiling the shader objects with **glCompileShader**, and successfully linking the program object with **glLinkProgram**. These executables are made part of current state when **glUseProgram** is called. Program objects can be deleted with **glDeleteProgram**. The memory associated with the program object is deleted when it is no longer part of current rendering state for any context.

NOTES

glCreateProgram is available only if the GL version is 2.0 or greater.

Like display lists and texture objects, the namespace for program objects may be shared across a set of contexts, as long as the server sides of the contexts share the same address space. If the namespace is shared across contexts, any attached objects and the data associated with those attached objects are shared as well.

Applications are responsible for synchronizing across API calls when objects are accessed from different execution threads.

ERRORS

This function returns 0 if an error occurs creating the program object.

GL_INVALID_OPERATION is generated if **glCreateProgram** is executed between the execution of **glBegin** and the corresponding execution of **glEnd**.

ASSOCIATED GETS

glGet with the argument GL_CURRENT_PROGRAM

glGetActiveAttrib with a valid program object and the index of an active attribute variable

glGetActiveUniform with a valid program object and the index of an active uniform variable

glGetAttachedShaders with a valid program object

glGetAttribLocation with a valid program object and the name of an attribute variable

glGetProgram with a valid program object and the parameter to be queried

glGetProgramInfoLog with a valid program object

glGetUniform with a valid program object and the location of a uniform variable

glGetUniformLocation with a valid program object and the name of a uniform variable

glIsProgram

SEE ALSO

glAttachShader, **glBindAttribLocation**, **glCreateShader**, **glDeleteProgram**, **glDetachShader**, **glLinkProgram**, **glUniform**, **glUseProgram**, **glValidateProgram**

glCreateShader

NAME

glCreateShader—Creates a shader object

C SPECIFICATION

```
GLuint glCreateShader(GLenum shaderType)
```

PARAMETERS

shaderType   Specifies the type of shader to be created. Must be either GL_VERTEX_SHADER or GL_FRAGMENT_SHADER.

DESCRIPTION

glCreateShader creates an empty shader object and returns a nonzero value by which it can be referenced. A shader object maintains the source code strings that define a shader. *shaderType* specifies the type of shader to be created. Two types of shaders are supported. A shader of type GL_VERTEX_SHADER is a shader that is intended to run on the programmable vertex processor and replace the fixed functionality vertex processing in OpenGL. A shader of type GL_FRAGMENT_SHADER is a shader that is intended to run on the programmable fragment processor and replace the fixed functionality fragment processing in OpenGL.

When created, a shader object's GL_SHADER_TYPE parameter is set to either GL_VERTEX_SHADER or GL_FRAGMENT_SHADER, depending on the value of *shaderType*.

NOTES

glCreateShader is available only if the GL version is 2.0 or greater.

Like display lists and texture objects, the namespace for shader objects may be shared across a set of contexts, as long as the server sides of the contexts share the same address space. If the namespace is shared across contexts, any attached objects and the data associated with those attached objects are shared as well.

Applications are responsible for providing the synchronization across API calls when objects are accessed from different execution threads.

ERRORS

This function returns 0 if an error occurs creating the shader object.

GL_INVALID_ENUM is generated if *shaderType* is not an accepted value.

GL_INVALID_OPERATION is generated if **glCreateShader** is executed between the execution of **glBegin** and the corresponding execution of **glEnd**.

ASSOCIATED GETS

glGetShader with a valid shader object and the parameter to be queried

glGetShaderInfoLog with a valid shader object

glGetShaderSource with a valid shader object

glIsShader

SEE ALSO

glAttachShader, glCompileShader, glCreateProgram, glDeleteShader, glDetachShader, glShaderSource

glDeleteProgram

NAME

glDeleteProgram—Deletes a program object

C SPECIFICATION

```
void glDeleteProgram(GLuint program)
```

PARAMETERS

program   Specifies the program object to be deleted

DESCRIPTION

glDeleteProgram frees the memory and invalidates the name associated with the program object specified by *program*. This command effectively undoes the effects of a call to **glCreateProgram**.

If a program object is in use as part of current rendering state, it is flagged for deletion but is not deleted until it is no longer part of the current state for any rendering context. If a program object to be deleted has shader objects attached to it, those shader objects are automatically detached but not deleted unless they have already been flagged for deletion by a previous call to **glDeleteShader**. A value of 0 for *program* is silently ignored.

To determine whether a program object has been flagged for deletion, call **glGetProgram** with arguments *program* and GL_DELETE_STATUS.

NOTES

glDeleteProgram is available only if the GL version is 2.0 or greater.

ERRORS

GL_INVALID_VALUE is generated if *program* is not a value generated by OpenGL.

GL_INVALID_OPERATION is generated if **glDeleteProgram** is executed between the execution of **glBegin** and the corresponding execution of **glEnd**.

ASSOCIATED GETS

glGet with argument GL_CURRENT_PROGRAM

glGetProgram with arguments *program* and GL_DELETE_STATUS

glIsProgram

SEE ALSO

glCreateProgram, **glCreateShader**, **glDetachShader**, **glUseProgram**

glDeleteShader

NAME

glDeleteShader—Deletes a shader object

C SPECIFICATION

```
void glDeleteShader(GLuint shader)
```

PARAMETERS

shader   Specifies the shader object to be deleted

DESCRIPTION

glDeleteShader frees the memory and invalidates the name associated with the shader object specified by *shader*. This command effectively undoes the effects of a call to **glCreateShader.**

If a shader object to be deleted is attached to a program object, it is flagged for deletion but is not deleted until it is no longer attached to any program object, for any rendering context (i.e., it must be detached from wherever it was attached before it can be deleted). A value of 0 for *shader* is silently ignored.

To determine whether an object has been flagged for deletion, call **glGetShader** with arguments *shader* and GL_DELETE_STATUS.

NOTES

glDeleteShader is available only if the GL version is 2.0 or greater.

ERRORS

GL_INVALID_VALUE is generated if *shader* is not a value generated by OpenGL.

GL_INVALID_OPERATION is generated if **glDeleteShader** is executed between the execution of **glBegin** and the corresponding execution of **glEnd.**

ASSOCIATED GETS

glGetAttachedShaders with the program object to be queried

glGetShader with arguments *shader* and GL_DELETE_STATUS

glIsShader

SEE ALSO

glCreateProgram, glCreateShader, glDetachShader, glUseProgram

glDetachShader

NAME

glDetachShader—Detaches a shader object from a program object to which it is attached

C SPECIFICATION

```
void glDetachShader(GLuint program,
                    GLuint shader)
```

PARAMETERS

program   Specifies the program object from which to detach the shader object

shader   Specifies the shader object to be detached

DESCRIPTION

glDetachShader detaches the shader object specified by *shader* from the program object specified by *program*. This command undoes the effect of the command **glAttachShader**.

If *shader* has already been flagged for deletion by a call to **glDeleteShader** and it is not attached to any other program object, it is deleted after it has been detached.

NOTES

glDetachShader is available only if the GL version is 2.0 or greater.

ERRORS

GL_INVALID_VALUE is generated if either *program* or *shader* is a value that was not generated by OpenGL.

GL_INVALID_OPERATION is generated if *program* is not a program object.

GL_INVALID_OPERATION is generated if *shader* is not a shader object.

GL_INVALID_OPERATION is generated if *shader* is not attached to *program*.

GL_INVALID_OPERATION is generated if **glDetachShader** is executed between the execution of **glBegin** and the corresponding execution of **glEnd**.

ASSOCIATED GETS

glGetAttachedShaders with the handle of a valid program object

glGetShader with arguments *shader* and GL_DELETE_STATUS

glIsProgram

glIsShader

SEE ALSO

glAttachShader

glDrawBuffers

NAME

glDrawBuffers—Specifies a list of color buffers to be drawn into

C SPECIFICATION

```
void glDrawBuffers(GLsizei n,
                   const GLenum *bufs)
```

PARAMETERS

n   Specifies the number of buffers in *bufs*

bufs   Points to an array of symbolic constants specifying the buffers into which fragment colors or data values will be written

DESCRIPTION

glDrawBuffers defines an array of buffers into which fragment color values or fragment data will be written. If no fragment shader is active, rendering operations generate only one fragment color per fragment, and that fragment is written into each of the buffers specified by *bufs*. If a fragment shader is active and it writes a value to the output variable *gl_FragColor*, then that value is written into each of the buffers specified by *bufs*. If a fragment shader is active and it writes a value to one or more elements of the output array variable *gl_FragData[]*, then the value of *gl_FragData[0]* is written into the first buffer specified by *bufs*, the value of *gl_FragData[1]* is written into the second buffer specified by *bufs*, and so on, up to *gl_FragData[n-1]*. The draw buffer used for *gl_FragData[n]* and beyond is implicitly set to be GL_NONE.

The symbolic constants contained in *bufs* may be any of the following:

GL_NONE
> The fragment color/data value is not written into any color buffer.

GL_FRONT_LEFT
> The fragment color/data value is written into the front-left color buffer.

GL_FRONT_RIGHT
> The fragment color/data value is written into the front-right color buffer.

GL_BACK_LEFT
> The fragment color/data value is written into the back-left color buffer.

GL_BACK_RIGHT
> The fragment color/data value is written into the back-right color buffer.

GL_AUXi
> The fragment color/data value is written into auxiliary buffer i.

Except for GL_NONE, the preceding symbolic constants may not appear more than once in *bufs*. The maximum number of draw buffers supported is implementation dependent and can be queried by calling **glGet** with the argument GL_MAX_DRAW_BUFFERS. The number of auxiliary buffers can be queried by calling **glGet** with the argument GL_AUX_BUFFERS.

NOTES

glDrawBuffers is available only if the GL version is 2.0 or greater.

It is always the case that GL_AUXi = GL_AUX0 + i.

The symbolic constants GL_FRONT, GL_BACK, GL_LEFT, GL_RIGHT, and GL_FRONT_AND_BACK are not allowed in the *bufs* array since they may refer to multiple buffers.

If a fragment shader writes to neither *gl_FragColor* nor *gl_FragData*, the values of the fragment colors following shader execution are undefined. For each fragment generated in this situation, a different value may be written into each of the buffers specified by *bufs*.

ERRORS

GL_INVALID_ENUM is generated if one of the values in *bufs* is not an accepted value.

GL_INVALID_ENUM is generated if *n* is less than 0.

GL_INVALID_OPERATION is generated if a symbolic constant other than GL_NONE appears more than once in *bufs*.

GL_INVALID_OPERATION is generated if any entry in *bufs* (other than GL_NONE) indicates a color buffer that does not exist in the current GL context.

GL_INVALID_VALUE is generated if *n* is greater than GL_MAX_DRAW_BUFFERS.

GL_INVALID_OPERATION is generated if **glDrawBuffers** is executed between the execution of **glBegin** and the corresponding execution of **glEnd**.

ASSOCIATED GETS

glGet with argument GL_MAX_DRAW_BUFFERS

glGet with argument GL_DRAW_BUFFERSi where *i* indicates the number of the draw buffer whose value is to be queried

SEE ALSO

glBlendFunc, **glColorMask**, **glDrawBuffer**, **glIndexMask**, **glLogicOp**, **glReadBuffer**

glEnableVertexAttribArray

NAME

glEnableVertexAttribArray, **glDisableVertexAttribArray**—Enable or disable a generic vertex attribute array

C SPECIFICATION

```
void glEnableVertexAttribArray(GLuint index)
void glDisableVertexAttribArray(GLuint index)
```

PARAMETERS

index   Specifies the index of the generic vertex attribute to be enabled or disabled

DESCRIPTION

glEnableVertexAttribArray enables the generic vertex attribute array specified by *index*. **glDisableVertexAttribArray** disables the generic vertex attribute array specified by *index*. By default, all client-side capabilities are disabled, including all generic vertex attribute arrays. If enabled, the values in the generic vertex attribute array are accessed and used for rendering when calls are made to vertex array commands such as **glDrawArrays**, **glDrawElements**, **glDrawRangeElements**, **glArrayElement**, **glMultiDrawElements**, or **glMultiDraw-Arrays**.

NOTES

glEnableVertexAttribArray and **glDisableVertexAttribArray** are available only if the GL version is 2.0 or greater.

ERRORS

GL_INVALID_VALUE is generated if *index* is greater than or equal to GL_MAX_VERTEX_ATTRIBS.

GL_INVALID_OPERATION is generated if either **glEnableVertexAttribArray** or **glDisableVertexAttribArray** is executed between the execution of **glBegin** and the corresponding execution of **glEnd**.

ASSOCIATED GETS

glGet with argument GL_MAX_VERTEX_ATTRIBS

glGetVertexAttrib with arguments *index* and GL_VERTEX_ATTRIB_ARRAY_ENABLED

glGetVertexAttribPointer with arguments *index* and GL_VERTEX_ATTRIB_ARRAY_POINTER

SEE ALSO

glArrayElement, **glBindAttribLocation**, **glDrawArrays**, **glDrawElements**, **glDrawRangeElements**, **glMultiDrawArrays**, **glMultiDrawElements**, **glPopClientAttrib**, **glPushClientAttrib**, **glVertexAttrib**, **glVertexAttribPointer**

glGetActiveAttrib

NAME

glGetActiveAttrib—Returns information about an active attribute variable for the specified program object

C SPECIFICATION

```
void glGetActiveAttrib(GLuint program,
                       GLuint index,
                       GLsizei bufSize,
                       GLsizei *length,
                       GLint *size,
                       GLenum *type,
                       GLchar *name)
```

PARAMETERS

program	Specifies the program object to be queried
index	Specifies the index of the attribute variable to be queried
bufSize	Specifies the maximum number of characters OpenGL is allowed to write in the character buffer indicated by *name*
length	Returns the number of characters actually written by OpenGL in the string indicated by *name* (excluding the null terminator) if a value other than NULL is passed
size	Returns the size of the attribute variable
type	Returns the data type of the attribute variable
name	Returns a null-terminated string containing the name of the attribute variable

DESCRIPTION

glGetActiveAttrib returns information about an active attribute variable in the program object specified by *program*. The number of active attributes can be obtained by calling **glGetProgram** with the value GL_ACTIVE_ATTRIBUTES. A value of 0 for *index* selects the first active attribute variable. Permissible values for *index* range from 0 to the number of active attribute variables minus 1.

A vertex shader may use built-in attribute variables, user-defined attribute variables, or both. Built-in attribute variables have a prefix of "gl_" and reference conventional OpenGL vertex attributes (e.g., *gl_Vertex*, *gl_Normal*; see the OpenGL Shading Language specification for a complete list). User-defined attribute variables have arbitrary names and obtain their values through numbered generic vertex attributes. An attribute variable (either built-in or user-defined) is considered active if during the link operation, the determination is made that the attribute variable can be accessed during program execution. Therefore, *program* should have previously been the target of a call to **glLinkProgram**, but it is not necessary for it to have been linked successfully.

The size of the character buffer required to store the longest attribute variable name in *program* can be obtained by calling **glGetProgram** with the value GL_ACTIVE_ATTRIBUTE_MAX_LENGTH. This value should be used to allocate a buffer of sufficient size to store the returned attribute name. The size of this character buffer is passed in *bufSize*, and a pointer to this character buffer is passed in *name*.

glGetActiveAttrib returns the name of the attribute variable indicated by *index*, storing it in the character buffer specified by *name*. The string returned is null terminated. The actual number of characters written into this buffer is returned in *length*, and this count does not include the null termination character. If the length of the returned string is not required, a value of NULL can be passed in the *length* argument.

The *type* argument returns a pointer to the attribute variable's data type. The symbolic constants GL_FLOAT, GL_FLOAT_VEC2, GL_FLOAT_VEC3, GL_FLOAT_VEC4, GL_FLOAT_MAT2, GL_FLOAT_MAT3, and GL_FLOAT_MAT4 may be returned. The *size* argument returns the size of the attribute, in units of the type returned in *type*.

The list of active attribute variables may include both built-in attribute variables (which begin with the prefix "gl_") as well as user-defined attribute variable names.

This function returns as much information as it can about the specified active attribute variable. If no information is available, *length* is 0, and *name* is an empty string. This situation could occur if this function is called after a link operation that failed. If an error occurs, the return values *length*, *size*, *type*, and *name* are unmodified.

NOTES

glGetActiveAttrib is available only if the GL version is 2.0 or greater.

ERRORS

GL_INVALID_VALUE is generated if *program* is not a value generated by OpenGL.

GL_INVALID_OPERATION is generated if *program* is not a program object.

GL_INVALID_VALUE is generated if *index* is greater than or equal to the number of active attribute variables in *program*.

GL_INVALID_OPERATION is generated if **glGetActiveAttrib** is executed between the execution of **glBegin** and the corresponding execution of **glEnd**.

GL_INVALID_VALUE is generated if *bufSize* is less than 0.

ASSOCIATED GETS

glGet with argument GL_MAX_VERTEX_ATTRIBS

glGetProgram with argument GL_ACTIVE_ATTRIBUTES or GL_ACTIVE_ATTRIBUTE_MAX_LENGTH

glIsProgram

SEE ALSO

glBindAttribLocation, **glLinkProgram**, **glVertexAttrib**, **glVertexAttribPointer**

glGetActiveUniform

NAME

glGetActiveUniform—Returns information about an active uniform variable for the specified program object

C SPECIFICATION

```
void glGetActiveUniform(GLuint program,
                        GLuint index,
                        GLsizei bufSize,
                        GLsizei *length,
                        GLint *size,
                        GLenum *type,
                        GLchar *name)
```

PARAMETERS

program	Specifies the program object to be queried
index	Specifies the index of the uniform variable to be queried
bufSize	Specifies the maximum number of characters OpenGL is allowed to write in the character buffer indicated by *name*
length	Returns the number of characters actually written by OpenGL in the string indicated by *name* (excluding the null terminator) if a value other than NULL is passed
size	Returns the size of the uniform variable
type	Returns the data type of the uniform variable
name	Returns a null-terminated string containing the name of the uniform variable

DESCRIPTION

glGetActiveUniform returns information about an active uniform variable in the program object specified by *program*. The number of active uniform variables can be obtained by calling **glGetProgram** with the value GL_ACTIVE_UNIFORMS. A value of 0 for *index* selects the first active uniform variable. Permissible values for *index* range from 0 to the number of active uniform variables minus 1.

Shaders may use built-in uniform variables, user-defined uniform variables, or both. Built-in uniform variables have a prefix of "gl_" and reference existing OpenGL state or values derived from such state (e.g., *gl_Fog*, *gl_ModelViewMatrix*; see the OpenGL Shading Language specification for a complete list). User-defined uniform variables have arbitrary names and obtain their values from the application through calls to **glUniform.** A uniform variable (either built-in or user-defined) is considered active if during the link operation, a determination is made that the uniform variable can be accessed during program execution. Therefore, *program* should have previously been the target of a call to **glLinkProgram,** but it is not necessary for it to have been linked successfully.

The size of the character buffer required to store the longest uniform variable name in *program* can be obtained by calling **glGetProgram** with the value GL_ACTIVE_UNIFORM_MAX_LENGTH. This value should be used to allocate a buffer of sufficient size to store the returned uniform variable name. The size of this character buffer is passed in *bufSize*, and a pointer to this character buffer is passed in *name*.

glGetActiveUniform returns the name of the uniform variable indicated by *index*, storing it in the character buffer specified by *name.* The string returned is null terminated. The actual number of characters written into this buffer is returned in *length*, and this count does not include the null termination character. If the length of the returned string is not required, a value of NULL can be passed in the *length* argument.

The *type* argument returns a pointer to the uniform variable's data type. The symbolic constants GL_FLOAT, GL_FLOAT_VEC2, GL_FLOAT_VEC3, GL_FLOAT_VEC4, GL_INT, GL_INT_VEC2, GL_INT_VEC3, GL_INT_VEC4, GL_BOOL, GL_BOOL_VEC2, GL_BOOL_VEC3, GL_BOOL_VEC4, GL_FLOAT_MAT2, GL_FLOAT_MAT3, GL_FLOAT_MAT4, GL_SAMPLER_1D, GL_SAMPLER_2D, GL_SAMPLER_3D, GL_SAMPLER_CUBE, GL_SAMPLER_1D_SHADOW, or GL_SAMPLER_2D_SHADOW may be returned.

If one or more elements of an array are active, the name of the array is returned in *name*, the type is returned in *type*, and the *size* parameter returns the highest array element index used, plus one, as determined by the compiler and/or linker. Only one active uniform variable is reported for a uniform array.

Uniform variables that are declared as structures or arrays of structures are not returned directly by this function. Instead, each of these uniform variables is reduced to its fundamental components containing the "." and "[]" operators such that each of the names is valid as an argument to **glGetUniformLocation**. Each of these reduced uniform variables is counted as one active uniform variable and is assigned an index. A valid name cannot be a structure, an array of structures, or a subcomponent of a vector or matrix.

The size of the uniform variable is returned in *size.* Uniform variables other than arrays have a size of 1. Structures and arrays of structures are reduced as described earlier, such that each of the names returned is a data type in the earlier list. If this reduction results in an array, the size returned is as described for uniform arrays; otherwise, the size returned is 1.

The list of active uniform variables may include both built-in uniform variables (which begin with the prefix "gl_") as well as user-defined uniform variable names.

This function returns as much information as it can about the specified active uniform variable. If no information is available, *length* is 0, and *name* is an empty string. This situation could occur if this function is called after a link operation that failed. If an error occurs, the return values *length*, *size*, *type*, and *name* are unmodified.

NOTES

glGetActiveUniform is available only if the GL version is 2.0 or greater.

ERRORS

GL_INVALID_VALUE is generated if *program* is not a value generated by OpenGL.

GL_INVALID_OPERATION is generated if *program* is not a program object.

GL_INVALID_VALUE is generated if *index* is greater than or equal to the number of active uniform variables in *program*.

GL_INVALID_OPERATION is generated if **glGetActiveUniform** is executed between the execution of **glBegin** and the corresponding execution of **glEnd**.

GL_INVALID_VALUE is generated if *bufSize* is less than 0.

ASSOCIATED GETS

glGet with argument GL_MAX_VERTEX_UNIFORM_COMPONENTS or GL_MAX_ FRAGMENT_UNIFORM_COMPONENTS

glGetProgram with argument GL_ACTIVE_UNIFORMS or GL_ACTIVE_ UNIFORM_MAX_LENGTH

glIsProgram

SEE ALSO

glGetUniform, **glGetUniformLocation**, **glLinkProgram**, **glUniform**, **glUseProgram**

glGetAttachedShaders

NAME

glGetAttachedShaders—Returns the handles of the shader objects attached to a program object

C SPECIFICATION

```
void glGetAttachedShaders(GLuint program,
                          GLsizei maxCount,
                          GLsizei *count,
                          GLuint *shaders)
```

PARAMETERS

program	Specifies the program object to be queried
maxCount	Specifies the size of the array for storing the returned object names
count	Returns the number of names actually returned in *objects*
shaders	Specifies an array that is used to return the names of attached shader objects

DESCRIPTION

glGetAttachedShaders returns the names of the shader objects attached to *program*. The names of shader objects that are attached to *program* are returned in *shaders*. The actual number of shader names written into *shaders* is returned in *count*. If no shader objects are attached to *program*, *count* is set to 0. The maximum number of shader names that may be returned in *shaders* is specified by *maxCount*.

If the number of names actually returned is not required (for instance, if it has just been obtained with **glGetProgram**), a value of NULL may be passed for count. If no shader objects are attached to *program*, a value of 0 is returned in *count*. The actual number of attached shaders can be obtained by calling **glGetProgram** with the value GL_ATTACHED_SHADERS.

NOTES

glGetAttachedShaders is available only if the GL version is 2.0 or greater.

ERRORS

GL_INVALID_VALUE is generated if *program* is not a value generated by OpenGL.

GL_INVALID_OPERATION is generated if *program* is not a program object.

GL_INVALID_VALUE is generated if *maxCount* is less than 0.

GL_INVALID_OPERATION is generated if **glGetAttachedShaders** is executed between the execution of **glBegin** and the corresponding execution of **glEnd**.

ASSOCIATED GETS

glGetProgram with argument GL_ATTACHED_SHADERS

glIsProgram

SEE ALSO

glAttachShader, **glDetachShader**

glGetAttribLocation

NAME

glGetAttribLocation—Returns the location of an attribute variable

C SPECIFICATION

```
GLint glGetAttribLocation(GLuint program,
                          const GLchar *name)
```

PARAMETERS

program   Specifies the program object to be queried

name   Points to a null-terminated string containing the
               name of the attribute variable whose location is to be
               queried

DESCRIPTION

glGetAttribLocation queries the previously linked program object specified by *program* for the attribute variable specified by *name* and returns the index of the generic vertex attribute that is bound to that attribute variable. If *name* is a matrix attribute variable, the index of the first column of the matrix is returned. If the named attribute variable is not an active attribute in the specified program object or if *name* starts with the reserved prefix "gl_", a value of –1 is returned.

The association between an attribute variable name and a generic attribute index can be specified at any time with **glBindAttribLocation**. Attribute bindings do not take effect until **glLinkProgram** is called. After a program object has been linked successfully, the index values for attribute variables remain fixed until the next link command occurs. The attribute bindings can be queried only after a link if the link was successful. **glGetAttribLocation** returns the binding that actually went into effect the last time **glLinkProgram** was called for the specified program object. Attribute bindings that have been specified since the last link operation are not returned by **glGetAttribLocation**.

NOTES

glGetAttribLocation is available only if the GL version is 2.0 or greater.

ERRORS

GL_INVALID_OPERATION is generated if *program* is not a value generated by OpenGL.

GL_INVALID_OPERATION is generated if *program* is not a program object.

GL_INVALID_OPERATION is generated if *program* has not been successfully linked.

GL_INVALID_OPERATION is generated if **glGetAttribLocation** is executed between the execution of **glBegin** and the corresponding execution of **glEnd**.

ASSOCIATED GETS

glGetActiveAttrib with argument *program* and the index of an active attribute

glIsProgram

SEE ALSO

glBindAttribLocation, glLinkProgram, glVertexAttrib, glVertexAttribPointer

glGetProgram

NAME

glGetProgramiv—Returns a parameter from a program object

C SPECIFICATION

```
void glGetProgramiv(GLuint program,
                    GLenum pname,
                    GLint *params)
```

PARAMETERS

program   Specifies the program object to be queried.

pname   Specifies the object parameter. Accepted symbolic
                names are GL_DELETE_STATUS, GL_LINK_STATUS,
                GL_VALIDATE_STATUS, GL_INFO_LOG_LENGTH,
                GL_ATTACHED_SHADERS, GL_ACTIVE_ATTRIBUTES,
                GL_ACTIVE_ATTRIBUTE_MAX_LENGTH, GL_ACTIVE_
                UNIFORMS, and GL_ACTIVE_UNIFORM_MAX_LENGTH.

params   Returns the requested object parameter.

DESCRIPTION

glGetProgram returns in *params* the value of a parameter for a specific
program object. The following parameters are defined:

GL_DELETE_STATUS
> *params* returns GL_TRUE if *program* is currently flagged for deletion,
> and GL_FALSE otherwise.

GL_LINK_STATUS
> *params* returns GL_TRUE if the last link operation on *program* was
> successful, and GL_FALSE otherwise.

GL_VALIDATE_STATUS
> *params* returns GL_TRUE or if the last validation operation on
> *program* was successful, and GL_FALSE otherwise.

GL_INFO_LOG_LENGTH

> *params* returns the number of characters in the information log for *program* including the null termination character (i.e., the size of the character buffer required to store the information log). If *program* has no information log, a value of 0 is returned.

GL_ATTACHED_SHADERS

> *params* returns the number of shader objects attached to *program*.

GL_ACTIVE_ATTRIBUTES

> *params* returns the number of active attribute variables for *program*.

GL_ACTIVE_ATTRIBUTE_MAX_LENGTH

> *params* returns the length of the longest active attribute name for *program*, including the null termination character (i.e., the size of the character buffer required to store the longest attribute name). If no active attributes exist, 0 is returned.

GL_ACTIVE_UNIFORMS

> *params* returns the number of active uniform variables for *program*.

GL_ACTIVE_UNIFORM_MAX_LENGTH

> *params* returns the length of the longest active uniform variable name for *program*, including the null termination character (i.e., the size of the character buffer required to store the longest uniform variable name). If no active uniform variables exist, 0 is returned.

NOTES

glGetProgram is available only if the GL version is 2.0 or greater.

If an error is generated, no change is made to the contents of *params*.

ERRORS

GL_INVALID_VALUE is generated if *program* is not a value generated by OpenGL.

GL_INVALID_OPERATION is generated if *program* does not refer to a program object.

GL_INVALID_ENUM is generated if *pname* is not an accepted value.

GL_INVALID_OPERATION is generated if **glGetProgram** is executed between the execution of **glBegin** and the corresponding execution of **glEnd**.

ASSOCIATED GETS

glGetActiveAttrib with argument *program*

glGetActiveUniform with argument *program*

glGetAttachedShaders with argument *program*

glGetProgramInfoLog with argument *program*

glIsProgram

SEE ALSO

glAttachShader, **glCreateProgram**, **glDeleteProgram**, **glGetShader**, **glLinkProgram**, **glValidateProgram**

glGetProgramInfoLog

NAME

glGetProgramInfoLog—Returns the information log for a program object

C SPECIFICATION

```
void glGetProgramInfoLog(GLuint program,
                         GLsizei maxLength,
                         GLsizei *length,
                         GLchar *infoLog)
```

PARAMETERS

program   Specifies the program object whose information log is
                to be queried

maxLength   Specifies the size of the character buffer for storing the
                returned information log

length   Returns the length of the string returned in *infoLog*
                (excluding the null terminator)

infoLog   Specifies an array of characters that is used to return
                the information log

DESCRIPTION

glGetProgramInfoLog returns the information log for the specified program
object. The information log for a program object is modified when the
program object is linked or validated. The string that is returned is null
terminated.

glGetProgramInfoLog returns in *infoLog* as much of the information log as it
can, up to a maximum of *maxLength* characters. The number of characters
actually returned, excluding the null termination character, is specified by
length. If the length of the returned string is not required, a value of NULL
can be passed in the *length* argument. The size of the buffer required to store
the returned information log can be obtained by calling **glGetProgram** with
the value GL_INFO_LOG_LENGTH.

The information log for a program object is either an empty string, a string containing information about the last link operation, or a string containing information about the last validation operation. It may contain diagnostic messages, warning messages, and other information. When a program object is created, its information log is a string of length 0.

NOTES

glGetProgramInfoLog is available only if the GL version is 2.0 or greater.

The information log for a program object is the OpenGL implementor's primary mechanism for conveying information about linking and validating. Therefore, the information log can be helpful to application developers during the development process, even when these operations are successful. Application developers should not expect different OpenGL implementations to produce identical information logs.

ERRORS

GL_INVALID_VALUE is generated if *program* is not a value generated by OpenGL.

GL_INVALID_OPERATION is generated if *program* is not a program object.

GL_INVALID_VALUE is generated if *maxLength* is less than 0.

GL_INVALID_OPERATION is generated if **glGetProgramInfoLog** is executed between the execution of **glBegin** and the corresponding execution of **glEnd**.

ASSOCIATED GETS

glGetProgram with argument GL_INFO_LOG_LENGTH

glIsProgram

SEE ALSO

glCompileShader, **glGetShaderInfoLog**, **glLinkProgram**, **glValidateProgram**

glGetShader

NAME

glGetShaderiv—Returns a parameter from a shader object

C SPECIFICATION

```
void glGetShaderiv(GLuint shader,
                   GLenum pname,
                   GLint *params)
```

PARAMETERS

shader   Specifies the shader object to be queried.

pname   Specifies the object parameter. Accepted symbolic
                names are GL_SHADER_TYPE, GL_DELETE_STATUS,
                GL_COMPILE_STATUS, GL_INFO_LOG_LENGTH,
                GL_SHADER_SOURCE_LENGTH.

params   Returns the requested object parameter.

DESCRIPTION

glGetShader returns in *params* the value of a parameter for a specific shader
object. The following parameters are defined:

GL_SHADER_TYPE
        params returns GL_VERTEX_SHADER if *shader* is a vertex shader
        object, and GL_FRAGMENT_SHADER if *shader* is a fragment shader
        object.

GL_DELETE_STATUS
        params returns GL_TRUE if *shader* is currently flagged for deletion,
        and GL_FALSE otherwise.

GL_COMPILE_STATUS
        params returns GL_TRUE if the last compile operation on *shader*
        was successful, and GL_FALSE otherwise.

GL_INFO_LOG_LENGTH
        params returns the number of characters in the information log for
        shader including the null termination character (i.e., the size of the
        character buffer required to store the information log). If *shader*
        has no information log, a value of 0 is returned.

GL_SHADER_SOURCE_LENGTH

params returns the length of the concatenation of the source strings that make up the shader source for the *shader*, including the null termination character (i.e., the size of the character buffer required to store the shader source). If no source code exists, 0 is returned.

NOTES

glGetShader is available only if the GL version is 2.0 or greater.

If an error is generated, no change is made to the contents of *params*.

ERRORS

GL_INVALID_VALUE is generated if *shader* is not a value generated by OpenGL.

GL_INVALID_OPERATION is generated if *shader* does not refer to a shader object.

GL_INVALID_ENUM is generated if *pname* is not an accepted value.

GL_INVALID_OPERATION is generated if **glGetShader** is executed between the execution of **glBegin** and the corresponding execution of **glEnd**.

ASSOCIATED GETS

glGetShaderInfoLog with argument *shader*

glGetShaderSource with argument *shader*

glIsShader

SEE ALSO

glCompileShader, glCreateShader, glDeleteShader, glGetProgram, glShaderSource

glGetShaderInfoLog

NAME

glGetShaderInfoLog—Returns the information log for a shader object

C SPECIFICATION

```
void glGetShaderInfoLog(GLuint shader,
                        GLsizei maxLength,
                        GLsizei *length,
                        GLchar *infoLog)
```

PARAMETERS

shader	Specifies the shader object whose information log is to be queried
maxLength	Specifies the size of the character buffer for storing the returned information log
length	Returns the length of the string returned in *infoLog* (excluding the null terminator)
infoLog	Specifies an array of characters that returns the information log

DESCRIPTION

glGetShaderInfoLog returns the information log for the specified shader object. The information log for a shader object is modified when the shader is compiled. The string that is returned is null terminated.

glGetShaderInfoLog returns in *infoLog* as much of the information log as it can, up to a maximum of *maxLength* characters. The number of characters actually returned, excluding the null termination character, is specified by *length*. If the length of the returned string is not required, a value of NULL can be passed in the *length* argument. The size of the buffer required to store the returned information log can be obtained by calling **glGetShader** with the value GL_INFO_LOG_LENGTH.

The information log for a shader object is a string that may contain diagnostic messages, warning messages, and other information about the last compile operation. When a shader object is created, its information log is a string of length 0.

NOTES

glGetShaderInfoLog is available only if the GL version is 2.0 or greater.

The information log for a shader object is the OpenGL implementor's primary mechanism for conveying information about the compilation process. Therefore, the information log can be helpful to application developers during the development process, even when compilation is successful. Application developers should not expect different OpenGL implementations to produce identical information logs.

ERRORS

GL_INVALID_VALUE is generated if *shader* is not a value generated by OpenGL.

GL_INVALID_OPERATION is generated if *shader* is not a shader object.

GL_INVALID_VALUE is generated if *maxLength* is less than 0.

GL_INVALID_OPERATION is generated if **glGetShaderInfoLog** is executed between the execution of **glBegin** and the corresponding execution of **glEnd**.

ASSOCIATED GETS

glGetShader with argument GL_INFO_LOG_LENGTH

glIsShader

SEE ALSO

glCompileShader, **glGetProgramInfoLog**, **glLinkProgram**, **glValidateProgram**

glGetShaderSource

NAME

glGetShaderSource—Returns the source code string from a shader object

C SPECIFICATION

```
void glGetShaderSource(GLuint shader,
                       GLsizei bufSize,
                       GLsizei *length,
                       GLchar *source)
```

PARAMETERS

shader   Specifies the shader object to be queried

bufSize   Specifies the size of the character buffer for storing the returned source code string

length   Returns the length of the string returned in *source* (excluding the null terminator)

source   Specifies an array of characters that is used to return the source code string

DESCRIPTION

glGetShaderSource returns the concatenation of the source code strings from the shader object specified by *shader*. The source code strings for a shader object are the result of a previous call to **glShaderSource**. The string returned by the function is null terminated.

glGetShaderSource returns in *source* as much of the source code string as it can, up to a maximum of *bufSize* characters. The number of characters actually returned, excluding the null termination character, is specified by *length*. If the length of the returned string is not required, a value of NULL can be passed in the *length* argument. The size of the buffer required to store the returned source code string can be obtained by calling **glGetShader** with the value GL_SHADER_SOURCE_LENGTH.

NOTES

glGetShaderSource is available only if the GL version is 2.0 or greater.

ERRORS

GL_INVALID_VALUE is generated if *shader* is not a value generated by OpenGL.

GL_INVALID_OPERATION is generated if *shader* is not a shader object.

GL_INVALID_VALUE is generated if *bufSize* is less than 0.

GL_INVALID_OPERATION is generated if **glGetShaderSource** is executed between the execution of **glBegin** and the corresponding execution of **glEnd**.

ASSOCIATED GETS

glGetShader with argument GL_SHADER_SOURCE_LENGTH

glIsShader

SEE ALSO

glCreateShader, glShaderSource

glGetUniform

NAME

glGetUniformfv, **glGetUniformiv**—Return the value of a uniform variable

C SPECIFICATION

```
void glGetUniformfv(GLuint program,
                    GLint location,
                    GLfloat *params)

void glGetUniformiv(GLuint program,
                    GLint location,
                    GLint *params)
```

PARAMETERS

program   Specifies the program object to be queried

location   Specifies the location of the uniform variable to be
              queried

params   Returns the value of the specified uniform variable

DESCRIPTION

glGetUniform returns in *params* the value or values of the specified uniform
variable. The type of the uniform variable specified by *location* determines
the number of values returned. If the uniform variable is defined in the
shader as a Boolean, int, or float, a single value is returned. If it is defined as
a vec2, ivec2, or bvec2, two values are returned. If it is defined as a vec3,
ivec3, or bvec3, three values are returned, and so on. To query values stored
in uniform variables declared as arrays, call **glGetUniform** for each element of
the array. To query values stored in uniform variables declared as structures,
call **glGetUniform** for each field in the structure. The values for uniform variables declared as a matrix are returned in column major order.

The locations assigned to uniform variables are not known until the
program object is linked. After linking has occurred, the command
glGetUniformLocation obtains the location of a uniform variable. This location value can then be passed to **glGetUniform** to query the current value of
the uniform variable. After a program object has been linked successfully,

the index values for uniform variables remain fixed until the next link command occurs. The uniform variable values can be queried only after a link if the link was successful.

NOTES

glGetUniform is available only if the GL version is 2.0 or greater.

If an error is generated, no change is made to the contents of *params*.

ERRORS

GL_INVALID_VALUE is generated if *program* is not a value generated by OpenGL.

GL_INVALID_OPERATION is generated if *program* is not a program object.

GL_INVALID_OPERATION is generated if *program* has not been successfully linked.

GL_INVALID_OPERATION is generated if *location* does not correspond to a valid uniform variable location for the specified program object.

GL_INVALID_OPERATION is generated if **glGetUniform** is executed between the execution of **glBegin** and the corresponding execution of **glEnd**.

ASSOCIATED GETS

glGetActiveUniform with arguments *program* and the index of an active uniform variable

glGetProgram with arguments *program* and GL_ACTIVE_UNIFORMS or GL_ACTIVE_UNIFORM_MAX_LENGTH

glGetUniformLocation with arguments *program* and the name of a uniform variable

glIsProgram

SEE ALSO

glCreateProgram, glLinkProgram, glUniform

glGetUniformLocation

NAME

glGetUniformLocation—Returns the location of a uniform variable

C SPECIFICATION

```
GLint glGetUniformLocation(GLuint program,
                          const GLchar *name)
```

PARAMETERS

program   Specifies the program object to be queried

name   Points to a null-terminated string containing the
                   name of the uniform variable whose location is to
                   be queried

DESCRIPTION

glGetUniformLocation returns an integer that represents the location of a specific uniform variable within a program object. *name* must be a null-terminated string that contains no white space. *name* must be an active uniform variable name in *program* that is not a structure, an array of structures, or a subcomponent of a vector or a matrix. This function returns –1 if *name* does not correspond to an active uniform variable in *program* or if *name* starts with the reserved prefix "gl_".

Uniform variables that are structures or arrays of structures may be queried with **glGetUniformLocation** for each field within the structure. The array element operator "[]" and the structure field operator "." may be used in *name* to select elements within an array or fields within a structure. The result of using these operators is not allowed to be another structure, an array of structures, or a subcomponent of a vector or a matrix. Except if the last part of *name* indicates a uniform variable array, the location of the first element of an array can be retrieved with the name of the array or with the name appended by "[0]".

The actual locations assigned to uniform variables are not known until the program object is linked successfully. After linking has occurred, the command **glGetUniformLocation** obtains the location of a uniform variable. This location value can then be passed to **glUniform** to set the value of the uniform variable or to **glGetUniform** to query the current value of the uniform variable. After a program object has been linked successfully, the index values for uniform variables remain fixed until the next link command occurs. Uniform variable locations and values can be queried after a link only if the link was successful.

NOTES

glGetUniformLocation is available only if the GL version is 2.0 or greater.

ERRORS

GL_INVALID_VALUE is generated if *program* is not a value generated by OpenGL.

GL_INVALID_OPERATION is generated if *program* is not a program object.

GL_INVALID_OPERATION is generated if *program* has not been successfully linked.

GL_INVALID_OPERATION is generated if **glGetUniformLocation** is executed between the execution of **glBegin** and the corresponding execution of **glEnd**.

ASSOCIATED GETS

glGetActiveUniform with arguments *program* and the index of an active uniform variable

glGetProgram with arguments *program* and GL_ACTIVE_UNIFORMS or GL_ACTIVE_UNIFORM_MAX_LENGTH

glGetUniform with arguments *program* and the name of a uniform variable

glsProgram

SEE ALSO

glLinkProgram, glUniform

glGetVertexAttrib

NAME

glGetVertexAttribdv, **glGetVertexAttribfv**, **glGetVertexAttribiv**—Return a generic vertex attribute parameter

C SPECIFICATION

```
void glGetVertexAttribdv(GLuint index,
                         GLenum pname,
                         GLdouble *params)

void glGetVertexAttribfv(GLuint index,
                         GLenum pname,
                         GLfloat *params)

void glGetVertexAttribiv(GLuint index,
                         GLenum pname,
                         GLint *params)
```

PARAMETERS

index	Specifies the generic vertex attribute to be queried.
pname	Specifies the symbolic name of the vertex attribute parameter to be queried. GL_VERTEX_ATTRIB_ARRAY_ENABLED, GL_VERTEX_ATTRIB_ARRAY_SIZE, GL_VERTEX_ATTRIB_ARRAY_STRIDE, GL_VERTEX_ATTRIB_ARRAY_TYPE, GL_VERTEX_ATTRIB_ARRAY_NORMALIZED, and GL_CURRENT_VERTEX_ATTRIB are accepted.
params	Returns the requested data.

DESCRIPTION

glGetVertexAttrib returns in params the value of a generic vertex attribute parameter. The generic vertex attribute to be queried is specified by *index*, and the parameter to be queried is specified by *pname*.

The accepted parameter names are as follows:

GL_VERTEX_ATTRIB_ARRAY_ENABLED

> *params* returns a single value that is nonzero (true) if the vertex attribute array for *index* is enabled and 0 (false) if it is disabled. The initial value is GL_FALSE.

GL_VERTEX_ATTRIB_ARRAY_SIZE

> *params* returns a single value, the size of the vertex attribute array for *index*. The size is the number of values for each element of the vertex attribute array, and it is 1, 2, 3, or 4. The initial value is 4.

GL_VERTEX_ATTRIB_ARRAY_STRIDE

> *params* returns a single value, the array stride for (number of bytes between successive elements in) the vertex attribute array for *index*. A value of 0 signifies that the array elements are stored sequentially in memory. The initial value is 0.

GL_VERTEX_ATTRIB_ARRAY_TYPE

> *params* returns a single value, a symbolic constant indicating the array type for the vertex attribute array for *index*. Possible values are GL_BYTE, GL_UNSIGNED_BYTE, GL_SHORT, GL_UNSIGNED_SHORT, GL_INT, GL_UNSIGNED_INT, GL_FLOAT, and GL_DOUBLE. The initial value is GL_FLOAT.

GL_VERTEX_ATTRIB_ARRAY_NORMALIZED

> *params* returns a single value that is non-zero (true) if fixed-point data types for the vertex attribute array indicated by *index* are normalized when they are converted to floating point, and 0 (false) otherwise. The initial value is GL_FALSE.

GL_CURRENT_VERTEX_ATTRIB

> *params* returns four values that represent the current value for the generic vertex attribute specified by *index*. Generic vertex attribute 0 is unique in that it has no current state, so an error is generated if *index* is 0. The initial value for all other generic vertex attributes is (0,0,0,1).

All the parameters except GL_CURRENT_VERTEX_ATTRIB represent client-side state.

NOTES

glGetVertexAttrib is available only if the GL version is 2.0 or greater.

If an error is generated, no change is made to the contents of *params*.

ERRORS

GL_INVALID_VALUE is generated if *index* is greater than or equal to GL_MAX_VERTEX_ATTRIBS.

GL_INVALID_ENUM is generated if *pname* is not an accepted value.

GL_INVALID_OPERATION is generated if *index* is 0 and *pname* is GL_CURRENT_VERTEX_ATTRIB.

ASSOCIATED GETS

glGet with argument GL_MAX_VERTEX_ATTRIBS

glGetVertexAttribPointer with arguments *index* and GL_VERTEX_ATTRIB_ARRAY_POINTER

SEE ALSO

glBindAttribLocation, **glDisableVertexAttribArray**, **glEnableVertexAttribArray**, **glVertexAttrib**, **glVertexAttribPointer**

glGetVertexAttribPointer

NAME

glGetVertexAttributePointerv—Returns the address of the specified pointer

C SPECIFICATION

```
void glGetVertexAttribPointerv(GLuint index,
                               GLenum pname,
                               GLvoid **pointer)
```

PARAMETERS

index   Specifies the generic vertex attribute to be queried.

pname   Specifies the symbolic name of the generic vertex attri-
                  bute parameter to be queried. Must be GL_VERTEX_
                  ATTRIB_ARRAY_POINTER.

params   Returns the requested data.

DESCRIPTION

glGetVertexAttribPointer returns pointer information. *index* is the generic
vertex attribute to be queried, *pname* is a symbolic constant indicating the
pointer to be returned, and *params* is a pointer to a location in which to
place the returned data. The accepted parameter names are as follows:

GL_VERTEX_ATTRIB_ARRAY_POINTER
>   *params* returns a single value that is a pointer to the vertex
>   attribute array for the generic vertex attribute specified by *index*.

NOTES

glGetVertexAttribPointer is available only if the GL version is 2.0 or greater.

The pointer returned is client-side state.

The initial value for each pointer is NULL.

ERRORS

GL_INVALID_VALUE is generated if *index* is greater than or equal to GL_MAX_VERTEX_ATTRIBS.

GL_INVALID_ENUM is generated if *pname* is not an accepted value.

ASSOCIATED GETS

glGet with argument GL_MAX_VERTEX_ATTRIBS

glGetVertexAttrib with arguments *index* and the name of a generic vertex attribute parameter

SEE ALSO

glVertexAttribPointer

glIsProgram

NAME

glIsProgram—Determines whether a name corresponds to a program object

C SPECIFICATION

```
GLboolean glIsProgram(GLuint program)
```

PARAMETERS

program   Specifies a potential program object

DESCRIPTION

glIsProgram returns GL_TRUE if *program* is the name of a program object. If *program* is zero or a nonzero value that is not the name of a program object, **glIsProgram** returns GL_FALSE.

NOTES

glIsProgram is available only if the GL version is 2.0 or greater.

No error is generated if *program* is not a valid program object name.

ERRORS

GL_INVALID_OPERATION is generated if **glIsProgram** is executed between the execution of **glBegin** and the corresponding execution of **glEnd**.

ASSOCIATED GETS

glGet with the argument GL_CURRENT_PROGRAM

glGetActiveAttrib with arguments *program* and the index of an active attribute variable

glGetActiveUniform with arguments *program* and the index of an active uniform variable

glGetAttachedShaders with argument *program*

glGetAttribLocation with arguments *program* and the name of an attribute variable

glGetProgram with arguments *program* and the parameter to be queried

glGetProgramInfoLog with argument *program*

glGetUniform with arguments *program* and the location of a uniform variable

glGetUniformLocation with arguments *program* and the name of a uniform variable

SEE ALSO

glAttachShader, **glBindAttribLocation**, **glCreateProgram**, **glDeleteProgram**, **glDetachShader**, **glLinkProgram**, **glUniform**, **glUseProgram**, **glValidateProgram**

glIsShader

NAME

glIsShader—Determines whether a name corresponds to a shader object

C SPECIFICATION

```
GLboolean glIsShader(GLuint shader)
```

PARAMETERS

shader   Specifies a potential shader object

DESCRIPTION

glIsShader returns GL_TRUE if *shader* is the name of a shader object. If *shader* is zero or a nonzero value that is not the name of a shader object, **glIsShader** returns GL_FALSE.

NOTES

glIsShader is available only if the GL version is 2.0 or greater.

No error is generated if *shader* is not a valid shader object name.

ERRORS

GL_INVALID_OPERATION is generated if **glIsShader** is executed between the execution of **glBegin** and the corresponding execution of **glEnd**.

ASSOCIATED GETS

glGetAttachedShaders with a valid program object

glGetShader with arguments *shader* and a parameter to be queried

glGetShaderInfoLog with argument *object*

glGetShaderSource with argument *object*

SEE ALSO

glAttachShader, glCompileShader, glCreateShader, glDeleteShader, glDetachShader, glLinkProgram, glShaderSource

glLinkProgram

NAME

glLinkProgram—Links a program object

C SPECIFICATION

```
void glLinkProgram(GLuint program)
```

PARAMETERS

program   Specifies the handle of the program object to be linked

DESCRIPTION

glLinkProgram links the program object specified by *program.* If any shader objects of type GL_VERTEX_SHADER are attached to *program*, they are used to create an executable that will run on the programmable vertex processor. If any shader objects of type GL_FRAGMENT_SHADER are attached to *program*, they are used to create an executable that will run on the program-mable fragment processor.

The status of the link operation is stored as part of the program object's state. This value is set to GL_TRUE if the program object was linked without errors and is ready for use, and GL_FALSE otherwise. It can be queried by calling **glGetProgram** with arguments *program* and GL_LINK_STATUS.

As a result of a successful link operation, all active user-defined uniform variables belonging to *program* are initialized to 0, and each of the program object's active uniform variables is assigned a location that can be queried with **glGetUniformLocation**. Also, any active user-defined attribute variables that have not been bound to a generic vertex attribute index are bound to one at this time.

Linking of a program object can fail for a number of reasons as specified in the OpenGL Shading Language Specification. The following lists some of the conditions that cause a link error:

- The number of active attribute variables supported by the implementa-tion has been exceeded.

- The storage limit for uniform variables has been exceeded.

- The number of active uniform variables supported by the implementation has been exceeded.

- The **main** function is missing for the vertex shader or the fragment shader.

- A varying variable actually used in the fragment shader is not declared in the same way (or is not declared at all) in the vertex shader.

- A reference to a function or variable name is unresolved.

- A shared global is declared with two different types or two different initial values.

- One or more of the attached shader objects has not been successfully compiled.

- Binding a generic attribute matrix caused some rows of the matrix to fall outside the allowed maximum of GL_MAX_VERTEX_ATTRIBS.

- Not enough contiguous vertex attribute slots could be found to bind attribute matrices.

When a program object has been successfully linked, the program object can be made part of current state with **glUseProgram**. Whether or not the link operation was successful, the program object's information log is overwritten. The information log can be retrieved with **glGetProgramInfoLog**.

glLinkProgram also installs the generated executables as part of the current rendering state if the link operation was successful and the specified program object is already currently in use as a result of a previous call to **glUseProgram**. If the program object currently in use is relinked unsuccessfully, its link status is set to GL_FALSE, but the executables and associated state remain part of the current state until a subsequent call to **glUseProgram** removes it from use. After it is removed from use, it cannot be made part of current state until it has been successfully relinked.

If *program* contains shader objects of type GL_VERTEX_SHADER but does not contain shader objects of type GL_FRAGMENT_SHADER, the vertex shader is linked against the implicit interface for fixed functionality fragment processing. Similarly, if *program* contains shader objects of type GL_FRAGMENT_SHADER but does not contain shader objects of type GL_VERTEX_SHADER, the fragment shader is linked against the implicit interface for fixed functionality vertex processing.

The program object's information log is updated, and the program is generated at the time of the link operation. After the link operation, applications are free to modify attached shader objects, compile attached shader objects, detach shader objects, delete shader objects, and attach additional shader objects. None of these operations affect the information log or the program that is part of the program object.

NOTES

glLinkProgram is available only if the GL version is 2.0 or greater.

If the link operation is unsuccessful, any information about a previous link operation on *program* is lost (i.e., a failed link does not restore the old state of *program*). Certain information can still be retrieved from *program* even after an unsuccessful link operation. See, for instance, **glGetActiveAttrib** and **glGetActiveUniform**.

ERRORS

GL_INVALID_VALUE is generated if *program* is not a value generated by OpenGL.

GL_INVALID_OPERATION is generated if *program* is not a program object.

GL_INVALID_OPERATION is generated if **glLinkProgram** is executed between the execution of **glBegin** and the corresponding execution of **glEnd**.

ASSOCIATED GETS

glGet with the argument GL_CURRENT_PROGRAM

glGetActiveAttrib with argument *program* and the index of an active attribute variable

glGetActiveUniform with argument *program* and the index of an active uniform variable

glGetAttachedShaders with argument *program*

glGetAttribLocation with argument *program* and an attribute variable name

glGetProgram with arguments *program* and GL_LINK_STATUS

glGetProgramInfoLog with argument *program*

glGetUniform with argument *program* and a uniform variable location

glGetUniformLocation with argument *program* and a uniform variable name

glIsProgram

SEE ALSO

glAttachShader, glBindAttribLocation, glCompileShader, glCreateProgram, glDeleteProgram, glDetachShader, glUniform, glUseProgram, glValidateProgram

glShaderSource

NAME

glShaderSource—Replaces the source code in a shader object

C SPECIFICATION

```
void glShaderSource(GLuint shader,
                    GLsizei count,
                    const GLchar **string,
                    const GLint *length)
```

PARAMETERS

shader   Specifies the handle of the shader object whose source
             code is to be replaced

count   Specifies the number of elements in the *string* and
             length arrays

string   Specifies an array of pointers to strings containing the
             source code to be loaded into the shader

length   Specifies an array of string lengths

DESCRIPTION

glShaderSource sets the source code in *shader* to the source code in the array
of strings specified by *string*. Any source code previously stored in the shader
object is completely replaced. The number of strings in the array is specified
by *count*. If *length* is NULL, each string is assumed to be null terminated. If
length is a value other than NULL, it points to an array containing a string
length for each of the corresponding elements of *string*. Each element in the
length array may contain the length of the corresponding string (the null
character is not counted as part of the string length) or a value less than 0
to indicate that the string is null terminated. The source code strings are not
scanned or parsed at this time; they are simply copied into the specified
shader object.

NOTES

glShaderSource is available only if the GL version is 2.0 or greater.

OpenGL copies the shader source code strings when **glShaderSource** is called, so an application can free its copy of the source code strings immediately after the function returns.

ERRORS

GL_INVALID_VALUE is generated if *shader* is not a value generated by OpenGL.

GL_INVALID_OPERATION is generated if *shader* is not a shader object.

GL_INVALID_VALUE is generated if *count* is less than 0.

GL_INVALID_OPERATION is generated if **glShaderSource** is executed between the execution of **glBegin** and the corresponding execution of **glEnd**.

ASSOCIATED GETS

glGetShader with arguments *shader* and GL_SHADER_SOURCE_LENGTH

glGetShaderSource with argument *shader*

glIsShader

SEE ALSO

glCompileShader, glCreateShader, glDeleteShader

glUniform

NAME

glUniform1f, **glUniform2f**, **glUniform3f**, **glUniform4f**, **glUniform1i**, **glUniform2i**, **glUniform3i**, **glUniform4i**, **glUniform1fv**, **glUniform2fv**, **glUniform3fv**, **glUniform4fv**, **glUniform1iv**, **glUniform2iv**, **glUniform3iv**, **glUniform4iv**, **glUniformMatrix2fv**, **glUniformMatrix3fv**, **glUniformMatrix4fv**—Specify the value of a uniform variable for the current program object

C SPECIFICATION

```
void glUniform1f(GLint location,
                 GLfloat v0)
void glUniform2f(GLint location,
                 GLfloat v0,
                 GLfloat v1)
void glUniform3f(GLint location,
                 GLfloat v0,
                 GLfloat v1,
                 GLfloat v2)
void glUniform4f(GLint location,
                 GLfloat v0,
                 GLfloat v1,
                 GLfloat v2,
                 GLfloat v3)

void glUniform1i(GLint location,
                 GLint v0)
void glUniform2i(GLint location,
                 GLint v0,
                 GLint v1)
void glUniform3i(GLint location,
                 GLint v0,
                 GLint v1,
                 GLint v2)
void glUniform4i(GLint location,
                 GLint v0,
                 GLint v1,
                 GLint v2,
                 GLint v3)
```

PARAMETERS

location   Specifies the location of the uniform variable to be
                    modified

v0, v1, v2, v3   Specify the new values to be used for the specified
                    uniform variable

C SPECIFICATION

```
void glUniform1fv(GLint location,
                  GLsizei count,
                  const GLfloat *value)
void glUniform2fv(GLint location,
                  GLsizei count,
                  const GLfloat *value)
void glUniform3fv(GLint location,
                  GLsizei count,
                  const GLfloat *value)
void glUniform4fv(GLint location,
                  GLsizei count,
                  const GLfloat *value)

void glUniform1iv(GLint location,
                  GLsizei count,
                  const GLint *value)
void glUniform2iv(GLint location,
                  GLsizei count,
                  const GLint *value)
void glUniform3iv(GLint location,
                  GLsizei count,
                  const GLint *value)
void glUniform4iv(GLint location,
                  GLsizei count,
                  const GLint *value)
```

PARAMETERS

location   Specifies the location of the uniform value to be modified

count   Specifies the number of elements that are to be modified (this should be 1 if the targeted uniform variable is not an array, 1 or more if it is an array)

value   Specifies a pointer to an array of *count* values that are used to update the specified uniform variable

C SPECIFICATION

```
void glUniformMatrix2fv(GLint location,
                        GLsizei count,
                        GLboolean transpose,
                        const GLfloat *value)
void glUniformMatrix3fv(GLint location,
                        GLsizei count,
                        GLboolean transpose,
                        const GLfloat *value)
void glUniformMatrix4fv(GLint location,
                        GLsizei count,
                        GLboolean transpose,
                        const GLfloat *value)
```

PARAMETERS

location   Specifies the location of the uniform value to be modified

count   Specifies the number of elements that are to be modified (this should be 1 if the targeted uniform variable is not an array, 1 or more if it is an array)

transpose   Specifies whether to transpose the matrix as the values are loaded into the uniform variable

value   Specifies a pointer to an array of *count* values that are used to update the specified uniform variable

DESCRIPTION

glUniform modifies the value of a uniform variable or a uniform variable array. The location of the uniform variable to be modified is specified by *location*, which should be a value returned by **glGetUniformLocation**. **glUniform** operates on the program object that was made part of current state with **glUseProgram**.

The commands **glUniform{1|2|3|4}{f|i}** change the value of the uniform variable specified by *location*, using the values passed as arguments. The number specified in the command should match the number of components in the data type of the specified uniform variable (e.g., **1** for float, int, bool; **2** for vec2, ivec2, bvec2). The suffix **f** means that floating-point values are being passed; the suffix **i** means that integer values are being passed, and this type should also match the data type of the specified uniform variable. The **i** variants of this function provide values for uniform variables defined as int, ivec2, ivec3, ivec4, or arrays of these. The **f** variants provide values for uniform variables of type float, vec2, vec3, vec4, or arrays of these. Either the **i** or the **f** variants can provide values for uniform variables of type bool, bvec2, bvec3, bvec4, or arrays of these. The uniform variable is set to false if the input value is 0 or 0.0f, and it is set to true otherwise.

All active uniform variables defined in a program object are initialized to 0 when the program object is linked successfully. They retain the values assigned to them with **glUniform** until the next successful link operation occurs on the program object, when they are once again initialized to 0.

The commands **glUniform{1|2|3|4}{f|i}v** modify a single uniform variable or a uniform variable array. These commands pass a count and a pointer to the values to be loaded into a uniform variable or a uniform variable array. Use a count of 1 if modifying the value of a single uniform variable, and a count of 1 or greater if modifying an entire array or part of an array. When n elements starting at an arbitrary position m in a uniform variable array are loaded, elements $m + n - 1$ in the array are replaced with the new values. If $m + n - 1$ is larger than the size of the uniform variable array, values for all array elements beyond the end of the array are ignored. The number specified in the name of the command indicates the number of components for each element in *value*, and it should match the number of components in the data type of the specified uniform variable (e.g., **1** for float, int, bool; **2** for vec2, ivec2, bvec2). The data type specified in the name of the command must match the data type for the specified uniform variable as described previously for **glUniform{1|2|3|4}{f|i}**.

For uniform variable arrays, each element of the array is considered to be of the type indicated in the name of the command (e.g., **glUniform3f** or **glUniform3fv** can be used to load a uniform variable array of type vec3). The number of elements of the uniform variable array to be modified is specified by *count*.

The commands **glUniformFloatMatrix{2|3|4}fv** modify a matrix or an array of matrices. The number in the command name is interpreted as the dimensionality of the matrix. The number **2** indicates a 2×2 matrix (i.e., 4 values), the number **3** indicates a 3×3 matrix (i.e., 9 values), and the number **4** indicates a 4×4 matrix (i.e., 16 values). If *transpose* is GL_FALSE, each matrix is assumed to be supplied in column major order. If *transpose* is GL_TRUE, each matrix is assumed to be supplied in row major order. The *count* argument specifies the number of matrices to be passed. Use a count of 1 if modifying the value of a single matrix, and use a count greater than 1 if modifying an array of matrices.

NOTES

glUniform is available only if the GL version is 2.0 or greater.

glUniform1i and **glUniform1iv** are the only two functions that may load uniform variables defined as sampler types. Loading samplers with any other function results in a GL_INVALID_OPERATION error.

If *count* is greater than 1 and the indicated uniform variable is not an array, a GL_INVALID_OPERATION error is generated, and the specified uniform variable remains unchanged.

Other than the preceding exceptions, if the type and size of the uniform variable as defined in the shader do not match the type and size specified in the name of the command used to load a value for the uniform variable, a GL_INVALID_OPERATION error is generated, and the specified uniform variable remains unchanged.

If *location* is a value other than −1 and it does not represent a valid uniform variable location in the current program object, an error is generated, and no changes are made to the uniform variable storage of the current program object. If *location* is equal to −1, the data passed in is silently ignored, and the specified uniform variable is unchanged.

ERRORS

GL_INVALID_OPERATION is generated if there is no current program object.

GL_INVALID_OPERATION is generated if the size of the uniform variable declared in the shader does not match the size indicated by the **glUniform** command.

GL_INVALID_OPERATION is generated if one of the integer variants of this function loads a uniform variable of type float, vec2, vec3, vec4, or an array of these, or if one of the floating-point variants of this function loads a uniform variable of type int, ivec2, ivec3, or ivec4, or an array of these.

GL_INVALID_OPERATION is generated if *location* is an invalid uniform location for the current program object and *location* is not equal to −1.

GL_INVALID_VALUE is generated if *count* is less than 0.

GL_INVALID_OPERATION is generated if *count* is greater than 1 and the indicated uniform variable is not an array variable.

GL_INVALID_OPERATION is generated if a sampler is loaded with a command other than **glUniform1i** and **glUniform1iv**.

GL_INVALID_OPERATION is generated if **glUniform** is executed between the execution of **glBegin** and the corresponding execution of **glEnd**.

ASSOCIATED GETS

glGet with the argument GL_CURRENT_PROGRAM

glGetActiveUniform with the handle of a program object and the index of an active uniform variable

glGetUniform with the handle of a program object and the location of a uniform variable

glGetUniformLocation with the handle of a program object and the name of a uniform variable

SEE ALSO

glLinkProgram, glUseProgram

glUseProgram

NAME

glUseProgram—Installs a program object as part of current rendering state

C SPECIFICATION

```
void glUseProgram(GLuint program)
```

PARAMETERS

program　　　　　Specifies the handle of the program object whose
executables are to be used as part of current
rendering state

DESCRIPTION

glUseProgram installs the program object specified by *program* as part of
current rendering state. Creating one or more executables in a program
object involves successfully attaching shader objects to it with **glAttach-
Shader,** successfully compiling the shader objects with **glCompileShader,**
and successfully linking the program object with **glLinkProgram.**

A program object contains an executable that will run on the vertex
processor if it contains one or more shader objects of type GL_VERTEX_
SHADER that have been successfully compiled and linked. Similarly, a
program object contains an executable that will run on the fragment
processor if it contains one or more shader objects of type GL_FRAGMENT_
SHADER that have been successfully compiled and linked.

Successfully installing an executable on a programmable processor disables
the corresponding fixed functionality of OpenGL. Specifically, if an executable is installed on the vertex processor, the OpenGL fixed functionality is
disabled as follows:

- The modelview matrix is not applied to vertex coordinates.

- The projection matrix is not applied to vertex coordinates.

- The texture matrices are not applied to texture coordinates.

- Normals are not transformed to eye coordinates.

- Normals are not rescaled or normalized.

- Normalization of GL_AUTO_NORMAL evaluated normals is not performed.

- Texture coordinates are not generated automatically.

- Per-vertex lighting is not performed.

- Color material computations are not performed.

- Color index lighting is not performed.

This list also applies to setting the current raster position.

The executable that is installed on the vertex processor is expected to implement any or all of the desired functionality from the preceding list. Similarly, if an executable is installed on the fragment processor, the OpenGL fixed functionality is disabled as follows:

- Texture environment and texture functions are not applied.

- Texture application is not applied.

- Color sum is not applied.

- Fog is not applied.

Again, the fragment shader that is installed is expected to implement any or all of the desired functionality from the preceding list.

While a program object is in use, applications are free to modify attached shader objects, compile attached shader objects, attach additional shader objects, and detach or delete shader objects. None of these operations affect the executables that are part of the current state. However, relinking the program object that is currently in use installs the program object as part of the current rendering state if the link operation was successful (see **glLinkProgram**). If the program object currently in use is relinked unsuccessfully, its link status is set to GL_FALSE, but the executables and associated state remain part of the current state until a subsequent call to **glUseProgram** removes the program object from use. After it is removed from use, it cannot be made part of current state until it has been successfully relinked.

If *program* contains shader objects of type GL_VERTEX_SHADER but does not contain shader objects of type GL_FRAGMENT_SHADER, an executable is installed on the vertex processor, but fixed functionality is used for fragment processing. Similarly, if *program* contains shader objects of type GL_FRAGMENT_SHADER but does not contain shader objects of type

GL_VERTEX_SHADER, an executable is installed on the fragment processor, but fixed functionality is used for vertex processing. If *program* is 0, the programmable processors are disabled, and fixed functionality is used for both vertex and fragment processing.

NOTES

glUseProgram is available only if the GL version is 2.0 or greater.

While a program object is in use, the state that controls the disabled fixed functionality may also be updated with the normal OpenGL calls.

Like display lists and texture objects, the namespace for program objects may be shared across a set of contexts, as long as the server sides of the contexts share the same address space. If the namespace is shared across contexts, any attached objects and the data associated with those attached objects are shared as well.

Applications are responsible for synchronizing across API calls when objects are accessed from different execution threads.

ERRORS

GL_INVALID_VALUE is generated if *program* is neither 0 nor a value generated by OpenGL.

GL_INVALID_OPERATION is generated if *program* is not a program object.

GL_INVALID_OPERATION is generated if *program* could not be made part of current state.

GL_INVALID_OPERATION is generated if **glUseProgram** is executed between the execution of **glBegin** and the corresponding execution of **glEnd**.

ASSOCIATED GETS

glGet with the argument GL_CURRENT_PROGRAM

glGetActiveAttrib with a valid program object and the index of an active attribute variable

glGetActiveUniform with a valid program object and the index of an active uniform variable

glGetAttachedShaders with a valid program object

glGetAttribLocation with a valid program object and the name of an attribute variable

glGetProgram with a valid program object and the parameter to be queried

glGetProgramInfoLog with a valid program object

glGetUniform with a valid program object and the location of a uniform variable

glGetUniformLocation with a valid program object and the name of a uniform variable

glIsProgram

SEE ALSO

glIAttachShader, **glBindAttribLocation**, **glCompileShader**, **glCreateProgram**, **glDeleteProgram**, **glDetachShader**, **glLinkProgram**, **glUniform**, **glValidateProgram**, **glVertexAttrib**

glValidateProgram

NAME

glValidateProgram—Validates a program object

C SPECIFICATION

```
void glValidateProgram(GLuint program)
```

PARAMETERS

program   Specifies the handle of the program object to be
                     validated

DESCRIPTION

glValidateProgram checks to see whether the executables contained in
program can execute given the current OpenGL state. The information
generated by the validation process is stored in *program*'s information log.
The validation information may consist of an empty string, or it may be a
string containing information about how the current program object interacts with the rest of current OpenGL state. This function provides a way for
OpenGL implementors to convey more information about why the current
program is inefficient, suboptimal, failing to execute, and so on.

The status of the validation operation is stored as part of the program
object's state. This value is set to GL_TRUE if the validation succeeded, and
GL_FALSE otherwise. It can be queried by calling **glGetProgram** with arguments *program* and GL_VALIDATE_STATUS. If validation is successful, *program*
is guaranteed to execute given the current state. Otherwise, *program* is guaranteed to not execute.

This function is typically useful only during application development. The
informational string stored in the information log is completely implementation dependent; therefore, different OpenGL implementations cannot be
expected to produce identical information strings.

NOTES

glValidateProgram is available only if the GL version is 2.0 or greater.

This function mimics the validation operation that OpenGL implementations
must perform when rendering commands are issued while programmable

shaders are part of current state. The error GL_INVALID_OPERATION is generated by **glBegin**, **glRasterPos**, or any command that performs an implicit call to **glBegin** if

- any two active samplers in the current program object are of different types but refer to the same texture image unit;

- any active sampler in the current program object refers to a texture image unit in which fixed function fragment processing accesses a texture target that does not match the sampler type; or

- the sum of the number of active samplers in the program and the number of texture image units enabled for fixed function fragment processing exceeds the combined limit on the total number of texture image units allowed.

Difficulties or performance degradation may occur if applications try to catch these errors when issuing rendering commands. Therefore, applications are advised to make calls to **glValidateProgram** to detect these issues during application development.

ERRORS

GL_INVALID_VALUE is generated if *program* is not a value generated by OpenGL.

GL_INVALID_OPERATION is generated if *program* is not a program object.

GL_INVALID_OPERATION is generated if **glValidateProgram** is executed between the execution of **glBegin** and the corresponding execution of **glEnd**.

ASSOCIATED GETS

glGetProgram with arguments *program* and GL_VALIDATE_STATUS

glGetProgramInfoLog with argument *program*

glIsProgram

SEE ALSO

glLinkProgram, **glUseProgram**

glVertexAttrib

NAME

glVertexAttrib1f, glVertexAttrib1s, glVertexAttrib1d, glVertexAttrib2f, glVertexAttrib2s, glVertexAttrib2d, glVertexAttrib3f, glVertexAttrib3s, glVertexAttrib3d, glVertexAttrib4f, glVertexAttrib4s, glVertexAttrib4d, glVertexAttrib4Nub, glVertexAttrib1fv, glVertexAttrib1sv, glVertexAttrib1dv, glVertexAttrib2fv, glVertexAttrib2sv, glVertexAttrib2dv, glVertexAttrib3fv, glVertexAttrib3sv, glVertexAttrib3dv, glVertexAttrib4fv, glVertexAttrib4sv, glVertexAttrib4dv, glVertexAttrib4iv, glVertexAttrib4bv, glVertexAttrib4ubv, glVertexAttrib4usv, glVertexAttrib4uiv, glVertexAttrib4Nbv, glVertexAttrib4Nsv, glVertexAttrib4Niv, glVertexAttrib4Nubv, glVertexAttrib4Nusv, glVertexAttrib4Nuiv—Specify the value of a generic vertex attribute

C SPECIFICATION

```
void glVertexAttrib1f(GLuint index,
                      GLfloat v0)
void glVertexAttrib1s(GLuint index,
                      GLshort v0)
void glVertexAttrib1d(GLuint index,
                      GLdouble v0)

void glVertexAttrib2f(GLuint index,
                      GLfloat v0,
                      GLfloat v1)
void glVertexAttrib2s(GLuint index,
                      GLshort v0,
                      GLshort v1)
void glVertexAttrib2d(GLuint index,
                      GLdouble v0,
                      GLdouble v1)

void glVertexAttrib3f(GLuint index,
                      GLfloat v0,
                      GLfloat v1,
                      GLfloat v2)
void glVertexAttrib3s(GLuint index,
                      GLshort v0,
                      GLshort v1,
                      GLshort v2)
```

```
void glVertexAttrib3d(GLuint index,
                      GLdouble v0,
                      GLdouble v1,
                      GLdouble v2)

void glVertexAttrib4f(GLuint index,
                      GLfloat v0,
                      GLfloat v1,
                      GLfloat v2,
                      GLfloat v3)
void glVertexAttrib4s(GLuint index,
                      GLshort v0,
                      GLshort v1,
                      GLshort v2,
                      GLshort v3)
void glVertexAttrib4d(GLuint index,
                      GLdouble v0,
                      GLdouble v1,
                      GLdouble v2,
                      GLdouble v3)

void glVertexAttrib4Nub(GLuint index,
                        GLubyte v0,
                        GLubyte v1,
                        GLubyte v2,
                        GLubyte v3)
```

PARAMETERS

index   Specifies the index of the generic vertex attribute to be modified

v0, v1, v2, v3   Specify the new values to be used for the specified vertex attribute

C SPECIFICATION

```
void glVertexAttrib1fv(GLuint index, const GLfloat *v)
void glVertexAttrib1sv(GLuint index, const GLshort *v)
void glVertexAttrib1dv(GLuint index, const GLdouble *v)

void glVertexAttrib2fv(GLuint index, const GLfloat *v)
void glVertexAttrib2sv(GLuint index, const GLshort *v)
void glVertexAttrib2dv(GLuint index, const GLdouble *v)

void glVertexAttrib3fv(GLuint index, const GLfloat *v)
void glVertexAttrib3sv(GLuint index, const GLshort *v)
void glVertexAttrib3dv(GLuint index, const GLdouble *v)

void glVertexAttrib4fv(GLuint index, const GLfloat *v)
void glVertexAttrib4sv(GLuint index, const GLshort *v)
void glVertexAttrib4dv(GLuint index, const GLdouble *v)
void glVertexAttrib4iv(GLuint index, const GLint *v)
void glVertexAttrib4bv(GLuint index, const GLbyte *v)

void glVertexAttrib4ubv(GLuint index, const GLubyte *v)
void glVertexAttrib4usv(GLuint index, const GLushort *v)
void glVertexAttrib4uiv(GLuint index, const GLuint *v)

void glVertexAttrib4Nbv(GLuint index, const GLbyte *v)
void glVertexAttrib4Nsv(GLuint index, const GLshort *v)
void glVertexAttrib4Niv(GLuint index, const GLint *v)
void glVertexAttrib4Nubv(GLuint index, const GLubyte *v)
void glVertexAttrib4Nusv(GLuint index, const GLushort *v)
void glVertexAttrib4Nuiv(GLuint index, const GLuint *v)
```

PARAMETERS

index   Specifies the index of the generic vertex attribute to be modified

v   Specifies a pointer to an array of values to be used for the generic vertex attribute

DESCRIPTION

OpenGL defines a number of standard vertex attributes that applications can modify with standard API entry points (color, normal, texture coordinates, etc.). The **glVertexAttrib** family of entry points allows an application to pass generic vertex attributes into numbered locations.

Generic attributes are defined as four-component values that are organized into an array. The first entry of this array is numbered 0, and the size of the array is specified by the implementation-dependent constant GL_MAX_VERTEX_ATTRIBS. Individual elements of this array can be modified with a **glVertexAttrib** call that specifies the index of the element to be modified and a value for that element.

These commands can specify one, two, three, or all four components of the generic vertex attribute specified by *index*. A **1** in the command name means that only one value is passed and that it modifies the first component of the generic vertex attribute. The second and third components are set to 0, and the fourth component is set to 1. Similarly, a **2** in the command name means that values are provided for the first two components, the third component is set to 0, and the fourth component is set to 1. A **3** in the command name means that values are provided for the first three components and that the fourth component is set to 1, and a **4** in the command name means that values are provided for all four components.

The letters **s**, **f**, **i**, **d**, **ub**, **us**, and **ui** specify whether the arguments are of type short, float, int, double, unsigned byte, unsigned short, or unsigned int. When **v** is appended to the name, the commands can take a pointer to an array of such values. The letter **N** in a command name means that the arguments are passed as fixed-point values that are scaled to a normalized range according to the component conversion rules defined by the OpenGL specification. Signed values are understood to represent fixed-point values in the range [–1,1], and unsigned values are understood to represent fixed-point values in the range [0,1].

OpenGL Shading Language attribute variables are allowed to be of type mat2, mat3, or mat4. Attributes of these types can be loaded by the **glVertexAttrib** entry points. Matrices must be loaded into successive generic attribute slots in column major order, with one column of the matrix in each generic attribute slot.

A user-defined attribute variable declared in a vertex shader can be bound to a generic attribute index with **glBindAttribLocation**. Such binding allows an application to use more descriptive variable names in a vertex shader. A subsequent change to the specified generic vertex attribute is immediately reflected as a change to the corresponding attribute variable in the vertex shader.

The binding between a generic vertex attribute index and a user-defined attribute variable in a vertex shader is part of the state of a program object, but the current value of the generic vertex attribute is not. The value of each generic vertex attribute is part of current state, just like standard vertex attributes, and it is maintained even if a different program object is used.

An application may freely modify generic vertex attributes that are not bound to a named vertex shader attribute variable. These values are simply maintained as part of current state and are not accessed by the vertex shader. If a generic vertex attribute bound to an attribute variable in a vertex shader is not updated while the vertex shader is executing, the vertex shader repeatedly uses the current value for the generic vertex attribute.

The generic vertex attribute with index 0 is the same as the vertex position attribute previously defined by OpenGL. A **glVertex2**, **glVertex3**, or **glVertex4** command is completely equivalent to the corresponding **glVertexAttrib** command with an index argument of 0. A vertex shader can access generic vertex attribute 0 by using the built-in attribute variable *gl_Vertex*. There are no current values for generic vertex attribute 0. This is the only generic vertex attribute with this property; calls to set other standard vertex attributes can be freely mixed with calls to set any of the other generic vertex attributes.

NOTES

glVertexAttrib is available only if the GL version is 2.0 or greater.

Generic vertex attributes can be updated at any time. In particular, **glVertexAttrib** can be called between a call to **glBegin** and the corresponding call to **glEnd**.

An application can bind more than one attribute name to the same generic vertex attribute index. This is referred to as aliasing, and it is allowed only if just one of the aliased attribute variables is active in the vertex shader or if no path through the vertex shader consumes more than one of the attributes aliased to the same location. OpenGL implementations are not required to do error checking to detect aliasing; they are allowed to assume that aliasing does not occur, and they are allowed to employ optimizations that work only in the absence of aliasing.

There is no provision for binding standard vertex attributes; therefore, it is not possible to alias generic attributes with standard attributes.

ERRORS

GL_INVALID_VALUE is generated if *index* is greater than or equal to GL_MAX_VERTEX_ATTRIBS.

ASSOCIATED GETS

glGet with the argument GL_CURRENT_PROGRAM

glGetActiveAttrib with argument *program* and the index of an active attribute variable

glGetAttribLocation with argument *program* and an attribute variable name

glGetVertexAttrib with arguments GL_CURRENT_VERTEX_ATTRIB and *index*

SEE ALSO

glBindAttribLocation, glVertex, glVertexAttribPointer

glVertexAttribPointer

NAME

glVertexAttribPointer—Defines a generic vertex attribute array

C SPECIFICATION

```
void glVertexAttribPointer(GLuint index,
                           GLint size,
                           GLenum type,
                           GLboolean normalized,
                           GLsizei stride,
                           const GLvoid *pointer)
```

PARAMETERS

index	Specifies the index of the generic vertex attribute to be modified.
size	Specifies the number of values for each element of the generic vertex attribute array. Must be 1, 2, 3, or 4.
type	Specifies the data type of each component in the array. Symbolic constants GL_BYTE, GL_UNSIGNED_BYTE, GL_SHORT, GL_UNSIGNED_SHORT, GL_INT, GL_UNSIGNED_INT, GL_FLOAT, and GL_DOUBLE are accepted.
normalized	Specifies whether fixed-point data values should be normalized (GL_TRUE) or converted directly as fixed-point values (GL_FALSE) when they are accessed.
stride	Specifies the byte offset between consecutive attribute values. If *stride* is 0 (the initial value), the attribute values are understood to be tightly packed in the array.
pointer	Specifies a pointer to the first component of the first attribute value in the array.

DESCRIPTION

glVertexAttribPointer specifies the location and data format of an array of generic vertex attribute values to use when rendering. *size* specifies the number of components per attribute and must be 1, 2, 3, or 4. *type* specifies the data type of each component, and *stride* specifies the byte stride from one attribute to the next, allowing attribute values to be intermixed with other attribute values or stored in a separate array. A value of 0 for *stride* means that the values are stored sequentially in memory with no gaps between successive elements. If set to GL_TRUE, *normalized* means that values stored in an integer format are to be mapped to the range [–1,1] (for signed values) or [0,1] (for unsigned values) when they are accessed and converted to floating point. Otherwise, values are converted to floats directly without normalization.

When a generic vertex attribute array is specified, *size*, *type*, *normalized*, *stride*, and *pointer* are saved as client-side state.

To enable and disable the generic vertex attribute array, call **glEnableVertexAttribArray** and **glDisableVertexAttribArray** with *index*. If enabled, the generic vertex attribute array is used when **glDrawArrays**, **glDrawElements**, **glDrawRangeElements**, **glArrayElement**, **glMultiDrawElements**, or **glMultiDrawArrays** is called.

NOTES

glVertexAttribPointer is available only if the GL version is 2.0 or greater.

Each generic vertex attribute array is initially disabled and is not accessed when **glDrawArrays**, **glDrawElements**, **glDrawRangeElements**, **glArrayElement**, **glMultiDrawElements**, or **glMultiDrawArrays** is called.

Execution of **glVertexAttribPointer** is not allowed between the execution of **glBegin** and **glEnd**, but an error may or may not be generated. If no error is generated, the operation is undefined.

glVertexAttribPointer is typically implemented on the client side.

Generic vertex attribute array parameters are client-side state and are therefore not saved or restored by **glPushAttrib** and **glPopAttrib**. Use **glPushClientAttrib** and **glPopClientAttrib** instead.

ERRORS

GL_INVALID_VALUE is generated if *index* is greater than or equal to GL_MAX_VERTEX_ATTRIBS.

GL_INVALID_VALUE is generated if *size* is not 1, 2, 3, or 4.

GL_INVALID_ENUM is generated if *type* is not an accepted value.

GL_INVALID_VALUE is generated if *stride* is negative.

ASSOCIATED GETS

glGet with argument GL_MAX_VERTEX_ATTRIBS

glGetVertexAttrib with arguments *index* and the name of a vertex attribute parameter

glGetVertexAttribPointer with arguments *index* and GL_VERTEX_ATTRIB_ARRAY_POINTER

SEE ALSO

glArrayElement, **glBindAttribLocation**, **glDisableVertexAttribArray**, **glDrawArrays**, **glDrawElements**, **glDrawRangeElements**, **glEnableVertexAttribArray**, **glMultiDrawArrays**, **glMultiDrawElements**, **glPopClientAttrib**, **glPushClientAttrib**, **glVertexAttrib**

OpenGL 1.5 to OpenGL 2.0 GLSL Migration Guide

The OpenGL Shading Language was initially supported through ARB extensions to OpenGL 1.5. The following table (originally compiled by Teri Morrison) documents the mapping of OpenGL 1.5 ARB extension API entry points to the OpenGL 2.0 API entry points.

glAttachObjectARB	Renamed to **glAttachShader**. Input arguments *program* and *shader* were changed from GLhandleARB to GLuint.
glBindAttribLocationARB	Renamed to **glBindAttribLocation**. Input argument *program* was changed from GLhandleARB to GLuint. Input argument *name* was changed from const GLcharARB* to const GLchar*.
glCompileShaderARB	Renamed to **glCompileShader**. Input argument *shader* was changed from GLhandleARB to GLuint.
glCreateProgramObjectARB	Renamed to **glCreateProgram**. Function return value was changed from GLhandleARB to GLuint.
glCreateShaderObjectARB	Renamed to **glCreateShader**. Function return value was changed from GLhandleARB to GLuint.
glDeleteObjectARB	Split into two functions, **glDeleteProgram** and **glDeleteShader**. Input argument *object* was changed from GLhandleARB to GLuint. Additional error checking was added to ensure that the input argument in the new function (*program* or *shader*) is the proper object type.
glDetachObjectARB	Renamed to **glDetachShader**. Input arguments *program* and *shader* were changed from GLhandleARB to GLuint.

glDisableVertexAttribArrayARB   Renamed to **glDisableVertexAttribArray**.

glEnableVertexAttribArrayARB   Renamed to **glEnableVertexAttribArray**.

glGetActiveAttribARB   Renamed to **glGetActiveAttrib**. Input argument *program* was changed from GLhandleARB to GLuint. Input argument *name* was changed from GLcharARB* to GLchar*.

glGetActiveUniformARB   Renamed to **glGetActiveUniform**. Input argument *program* was changed from GLhandleARB to GLuint. Input argument *name* was changed from GLcharARB* to GLchar*.

glGetAttachedObjectsARB   Renamed to **glGetAttachedShaders**. Input argument *program* was changed from GLhandleARB to GLuint. Input argument *objects* was changed from GLhandleARB* to GLuint*.

glGetAttribLocationARB   Renamed to **glGetAttribLocation**. Input argument *program* was changed from GLhandleARB to GLuint. Input argument *name* was changed from const GLcharARB* to const GLchar*.

glGetHandleARB   Replaced by calling **glGet** with the symbolic constant GL_CURRENT_PROGRAM.

glGetInfoLogARB   Split into two functions, **glGetProgramInfoLog** and **glGetShaderInfoLog**. Input argument *object* was changed from GLhandleARB to GLuint. Output argument *infoLog* was changed from const GLcharARB* to const GLchar*. New error checking was added to ensure that the input argument in the new function *(program* or *shader)* is the proper object type.

glGetObjectParameterARB	Split into two functions, **glGetProgram** and **glGetShader**. Input argument *object* was changed from GLhandleARB to GLuint. Additional error checking was added to ensure that the input argument in the new function *(program* or *shader)* is the proper object type. In OpenGL 2.0 there is no equivalent for the floating-point version of the ARB function **glGetObjectParameterfvARB**.
glGetShaderSourceARB	Renamed to **glGetShaderSource**. Input argument *shader* was changed from GLhandleARB to GLuint. Output argument *source* was changed from const GLcharARB* to const GLchar*.
glGetUniformARB	Renamed to **glGetUniform**. Input argument *program* was changed from GLhandleARB to GLuint.
glGetUniformLocationARB	Renamed to **glGetUniformLocation**. Input argument *program* was changed from GLhandleARB to GLuint. Input argument *name* was changed from const GLcharARB* to const GLchar*.
glGetVertexAttribARB	Renamed to **glGetVertexAttrib**.
glGetVertexAttribPointerARB	Renamed to **glGetVertexAttribPointer**.
glLinkProgramARB	Renamed to **glLinkProgram**. Input argument *program* was changed from GLhandleARB to GLuint.
glShaderSourceARB	Renamed to **glShaderSource**. Input argument *shader* was changed from GLhandleARB to GLuint. Input argument *strings* was changed from const GLcharARB** to const GLchar**.
glUniformARB	Renamed to **glUniform**.

glUseProgramObjectARB	Renamed to **glUseProgram**. Input argument *program* was changed from GLhandleARB to GLuint.
glValidateProgramARB	Renamed to **glValidateProgram**. Input argument *program* was changed from GLhandleARB to GLuint.
glVertexAttribARB	Renamed to **glVertexAttrib**.
glVertexAttribPointerARB	Renamed to **glVertexAttribPointer**.
New functions	The functions **glIsProgram** and **glIsShader** were added in OpenGL 2.0 and have no equivalent in the ARB extensions that support GLSL.
	The function **glDrawBuffers** was promoted to OpenGL 2.0 from the ARB_draw_buffers extension specification, where it was called **glDrawBuffersARB**.

Afterword

Writing a book requires a lot of time and effort. Sometimes authors refer to the finished product as "a labor of love." I have to say that, for me, writing this book has been "a labor of fun."

I have been fortunate to participate in a major architectural revolution in computer graphics hardware. In the last few years, consumer graphics hardware has undergone a sea change—from pure fixed functionality to almost complete user programmability. In many ways, this time feels like the late 1970s and early 1980s, when significant advances were being made in computer graphics at places like the University of Utah, NYU, Lucasfilm, JPL, UNC, and Cornell. The difference this time is that graphics hardware is now cheap enough and fast enough that you don't have to work at a research institute or attend an elite graduate school to play with it. You can explore the brave new world on your own personal computer.

It is relatively rare to participate in establishing even one industry standard, but I have had the good fortune to play a role in the definition of three important graphics standards. First was PEX in the late 1980s. Next was OpenGL in the early 1990s and, now, the OpenGL Shading Language in the first years of the new millennium. These efforts have been gratifying to me because they provide graphics hardware capabilities to people in an industry-standard way. Applications written to a standard are portable, and therefore the technology they are built on is accessible to a wider audience.

It's been a labor of fun because it is a lot of fun and truly remarkable to be one of the first people to implement classic rendering algorithms by using a high-level language on low-cost but high-performance graphics hardware. When our team first got the brick shader running on 3Dlabs Wildcat VP graphics hardware, it was a jaw-dropping "Wow!" moment. A similar feeling occurred when I got a shader I was developing to run successfully for the first time or saw, working for the first time, a shader written by someone else in the group. It seems to me that this feeling must be similar to that felt by the graphics pioneers twenty to twenty-five years ago when they got the first successful results from their new algorithms. And it is great fun to hear from end users who experience those same sorts of jaw-dropping "Wow!" moments.

Because of the architectural revolution in consumer graphics hardware, today people like you and me can quickly and easily write shaders that implement the rendering algorithms devised twenty years ago by the pioneers of computer graphics. To implement bump mapping, we looked up Blinn's 1978 paper, and to implement particle systems, we looked at Reeves's 1983 paper. I chuckled to myself when I saw the hand-drawn diagrams in Alvy Ray Smith's 1983 memo on digital filtering. Images that took hours to generate take milliseconds to render today. And shader code that took weeks to develop can now be written in minutes with a high-level shading language developed specifically for this task. It is mind-boggling to think how painstaking it must have been for Mandelbrot to generate images of his famous set in the late 1970s, compared to how easy it is to do today with the OpenGL Shading Language.

And part of the reason that I've so enjoyed writing this book is that I know there are significant new discoveries to be made in the area of computer graphics. If someone like me can simply and easily implement rendering algorithms that previously could run only on software on CPUs, imagine how much more is possible with the programmable graphics hardware that is available today. The availability of low-cost programmable graphics hardware makes it possible for many more people to experiment with new rendering techniques. Algorithms of much higher complexity can be developed. And I know that some of you out there will invent some exciting new rendering techniques when using the OpenGL Shading Language. This technology is moving rapidly to handheld devices such as PDAs and cell phones. A version of the OpenGL Shading Language for embedded devices was approved as part of OpenGL ES in the summer of 2005. That means that millions of devices will soon be running applications that use GLSL to unlock the power of the underlying programmable graphics hardware.

My mission in writing this book has been to educate you and, perhaps more important, to try to open your eyes to the rendering possibilities that exist beyond the fixed functionality with which we've been shackled for so many years. In my view, there's no longer any reason to continue to use the fixed functionality of OpenGL. Everyone should be writing shaders to render things the way they want instead of the way the fixed functionality graphics hardware has allowed. I encourage you to think outside the box, explore new ways of getting pixels on the screen, and share your discoveries with others. If you want, you can send your discoveries to me at randi@3dshaders.com and I'll make them available to others on my Web site.

Keep on pushing the pixels, and best of luck in all your rendering endeavors!

> —Randi Rost,
> Fort Collins, CO
> June 2003, 1st edition
> August 2005, 2nd edition

The path to the OpenGL Shading Language began in the hot, crowded ballroom of the Wilshire Grand at the OpenGL Birds of a Feather at SIGGRAPH 2001 in Los Angeles. By June of 2002, the "arb-gl2" workgroup formed, and I was privileged to be elected the chair of the group. The first draft of the OpenGL Shading Language specification was published February 27, 2003, followed in an astonishingly short time by the first edition of this book.

It is the collaboration of the people who work together on the OpenGL Architecture Review Board (ARB) who create and continue to evolve the OpenGL Shading Language. These people share their gifts of intelligence, passion, and endurance. It is a joy to work with these colleagues, no matter who signs their paychecks.

What a journey we are on together!

> —Bill Licea-Kane,
> Boston, MA
> April 2009, 3rd edition

Glossary

1D TEXTURE—A one-dimensional (width only) array of values stored in texture memory.

2D TEXTURE—A two-dimensional (width and height) array of values stored in texture memory.

3D TEXTURE—A three-dimensional (width, height, and depth) array of values stored in texture memory.

ACCUMULATION BUFFER—An OpenGL offscreen memory buffer that can accumulate the results of multiple rendering operations. This buffer often has more bits per pixel than the other offscreen memory buffers in order to support such accumulation operations.

ACTIVE ATTRIBUTES—In variables that can be accessed when a vertex shader is executed. (It is allowed to have in variables that are defined but never used within a vertex shader.)

ACTIVE SAMPLERS—Samplers that can be accessed when a program is executed.

ACTIVE TEXTURE UNIT—The texture unit currently defined as the target of commands that modify texture access state such as the current 1D/2D/3D/cube map texture, texture unit enable/disable, texture environment state, and so on.

ACTIVE UNIFORMS—Uniform variables that can be accessed when a shader is executed, including built-in uniform variables and user-defined uniform variables. (It is allowed to have uniform variables that are defined but never used within a shader.)

ALIASING—Artifacts caused by insufficient sampling or inadequate representation of high-frequency components in a computer graphics image. These artifacts are also commonly referred to as "jaggies."

ALPHA—The fourth component of a color value (after red, green, and blue). Alpha indicates the opacity of a pixel (1.0 means the pixel is fully opaque; 0.0 means the pixel is fully transparent). Alpha is used in color blending operations.

ALPHA TEST—An OpenGL pipeline stage that discards fragments depending on the outcome of a comparison between the current fragment's alpha value and a constant reference alpha value.

AMBIENT OCCLUSION—A technique for producing more realistic lighting and shadowing effects that uses a precomputed occlusion (or accessibility) factor to scale the diffuse illumination at each point on the surface of an object.

AMPLITUDE—The distance of a function's maximum or minimum from the mean of the function.

ANISOTROPIC—Something with properties that differ when measured in different directions, such as the property of a material (anisotropic reflection) or a characteristic of an algorithm (anisotropic texture filtering). Contrast with ISOTROPIC.

ANTIALIASING—The effort to reduce or eliminate artifacts caused by insufficient sampling or inadequate representation of high-frequency components in a computer graphics image.

APPLICATION PROGRAMMING INTERFACE (API)—A source-level interface provided for use by applications.

AREA SAMPLING—An antialiasing technique that considers the area of the primitive being sampled. This method usually produces better results than either point sampling or supersampling, but it can be more expensive to compute.

ATTENUATION—In the lighting computation, the effect of light intensity diminishing as a function of distance from the light source.

ATTRIBUTE ALIASING—Binding more than one user-defined in variable to the same generic vertex attribute index. This binding is allowed only if just one of the aliased attributes is active in the executable program or if no path through the shader consumes more than one in variable of a set of in variables aliased to the same location.

ATTRIBUTE VARIABLE—An OpenGL Shading Language variable that is qualified with the **in** keyword. Attribute variables contain the values that an application passes through the OpenGL API by using generic, numbered vertex attributes. With attribute variables, a vertex shader can obtain unique data at every vertex. These variables are read-only and can be defined only in vertex shaders. Attribute variables are used to pass frequently changing data to a shader.

AUXILIARY BUFFER—A region of offscreen memory that stores arbitrary or generic data, for example, intermediate results from a multipass rendering algorithm. A framebuffer may have more than one associated auxiliary buffer.

BENT NORMAL—A surface attribute that represents the average direction of the available light that is received at that point on the surface. This value is computed as follows: Cast rays from the point on the surface in the hemisphere indicated by the surface normal and then average all rays that are unoccluded by other parts of the model.

BIDIRECTIONAL REFLECTANCE DISTRIBUTION FUNCTION (BRDF)—A model for computing the reflection from a surface. The elevation and azimuth angles of the incoming and outgoing energy directions are used to compute the relative amount of energy reflected in the outgoing direction. Measurements of real-world materials can be used in this computation to create a more realistic looking surface. BRDFs can more accurately render materials with anisotropic reflection properties.

BRDF—See BIDIRECTIONAL REFLECTANCE DISTRIBUTION FUNCTION.

BUFFERS—Regions of memory on the graphics accelerator devoted to storing a particular type of data. A color buffer stores color values, a depth buffer stores depth values, etc.

BUMP MAP—A two-dimensional array of normal perturbation values that can be stored in texture memory.

BUMP MAPPING—A rendering technique that simulates the appearance of bumps, wrinkles, or other surface irregularities by perturbing surface normals before lighting calculations are performed.

CALL BY VALUE-RETURN—A subroutine calling convention whereby input parameters are copied into the function at call time and output parameters are copied back to the caller before the function exits.

CHROMATIC ABERRATION—The tendency of a lens to bend light of different colors by unequal amounts because of differences in the indices of refraction of the constituent wavelengths of the light.

CHROMATIC DISPERSION—The effect of distributing a light source into its constituent wavelengths, for example, by passing it through a prism.

CLIP SPACE—See CLIPPING COORDINATE SYSTEM.

CLIPPING—The process of comparing incoming graphics primitives to one or more reference planes and discarding any portion of primitives that are deemed to be outside those reference planes.

CLIPPING COORDINATE SYSTEM—The coordinate system in which view-volume clipping occurs. Graphics primitives are transformed from the eye coordinate system into the clipping coordinate system by the projection matrix.

COLOR SUM—The OpenGL pipeline stage that adds together the primary color and the secondary color. This stage occurs after texturing to allow a specular highlight that is the color of the light source to be applied on top of the textured surface.

COMPILER FRONT END—The part of the compiler that performs lexical, syntactical, and semantic analysis of source code and produces a binary representation of the code that is suitable for consumption by subsequent phases of compilation.

CONSTRUCTOR—A programming language feature for initializing aggregate data types or converting between data types.

CONTROL TEXTURE—A texture map whose primary function is to provide values that determine the behavior of a rendering algorithm rather than provide data for the rendering process.

CONVOLUTION—The weighted average of a function over a specified interval.

CONVOLUTION FILTER—See CONVOLUTION KERNEL.

CONVOLUTION KERNEL—The values that are used for weighting in a convolution operation.

CUBE MAP—A texture map comprising six 2D textures that correspond to faces on a cube. The faces are identified by their axial direction ($\pm x$, $\pm y$, $\pm z$), and the proper face is automatically selected when a texture access is performed.

CUBE MAPPING—The process of accessing the proper face of a cube map texture to retrieve the value that will be used in texture application. Cube mapping is one method for performing environment mapping.

CULLING—The act of discarding graphics primitives according to a particular criterion, such as whether the primitives are back facing with respect to the current viewing position.

DEFERRED SHADING—A shading algorithm that first identifies the visible surfaces in a scene and then applies a shading effect only to those visible surfaces.

DEPENDENT TEXTURE READ—A texture access operation that depends on values obtained from a previous texture-access operation.

DEPTH BUFFER—An OpenGL offscreen memory buffer that maintains depth values. This buffer stores the depth of the topmost visible graphics primitive at each pixel. In conjunction with the depth test operation, this buffer can perform hidden surface elimination.

DEPTH-CUING—A graphics rendering technique that alters the appearance of a graphics primitive according to its distance from the viewer. Depth-cuing is often used to fade the color of distant primitives to the background color to make them appear more distant.

DEPTH MAP—See SHADOW MAP.

DEPTH TEST—An OpenGL pipeline stage that compares the depth associated with the incoming fragment with the depth value retrieved from the framebuffer. If the test fails, the fragment is discarded.

DIFFRACTION—The change in the directions and intensities of a group of waves (e.g., light waves) as they pass by an obstacle or pass through an aperture.

DIFFRACTION GRATING—A glass or metal surface with large numbers of small, parallel, equally spaced grooves or slits that produces a diffraction effect.

DISPLAY MEMORY—Framebuffer memory that is allocated to maintaining the image displayed on the computer monitor or LCD. Display memory is read many times per second (the refresh rate) and updates the visible display surface.

DOUBLE BUFFERING—A graphics rendering technique that involves rendering to a back buffer while displaying a front buffer. When rendering is completed, the two buffers are swapped. In this way, the end user never sees partially complete images, and animation can be smoother and more realistic.

DRIVER—A piece of software that interacts with the native operating system and controls a specific piece of hardware in the system.

ENVIRONMENT MAPPING—A rendering technique that involves saving the scene surrounding an object as one or more specialized texture maps and then, when rendering the object, accessing these texture maps to compute accurate reflections of that environment.

EQUIRECTANGULAR TEXTURE MAP—A rectangular 2D texture that can be used as an environment map. The texture spans 360° horizontally and 180° vertically. Significant distortion occurs toward the top and bottom of the texture. Also known as a LATITUDE-LONGITUDE (or LAT-LONG) TEXTURE MAP.

EXECUTABLE—The machine code intended for execution on the vertex processor or the fragment processor.

EYE COORDINATE SYSTEM—The coordinate system that is defined to have the eye (viewing) position at the origin. Graphics primitives are transformed by the modelview matrix from the modeling (or object) coordinate system into the eye coordinate system.

EYE SPACE—see EYE COORDINATE SYSTEM.

FILTERING—The process of calculating a single value according to the values of multiple samples in the neighborhood of that value.

FIXED FUNCTIONALITY—The term used to describe portions of the OpenGL pipeline that are not programmable. These portions of OpenGL operate in a fixed fashion, and the behavior can be altered only when a predefined set of state variables is changed through the OpenGL API.

FLAT SHADING—The term used to describe the application of a single value of one vertex to the extent of a primitive (contrast with SMOOTH SHADING).

FOG—A rendering technique that simulates atmospheric effects due to particulates such as those contained in clouds and smog. Fog is computed by attenuation of the object color as a function of distance from the viewer.

FRACTAL—A geometrically complex object, the complexity of which arises through the repetition of a given form over a range of scales. (*Ken Musgrave*)

FRAGMENT—The set of data that is generated by rasterization and that represents the information necessary to update a single framebuffer location. A fragment consists of a window coordinate position and associated data such as color, depth, texture coordinates, and the like.

FRAGMENT PROCESSING—An OpenGL pipeline stage that defines the operations that occur to a fragment produced by rasterization before the back-end processing stages. For OpenGL fixed functionality, fragment processing operations included texture access, texture application, fog, and color sum. For the OpenGL programmable fragment processor, any type of per-fragment processing may be performed.

FRAGMENT PROCESSOR—A programmable unit that replaces the traditional fixed functionality fragment processing stage of OpenGL. Fragment shaders are executed on the fragment processor.

FRAGMENT SHADER—A program written in the OpenGL Shading Language for execution on the fragment processor. The fragment shader's **main** function is executed once for each fragment generated by rasterization and can be programmed to perform both traditional operations (texture access, texture application, fog) and nontraditional operations.

FRAMEBUFFER—The region of graphics memory that stores the results of OpenGL rendering operations. Part of the framebuffer (the front buffer) is visible on the display device, and part of it is not.

FRAMEBUFFER OPERATIONS—An OpenGL pipeline stage containing operations that control or affect the whole framebuffer (e.g., buffer masking operations, buffer clear operations).

FREQUENCY—The measure of periodicity in a function (i.e., how often the pattern of a function repeats).

FRESNEL EFFECT—The result of transparent materials causing light to be both reflected and refracted, with the amount of light reflected and refracted depending on the viewing angle.

FRUSTUM—See VIEW FRUSTUM.

FRUSTUM CLIPPING—An OpenGL pipeline stage that clips primitives to the view frustum.

GEOMETRIC PRIMITIVE—A point, line, or polygon.

GLOSS MAP—A texture map that controls the reflective characteristics of a surface rather than supply image data for the texturing operation.

GLYPH BOMBING—TEXTURE BOMBING using character glyphs from a texture map.

GOOCH SHADING—A non-photorealistic rendering technique that attempts to duplicate the look of a technical illustration. This technique is also called a low dynamic range artistic tone algorithm.

GOURAUD SHADING—See SMOOTH SHADING.

GRADIENT—The measure of how rapidly a function is changing in a particular direction. Properly, this is a vector (see GRADIENT VECTOR). More commonly, the magnitude of the gradient vector for the function $f(x,y)$ in a particular direction is referred to as the gradient of the function $f(x,y)$ in that direction.

GRADIENT NOISE—See PERLIN NOISE.

GRADIENT VECTOR—A vector that defines the rate of change of a function in all directions. The gradient vector for the function $f(x,y)$ contains two components: the partial derivative of f with respect to x and the partial derivative of f with respect to y.

GRAPHICS ACCELERATOR—Hardware dedicated to the process of rendering and displaying graphics.

GRAPHICS CONTEXT—The OpenGL data structure that contains the state needed to control the operation of the rendering pipeline.

GRAPHICS PROCESSING PIPELINE—The sequence of operations that occurs when geometry or image data defined by an application is transformed into something that is stored in the framebuffer. This processing is divided into stages that occur in a specific order. Each stage has defined inputs and outputs and can be precisely described.

HEMISPHERE LIGHTING—The process of illuminating scenes and objects by modeling global illumination as two hemispheres, one representing the color of the sky and the other representing the color of the ground (or shadows). Computing the illumination at any surface point is done by integrating the light from the visible hemisphere at that point.

IMAGE-BASED LIGHTING—The process of illuminating scenes and objects with images of light captured from the real world.

IMAGING SUBSET—A collection of imaging-related functionality that was added to OpenGL as an optional subset in OpenGL 1.2. The imaging subset supports color matrix, convolution, histogram, and various blending operations. Graphics hardware vendors are not required to support this functionality as part of their OpenGL implementation.

IMMEDIATE MODE—A mode of rendering in which graphics commands are executed when they are specified.

INDEX OF REFRACTION—The property of a material that defines the ratio of the speed of light in a vacuum to the speed of light in that material.

ISOTROPIC—Something with properties that are the same along a pair of orthogonal axes from which they are measured (i.e., rotationally invariant). Contrast with ANISOTROPIC.

KEY-FRAME INTERPOLATION—An animation technique that produces "in-between" results based on interpolation between two key frames. This technique can save time and effort because the objects in the scene do not need to be painstakingly animated for every frame, only for those frames that provide the key to the overall animation sequence.

L-VALUE—An expression identifying an object in memory that can be written to. For example, variables that are writable are l-values. Array indexing and structure member selection are expressions that can result in l-values.

LACUNARITY—The frequency multiplier (or gap) between successive iterations of a summed noise (fractal) function.

LATITUDE-LONGITUDE TEXTURE MAP—see EQUIRECTANGULAR TEXTURE MAP.

LEVEL-OF-DETAIL—The value that selects a mipmap level from a mipmap texture. Incrementing the level-of-detail by 1 results in the selection of a mipmap level that is half the resolution of the previous one. Thus, increasing the value used for level-of-detail results in the selection of mipmap levels that contain smaller and smaller textures (suitable for use on smaller and smaller objects on the screen).

LEXICAL ANALYSIS—The process of scanning the input text to produce a sequence of tokens (or terminal symbols) for the syntactical analysis phase that follows. Characters or tokens that are not part of the language can be identified as errors during this process. Sometimes this process is referred to as scanning.

LIGHT PROBE—A device or a system that captures an omnidirectional, high dynamic range image of light from a real-world scene.

LIGHT PROBE IMAGE—An omnidirectional, high dynamic range image of light captured from the real world.

LOOKAT POINT—The lookat point is a reference point indicating the center of the scene.

LOW-PASS FILTERING—A method of filtering that eliminates high frequencies but leaves low frequencies unmodified. Low-pass filters are sometimes called SMOOTHING FILTERS because high frequencies are blurred (smoothed).

MIPMAP LEVEL—A specific texel array within a mipmap texture.

MIPMAP TEXTURE—An ordered set of texel arrays representing the same image. Typically, each array has a resolution that is half the previous one in each dimension.

MODEL SPACE—See MODELING COORDINATE SYSTEM.

MODEL TRANSFORMATION MATRIX—The matrix that transforms coordinates from the modeling coordinate system into the world coordinate system. In OpenGL, this matrix is not available separately; it is always part of the modelview matrix.

MODELING—The process of defining a numerical representation of an object that is to be rendered, for instance, defining the Bezier curves that specify a teapot, or the vertex positions, colors, surface normals, and texture coordinates that define a bowling pin.

MODELING COORDINATE SYSTEM—A coordinate system that is defined in a way that makes it convenient to specify and orient a single object. Also known as the OBJECT COORDINATE SYSTEM or OBJECT SPACE.

MODELING TRANSFORMATION—The transformation that takes coordinates from the modeling coordinate system into the world coordinate system.

MODELVIEW MATRIX—The matrix that transforms coordinates from the modeling coordinate system into the eye coordinate system.

MODELVIEW-PROJECTION MATRIX—The matrix that transforms coordinates from the modeling coordinate system into the clipping coordinate system.

MULTIFRACTAL—A function whose fractal dimension varies according to location.

MULTISAMPLE BUFFER—A region of offscreen memory that can perform supersampling by maintaining more than one sample per pixel and automatically averaging the samples to produce the final, antialiased image.

NEIGHBORHOOD AVERAGING—An image processing technique that low-pass filters (smooths) an image by computing the weighted average of pixels in close proximity to one another.

NOISE—A continuous, irregular function with a defined range that creates complex and interesting patterns.

NON-PHOTOREALISTIC RENDERING (NPR)—A class of rendering techniques whose purpose is to achieve something other than the most realistic result possible. Such techniques may strive to achieve a painterly or hand-drawn appearance, the look of a technical illustration, or a cartoonlike appearance. Hatching and Gooch shading are examples of NPR techniques.

NORMAL MAP—A texture map that contains normals rather than image data.

NORMALIZED DEVICE COORDINATE SPACE—The coordinate space that contains the view volume in an axis-aligned cube with a minimum corner at $(-1,-1,-1)$ and a maximum corner at $(1,1,1)$.

NPR—See NON-PHOTOREALISTIC RENDERING.

OBJECT COORDINATE SYSTEM—See MODELING COORDINATE SYSTEM.

OBJECT SPACE—See MODELING COORDINATE SYSTEM.

OCTAVE—Two frequencies that are related by a ratio of 2:1.

OFFSCREEN MEMORY—Framebuffer memory that stores things, such as depth buffers and textures, that are never directly visible on the display screen (contrast with DISPLAY MEMORY).

OPENGL SHADER—A term applied to a shader written in the OpenGL Shading Language to differentiate from a shader written in another shading language.

OPENGL SHADING LANGUAGE—The high-level programming language defined to allow application writers to write programs that execute on the programmable processors defined within OpenGL.

OPENGL SHADING LANGUAGE API—The set of function calls added to OpenGL to allow OpenGL shaders to be created, deleted, queried, compiled, linked, and used.

PARSING—See SYNTACTIC ANALYSIS.

PARTICLE SYSTEM—A rendering primitive that consists of a large number of points or short lines that are suitable for rendering a class of objects with ill-defined boundaries (e.g., fire, sparks, liquid sprays).

PER-FRAGMENT OPERATIONS—An OpenGL pipeline stage that occurs after fragment processing and before framebuffer operations. It includes a variety of tests, such as the stencil, alpha, and depth tests, aimed at determining whether the fragment should be used to update the framebuffer.

PERLIN NOISE—A noise function that is defined to have a value of 0 for integer input values and whose variability is introduced by defining pseudorandom gradient values at each of those points. Also called GRADIENT NOISE.

PHOTOREALISM—The effort to use computer graphics to model, render, and animate a scene in such a way that it is indistinguishable from a photograph or film sequence of the same scene in real life.

PIXEL GROUP—A value that will ultimately be used to update the framebuffer (i.e., a color, depth, or stencil value).

PIXEL OWNERSHIP TEST—An OpenGL pipeline stage that decides whether a fragment can be used to update the framebuffer or whether the targeted framebuffer location belongs to another window or to another OpenGL graphics context.

PIXEL PACKING—An OpenGL pipeline stage that writes pixels retrieved from OpenGL into application-controlled memory.

PIXEL RECTANGLE—A rectangular array of pixels (i.e., an image).

PIXEL TRANSFER—An OpenGL pipeline stage that processes pixel data while it is being transferred within OpenGL. At this stage, operations can occur for the following: scaling and biasing, lookup table, convolution, histogram, color matrix, and the like.

PIXEL UNPACKING—An OpenGL pipeline stage that reads pixels (i.e., image data) from application-controlled memory and sends them on for further processing by OpenGL.

POINT SAMPLING—The process of determining the value at each pixel by sampling the function at just one point. This is the typical behavior of graphics hardware and many graphics algorithms, and it can lead to aliasing artifacts. Contrast with SUPERSAMPLING and AREA SAMPLING.

POINT SPRITE—A screen-aligned quadrilateral that has texture coordinates and that is drawn by rasterizing a single point primitive. Normally, points are drawn as a single pixel or as a round circle. A point sprite can be used to draw an image stored in a texture map at each point position.

POLYNOMIAL TEXTURE MAP (PTM)—A light-dependent texture map that can reconstruct the color of a surface under varying lighting conditions.

PRIMITIVE ASSEMBLY—An OpenGL pipeline stage that occurs after vertex processing and that assembles individual vertex values into a primitive. The primary function of this stage is to buffer vertex values until enough accumulate to define the desired primitive. Points require one vertex, lines require two, triangles require three, and so on.

PRIMITIVES—In OpenGL parlance, things that can be rendered: points, lines, polygons, bitmaps, and images.

PROCEDURAL TEXTURE SHADER—A shader that produces its results primarily by synthesizing rather than by relying heavily on precomputed values.

PROCEDURAL TEXTURING—The process of computing a texture primarily by synthesizing rather than by relying heavily on precomputed values.

PROGRAM—The set of executables that result from successful linking of a program object. This program can be installed as part of OpenGL's current state to provide programmable vertex and fragment processing.

PROGRAM OBJECT—An OpenGL-managed data structure that serves as a container object for one or more shader objects. Program objects are used when shaders are linked. Linking a program object results in one or more executables that are part of the program object and that can be installed as part of current state.

PROJECTION MATRIX—The matrix that transforms coordinates from the eye coordinate system to the clipping coordinate system.

PROJECTION TRANSFORMATION—The transformation that takes coordinates from the eye coordinate system into the clipping coordinate system.

PTM—See POLYNOMIAL TEXTURE MAP.

PULSE TRAIN—A periodic function that varies abruptly between two values (i.e., a square wave).

R-VALUE—An expression identifying a declared or temporary object in memory that can be read—for example, a variable name is an r-value, but function names are not. Expressions result in r-values.

RASTER POSITION—A piece of OpenGL state that positions bitmap and image write operations.

RASTERIZATION—The process of converting graphics primitives such as points, lines, polygons, bitmaps, and images into fragments.

READ CONTROL—An OpenGL pipeline stage that contains state to define the region of framebuffer memory that is read during pixel read operations.

RENDERING—The process of converting geometry or image data defined by an application into something that is stored in the framebuffer.

RENDERING PIPELINE—See GRAPHICS PROCESSING PIPELINE.

SAMPLER—An opaque data type in the OpenGL Shading Language that stores the information needed to access a particular texture from within a shader.

SCANNING—See LEXICAL ANALYSIS.

SCENE GRAPH—Either a hierarchical data structure containing a description of a scene to be rendered or a rendering engine for traversing and rendering such data structures.

SCISSOR TEST—An OpenGL pipeline stage that, when enabled, allows drawing operations to occur only within a specific rectangular region that has been defined in window coordinates.

SEMANTIC ANALYSIS—The process of determining whether the input text conforms to the semantic rules defined or implied by a programming language. Semantic errors in the input text can be identified during this phase of compilation.

SHADER—Source code written in the OpenGL Shading Language that is intended for execution on one of OpenGL's programmable processors.

SHADER OBJECT—An OpenGL-managed data structure that stores the source code and the compiled code for a shader written in the OpenGL Shading Language. Shader objects can be compiled, and compiled shader objects can be linked to produce executable code (see PROGRAM OBJECT).

SHADOW MAP—A texture created by rendering a scene from the point of view of a light source. This texture is then used during a final rendering pass to determine the parts of the scene that are in shadow. Also known as a DEPTH MAP.

SHADOW MAPPING—An algorithm that computes shadows by rendering the scene once for each shadow-causing light source in the scene and once for the final rendering of the scene, including shadows. The per-light rendering passes are rendered from the light source's point of view and create shadow maps. These textures are then accessed on the final pass to determine the parts of the scene that are in shadow.

SMOOTH SHADING—The term used to describe the application of linearly interpolated vertex values across the extent of a primitive (contrast with FLAT SHADING). Also called GOURAUD SHADING.

SMOOTHING FILTERS—See LOW-PASS FILTERING.

SPHERE MAPPING—A method for performing environment mapping that simulates the projection of the environment onto a sphere surrounding the object to be rendered. The mapped environment is treated as a 2D texture map and accessed with the polar coordinates of the reflection vector.

STENCIL BUFFER—An offscreen region of framebuffer memory that can be used with the stencil test to mask regions. A complex shape can be stored in the stencil buffer, and subsequent drawing operations can use the contents of the stencil buffer to determine whether to update each pixel.

STENCIL TEST—An OpenGL pipeline stage that conditionally eliminates a pixel according to the results of a comparison between the value stored in the stencil buffer and a reference value. Applications can specify the action taken when the stencil test fails, the action taken when the stencil test passes and the depth test fails, and the action to be taken when both the stencil test and the depth test pass.

SUPERSAMPLING—A rendering technique that involves taking two or more point samples per pixel and then filtering these values to determine the value to be used for the pixel. Supersampling does not eliminate aliasing but can reduce it to the point at which it is no longer objectionable.

SURFACE-LOCAL COORDINATE SPACE—A coordinate system that assumes that each point on a surface is at (0,0,0) and that the unperturbed surface normal at each point is (0,0,1).

SWIZZLE—To duplicate or switch around the order of the components of a vector (e.g., to create a value that contains alpha, green, blue, red from one that contains red, green, blue, alpha).

SYNTACTIC ANALYSIS—The process of determining whether the structure of an input text is valid according to the grammar that defines the language. Syntax errors in the input text can be identified during this phase of compilation. Sometimes referred to as parsing.

TANGENT SPACE—A particular surface-local coordinate system that is defined with a tangent vector as one of the basis vectors.

T&L—See TRANSFORMATION AND LIGHTING.

TEMPORAL ALIASING—Aliasing artifacts that are caused by insufficient sampling in the time domain or inadequate representation of objects that are in motion.

TEXEL—A single pixel in a texture map.

TEXTURE ACCESS—The process of reading from a texture map in texture memory, including the filtering that occurs, the level-of-detail calculation for mipmap textures, and so on.

TEXTURE APPLICATION—The process of using the value read from texture memory to compute the color of a fragment. OpenGL's fixed functionality has fixed formulas for this process, but with programmability, this operation has become much more general.

TEXTURE BOMBING—The process of applying irregularly spaced decorative elements (stars, polka dots, character glyphs, etc.) to an object's surface. Decorative elements can be computed procedurally or obtained from a texture map. They can also be randomly scaled and rotated to add further interest.

TEXTURE MAPPING—The combination of texture access and texture application. Traditionally, this mapping involves reading image data from a texture map stored in texture memory and using it as the color for the primitive being rendered. With programmability, this operation has become much more general.

TEXTURE MEMORY—A region of memory on the graphics accelerator that is used for storing textures.

TEXTURE OBJECT—The OpenGL-managed data structure that contains information that describes a texture map, including the texels that define the texture, the wrapping behavior, the filtering method, and so on.

TEXTURE UNIT—An OpenGL abstraction for the graphics hardware that performs texture access and texture application. Since version 1.2, OpenGL has allowed the possibility of more than one texture unit, thus allowing access to more than one texture at a time.

TRANSFORMATION AND LIGHTING (T&L)—The process of converting vertex positions from object coordinates into window coordinates, and for converting vertex colors into colors that are displayable on the screen, taking into account the effects of simulated light sources.

TURBULENCE—A variation of Perlin noise that sums noise functions of different frequencies. These frequencies include an absolute value function to introduce discontinuities to the function in order to give the appearance of turbulent flow.

UNIFORM VARIABLE—An OpenGL Shading Language variable that is qualified with the **uniform** keyword. The values for these variables are provided by the application or through OpenGL state. They are read-only from within a shader and may be accessed from either vertex shaders or fragment shaders. They pass data that changes relatively infrequently.

UNSHARP MASKING—A method of sharpening an image by subtracting a blurred version of the image from itself.

USER CLIPPING—An OpenGL operation that compares graphics primitives to user-specified clip distances and discards everything that is deemed to be outside the intersection of those clip distances.

VALUE NOISE—A noise function that is defined as follows: Assign pseudorandom values in a defined range (e.g., [0,1] or [–1,1]) to each integer input value and then smoothly interpolate between those values.

VARYING VARIABLE—An OpenGL Shading Language variable that is qualified with the **varying** keyword. These variables are defined at each vertex and interpolated across a graphics primitive to produce a perspective-correct value at each fragment. They must be declared in both the vertex shader and the fragment shader with the same type. They are the output values from vertex shaders and the input values for fragment shaders.

VERTEX—A point in three-dimensional space.

VERTEX ATTRIBUTES—Values that are associated with a vertex. OpenGL defines both standard and generic vertex attributes. Standard attributes include vertex position, color, normal, and texture coordinates. Generic vertex attributes can be defined to be arbitrary data values that are passed to OpenGL for each vertex.

VERTEX PROCESSING—An OpenGL pipeline stage that defines the operations that occur to each vertex from the time the vertex is provided to OpenGL until the primitive assembly stage. For OpenGL fixed functionality, this processing included transformation, lighting, texture coordinate generation, and other operations. For the OpenGL programmable vertex processor, any type of per-vertex processing may be performed.

VERTEX PROCESSOR—A programmable unit that replaces the traditional fixed functionality vertex processing stage of OpenGL. Vertex shaders are executed on the vertex processor.

VERTEX SHADER—A program written in the OpenGL Shading Language that executes on the vertex processor. The vertex shader's **main** function is executed once for each vertex provided to OpenGL and can be programmed to perform both traditional operations (transformation, lighting) and nontraditional operations.

VIEW FRUSTUM—The view volume after it has been warped by the perspective division calculation.

VIEW VOLUME—The volume in the clipping coordinate system whose coordinates x, y, z, and w all satisfy the conditions that $-w \leq x \leq w$, $-w \leq y \leq w$, and $-w \leq z \leq w$. Any portion of a geometric primitive that extends beyond this volume will be clipped.

VIEWING MATRIX—The matrix that transforms coordinates from the world coordinate system into the eye coordinate system. In OpenGL, this matrix is not available separately; it is always part of the modelview matrix.

VIEWING TRANSFORMATION—The transformation that takes coordinates from the world coordinate system into the eye coordinate system.

VIEWPORT TRANSFORMATION—The transformation that takes coordinates from the normalized device coordinate system into the window coordinate system.

WINDOW COORDINATE SYSTEM—The coordinate system used to identify pixels within a window on the display device. In this coordinate system, x values range from 0 to the width of the window minus 1, and y values range from 0 to the height of the window minus 1. OpenGL defines the pixel with window coordinates (0,0) to be the pixel at the lower-left corner of the window.

WORLD COORDINATE SYSTEM—A coordinate system that is defined in a way that is convenient for the placement and orientation of all of the objects in a scene.

WORLD SPACE—See WORLD COORDINATE SYSTEM.

Further Reading

This section contains references to other useful papers, articles, books, and Web sites. Over the course of time, some Web addresses may change. Please see this book's companion Web site at http://3dshaders.com for current links.

Former 3Dlabs developer Web site: now at http://3dshaders.com

Abram, G. D., and T. Whitted, *Building Block Shaders*, Computer Graphics (SIGGRAPH '90 Proceedings), pp. 283–288, August 1990.

Akenine-Möller, Tomas, and E. Haines, *Real-Time Rendering, Second Edition*, AK Peters, Ltd., Natick, Massachusetts, 2002. www.realtimerendering.com

Apodaca, Anthony A., and Larry Gritz, *Advanced RenderMan: Creating CGI for Motion Pictures*, Morgan Kaufmann Publishers, San Francisco, 1999. www.renderman.org/RMR/Books/arman/materials.html

Arvo, James, ed., *Graphics Gems II*, Academic Press, San Diego, 1991. www.acm.org/pubs/tog/GraphicsGems

ATI developer Web site. www.ati.com/developer

Baker, Dan, and C. Boyd, *Advanced Shading and Lighting*, Microsoft Corp. Meltdown 2001 Presentation. www.microsoft.com/mscorp/corpevents/meltdown2001/ppt/DXGLighting.ppt

Baldwin, Dave, *OpenGL 2.0 Shading Language White Paper*, Version 1.0, 3Dlabs, October, 2001.

Barzel, Ronen, *Lighting Controls for Computer Cinematography*, Journal of Graphics Tools, 2(1), 1997, pp. 1–20.

Blinn, James, *Models of Light Reflection for Computer Synthesized Pictures*, Computer Graphics (SIGGRAPH '77 Proceedings), pp. 192–198, July 1977.

———, *Simulation of Wrinkled Surfaces*, Computer Graphics (SIGGRAPH '78 Proceedings), pp. 286–292, August 1978.

———, *Light Reflection Functions for Simulation of Clouds and Dusty Surfaces*, Computer Graphics (SIGGRAPH '82 Proceedings), pp. 21–29, July 1982.

Blinn, James, and M. E. Newell, *Texture and Reflection in Computer Generated Images*, Communications of the ACM, vol. 19, no. 10, pp. 542–547, October 1976.

Bunnell, Michael, *Dynamic Ambient Occlusion and Indirect Lighting*, in *GPU Gems 2: Programming Techniques for High-Performance Graphics and General-Purpose Computation*, Editor: Matt Pharr, Addison-Wesley, Reading, Massachusetts, 2005. http://download.nvidia.com/developer/GPU_Gems_2/GPU_Gems2_ch14.pdf

Bunnell, Michael, and Fabio Pellacini, *Shadow Map Antialiasing*, in *GPU Gems: Programming Techniques, Tips, and Tricks for Real-Time Graphics*, Editor: Randima Fernando, Addison-Wesley, Reading, Massachusetts, 2004. http://developer.nvidia.com/object/gpu_gems_home.html

Cabral, B., N. Max, and R. Springmeyer, *Bidirectional Reflection Functions from Surface Bump Maps*, Computer Graphics (SIGGRAPH '87 Proceedings), pp. 273–281, July 1987.

Card, Drew, and Jason L. Mitchell, *Non-Photorealistic Rendering with Pixel and Vertex Shaders*, in Engel, Wolfgang, ed., ShaderX, Wordware, May 2002. www.shaderx.com

Cook, Robert L., *Shade Trees*, Computer Graphics (SIGGRAPH '84 Proceedings), pp. 223–231, July 1984.

———, *Stochastic Sampling in Computer Graphics*, ACM Transactions on Graphics, vol. 5, no. 1, pp. 51–72, January 1986.

Cook, Robert L., and Kenneth E. Torrance, *A Reflectance Model for Computer Graphics*, Computer Graphics (SIGGRAPH '81 Proceedings), pp. 307–316, July 1981.

———, *A Reflectance Model for Computer Graphics*, ACM Transactions on Graphics, vol. 1, no. 1, pp. 7–24, January 1982.

Cornell University Program of Computer Graphics Measurement Data. www.graphics.cornell.edu/online/measurements

Crow, Franklin C., *The Aliasing Problem in Computer-Generated Shaded Images*, Communications of the ACM, vol. 20, no. 11, pp. 799–805, November 1977.

———, *Shadow Algorithms for Computer Graphics*, Computer Graphics (SIGGRAPH '77 Proceedings), vol. 11, no. 2, pp. 242–248, July 1977.

———, *Summed-Area Tables for Texture Mapping*, Computer Graphics (SIGGRAPH '84 Proceedings), pp. 207–212, July 1984.

Curtis, Cassidy J., *Loose and Sketchy Animation*, SIGGRAPH '98 Technical Sketch, p. 317, 1998. www.otherthings.com/uw/loose/sketch.html

Curtis, Cassidy J., Sean E. Anderson, Kurt W. Fleischer, and David H. Salesin, *Computer-Generated Watercolor*, Computer Graphics (SIGGRAPH '97 Proceedings), pp. 421–430, August 1997. http://grail.cs.washington.edu/projects/watercolor

Dawson, Bruce, *What Happened to My Colours!?!* Game Developers Conference, pp. 251–268, March 2001. www.gdconf.com/archives/2001/ dawson.doc

Debevec, Paul, *Image-Based Lighting*, IEEE Computer Graphics and Applications, vol. 22, no. 2, pp. 26–34. www.debevec.org/CGAIBL2/ibl-tutorial-cga2002.pdf

Debevec, Paul, personal Web site. www.debevec.org

Debevec, Paul, *Rendering Synthetic Objects into Real Scenes: Bridging Traditional and Image-Based Graphics with Global Illumination and High Dynamic Range Photography*, Computer Graphics (SIGGRAPH '98 Proceedings), pp. 189–198. http://athens.ict.usc.edu/Research/IBL

Debevec, Paul, and J. Malik, *Recovering High Dynamic Range Radiance Maps from Photographs*, Computer Graphics (SIGGRAPH '97 Proceedings), pp. 369–378. www.debevec.org/Research/HDR

Delphi3D Web site. http://delphi3d.net

DeLoura, Mark, ed., *Game Programming Gems*, Charles River Media, Hingham, Massachusetts, 2000.

———, *Game Programming Gems II*, Charles River Media, Hingham, Massachusetts, 2001.

———, *Game Programming Gems III*, Charles River Media, Hingham, Massachusetts, 2002.

Derbyshire, Paul, *PGD's Quick Guide to the Mandelbrot Set*, personal Web site. www.globalserve.net/~derbyshire/manguide.html (defunct)

Dippé, Mark A. Z., and Erling Henry Wold, *Antialiasing Through Stochastic Sampling*, Computer Graphics (SIGGRAPH '85 Proceedings), pp. 69–78, July 1985.

Duff, Tom, *Compositing 3-D Rendered Images*, Computer Graphics (SIGGRAPH '85 Proceedings), pp. 41–44, July 1985.

Ebert, David S., John Hart, Bill Mark, F. Kenton Musgrave, Darwyn Peachey, Ken Perlin, and Steven Worley, *Texturing and Modeling: A Procedural Approach, Third Edition*, Morgan Kaufmann Publishers, San Francisco, 2002. www.texturingandmodeling.com

Fernando, Randima, and Mark J. Kilgard, *The Cg Tutorial: The Definitive Guide to Programmable Real-Time Graphics*, Addison-Wesley, Boston, Massachusetts, 2003.

Foley, J. D., A. van Dam, S.K. Feiner, and J. F. Hughes, *Computer Graphics: Principles and Practice in C, Second Edition*, Addison-Wesley, Reading, Massachusetts, 1996.

Foley, J. D., A. van Dam, S.K. Feiner, J. F. Hughes, and R.L. Philips, *Introduction to Computer Graphics*, Addison-Wesley, Reading, Massachusetts, 1994.

Fosner, Ron, *Real-Time Shader Programming, Covering DirectX 9.0*, Morgan Kaufmann Publishers, San Francisco, 2003.

Freudenberg, Bert, *A Non-Photorealistic Fragment Shader in OpenGL 2.0,* SIGGRAPH 2002 Exhibition, San Antonio, Texas, July 2002. http://isgwww.cs.uni-magdeburg.de/~bert/publications

———, *Stroke-based Real-Time Halftoning Rendering*, Ph.D. thesis, University of Magdeburg, submitted in 2003.

Freudenberg, Bert, and Maic Masuch, *Non-Photorealistic Shading in an Educational Game Engine,* SIGGRAPH and Eurographics Campfire, Snowbird, Utah, June 1–June 4, 2002. http://isgwww.cs.uni-magdeburg.de/~bert/publications

Freudenberg, Bert, Maic Masuch, and Thomas Strothotte, *Walk-Through Illustrations: Frame-Coherent Pen-and-Ink Style in a Game Engine*, Computer Graphics Forum, vol. 20 (2001), no. 3, Manchester, U.K. http://isgwww.cs.uni-magdeburg.de/~bert/publications

———, *Real-Time Halftoning: A Primitive For Non-Photorealistic Shading*, Rendering Techniques 2002, Proceedings 13th Eurographics Workshop, pp. 227–231, 2002. http://isgwww.cs.uni-magdeburg.de/~bert/publications

Glaeser, Georg, *Reflections on Spheres and Cylinders of Revolution*, Journal for Geometry and Graphics, Volume 3 (1999), No. 2, pp. 121–139. www.heldermann-verlag.de/jgg/jgg01_05/jgg0312.pdf

Glanville, Steve, *Texture Bombing*, in *GPU Gems: Programming Techniques, Tips, and Tricks for Real-Time Graphics*, Editor: Randima Fernando, Addison-Wesley, Reading, Massachusetts, 2004. http://developer.nvidia.com/object/gpu_gems_home.html

Glassner, Andrew S., ed., *Graphics Gems*, Academic Press, San Diego, 1990. www.acm.org/pubs/tog/GraphicsGems

Glassner, Andrew S., *Principles of Digital Image Synthesis*, vol. 1, Morgan Kaufmann Publishers, San Francisco, 1995.

———, *Principles of Digital Image Synthesis*, vol. 2, Morgan Kaufmann Publishers, San Francisco, 1995.

Gonzalez, Rafael C., and Richard E. Woods, *Digital Image Processing, Second Edition*, Prentice Hall, Upper Saddle River, New Jersey, 2002.

Gooch, Amy, *Interactive Non-Photorealistic Technical Illustration*, Master's thesis, University of Utah, December 1998. www.cs.utah.edu/~gooch/publication.html

Gooch, Amy, Bruce Gooch, Peter Shirley, and Elaine Cohen, *A Non-Photorealistic Lighting Model for Automatic Technical Illustration*, Computer Graphics (SIGGRAPH '98 Proceedings), pp. 447–452, July 1998. www.cs.utah.edu/~gooch/publication.html

Gooch, Bruce, and Amy Gooch, *Non-Photorealistic Rendering*, AK Peters Ltd., Natick, Massachusetts, 2001. www.cs.utah.edu/~gooch/book.html

Gooch, Bruce, Peter-Pike J. Sloan, Amy Gooch, Peter Shirley, and Richard Riesenfeld, *Interactive Technical Illustration*, Proceedings 1999 Symposium on Interactive 3D Graphics, pp. 31–38, April 1999. www.cs.utah.edu/~gooch/publication.html

Goral, Cindy M., K. Torrance, D. Greenberg, and B. Battaile, *Modeling the Interaction of Light Between Diffuse Surfaces*, Computer Graphics (SIGGRAPH '84 Proceedings), pp. 213–222, July 1984.

Gouraud, H., *Continuous Shading of Curved Surfaces*, IEEE Transactions on Computers, vol. C-20, pp. 623–629, June 1971.

GPU Gems: Programming Techniques, Tips, and Tricks for Real-Time Graphics, Editor: Randima Fernando, Addison-Wesley, Reading, Massachusetts, 2004. http://developer.nvidia.com/object/gpu_gems_home.html

GPU Gems 2: Programming Techniques for High-Performance Graphics and General-Purpose Computation, Editor: Matt Pharr, Addison-Wesley, Reading, Massachusetts, 2005. http://developer.nvidia.com/object/gpu_gems_2_home.html

Green, Robin, *Spherical Harmonic Lighting: The Gritty Details*, GDC 2003 Presentation. www.research.scea.com/gdc2003/spherical-harmonic-lighting.html

Greene, Ned, *Environment Mapping and Other Applications of World Projections*, IEEE Computer Graphics and Applications, vol. 6, no. 11, pp. 21–29, November 1986.

Gritz, Larry, *LGAntialiasedChecks.sl*, RenderMan Repository Web site. www.renderman.org/RMR/Shaders/LGShaders/index.html

Gruschel, Jens, *Blend Modes*, Pegtop Software Web site. www.pegtop.net/delphi/blendmodes

Haeberli, Paul, *Paint by Numbers: Abstract Image Representation*, Computer Graphics (SIGGRAPH '90 Proceedings), pp. 207–214, August 1990.

——, *Matrix Operations for Image Processing*, Silicon Graphics Inc., 1993. www.sgi.com/grafica/matrix

Haeberli, Paul, and Douglas Voorhies, *Image Processing by Interpolation and Extrapolation*, IRIS Universe Magazine, no. 28, Silicon Graphics, August 1994. http:/www.sgi.com/grafica/interp

Haeberli, Paul, and Kurt Akeley, *The Accumulation Buffer: Hardware Support for High-Quality Rendering*, Computer Graphics (SIGGRAPH '90 Proceedings), pp. 289–298, August 1990.

Haeberli, Paul, and Mark Segal, *Texture Mapping as a Fundamental Drawing Primitive*, 4th Eurographics Workshop on Rendering, pp. 259–266, 1993. www.sgi.com/grafica/texmap

Haines, Eric, *Real-Time Shadows*, GDC 2001 Presentation. www.gdconf.com/archives/2001/haines.pdf

Hall, Roy, *Illumination and Color in Computer Generated Imagery*, Springer-Verlag, New York, 1989.

Hanrahan, Pat, and Wolfgang Krueger, *Reflection From Layered Surfaces Due to Subsurface Scattering*, Computer Graphics (SIGGRAPH '93 Proceedings), pages 165–174, August 1993. www.graphics.stanford.edu/papers/subsurface

Hanrahan, Pat, and J. Lawson, *A Language for Shading and Lighting Calculations*, Computer Graphics (SIGGRAPH '90 Proceedings), pp. 289–298, August 1990.

Hart, Evan, Dave Gosselin, and John Isidoro, *Vertex Shading with Direct3D and OpenGL*, Game Developers Conference, San Jose, March 2001. www.ati.com/developer/ATIGDC2001Vertex.PDF

Hart, John C., *Perlin Noise Pixel Shaders*, ACM SIGGRAPH/Eurographics Workshop on Graphics Hardware, pp. 87–94, August 2001. http://graphics.cs.uiuc.edu/~jch/papers/pixelnoise.pdf

Heckbert, Paul S., *Survey of Texture Mapping*, IEEE Computer Graphics and Applications, vol. 6, no. 11, pp. 56–67, November 1986. www.cs.cmu.edu/~ph

———, *Fundamentals of Texture Mapping and Image Warping*, Report No. 516, Computer Science Division, University of California, Berkeley, June 1989. www.cs.cmu.edu/~ph

———, ed., *Graphics Gems IV*, Academic Press, San Diego, 1994. www.acm.org/pubs/tog/GraphicsGems

Heidrich, Wolfgang, and Hans-Peter Seidel, *View-Independent Environment Maps*, ACM SIGGRAPH/Eurographics Workshop on Graphics Hardware, pp. 39–45, August 1998.

———, *Realistic, Hardware-Accelerated Shading and Lighting*, Computer Graphics (SIGGRAPH '99 Proceedings), pp. 171–178, August 1999. www.cs.ubc.ca/~heidrich/Papers

Heidrich, Wolfgang, *Environment Maps and Their Applications*, SIGGRAPH 2000, Course 27, course notes. www.csee.umbc.edu/~olano/s2000c27/envmap.pdf

Hertzmann, Aaron, *Painterly Rendering with Curved Brush Strokes of Multiple Sizes*, Computer Graphics (SIGGRAPH '98 Proceedings), pp. 453–460, 1998. http://mrl.nyu.edu/publications/painterly98

———, *Introduction to 3D Non-Photorealistic Rendering: Silhouettes and Outlines*, SIGGRAPH '99 Non-Photorealistic Rendering course notes, 1999. www.mrl.nyu.edu/~hertzman/hertzmann-intro3d.pdf

Hewlett-Packard, *Polynomial Texture Mapping*, Web site. www.hpl.hp.com/ptm

Hoffman, Nathaniel, and A. Preetham, *Rendering Outdoor Light Scattering in Real Time*, Game Developers Conference 2002. www.ati.com/developer/dx9/ATI-LightScattering.pdf

Hook, Brian, *Multipass Rendering and the Magic of Alpha Blending*, Game Developer, vol. 4, no. 5, pp. 12–19, August 1997.

Hughes, John F., and Tomas Möller, *Building an Orthonormal Basis from a Unit Vector*, Journal of Graphics Tools, vol. 4, no. 4, pp. 33–35, 1999. www.acm.org/jgt/papers/HughesMoller99

International Lighting Vocabulary, Publication CIE No. 17.4, Joint publication IEC (International Electrotechnical Commission) and CIE (Committee Internationale de L'Èclairage), Geneva, 1987. www.cie.co.at/framepublications.html

ITU-R Recommendation BT.709, *Basic Parameter Values for the HDTV Standard for the Studio and for International Programme Exchange*, [formerly CCIR Rec. 709], Geneva, ITU, 1990.

Kajiya, James T., *Anisotropic Reflection Models*, Computer Graphics (SIGGRAPH '85 Proceedings), pp. 15–21, July 1985.

———, *The Rendering Equation*, Computer Graphics (SIGGRAPH '86 Proceedings), pp. 143–150, August 1986.

Kaplan, Matthew, Bruce Gooch, and Elaine Cohen, *Interactive Artistic Rendering*, Proceedings of the First International Symposium on Non-Photorealistic Animation and Rendering (NPAR), pp. 67–74, June 2000. www.cs.utah.edu/npr/utah_papers.html

Kautz, Jan, and Michael D. McCool, *Interactive Rendering with Arbitrary BRDFs Using Separable Approximations*, 10th Eurographics Workshop on Rendering, pp. 281–292, June 1999. www.mpi-sb.mpg.de/~jnkautz/publications

———, *Approximation of Glossy Reflection with Prefiltered Environment Maps*, Graphics Interface 2000, pp. 119–126, May 2000. www.mpi-sb.mpg.de/~jnkautz/publications

Kautz, Jan, P.-P. Vázquez, W. Heidrich, and H.-P. Seidel, *A Unified Approach to Prefiltered Environment Maps*, 11th Eurographics Workshop on Rendering, pp. 185–196, June 2000. www.mpi-sb.mpg.de/~jnkautz/publications

Kautz, Jan, and Hans-Peter Seidel, *Hardware Accelerated Displacement Mapping for Image Based Rendering*, Graphics Interface 2001, pp. 61–70, May 2001.

———, *Towards Interactive Bump Mapping with Anisotropic Shift-Variant BRDFs*, ACM SIGGRAPH/Eurographics Workshop on Graphics Hardware, pp. 51–58, 2000. www.mpi-sb.mpg.de/~jnkautz/projects/anisobumpmaps

Kautz, Jan, Chris Wynn, Jonathan Blow, Chris Blasband, Anis Ahmad, and Michael McCool, *Achieving Real-Time Realistic Reflectance, Part 1*, Game Developer, vol. 8, no. 1, pp. 32–37, January 2001.

————, *Achieving Real-Time Realistic Reflectance, Part 2*, Game Developer, vol. 8, no. 2, pp. 38–44, February 2001. www.gdmag.com/code.htm

Kerlow, Isaac V., *The Art of 3-D: Computer Animation and Imaging, Second Edition*, John Wiley & Sons, New York, 2000.

Kernighan, Brian, and Dennis Ritchie, *The C Programming Language, Second Edition*, Prentice Hall, Englewood Cliffs, New Jersey, 1988.

Kessenich, John, Dave Baldwin, and Randi Rost, *The OpenGL Shading Language, Version 1.10*, 3Dlabs, April 2004. www.opengl.org/documentation/spec.html

Kilgard, Mark J., *A Practical and Robust Bump-mapping Technique for Today's GPUs*, Game Developers Conference, NVIDIA White Paper, 2000. http://developer.nvidia.com/object/Practical_Bumpmapping_Tech.html

Kirk, David, ed., *Graphics Gems III*, Academic Press, San Diego, 1992. www.acm.org/pubs/tog/GraphicsGems

Lander, Jeff, *Collision Response: Bouncy, Trouncy, Fun*, Game Developer, vol. 6, no. 3, pp. 15–19, March 1999. www.darwin3d.com/gdm1999.htm

————, *The Era of Post-Photorealism*, Game Developer, vol. 8, no. 6, pp. 18–22, June 2001.

————, *Graphics Programming and the Tower of Babel*, Game Developer, vol. 8, no. 3, pp. 13–16, March 2001. www.gdmag.com/code.htm

————, *Haunted Trees for Halloween*, Game Developer Magazine, vol. 7, no. 11, pp. 17–21, November 2000. www.gdmag.com/code.htm

————, *A Heaping Pile of Pirate Booty*, Game Developer, vol. 8, no. 4, pp. 22–30, April 2001.

————, *Images from Deep in the Programmer's Cave*, Game Developer, vol. 8, no. 5, pp. 23–28, May 2001. www.gdmag.com/code.htm

————, *The Ocean Spray in Your Face*, Game Developer, vol. 5, no. 7, pp. 13–19, July 1998. www.darwin3d.com/gdm1998.htm

————, *Physics on the Back of a Cocktail Napkin*, Game Developer, vol. 6, no. 9, pp. 17–21, September 1999. www.darwin3d.com/gdm1999.htm

————, *Return to Cartoon Central*, Game Developer Magazine, vol. 7, no. 8, pp. 9–14, August 2000. www.gdmag.com/code.htm

————, *Shades of Disney: Opaquing a 3D World*, Game Developer Magazine, vol. 7, no. 3, pp. 15–20, March 2000. www.darwin3d.com/gdm2000.htm

————, *Skin Them Bones: Game Programming for the Web Generation*, Game Developer, vol. 5, no. 5, pp. 11–16, May 1998. www.darwin3d.com/gdm1998.htm

————, *Slashing Through Real-Time Character Animation*, Game Developer, vol. 5, no. 4, pp. 13–15, April 1998. www.darwin3d.com/gdm1998.htm

————, *That's a Wrap: Texture Mapping Methods*, Game Developer Magazine, vol. 7, no. 10, pp. 21–26, October 2000. www.gdmag.com/code.htm

————, *Under the Shade of the Rendering Tree*, Game Developer Magazine, vol. 7, no. 2, pp. 17–21, February 2000. www.darwin3d.com/gdm2000.htm

Landis, Hayden, *Production-Ready Global Illumination*, SIGGRAPH 2002 Course Notes, course 16, RenderMan In Production. www.debevec.org/HDRI2004/landis-S2002-course16-prodreadyGI.pdf

Lasseter, John, *Principles of Traditional Animation Applied to 3D Computer Animation*, Computer Graphics, (SIGGRAPH '87 Proceedings) pp. 35–44, July 1987.

————, *Tricks to Animating Characters with a Computer*, SIGGRAPH '94, Course 1, course notes. www.siggraph.org/education/materials/HyperGraph/animation/character_animation/principles/lasseter_s94.htm

Lichtenbelt, Barthold, *Integrating the OpenGL Shading Language*, 3Dlabs internal white paper, July 2003.

Lindbloom, Bruce J., *Accurate Color Reproduction for Computer Graphics Applications*, Computer Graphics (SIGGRAPH '89 Proceedings), pp. 117–126, July 1989.

————, personal Web site, 2003. www.brucelindbloom.com

Litwinowicz, Peter, *Processing Images and Video for an Impressionist Effect*, Computer Graphics (SIGGRAPH '97 Proceedings), pp. 407–414, August 1997.

Lorensen, William E., and Harvey E. Cline, *Marching Cubes: A High Resolution 3D Surface Construction Algorithm*, Computer Graphics (SIGGRAPH '87 Proceedings), pp. 163–169, July 1987.

Lowell, Ross, *Matters of Light & Depth*, Lowel-Light Manufacturing, 1992.

Malzbender, Tom, Dan Gelb, and Hans Wolters, *Polynomial Texture Maps*, Computer Graphics (SIGGRAPH 2001 Proceedings), pp. 519–528, August 2001. www.hpl.hp.com/research/ptm/papers/ptm.pdf

Mandelbrot, Benoit B., *The Fractal Geometry of Nature, Updated and Augmented*, W. H. Freeman and Company, New York, 1983.

Mark, William R., *Real-Time Shading: Stanford Real-Time Procedural Shading System*, SIGGRAPH 2001, Course 24, course notes, 2001. http://graphics.stanford.edu/projects/shading/pubs/sigcourse2001.pdf

Mark, William R., R. Steven Glanville, Kurt Akeley, and Mark Kilgard, *Cg: A System for Programming Graphics Hardware in a C-like Language*, Computer Graphics (SIGGRAPH 2003 Proceedings), pp. 896–907, July 2003. www.cs.utexas.edu/users/billmark/papers/Cg

Markosian, Lee, Michael A. Kowalski, Daniel Goldstein, Samuel J. Trychin, John F. Hughes, and Lubomir D. Bourdev, *Real-time Nonphotorealistic Rendering*, Computer Graphics (SIGGRAPH '97 Proceedings), pp. 415–420, August 1997. www.eecs.umich.edu/~sapo/pubs

McCool, Michael D., *SMASH: A Next-Generation API for Programmable Graphics Accelerators*, Technical Report CS-2000-14, University of Waterloo, August 2000. www.cgl.uwaterloo.ca/Projects/rendering/Papers/smash.pdf

McCool, Michael D., Jason Ang, and Anis Ahmad, *Homomorphic Factorization of BRDFs for High-performance Rendering*, Computer Graphics (SIGGRAPH 2001 Proceedings), pp. 171–178, August 2001. www.cgl.uwaterloo.ca/Projects/rendering/Papers

McReynolds, Tom, David Blythe, Brad Grantham, and Scott Nelson, *Advanced Graphics Programming Techniques Using OpenGL*, SIGGRAPH '99 course notes, 1999. www.opengl.org/resources/tutorials/sig99/advanced99/notes/notes.html

McReynolds, Tom, and David Blythe, *Advanced Graphics Programming Techniques Using OpenGL*, Morgan Kaufmann Publishers, San Francisco, 2005.

Meier, Barbara J, *Painterly Rendering for Animation*, Computer Graphics (SIGGRAPH '96 Proceedings), pp. 477–484, August 1996. www.cs.virginia.edu/~dbrogan/CS551.851.animation.sp.2000/Papers/p477-meier.pdf

Microsoft, *Advanced Shading and Lighting*, Meltdown 2001, July 2001. www.microsoft.com/mscorp/corpevents/meltdown2001/presentations.asp

———, *DirectX 9.0 SDK*, 2003. http://msdn.microsoft.com/directx

Mitchell, Jason L., *Advanced Vertex and Pixel Shader Techniques*, European Game Developers Conference, London, September 2001. www.pixelmaven.com/jason

———, *Image Processing with Pixel Shaders in Direct3D*, in Engel, Wolfgang, ed., ShaderX, Wordware, May 2002. www.pixelmaven.com/jason

Muchnick, Steven, *Advanced Compiler Design and Implementation*, Morgan Kaufmann Publishers, San Francisco, 1997.

Myler, Harley R., and Arthur R. Weeks, *The Pocket Handbook of Image Processing Algorithms in C*, Prentice Hall, Upper Saddle River, NJ, 1993.

NASA, *Earth Observatory*, Web site. http://earthobservatory.nasa.gov/Newsroom/BlueMarble

Nishita, Tomoyuki, Takao Sirai, Katsumi Tadamura, and Eihachiro Nakamae, *Display of the Earth Taking into Account Atmospheric Scattering*, Computer Graphics (SIGGRAPH '93 Proceedings), pp. 175–182, August 1993. http://nis-lab.is.s.u-tokyo.ac.jp/~nis/abs_sig.html#sig93

NVIDIA developer Web site. http://developer.nvidia.com

NVIDIA Corporation, Cg Toolkit, Release 1.4, software and documentation. http://developer.nvidia.com/object/cg_toolkit.html

Olano, Marc, and Anselmo Lastra, *A Shading Language on Graphics Hardware: The PixelFlow Shading System*, Computer Graphics (SIGGRAPH '98 Proceedings), pp. 159–168, July 1998. www.csee.umbc.edu/~olano/papers

Olano, Marc, John Hart, Wolfgang Heidrich, and Michael McCool, *Real-Time Shading*, AK Peters, Ltd., Natick, Massachusetts, 2002.

OpenGL Architecture Review Board, *ARB_fragment_program Extension Specification*, OpenGL Extension Registry. http://oss.sgi.com/projects/ogl-sample/registry

————, *ARB_fragment_shader Extension Specification*, OpenGL Extension Registry. http://oss.sgi.com/projects/ogl-sample/registry

————, *ARB_shader_objects Extension Specification*, OpenGL Extension Registry. http://oss.sgi.com/projects/ogl-sample/registry

————, *ARB_vertex_program Extension Specification*, OpenGL Extension Registry. http://oss.sgi.com/projects/ogl-sample/registry

————, *ARB_vertex_shader Extension Specification*, OpenGL Extension Registry. http://oss.sgi.com/projects/ogl-sample/registry

————, *OpenGL Reference Manual, Fourth Edition: The Official Reference to OpenGL, Version 1.4*, Editor: Dave Shreiner, Addison-Wesley, Reading, Massachusetts, 2004.

OpenGL, official Web site. http://opengl.org

OpenGL Performer Web site. www.sgi.com/products/software/performer/

OpenSceneGraph Web site. www.openscenegraph.org/

OpenSG Web site. www.opensg.org

Owen, G. Scott, *Computer Animation*, Web site. www.siggraph.org/education/materials/HyperGraph/animation/anim0.htm

Pandromeda Web site. www.pandromeda.com

Parent, Rick, *Computer Animation: Algorithms and Techniques*, Morgan Kaufmann Publishers, San Francisco, 2001.

Peachey, Darwyn, *Solid Texturing of Complex Surfaces*, Computer Graphics (SIGGRAPH '85 Proceedings), pp. 279–286, July 1985.

Peeper, Craig, and Jason Mitchell, *Introduction to the DirectX 9 High-Level Shader Language*, in *ShaderX2 : Shader Programming Tips and Tricks with DirectX 9.0*, Editor: Wolfgang Engel, Wordware Publishing, 2003. www.ati.com/developer/ShaderX2_IntroductionToHLSL.pdf

Peercy, Mark S., Marc Olano, John Airey, and P. Jeffrey Ungar, *Interactive Multi-Pass Programmable Shading*, Computer Graphics (SIGGRAPH 2000 Proceedings), pp. 425–432, July 2000. www.csee.umbc.edu/~olano/papers

Peitgen, Heinz-Otto, and P. H. Richter, *The Beauty of Fractals, Images of Complex Dynamical Systems*, Springer Verlag, Berlin Heidelberg, 1986.

Peitgen, Heinz-Otto, D. Saupe, M. F. Barnsley, R. L. Devaney, B. B. Mandelbrot, and R. F. Voss, *The Science of Fractal Images*, Springer Verlag, New York, 1988.

Perlin, Ken, *An Image Synthesizer*, Computer Graphics (SIGGRAPH '85 Proceedings), pp. 287–296, July 1985.

———, *Implementing Improved Perlin Noise* in *GPU Gems: Programming Techniques, Tips, and Tricks for Real-Time Graphics*, Editor: Randima Fernando, Addison-Wesley, Reading, Massachusetts, 2004. http://developer.nvidia.com/object/gpu_gems_home.html

———, *Improving Noise*, Computer Graphics (SIGGRAPH 2002 Proceedings), pp. 681–682, July 2002. http://mrl.nyu.edu/perlin/paper445.pdf

———, personal Web site. www.noisemachine.com

———, personal Web site. http://mrl.nyu.edu/~perlin

Pharr, Matt, and Simon Green, *Ambient Occlusion,* in *GPU Gems: Programming Techniques, Tips, and Tricks for Real-Time Graphics*, Editor: Randima Fernando, Addison-Wesley, Reading, Massachusetts, 2004. http://developer.nvidia.com/object/gpu_gems_home.html

Pharr, Matt, and Greg Humphreys, *Physically Based Rendering: From Theory to Implementation*, Morgan Kaufmann, San Francisco, 2004. http://pbrt.org/

Phong, Bui Tuong, *Illumination for Computer Generated Pictures*, Communications of the ACM, vol. 18, no. 6, pp. 311–317, June 1975.

Pixar, *The RenderMan Interface Specification*, Version 3.2, Pixar, July 2000. https://renderman.pixar.com/products/rispec/index.htm

Porter, Thomas, and Tom Duff, *Compositing Digital Images*, Computer Graphics (SIGGRAPH '84 Proceedings), pp. 253–259, July 1984.

Poulin, P., and A. Fournier, *A Model for Anisotropic Reflection*, Computer Graphics (SIGGRAPH '90 Proceedings), pp. 273–282, August 1990.

Poynton, Charles A., *Frequently Asked Questions about Color*, 1997. www.poynton.com/Poynton-color.html

———, *Frequently Asked Questions about Gamma*, 1997. www.poynton.com/Poynton-color.html

———, *A Technical Introduction to Digital Video*, John Wiley & Sons, New York, 1996.

Praun, Emil, Adam Finkelstein, and Hugues Hoppe, *Lapped Textures*, Computer Graphics (SIGGRAPH 2000 Proceedings), pp. 465–470, July 2000. www.cs.princeton.edu/gfx/proj/lapped_tex

Praun, Emil, Hugues Hoppe, Matthew Webb, and Adam Finkelstein, *Real-time Hatching*, Computer Graphics (SIGGRAPH 2000 Proceedings), pp. 581–586, August 2001. www.cs.princeton.edu/gfx/proj/hatching

Proakis, John G., and Dimitris G. Manolakis, *Digital Signal Processing: Principles, Algorithms, and Applications, Third Edition*, Prentice Hall, Upper Saddle River, New Jersey, 1995.

Proudfoot, Kekoa, William R. Mark, Svetoslav Tzvetkov, and Pat Hanrahan, *A Real-Time Procedural Shading System for Programmable Graphics Hardware*, Computer Graphics (SIGGRAPH 2001 Proceedings), pp. 159–170, August 2001. http://graphics.stanford.edu/projects/shading/pubs/sig2001

Purcell, Timothy J., Ian Buck, William R. Mark, and Pat Hanrahan, *Ray Tracing on Programmable Graphics Hardware*, Computer Graphics (SIGGRAPH 2002 Proceedings), July 2002. www-graphics.stanford.edu/papers/rtongfx

Ramamoorthi, Ravi, and P. Hanrahan, *An Efficient Representation for Irradiance Environment Maps*, Computer Graphics (SIGGRAPH 2001 Proceedings), pp. 497–500, August 2001. www1.cs.columbia.edu/~ravir/papers/envmap/index.html

Raskar, Ramesh, and Michael Cohen, *Image Precision Silhouette Edges*, Proceedings 1999 Symposium on Interactive 3D Graphics, pp. 135–140, April 1999. www.cs.unc.edu/~raskar/NPR

Raskar, Ramesh, *Hardware Support for Non-photorealistic Rendering*, ACM SIGGRAPH/Eurographics Workshop on Graphics Hardware, pp. 41–46, 2001. www.cs.unc.edu/~raskar/HWWS

Reeves, William T., *Particle Systems—A Technique for Modeling a Class of Fuzzy Objects*, ACM Transactions on Graphics, vol. 2, no. 2, pp. 91–108, April 1983.

Reeves, William T., and Ricki Blau, *Approximate and Probabilistic Algorithms for Shading and Rendering Structured Particle Systems*, Computer Graphics (SIGGRAPH '85 Proceedings), pp. 313–322, July 1985.

Reeves, William T., David H. Salesin, and Robert L. Cook, *Rendering Antialiased Shadows with Depth Maps*, Computer Graphics (SIGGRAPH '87 Proceedings), pp. 283–291, July 1987.

Reynolds, Craig, *Stylized Depiction in Computer Graphics*, Web site. www.red3d.com/cwr/npr

Rost, Randi J., *The OpenGL Shading Language*, SIGGRAPH 2002, Course 17, course notes. http://3dshaders.com/pubs

———, *Using OpenGL for Imaging*, SPIE Medical Imaging '96 Image Display Conference, February 1996. http://3dshaders.com/pubs

Salisbury, Michael, Sean E. Anderson, Ronen Barzel, and David H. Salesin, *Interactive Pen-and-Ink Illustration*, Computer Graphics (SIGGRAPH '94 Proceedings), pp. 101–108, July 1994. http://grail.cs.washington.edu/pub

Salisbury, Michael, *Image-Based Pen-and-Ink Illustration*, Ph.D. thesis, University of Washington, 1997. http://grail.cs.washington.edu/theses

Saito, Takafumi, and Tokiichiro Takahashi, *Comprehensible Rendering of 3-D Shapes*, Computer Graphics (SIGGRAPH '90 Proceedings), pp. 197–206, August 1990.

Schlick, Christophe, *An Inexpensive BRDF Model for Physically Based Rendering*, Eurographics '94, published in Computer Graphics Forum, vol. 13., no. 3, pp. 149–162, September 1994.

Schneider, Philip, and David Eberly, *Geometric Tools for Computer Graphics*, Morgan Kaufmann Publishers, San Francisco, 2002.

Segal, Mark, C. Korobkin, R. van Widenfelt, J. Foran, and P. Haeberli, *Fast Shadows and Lighting Effects Using Texture Mapping*, Computer Graphics (SIGGRAPH '92 Proceedings), pp. 249–252, July 1992.

Segal, Mark, and Kurt Akeley, *The Design of the OpenGL Graphics Interface*, Silicon Graphics Inc., 1994.
wwws.sun.com/software/graphics/opengl/OpenGLdesign.pdf

———, *The OpenGL Graphics System: A Specification (Version 2.0)*, Editor (v1.1): Chris Frazier, (v1.2–1.5): Jon Leech, (v2.0): Jon Leech and Pat Brown, September 2004. www.opengl.org/documentation/spec.html

SGI OpenGL Web site. www.sgi.com/software/opengl

SGI OpenGL Shader Web site. www.sgi.com/software/shader (defunct)

ShaderX2 : Shader Programming Tips and Tricks with DirectX 9.0, Editor: Wolfgang Engel, Wordware Publishing, 2003. www.shaderx2.com

Shishkovtsov, Oles, *Deferred Shading in S.T.A.L.K.E.R.*, in *GPU Gems 2: Programming Techniques for High-Performance Graphics and General-Purpose Computation*, Editor: Matt Pharr, Addison-Wesley, Reading, Massachusetts, 2005. http://developer.nvidia.com/object/gpu_gems_2_home.html

Shreiner, Dave, and The Khronos OpenGL ARB Working Group, *OpenGL Programming Guide, Seventh Edition: The Official Guide to Learning OpenGL, Versions 3.0 and 3.1*, Addison-Wesley, Boston, Massachusetts, 2010.

SIGGRAPH Proceedings, Web site of online materials. http://portal.acm.org.

Sillion, François, and Claude Puech, *Radiosity and Global Illumination*, Morgan Kaufmann Publishers, San Francisco, 1994.

Sloup, Jaroslav, *Physically-based Simulation: A Survey of the Modelling and Rendering of the Earth's Atmosphere*, Proceedings of the 18th Spring Conference on Computer Graphics, pp. 141–150, April 2002. http://sgi.felk.cvut.cz/~sloup/html/research/project

Smith, Alvy Ray, *Color Gamut Transform Pairs*, Computer Graphics (SIGGRAPH '78 Proceedings), pp. 12–19, August 1978. www.alvyray.com

———, *Digital Filtering Tutorial for Computer Graphics*, Lucasfilm Technical Memo 27, revised March 1983. www.alvyray.com/memos/default.htm

———, *Digital Filtering Tutorial, Part II*, Lucasfilm Technical Memo 27, revised March 1983. www.alvyray.com/memos/default.htm

———, *A Pixel Is Not a Little Square, A Pixel Is Not a Little Square, A Pixel Is Not a Little Square! (And a Voxel is Not a Little Cube)*, Technical Memo 6, Microsoft Research, July 1995. www.alvyray.com/memos/default.htm

SMPTE RP 177–1993, *Derivation of Basic Television Color Equations.*

Stam, Jos, *Diffraction Shaders*, Computer Graphics (SIGGRAPH '99 Proceedings), pp. 101–110, August 1999. www.dgp.toronto.edu/people/stam/reality/Research/pdf/diff.pdf

———, *Simulating Diffraction*, in *GPU Gems: Programming Techniques, Tips, and Tricks for Real-Time Graphics*, Editor: Randima Fernando, Addison-Wesley, Reading, Massachusetts, 2004. http://developer.nvidia.com/object/gpu_gems_home.html

Stokes, Michael, Matthew Anderson, Srinivasan Chandrasekar, and Ricardo Motta, *A Standard Default Color Space for the Internet—sRGB*, Version 1.10, November 1996. www.color.org/sRGB.html

Stone, Maureen, *A Survey of Color for Computer Graphics*, Course 4 at SIGGRAPH 2001, August 2001. www.stonesc.com

Strothotte, Thomas, and S. Schlectweg, *Non-Photorealistic Computer Graphics, Modeling, Rendering, and Animation*, Morgan Kaufmann Publishers, San Francisco, 2002.

Stroustrup, Bjarne, *The C++ Programming Language (Special 3rd Edition)*, Addison-Wesley, Reading, Massachusetts, 2000.

Taylor, Philip, *Per-Pixel Lighting*, Microsoft Corp., November 2001.

Thomas, Frank, and Ollie Johnston, *Disney Animation—The Illusion of Life*, Abbeville Press, New York, 1981.

———, *The Illusion of Life—Disney Animation, Revised Edition*, Hyperion, 1995.

Torrance, K., and E. Sparrow, *Theory for Off-Specular Reflection from Roughened Surfaces*, J. Optical Society of America, vol. 57, September 1967.

Tufte, Edward, *Visual Explanations*, Graphics Press, Cheshire, Connecticut, 1997.

Upstill, Steve, *The RenderMan Companion: A Programmer's Guide to Realistic Computer Graphics*, Addison-Wesley, Reading, Massachusetts, 1990.

Verbeck, Channing P., and D. Greenberg, *A Comprehensive Light Source Description for Computer Graphics*, IEEE Computer Graphics and Applications, vol. 4, no. 7, July 1984, pp. 66–75.

Ward, Gregory, *Measuring and Modeling Anisotropic Reflection*, Computer Graphics (SIGGRAPH '92 Proceedings), pp. 265–272, July 1992. http://radsite.lbl.gov/radiance/papers/sg92/paper.html

Watt, Alan H., and Mark Watt, *Advanced Animation and Rendering Techniques: Theory and Practice*, Addison-Wesley, Reading, Massachusetts, 1992.

Whitted, Turner, *An Improved Illumination Model for Shaded Display*, Communications of the ACM vol. 23, no. 6, pp. 343–349, 1980.

Williams, Lance, *Pyramidal Parametrics*, Computer Graphics (SIGGRAPH '83 Proceedings), pp. 1–11, July 1983.

Winkenbach, Georges, and David Salesin, *Computer-Generated Pen-and-Ink Illustration*, Computer Graphics (SIGGRAPH '94 Proceedings), pp. 91–100, July 1994. http://grail.cs.washington.edu/pub

Winkenbach, Georges, *Computer-Generated Pen-and-Ink Illustration*, Ph.D. Dissertation, University of Washington, 1996. http://grail.cs.washington.edu/theses

Wolberg, George, *Digital Image Warping*, Wiley-IEEE Press, 2002.

Woo, Andrew, P. Poulin, and A. Fournier, *A Survey of Shadow Algorithms*, IEEE Computer Graphics and Applications, vol. 10, no. 6, pp.13–32, November 1990.

Worley, Steven, *A Cellular Texture Basis Function*, Computer Graphics (SIGGRAPH '96 Proceedings), pp. 291–294, August 1996.

Wright, Richard, *Understanding and Using OpenGL Texture Objects*, Gamasutra, July 23, 1999. www.gamasutra.com/features/19990723/opengl_texture_objects_01.htm

Wright, Richard, and Benjamin Lipchak, *OpenGL SuperBible, Third Edition,* Sams Publishing, 2005. www.starstonesoftware.com/OpenGL/opengl_superbbile.htm

Zhukov, Sergei, A. Iones, G. Kronin, *An Ambient Light Illumination Model*, Proceedings of Eurographics Rendering Workshop '98.

Zwillinger, Dan, *CRC Standard Mathematical Tables and Formulas*, 30th Edition, CRC Press, 1995. http://geom.math.uiuc.edu/docs/reference/CRC-formulas/

Index

OpenGL® Titles from Addison-Wesley

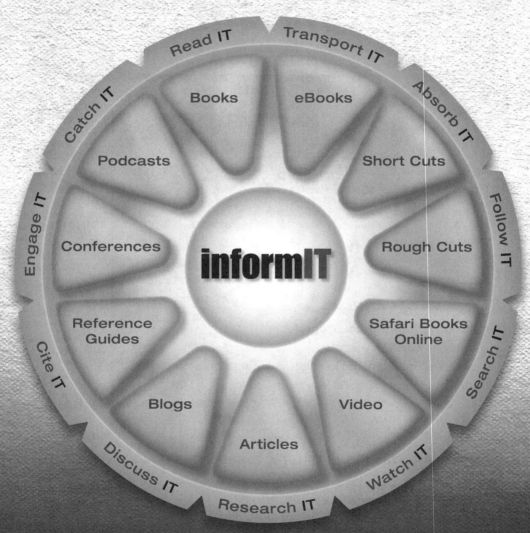